Network Optimization:
Continuous and Discrete Models

Dimitri P. Bertsekas

Massachusetts Institute of Technology

WWW site for book information and orders

http://world.std.com/~athenasc/index.html

 Athena Scientific, Belmont, Massachusetts

Athena Scientific
Post Office Box 391
Belmont, Mass. 02178-9998
U.S.A.

Email: athenasc@world.std.com
WWW: http://world.std.com/~athenasc/index.html

Cover Design: *Ann Gallager*

Publisher's Cataloging-in-Publication Data

Bertsekas, Dimitri P.
Network Optimization: Continuous and Discrete Models
Includes bibliographical references and index
1. Network analysis (Planning). 2. Mathematical Optimization. I. Title.
T57.85.B44 1998   658.4'032-dc20   98-70298

ISBN 1-886529-02-7

ABOUT THE AUTHOR

Dimitri Bertsekas studied Mechanical and Electrical Engineering at the National Technical University of Athens, Greece, and obtained his Ph.D. in system science from the Massachusetts Institute of Technology. He has held faculty positions with the Engineering-Economic Systems Dept., Stanford University and the Electrical Engineering Dept. of the University of Illinois, Urbana. He is currently Professor of Electrical Engineering and Computer Science at the Massachusetts Institute of Technology. He consults regularly with private industry and has held editorial positions in several journals. He has been elected Fellow of the IEEE.

Professor Bertsekas has done research in a broad variety of subjects from optimization theory, control theory, parallel and distributed computation, data communication networks, and systems analysis. He has written numerous papers in each of these areas.

Other books by the author:

1) *Dynamic Programming and Stochastic Control*, Academic Press, 1976.
2) *Stochastic Optimal Control: The Discrete-Time Case*, Academic Press, 1978; republished by Athena Scientific, 1997 (with S. E. Shreve; translated in Russian).
3) *Constrained Optimization and Lagrange Multiplier Methods*, Academic Press, 1982; republished by Athena Scientific, 1996 (translated in Russian).
4) *Dynamic Programming: Deterministic and Stochastic Models*, Prentice-Hall, 1987.
5) *Data Networks*, Prentice-Hall, 1987; 2nd Edition 1992 (with R. G. Gallager; translated in Russian and Japanese).
6) *Parallel and Distributed Computation: Numerical Methods*, Prentice-Hall, 1989; republished by Athena Scientific, 1997 (with J. N. Tsitsiklis).
7) *Linear Network Optimization: Algorithms and Codes*, M.I.T. Press, 1991.
8) *Dynamic Programming and Optimal Control*, (2 Vols.), Athena Scientific, 1995.
9) *Nonlinear Programming*, Athena Scientific, 1995.
10) *Neuro-Dynamic Programming*, Athena Scientific, 1996 (with J. N. Tsitsiklis).

OPTIMIZATION AND NEURAL COMPUTATION SERIES

1. Dynamic Programming and Optimal Control, Vols. I and II, by Dimitri P. Bertsekas, 1995, ISBN 1-886529-11-6, 704 pages

2. Nonlinear Programming, by Dimitri P. Bertsekas, 1995, ISBN 1-886529-14-0, 656 pages

3. Neuro-Dynamic Programming, by Dimitri P. Bertsekas and John N. Tsitsiklis, 1996, ISBN 1-886529-10-8, 512 pages

4. Constrained Optimization and Lagrange Multiplier Methods, by Dimitri P. Bertsekas, 1996, ISBN 1-886529-04-3, 410 pages

5. Stochastic Optimal Control: The Discrete-Time Case by Dimitri P. Bertsekas and Steven E. Shreve, 1996, ISBN 1-886529-03-5, 330 pages

6. Introduction to Linear Optimization by Dimitris Bertsimas and John N. Tsitsiklis, 1997, ISBN 1-886529-19-1, 608 pages

7. Parallel and Distributed Computation: Numerical Methods by Dimitri P. Bertsekas and John N. Tsitsiklis, 1997, ISBN 1-886529-01-9, 718 pages

8. Network Optimization: Continuous and Discrete Models by Dimitri P. Bertsekas, 1998, ISBN 1-886529-02-7, 608 pages

Contents

Preface

Network optimization lies in the middle of the great divide that separates the two major types of optimization problems, continuous and discrete. The ties between linear programming and combinatorial optimization can be traced to the representation of the constraint polyhedron as the convex hull of its extreme points. When a network is involved, however, these ties become much stronger because the extreme points of the polyhedron are integer and represent solutions of combinatorial problems that are seemingly unrelated to linear programming. Because of this structure and also because of their intuitive character, network models provide ideal vehicles for explaining many of the fundamental ideas in both continuous and discrete optimization.

Aside from their interesting methodological characteristics, network models are also used extensively in practice, in an ever expanding spectrum of applications. Indeed collectively, network problems such as shortest path, assignment, max-flow, transportation, transhipment, spanning tree, matching, traveling salesman, generalized assignment, vehicle routing, and multicommodity flow constitute the most common class of practical optimization problems. There has been steady progress in the solution methodology of network problems, and in fact the progress has accelerated in the last fifteen years thanks to algorithmic and technological advances.

The purpose of this book is to provide a fairly comprehensive and up-to-date development of linear, nonlinear, and discrete network optimization problems. The interplay between continuous and discrete structures has been highlighted, the associated analytical and algorithmic issues have been treated quite extensively, and a guide to important network models and applications has been provided.

Regarding continuous network optimization, we focus on two ideas, which are also fundamental in general mathematical programming: *duality* and *iterative cost improvement*. We provide an extensive treatment of iterative algorithms for the most common linear cost problem, the minimum cost flow or transhipment problem, and for its convex cost extensions. The discussion of duality is comprehensive: it starts with linear network programming duality, and culminates with Rockafellar's development of monotropic programming duality.

Regarding discrete network optimization, we illustrate problem formulation through major paradigms such as traveling salesman, generalized assignment, spanning tree, matching, and routing. This is essential because the structure of discrete optimization problems is far less streamlined than the structure of their continuous counterparts, and familiarity with important types of problems is important for modeling, analysis, and algorithmic solution. We also develop the main algorithmic approaches, including branch-and-bound, Lagrangian relaxation, Dantzig-Wolfe decomposition, heuristics, and local search methods.

This is meant to be an introductory book that covers a very broad variety of topics. It is thus inevitable that some topics have been treated in less detail than others. The choices made reflect in part personal taste and expertise, and in part a preference for simple models that can help most effectively the reader develop insight. At the same time, our analysis and presentation aims to enhance the reader's mathematical modeling ability in two ways: by delineating the range of problems for which various algorithms are applicable and efficient, and by providing many examples of problem formulation.

The chapter-by-chapter description of the book follows:

Chapter 1: This is an introductory chapter that establishes terminology and basic notions about graphs, discusses some examples of network models, and provides some orientation regarding linear network optimization algorithms.

Chapter 2: This chapter provides an extensive treatment of shortest path problems. It covers the major methods, and discusses their theoretical and practical performance.

Chapter 3: This chapter focuses on the max-flow problem and develops the class of augmenting path algorithms for its solution. In addition to the classical variants of the Ford-Fulkerson method, a recent algorithm based on auction ideas is discussed.

Chapter 4: The minimum cost flow problem (linear cost, single commodity, no side constraints) and its equivalent variants are introduced here. Subsequently, the basic duality theory for the problem is developed and interpreted.

Chapter 5: This chapter focuses on simplex methods for the minimum cost flow problem. The basic results regarding the integrality of solutions are developed here constructively, using the simplex method. Furthermore, the duality theory of Chapter 4 is significantly strengthened.

Chapter 6: This chapter develops dual ascent methods, including primal-dual, sequential shortest path, and relaxation methods.

Chapter 7: This chapter starts with the auction algorithm for the assignment problem, and proceeds to show how this algorithm can be extended to more complex problems. In this way, preflow-push methods for the max-flow problem and the ϵ-relaxation method for the minimum cost flow problem are obtained. Several additional variants of auction algorithms are developed.

Chapter 8: This is an important chapter that marks the transition from linear to nonlinear network optimization. The primary focus is on continuous (convex) problems, and their associated broad variety of structures and methodology. In particular, there is an overview of the types of algorithms from nonlinear programming that are useful in connection with various convex network problems. There is also some discussion of discrete (integer) problems with an emphasis on their ties with continuous problems.

Chapter 9: This is a fairly sophisticated chapter that is directed primarily towards the advanced and/or research-oriented reader. It deals with separable convex problems, discusses their connection with classical network equilibrium problems, and develops their rich theoretical structure. The salient features of this structure are a particularly sharp duality theory, and a combinatorial connection of descent directions with the finite set of elementary vectors of the subspace defined by the conservation of flow constraints. Besides treating convex separable network problems, this chapter provides an introduction to monotropic programming, which is the largest class of nonlinear programming problems that possess the strong duality and combinatorial properties of linear programs. This chapter also develops auction algorithms for convex separable problems and provides an analysis of their running time.

Chapter 10: This chapter deals with the basic methodological approaches for integer-constrained problems. There is a treatment of exact methods such as branch-and-bound, and the associated methods of Lagrangian relaxation, subgradient optimization, and cutting plane. There is also a description of approximate methods based on local search, such as genetic algorithms, tabu search, and simulated annealing. Finally, there is a discussion of rollout algorithms, a relatively new and broadly applicable class of approximate methods, which can be used in place of, or in conjunction with local search.

The book can be used for a course on network optimization or for part of a course on introductory optimization at the first-year graduate level. With the exception of some of the material in Chapter 9, the prerequisites are fairly elementary. The main one is a certain degree of mathematical maturity, as provided for example by a rigorous mathematics course beyond the calculus level. One may cover most of the book in a course on linear and nonlinear network optimization. A shorter version of this course may consist of Chapters 1-5, and 8. Alternatively, one may teach a course that focuses on linear and discrete network optimization, using Chapters 1-5, a small part of Chapter 8, and Chapter 10. Actually, in these chapter sequences, it is not essential to cover Chapter 5, if one is content with weaker versions of duality results (given in Chapter 4) and one establishes the integrality properties of optimal solutions with a line of argument such as the one given in Exercise 1.34. The following figure illustrates the chapter dependencies.

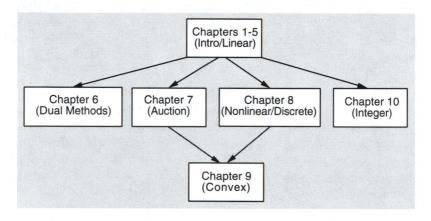

The book contains a large number of examples and exercises, which should enhance its suitability for classroom instruction. Some of the exercises are theoretical in nature and supplement substantially the main text. Solutions to a subset of these (as well as errata and additional material) will be posted and periodically updated on the book's web page:

http://world.std.com/~ athenasc/netsbook.html

Also, the author's web page

http://web.mit.edu/dimitrib/www/home.html

contains listings of FORTRAN codes implementing many of the algorithms discussed in the book.

There is a very extensive literature on continuous and discrete network optimization, and to give a complete bibliography and a historical account of the research that led to the present form of the subject would have been impossible. Thus I have not attempted to compile a comprehensive list of original contributions to the field. I have cited sources that I have used extensively, that provide important extensions to the material of the book, that survey important topics, or that are particularly well suited for further reading. I have also cited selectively a few sources that are historically significant, but the reference list is far from exhaustive in this respect. Generally, to aid researchers in the field, I have preferred to cite surveys and textbooks for subjects that are relatively mature, and to give a larger number of references for relatively recent developments.

A substantial portion of this book is based on the author's research on network optimization over the last twenty years. I was fortunate to have several outstanding collaborators in this research, and I would like to mention those with whom I have worked extensively. Eli Gafni assisted with the computational experimentation using the auction algorithm and the relaxation method for assignment problems in 1979. The idea of ϵ-scaling arose during my interactions with Eli at that time. Furthermore, Eli collaborated extensively with me on various routing methods for data networks, including projection methods for convex multicommodity flow problems. Paul Tseng worked with me on network optimization starting in 1982. Together we developed the RELAX codes, we developed several extensions to the basic relaxation method and we collaborated closely on a broad variety of other subjects, including the recent auction algorithms for convex network problems and network problems with gains. David Castanon has worked extensively with me on a broad variety of algorithms for assignment, transportation, and minimum cost flow problems, for both serial and parallel computers, since 1987. John Tsitsiklis has been my coauthor and close collaborator for many years on a variety of optimization and large scale computation topics, including some that deal with networks. In addition to Eli, Paul, David, and John, I have had substantial research collaborations with several colleagues, the results of which have been reflected in this book. In this regard, I would like to mention Jon Eckstein, Bob Gallager, Francesca Guerriero, Roberto Musmanno, Stefano Pallottino, and Maria-Grazia Scutellà. Several colleagues proofread portions of the book, and contributed greatly with their suggestions. David Castanon, Stefano Pallottino, Steve Patek, Serap Savari, Paul Tseng, and John Tsitsiklis were particularly helpful in this regard. The research support of NSF under grants from the DDM and the CCI divisions are very much appreciated. My family has been a source of stability and loving support, without which the book would not have been written.

Dimitri P. Bertsekas
Cambridge, Mass.
Spring 1998

1

Introduction

Contents

Network flow problems are one of the most important and most frequently encountered class of optimization problems. They arise naturally in the analysis and design of large systems, such as communication, transportation, and manufacturing networks. They can also be used to model important classes of combinatorial problems, such as assignment, shortest path, and traveling salesman problems.

Loosely speaking, network flow problems consist of supply and demand points, together with several routes that connect these points and are used to transfer the supply to the demand. These routes may contain intermediate transshipment points. Often, the supply, demand, and transshipment points can be modeled by the nodes of a graph, and the routes can be modeled by the paths of the graph. Furthermore, there may be multiple "types" of supply/demand (or "commodities") sharing the routes. There may also be some constraints on the characteristics of the routes, such as their carrying capacities, and some costs associated with using particular routes. Such situations are naturally modeled as network optimization problems whereby, roughly speaking, we try to select routes that minimize the cost of transfer of the supply to the demand.

This book deals with a broad spectrum of network optimization problems, involving linear and nonlinear cost functions. We pay special attention to four major classes of problems:

(a) The *transshipment* or *minimum cost flow problem*, which involves a single commodity and a linear cost function. This problem has several important special cases, such as the shortest path, the max-flow, the assignment, and the transportation problems.

(b) The *single commodity network flow problem with convex cost*. This problem is identical to the preceding transshipment problem, except that the cost function is convex rather than linear.

(c) The *multicommodity network flow problem with linear or convex cost*. This problem generalizes the preceding two classes of problems to the case of multiple commodities.

(d) *Discrete network optimization problems*. These are problems where the quantities transferred along the routes of the network are restricted to take one of a finite number of values. Many combinatorial optimization problems can be modeled in this way, including some problems where the network structure is not immediately apparent. Some discrete optimization problems are computationally very difficult, and in practice can only be solved approximately. Their algorithmic solution often involves the solution of "continuous" subproblems that belong to the preceding three classes.

All of the network flow problems above can be mathematically modeled in terms of graph-related notions. In Section 1.1, we introduce the associated notation and terminology. In Section 1.2, we provide mathematical formulations and practical examples of network optimization models. Finally, in Section 1.3, we give an overview of some of the types of computational algorithms that we develop in subsequent chapters.

1.1 GRAPHS AND FLOWS

In this section, we introduce some of the basic definitions relating to graphs, paths, flows, and other related notions. Graph concepts are fairly intuitive, and can be understood in terms of suggestive figures, but often involve hidden subtleties. Thus the reader may wish to revisit the present section and pay close attention to some of the fine points of the definitions.

A *directed graph*, $\mathcal{G} = (\mathcal{N}, \mathcal{A})$, consists of a set $\mathcal{N}$ of *nodes* and a set $\mathcal{A}$ of pairs of distinct nodes from $\mathcal{N}$ called *arcs*. The numbers of nodes and arcs are denoted by N and A, respectively, and it is assumed throughout that $1 \leq N < \infty$ and $0 \leq A < \infty$. An arc (i, j) is viewed as an ordered pair, and is to be distinguished from the pair (j, i). If (i, j) is an arc, we say that (i, j) is *outgoing* from node i and *incoming* to node j; we also say that j is an *outward neighbor* of i and that i is an *inward neighbor* of j. We say that arc (i, j) is *incident* to i and to j, and that i is the *start* node and j is the *end* node of the arc. We also say that i and j are the *end nodes* of arc (i, j). The *degree* of a node i is the number of arcs that are incident to i. A graph is said to be *complete* if it contains all possible arcs; that is, if there exists an arc for each ordered pair of nodes.

We do not exclude the possibility that there is a separate arc connecting a pair of nodes in each of the two directions. However, we do not allow more than one arc between a pair of nodes in the same direction, so that we can refer unambiguously to the arc with start i and end j as arc (i, j). This is done for notational convenience.† Our analysis can be simply extended to handle multiple arcs with start i and end j; the extension is based on modifying the graph by introducing for each such arc, an additional node, call it n, together with the two arcs (i, n) and (n, j). On occasion, we will pause to provide examples of this type of extension.

We note that much of the literature of graph theory distinguishes between *directed* graphs where an arc (i, j) is an ordered pair to be distinguished from arc (j, i), and *undirected* graphs where an arc is associated with a pair of nodes regardless of order. One may use directed graphs, even in contexts where the use of undirected graphs would be appropriate and conceptually simpler. For this, one may need to replace an undirected arc (i, j) with two directed arcs (i, j) and (j, i) having identical characteristics.

---

† Some authors use a single symbol, such as a, to denote an arc, and use something like $s(a)$ and $e(a)$ to denote the start and end nodes of a, respectively. This notational method allows the existence of multiple arcs with the same start and end nodes, but is also more cumbersome and less suggestive.

We have chosen to deal exclusively with directed graphs because in our
development there are only a few occasions where undirected graphs are
convenient. Thus, *all our references to a graph implicitly assume that the
graph is directed*. In fact we often omit the qualifier "directed" and refer
to a directed graph simply as a *graph*.

1.1.1   Paths and Cycles

A *path* P in a directed graph is a sequence of nodes $(n_1, n_2, \ldots, n_k)$ with
$k \geq 2$ and a corresponding sequence of $k-1$ arcs such that the ith arc in the
sequence is either (n_i, n_{i+1}) (in which case it is called a *forward* arc of the
path) or (n_{i+1}, n_i) (in which case it is called a *backward* arc of the path).
Nodes n_1 and n_k are called the *start node* (or *origin*) and the *end node* (or
destination) of P, respectively. A path is said to be *forward* (or *backward*)
if all of its arcs are forward (respectively, backward) arcs. We denote by
P^+ and P^- the sets of forward and backward arcs of P, respectively.

   A *cycle* is a path for which the start and end nodes are the same. A
path is said to be *simple* if it contains no repeated arcs and no repeated
nodes, except that the start and end nodes could be the same (in which
case the path is called a *simple cycle*). A *Hamiltonian cycle* is a simple
forward cycle that contains all the nodes of the graph. These definitions
are illustrated in Fig. 1.1. We mention that some authors use a slightly
different terminology: they use the term "walk" to refer to a path and they
use the term "path" to refer to a simple path.

   Note that the sequence of nodes $(n_1, n_2, \ldots, n_k)$ is not sufficient to
specify a path; the sequence of arcs may also be important, as Fig. 1.1(c)
shows. The difficulty arises when for two successive nodes n_i and n_{i+1} of
the path, both (n_i, n_{i+1}) and (n_{i+1}, n_i) are arcs, so there is ambiguity as
to which of the two is the corresponding arc of the path. If a path is known
to be forward or is known to be backward, it is uniquely specified by the
sequence of its nodes. Otherwise, however, the intended sequence of arcs
must be explicitly defined.

   A graph that contains no simple cycles is said to be *acyclic*. A graph
is said to be *connected* if for each pair of nodes i and j, there is a path
starting at i and ending at j; it is said to be *strongly connected* if for each
pair of nodes i and j, there is a forward path starting at i and ending
at j. Thus, for example, the graph of Fig. 1.1(b) is connected but not
strongly connected. It can be shown that if a graph is connected and each
of its nodes has even degree, there is a cycle (not necessarily forward) that
contains all the arcs of the graph exactly once (see Exercise 1.5). Such
a cycle is called an *Euler cycle*, honoring the historically important work
of Euler; see the discussion in Section 10.1 about the Königsberg bridge
problem. Figure 1.2 gives an example of an Euler cycle.

   We say that a graph $\mathcal{G}' = (\mathcal{N}', \mathcal{A}')$ is a *subgraph* of a graph $\mathcal{G} = (\mathcal{N}, \mathcal{A})$
if $\mathcal{N}' \subset \mathcal{N}$ and $\mathcal{A}' \subset \mathcal{A}$. A *tree* is a connected acyclic graph. A *spanning*

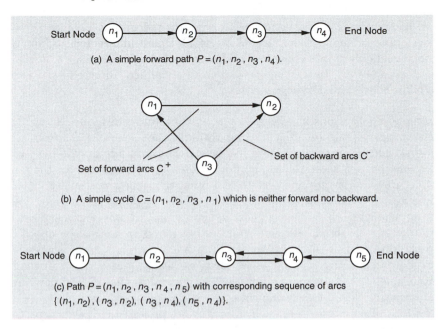

Start Node n_1 $\longrightarrow$ n_2 $\longrightarrow$ n_3 $\longrightarrow$ n_4 End Node

(a) A simple forward path $P = (n_1, n_2, n_3, n_4)$.

Set of forward arcs C^+

Set of backward arcs C^-

(b) A simple cycle $C = (n_1, n_2, n_3, n_1)$ which is neither forward nor backward.

Start Node n_1 $\longrightarrow$ n_2 $\longrightarrow$ n_3 $\longleftarrow$ n_4 $\longleftarrow$ n_5 End Node

(c) Path $P = (n_1, n_2, n_3, n_4, n_5)$ with corresponding sequence of arcs
$\{(n_1, n_2), (n_3, n_2), (n_3, n_4), (n_5, n_4)\}$.

Figure 1.1: Illustration of various types of paths and cycles. The cycle in (b) is not a Hamiltonian cycle; it is simple and contains all the nodes of the graph, but it is not forward. Note that for the path (c), in order to resolve ambiguities, it is necessary to specify the sequence of arcs of the path (rather than just the sequence of nodes) because both (n_3, n_4) and (n_4, n_3) are arcs.

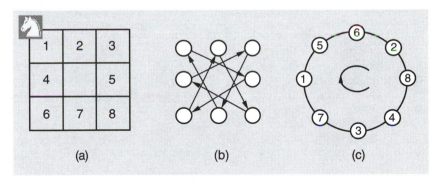

(a)   (b)   (c)

Figure 1.2: Example of an Euler cycle. Consider a 3×3 chessboard, where the middle square has been deleted. A knight starting at one of the squares of the board can visit every other square exactly once and return to the starting square as shown in the graph (b), or equivalently in (c). In the process, the knight will make all the possible moves (in one direction only), or equivalently, it will cross every arc of the graph in (b) exactly once. The knight's tour is an Euler cycle for the graph of (b).

tree of a graph $\mathcal{G}$ is a subgraph of $\mathcal{G}$, which is a tree and includes all the nodes of $\mathcal{G}$. It can be shown [Exercise 1.14(c)] that a subgraph is a spanning tree if and only if it is connected and it contains $N - 1$ arcs.

1.1.2   Flow and Divergence

In many applications involving graphs, it is useful to introduce a variable that measures the quantity flowing through each arc, like for example, electric current in an electric circuit, or water flow in a hydraulic network. We refer to such a variable as the *flow of an arc*. Mathematically, the flow of an arc (i, j) is simply a scalar (real number), which we usually denote by x_{ij}. It is convenient to allow negative as well as positive values for flow. In applications, a negative arc flow indicates that whatever is represented by the flow (material, electric current, etc.), moves in a direction opposite to the direction of the arc. We can always change the sign of a negative arc flow to positive as long as we change the arc direction, so in many situations we can assume without loss of generality that all arc flows are nonnegative. For the development of a general methodology, however, this device is often cumbersome, which is why we prefer to simply accept the possibility of negative arc flows.

Given a graph $(\mathcal{N}, \mathcal{A})$, a set of flows $\{x_{ij} \mid (i, j) \in \mathcal{A}\}$ is referred to as a *flow vector*. The *divergence vector* y associated with a flow vector x is the N-dimensional vector with coordinates

$$y_i = \sum_{\{j \mid (i,j) \in \mathcal{A}\}} x_{ij} - \sum_{\{j \mid (j,i) \in \mathcal{A}\}} x_{ji}, \qquad \forall \, i \in \mathcal{N}. \tag{1.1}$$

Thus, y_i is the total flow departing from node i less the total flow arriving at i; it is referred to as the *divergence of i*.

We say that node i is a *source* (respectively, *sink*) for the flow vector x if $y_i > 0$ (respectively, $y_i < 0$). If $y_i = 0$ for all $i \in \mathcal{N}$, then x is called a *circulation*. These definitions are illustrated in Fig. 1.3. Note that by adding Eq. (1.1) over all $i \in \mathcal{N}$, we obtain

$$\sum_{i \in \mathcal{N}} y_i = 0.$$

Every divergence vector y must satisfy this equation.

The flow vectors x that we will consider will often be constrained to lie between given lower and upper bounds of the form

$$b_{ij} \le x_{ij} \le c_{ij}, \qquad \forall \, (i, j) \in \mathcal{A}.$$

Given a flow vector x that satisfies these bounds, we say that a path P is *unblocked with respect to x* if, roughly speaking, we can send some positive flow along P without violating the bound constraints; that is, if flow can

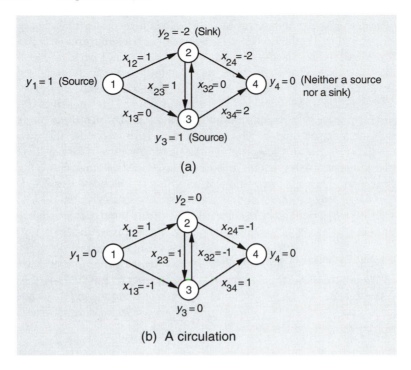

Figure 1.3: Illustration of flows x_{ij} and the corresponding divergences y_i. The flow in (b) is a circulation because $y_i = 0$ for all i.

be increased on the set P^+ of the forward arcs of P, and can be decreased on the set P^- of the backward arcs of P:

$$x_{ij} < c_{ij}, \quad \forall\, (i,j) \in P^+, \qquad b_{ij} < x_{ij}, \quad \forall\, (i,j) \in P^-.$$

For example, in Fig. 1.3(a), suppose that all arcs (i,j) have flow bounds $b_{ij} = -2$ and $c_{ij} = 2$. Then the path consisting of the sequence of nodes $(1, 2, 4)$ is unblocked, while the reverse path $(4, 2, 1)$ is not unblocked.

1.1.3   Path Flows and Conformal Decomposition

A *simple path flow* is a flow vector that corresponds to sending a positive amount of flow along a simple path; more precisely, it is a flow vector x with components of the form

$$x_{ij} = \begin{cases} a & \text{if } (i,j) \in P^+, \\ -a & \text{if } (i,j) \in P^-, \\ 0 & \text{otherwise,} \end{cases} \tag{1.2}$$

where a is a positive scalar, and P^+ and P^- are the sets of forward and backward arcs, respectively, of some simple path P. Note that the path P may be a cycle, in which case x is also called a *simple cycle flow*.

It is often convenient to break down a flow vector into the sum of simple path flows. This leads to the notion of a conformal realization, which we proceed to discuss.

We say that a path P *conforms* to a flow vector x if $x_{ij} > 0$ for all forward arcs (i, j) of P and $x_{ij} < 0$ for all backward arcs (i, j) of P, and furthermore either P is a cycle or else the start and end nodes of P are a source and a sink of x, respectively. Roughly, a path conforms to a flow vector if it "carries flow in the forward direction," i.e., in the direction from the start node to the end node. In particular, for a forward cycle to conform to a flow vector, all its arcs must have positive flow. For a forward path which is not a cycle to conform to a flow vector, its arcs must have positive flow, and in addition the start and end nodes must be a source and a sink, respectively; for example, in Fig. 1.3(a), the path consisting of the sequence of arcs (1,2), (2,3), (3,4) does not conform to the flow vector shown, because node 4, the end node of the path, is not a sink.

We say that a simple path flow x^s *conforms* to a flow vector x if the path P corresponding to x^s via Eq. (1.2) conforms to x. This is equivalent to requiring that

$$0 < x_{ij} \qquad \text{for all arcs } (i, j) \text{ with } 0 < x_{ij}^s,$$

$$x_{ij} < 0 \qquad \text{for all arcs } (i, j) \text{ with } x_{ij}^s < 0,$$

and that either P is a cycle or else the start and end nodes of P are a source and a sink of x, respectively.

An important fact is that any flow vector can be decomposed into a set of conforming simple path flows, as illustrated in Fig. 1.4. We state this as a proposition. The proof is based on an algorithm that can be used to construct the conforming components one by one (see Exercise 1.2).

Proposition 1.1: (Conformal Realization Theorem) A nonzero flow vector x can be decomposed into the sum of t simple path flow vectors $x^1, x^2, \ldots, x^t$ that conform to x, with t being at most equal to the sum of the numbers of arcs and nodes $A + N$. If x is integer, then $x^1, x^2, \ldots, x^t$ can also be chosen to be integer. If x is a circulation, then $x^1, x^2, \ldots, x^t$ can be chosen to be simple cycle flows, and $t \leq A$.

1.2 NETWORK FLOW MODELS – EXAMPLES

In this section we introduce some of the major classes of problems that will be discussed in this book. We begin with the *minimum cost flow problem*, which, together with its special cases, will be the subject of the following six chapters.

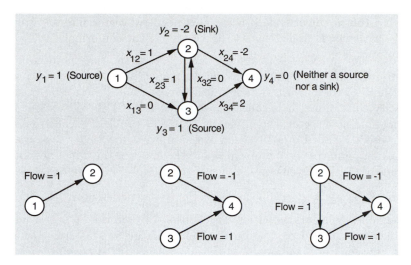

Figure 1.4: Decomposition of a flow vector x into three simple path flows conforming to x. Consistent with the definition of conformance of a path flow, each arc (i, j) of the three component paths carries positive (or negative) flow only if $x_{ij} > 0$ (or $x_{ij} < 0$, respectively). The first two paths [(1, 2) and (3, 4, 2)] are not cycles, but they start at a source and end at a sink, as required. Arcs $(1, 3)$ and $(3, 2)$ do not belong to any of these paths because they carry zero flow. In this example, the decomposition is unique, but in general this need not be the case.

1.2.1 The Minimum Cost Flow Problem

This problem is to find a set of arc flows that minimize a linear cost function, subject to the constraints that they produce a given divergence vector and they lie within some given bounds; that is,

$$\text{minimize} \quad \sum_{(i,j)\in\mathcal{A}} a_{ij}x_{ij} \tag{1.3}$$

subject to the constraints

$$\sum_{\{j|(i,j)\in\mathcal{A}\}} x_{ij} - \sum_{\{j|(j,i)\in\mathcal{A}\}} x_{ji} = s_i, \qquad \forall\, i \in \mathcal{N}, \tag{1.4}$$

$$b_{ij} \leq x_{ij} \leq c_{ij}, \qquad \forall\, (i, j) \in \mathcal{A}, \tag{1.5}$$

where a_{ij}, b_{ij}, c_{ij}, and s_i are given scalars. We use the following terminology:

  a_{ij}: the *cost coefficient* (or simply *cost*) of (i, j),

  b_{ij} and c_{ij}: the *flow bounds* of (i, j),

  $[b_{ij}, c_{ij}]$: the *feasible flow range* of (i, j),

s_i: the *supply* of node i (when s_i is negative, the scalar $-s_i$ is called the *demand* of i).

We also refer to the constraints (1.4) and (1.5) as the *conservation of flow constraints*, and the *capacity constraints*, respectively. A flow vector satisfying both of these constraints is called *feasible*, and if it satisfies just the capacity constraints, it is called *capacity-feasible*. If there exists at least one feasible flow vector, the minimum cost flow problem is called *feasible*; otherwise it is called *infeasible*. On occasion, we will consider the variation of the minimum cost flow problem where the lower or the upper flow bound of some of the arcs is either $-\infty$ or ∞, respectively. In these cases, we will explicitly state so.

For a typical application of the minimum cost flow problem, think of the nodes as locations (cities, warehouses, or factories) where a certain product is produced or consumed. Think of the arcs as transportation links between the locations, each with transportation cost a_{ij} per unit transported. The problem then is to move the product from the production points to the consumption points at minimum cost while observing the capacity constraints of the transportation links.

However, the minimum cost flow problem has many applications that are well beyond the transportation context just described, as will be seen from the following examples. These examples illustrate how some important discrete/combinatorial problems can be modeled as minimum cost flow problems, and highlight the important connection between continuous and discrete network optimization.

Example 1.1. The Shortest Path Problem

Suppose that each arc (i, j) of a graph is assigned a scalar cost a_{ij}, and suppose that we define the cost of a forward path to be the sum of the costs of its arcs. Given a pair of nodes, the shortest path problem is to find a forward path that connects these nodes and has minimum cost. An analogy here is made between arcs and their costs, and roads in a transportation network and their lengths, respectively. Within this transportation context, the problem becomes one of finding the shortest route between two geographical points. Based on this analogy, the problem is referred to as the *shortest path problem*, and the arc costs and path costs are commonly referred to as the *arc lengths* and *path lengths*, respectively.

The shortest path problem arises in a surprisingly large number of contexts. For example in a data communication network, a_{ij} may denote the average delay of a packet to cross the communication link (i, j), in which case a shortest path is a minimum average delay path that can be used for routing the packet from its origin to its destination. As another example, if p_{ij} is the probability that a given arc (i, j) in a communication network is usable, and each arc is usable independently of all other arcs, then the product of the probabilities of the arcs of a path provides a measure of reliability of the path. With this in mind, it is seen that finding the most reliable path connecting two nodes is equivalent to finding the shortest path between the two nodes with arc lengths $(-\ln p_{ij})$.

The shortest path problem also arises often as a subroutine in algorithms that solve other more complicated problems. Examples are the primal-dual algorithm for solving the minimum cost flow problem (see Chapter 6), and the conditional gradient and projection algorithms for solving multicommodity flow problems (see Chapter 8).

It is possible to cast the problem of finding a shortest path from node s to node t as the following minimum cost flow problem:

$$
\begin{aligned}
\text{minimize} \quad & \sum_{(i,j)\in\mathcal{A}} a_{ij}x_{ij} \\
\text{subject to} \quad & \sum_{\{j|(i,j)\in\mathcal{A}\}} x_{ij} - \sum_{\{j|(j,i)\in\mathcal{A}\}} x_{ji} = \begin{cases} 1 & \text{if } i = s, \\ -1 & \text{if } i = t, \\ 0 & \text{otherwise}, \end{cases} \\
& 0 \le x_{ij}, \quad \forall\, (i,j) \in \mathcal{A}.
\end{aligned}
\tag{1.6}
$$

To see this, let us associate with any forward path P from s to t the flow vector x with components given by

$$
x_{ij} = \begin{cases} 1 & \text{if } (i,j) \text{ belongs to } P, \\ 0 & \text{otherwise.} \end{cases}
\tag{1.7}
$$

Then x is feasible for problem (1.6) and the cost of x is equal to the length of P. Thus, if a vector x of the form (1.7) is an optimal solution of problem (1.6), the corresponding path P is shortest.

Conversely, it can be shown that if problem (1.6) has at least one optimal solution, then it has an optimal solution of the form (1.7), with a corresponding path P that is shortest. This is not immediately apparent, but its proof can be traced to a remarkable fact that we will show in Chapter 5 about minimum cost flow problems with node supplies and arc flow bounds that are integer: such problems, if they have an optimal solution, they have an *integer* optimal solution, that is, a set of optimal arc flows that are integer (an alternative proof of this fact is sketched in Exercise 1.34). From this it follows that if problem (1.6) has an optimal solution, it has one with arc flows that are 0 or 1, and which is of the form (1.7) for some path P. This path is shortest because its length is equal to the optimal cost of problem (1.6), so it must be less or equal to the cost of any other flow vector of the form (1.7), and therefore also less or equal to the length of any other path from s to t. Thus the shortest path problem is essentially equivalent with the minimum cost flow problem (1.6).

Example 1.2. The Assignment Problem

Suppose that there are n persons and n objects that we have to match on a one-to-one basis. There is a benefit or value a_{ij} for matching person i with object j, and we want to assign persons to objects so as to maximize the total

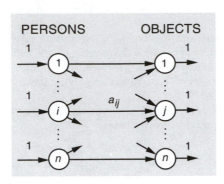

Figure 1.5: The graph representation of an assignment problem.

benefit. There is also a restriction that person i can be assigned to object j
only if (i,j) belongs to a given set of pairs $\mathcal{A}$. Mathematically, we want to find
a set of person-object pairs $(1,j_1),\ldots,(n,j_n)$ from $\mathcal{A}$ such that the objects
$j_1,\ldots,j_n$ are all distinct, and the total benefit $\sum_{i=1}^{n} a_{ij_i}$ is maximized.

The assignment problem is important in many practical contexts. The
most obvious ones are resource allocation problems, such as assigning em-
ployees to jobs, machines to tasks, etc. There are also situations where the
assignment problem appears as a subproblem in methods for solving various
complex combinatorial problems (see Chapter 10).

We may associate any assignment with the set of variables $\{x_{ij} \mid (i,j) \in \mathcal{A}\}$, where $x_{ij} = 1$ if person i is assigned to object j and $x_{ij} = 0$ otherwise.
The value of this assignment is $\sum_{(i,j)\in\mathcal{A}} a_{ij}x_{ij}$. The restriction of one object
per person can be stated as $\sum_{j} x_{ij} = 1$ for all i and $\sum_{i} x_{ij} = 1$ for all j. We
may then formulate the assignment problem as the linear program

$$
\begin{aligned}
\text{maximize} \quad & \sum_{(i,j)\in\mathcal{A}} a_{ij}x_{ij} \\
\text{subject to} \quad & \sum_{\{j|(i,j)\in\mathcal{A}\}} x_{ij} = 1, \qquad \forall\, i = 1,\ldots,n, \\
& \sum_{\{i|(i,j)\in\mathcal{A}\}} x_{ij} = 1, \qquad \forall\, j = 1,\ldots,n, \\
& 0 \le x_{ij} \le 1, \qquad \forall\, (i,j) \in \mathcal{A}.
\end{aligned}
\tag{1.8}
$$

Actually we should further restrict x_{ij} to be either 0 or 1. However, as we
will show in Chapter 5, the above linear program has the property that if it
has a feasible solution at all, then it has an optimal solution where all x_{ij}
are either 0 or 1 (compare also with the discussion in the preceding example
and Exercise 1.34). In fact, the set of its optimal solutions includes all the
optimal assignments.

We now argue that the assignment/linear program (1.8) is a minimum
cost flow problem involving the graph shown in Fig. 1.5. Here, there are
$2n$ nodes divided into two groups: n corresponding to persons and n corresponding to objects. Also, for every possible pair $(i,j) \in \mathcal{A}$, there is an arc
connecting person i with object j. The variable x_{ij} is the flow of arc (i,j).

The constraint

$$\sum_{\{j|(i,j)\in\mathcal{A}\}} x_{ij} = 1$$

indicates that the divergence of person/node i should be equal to 1, while the constraint

$$\sum_{\{i|(i,j)\in\mathcal{A}\}} x_{ij} = 1$$

indicates that the divergence of object/node j should be equal to -1. Finally, we may view $(-a_{ij})$ as the cost coefficient of the arc (i,j) (by reversing the sign of a_{ij}, we convert the problem from a maximization to a minimization problem).

Example 1.3. The Max-Flow Problem

In the max-flow problem, we have a graph with two special nodes: the *source*, denoted by s, and the *sink*, denoted by t. Roughly, the objective is to move as much flow as possible from s into t while observing the capacity constraints. More precisely, we want to find a flow vector that makes the divergence of all nodes other than s and t equal to 0 while maximizing the divergence of s.

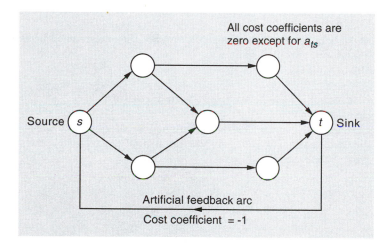

Figure 1.6: The minimum cost flow representation of a max-flow problem. At the optimum, the flow x_{ts} equals the maximum flow that can be sent from s to t through the subgraph obtained by deleting the artificial arc (t,s).

The max-flow problem arises in many practical contexts, such as calculating the throughput of a highway system or a communication network. It also arises often as a subproblem in more complicated problems or algorithms; in particular, it bears a fundamental connection to the question of existence of a feasible solution of a general minimum cost flow problem (see our discussion in Chapter 3). Finally, several discrete/combinatorial optimization problems can be formulated as max-flow problems (see the Exercises in Chapter 3).

We formulate the problem as a special case of the minimum cost flow problem by assigning cost 0 to all arcs and by introducing an artificial arc (t, s) with cost -1, as shown in Fig. 1.6. Mathematically, the problem is:

maximize x_{ts}

subject to

$$\sum_{\{j|(i,j)\in\mathcal{A}\}} x_{ij} - \sum_{\{j|(j,i)\in\mathcal{A}\}} x_{ji} = 0, \qquad \forall\ i \in \mathcal{N} \text{ with } i \neq s \text{ and } i \neq t,$$

$$\sum_{\{j|(s,j)\in\mathcal{A}\}} x_{sj} = \sum_{\{i|(i,t)\in\mathcal{A}\}} x_{it} = x_{ts},$$

$$b_{ij} \leq x_{ij} \leq c_{ij}, \qquad \forall\ (i,j) \in \mathcal{A} \text{ with } (i,j) \neq (t,s).$$

Viewing the problem as a maximization is consistent with its intuitive interpretation. Alternatively, we could write the problem as a minimization of $-x_{ts}$ subject to the same constraints. Also, we could introduce upper and lower bounds on x_{ts},

$$\sum_{\{i|(i,t)\in\mathcal{A}\}} b_{it} \leq x_{ts} \leq \sum_{\{i|(i,t)\in\mathcal{A}\}} c_{it},$$

but these bounds are actually redundant since they are implied by the other upper and lower arc flow bounds.

Example 1.4. The Transportation Problem

This problem is the same as the assignment problem except that the node supplies need not be 1 or -1, and the numbers of sources and sinks need not be equal. It has the form

$$
\begin{aligned}
\text{minimize} \quad & \sum_{(i,j)\in\mathcal{A}} a_{ij} x_{ij} \\
\text{subject to} \quad & \sum_{\{j|(i,j)\in\mathcal{A}\}} x_{ij} = \alpha_i, \qquad \forall\ i = 1, \ldots, m, \\
& \sum_{\{i|(i,j)\in\mathcal{A}\}} x_{ij} = \beta_j, \qquad \forall\ j = 1, \ldots, n, \\
& 0 \leq x_{ij} \leq \min\{\alpha_i, \beta_j\}, \qquad \forall\ (i,j) \in \mathcal{A}.
\end{aligned}
\tag{1.9}
$$

Here α_i and β_j are positive scalars, which for feasibility must satisfy

$$\sum_{i=1}^{m} \alpha_i = \sum_{j=1}^{n} \beta_j,$$

(add the conservation of flow constraints). In an alternative formulation, the upper bound constraint $x_{ij} \leq \min\{\alpha_i, \beta_j\}$ could be discarded, since it is implied by the conservation of flow and the nonnegativity constraints.

As a practical example of a transportation problem that has a combinatorial flavor, suppose that we have m communication terminals, each to be connected to one of n traffic concentrators. We introduce variables x_{ij}, which take the value 1 if terminal i is connected to concentrator j. Assuming that concentrator j can be connected to no more than b_j terminals, we obtain the constraints

$$\sum_{i=1}^{m} x_{ij} \leq b_j, \qquad \forall\, j = 1, \dots, n.$$

Also, since each terminal must be connected to exactly one concentrator, we have the constraints

$$\sum_{j=1}^{n} x_{ij} = 1, \qquad \forall\, i = 1, \dots, m.$$

Assuming that there is a cost a_{ij} for connecting terminal i to concentrator j, the problem is to find the connection of minimum cost, that is, to minimize

$$\sum_{i=1}^{m} \sum_{j=1}^{n} a_{ij} x_{ij}$$

subject to the preceding constraints. This problem is not yet a transportation problem of the form (1.9) for two reasons:

(a) The arc flows x_{ij} are constrained to be 0 or 1.

(b) The constraints $\sum_{i=1}^{m} x_{ij} \leq b_j$ are not equality constraints, as required in problem (1.9).

It turns out, however, that we can ignore the 0-1 constraint on x_{ij}. As discussed in connection with the shortest path and assignment problems, even if we relax this constraint and replace it with the capacity constraint $0 \leq x_{ij} \leq 1$, there is an optimal solution such that each x_{ij} is either 0 or 1. Furthermore, to convert the inequality constraints to equalities, we can introduce a total of $\sum_{j=1}^{n} b_j - m$ "dummy" terminals that can be connected at zero cost to all of the concentrators. In particular, we introduce a special supply node 0 together with the constraint

$$\sum_{j=1}^{n} x_{0j} = \sum_{j=1}^{n} b_j - m,$$

and we change the inequality constraints $\sum_{j=1}^{n} x_{ij} \leq b_j$ to

$$x_{0j} + \sum_{i=1}^{m} x_{ij} = b_j.$$

The resulting problem has the transportation structure of problem (1.9), and is equivalent to the original problem.

1.2.2   Network Flow Problems with Convex Cost

A more general version of the minimum cost flow problem arises when the cost function is convex rather than linear. An important special case is the problem

$$\text{minimize} \quad \sum_{(i,j)\in\mathcal{A}} f_{ij}(x_{ij})$$

$$\text{subject to} \quad \sum_{\{j|(i,j)\in\mathcal{A}\}} x_{ij} - \sum_{\{j|(j,i)\in\mathcal{A}\}} x_{ji} = s_i, \qquad \forall\, i \in \mathcal{N},$$

$$x_{ij} \in X_{ij}, \qquad \forall\, (i,j) \in \mathcal{A},$$

where f_{ij} is a convex function of the flow x_{ij} of arc (i,j), s_i are given scalars, and X_{ij} are convex intervals of real numbers, such as for example

$$X_{ij} = [b_{ij}, c_{ij}],$$

where b_{ij} and c_{ij} are given scalars. We refer to this as the *separable convex cost network flow problem*, because the cost function separates into the sum of cost functions, one per arc. This problem will be discussed in detail in Chapters 8 and 9.

Example 1.5.   The Matrix Balancing Problem

Here the problem is to find an $m \times n$ matrix X that has given row sums and column sums, and approximates a given $m \times n$ matrix M in some optimal manner. We can formulate such a problem in terms of a graph consisting of m sources and n sinks. In this graph, the set of arcs consists of the pairs (i,j) for which the corresponding entry x_{ij} of the matrix X is allowed to be nonzero. The given row sums r_i and the given column sums c_j are expressed as the constraints

$$\sum_{\{j|(i,j)\in A\}} x_{ij} = r_i, \qquad i = 1,\ldots,m,$$

$$\sum_{\{i|(i,j)\in A\}} x_{ij} = c_j, \qquad j = 1,\ldots,n.$$

There may be also bounds for the entries x_{ij} of X. Thus, the structure of this problem is similar to the structure of a transportation problem. The cost function to be optimized has the form

$$\sum_{(i,j)\in A} f_{ij}(x_{ij}),$$

and expresses the objective of making the entries of X close to the corresponding entries of the given matrix M. A commonly used example is the quadratic function

$$f_{ij}(x_{ij}) = \sum_{(i,j)\in A} w_{ij}(x_{ij} - m_{ij})^2,$$

where w_{ij} are given positive scalars.

Another interesting cost function is the logarithmic

$$f_{ij}(x_{ij}) = x_{ij}\left[\ln\left(\frac{x_{ij}}{m_{ij}}\right) - 1\right],$$

where we assume that $m_{ij} > 0$ for all $(i,j) \in A$. Note that this function is not defined for $x_{ij} \le 0$, so to obtain a problem that fits our framework, we must use a constraint interval of the form $X_{ij} = (0, \infty)$ or $X_{ij} = (0, c_{ij}]$, where c_{ij} is a positive scalar.

An example of a practical problem that can be addressed using the preceding optimization model is to predict the distribution matrix X of telephone traffic between m origins and n destinations. Here we are given the total supplies r_i of the origins and the total demands c_j of the destinations, and we are also given some matrix M that defines a nominal traffic pattern obtained from historical data.

There are other types of network flow problems with convex cost that often arise in practice. We generically represent such problems in the form

$$\text{minimize}\ \ f(x)$$
$$\text{subject to}\ \ x \in F$$

where F is a convex subset of flow vectors in a graph and f is a convex function over the set F. We will discuss in some detail various classes of problems of this type in Chapter 8, and we will see that they arise in several different ways; for example, the cost function may be *nonseparable* because of coupling of the costs of several arc flows, and/or there may be *side constraints*, whereby the flows of several arcs are jointly restricted by the availability of resource. An important example is multicommodity flow problems, which we discuss next.

1.2.3   Multicommodity Flow Problems

Multicommodity network flow problems involve several flow "types" or *commodities*, which simultaneously use the network and are coupled through either the arc flow bounds, or through the cost function. Important examples of such problems arise in communication, transportation, and manufacturing networks. For example, in communication networks the commodities are the streams of different classes of traffic (telephone, data,

video, etc.) that involve different origin-destination pairs. Thus there is
a separate commodity per class of traffic and origin-destination pair. The
following example introduces this context. In Chapter 8, we will discuss
similar and/or more general multicommodity network flow problems that
arise in other practical contexts.

Example 1.6. Routing in Data Networks

We are given a directed graph, which is viewed as a model of a data communication network. We are also given a set of ordered node pairs (i_m, j_m),
$m = 1, \ldots, M$, referred to as *origin-destination (OD) pairs*. The nodes i_m
and j_m are referred to as the *origin* and the *destination* of the OD pair. For
each OD pair (i_m, j_m), we are given a scalar r_m that represents its input
traffic. In the context of routing of data in a communication network, r_m
(measured for example in bits/second) is the arrival rate of traffic entering
the network at node i_m and exiting at node j_m. The routing objective is to
divide each r_m among the many paths from the origin i_m to the destination
j_m in a way that the resulting total arc flow pattern minimizes a suitable cost
function (see Fig. 1.7).

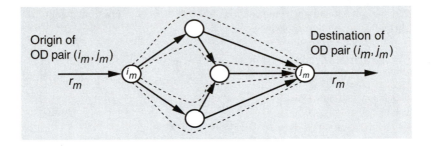

Figure 1.7: Illustration of how the input r_m of the OD pair (i_m, j_m) is
divided into nonnegative path flows that start at i_m and end at j_m. The
flows of the different OD pairs interact by sharing the arcs of the network.

If we denote by $x_{ij}(m)$ the flow on arc (i, j) of OD pair (i_m, j_m), we
have the conservation of flow constraints

$$\sum_{\{j | (i,j) \in \mathcal{A}\}} x_{ij}(m) - \sum_{\{j | (j,i) \in \mathcal{A}\}} x_{ji}(m) = \begin{cases} r_m & \text{if } i = i_m, \\ -r_m & \text{if } i = j_m, \\ 0 & \text{otherwise}, \end{cases} \quad \forall \, i \in \mathcal{N},$$

for each $m = 1, \ldots, M$. Furthermore, the flows $x_{ij}(m)$ are required to be
nonnegative, and possibly to satisfy additional constraints, such as upper
bounds. The cost function often has the form

$$f(x) = \sum_{(i,j) \in \mathcal{A}} f_{ij}(y_{ij}),$$

where f_{ij} is a function of the *total flow* of arc (i, j)

$$y_{ij} = \sum_{m=1}^{M} x_{ij}(m).$$

Such a cost function is often based on a queueing model of average delay (see for example the data network textbook by Bertsekas and Gallager [1992]).

1.2.4   Discrete Network Optimization Problems

Many linear or convex network flow problems, in addition to the conservation of flow constraints and arc flow bounds, involve some additional constraints. In particular, there may be constraints that couple the flows of different arcs, and there may also be *integer constraints* on the arc flows, such as for example that each arc flow be either 0 or 1. Several famous combinatorial optimization problems, such as the following one, are of this type.

Example 1.7. The Traveling Salesman Problem

This problem refers to a salesman who wants to find a minimum mileage/cost tour that visits each of N given cities exactly once and returns to the city he started from. To convert this to a network flow problem, we associate a node with each city $i = 1, \ldots, N$, and we introduce an arc (i, j) with traversal cost a_{ij} for each ordered pair of nodes i and j. A *tour* is synonymous to a Hamiltonian cycle, which was earlier defined to be a simple forward cycle that contains all the nodes of the graph. Equivalently, a tour is a connected subgraph that consists of N arcs, such that there is exactly one incoming and one outgoing arc for each node $i = 1, \ldots, N$. The problem is to find a tour with minimum sum of arc costs.

To formulate this problem as a network flow problem, we denote by x_{ij} the flow of arc (i, j) and we require that this flow is either 1 or 0, indicating that the arc is or is not part of the tour, respectively. The cost of a tour T is then

$$\sum_{(i,j)\in T} a_{ij} x_{ij}.$$

The constraint that each node has a single incoming and a single outgoing arc on the tour is expressed by the following two conservation of flow equations:

$$\sum_{\substack{j=1,\ldots,N \\ j \neq i}} x_{ij} = 1, \qquad i = 1, \ldots, N,$$

$$\sum_{\substack{i=1,\ldots,N \\ i \neq j}} x_{ij} = 1, \qquad j = 1, \ldots, N.$$

There is one additional connectivity constraint:

the subgraph with node set $\mathcal{N}$ and arc set $\{(i,j) \mid x_{ij} = 1\}$ is connected.

If this constraint was not present, the problem would be an ordinary assignment problem. Unfortunately, this constraint is essential, since without it, there would be feasible solutions involving multiple disconnected cycles.

Despite the similarity, the traveling salesman problem is far more difficult than the assignment problem. Solving problems having a mere few hundreds of nodes can be very challenging. By contrast, assignment problems with hundreds of thousands of nodes can be solved in reasonable time with the presently available methodology.

Actually, we have already described some discrete/combinatorial problems that fall within the framework of the minimum cost flow problem, such as shortest path and assignment (cf. Examples 1.1 and 1.2). These problems require that the arc flows be 0 or 1, but, as mentioned earlier, we can neglect these 0-1 constraints because it turns out that even if we relax them and replace them with flow bound intervals $[0, 1]$, we can obtain optimal flows that are 0 or 1 (for a proof, see Section 5.2 or Exercise 1.34).

On the other hand, once we deviate from the minimum cost flow structure and we impose additional constraints or use a nonlinear cost function, the integer character of optimal solutions is lost, and all integer constraints must be explicitly imposed. This often complicates dramatically the solution process, and in fact it may be practically impossible to obtain an exactly optimal solution. As we will discuss in Chapter 10, there are several approximate solution approaches that are based on simplified versions of the problem, such as relaxing the integer constraints. These simplified problems can often be addressed with the efficient minimum cost flow algorithms that we will develop in Chapters 2-7.

1.3 NETWORK FLOW ALGORITHMS – AN OVERVIEW

This section, which may be skipped without loss of continuity, provides a broad classification of the various classes of algorithms for linear and convex network optimization problems. It turns out that these algorithms rely on just a few basic ideas, so they can be easily grouped in a few major categories. By contrast, there is a much larger variety of algorithmic ideas for discrete optimization problems. For this reason, we postpone the corresponding discussion for Chapter 10.

Network optimization problems typically cannot be solved analytically. Usually they must be addressed computationally with one of several available algorithms. One possibility, for linear and convex problems, is to use a general purpose linear or nonlinear programming algorithm. However, the network structure can be exploited to speed up the solution by using either an adaptation of a general purpose algorithm such as the simplex method, or by using a specialized network optimization algorithm. In practice, network optimization problems can often be solved hundreds and even thousands of times faster than general linear or convex programs of comparable dimension.

The algorithms for linear and convex network problems that we will discuss in this book can be grouped in three main categories:

(a) *Primal cost improvement.* Here we try to iteratively improve the cost to its optimal value by constructing a corresponding sequence of feasible flows.

(b) *Dual cost improvement.* Here we define a problem related to the original network flow problem, called the *dual problem*, whose variables are called *prices*. We then try to iteratively improve the dual cost to its optimal value by constructing a corresponding sequence of prices. Dual cost improvement algorithms also iterate on flows, which are related to the prices through a property called *complementary slackness*.

(c) *Auction.* Here we generate a sequence of prices in a way that is reminiscent of real-life auctions. Strictly speaking, there is no primal or dual cost improvement here, although we will show that auction can be viewed as an approximate dual cost improvement process. In addition to prices, auction algorithms also iterate on flows, which are related to prices through a property called ϵ-*complementary slackness*; this is an approximate form of the complementary slackness property mentioned above.

All of the preceding types of algorithms can be used to solve both linear and convex network problems (although the structure of the given problem may favor significantly the use of some types of methods over others). For simplicity, in this chapter we will explain these ideas primarily through the assignment problem, deferring a more detailed development to subsequent chapters. Our illustrations, however, are relevant to the general minimum cost flow problem and to its convex cost extensions. Some of our explanations are informal. Precise statements of algorithms and results will be given in subsequent chapters.

1.3.1   Primal Cost Improvement

Primal cost improvement algorithms for the minimum cost flow problem start from an initial feasible flow vector and then generate a sequence of feasible flow vectors, each having a better cost than the preceding one. Let us derive an important characterization of the differences between successive vectors, which is the basis for algorithms as well as for optimality conditions.

Let x and $\overline{x}$ be two feasible flow vectors, and consider their difference $z = \overline{x} - x$. This difference must be a circulation with components

$$z_{ij} = \overline{x}_{ij} - x_{ij},$$

since both x and $\overline{x}$ are feasible. Furthermore, if the cost of $\overline{x}$ is smaller than the cost of x, the circulation z must have negative cost, i.e.,

$$\sum_{(i,j)\in\mathcal{A}} a_{ij} z_{ij} < 0.$$

We can decompose z into the sum of simple cycle flows by using the conformal realization theorem (Prop. 1.1). In particular, for some positive integer K, we have

$$z = \sum_{k=1}^{K} w^k \xi^k,$$

where w^k are positive scalars, and ξ^k are simple cycle flows whose nonzero components ξ_{ij}^k are 1 or -1, depending on whether $z_{ij} > 0$ or $z_{ij} < 0$, respectively. It is seen that the cost of z is

$$\sum_{(i,j)\in\mathcal{A}} a_{ij} z_{ij} = \sum_{k=1}^{K} w^k c^k,$$

where c^k is the cost of the simple cycle flow ξ^k. Thus, since the scalars w^k are positive, if the cost of z is negative, at least one c^k must be negative. Note that if C_k is the cycle corresponding to ξ^k, we have

$$c^k = \sum_{(i,j)\in\mathcal{A}} a_{ij} \xi_{ij}^k = \sum_{(i,j)\in C_k^+} a_{ij} - \sum_{(i,j)\in C_k^-} a_{ij},$$

where C_k^+ and C_k^- are the sets of forward and backward arcs of the cycle C_k, respectively. We refer to the expression in the right-hand side above as the *cost of the cycle* C_k.

The preceding argument has shown that *if x is feasible but not optimal, and $\overline{x}$ is feasible and has smaller cost than x, then at least one of the cycles corresponding to a conformal decomposition of the circulation $\overline{x} - x$ as above has negative cost*. This is used to prove the following important optimality condition.

Proposition 1.2: Consider the minimum cost flow problem. A flow vector x^* is optimal if and only if x^* is feasible and every simple cycle C that is unblocked with respect to x^* has nonnegative cost; that is,

$$\sum_{(i,j)\in C^+} a_{ij} - \sum_{(i,j)\in C^-} a_{ij} \geq 0.$$

Proof: Let x^* be an optimal flow vector and let C be a simple cycle that is unblocked with respect to x^*. Then there exists an $\epsilon > 0$ such that increasing (decreasing) the flow of arcs of C^+ (of C^-, respectively) by ϵ results in a feasible flow that has cost equal to the cost of x^* plus ϵ times the cost of C. Thus, since x^* is optimal, the cost of C must be nonnegative.

Conversely, suppose, to arrive at a contradiction, that x^* is feasible and has the nonnegative cycle property stated in the proposition, but is not optimal. Let $\overline{x}$ be a feasible flow vector with cost smaller that the one of x^*, and consider a conformal decomposition of the circulation $z = \overline{x} - x^*$. From the discussion preceding the proposition, we see that there is a simple cycle C with negative cost, such that $x_{ij}^* < \overline{x}_{ij}$ for all $(i, j) \in C^+$, and such that $x_{ij}^* > \overline{x}_{ij}$ for all $(i, j) \in C^-$. Since $\overline{x}$ is feasible, we have $b_{ij} \leq \overline{x}_{ij} \leq c_{ij}$ for all (i, j). It follows that $x_{ij}^* < c_{ij}$ for all $(i, j) \in C^+$, and $x_{ij}^* > b_{ij}$ for all $(i, j) \in C^-$, so that C is unblocked with respect to x^*. This contradicts the hypothesis that every simple cycle that is unblocked with respect to x^* has nonnegative cost.   **Q.E.D.**

Most primal cost improvement algorithms (including for example the simplex method, to be discussed in Chapter 5) are based on the preceding proposition. They employ various mechanisms to construct negative cost cycles along which flow is pushed without violating the bound constraints. The idea of improving the cost by pushing flow along a suitable cycle often has an intuitive meaning as we illustrate in the context of the assignment problem.

Example 1.7. Multi-Person Exchanges in Assignment

Consider the $n \times n$ assignment problem (cf. Example 1.2) and suppose that we have a feasible assignment, that is, a set of n pairs (i, j) involving each person i exactly once and each object j exactly once. In order to improve this assignment, we could consider a *two-person exchange*, that is, replacing two pairs (i_1, j_1) and (i_2, j_2) from the assignment with the pairs (i_1, j_2) and (i_2, j_1). The resulting assignment will still be feasible, and it will have a higher value if and only if

$$a_{i_1 j_2} + a_{i_2 j_1} > a_{i_1 j_1} + a_{i_2 j_2}.$$

We note here that, in the context of the minimum cost flow representation of the assignment problem, a two-person exchange can be identified with a cycle involving the four arcs (i_1, j_1), (i_2, j_2), (i_1, j_2), and (i_2, j_1). Furthermore, this cycle is the difference between the assignment before and the assignment after the exchange, while the preceding inequality is equivalent to the cycle having a positive value.

Unfortunately, it may be impossible to improve the current assignment by a two-person exchange, even if the assignment is not optimal; see Fig. 1.8. An improvement, however, is possible by means of a k-*person exchange*, for some $k \geq 2$, where a set of pairs $(i_1, j_1), \ldots, (i_k, j_k)$ from the current assignment is replaced by the pairs $(i_1, j_2), \ldots, (i_{k-1}, j_k), (i_k, j_1)$. To see this,

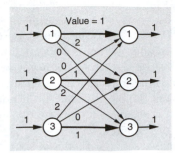

Figure 1.8: An example of a nonoptimal feasible assignment that cannot be improved by a two-person exchange. The value of each pair is shown next to the corresponding arc. Here, the value of the assignment $\{(1,1),(2,2),(3,3)\}$ is left unchanged at 3 by any two-person exchange. Through a three-person exchange, however, we obtain the optimal assignment, $\{(1,2),(2,3),(3,1)\}$, which has value 6.

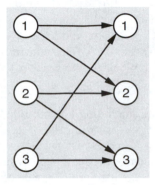

Figure 1.9: Illustration of the correspondence of a k-person exchange to a simple cycle. This is the same example as in the preceding figure. The backward arcs of the cycle are $(1,1)$, $(2,2)$, and $(3,3)$, and correspond to the current assignment pairs. The forward arcs of the cycle are $(1,2)$, $(2,3)$, and $(3,1)$, and correspond to the new assignment pairs. This three-person exchange is value-improving because the sum of the values of the forward arcs $(2+2+2)$ is greater than the sum of the values of the backward arcs $(1+1+1)$.

note that in the context of the minimum cost flow representation of the assignment problem, a k-person exchange corresponds to a simple cycle with k forward arcs (corresponding to the new assignment pairs) and k backward arcs (corresponding to the current assignment pairs that are being replaced); see Fig. 1.9. Thus, performing a k-person exchange is equivalent to pushing one unit of flow along the corresponding simple cycle. The k-person exchange improves the assignment if and only if

$$a_{i_k j_1} + \sum_{m=1}^{k-1} a_{i_m j_{m+1}} - \sum_{m=1}^{k} a_{i_m j_m},$$

which is equivalent to the corresponding cycle having positive value. Furthermore, by Prop. 1.2, a cost improving cycle exists if the flow corresponding to the current assignment is not optimal.

1.3.2   Dual Cost Improvement

Duality theory deals with the relation between the original network optimization problem and another optimization problem called the *dual*. To develop an intuitive understanding of duality, we will focus on an $n \times n$ assignment problem (cf. Example 1.2) and consider a closely related economic equilibrium problem. In particular, let us consider matching the n objects with the n persons through a market mechanism, viewing each person as an economic agent acting in his/her own best interest. Suppose that object j has a price p_j and that the person who receives the object must pay the price p_j. Then the net value of object j for person i is $a_{ij} - p_j$, and each person i will logically want to be assigned to an object j_i with maximal value, that is, with

$$a_{ij_i} - p_{j_i} = \max_{j \in A(i)} \{a_{ij} - p_j\}, \qquad (1.10)$$

where

$$A(i) = \{j \mid (i,j) \in \mathcal{A}\}$$

is the set of objects that can be assigned to person i. When this condition holds for all persons i, we say that the assignment and the price vector $p = (p_1, \ldots, p_n)$ satisfy *complementary slackness* (CS for short); this name is standard in linear programming. The economic system is then at equilibrium, in the sense that no person would have an incentive to unilaterally seek another object. Such equilibrium conditions are naturally of great interest to economists, but there is also a fundamental relation with the assignment problem. We have the following proposition.

Proposition 1.3: If a feasible assignment and a set of prices satisfy the complementary slackness condition (1.10) for all persons i, then the assignment is optimal and the prices are an optimal solution of a dual problem, which is to minimize over $p = (p_1, \ldots, p_n)$ the cost function

$$\sum_{i=1}^{n} q_i(p) + \sum_{j=1}^{n} p_j,$$

where the functions q_i are given by

$$q_i(p) = \max_{j \in A(i)} \{a_{ij} - p_j\}, \qquad i = 1, \ldots, n.$$

Furthermore, the value of the optimal assignment and the optimal cost of the dual problem are equal.

Proof: The total value of any feasible assignment $\{(i, k_i) \mid i = 1, \ldots, n\}$ satisfies

$$\sum_{i=1}^{n} a_{ik_i} \leq \sum_{i=1}^{n} \max_{j \in A(i)} \{a_{ij} - p_j\} + \sum_{j=1}^{n} p_j, \qquad (1.11)$$

for any set of prices $\{p_j \mid j = 1, \ldots, n\}$, since the first term of the right-hand side is no less than

$$\sum_{i=1}^{n} (a_{ik_i} - p_{k_i}),$$

while the second term is equal to $\sum_{i=1}^{n} p_{k_i}$. On the other hand, the given assignment and set of prices, denoted by $\{(i, j_i) \mid i = 1, \ldots, n\}$ and $\{\overline{p}_j \mid j = 1, \ldots, n\}$, respectively, satisfy the CS conditions, so we have

$$a_{ij_i} - \overline{p}_{j_i} = \max_{j \in A(i)} \{a_{ij} - \overline{p}_j\}, \qquad i = 1, \ldots, n.$$

By adding this relation over all i, we have

$$\sum_{i=1}^{n} \left(\max_{j \in A(i)} \{a_{ij} - \overline{p}_j\} + \overline{p}_{j_i} \right) = \sum_{i=1}^{n} a_{ij_i}$$

and by using Eq. (1.11), we obtain

$$\sum_{i=1}^{n} a_{ik_i} \leq \sum_{i=1}^{n} \left(\max_{j \in A(i)} \{a_{ij} - \overline{p}_j\} + \overline{p}_{j_i} \right)$$

$$= \sum_{i=1}^{n} a_{ij_i}$$

$$\leq \sum_{i=1}^{n} \max_{j \in A(i)} \{a_{ij} - p_j\} + \sum_{j=1}^{n} p_j,$$

for every feasible assignment $\{(i, k_i) \mid i = 1, \ldots, n\}$ and every set of prices $\{p_j \mid j = 1, \ldots, n\}$. Therefore, the assignment $\{(i, j_i) \mid i = 1, \ldots, n\}$ is optimal for the primal problem, and the set of prices $\{\overline{p}_j \mid j = 1, \ldots, n\}$ is optimal for the dual problem. Furthermore, the two optimal values are equal. **Q.E.D.**

In analogy with primal cost improvement algorithms, one may start with a price vector and try to successively obtain new price vectors with improved dual cost. The major algorithms of this type involve price changes of the form

$$p_i := \begin{cases} p_i + \gamma & \text{if } i \in S, \\ p_i & \text{if } i \notin S, \end{cases} \tag{1.12}$$

where S is a connected subset of nodes, and γ is some positive scalar that is small enough to ensure that the new price vector has an improved dual cost.

The existence of a node subset S that results in cost improvement at a nonoptimal price vector, as described above, will be shown in Chapter 6.

This is an important and remarkable result, which may be viewed as a dual version of the result of Prop. 1.2 (at a nonoptimal flow vector, there exists at least one unblocked simple cycle with negative cost). In fact both results are special cases of a more general theorem concerning elementary vectors of subspaces, which is central in the theory of *monotropic programming* (see Chapter 9).

Most dual cost improvement methods, simultaneously with changing p along a direction of dual cost improvement, also iterate on a flow vector x satisfying CS together with p. They terminate when x becomes feasible, at which time, by Prop. 1.3, the pair (x, p) must consist of a primal and a dual optimal solution.

In Chapter 6 we will discuss two main methods that select subsets S and corresponding directions of dual cost improvement in different ways:

(a) In the *primal-dual method*, the direction has a *steepest ascent property*, that is, it provides the maximal rate of improvement of the dual cost per unit change in the price vector.

(b) In the *relaxation (or coordinate ascent) method*, the direction is computed so that it has a small number of nonzero elements (i.e., the set S has few nodes). Such a direction may not be optimal in terms of rate of dual cost improvement, but can typically be computed much faster than the steepest ascent direction. Often the direction has only one nonzero element, in which case only one node price coordinate is changed; this motivates the name "coordinate ascent." Note, however, that coordinate ascent directions cannot be used exclusively to improve the dual cost, as is shown in Fig. 1.10.

1.3.3 Auction

Our third type of algorithm represents a significant departure from the cost improvement idea; at any one iteration, it may deteriorate both the primal and the dual cost, although in the end it does find an optimal primal solution. It is based on an approximate version of complementary slackness, called ϵ-*complementary slackness*, and while it implicitly tries to solve a dual problem, it actually attains a dual solution that is not quite optimal. This subsection introduces the main ideas underlying auction algorithms. Chapters 7 and 9 provide a detailed discussion for the minimum cost flow problem and for the separable convex cost problem, respectively.

Naive Auction

Let us return to the assignment problem, and consider a natural process for finding an equilibrium assignment and price vector. We will call this process the *naive auction algorithm*, because it has a serious flaw, as will be

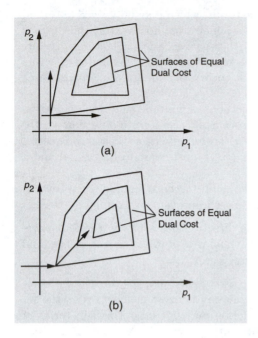

Figure 1.10: (a) The difficulty with using exclusively coordinate ascent iterations to solve the dual problem. Because the dual cost is piecewise linear, it may be impossible to improve it at some corner points by changing any *single* price coordinate. (b) As will be discussed in Chapter 6, a dual cost improvement is possible by changing several price coordinates by equal amounts, as in Eq. (1.12).

seen shortly. Nonetheless, this flaw will help motivate a more sophisticated and correct algorithm.

The naive auction algorithm proceeds in iterations and generates a sequence of price vectors and partial assignments. By a *partial assignment* we mean an assignment where only a subset of the persons have been matched with objects. A partial assignment should be contrasted with a *feasible* or *complete* assignment where all the persons have been matched with objects on a one-to-one basis. At the beginning of each iteration, the CS condition [cf. Eq. (1.10)]

$$a_{ij_i} - p_{j_i} = \max_{j \in A(i)} \{a_{ij} - p_j\}$$

is satisfied for all pairs (i, j_i) of the partial assignment. If all persons are assigned, the algorithm terminates. Otherwise some person who is unassigned, say i, is selected. This person finds an object j_i which offers maximal value, that is,

$$j_i = \arg \max_{j \in A(i)} \{a_{ij} - p_j\},$$

and then:

(a) Gets assigned to the best object j_i; the person who was assigned to j_i at the beginning of the iteration (if any) becomes unassigned.

(b) Sets the price of j_i to the level at which he/she is indifferent between j_i and the second best object; that is, he/she sets p_{j_i} to

$$p_{j_i} + \gamma_i,$$

where

$$\gamma_i = v_i - w_i, \tag{1.13}$$

v_i is the best object value,

$$v_i = \max_{j \in A(i)} \{a_{ij} - p_j\}, \tag{1.14}$$

and w_i is the second best object value,

$$w_i = \max_{j \in A(i),\, j \neq j_i} \{a_{ij} - p_j\}. \tag{1.15}$$

(Note that as p_{j_i} is increased, the value $a_{ij_i} - p_{j_i}$ offered by object j_i to person i is decreased. γ_i is the largest increment by which p_{j_i} can be increased, while maintaining the property that j_i offers maximal value to i.)

This process is repeated in a sequence of iterations until each person has been assigned to an object.

We may view this process as an auction where at each iteration the bidder i raises the price of a preferred object by the *bidding increment* γ_i. Note that γ_i cannot be negative, since $v_i \geq w_i$ [compare Eqs. (1.14)and (1.15)], so the object prices tend to increase. The choice γ_i is illustrated in Fig. 1.11. Just as in a real auction, bidding increments and price increases spur competition by making the bidder's own preferred object less attractive to other potential bidders.

ϵ-Complementary Slackness

Unfortunately, the naive auction algorithm does not always work (although it is an excellent initialization procedure for other methods, such as primal-dual or relaxation, and it is useful in other specialized contexts). The difficulty is that the bidding increment γ_i is 0 when two or more objects are tied in offering maximum value for the bidder i. As a result, a situation may be created where several persons contest a smaller number of equally desirable objects without raising their prices, thereby creating a never ending cycle; see Fig. 1.12.

To break such cycles, we introduce a perturbation mechanism, motivated by real auctions where each bid for an object must raise its price by a minimum positive increment, and bidders must on occasion take risks to win their preferred objects. In particular, let us fix a positive scalar ϵ, and

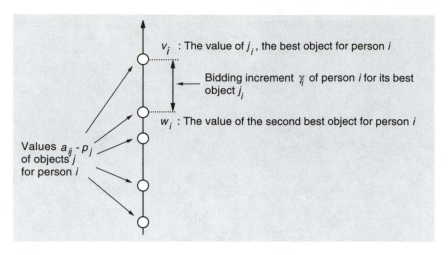

Figure 1.11: In the naive auction algorithm, even after the price of the best object j_i is increased by the bidding increment γ_i, j_i continues to be the best object for the bidder i, so CS is satisfied at the end of the iteration. However, we have $\gamma_i = 0$ if there is a tie between two or more objects that are most preferred by i.

say that a partial assignment and a price vector p satisfy ϵ-*complementary slackness* (ϵ-*CS for short*) if

$$a_{ij} - p_j \geq \max_{k \in A(i)} \{a_{ik} - p_k\} - \epsilon$$

for all assigned pairs (i, j). In words, to satisfy ϵ-CS, all assigned persons of the partial assignment must be assigned to objects that are within ϵ of being best.

The Auction Algorithm

We now reformulate the previous auction process so that the bidding increment is always at least equal to ϵ. The resulting method, the *auction algorithm*, is the same as the naive auction algorithm, except that the bidding increment γ_i is

$$\gamma_i = v_i - w_i + \epsilon \qquad (1.16)$$

rather than $\gamma_i = v_i - w_i$ as in Eq. (1.13). With this choice, the ϵ-CS condition is satisfied, as illustrated in Fig. 1.13. The particular increment $\gamma_i = v_i - w_i + \epsilon$ used in the auction algorithm is the maximum amount with this property. Smaller increments γ_i would also work as long as $\gamma_i \geq \epsilon$, but using the largest possible increment accelerates the algorithm. This is consistent with experience from real auctions, which tend to terminate faster when the bidding is aggressive.

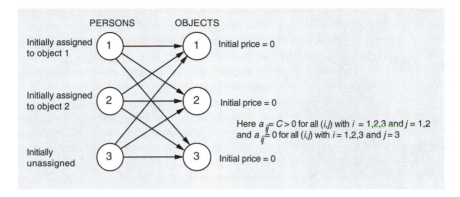

At Start of Iteration #	Object Prices	Assigned Pairs	Bidder	Preferred Object	Bidding Increment
1	0,0,0	(1,1), (2,2)	3	2	0
2	0,0,0	(1,1), (3,2)	2	2	0
3	0,0,0	(1,1), (2,2)	3	2	0

Figure 1.12: Illustration of how the naive auction algorithm may never terminate for a problem involving three persons and three objects. Here objects 1 and 2 offer benefit $C > 0$ to all persons, and object 3 offers benefit 0 to all persons. The algorithm cycles as persons 2 and 3 alternately bid for object 2 without changing its price because they prefer equally object 1 and object 2.

It can be shown that this reformulated auction process terminates, necessarily with a feasible assignment and a set of prices that satisfy ϵ-CS. To get a sense of this, note that if an object receives a bid during m iterations, its price must exceed its initial price by at least $m\epsilon$. Thus, for sufficiently large m, the object will become "expensive" enough to be judged "inferior" to some object that has not received a bid so far. It follows that only for a limited number of iterations can an object receive a bid while some other object still has not yet received any bid. On the other hand, once every object has received at least one bid, the auction terminates. (This argument assumes that any person can bid for any object, but it can be generalized to the case where the set of feasible person-object pairs is limited, as long as at least one feasible assignment exists; see Prop. 7.2 in Chapter 7.) Figure 1.14 shows how the auction algorithm, based on the bidding increment $\gamma_i = v_i - w_i + \epsilon$ [see Eq. (1.16)], overcomes the cycling difficulty in the example of Fig. 1.12.

When the auction algorithm terminates, we have an assignment satisfying ϵ-CS, but is this assignment optimal? The answer depends strongly

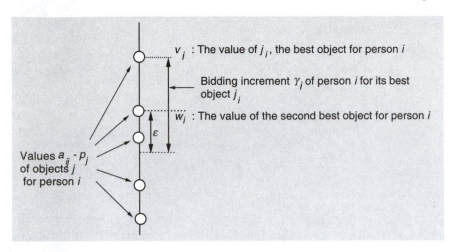

v_i : The value of j_i, the best object for person i

Bidding increment γ_i of person i for its best object j_i

w_i : The value of the second best object for person i

Values a_{ij} - p_j of objects j for person i

Figure 1.13: In the auction algorithm, even after the price of the preferred object j_i is increased by the bidding increment γ_i, j_i will be within ϵ of being most preferred, so the ϵ-CS condition holds at the end of the iteration.

on the size of ϵ. In a real auction, a prudent bidder would not place an excessively high bid for fear of winning the object at an unnecessarily high price. Consistent with this intuition, we can show that if ϵ is small, then the final assignment will be "almost optimal." In particular, we will show that *the total benefit of the final assignment is within $n\epsilon$ of being optimal.* The idea is that a feasible assignment and a set of prices satisfying ϵ-CS may be viewed as satisfying CS for a *slightly different* problem, where all benefits a_{ij} are the same as before except the benefits of the n assigned pairs, which are modified by no more than ϵ.

Proposition 1.4: A feasible assignment satisfying ϵ-complementary slackness, together with some price vector, attains within $n\epsilon$ the optimal primal value. Furthermore, the price vector attains within $n\epsilon$ the optimal dual cost.

Proof: Let A^* be the optimal total assignment benefit

$$A^* = \max_{\substack{k_i,\, i=1,\ldots,n \\ k_i \neq k_m \text{ if } i \neq m}} \sum_{i=1}^{n} a_{ik_i}$$

and let D^* be the optimal dual cost (cf. Prop. 1.3):

$$D^* = \min_{\substack{p_j \\ j=1,\ldots,n}} \left\{ \sum_{i=1}^{n} \max_{j \in A(i)} \left\{ a_{ij} - p_j \right\} + \sum_{j=1}^{n} p_j \right\}.$$

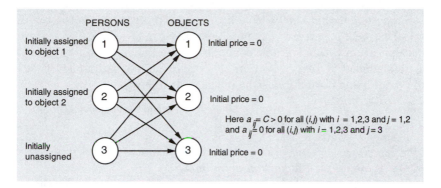

At Start of Iteration #	Object Prices	Assigned Pairs	Bidder	Preferred Object	Bidding Increment
1	0,0,0	(1,1), (2,2)	3	2	ϵ
2	0,ϵ,0	(1,1), (3,2)	2	1	2ϵ
3	$2\epsilon,\epsilon$,0	(2,1), (3,2)	1	2	2ϵ
4	$2\epsilon,3\epsilon$,0	(1,2), (2,1)	3	1	2ϵ
5	$4\epsilon,3\epsilon$,0	(1,2), (3,1)	2	2	2ϵ
6	$\cdots$	$\cdots$	$\cdots$	$\cdots$	$\cdots$

Figure 1.14: Illustration of how the auction algorithm, by making the bidding increment at least ϵ, overcomes the cycling difficulty for the example of Fig. 1.12. The table shows one possible sequence of bids and assignments generated by the auction algorithm, starting with all prices equal to 0 and with the partial assignment $\{(1,1),(2,2)\}$. At each iteration except the last, the person assigned to object 3 bids for either object 1 or 2, increasing its price by ϵ in the first iteration and by 2ϵ in each subsequent iteration. In the last iteration, after the prices of 1 and 2 reach or exceed C, object 3 receives a bid and the auction terminates.

If $\{(i, j_i) \mid i = 1, \ldots, n\}$ is the given assignment satisfying the ϵ-CS condition together with a price vector $\bar{p}$, we have

$$\max_{j \in A(i)} \{a_{ij} - \bar{p}_j\} - \epsilon \leq a_{ij_i} - \bar{p}_{j_i}.$$

By adding this relation over all i, we see that

$$D^* \leq \sum_{i=1}^{n} \left(\max_{j \in A(i)} \{a_{ij} - \bar{p}_j\} + \bar{p}_{j_i} \right) \leq \sum_{i=1}^{n} a_{ij_i} + n\epsilon \leq A^* + n\epsilon.$$

Since we showed in Prop. 1.3 that $A^* = D^*$, it follows that the total assignment benefit $\sum_{i=1}^{n} a_{ij_i}$ is within $n\epsilon$ of the optimal value A^*, while the dual cost of $\bar{p}$ is within $n\epsilon$ of the optimal dual cost.   **Q.E.D.**

Suppose now that the benefits a_{ij} are all integer, which is the typical practical case. (If a_{ij} are rational numbers, they can be scaled up to integer by multiplication with a suitable common number.) Then the total benefit of any assignment is integer, so if $n\epsilon < 1$, any complete assignment that is within $n\epsilon$ of being optimal must be optimal. It follows that *if*

$$\epsilon < \frac{1}{n}$$

and the benefits a_{ij} are all integer, then the assignment obtained upon termination of the auction algorithm is optimal.

Figure 1.15 shows the sequence of generated object prices for the example of Fig. 1.12 in relation to the contours of the dual cost function. It can be seen from this figure that each bid has the effect of setting the price of the object receiving the bid nearly equal (within ϵ) to the price that minimizes the dual cost with respect to that price, with all other prices held fixed (this will be shown rigorously in Section 7.1). Successive minimization of a cost function along single coordinates is a central feature of coordinate descent and relaxation methods, which are popular for unconstrained minimization of smooth functions and for solving systems of smooth equations. Thus, the auction algorithm can be interpreted as an approximate coordinate descent method; as such, it is related to the relaxation method discussed in the previous subsection.

Scaling

Figure 1.15 also illustrates a generic feature of auction algorithms. The amount of work needed to solve the problem can depend strongly on the value of ϵ and on the maximum absolute object benefit

$$C = \max_{(i,j)\in\mathcal{A}} |a_{ij}|.$$

Basically, for many types of problems, the number of iterations up to termination tends to be proportional to C/ϵ. This can be seen from the figure, where the total number of iterations is roughly C/ϵ, starting from zero initial prices.

Note also that there is a dependence on the initial prices; if these prices are "near optimal," we expect that the number of iterations needed to solve the problem will be relatively small. This can be seen from Fig. 1.15; if the initial prices satisfy $p_1 \approx p_3 + C$ and $p_2 \approx p_3 + C$, the number of iterations up to termination is quite small.

The preceding observations suggest the idea of ϵ-*scaling*, which consists of applying the algorithm several times, starting with a large value of ϵ and successively reducing ϵ until it is less than some critical value (for example, $1/n$, when a_{ij} are integer). Each application of the algorithm provides good initial prices for the next application. This is a common idea

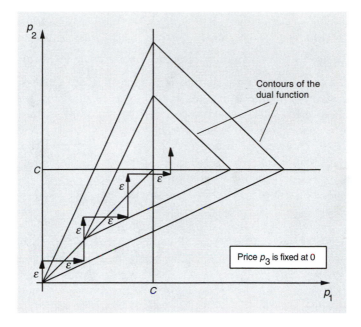

Figure 1.15: A sequence of prices p_1 and p_2 generated by the auction algorithm for the example of Figs. 1.12 and 1.14. The figure shows the equal dual cost surfaces in the space of p_1 and p_2, with p_3 fixed at 0. The arrows indicate the price iterates as given by the table of Fig. 1.14. Termination occurs when the prices reach an ϵ-neighborhood of the point (C, C), and object 3 becomes "sufficiently inexpensive" to receive a bid and to get assigned. The total number of iterations is roughly C/ϵ, starting from zero initial prices.

in nonlinear programming; it is encountered, for example, in barrier and penalty function methods (see Section 8.8). In practice, scaling is typically beneficial, and accelerates the termination of the auction algorithm.

1.3.4   Good, Bad, and Polynomial Algorithms

We have discussed several types of methods, so the natural question arises: is there a best method and what criterion should we use to rank methods?

A practitioner who has a specific type of problem to solve, perhaps repeatedly, with the data and size of the problem within some limited range, will usually be interested in one or more of the following:

(a) Fast solution time.

(b) Flexibility to use good starting solutions (which the practitioner can usually provide, based on his/her knowledge of the problem, or based on a known solution of some similar problem).

(c) The ability to perform sensitivity analysis (resolve the problem with slightly different problem data) quickly.

(d) The ability to take advantage of parallel computing hardware.

Given the diversity of these considerations, it is not surprising that there is no algorithm that will dominate the others in all or even most practical situations. Otherwise expressed, every type of algorithm that we will discuss is best given the right type of practical situation. Thus, to make intelligent choices, the practitioner needs to understand the properties of different algorithms relating to speed of convergence, flexibility, parallelization, and suitability for specific problem structures. For challenging problems, the choice of algorithm is often settled by experimentation with several candidates.

A theoretical analyst may also have difficulty ranking different algorithms for specific types of problems. The most common approach for this purpose is worst-case computational complexity analysis. For example, for the minimum cost flow problem, one tries to bound the number of elementary numerical operations needed by a given algorithm with some measure of the "problem size," that is, with some expression of the form

$$K f(N, A, C, U, S),$$

where

     N is the number of nodes,

     A is the number of arcs,

     C is the arc cost range $\max_{(i,j) \in \mathcal{A}} |a_{ij}|$,

     U is the maximum arc flow range $\max_{(i,j) \in \mathcal{A}} (c_{ij} - b_{ij})$,

     S is the supply range $\max_{i \in \mathcal{N}} |s_i|$,

     f is some known function,

     K is a (usually unknown) constant.

If a bound of this form can be found, we say that the *running time* or *operation count of the algorithm is* $O(f(N, A, C, U, S))$. If $f(N, A, C, U, S)$ can be written as a polynomial function of the number of bits needed to express the problem data, the algorithm is said to be *polynomial*. Examples of polynomial complexity bounds are $O(N^\alpha A^\beta)$ and $O(N^\alpha A^\beta \log C)$, where α and β are positive integers, and the numbers a_{ij} are assumed integer. The bound $O(N^\alpha A^\beta)$ is sometimes said to be *strongly polynomial* because it involves only the graph size parameters. A bound of the form $O(N^\alpha A^\beta C)$ is not polynomial, even assuming that the a_{ij} are integer, because C is not a polynomial expression of $\log C$, the number of bits needed to express a single number a_{ij}. Bounds like $O(N^\alpha A^\beta C)$, which are polynomial in the problem data rather than in the number of bits needed to express the data, are called *pseudopolynomial*.

A common assumption in theoretical computer science is that polynomial algorithms are "better" than pseudopolynomial, and pseudopolynomial algorithms are "better" than exponential [for example, those with a bound of the form $K2^{g(N,A)}$, where g is a polynomial in N and A]. Furthermore, it is thought that two polynomial algorithms can be compared in terms of the degree of the polynomial bound; e.g., an $O(N^2)$ algorithm is "better" than an $O(N^3)$ algorithm. Unfortunately, quite often this assumption is not supported by computational practice in linear programming and network optimization. Pseudopolynomial and even exponential algorithms are often faster in practice than polynomial ones. In fact, the simplex method for general linear programs is an exponential algorithm, as shown by Klee and Minty [1972] (see also the textbooks by Chvatal [1983], or Bertsimas and Tsitsiklis [1997]), and yet it is used widely, because of its excellent practical properties.

There are two main reasons why worst-case complexity estimates may fail to predict the practical performance of network flow algorithms. First, the estimates, even if they are tight, may be very pessimistic as they may correspond to problem instances that are highly unlikely in practice. (Average complexity estimates would be more appropriate for such situations. However, obtaining these is usually hard, and the statistical assumptions underlying them may be inappropriate for many types of practical problems.) Second, worst-case complexity estimates involve the (usually unknown) constant K, which may dominate the estimate for all except for unrealistically large problem sizes. Thus, a comparison between two algorithms that is based on the size-dependent terms of running time estimates, and does not take into account the corresponding constants may be unreliable.

Despite its shortcomings, computational complexity analysis is valuable because it often illuminates the computational bottlenecks of many algorithms and motivates the use of efficient data structures. For this reason, throughout the book, we will comment on available complexity results, we will prove some of the most important estimates, and we will try to relate these estimates to computational practice. For some classes of problems, however, it turns out that the methods with the best computational complexity are impractical, because they are either too complicated or too slow in practice. In such cases, we will refer to the literature, without providing a detailed discussion.

1.4 NOTES, SOURCES, AND EXERCISES

Network problems are discussed in many books (Berge [1962], Berge and Ghouila-Houri [1962], Ford and Fulkerson [1962], Dantzig [1963], Busacker and Saaty [1965], Hu [1969], Iri [1969], Frank and Frisch 1970], Christofides

[1975], Zoutendijk [1976], Minieka [1978], Jensen and Barnes [1980], Kennington and Helgason [1980], Papadimitriou and Steiglitz [1982], Chvatal [1983], Gondran and Minoux [1984], Luenberger [1984], Rockafellar [1984], Bazaraa, Jarvis, and Sherali [1990], Bertsekas [1991a], Murty [1992], Bertsimas and Tsitsiklis [1997]). Several of these books discuss linear programming first and develop linear network optimization as a special case. An alternative approach that relies heavily on duality, is given by Rockafellar [1984]. The conformal realization theorem (Prop. 1.1) has been developed in different forms in several sources, including Ford and Fulkerson [1962], Busacker and Saaty [1965], and Rockafellar [1984].

The primal cost improvement approach for network optimization was initiated by Dantzig [1951], who specialized the simplex method to the transportation problem. The extensive subsequent work using this approach is surveyed at the end of Chapter 5.

The dual cost improvement approach was initiated by Kuhn [1955] who proposed the *Hungarian method* for the assignment problem. (The name of the algorithm honors its connection with the research of the Hungarian mathematicians Egervary [1931] and König [1931].) Work using this approach is surveyed in Chapter 6.

The auction approach was initiated in Bertsekas [1979a] for the assignment problem, and in Bertsekas [1986a], [1986b] for the minimum cost flow problem. Work using this approach is surveyed at the end of Chapter 7.

EXERCISES

1.1

Consider the graph and the flow vector of Fig. 1.16.

(a) Enumerate the simple paths and the simple forward paths that start at node 1.

(b) Enumerate the simple cycles and the simple forward cycles of the graph.

(c) Is the graph connected? Is it strongly connected?

(d) Calculate the divergences of all the nodes and verify that they add to 0.

(e) Give an example of a simple path flow that starts at node 1, ends at node 5, involves four arcs, and conforms to the given flow vector.

(f) Suppose that all arcs have arc flow bounds -1 and 5. Enumerate all the simple paths that start at node 1, end at node 5, and are unblocked with respect to the given flow vector.

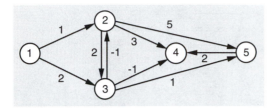

Figure 1.16: Flow vector for Exercise 1.1. The arc flows are the numbers shown next to the arcs.

1.2 (Proof of the Conformal Realization Theorem)

Prove the conformal realization theorem (Prop. 1.1) by completing the details of the following argument. Assume first that x is a circulation. Consider the following procedure by which given x, we obtain a simple cycle flow x' that conforms to x and satisfies

$$0 \le x'_{ij} \le x_{ij} \qquad \text{for all arcs } (i,j) \text{ with } 0 \le x_{ij},$$
$$x_{ij} \le x'_{ij} \le 0 \qquad \text{for all arcs } (i,j) \text{ with } x_{ij} \le 0,$$
$$x_{ij} = x'_{ij} \qquad \text{for at least one arc } (i,j) \text{ with } x_{ij} \ne 0;$$

(see Fig. 1.17). Choose an arc (i,j) with $x_{ij} \ne 0$. Assume that $x_{ij} > 0$. (A similar procedure can be used when $x_{ij} < 0$.) Construct a sequence of node subsets $T_0, T_1, \ldots$, as follows: Take $T_0 = \{j\}$. For $k = 0, 1, \ldots$, given T_k, let

$$T_{k+1} = \big\{ n \notin \cup_{p=0}^{k} T_p \mid \text{ there is a node } m \in T_k, \text{ and either an arc } (m,n)$$
$$\text{such that } x_{mn} > 0 \text{ or an arc } (n,m) \text{ such that } x_{nm} < 0 \big\},$$

and mark each node $n \in T_{k+1}$ with the label "(m,n)" or "(n,m)," where m is a node of T_k such that $x_{mn} > 0$ or $x_{nm} < 0$, respectively. The procedure terminates when T_{k+1} is empty.

At the end of the procedure, trace labels backward from i until node j is reached. (How do we know that i belongs to one of the sets T_k?) In particular, let "(i_1, i)" or "(i, i_1)" be the label of i, let "(i_2, i_1)" or "(i_1, i_2)" be the label of i_1, etc., until a node i_k with label "(i_k, j)" or "(j, i_k)" is found. The cycle $C = (j, i_k, i_{k-1}, \ldots, i_1, i, j)$ is simple, it contains (i,j) as a forward arc, and is such that all its forward arcs have positive flow and all its backward arcs have negative flow. Let $a = \min_{(m,n) \in C} |x_{mn}| > 0$. Then the simple cycle flow x', where

$$x'_{ij} = \begin{cases} a & \text{if } (i,j) \in C^+, \\ -a & \text{if } (i,j) \in C^-, \\ 0 & \text{otherwise,} \end{cases}$$

has the required properties.

Now subtract x' from x. We have $x_{ij} - x'_{ij} > 0$ only for arcs (i,j) with $x_{ij} > 0$, $x_{ij} - x'_{ij} < 0$ only for arcs (i,j) with $x_{ij} < 0$, and $x_{ij} - x'_{ij} = 0$ for at

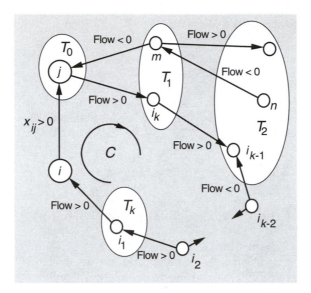

Figure 1.17: Construction of a cycle of arcs with nonzero flow used in the proof of the conformal realization theorem.

least one arc (i, j) with $x_{ij} \neq 0$. If x is integer, then x' and $x - x'$ will also be integer. We then repeat the process (for at most A times) with the circulation x replaced by the circulation $x - x'$ and so on, until the zero flow is obtained.

If x is not a circulation, we form an enlarged graph by introducing a new node s and by introducing for each node $i \in \mathcal{N}$ an arc (s, i) with flow x_{si} equal to the divergence y_i. The resulting flow vector is seen to be a circulation in the enlarged graph (why?). This circulation, by the result just shown, can be decomposed into at most $A + N$ simple cycle flows of the enlarged graph, conforming to the flow vector. Out of these cycle flows, we consider those containing node s, and we remove s and its two incident arcs while leaving the other cycle flows unchanged. As a result we obtain a set of at most $A+N$ path flows of the original graph, which add up to x. These path flows also conform to x, as required.

1.3

Use the algorithm of Exercise 1.2 to decompose the flow vector of Fig. 1.16 into conforming simple path flows.

1.4 (Path Decomposition Theorem)

(a) Use the conformal realization theorem (Prop. 1.1) to show that a forward path P can be decomposed into a (possibly empty) collection of simple forward cycles, together with a simple forward path that has the same start node and end node as P. (Here "decomposition" means that the union of the arcs of the component paths is equal to the set of arcs of P with the multiplicity of repeated arcs properly accounted for.)

(b) Suppose that a graph is strongly connected and that a length a_{ij} is given for every arc (i, j). Show that if all forward cycles have nonnegative length, then there exists a shortest path from any node s to any node t. Show also that if there exists a shortest path from some node s to some node t, then all forward cycles have nonnegative length. Why is the connectivity assumption needed?

1.5 (Cycle Decomposition - Euler Cycles)

Consider a graph such that each of the nodes has even degree.

(a) Give an algorithm to decompose the graph into a collection of simple cycles that are disjoint, in the sense that they share no arcs (although they may share some nodes). (Here "decomposition" means that the union of the arcs of the component cycles is equal to the set of arcs of the graph.) *Hint:* Given a connected graph where each of the nodes has even degree, the deletion of the arcs of any cycle creates some connected subgraphs where each of the nodes has even degree (including possibly some isolated nodes).

(b) Assume in addition that the graph is connected. Show that there is an Euler cycle, i.e., a cycle that contains all the arcs of a graph exactly once. *Hint:* Apply the decomposition of part (a), and successively merge an Euler cycle of a subgraph with a simple cycle.

1.6

In the graph of Fig. 1.16, consider the graph obtained by deleting node 1 and arcs $(1, 2)$, $(1, 3)$, and $(5, 4)$. Decompose this graph into a collection of simple cycles that are disjoint (cf. Exercise 1.5) and construct an Euler cycle.

1.7

(a) Consider an $n \times n$ chessboard, and a rook that is allowed to make the standard moves along the rows and columns. Show that the rook can start at a given square and return to that square after making each of the possible legal moves exactly once and in one direction only [of the two moves (a, b) and (b, a) only one should be made]. *Hint:* Construct an Euler cycle in a suitable graph.

(b) Consider an $n \times n$ chessboard with n even, and a bishop that is allowed to make two types of moves: legal moves (which are the standard moves along the diagonals of its color), and illegal moves (which go from any square of its color to any other square of its color). Show that the bishop can start at a given square and return to that square after making each of the possible legal moves exactly once and in one direction only, plus $n^2/4$ illegal moves.

For every square of its color, there should be exactly one illegal move that either starts or ends at that square.

1.8 (Forward Euler Cycles)

Consider a graph and the question whether there exists a forward cycle that passes through each arc of the graph exactly once. Show that such a cycle exists if and only if the graph is connected and the number of incoming arcs to each node is equal to the number of outgoing arcs from the node.

1.9

Consider an $n \times n$ chessboard with $n \geq 4$. Show that a knight starting at any square can visit every other square, with a move sequence that contains every possible move exactly once [a move (a, b) as well as its reverse (b, a) should be made]. Interpret this sequence as a forward Euler cycle in a suitable graph (cf. Exercise 1.8).

1.10 (Euler Paths)

Consider a graph and the question whether there exists a path that passes through each arc of the graph exactly once. Show that such a path exists if and only if the graph is connected, and either the degrees of all the nodes are even, or else the degrees of all the nodes except two are even.

1.11

In shatranj, the old version of chess, the firz (or vizier, the predecessor to the modern queen) can move one square diagonally in each direction. Show that starting at a corner of an $n \times n$ chessboard where n is even, the firz can reach the opposite corner after making each of the possible moves along its diagonals exactly once and in one direction only [of the two moves (a, b) and (b, a) only one should be made].

1.12

Show that the number of nodes with odd degree in a graph is even.

1.13

Assume that all the nodes of a graph have degree greater than one. Show that the graph must contain a cycle.

1.14

(a) Show that every tree with at least two nodes has at least two nodes with degree one.

(b) Show that a graph is a tree if and only if it is connected and the number of arcs is one less than the number of nodes.

1.15

Consider a volleyball net that consists of a mesh with m squares on the horizontal dimension and n squares on the vertical. What is the maximum number of strings that can be cut before the net falls apart into two pieces.

1.16 (Checking Connectivity)

Consider a graph with A arcs.

(a) Devise an algorithm with $O(A)$ running time that checks whether the graph is connected, and if it is connected, simultaneously constructs a path connecting any two nodes. *Hint*: Start at a node, mark its neighbors, and continue.

(b) Repeat part (a) for the case where we want to check strong connectedness.

(c) Devise an algorithm with $O(A)$ running time that checks whether there exists a cycle that contains two given nodes.

(d) Repeat part (c) for the case where the cycle is required to be forward.

1.17 (Inequality Constrained Minimum Cost Flows)

Consider the following variant of the minimum cost flow problem:

$$\text{minimize} \quad \sum_{(i,j)\in\mathcal{A}} a_{ij}x_{ij}$$

$$\text{subject to} \quad \underline{s}_i \le \sum_{\{j|(i,j)\in\mathcal{A}\}} x_{ij} - \sum_{\{j|(j,i)\in\mathcal{A}\}} x_{ji} \le \overline{s}_i, \qquad \forall\, i \in \mathcal{N},$$

$$b_{ij} \le x_{ij} \le c_{ij}, \qquad \forall\, (i,j) \in \mathcal{A},$$

where the bounds $\underline{s}_i$ and $\overline{s}_i$ on the divergence of node i are given. Show that this problem can be converted to a standard (equality constrained) minimum cost flow problem by adding an extra node A and an arc (A, i) from this node to every other node i, with feasible flow range $[0, \overline{s}_i - \underline{s}_i]$.

1.18 (Node Throughput Constraints)

Consider the minimum cost flow problem with the additional constraints that the total flow of the outgoing arcs from each node i must lie within a given range $[\underline{t}_i, \bar{t}_i]$, that is,

$$\underline{t}_i \le \sum_{\{j|(i,j)\in\mathcal{A}\}} x_{ij} \le \bar{t}_i.$$

Convert this problem into the standard form of the minimum cost flow problem by splitting each node into two nodes with a connecting arc.

1.19 (Piecewise Linear Arc Costs)

Consider the minimum cost flow problem with the difference that, instead of the linear form $a_{ij}x_{ij}$, each arc's cost function has the piecewise linear form

$$f_{ij}(x_{ij}) = \begin{cases} a_{ij}^1 x_{ij} & \text{if } b_{ij} \le x_{ij} \le m_{ij}, \\ a_{ij}^1 m_{ij} + a_{ij}^2 (x_{ij} - m_{ij}) & \text{if } m_{ij} \le x_{ij} \le c_{ij}, \end{cases}$$

where m_{ij}, a_{ij}^1, and a_{ij}^2 are given scalars satisfying $b_{ij} \le m_{ij} \le c_{ij}$ and $a_{ij}^1 \le a_{ij}^2$.

(a) Show that the problem can be converted to a linear minimum cost flow problem where each arc (i,j) is replaced by two arcs with arc cost coefficients a_{ij}^1 and a_{ij}^2, and arc flow ranges $[b_{ij}, m_{ij}]$ and $[0, c_{ij} - m_{ij}]$, respectively.

(b) Generalize to the case of piecewise linear cost functions with more than two pieces.

1.20 (Asymmetric Assignment and Transportation Problems)

Consider an assignment problem where the number of objects is larger than the number of persons, and we require that each person be assigned to one object. The associated linear program (cf. Example 1.2) is

$$\text{maximize} \quad \sum_{(i,j)\in\mathcal{A}} a_{ij}x_{ij}$$

$$\text{subject to} \quad \sum_{\{j|(i,j)\in\mathcal{A}\}} x_{ij} = 1, \quad \forall\, i = 1,\ldots,m,$$

$$\sum_{\{i|(i,j)\in\mathcal{A}\}} x_{ij} \le 1, \quad \forall\, j = 1,\ldots,n,$$

$$0 \le x_{ij} \le 1, \quad \forall\, (i,j) \in \mathcal{A},$$

where $m < n$.

(a) Show how to formulate this problem as a minimum cost flow problem by introducing extra arcs and nodes.

(b) Repeat part (a) for the case where there may be some persons that are left unassigned; that is, the constraint $\sum_{\{j|(i,j)\in\mathcal{A}\}} x_{ij} = 1$ is replaced by $\sum_{\{j|(i,j)\in\mathcal{A}\}} x_{ij} \leq 1$. Give an example of a problem with $a_{ij} > 0$ for all $(i,j) \in \mathcal{A}$, which is such that in the optimal assignment some persons are left unassigned, even though there exist feasible assignments that assign every person to some object.

(c) Formulate an asymmetric transportation problem where the total supply is less than the total demand, but some demand may be left unsatisfied, and appropriately modify your answers to parts (a) and (b).

1.21 (Bipartite Matching)

Bipartite matching problems are assignment problems where the coefficients (i,j) are all equal to 1. In such problems, we want to maximize the cardinality of the assignment, that is, the number of assigned pairs (i,j). Formulate a bipartite matching problem as an equivalent max-flow problem.

1.22 (Production Planning)

Consider a problem of scheduling production of a certain item to meet a given demand over N time periods. Let us denote:

x_i: The amount of product stored at the beginning of period i, where $i = 0, \ldots, N-1$. There is a nonnegativity constraint on x_i.

u_i: The amount of product produced during period i. There is a constraint $0 \leq u_i \leq c_i$, where the scalar c_i is given for each i.

d_i: The amount of product demanded during period i. This is a given scalar for each i.

The amount of product stored evolves according to the equation

$$x_{i+1} = x_i + u_i - d_i, \qquad i = 0, \ldots, N-1.$$

Given x_0, we want to find a feasible production sequence $\{u_0, \ldots, u_{N-1}\}$ that minimizes

$$\sum_{i=0}^{N-1} (a_i x_i + b_i u_i),$$

where a_i and b_i are given scalars for each i. Formulate this problem as a minimum cost flow problem. *Hint:* For each i, introduce a node that connects to a special artificial node.

1.23 (Capacity Expansion)

The capacity of a certain facility is to be expanded over N time periods by adding an increment $u_i \in [0, c_i]$ at time period $i = 0, \ldots, N-1$, where c_i is a given scalar. Thus, if x_i is the capacity at the beginning of period i, we have

$$x_{i+1} = x_i + u_i, \qquad i = 0, \ldots, N-1.$$

Given x_0, consider the problem of finding u_i, $i = 0, \ldots, N - 1$, such that each x_i lies within a given interval $[\underline{x}_i, \bar{x}_i]$ and the cost

$$\sum_{i=0}^{N-1} (a_i x_i + b_i u_i)$$

is minimized, where a_i and b_i are given scalars for each i. Formulate the problem as a minimum cost flow problem.

1.24 (Dynamic Transhipment Problems)

Consider a transhipment context for the minimum cost flow problem where the problem is to optimally transfer flow from some supply points to some demand points over arcs of limited capacity. In a dynamic version of this context, the transfer is to be performed over N time units, and transferring flow along an arc (i, j) requires time τ_{ij}, which is a given positive integer number of time units. This means that at each time $t = 0, \ldots, N - \tau_{ij}$, we may send from node i along arc (i, j) a flow $x_{ij} \in [0, c_{ij}]$, which will arrive at node j at time $t + \tau_{ij}$. Formulate this problem as a minimum cost flow problem involving a copy of the given graph for each time period.

1.25 (Concentrator Assignment)

We have m communication terminals, each to be connected to one out of a given collection of concentrators. Suppose that there is a cost a_{ij} for connecting terminal i to concentrator j, and that each concentrator j has an upper bound b_j on the number of terminals it can be connected to. Also, each terminal i can be connected to only a given subset of concentrators.

(a) Formulate the problem of finding the minimum cost connection of terminals to concentrators as a minimum cost flow problem. *Hint*: You may use the fact that there exists an integer optimal solution to a minimum cost flow problem with integer supplies and arc flow bounds. (This will be shown in Chapter 5.)

(b) Suppose that a concentrator j can operate in an overload condition with a number of connected terminals greater than b_j, up to a number $\bar{b}_j > b_j$. In this case, however, the cost per terminal connected becomes $\bar{a}_{ij} > a_{ij}$. Repeat part (a).

(c) Suppose that when no terminals are connected to concentrator j there is a given cost savings $c_j > 0$. Can you still formulate the problem as a minimum cost flow problem?

1.26

Consider a round-robin chess tournament involving n players that play each other once. A win scores 1 for the winner and 0 for the loser, while a draw scores 1/2 for each player. We are given a set of final scores $(s_1, \ldots, s_n)$ for the players, from the range $[0, n-1]$, whose sum is $n(n-1)/2$, and we want to check whether these scores are feasible [for example, in a four-player tournament, a set of final scores of $(3, 3, 0, 0)$ is impossible]. Show that this is equivalent to checking feasibility of some transportation problem.

1.27 (k-Color Problem)

Consider the k-color problem, which is to assign one out of k colors to each node of a graph so that for every arc (i, j), nodes i and j have different colors.

(a) Suppose we want to choose the colors of countries in a world map so that no two adjacent countries have the same color. Show that if the number of available colors is k, the problem can be formulated as a k-color problem.

(b) Show that the k-color problem has a solution if and only if the number of nodes can be partitioned in k or less disjoint subsets such that there is no arc connecting a pair of nodes from the same subset.

(c) Show that when the graph is a tree, the 2-color problem has a solution. *Hint*: First color some node i and then color the remaining nodes based on their "distance" from i.

(d) Show that if each node has at most $k - 1$ neighbors, the k-color problem has a solution.

1.28 (k-Coloring and Parallel Computation)

Consider the n-dimensional vector $x = (x_1, \ldots, x_n)$ and an iteration of the form

$$x_j := f_j(x), \qquad j = 1, \ldots, n,$$

where $f = (f_1, \ldots, f_n)$ is a given function. The *dependency graph* of f has nodes $1, \ldots, n$ and an arc set such that (i, j) is an arc if the function f_j exhibits a dependence on the component x_i. Consider an ordering $j_1, \ldots, j_n$ of the indices $1, \ldots, n$, and a partition of $\{j_1, \ldots, j_n\}$ into disjoint subsets $J_1, \ldots, J_M$ such that:

(1) For all k, if $j_k \in J_m$, then $j_{k+1} \in J_m \cup \cdots \cup J_M$.

(2) If $j_p, j_q \in J_m$ and $p < q$, then f_{j_q} does not depend on x_{j_p}.

Show that such an ordering and partition exist if and only if the nodes of the dependency graph can be colored with M colors so that there exists no forward cycle with all the nodes on the cycle having the same color. *Note*: This is challenging (see Bertsekas and Tsitsiklis [1989], Section 1.2.4, for discussion and analysis). An ordering and partition of this type can be used to execute Gauss-Seidel iterations in M parallel steps.

1.29 (Replacing Arc Costs with Reduced Costs)

Consider the minimum cost flow problem and let p_j be a scalar price for each node j. Show that if the arc cost coefficients a_{ij} are replaced by $a_{ij} + p_j - p_i$, we obtain a problem that is equivalent to the original (except for a scalar shift in the cost function value).

1.30

Consider the assignment problem.

  (a) Show that every k-person exchange can be accomplished with a sequence of $k-1$ successive two-person exchanges.

  (b) In light of the result of part (a), how do you explain that a nonoptimal assignment may not be improvable by any two-person exchange?

1.31 (Dual Cost Improvement Directions)

Consider the assignment problem. Let p_j denote the price of object j, let T be a subset of objects, and let

$$S = \left\{ i \mid \text{the maximum of } a_{ij} - p_j \text{ over } j \in A(i) \right.$$
$$\left. \text{is attained by some element of } T \right\}.$$

Assume that:

  (1) For each $i \in S$, the maximum of $a_{ij} - p_j$ over $j \in A(i)$ is attained only by elements of T.

  (2) S has more elements than T.

Show that the direction $d = (d_1, \ldots, d_n)$, where $d_j = 1$ if $j \in T$ and $d_j = 0$ if $j \notin T$, is a direction of dual cost improvement. *Note*: Directions of this type are used by the most common dual cost improvement algorithms for the assignment problem.

1.32

Use ϵ-CS to verify that the assignment of Fig. 1.18 is optimal and obtain a bound on how far from optimal the given price vector is. State the dual problem and verify the correctness of the bound by comparing the dual value of the price vector with the optimal dual value.

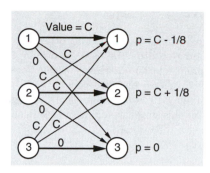

Figure 1.18: Graph of an assignment problem. Objects 1 and 2 have value C for all persons. Object 3 has value 0 for all persons. Object prices are as shown. The thick lines indicate the given assignment.

1.33 (Generic Negative Cycle Algorithm)

Consider the following minimum cost flow problem

$$\text{minimize} \quad \sum_{(i,j)\in\mathcal{A}} a_{ij} x_{ij}$$

$$\text{subject to} \quad \sum_{\{j|(i,j)\in\mathcal{A}\}} x_{ij} - \sum_{\{j|(j,i)\in\mathcal{A}\}} x_{ji} = s_i, \quad \forall\, i \in \mathcal{N},$$

$$0 \le x_{ij} \le c_{ij}, \quad \forall\, (i,j) \in \mathcal{A},$$

and assume that the problem has at least one feasible solution. Consider first the circulation case where $s_i = 0$ for all $i \in \mathcal{N}$. Construct a sequence of flow vectors $x^0, x^1, \ldots$ as follows: Start with $x^0 = 0$. Given x^k, stop if x^k is optimal, and otherwise find a simple cycle C^k that is unblocked with respect to x^k and has negative cost (cf. Prop. 1.2). Increase (decrease) the flow of the forward (backward, respectively) arcs of C^k by the maximum possible increment.

(a) Show that the cost of x^{k+1} is smaller than the cost of x^k by an amount that is proportional to the cost of the cycle C^k and to the increment of the corresponding flow change.

(b) Assume that the flow increment at each iteration is greater or equal to some scalar $\delta > 0$. Show that the algorithm must terminate after a finite number of iterations with an optimal flow vector. *Note*: The assumption of existence of such a δ is essential (see Exercise 3.7 in Chapter 3).

(c) Extend parts (a) and (b) to the general case where we may have $s_i \ne 0$ for some i, by converting the problem to the circulation format (a method for doing this is given in Section 4.1.3).

1.34 (Integer Optimal Solutions of Min-Cost Flow Problems)

Consider the minimum cost flow problem of Exercise 1.33, where the upper bounds c_{ij} are given positive integers and the supplies s_i are given integers. Assume that the problem has at least one feasible solution. Show that there exists an optimal flow vector that is integer. *Hint*: Show that the flow vectors generated by the negative cycle algorithm of Exercise 1.33 are integer.

1.35 (The Original Hamiltonian Cycle)

The origins of the traveling salesman problem can be traced (among others) to the work of the Irish mathematician Sir William Hamilton. In 1856, he developed a system of commutative algebra, which inspired a puzzle marketed as the "Icosian Game." The puzzle is to find a cycle that passes exactly once through each of the 20 nodes of the graph shown in Fig. 1.19, which represents a regular dodecahedron. Find a Hamiltonian cycle on this graph using as first four nodes the ones marked 1-4 (all arcs are considered bidirectional).

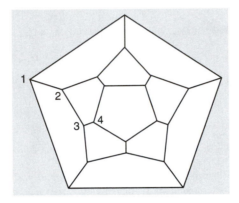

Figure 1.19: Graph for the Icosian Game (cf. Exercise 1.35). The arcs and nodes correspond to the edges and vertices of the regular dodecahedron, respectively. The name "icosian" comes from the Greek word "icosi," which means twenty. Adjacent nodes of the dodecahedron correspond to adjacent faces of the regular icosahedron.

1.36 (Hamiltonian Cycle on the Hypercube)

The hypercube of dimension n is a graph with 2^n nodes, each corresponding to an n-bit string where each bit is either a 0 or a 1. There is a bidirectional arc connecting every pair of nodes whose n-bit strings differ by a single bit. Show that for every $n \geq 2$, the hypercube contains a Hamiltonian cycle. *Hint*: Use induction.

1.37 (Hardy's Theorem)

Let $\{a_1, \ldots, a_n\}$ and $\{b_1, \ldots, b_n\}$ be monotonically nondecreasing sequences of numbers. Consider the problem of associating with each $i = 1, \ldots, n$ a distinct index j_i in a way that maximizes $\sum_{i=1}^{n} a_i b_{j_i}$. Formulate this as an assignment problem and show that it is optimal to select $j_i = i$ for all i. *Hint*: Use the complementary slackness conditions with prices defined by $p_1 = 0$ and $p_k = p_{k-1} + a_k(b_k - b_{k-1})$ for $k = 2, \ldots, n$.

2

The Shortest Path Problem

Contents

The shortest path problem is a classical and important combinatorial problem that arises in many contexts. We are given a directed graph $(\mathcal{N}, \mathcal{A})$ with nodes numbered $1, \ldots, N$. Each arc $(i, j) \in \mathcal{A}$ has a cost or "length" a_{ij} associated with it. The length of a forward path $(i_1, i_2, \ldots, i_k)$ is the length of its arcs

$$\sum_{n=1}^{k-1} a_{i_n i_{n+1}}.$$

This path is said to be *shortest* if it has minimum length over all forward paths with the same origin and destination nodes. The length of a shortest path is also called the *shortest distance*. The shortest path problem deals with finding shortest distances between selected pairs of nodes. [Note that here we are optimizing over forward paths; when we refer to a path (or a cycle) in connection with the shortest path problem, we implicitly assume that the path (or the cycle) is forward.]

The range of applications of the shortest path problem is very broad. In the next section, we will provide some representative examples. We will then develop a variety of algorithms. Most of these algorithms can be viewed as primal cost or dual cost improvement algorithms for an appropriate special case of the minimum cost flow problem, as we will see later. However, the shortest path problem is simple, so we will discuss it based on first principles, and without much reference to cost improvement. This serves a dual purpose. First, it provides an opportunity to illustrate some basic graph concepts in the context of a problem that is simple and rich in intuition. Second, it allows the early development of some ideas and results that will be used later in a variety of other algorithmic contexts.

2.1 PROBLEM FORMULATION AND APPLICATIONS

The shortest path problem appears in a large variety of contexts. We discuss a few representative applications.

Example 2.1. Routing in Data Networks

Data network communication involves the use of a network of computers (nodes) and communication links (arcs) that transfer packets (groups of bits) from their origins to their destinations. The most common method for selecting the path of travel (or route) of packets is based on a shortest path formulation. In particular, each communication link is assigned a positive scalar which is viewed as its length. A shortest path routing algorithm routes each packet along a minimum length (or shortest) path between the origin and destination nodes of the packet.

There are several possibilities for selecting the link lengths. The simplest is for each link to have unit length, in which case a shortest path is

simply a path with minimum number of links. More generally, the length
of a link, may depend on its transmission capacity and its projected traffic
load. The idea here is that a shortest path should contain relatively few and
uncongested links, and therefore be desirable for routing. Sophisticated routing algorithms also allow the length of each link to change over time and to
depend on the prevailing congestion level of the link. Then a shortest path
may adapt to temporary overloads and route packets around points of congestion. Within this context, the shortest path routing algorithm operates
continuously, solving the shortest path problem with lengths that vary over
time.

A peculiar feature of shortest path routing algorithms is that they are
often implemented using distributed and asynchronous communication and
computation. In particular, each node of the communication network mon-
itors the traffic conditions of its adjacent links, calculates estimates of its
shortest distances to various destinations, and passes these estimates to other
nodes who adjust their own estimates, etc. This process is based on standard shortest path algorithms that will be discussed in this chapter, but it
is also executed asynchronously, and with out-of-date information because of
communication delays between the nodes. Despite this fact, it turns out that
these distributed asynchronous algorithms maintain much of the validity of
their synchronous counterparts (see the textbooks by Bertsekas and Tsitsiklis
[1989], and Bertsekas and Gallager [1992] for related analysis).

There is an important connection between shortest path problems
and problems of deterministic discrete-state dynamic programming, which
involve sequential decision making over a finite number of time periods.
The following example shows that dynamic programming problems can be
formulated as shortest path problems. The reverse is also possible; that is,
any shortest path problem can be formulated as a dynamic programming
problem (see e.g., Bertsekas [1995a], Ch. 2).

Example 2.2. Dynamic Programming

Here we have a discrete-time dynamic system involving N stages. The state
of the system at the start of the kth stage is denoted by x_k and takes values
in a given finite set, which may depend on the index k. The initial state x_0 is
given. During the kth stage, the state of the system changes from x_k to x_{k+1}
according to an equation of the form

$$x_{k+1} = f_k(x_k, u_k), \tag{2.1}$$

where u_k is a control that takes values from a given finite set, which may
depend on the index k. This transition involves a cost $g_k(x_k, u_k)$. The final
transition from x_{N-1} to x_N, involves an additional terminal cost $G(x_N)$.
Here, the functions f_k, g_k, and G are given.

Given a control sequence $(u_0, \ldots, u_{N-1})$, the corresponding state sequence $(x_0, \ldots, x_N)$ is determined from the given initial state x_0 and the
system of Eq. (2.1). The objective in dynamic programming is to find a

control sequence and a corresponding state sequence such that the total cost

$$G(x_N) + \sum_{k=0}^{N-1} g_k(x_k, u_k)$$

is minimized.

For an example, consider an inventory system that operates over N time periods, and let x_k and u_k denote the number of items held in stock and number of items purchased at the beginning of period k, respectively. We require that u_k be an integer from a given range $[0, r_k]$. We assume that the stock evolves according to the equation

$$x_{k+1} = x_k + u_k - v_k,$$

where v_k is a known integer demand for period k; this is the system equation [cf. Eq. (2.1)]. A negative x_k here indicates unsatisfied demand that is backordered. A common type of cost used in inventory problems has the form

$$g_k(x_k, u_k) = h_k(x_k) + c_k u_k,$$

where c_k is a given cost per unit stock at period k, and $h_k(x_k)$ is a cost either for carrying excess inventory ($x_k > 0$) or for backordering demand ($x_k < 0$). For example $h_k(x_k) = \max\{a_k x_k, -b_k x_k\}$ or $h_k(x_k) = d_k x_k^2$, where a_k, b_k, and d_k are positive scalars, are both reasonable choices for cost function. Finally, we could take $G(x_N) = 0$ to indicate that the final stock x_N has no value [otherwise $G(x_N)$ indicates the cost (or negative salvage value) of x_N]. The objective in this problem is roughly to determine the sequence of purchases over time to minimize the costs of excess inventory and backordering demand over the N time periods.

To convert the dynamic programming problem to a shortest path problem, we introduce a graph such as the one of Fig. 2.1, where the arcs correspond to transitions between states at successive stages and each arc has a cost associated with it. To handle the final stage, we also add an artificial terminal node t. Each state x_N at stage N is connected to the terminal node t with an arc having cost $G(x_N)$. Control sequences correspond to paths originating at the initial state x_0 and terminating at one of the nodes corresponding to the final stage N. The optimal control sequence corresponds to a shortest path from node x_0 to node t. For an extensive treatment of dynamic programming and associated shortest path algorithms we refer to Bertsekas [1995a].

Shortest path problems arise often in contexts of scheduling and sequencing. The following two examples are typical.

Example 2.3. Project Management

Consider the planning of a project involving several activities, some of which must be completed before others can begin. The duration of each activity is

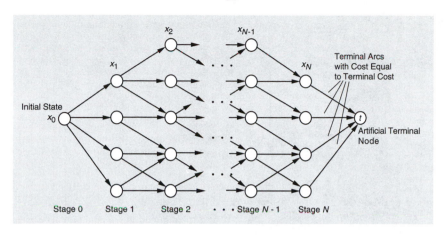

Figure 2.1: Converting a deterministic finite-state N-stage dynamic programming problem to a shortest path problem. Nodes correspond to states. An arc with start and end nodes x_k and x_{k+1}, respectively, corresponds to a transition of the form $x_{k+1} = f_k(x_k, u_k)$. The length of this arc is equal to the cost of the corresponding transition $g_k(x_k, u_k)$. The problem is equivalent to finding a shortest path from the initial state/node x_0 to the artificial terminal node t. Note that the state space and the possible transitions between states may depend on the stage index k.

known in advance. We want to find the time required to complete the project, as well as the *critical* activities, those that even if slightly delayed will result in a corresponding delay of completion of the overall project.

The problem can be represented by a graph where nodes represent completion of some phase of the project (cf. Fig. 2.2). An arc (i, j) represents an activity that starts once phase i is completed and has known duration $t_{ij} > 0$. A phase (node) j is completed when all activities or arcs (i, j) that are incoming to j are completed. Two special nodes 1 and N represent the start and end of the project, respectively. Node 1 has no incoming arcs, while node N has no outgoing arcs. Furthermore, there is at least one path from node 1 to every other node. An important characteristic of an activity network is that it is acyclic. This is inherent in the problem formulation and the interpretation of nodes as phase completions.

For any path $p = \{(1, j_1), (j_1, j_2,), \ldots, (j_k, i)\}$ from node 1 to a node i, let D_p be the duration of the path defined as the sum of durations of its activities; that is,

$$D_p = t_{ij_1} + t_{j_1 j_2} + \cdots + t_{j_k i}.$$

Then the time T_i required to complete phase i is

$$T_i = \max_{\substack{\text{paths } p \\ \text{from 1 to } i}} D_p.$$

The maximum above is attained by *some* path because there can be only a finite number of paths from 1 to i, since the network is acyclic. Thus to find

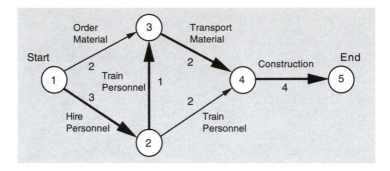

Figure 2.2: Example graph of an activity network. Arcs (i, j) represent activities and are labeled by the corresponding duration t_{ij}. Nodes represent completion of some phase of the project. A phase is completed if all activities associated with incoming arcs at the corresponding node are completed. The project is completed when all phases are completed. The project duration time is the longest sum of arc durations over paths that start at node 1 and end at node 5. The path of longest duration, also called a *critical path*, is shown with thick line. Because the graph is acyclic, finding this path is a shortest path problem with the length of each arc (i, j) being $-t_{ij}$. Activities on the critical path have the property that if any one of them is delayed, a corresponding delay of completion of the overall project will result.

T_i, we should find the *longest* path from 1 to i. Because the graph is acyclic, this problem may also be viewed as a shortest path problem with the length of each arc (i, j) being $-t_{ij}$. In particular, finding the duration of the project is equivalent to finding the shortest path from 1 to N. For further discussion of project management problems, we refer to the literature, e.g., the textbook by Elmaghraby [1978].

Example 2.4. The Paragraphing Problem

This problem arises in a word processing context, where we want to break down a given paragraph consisting of N words into lines for "optimal" appearance and readability. Suppose that we have a heuristic rule, which assigns to any sequence of words a cost that expresses the undesirability of grouping these words together in a line. Based on such a rule, we can assign a cost c_{ij} to a line starting with word i and ending with word $j - 1$ of the given paragraph. An optimally divided paragraph is one for which the sum of the costs of its lines is minimal.

We can formulate this as a shortest path problem. There are N nodes, which correspond to the N words of the paragraph, and there is an arc (i, j) with cost c_{ij} connecting any two words i and j with $i < j$. The arcs of the shortest path from node/word 1 to node/word N correspond to the lines of the optimally broken down paragraph.

The exercises contain a number of additional examples that illustrate the broad range of applications of the shortest path problem.

2.2 A GENERIC SHORTEST PATH ALGORITHM

The shortest path problem can be posed in a number of ways; for example, finding a shortest path from a single origin to a single destination, or finding a shortest path from each of several origins to each of several destinations. We focus initially on problems with a single origin and many destinations. For concreteness, we take the origin node to be node 1. The arc lengths a_{ij} are given scalars. They may be negative and/or noninteger, although on occasion we will assume in our analysis that they are nonnegative and/or integer, in which case we will state so explicitly.

In this section, we develop a broad class of shortest path algorithms for the single origin/all destinations problem. These algorithms maintain and adjust a vector $(d_1, d_2, \ldots, d_N)$, where each d_j, called the *label of node j*, is either a scalar or ∞. The use of labels is motivated by a simple optimality condition, which is given in the following proposition.

Proposition 2.1: Let $d_1, d_2, \ldots, d_N$ be scalars satisfying

$$d_j \leq d_i + a_{ij}, \qquad \forall \, (i,j) \in \mathcal{A}, \tag{2.2}$$

and let P be a path starting at a node i_1 and ending at a node i_k. If

$$d_j = d_i + a_{ij}, \qquad \text{for all arcs } (i,j) \text{ of } P, \tag{2.3}$$

then P is a shortest path from i_1 to i_k.

Proof: By adding Eq. (2.3) over the arcs of P, we see that the length of P is equal to the difference $d_{i_k} - d_{i_1}$ of labels of the end node and start node of P. By adding Eq. (2.2) over the arcs of any other path P' starting at i_1 and ending at i_k, we see that the length of P' must be no less than $d_{i_k} - d_{i_1}$. Therefore, P is a shortest path. **Q.E.D.**

The conditions (2.2) and (2.3) are called the *complementary slackness (CS) conditions for the shortest path problem.* This terminology is motivated by the connection of the shortest path problem with the minimum cost flow problem (cf. Section 1.2.1); we will see in Chapter 4 that the CS conditions of Prop. 2.1 are a special case of a general optimality condition (also called CS condition) for the equivalent minimum cost flow problem (in fact they are a special case of a corresponding CS condition for general linear programs; see e.g., Bertsimas and Tsitsiklis [1997], Dantzig [1963]). Furthermore, we will see that the scalars d_i in Prop. 2.1 are related to dual variables.

Let us now describe a prototype shortest path method that contains several interesting algorithms as special cases. In this method, we start with some vector of labels $(d_1, d_2, \ldots, d_N)$, we successively select arcs (i,j) that violate the CS condition (2.2), i.e., $d_j > d_i + a_{ij}$, and we set

$$d_j := d_i + a_{ij}.$$

This is continued until the CS condition $d_j \leq d_i + a_{ij}$ is satisfied for all arcs (i,j).

A key idea is that, in the course of the algorithm, d_i can be interpreted for all i as the length of some path P_i from 1 to i.† Therefore, if $d_j > d_i + a_{ij}$ for some arc (i,j), the path obtained by extending path P_i by arc (i,j), which has length $d_i + a_{ij}$, is a better path than the current path P_j, which has length d_j. Thus, the algorithm finds successively better paths from the origin to various destinations.

Instead of selecting arcs in arbitrary order to check violation of the CS condition, it is usually most convenient and efficient to select nodes, one-at-a-time according to some order, and simultaneously check violation of the CS condition for all of their outgoing arcs. The corresponding algorithm, referred to as *generic*, maintains a list of nodes V, called the *candidate list*, and a vector of labels $(d_1, d_2, \ldots, d_N)$, where each d_j is either a real number or ∞. Initially,

$$V = \{1\},$$

$$d_1 = 0, \qquad d_i = \infty, \qquad \forall\, i \neq 1.$$

The algorithm proceeds in iterations and terminates when V is empty. The typical iteration (assuming V is nonempty) is as follows:

Iteration of the Generic Shortest Path Algorithm

Remove a node i from the candidate list V. For each outgoing arc $(i,j) \in \mathcal{A}$, if $d_j > d_i + a_{ij}$, set

$$d_j := d_i + a_{ij}$$

and add j to V if it does not already belong to V.

---

† In the case of the origin node 1, we will interpret the label d_1 as either the length of a cycle that starts and ends at 1, or (in the case $d_1 = 0$) the length of the trivial "path" from 1 to itself.

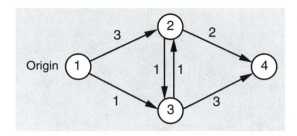

Iteration #	Candidate List V	Node Labels	Node out of V
1	$\{1\}$	$(0, \infty, \infty, \infty)$	1
2	$\{2,3\}$	$(0, 3, 1, \infty)$	2
3	$\{3,4\}$	$(0, 3, 1, 5)$	3
4	$\{4,2\}$	$(0, 2, 1, 4)$	4
5	$\{2\}$	$(0, 2, 1, 4)$	2
	$\varnothing$	$(0, 2, 1, 4)$	

Figure 2.3: Illustration of the generic shortest path algorithm. The numbers next to the arcs are the arc lengths. Note that node 2 enters the candidate list twice. If in iteration 2 node 3 was removed from V instead of node 2, each node would enter V only once. Thus, the order in which nodes are removed from V is significant.

It can be seen that, in the course of the algorithm, the labels are monotonically nonincreasing. Furthermore, we have

$$d_i < \infty \qquad \Longleftrightarrow \qquad i \text{ has entered } V \text{ at least once.}$$

Figure 2.3 illustrates the algorithm. The following proposition gives its main properties.

Proposition 2.2: Consider the generic shortest path algorithm.

(a) At the end of each iteration, the following conditions hold:

    (i) If $d_j < \infty$, then d_j is the length of some path that starts at 1 and ends at j.

    (ii) If $i \notin V$, then either $d_i = \infty$ or else

$$d_j \leq d_i + a_{ij}, \qquad \forall \, j \text{ such that } (i,j) \in \mathcal{A}.$$

(b) If the algorithm terminates, then upon termination, for all j with $d_j < \infty$, d_j is the shortest distance from 1 to j and

$$d_j = \begin{cases} \min_{(i,j) \in \mathcal{A}} \{d_i + a_{ij}\} & \text{if } j \neq 1, \\ 0 & \text{if } j = 1. \end{cases} \qquad (2.4)$$

Furthermore, upon termination we have $d_j = \infty$ if and only if there is no path from 1 to j.

(c) If the algorithm does not terminate, then there exists some node j and a sequence of paths that start at 1, end at j, and have lengths that diverge to $-\infty$.

(d) The algorithm terminates if and only if there is no path that starts at 1 and contains a cycle with negative length.

Proof: (a) We prove (i) by induction on the iteration count. Indeed, (i) holds at the end of the first iteration since the nodes $j \neq 1$ with $d_j < \infty$ are those for which $(1, j)$ is an arc and their labels are $d_j = a_{1j}$, while for the origin 1, we have $d_1 = 0$, which by convention is viewed as the length of the trivial "path" from 1 to itself. Suppose that (i) holds at the start of some iteration at which the node removed from V is i. Then $d_i < \infty$ (which is true for all nodes of V by the rules of the algorithm), and (by the induction hypothesis) d_i is the length of some path P_i starting at 1 and ending at i. When a label d_j changes as a result of the iteration, d_j is set to $d_i + a_{ij}$, which is the length of the path consisting of P_i followed by arc (i, j). Thus property (i) holds at the end of the iteration, completing the induction proof.

To prove (ii), note that for any i, each time i is removed from V, the condition $d_j \leq d_i + a_{ij}$ is satisfied for all $(i, j) \in \mathcal{A}$ by the rules of the algorithm. Up to the next entrance of i into V, d_i stays constant, while the labels d_j for all j with $(i, j) \in \mathcal{A}$ cannot increase, thereby preserving the condition $d_j \leq d_i + a_{ij}$.

(b) We first introduce the sets

$$I = \{i \mid d_i < \infty \text{ upon termination}\},$$

$$\bar{I} = \{i \mid d_i = \infty \text{ upon termination}\},$$

and we show that we have $j \in \bar{I}$ if and only if there is no path from 1 to j. Indeed, if $i \in I$, we have $d_i < \infty$ and therefore $d_j < \infty$ for all j such that (i, j) is an arc in view of condition (ii) of part (a), so that $j \in I$. It follows that there is no path from any node of I (and in particular, node 1) to any node of $\bar{I}$. Conversely, if there is no path from 1 to j, it follows from condition (i) of part (a) that we cannot have $d_j < \infty$ upon termination, so $j \in \overline{I}$.

We show now that for all $j \in I$, upon termination, d_j is the shortest distance from 1 to j and Eq. (2.4) holds. Indeed, conditions (i) and (ii) of part (a) imply that upon termination we have, for all $i \in I$,

$$d_j \leq d_i + a_{ij}, \qquad \forall \; j \text{ such that } (i,j) \in \mathcal{A}, \qquad (2.5)$$

while d_i is the length of some path from 1 to i, denoted P_i. Fix a node $m \in I$, and consider any path P from 1 to m. By adding the condition (2.5) over the arcs of P, we see that the length of P is no less than $d_m - d_1$, which is less or equal to d_m (we have $d_1 \leq 0$, since initially $d_1 = 0$ and all node labels are monotonically nonincreasing). Hence P_m is a shortest path from 1 to m and the shortest distance is d_m. Furthermore, the equality $d_j = d_i + a_{ij}$ must hold for all arcs (i,j) on the shortest paths P_m, $m \in I$, implying that $d_j = \min_{(i,j)\in\mathcal{A}}\{d_i + a_{ij}\}$ for all $j \in I$ with $j \neq 1$, while $d_1 = 0$.

(c) If the algorithm never terminates, some label d_j must decrease strictly an infinite number of times, generating a corresponding sequence of distinct paths P_j as per condition (i) of part (a). Each of these paths can be decomposed into a simple path from 1 to j plus a collection of simple cycles, as in Exercise 1.4 of Chapter 1. Since the number of simple paths from 1 to j is finite, and the length of P_j is monotonically decreasing, it follows that P_j eventually must involve a cycle with negative length. By replicating this cycle a sufficiently large number of times, one can obtain paths from 1 to j with arbitrarily small length.

(d) Using part (c), we have that the algorithm will terminate if and only if there is a lower bound on the length of all paths that start at node 1. Thus, the algorithm will terminate if and only if there is no path that starts at node 1 and contains a cycle with negative length.   **Q.E.D.**

When some arc lengths are negative, Prop. 2.2 points to a way to detect existence of a path that starts at the origin 1 and contains a cycle of negative length. If such a path exists, it can be shown under mild assumptions that the label of at least one node will diverge to $-\infty$ (see Exercise 2.32). We can thus monitor whether for some j we have

$$d_j < (N-1) \min_{(i,j)\in\mathcal{A}} a_{ij}.$$

When this condition occurs, the path from 1 to j whose length is equal to d_j [as per Prop. 2.2(a)] must contain a negative cycle [if it were simple, it would consist of at most $N-1$ arcs, and its length could not be smaller than $(N-1)\min_{(i,j)\in\mathcal{A}} a_{ij}$; a similar argument would apply if it were not simple but it contained only cycles of nonnegative length].

Bellman's Equation and Shortest Path Construction

When all cycles have nonnegative length and there exists a path from node 1 to every node j, then Prop. 2.2 shows that the generic algorithm terminates and that, upon termination, all labels are equal to the corresponding shortest distances, and satisfy $d_1 = 0$ and

$$d_j = \min_{(i,j) \in \mathcal{A}} \{d_i + a_{ij}\}, \qquad \forall \, j \neq 1. \tag{2.6}$$

This is known as *Bellman's equation* and it has an intuitive meaning: it indicates that the shortest distance from 1 to j is obtained by optimally choosing the predecessor i of node j in order to minimize the sum of the shortest distance from 1 to i and the length of arc (i, j). It also indicates that if P_j is a shortest path from 1 to j, and a node i belongs to P_j, then the portion of P_j from 1 to i, is a shortest path from 1 to i.

From Bellman's equation, we can obtain the shortest paths (in addition to the shortest path lengths) if all cycles not including node 1 have strictly positive length. To do this, select for each $j \neq 1$ one arc (i, j) that attains the minimum in $d_j = \min_{(i,j) \in \mathcal{A}} \{d_i + a_{ij}\}$ and consider the subgraph consisting of these $N - 1$ arcs; see Fig. 2.4. To find the shortest path to any node j, start from j and follow the corresponding arcs of the subgraph backward until node 1 is reached. Note that the same node cannot be reached twice before node 1 is reached, since a cycle would be formed that, on the basis of Eqs. (2.6), would have zero length. [To see this, let $(i_1, i_2, \ldots, i_k, i_1)$ be the cycle and add the equations

$$d_{i_1} = d_{i_2} + a_{i_2 i_1}$$

$$\cdots$$

$$d_{i_{k-1}} = d_{i_k} + a_{i_k i_{k-1}}$$

$$d_{i_k} = d_{i_1} + a_{i_1 i_k}$$

obtaining $a_{i_2 i_1} + \cdots + a_{i_k i_{k-1}} + a_{i_1 i_k} = 0$.] Since the subgraph is connected and has $N - 1$ arcs, it must be a spanning tree. We call this subgraph a *shortest path spanning tree*, and we note its special structure: it has a root (node 1) and every arc of the tree is directed away from the root. The preceding argument can also be used to show that Bellman's equation has no solution other than the shortest distances; see Exercise 2.5.

A shortest path spanning tree can also be constructed in the process of executing the generic shortest path algorithm by recording the arc (i, j) every time d_j is decreased to $d_i + a_{ij}$; see Exercise 2.4.

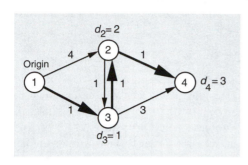

Figure 2.4: Example of construction of shortest path spanning tree. The arc lengths are shown next to the arcs, and the shortest distances are shown next to the nodes. For each $j \neq 1$, we select an arc (i, j) such that

$$d_j = d_i + a_{ij}$$

and we form the shortest path spanning tree. The arcs selected in this example are $(1, 3)$, $(3, 2)$, and $(2, 4)$.

Advanced Initialization

The generic algorithm need not be started with the initial conditions

$$V = \{1\}, \qquad d_1 = 0, \qquad d_i = \infty, \quad \forall \, i \neq 1,$$

in order to work correctly. Any set of labels $(d_1, \ldots, d_N)$ and candidate list V can be used initially, as long as they satisfy the conditions of Prop. 2.2(a). It can be seen that the proof of the remaining parts of Prop. 2.2 go through under these conditions.

In particular, the algorithm works correctly if the labels and the candidate list are initialized so that $d_1 = 0$ and:

(a) For each node i, d_i is either ∞ or else it is the length of a path from 1 to i.

(b) The candidate list V contains all nodes i such that

$$d_i + a_{ij} < d_j \text{ for some } (i, j) \in \mathcal{A}. \tag{2.7}$$

This kind of initialization is very useful in reoptimization contexts, where we have to solve a large number of similar problems that differ slightly from each other; for example they may differ by just a few arc lengths or they may have a slightly different node set. The lengths of the shortest paths of one problem can be used as the starting labels for another problem, and substantial computational savings may be obtained, because it is likely that many of the nodes will maintain their shortest path lengths and will never enter V.

Another important situation where an advanced initialization is very useful arises if, by using heuristics or an available solution of a similar shortest path problem, we can construct a set of "good" paths from node 1 to the other nodes. Then we can use the lengths of these paths as the initial labels in the generic shortest path algorithm and start with a candidate list consisting of the nodes where the CS condition is violated [cf. Eq. (2.7)].

Finally, let us note another technique that is sometimes useful in reoptimization settings. Suppose that we have some scalars $\delta_1, \ldots, \delta_N$ and we change the arc lengths to

$$\hat{a}_{ij} = a_{ij} + \delta_i - \delta_j.$$

Then it can be seen that the length of any path from a node m to a node n will be increased by $\delta_m - \delta_n$, while the shortest paths will be unaffected. Thus it may be advantageous to use the modified arc lengths $\hat{a}_{ij}$ instead of the original lengths a_{ij}, if this will enhance the application of a suitable shortest path algorithm. For example, we may be able with proper choice of δ_i, to reduce the arc cost range $\max_{(i,j)} |\hat{a}_{ij}|$ (this is helpful in some algorithms) or to make $\hat{a}_{ij}$ nonnegative (see Section 2.7 for an application of this idea).

Implementations of the Generic Algorithm

There are many implementations of the generic algorithm. They differ in how they select the node to be removed from the candidate list V, and they are broadly divided into two categories:

(a) *Label setting methods.* In these methods, the node i removed from V is a node with minimum label. Under the assumption that *all arc lengths are nonnegative*, these methods have a remarkable property: each node will enter V at most *once*, as we will show shortly; its label has its permanent or final value at the first time it is removed from V. The most time-consuming part of these methods is calculating the minimum label node in V at each iteration; there are several implementations, that use a variety of creative procedures to obtain this minimum.

(b) *Label correcting methods.* In these methods the choice of the node i removed from V is less sophisticated than in label setting methods, and requires less calculation. However, a node may enter V multiple times.

There are several worst-case complexity bounds for label setting and label correcting methods. The best bounds for the case of nonnegative arc lengths correspond to label setting methods. The best practical methods, however, are not necessarily the ones with the best complexity bounds, as will be discussed in the next two sections.

In practice, when the arc lengths are nonnegative, the best label setting methods and the best label correcting methods are competitive. As a general rule, a sparse graph favors the use of a label correcting over a label setting method for reasons that will be explained later (see the discussion at the end of Section 2.4). An important advantage of label correcting methods is that they are more general, since they do not require nonnegativity of the arc lengths.

2.3 LABEL SETTING (DIJKSTRA) METHODS

In this section we discuss various implementations of the label setting approach. The prototype label setting method, first published by Dijkstra [1959] but also discovered independently by several other researchers, is the special case of the generic algorithm where the node i removed from the candidate list V at each iteration has minimum label, that is,

$$d_i = \min_{j \in V} d_j.$$

For convenient reference, let us state this method explicitly.

Initially, we have

$$V = \{1\},$$

$$d_1 = 0, \qquad d_i = \infty, \quad \forall\, i \neq 1.$$

The method proceeds in iterations and terminates when V is empty. The typical iteration (assuming V is nonempty) is as follows:

Iteration of the Label Setting Method

Remove from the candidate list V a node i such that

$$d_i = \min_{j \in V} d_j.$$

For each outgoing arc $(i, j) \in \mathcal{A}$, if $d_j > d_i + a_{ij}$, set

$$d_j := d_i + a_{ij}$$

and add j to V if it does not already belong to V.

Figure 2.5 illustrates the label setting method. Some insight into the method can be gained by considering the set W of nodes that have already been in V but are not currently in V:

$$W = \{i \mid d_i < \infty, i \notin V\}.$$

We will prove later, in Prop. 2.3(a), that as a consequence of the policy of removing from V a minimum label node, W contains nodes with "small" labels throughout the algorithm, in the sense that

$$d_j \leq d_i, \qquad \text{if } j \in W \text{ and } i \notin W. \tag{2.8}$$

Using this property and the assumption $a_{ij} \geq 0$, it can be seen that when a node i is removed from V, we have, for all $j \in W$ for which (i, j) is an arc,

$$d_j \leq d_i + a_{ij}.$$

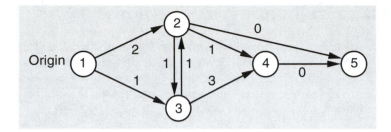

Iteration #	Candidate List V	Node Labels	Node out of V
1	$\{1\}$	$(0, \infty, \infty, \infty, \infty)$	1
2	$\{2, 3\}$	$(0, 2, 1, \infty, \infty)$	3
3	$\{2, 4\}$	$(0, 2, 1, 4, \infty)$	2
4	$\{4, 5\}$	$(0, 2, 1, 3, 2)$	5
5	$\{4\}$	$(0, 2, 1, 3, 2)$	4
	$\emptyset$	$(0, 2, 1, 3, 2)$	

Figure 2.5: Example illustrating the label setting method. At each iteration, the node with the minimum label is removed from V. Each node enters V only once.

Hence, once a node enters W, it stays in W and its label does not change further. Thus, W can be viewed as the set of *permanently labeled nodes*, that is, the nodes that have acquired a final label, which by Prop. 2.2, must be equal to their shortest distance from the origin.

The following proposition makes the preceding argument precise and proves some additional facts.

Proposition 2.3: Assume that all arc lengths are nonnegative.

(a) For any iteration of the label setting method, the following hold for the set

$$W = \{i \mid d_i < \infty, i \notin V\}. \qquad (2.9)$$

    (i) No node belonging to W at the start of the iteration will enter the candidate list V during the iteration.

    (ii) At the end of the iteration, we have $d_i \leq d_j$ for all $i \in W$ and $j \notin W$.

(iii) For each node j, consider simple paths that start at 1, end at j, and have all their other nodes in W at the end of the iteration. Then the label d_j at the end of the iteration is equal to the length of the shortest of these paths ($d_j = \infty$ if no such path exists).

(b) The label setting method will terminate, and all nodes with a final label that is finite will be removed from the candidate list V exactly once in order of increasing shortest distance from node 1; that is, if the final labels of i and j are finite and satisfy $d_i < d_j$, then i will be removed before j.

Proof: (a) Properties (i) and (ii) will be proved simultaneously by induction on the iteration count. Clearly (i) and (ii) hold for the initial iteration at which node 1 exits V and enters W.

Suppose that (i) and (ii) hold for iteration $k - 1$, and suppose that during iteration k, node i satisfies $d_i = \min_{j \in V} d_j$ and exits V. Let W and $\overline{W}$ be the set of Eq. (2.9) at the start and at the end of iteration k, respectively. Let d_j and $\overline{d}_j$ be the label of each node j at the start and at the end of iteration k, respectively. Since by the induction hypothesis we have $d_j \leq d_i$ for all $j \in W$, and $a_{ij} \geq 0$ for all arcs (i, j), it follows that $d_j \leq d_i + a_{ij}$ for all arcs (i, j) with $j \in W$. Hence, a node $j \in W$ cannot enter V at iteration k. This completes the induction proof of property (i), and shows that

$$\overline{W} = W \cup \{i\}.$$

Thus, at iteration k, the only labels that may change are the labels d_j of nodes $j \notin \overline{W}$ such that (i, j) is an arc; the label $\overline{d}_j$ at the end of the iteration will be $\min\{d_j, d_i + a_{ij}\}$. Since $a_{ij} \geq 0$, $d_i \leq d_j$ for all $j \notin W$, and $d_i = \overline{d}_i$, we must have $\overline{d}_i \leq \overline{d}_j$ for all $j \notin \overline{W}$. Since by the induction hypothesis we have $d_m \leq d_i$ and $d_m = \overline{d}_m$ for all $m \in \overline{W}$, it follows that $\overline{d}_m \leq \overline{d}_j$ for all $m \in \overline{W}$ and $j \notin \overline{W}$. This completes the induction proof of property (ii).

To prove property (iii), choose any node j and consider the subgraph consisting of the nodes $W \cup \{j\}$ together with the arcs that have both end nodes in $W \cup \{j\}$. Consider also a modified shortest path problem involving this subgraph, and the same origin and arc lengths as in the original shortest path problem. In view of properties (i) and (ii), the label setting method applied to the modified shortest path problem yields the same sequence of nodes exiting V and the same sequence of labels as when applied to the original problem up to the current iteration. By Prop. 2.2, the label setting method for the modified problem terminates with the labels equal to the shortest distances of the modified problem at the current iteration. This means that the labels at the end of the iteration have the property stated in the proposition.

(b) Since there is no cycle with negative length, by Prop. 2.2(d), we see that the label setting method will terminate. At each iteration the node removed from V is added to W, and according to property (i) (proved above), no node from W is ever returned to V. Therefore, each node with a final label that is finite will be removed from V and simultaneously entered in W exactly once, and, by the rules of the algorithm, its label cannot change after its entrance in W. Property (ii) then shows that each new node added to W has a label at least as large as the labels of the nodes already in W. Therefore, the nodes are removed from V in the order stated in the proposition.   **Q.E.D.**

2.3.1   Performance of Label Setting Methods

In label setting methods, the candidate list V is typically maintained with the help of some data structure that facilitates the removal and the addition of nodes, and also facilitates finding the minimum label node from the list. The choice of data structure is crucial for good practical performance as well as for good theoretical worst-case performance.

To gain some insight into this, we first consider a somewhat naive implementation that will serve as a yardstick for comparison. By Prop. 2.3, there will be exactly N iterations, and in each of these, the candidate list V will be searched for a minimum label node. Suppose this is done by examining all nodes in sequence, checking whether they belong to V, and finding one with minimum label among those who do. Searching V in this way requires $O(N)$ operations per iteration, for a total of $O(N^2)$ operations. Also during the algorithm, we must examine each arc (i, j) exactly once to check whether the condition $d_j > d_i + a_{ij}$ holds, and to set $d_j := d_i + a_{ij}$ if it does. This requires $O(A)$ operations, which is dominated by the preceding $O(N^2)$ estimate.

The $O(A)$ operation count for arc examination is unavoidable and cannot be reduced [each arc (i, j) must be checked at least once just to verify the optimality condition $d_j \leq d_i + a_{ij}$]. However, the $O(N^2)$ operation count for minimum label searching can be reduced considerably by using appropriate data structures. The best estimates of the worst-case running time that have been thus obtained are $O(A + N \log N)$ and $O(A + N\sqrt{\log C})$, where C is the arc length range $C = \max_{(i,j) \in \mathcal{A}} a_{ij}$; see Fredman and Tarjan [1984], and Ahuja, Mehlhorn, Orlin, and Tarjan [1990]. On the basis of present experience, however, the implementations that perform best in practice have considerable less favorable running time estimates. The explanation for this is that the $O(\cdot)$ estimates involve a different constant for each method and also correspond to worst-case problem instances. Thus, the worst-case complexity estimates may not provide a reliable practical comparison of various methods. We now discuss two of the most popular implementations of the label setting method.

2.3.2   The Binary Heap Method

Here the nodes are organized as a binary heap on the basis of label values and membership in V; see Fig. 2.6. The node at the top of the heap is the node of V that has minimum label, and the label of every node in V is no larger than the labels of all the nodes that are in V and are its descendants in the heap. Nodes that are not in V may be in the heap but may have no descendants that are in V.

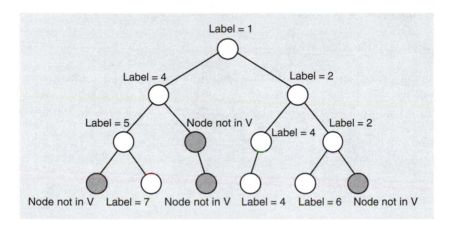

Figure 2.6: A binary heap organized on the basis of node labels is a binary balanced tree such that the label of each node of V is no larger than the labels of all its descendants that are in V. Nodes that are not in V may have no descendants that are in V. The topmost node, called the *root*, has the minimum label. The tree is balanced in that the numbers of arcs in the paths from the root to any nodes with no descendants differ by at most 1. If the label of some node decreases, the node must be moved upward toward the root, requiring $O(\log N)$ operations. [It takes $O(1)$ operations to compare the label of a node i with the label of one of its descendants j, and to interchange the positions of i and j if the label of j is smaller. Since there are $\log N$ levels in the tree, it takes at most $\log N$ such comparisons and interchanges to move a node upward to the appropriate position once its label is decreased.] Similarly, when the topmost node is removed from V, moving the node downward to the appropriate level in the heap requires at most $\log N$ steps and $O(\log N)$ operations. (Each step requires the interchange of the position of the node and the position of one of its descendants. The descendant must be in V for the step to be executed; if both descendants are in V, the one with smaller label is selected.)

At each iteration, the top node of the heap is removed from V. Furthermore, the labels of some nodes already in V may decrease, so these may have to be repositioned in the heap; also, some other nodes may enter

V for the first time and have to be inserted in the heap at the right place. It can be seen that each of these removals, repositionings, and insertions can be done in $O(\log N)$ time. There are a total of N removals and N node insertions, so the number of operations for maintaining the heap is $O\big((N + R)\log N\big)$, where R is the total number of node repositionings. There is at most one repositioning per arc, since each arc is examined at most once, so we have $R \leq A$ and the total operation count for maintaining the heap is $O(A \log N)$. This dominates the $O(A)$ operation count to examine all arcs, so the worst-case running time of the method is $O(A \log N)$. On the other hand, practical experience indicates that the number of node repositionings R is usually a small multiple of N, and considerably less than the upper bound A. Thus, the running time of the method in practice typically grows approximately like $O(A + N \log N)$.

2.3.3 Dial's Algorithm

This algorithm, due to Dial [1969], requires that all arc lengths are *nonnegative integers*. It uses a naive yet often surprisingly effective method for finding the minimum label node in V. The idea is to maintain for every possible label value, a list of the nodes that have that value. Since every finite label is equal to the length of some path with no cycles [Prop. 2.3(a), part (iii)], the possible label values range from 0 to $(N - 1)C$, where

$$C = \max_{(i,j)\in\mathcal{A}} a_{ij}.$$

Thus, we may scan the $(N - 1)C + 1$ possible label values (in ascending order) and look for a label value with nonempty list, instead of scanning the candidate list V.

To visualize the algorithm, it is useful to think of each integer in the range $[0, (N - 1)C]$ as some kind of container, referred to as a *bucket*. Each bucket b holds the nodes with label equal to b. Tracing steps, we see that the method starts with the origin node 1 in bucket 0 and all other buckets empty. At the first iteration, each node j with $(1, j) \in \mathcal{A}$ enters the candidate list V and is inserted in bucket a_{1j}. After we are done with bucket 0, we proceed to check bucket 1. If it is nonempty, we repeat the process, removing from V all nodes with label 1 and moving other nodes to smaller numbered buckets as required; if not, we check bucket 2, and so on. Figure 2.7 illustrates the method with an example.

Let us now consider the efficient implementation of the algorithm. We first note that a doubly linked list (see Fig. 2.8) can be used to maintain the set of nodes belonging to a given bucket, so that checking the emptiness of a bucket and inserting or removing a node from a bucket are easy, requiring $O(1)$ operations. With such a data structure, the time required for minimum label node searching is $O(NC)$, and the time required for adjusting node labels and repositioning nodes between buckets is $O(A)$. Thus the

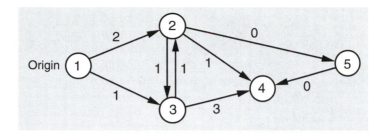

Iter. #	Cand. List V	Node Labels	Buck. 0	Buck. 1	Buck. 2	Buck. 3	Buck. 4	Out of V
1	$\{1\}$	$(0,\infty,\infty,\infty,\infty)$	1	–	–	–	–	1
2	$\{2,3\}$	$(0,2,1,\infty,\infty)$	1	3	2	–	–	3
3	$\{2,4\}$	$(0,2,1,4,\infty)$	1	3	2	–	4	2
4	$\{4,5\}$	$(0,2,1,3,2)$	1	3	2,5	4	–	5
5	$\{4\}$	$(0,2,1,2,2)$	1	3	2,4,5	–	–	4
	$\varnothing$	$(0,2,1,2,2)$	1	3	2,4,5	–	–	

Figure 2.7: An example illustrating Dial's method.

overall running time is $O(A + NC)$. The algorithm is pseudopolynomial, but for small values of C (much smaller than N) it performs very well in practice.

In problems where the minimum arc length

$$\bar{a} = \min_{(i,j)\in\mathcal{A}} a_{ij}$$

is greater than 1, the performance of the algorithm can be improved by using a device suggested by Denardo and Fox [1979]. The idea is that the label of a node cannot be reduced below $b + \bar{a}$ while searching bucket b, so that no new nodes will be added to buckets $b + 1, \ldots, b + \bar{a} - 1$ while searching bucket b. As a result, buckets $b, b+1, \ldots, b+\bar{a}-1$ can be lumped into a single bucket. To take advantage of this idea, we can use

$$\left\lceil \frac{(N-1)C+1}{\bar{a}} \right\rceil$$

buckets, and follow the strategy of placing node i into bucket b if

$$\bar{a}b \le d_i \le \bar{a}(b+1) - 1.$$

The running time of the algorithm is then reduced to $O\big(A + (NC/\bar{a})\big)$.

Bucket b	0	1	2	3	4	5	6	7	8
Contents of b	1	–	3,4,5	2,7	–	6	–	–	–
$FIRST(b)$	1	0	3	2	0	6	0	0	0

Node i	1	2	3	4	5	6	7
Label d_i	0	3	2	2	2	5	3
$NEXT(i)$	0	7	4	5	0	0	0
$PREVIOUS(i)$	0	0	0	1	4	0	2

Figure 2.8: Illustration of a doubly linked list data structure to maintain the candidate list V in buckets. In this example, the nodes in V are numbered $1, 2, \ldots, 7$, and the buckets are numbered $0, 1, \ldots, 8$. A node i belongs to bucket b if $d_i = b$.

As shown in the first table, for each bucket b we maintain the first node of the bucket in an array element $FIRST(b)$, where $FIRST(b) = 0$ if bucket b is empty.

As shown in the second table, for every node i we maintain two array elements, $NEXT(i)$ and $PREVIOUS(i)$, giving the next node and the preceding node, respectively, of node i in the bucket where i is currently residing [$NEXT(i) = 0$ or $PREVIOUS(i) = 0$ if i is the last node or the first node in its bucket, respectively].

Another useful idea is that it is sufficient to maintain only $C + 1$ buckets, rather than $(N - 1)C + 1$, thereby significantly saving in memory. The reason is that if we are currently searching bucket b, then all buckets beyond $b + C$ are known to be empty. To see this, note that the label d_j of any node j must be of the form $d_i + a_{ij}$, where i is a node that has already been removed from the candidate list. Since $d_i \le b$ and $a_{ij} \le C$, it follows that $d_j \le b + C$.

The idea of using buckets to maintain the nodes of the candidate list can be generalized considerably. In particular, buckets of width larger than $\max\{1, \min_{(i,j) \in \mathcal{A}} a_{ij}\}$ may be used. This results in fewer buckets to search over, thereby alleviating the $O(NC)$ bottleneck of the running time of the algorithm. There is a price for this, namely the need to search for a minimum label node within the current bucket. This search can be speeded up by using buckets with nonuniform widths, and by breaking down buckets of large width into buckets of smaller width at the right moment. With intelligent strategies of this type, one may obtain label setting methods with very good polynomial complexity bounds; see Johnson [1977], Denardo and Fox [1979], Ahuja, Mehlhorn, Orlin, and Tarjan [1990]. In practice, however, the simpler algorithm of Dial has been more popular than these methods.

2.4 LABEL CORRECTING METHODS

We now turn to the analysis of label correcting methods. In these methods, the selection of the node to be removed from the candidate list V is simpler and requires less overhead than in label setting methods, at the expense of multiple entrances of nodes in V. All of these methods use some type of queue to maintain the candidate list V. They differ in the way the queue is structured, and in the choice of the queue position into which nodes are inserted. In this section, we will discuss some of the most interesting possibilities.

2.4.1   The Bellman-Ford Method

The simplest label correcting method uses a first-in first-out rule to update the queue that is used to store the candidate list V. In particular, a node is always removed from the top of the queue, and a node, upon entrance in the candidate list, is placed at the bottom of the queue. Thus, it can be seen that the method operates in *cycles* of iterations: the first cycle consists of just iterating on node 1; in each subsequent cycle, the nodes that entered the candidate list during the preceding cycle, are removed from the list in the order that they were entered. We will refer to this method as the *Bellman-Ford method*, because it is closely related to a method proposed by Bellman [1957] and Ford [1956] based on dynamic programming ideas (see Exercise 2.6).

The complexity analysis of the method is based on the following property, which we will prove shortly:

Bellman-Ford Property

For each node i and integer $k \geq 1$, let

$d_i^k =$ Shortest distance from 1 to i using paths that have k arcs or less,

where $d_i^k = \infty$ if there is no path from 1 to i with k arcs or less. Then the label d_i at the end of the kth cycle of iterations of the Bellman-Ford method is less or equal to d_i^k.

In the case where all cycles have nonnegative length, the shortest distance of every node can be achieved with a path having $N - 1$ arcs or less, so the above Bellman-Ford property implies that the method finds all the shortest distances after at most $N - 1$ cycles. Since each cycle of iterations requires a total of $O(A)$ operations (each arc is examined at most once in each cycle), the running time of the Bellman-Ford method is $O(NA)$.

To prove the Bellman-Ford property, we first note that

$$d_j^{k+1} = \min\left\{d_j^k, \min_{(i,j)\in\mathcal{A}}\{d_i^k + a_{ij}\}\right\}, \qquad \forall\, j,\, k \geq 1, \qquad (2.10)$$

since d_j^{k+1} is either the length of a path from 1 to j with k arcs or less, in which case it is equal to d_j^k, or else it is the length of some path that starts at 1 goes to a predecessor node i with k arcs or less, and then goes to j using arc (i,j). We now prove the Bellman-Ford property by induction. At the end of the 1st cycle, we have for all i,

$$d_i = \begin{cases} 0 & \text{if } i = 1, \\ a_{1i} & \text{if } i \neq 1 \text{ and } (1,i) \in \mathcal{A}, \\ \infty & \text{if } i \neq 1 \text{ and } (1,i) \notin \mathcal{A}, \end{cases}$$

while

$$d_i^1 = \begin{cases} a_{1i} & \text{if } (1,i) \in \mathcal{A}, \\ \infty & \text{if } (1,i) \notin \mathcal{A}, \end{cases}$$

so that $d_i \leq d_i^1$ for all i. Let d_i and V be the node labels and the contents of the candidate list at the end of the kth cycle, respectively. Let also $\bar{d}_i$ be the node labels at the end of the $(k+1)$st cycle. We assume that $d_i \leq d_i^k$ for all i, and we will show that $\bar{d}_i \leq d_i^{k+1}$ for all i. Indeed, by condition (ii) of Prop. 2.2(a), we have

$$d_j \leq d_i + a_{ij}, \qquad \forall\, (i,j) \in \mathcal{A} \text{ with } i \notin V,$$

and since $\bar{d}_j \leq d_j$, it follows that

$$\bar{d}_j \leq d_i + a_{ij}, \qquad \forall\, (i,j) \in \mathcal{A} \text{ with } i \notin V. \qquad (2.11)$$

We also have

$$\bar{d}_j \leq d_i + a_{ij}, \qquad \forall\, (i,j) \in \mathcal{A} \text{ with } i \in V, \qquad (2.12)$$

since at the time when i is removed from V, its current label, call it $\tilde{d}_i$, satisfies $\tilde{d}_i \leq d_i$, and the label of j is set to $\tilde{d}_i + a_{ij}$ if it exceeds $\tilde{d}_i + a_{ij}$. By combining Eqs. (2.11) and (2.12), we see that

$$\bar{d}_j \leq \min_{(i,j)\in\mathcal{A}}\{d_i + a_{ij}\} \leq \min_{(i,j)\in\mathcal{A}}\{d_i^k + a_{ij}\}, \qquad \forall\, j, \qquad (2.13)$$

where the second inequality follows by the induction hypothesis. We also have $\overline{d}_j \leq d_j \leq d_j^k$ by the induction hypothesis, so Eq. (2.13) yields

$$\overline{d}_j \leq \min \left\{ d_j^k, \min_{(i,j) \in \mathcal{A}} \{ d_i^k + a_{ij} \} \right\} = d_j^{k+1},$$

where the last equality holds by Eq. (2.10). This completes the induction proof of the Bellman-Ford property.

The Bellman-Ford method can be used to detect the presence of a negative cycle. Indeed, from Prop. 2.2, we see that the method fails to terminate if and only if there exists a path that starts at 1 and contains a negative cycle. Thus in view of the Bellman-Ford property, such a path exists if and only if the algorithm has not terminated by the end of $N - 1$ cycles.

The best practical implementations of label correcting methods are more sophisticated than the Bellman-Ford method. Their worst-case running time is no better than the $O(NA)$ time of the Bellman-Ford method, and in some cases it is considerably slower. Yet their practical performance is often considerably better. We will discuss next three different types of implementations.

2.4.2   The D'Esopo-Pape Algorithm

In this method, a node is always removed from the top of the queue used to maintain the candidate list V. A node, upon entrance in the queue, is placed at the bottom of the queue if it has never been in the queue before; otherwise it is placed at the top.

The idea here is that when a node i is removed from the queue, its label affects the labels of a subset B_i of the neighbor nodes j with $(i,j) \in \mathcal{A}$. When the label of i changes again, it is likely that the labels of the nodes in B_i will require updating also. It is thus argued that it makes sense to place the node at the top of the queue so that the labels of the nodes in B_i get a chance to be updated as quickly as possible.

While this rationale is not quite convincing, it seems to work well in practice for a broad variety of problems, including types of problems where there are some negative arc lengths. On the other hand, special examples have been constructed (Kershenbaum [1981], Shier and Witzgall [1981]), where the D'Esopo-Pape algorithm performs very poorly. In particular, in these examples, the number of entrances of some nodes in the candidate list V is not polynomial. Computational studies have also shown that for some classes of problems, the practical performance of the D'Esopo-Pape algorithm can be very poor (Bertsekas [1993a]). Pallottino [1984], and Gallo and Pallottino [1988] give a polynomial variant of the algorithm, whose practical performance, however, is roughly similar to the one of the original version.

2.4.3   The SLF and LLL Algorithms

These methods are motivated by the hypothesis that when the arc lengths
are nonnegative, the queue management strategy should try to place nodes
with small labels near the top of the queue. For a supporting heuristic
argument, note that for a node j to reenter V, some node i such that
$d_i + a_{ij} < d_j$ must first exit V. Thus, the smaller d_j was at the previous
exit of j from V the less likely it is that $d_i + a_{ij}$ will subsequently become less
than d_j for some node $i \in V$ and arc (i, j). In particular, if $d_j \leq \min_{i \in V} d_i$
and the arc lengths a_{ij} are nonnegative, it is impossible that subsequent
to the exit of j from V we will have $d_i + a_{ij} < d_j$ for some $i \in V$.

We can think of Dijkstra's method as implicitly placing at the top of
an imaginary queue the node with the smallest label, thereby resulting in
the minimal number N of iterations. The methods of this section attempt
to emulate approximately the minimum label selection policy of Dijkstra's
algorithm with a much smaller computational overhead. They are primarily
suitable for the case of nonnegative arc lengths. While they will work even
when there are some negative arc lengths as per Prop. 2.2, there is no
reason to expect that in this case they will terminate faster (or slower)
than any of the other label correcting methods that we will discuss.

A simple strategy for placing nodes with small label near the top of the
queue is the *Small Label First method* (SLF for short). Here the candidate
list V is maintained as a double ended queue Q. At each iteration, the
node exiting V is the top node of Q. The rule for inserting new nodes is
given below:

SLF Strategy

Whenever a node j enters Q, its label d_j is compared with the label
d_i of the top node i of Q. If $d_j \leq d_i$, node j is entered at the top of
Q; otherwise j is entered at the bottom of Q.

The SLF strategy provides a rule for inserting nodes in Q, but always
removes (selects for iteration) nodes from the top of Q. A more sophisticated strategy is to make an effort to remove from Q nodes with small
labels. A simple possibility, called the *Large Label Last method* (LLL for
short) works as follows: At each iteration, when the node at the top of Q
has a larger label than the average node label in Q (defined as the sum of
the labels of the nodes in Q divided by the cardinality $|Q|$ of Q), this node
is not removed from Q, but is instead repositioned to the bottom of Q.

LLL Strategy

Let i be the top node of Q, and let

$$a = \frac{\sum_{j \in Q} d_j}{|Q|}.$$

If $d_i > a$, move i to the bottom of Q. Repeat until a node i such that $d_i \leq a$ is found and is removed from Q.

It is simple to combine the SLF queue insertion and the LLL node removal strategies, thereby obtaining a method referred to as SLF/LLL.

Experience suggests that, assuming nonnegative arc lengths, the SLF, LLL, and combined SLF/LLL algorithms perform substantially faster than the Bellman-Ford and the D'Esopo-Pape methods. The strategies are also well-suited for parallel computation (see Bertsekas, Guerriero, and Musmanno [1996]). The combined SLF/LLL method consistently requires a smaller number of iterations than either SLF or LLL, although the gain in number of iterations is sometimes offset by the extra overhead.

Regarding the theoretical worst-case performance of the SLF and the combined SLF/LLL algorithms, an example has been constructed by Chen and Powell [1997], showing that these algorithms do not have polynomial complexity in their pure form. However, nonpolynomial behavior seems to be an extremely rare phenomenon in practice. In any case, one may construct polynomial versions of the SLF and LLL algorithms, when the arc lengths are nonnegative. A simple approach is to first sort the outgoing arcs of each node by length. That is, when a node i is removed from Q, first examine the outgoing arc from i that has minimum length, then examine the arc of second minimum length, etc. This approach, due to Chen and Powell [1997], can be shown to have complexity $O(NA^2)$ (see Exercise 2.9). Note, however, that sorting the outgoing arcs of a node by length may involve significant overhead.

There is also another approach to construct polynomial versions of the SLF and LLL algorithms (as well as other label correcting methods), which leads to $O(NA)$ complexity, assuming nonnegative arc lengths. To see how this works, suppose that in the generic label correcting algorithm, there is a set of increasing iteration indices $t_1, t_2, \ldots, t_{n+1}$ such that $t_1 = 1$, and for $i = 1, \ldots, n$, all nodes that are in V at the start of iteration t_i are removed from V at least once prior to iteration t_{i+1}. Because all arc lengths are nonnegative, this guarantees that the minimum label node of V at the start of iteration t_i will never reenter V after iteration t_{i+1}. Thus the candidate list must have no more than $N - i$ nodes at the start of iteration t_{i+1}, and must become empty prior to iteration t_{N+1}. Thus, if the running time of the algorithm between iterations t_i and t_{i+1} is bounded by R, the total running time of the algorithm will be bounded by NR, and if R is polynomially bounded, the running time of the algorithm will also be polynomially bounded.

Specializing now to the SLF and LLL cases, assume that between iterations t_i and t_{i+1}, each node is inserted at the top of Q for a number of times that is bounded by a constant and that (in the case of SLF/LLL) the total number of repositionings is bounded by a constant multiple of A. Then it can be seen that the running time of the algorithm between iterations t_i and t_{i+1} is $O(A)$, and therefore the complexity of the algorithm is $O(NA)$.

To modify SLF or SLF/LLL so that they have an $O(NA)$ worst-case complexity, based on the preceding result, it is sufficient that we fix an integer $k > 1$, and that we separate the iterations of the algorithm in successive blocks of kN iterations each. We then impose an additional restriction that, within each block of kN iterations, each node can be inserted at most $k-1$ times at the top of Q [that is, after the $(k-1)$th insertion of a node to the top of Q within a given block of kN iterations, all subsequent insertions of that node within that block of kN iterations must be at the bottom of Q]. In the case of SLF/LLL, we also impose the additional restriction that the total number of repositionings within each block of kN iterations should be at most kA (that is, once the maximum number of kA repositionings is reached, the top node of Q is removed from Q regardless of the value of its label). The worst-case running time of the modified algorithms are then $O(NA)$. In practice, it is highly unlikely that the restrictions introduced into the algorithms to guarantee $O(NA)$ complexity will ever be exercised if k is larger than a small number such as 3 or 4.

2.4.4 The Threshold Algorithm

Similar to the SLF/LLL methods, the premise of this algorithm is also that, for nonnegative arc lengths, the number of iterations is reduced by removing from the candidate list V nodes with relatively small label. In the threshold algorithm, V is organized into two distinct queues Q' and Q'' using a *threshold* parameter s. The queue Q' contains nodes with "small" labels; that is, it contains only nodes whose labels are no larger than s. At each iteration, a node is removed from Q', and any node j to be added to the candidate list is inserted at the bottom of Q' or Q'' depending on whether $d_j \leq s$ or $d_j > s$, respectively. When the queue Q' is exhausted, the entire candidate list is repartitioned. The threshold is adjusted, and the queues Q' and Q'' are recalculated, so that Q' consists of the nodes with labels that are no larger than the new threshold.

To understand how the threshold algorithm works, consider the case of nonnegative arc lengths, and suppose that at time t the candidate list is repartitioned based on a new threshold value s, and that at some subsequent time $t' > t$ the queue Q' gets exhausted. Then at time t', all the nodes of the candidate list have label greater than s. In view of the nonnegativity of the arc lengths, this implies that all nodes with label less than or equal to s will not reenter the candidate list after time t'. In particular, all nodes that exited the candidate list between times t and t' become permanently labeled at time t' and never reenter the candidate list. We may thus interpret the threshold algorithm as a *block version of Dijkstra's method*, whereby a whole subset of nodes becomes permanently labeled when the queue Q' gets exhausted.

The preceding interpretation suggests that the threshold algorithm is suitable primarily for the case of nonnegative arc lengths (even though it will work in general). Furthermore, the performance of the algorithm is quite sensitive to the method used to adjust the threshold. For example, if s is taken to be equal to the current minimum label, the method is identical to Dijkstra's algorithm; if s is larger than all node labels, Q'' is empty and the algorithm reduces to the generic label correcting method. With an effective choice of threshold, the practical performance of the algorithm is very good. A number of heuristic approaches have been developed for selecting the threshold (see Glover, Klingman, and Phillips [1985], and Glover, Klingman, Phillips, and Schneider [1985]). If all arc lengths are nonnegative, a bound $O(NA)$ on the operation count of the algorithm can be shown; see Exercise 2.8(c).

Combinations of the Threshold and the SLF/LLL Methods

We mentioned earlier that the threshold algorithm may be interpreted as a block version of Dijkstra's method, whereby attention is restricted to the subset of nodes that belong to the queue Q', until this subset becomes permanently labeled. The algorithm used to permanently label the nodes of Q' is essentially the Bellman-Ford algorithm restricted to the subgraph defined by Q'. It is possible to use a different algorithm for this purpose, based for example on the SLF and LLL strategies. This motivates combinations of the threshold and the SLF/LLL algorithms.

In particular, the LLL strategy can be used when selecting a node to exit the queue Q' in the threshold algorithm (the top node of Q' is repositioned to the bottom of Q' if its label is found smaller than the average label in Q'). Furthermore, whenever a node enters the queue Q', it is added, according to the SLF strategy, at the bottom or the top of Q' depending on whether its label is greater than the label of the top node of Q' or not. The same policy is used when transferring to Q' the nodes of Q'' whose labels do not exceed the current threshold parameter. Thus the nodes of Q'' are transferred to Q' one-by-one, and they are added to the top or the bottom of Q' according to the SLF strategy. Finally, the SLF strategy is also followed when a node enters the queue Q''.

Generally, the threshold strategy and the SLF/LLL strategy are complementary and work synergistically. Computational experience suggests that their combination performs extremely well in practice, and typically results in an average number of iterations per node that is only slightly larger than the minimum of 1 achieved by Dijkstra's method. At the same time, these combined methods require considerably less overhead than Dijkstra's method.

2.4.5   Comparison of Label Setting and Label Correcting

Let us now try to compare the two major special cases of the generic algorithm, label setting and label correcting methods, assuming that the arc lengths are nonnegative.

We mentioned earlier that label setting methods offer a better guarantee of good performance than label correcting methods, because their worst-case running time is more favorable. In practice, however, there are several considerations that argue in favor of label correcting methods. One such consideration is that label correcting methods, because of their inherent flexibility, are better suited for exploiting advanced initialization.

Another consideration is that when the graph is acyclic, label correcting methods can be adapted to exploit the problem's structure, so that each node enters and exits the candidate list only once, thereby nullifying the major advantage of label setting methods (see Exercise 2.10). The corresponding running time is $O(A)$, which is the minimum possible. Note that an important class of problems involving an acyclic graph is dynamic programming (cf. Fig. 2.1).

A third consideration is that in practice, the graphs of shortest path problems are often sparse; that is, the number of arcs is much smaller than the maximum possible N^2. In this case, efficient label correcting methods tend to have a faster practical running time than label setting methods. To understand the reason, note that all shortest path methods require the unavoidable $O(A)$ operations needed to scan once every arc, plus some additional time which we can view as "overhead." The overhead of the popular label setting methods is roughly proportional to N in practice (perhaps times a slowly growing factor, like $\log N$), as argued earlier for the binary heap method and Dial's algorithm. On the other hand, the overhead of label correcting methods grows linearly with A (times a factor that likely grows slowly), because for the most popular methods, the average number of node entrances in the queue per node is typically not much larger than 1. Thus, we may conclude that the overhead ratio of label correcting to label setting methods is roughly

$$\frac{A}{N} \cdot (\text{a constant factor}).$$

The constant factor above depends on the particular method used and may vary slowly with the problem size, but is typically much less than 1. Thus, the overhead ratio favors label correcting methods for a sparse graph ($A << N^2$), and label setting methods for a dense graph ($A \approx N^2$). This is consistent with empirical observations.

Let us finally note that label setting methods can take better advantage of situations where only a small subset of the nodes are destinations, as will be seen in the next section. This is also true of the auction algorithms to be discussed in Section 2.6.

2.5 SINGLE ORIGIN/SINGLE DESTINATION METHODS

In this section, we discuss the adaptation of our earlier single origin/all destination algorithms to the case where there is only one destination, call it t, and we want to find the shortest distance from the origin node 1 to t. We could of course use our earlier all-destinations algorithms, but some improvements are possible.

2.5.1 Label Setting

Suppose that we use the label setting method. Then we can stop the method when the destination t becomes permanently labeled; further computation will not improve the label d_t (Exercise 2.13 sharpens this criterion in the case where $\min_{\{i|(i,t)\in\mathcal{A}\}} a_{ij} > 0$). If t is closer to the origin than many other nodes, the saving in computation time will be significant. Note that this approach can also be used when there are several destinations. The method is stopped when all destinations have become permanently labeled.

Another possibility is to use a *two-sided label setting method*; that is, a method that simultaneously proceeds from the origin to the destination *and* from the destination to the origin. In this method, we successively label permanently the closest nodes to the origin (with their shortest distance *from* the origin) and the closest nodes to the destination (with their shortest distance *to* the destination). It can be shown that when some node gets permanently labeled from both sides, the labeling can stop; by combining the forward and backward paths of each labeled node and by comparing the resulting origin-to-destination paths, one can obtain a shortest path. Exercise 2.14 develops in some detail this approach, which can often lead to a dramatic reduction in the total number of iterations. However, the approach does not work when there are multiple destinations.

2.5.2 Label Correcting

Unfortunately, when label correcting methods are used, it may not be easy to realize the savings just discussed in connection with label setting. The difficulty is that even after we discover several paths to the destination t (each marked by an entrance of t into V), we cannot be sure that better paths will not be discovered later. In the presence of additional problem structure, however, the number of times various nodes will enter V can be reduced considerably, as we now explain.

Suppose that at the start of the algorithm we have, for each node i, an *underestimate* u_i of the shortest distance from i to t (we require $u_t = 0$). For example, if all arc lengths are nonnegative we may take $u_i = 0$ for all i. (We do not exclude the possibility that $u_i = -\infty$ for some i, which corresponds to the case where no underestimate is available for the shortest distance of i.) The following is a modified version of the generic shortest path algorithm.

Initially
$$V = \{1\},$$
$$d_1 = 0, \qquad d_i = \infty, \qquad \forall\, i \neq 1.$$

The algorithm proceeds in iterations and terminates when V is empty. The typical iteration (assuming V is nonempty) is as follows.

Iteration of the Generic Single Origin/Single Destination Algorithm

Remove a node i from V. For each outgoing arc $(i, j) \in \mathcal{A}$, if

$$d_i + a_{ij} < \min\{d_j, d_t - u_j\},$$

set

$$d_j := d_i + a_{ij}$$

and add j to V if it does not already belong to V.

The preceding iteration is the same as the one of the all-destinations generic algorithm, except that the test $d_i + a_{ij} < d_j$ for entering a node j into V is replaced by the more stringent test $d_i + a_{ij} < \min\{d_j, d_t - u_j\}$. (In fact, when the trivial underestimate $u_j = -\infty$ is used for all $j \neq t$ the two iterations coincide.) To understand the idea behind the iteration, note that the label d_j corresponds at all times to the best path found thus far from 1 to j (cf. Prop. 2.2). Intuitively, the purpose of entering node j in V when its label is reduced is to generate shorter paths to the destination that pass through node j. If P_j is the path from 1 to j corresponding to $d_i + a_{ij}$, then $d_i + a_{ij} + u_j$ is an underestimate of the shortest path length among the collection of paths $\mathcal{P}_j$ that first follow path P_j to node j and then follow some other path from j to t. However, if

$$d_i + a_{ij} + u_j \geq d_t,$$

the current best path to t, which corresponds to d_t, is at least as short as any of the paths in the collection $\mathcal{P}_j$, which have P_j as their first component.

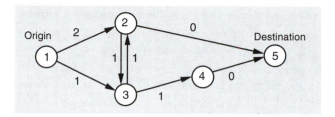

Iter. #	Candidate List V	Node Labels	Node out of V
1	$\{1\}$	$(0, \infty, \infty, \infty, \infty)$	1
2	$\{2, 3\}$	$(0, 2, 1, \infty, \infty)$	2
3	$\{3, 5\}$	$(0, 2, 1, \infty, 2)$	3
4	$\{5\}$	$(0, 2, 1, \infty, 2)$	5
	$\emptyset$	$(0, 2, 1, \infty, 2)$	

Figure 2.9: Illustration of the generic single origin/single destination algorithm. Here the destination is $t = 5$ and the underestimates of shortest distances to t are $u_i = 0$ for all i. Note that at iteration 3, when node 3 is removed from V, the label of node 4 is not improved to $d_4 = 2$ and node 4 is not entered in V. The reason is that $d_3 + a_{34}$ (which is equal to 2) is not smaller than $d_5 - u_4$ (which is also equal to 2). Note also that upon termination the label of a node other than t may not be equal to its shortest distance (e.g. d_4).

It is unnecessary to consider such paths, and for this reason node j need not be entered in V. In this way, the number of node entrances in V may be sharply reduced.

Figure 2.9 illustrates the algorithm. The following proposition proves its validity.

Proposition 2.4: Consider the generic single origin/single destination algorithm.

(a) At the end of each iteration, if $d_j < \infty$, then d_j is the length of some path that starts at 1 and ends at j.

(b) If the algorithm terminates, then upon termination, either $d_t < \infty$, in which case d_t is the shortest distance from 1 to t, or else there is no path from 1 to t.

(c) If the algorithm does not terminate, there exist paths of arbitrarily small length that start at 1.

Proof: (a) The proof is identical to the corresponding part of Prop. 2.2.

(b) If upon termination we have $d_t = \infty$, then the extra test $d_i + a_{ij} + u_j < d_t$ for entering V is always passed, so the algorithm generates the same label sequences as the generic (all destinations) shortest path algorithm. Therefore, Prop. 2.2(b) applies and shows that there is no path from 1 to t. It will thus be sufficient to prove this part assuming that we have $d_t < \infty$ upon termination.

Let $\bar{d}_j$ be the final values of the labels d_j obtained upon termination and suppose that $\bar{d}_t < \infty$. Assume, to arrive at a contradiction, that there is a path $P_t = (1, j_1, j_2, \ldots, j_k, t)$ that has length L_t with $L_t < \bar{d}_t$. For $m = 1, \ldots, k$, let L_{j_m} be the length of the path $P_m = (1, j_1, j_2, \ldots, j_m)$.

Let us focus on the node j_k preceding t on the path P_t. We claim that $L_{j_k} < \bar{d}_{j_k}$. Indeed, if this were not so, then j_k must have been removed at some iteration from V with a label d_{j_k} satisfying $d_{j_k} \leq L_{j_k}$. If d_t is the label of t at the start of that iteration, we would then have

$$d_{j_k} + a_{j_k t} \leq L_{j_k} + a_{j_k t} = L_t < \bar{d}_t \leq d_t,$$

implying that the label of t would be reduced at that iteration from d_t to $d_{j_k} + a_{j_k t}$, which is less than the final label $\bar{d}_t$ – a contradiction.

Next we focus on the node j_{k-1} preceding j_k and t on the path P_t. We use a similar (though not identical) argument to show that $L_{j_{k-1}} < \bar{d}_{j_{k-1}}$. Indeed, if this were not so, then j_{k-1} must have been removed at some iteration from V with a label $d_{j_{k-1}}$ satisfying $d_{j_{k-1}} \leq L_{j_{k-1}}$. If d_{j_k} and d_t are the labels of j_k and t at the start of that iteration, we would then have

$$d_{j_{k-1}} + a_{j_{k-1}j_k} \leq L_{j_{k-1}} + a_{j_{k-1}j_k} = L_{j_k} < \bar{d}_{j_k} \leq d_{j_k},$$

and since $L_{j_k} + u_{j_k} \leq L_t < \bar{d}_t \leq d_t$, we would also have

$$d_{j_{k-1}} + a_{j_{k-1}j_k} < d_t - u_{j_k}.$$

From the above two equations, it follows that the label of j_k would be reduced at that iteration from d_{j_k} to $d_{j_{k-1}} + a_{j_{k-1}t}$, which is less than the final label $\bar{d}_{j_k}$ – a contradiction.

Proceeding similarly, we obtain $L_{j_m} < \bar{d}_{j_m}$ for all $m = 1, \ldots, k$, and in particular $a_{1j_1} = L_{j_1} < \bar{d}_{j_1}$. Since

$$a_{1j_1} + u_{j_1} \leq L_t < \bar{d}_t,$$

and d_t is monotonically nonincreasing throughout the algorithm, we see that at the first iteration we will have $a_{1j_1} < \min\{d_{j_1}, d_t - u_{j_1}\}$, so j_1 will enter V with the label a_{1j_1}, which cannot be less than the final label $\bar{d}_{j_1}$. This is a contradiction; the proof of part (b) is complete.

(c) The proof is identical to the proof of Prop. 2.2(c). **Q.E.D.**

There are a number of possible implementations of the algorithm of this subsection, which parallel the ones given earlier for the many destinations problem. An interesting possibility to speed up the algorithm arises when an *overestimate* v_j of the shortest distance from j to t is known *a priori*. (We require that $v_t = 0$. Furthermore, we set $v_j = \infty$ if no overestimate is known for j.) The idea is that the method still works if the test $d_i + a_{ij} < d_t - u_j$ is replaced by the possibly sharper test $d_i + a_{ij} < D - u_j$, where D is any overestimate of the shortest distance from 1 to t with $D \leq d_t$ (check the proof of Prop. 2.4). We can obtain estimates D that may be strictly smaller than d_t by using the scalars v_j as follows: each time the label of a node j is reduced, we check whether $d_j + v_j < D$; if this is so, we replace D by $d_j + v_j$. In this way, we make the test for future admissibility into the candidate list V more stringent and save some unnecessary node entrances in V.

Advanced Initialization

We finally note that similar to the all-destinations case, the generic single origin/single destination method need not be started with the initial conditions

$$V = \{1\}, \qquad d_1 = 0, \qquad d_i = \infty, \quad \forall\, i \neq 1.$$

The algorithm works correctly using several other initial conditions. One possibility is to use for each node i, an initial label d_i that is either ∞ or else it is the length of a path from 1 to i, and to take $V = \{i \mid d_i < \infty\}$. A more sophisticated alternative is to initialize V so that it contains all nodes i such that

$$d_i + a_{ij} < \min\{d_j, d_t - u_j\} \text{ for some } (i,j) \in \mathcal{A}.$$

This kind of initialization can be extremely useful when a "good" path

$$P = (1, i_1, \ldots, i_k, t)$$

from 1 to t is known or can be found heuristically, and the arc lengths are nonnegative so that we can use the underestimate $u_i = 0$ for all i. Then we can initialize the algorithm with

$$d_i = \begin{cases} \text{Length of portion of path } P \text{ from 1 to } i & \text{if } i \in P, \\ \infty & \text{if } i \notin P, \end{cases}$$

$$V = \{1, i_1, \ldots, i_k\}.$$

If P is a near-optimal path and consequently the initial value d_t is near its final value, the test for future admissibility into the candidate list V will be relatively tight from the start of the algorithm and many unnecessary entrances of nodes into V may be saved. In particular, it can be seen that all nodes whose shortest distances from the origin are greater or equal to the length of P will never enter the candidate list.

2.6 AUCTION ALGORITHMS

In this section, we discuss another class of algorithms for finding a shortest path from an origin s to a destination t. These are called *auction* algorithms because they can be shown to be closely related to the naive auction algorithm for the assignment problem discussed in Section 1.3 (see Bertsekas [1991a], Section 4.3.3, or Bertsekas [1991b]). The main algorithm is very simple. It maintains a single path starting at the origin. At each iteration, the path is either *extended* by adding a new node, or *contracted* by deleting its terminal node. When the destination becomes the terminal node of the path, the algorithm terminates.

   To get an intuitive sense of the algorithm, think of a mouse moving in a graph-like maze, trying to reach a destination. The mouse criss-crosses the maze, either advancing or backtracking along its current path. Each time the mouse backtracks from a node, it records a measure of the desirability of revisiting and advancing from that node in the future (this will be represented by a suitable variable). The mouse revisits and proceeds forward from a node when the node's measure of desirability is judged superior to those of other nodes. The algorithm emulates efficiently this search process using simple data structures.

   The algorithm maintains a path $P = \big((s, i_1), (i_1, i_2), \ldots, (i_{k-1}, i_k)\big)$ with no cycles, and modifies P using two operations, *extension* and *contraction*. If i_{k+1} is a node not on P and (i_k, i_{k+1}) is an arc, an *extension of P by i_{k+1}* replaces P by the path $\big((s, i_1), (i_1, i_2), \ldots, (i_{k-1}, i_k), (i_k, i_{k+1})\big)$. If P does not consist of just the origin node s, a *contraction of P* replaces P by the path $\big((s, i_1), (i_1, i_2), \ldots, (i_{k-2}, i_{k-1})\big)$.

   We introduce a variable p_i for each node i, called the *price of node i*. We denote by p the price vector consisting of all node prices. The algorithm maintains a price vector p satisfying together with P the following property

$$p_i \leq a_{ij} + p_j, \qquad \text{for all arcs } (i, j), \tag{2.14}$$

$$p_i = a_{ij} + p_j, \qquad \text{for all arcs } (i, j) \text{ of } P. \tag{2.15}$$

If we view the prices p_i as the negative of the labels d_i that we used earlier, we see that the above conditions are equivalent to the CS conditions (2.2) and (2.4). Consequently, we will also refer to Eqs. (2.14) and (2.15) as the CS conditions. We assume that the initial pair (P, p) satisfies CS. This is not restrictive, since the default pair

$$P = (s), \qquad p_i = 0, \quad \text{for all } i$$

satisfies CS in view of the nonnegative arc length assumption. To define the algorithm we also need to assume that *all cycles have positive length*; Exercise 2.17 indicates how this assumption can be relaxed.

It can be shown that if a pair (P, p) satisfies the CS conditions, then the portion of P between node s and any node $i \in P$ is a shortest path from s to i, while $p_s - p_i$ is the corresponding shortest distance. To see this, note that by Eq. (2.15), $p_i - p_k$ is the length of the portion of P between i and k, and that every path connecting i to k must have length at least equal to $p_i - p_k$ [add Eq. (2.14) along the arcs of the path].

The algorithm proceeds in iterations, transforming a pair (P, p) satisfying CS into another pair satisfying CS. At each iteration, the path P is either extended by a new node or is contracted by deleting its terminal node. In the latter case the price of the terminal node is increased strictly. A degenerate case occurs when the path consists of just the origin node s; in this case the path is either extended or is left unchanged with the price p_s being strictly increased. The iteration is as follows.

Iteration of the Auction Algorithm

Let i be the terminal node of P. If

$$p_i < \min_{\{j \mid (i,j) \in \mathcal{A}\}} \{a_{ij} + p_j\},$$

go to Step 1; else go to Step 2.

Step 1 (Contract path): Set

$$p_i := \min_{\{j \mid (i,j) \in \mathcal{A}\}} \{a_{ij} + p_j\},$$

and if $i \neq s$, contract P. Go to the next iteration.

Step 2 (Extend path): Extend P by node j_i where

$$j_i = \arg \min_{\{j \mid (i,j) \in \mathcal{A}\}} \{a_{ij} + p_j\}$$

(ties are broken arbitrarily). If j_i is the destination t, stop; P is the desired shortest path. Otherwise, go to the next iteration.

It is easily seen that the algorithm maintains CS. Furthermore, the addition of the node j_i to P following an extension does not create a cycle, since otherwise, in view of the condition $p_i \leq a_{ij} + p_j$, for every arc (i, j) of the cycle we would have $p_i = a_{ij} + p_j$. By adding this equality along the cycle, we see that the length of the cycle must be zero, which is not possible by our assumptions.

Figure 2.10 illustrates the algorithm. It can be seen from the example of this figure that the terminal node traces the tree of shortest paths from the origin to the nodes that are closer to the origin than the given destination. This behavior is typical when the initial prices are all zero (see Exercise 2.19).

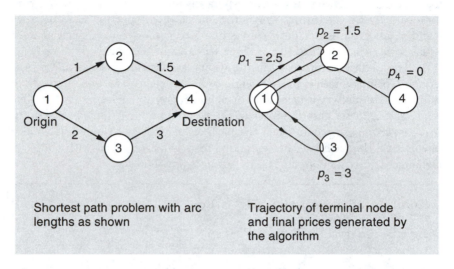

Shortest path problem with arc lengths as shown

Trajectory of terminal node and final prices generated by the algorithm

Iteration #	Path P prior to iteration	Price vector p prior to iteration	Type of action during iteration
1	(1)	(0, 0, 0, 0)	contraction at 1
2	(1)	(1, 0, 0, 0)	extension to 2
3	(1, 2)	(1, 0, 0, 0)	contraction at 2
4	(1)	(1, 1.5, 0, 0)	contraction at 1
5	(1)	(2, 1.5, 0, 0)	extension to 3
6	(1, 3)	(2, 1.5, 0, 0)	contraction at 3
7	(1)	(2, 1.5, 3, 0)	contraction at 1
8	(1)	(2.5, 1.5, 3, 0)	extension to 2
9	(1, 2)	(2.5, 1.5, 3, 0)	extension to 4
10	(1, 2, 4)	(2.5, 1.5, 3, 0)	stop

Figure 2.10: An example illustrating the auction algorithm starting with $P = (1)$ and $p = 0$.

There is an interesting interpretation of the CS conditions in terms of a mechanical model, due to Minty [1957]. Think of each node as a ball, and for every arc (i, j), connect i and j with a string of length a_{ij}. (This requires that $a_{ij} = a_{ji} > 0$, which we assume for the sake of the interpretation.) Let the resulting balls-and-strings model be at an arbitrary position in three-dimensional space, and let p_i be the vertical coordinate of node i. Then the CS condition $p_i - p_j \le a_{ij}$ clearly holds for all arcs (i, j), as illustrated in Fig. 2.11(b). If the model is picked up and left to hang from the origin node (by gravity – strings that are tight are perfectly vertical), then for all the tight strings (i, j) we have $p_i - p_j = a_{ij}$, so any tight chain of strings corresponds to a shortest path between the end nodes of the chain, as illustrated in Fig. 2.11(c). In particular, the length of the tight chain connecting the origin node s to any other node i is $p_s - p_i$ and is also equal to the shortest distance from s to i.

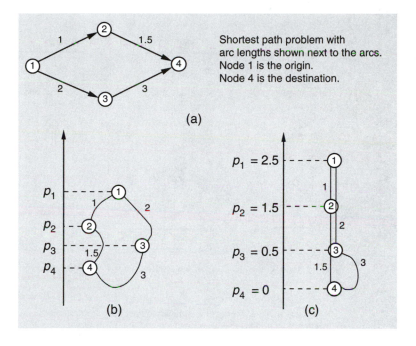

(a)

Shortest path problem with arc lengths shown next to the arcs. Node 1 is the origin. Node 4 is the destination.

(b)

(c)

Figure 2.11: Illustration of the CS conditions for the shortest path problem. If each node is a ball, and for every arc (i, j), nodes i and j are connected with a string of length a_{ij}, the vertical coordinates p_i of the nodes satisfy $p_i - p_j \le a_{ij}$, as shown in (b) for the problem given in (a). If the model is picked up and left to hang from the origin node s, then $p_s - p_i$ gives the shortest distance to each node i, as shown in (c).

The algorithm can also be interpreted in terms of the balls-and-strings model; it can be viewed as a process whereby nodes are raised in stages as illustrated in Fig. 2.12. Initially all nodes are resting on a flat surface. At each stage, we raise the *last* node in a tight chain that starts at the origin to the level at which at least one more string becomes tight.

The following proposition establishes the validity of the auction algorithm.

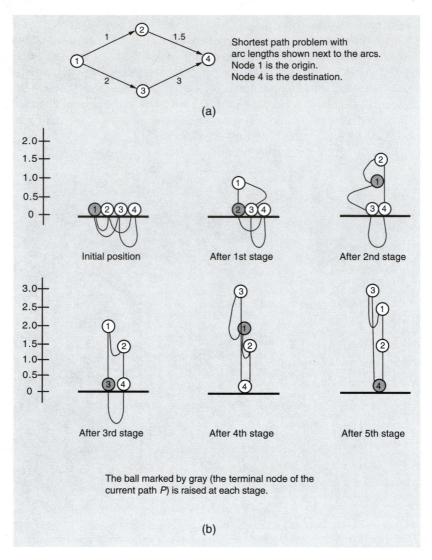

Figure 2.12: Illustration of the auction algorithm in terms of the balls-and-strings model for the problem shown in (a). The model initially rests on a flat surface, and various balls are then raised in stages. At each stage we raise a single ball $i \neq t$ (marked by gray), which is at a lower level than the origin s and can be reached from s through a sequence of tight strings; i should not have any tight string connecting it to another ball, which is at a lower level, that is, i should be the last ball in a tight chain hanging from s. (If s does not have any tight string connecting it to another ball, which is at a lower level, we use $i = s$.) We then raise i to the first level at which one of the strings connecting it to a ball at a lower level becomes tight. Each stage corresponds to a contraction plus all the extensions up to the next contraction. The ball i, which is being raised, corresponds to the terminal node of the current path P.

> **Proposition 2.5:** If there exists at least one path from the origin
> to the destination, the auction algorithm terminates with a shortest
> path from the origin to the destination. Otherwise the algorithm never
> terminates and $p_s \to \infty$.

Proof: We first show by induction that (P, p) satisfies the CS conditions

$$p_i \le a_{ij} + p_j, \qquad \text{for all arcs } (i, j), \qquad (2.16)$$

$$p_i = a_{ij} + p_j, \qquad \text{for all arcs } (i, j) \text{ of } P, \qquad (2.17)$$

throughout the algorithm. Indeed, the initial pair satisfies CS by assumption. Consider an iteration that starts with a pair (P, p) satisfying CS and produces a pair $(\overline{P}, \overline{p})$. Let i be the terminal node of P. If

$$p_i = a_{ij_i} + p_{j_i} = \min_{\{j \mid (i,j) \in \mathcal{A}\}} \{a_{ij} + p_j\}, \qquad (2.18)$$

then $\overline{P}$ is the extension of P by the node j_i and $\overline{p} = p$, implying that the CS condition (2.17) holds for all arcs of P as well as arc (i, j_i) [since j_i attains the minimum in Eq. (2.18)].

Suppose next that

$$p_i < \min_{\{j \mid (i,j) \in \mathcal{A}\}} \{a_{ij} + p_j\}.$$

Then if P is the degenerate path (s), the CS conditions hold vacuously. Otherwise, $\overline{P}$ is obtained by contracting P, and for all nodes $j \in \overline{P}$, we have $\overline{p}_j = p_j$, implying the CS conditions (2.16) and (2.17) for arcs outgoing from nodes of $\overline{P}$. Also, for the terminal node i, we have

$$\overline{p}_i = \min_{\{j \mid (i,j) \in \mathcal{A}\}} \{a_{ij} + p_j\},$$

implying the CS condition (2.16) for arcs outgoing from that node as well. Finally, since $\overline{p}_i > p_i$ and $\overline{p}_k = p_k$ for all $k \ne i$, we have $\overline{p}_k \le a_{kj} + \overline{p}_j$ for all arcs (k, j) outgoing from nodes $k \notin P$. This completes the induction proof that (P, p) satisfies CS throughout the algorithm.

Assume first that there is a path from node s to the destination t. By adding the CS condition (2.16) along that path, we see that $p_s - p_t$ is an underestimate of the (finite) shortest distance from s to t. Since p_s is monotonically nondecreasing, and p_t is fixed throughout the algorithm, it follows that p_s must stay bounded.

We next claim that p_i must stay bounded for all i. Indeed, in order to have $p_i \to \infty$, node i must become the terminal node of P infinitely often.

Each time this happens, $p_s - p_i$ is equal to the shortest distance from s to i, which is a contradiction since p_s is bounded.

We next show that the algorithm terminates. Indeed, it can be seen with a straightforward induction argument that for every node i, p_i is either equal to its initial value, or else it is the length of some path starting at i plus the initial price of the final node of the path; we call this the *modified length* of the path. Every path from s to i can be decomposed into a path with no cycles together with a finite number of cycles, each having positive length by assumption, so the number of distinct modified path lengths within any bounded interval is bounded. Now p_i was shown earlier to be bounded, and each time i becomes the terminal node by extension of the path P, p_i is strictly larger over the preceding time i became the terminal node of P, corresponding to a strictly larger modified path length. It follows that the number of times i can become a terminal node by extension of the path P is bounded. Since the number of path contractions between two consecutive path extensions is bounded by the number of nodes in the graph, the number of iterations of the algorithm is bounded, implying that the algorithm terminates.

Assume now that there is no path from node s to the destination. Then, the algorithm will never terminate, so by the preceding argument, some node i will become the terminal node by extension of the path P infinitely often and $p_i \to \infty$. At the end of iterations where this happens, $p_s - p_i$ must be equal to the shortest distance from s to i, implying that $p_s \to \infty$.   **Q.E.D.**

Nonpolynomial Behavior and Graph Reduction

A drawback of the auction algorithm as described above is that its running time can depend on the arc lengths. A typical situation arises in graphs involving a cycle with relatively small length, as illustrated in Fig. 2.13. It is possible to turn the algorithm into one that is polynomial, by using some variations of the algorithm. In these variations, in addition to the extension and contraction operations, an additional *reduction* operation is introduced whereby some unnecessary arcs of the graph are deleted. We briefly describe the simplest of these variations, and we refer to Bertsekas, Pallottino, and Scutellà [1995] for other more sophisticated variations and complexity analysis.

This variant of the auction algorithm has the following added feature: each time that a node j becomes the terminal node of the path P through an extension using arc (i, j), all incoming arcs (k, j) of j with $k \neq i$ are deleted from the graph. Also, each time that a node j with no outgoing arcs becomes the terminal node of P, the path P is contracted and the node j is deleted from the graph. It can be seen that the arc deletion process leaves the shortest distance from s to t unaffected, and that the

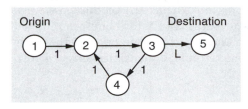

Figure 2.13: Example graph for which the number of iterations of the algorithm is not polynomially bounded. The lengths are shown next to the arcs and $L > 1$. By tracing the steps of the algorithm starting with $P = (1)$ and $p = 0$, we see that the price of node 3 will be first increased by 1 and then it will be increased by increments of 3 (the length of the cycle) as many times as is necessary for p_3 to reach or exceed L.

algorithm terminates either by finding a shortest path from s to t or by deleting s, depending on whether there exists at least one path from s to t or not. It can also be seen that this is also true even if there are cycles of zero length. Thus, in addition to addressing the nonpolynomial behavior, the graph reduction process deals effectively with the case where there are zero length cycles.

As an illustration, the reader may apply the algorithm with graph reduction to the example of Fig. 2.13. After the first iteration when node 2 becomes the terminal node of P for the first time, the arc $(4, 2)$ is deleted, and the cycle $(2, 3, 4, 2)$ that caused the nonpolynomial behavior is eliminated. Furthermore, once node 4 becomes the terminal node of P, it gets deleted because it no longer has any outgoing arcs. The number of iterations required is greatly reduced.

The effect of graph reduction may be enhanced by introducing a further idea due to Cerulli (see Cerulli, Festa, and Raiconi [1997a]). In particular, if in the process of eliminating arcs, a node i is left with only one outgoing arc (i, j), it may be "combined" with node j. This can be done efficiently, and may result in significant computational savings for some problem types (particularly those involving a sparse graph).

In addition to graph reduction, there are a number of ideas that can be used to implement efficiently the auction algorithm; see Bertsekas [1991b], Bertsekas, Pallottino, and Scutellà [1995], and Cerulli, Festa, and Raiconi [1997b].

The Case of Multiple Destinations or Multiple Origins

To solve the problem with multiple destinations and a single origin, one can simply run the algorithm until every destination becomes the terminal node of the path at least once. Also, to solve the problem with multiple origins and a single destination, one can combine several versions of the algorithm – one for each origin. However, the different versions can share a common price vector, since regardless of the origin considered, the condition $p_i \le a_{ij} + p_j$ is always maintained. There are several ways to operate such a method; they differ in the policy used for switching between different origins. One possibility is to run the algorithm for one origin and, after the shortest path is obtained, to switch to the next origin (without changing the price vector), and so on, until all origins are exhausted. Another possibility, which is probably preferable in most cases, is to rotate between different origins, switching from one origin to another, if a contraction at the origin occurs or the destination becomes the terminal node of the current path.

The Reverse Algorithm

For problems with one origin and one destination, a two-sided version of the algorithm is particularly effective. This method maintains, in addition to the path P, another path R that *ends at the destination*. To understand this version, we first note that in shortest path problems, one can exchange the role of origins and destinations by reversing the direction of all arcs. It is therefore possible to use a destination-oriented version of the auction algorithm that maintains a path R that *ends* at the destination and changes at each iteration by means of a contraction or an extension. This algorithm, called the *reverse algorithm*, is mathematically equivalent to the earlier (forward) auction algorithm. Initially, in the reverse algorithm, R is any path ending at the destination, and p is any price vector satisfying CS together with R; for example,

$$R = (t), \qquad p_i = 0, \quad \text{for all } i,$$

if all arc lengths are nonnegative.

Iteration of the Reverse Algorithm

Let j be the starting node of R. If

$$p_j > \max_{\{i|(i,j)\in\mathcal{A}\}} \{p_i - a_{ij}\},$$

go to Step 1; else go to Step 2.

Step 1: (Contract path) Set

$$p_j := \max_{\{i|(i,j)\in\mathcal{A}\}} \{p_i - a_{ij}\},$$

and if $j \neq t$, contract R, (that is, delete the starting node j of R). Go to the next iteration.

Step 2: (Extend path) Extend R by node i_j, (that is, make i_j the starting node of R, preceding j), where

$$i_j = \arg \max_{\{i \mid (i,j) \in \mathcal{A}\}} \{p_i - a_{ij}\}$$

(ties are broken arbitrarily). If i_j is the origin s, stop; R is the desired shortest path. Otherwise, go to the next iteration.

The reverse algorithm is most helpful when it is combined with the forward algorithm. In a combined algorithm, initially we have a price vector p, and two paths P and R, satisfying CS together with p, where P starts at the origin and R ends at the destination. The paths P and R are extended and contracted according to the rules of the forward and the reverse algorithms, respectively, and the combined algorithm terminates when P and R have a common node. Both P and R satisfy CS together with p throughout the algorithm, so when P and R meet, say at node i, the composite path consisting of the portion of P from s to i followed by the portion of R from i to t will be shortest.

Combined Forward/Reverse Auction Algorithm

Step 1: (Run forward algorithm) Execute several iterations of the forward algorithm (subject to the termination condition), at least one of which leads to an increase of the origin price p_s. Go to Step 2.

Step 2: (Run reverse algorithm) Execute several iterations of the reverse algorithm (subject to the termination condition), at least one of which leads to a decrease of the destination price p_t. Go to Step 1.

The combined forward/reverse algorithm can also be interpreted in terms of the balls-and-strings model of Fig. 2.11. Again, all nodes are resting initially on a flat surface. When the forward part of the algorithm is used, we raise nodes in stages as illustrated in Fig. 2.12. When the reverse part of the algorithm is used, we *lower* nodes in stages; at each stage, we lower the *top* node in a tight chain that ends at the destination to the level at which at least one more string becomes tight.

The combined forward/reverse auction algorithm can be easily extended to handle single-origin/many-destination problems. One may start the reverse portion of the algorithm from any destination for which a shortest path has not yet been found. Based on experiments with randomly generated problems, the combined forward/reverse auction algorithm (with graph reduction to eliminate nonpolynomial behavior) outperforms substantially and often dramatically its closest competitors for single-origin/few-destination problems (see Bertsekas [1991b], and Bertsekas, Pallottino, and Scutellà [1995]). The intuitive reason for this is that through the mechanism of the reverse portion of the algorithm, the selected destinations are reached by the forward portion faster than other nodes, thereby leading to faster termination.

2.7 MULTIPLE ORIGIN/MULTIPLE DESTINATION METHODS

In this section, we consider the all-pairs shortest path problem, where we want to find a shortest path from each node to each other node. The *Floyd-Warshall algorithm* is specifically designed for this problem, and it is not any faster when applied to the single destination problem. It starts with the initial condition

$$
D_{ij}^0 = \begin{cases} a_{ij} & \text{if } (i,j) \in \mathcal{A}, \\ \infty & \text{otherwise}, \end{cases}
$$

and generates sequentially for all $k = 0, 1, \ldots, N-1$, and all nodes i and j,

$$
D_{ij}^{k+1} = \begin{cases} \min\left\{ D_{ij}^k,\ D_{i(k+1)}^k + D_{(k+1)j}^k \right\} & \text{if } j \neq i, \\ \infty & \text{otherwise}. \end{cases}
$$

An induction argument shows that D_{ij}^k gives the shortest distance from node i to node j using only nodes from 1 to k as intermediate nodes. Thus, D_{ij}^N gives the shortest distance from i to j (with no restriction on the intermediate nodes). There are N iterations, each requiring $O(N^2)$ operations, for a total of $O(N^3)$ operations.

Unfortunately, the Floyd-Warshall algorithm cannot take advantage of sparsity of the graph. It appears that for sparse problems it is typically better to apply a single origin/all destinations algorithm separately for each origin. If all the arc lengths are nonnegative, a label setting method can be used separately for each origin. If there are negative arc lengths (but no negative length cycles), one can of course apply a label correcting method separately for each origin, but there is another alternative that results in a superior worst-case complexity. It is possible to apply a label correcting method only *once* to a single origin/all destinations problem and obtain an equivalent all-pairs shortest path problem with nonnegative arc lengths; the latter problem can be solved using N separate applications of a label setting method. This alternative is based on the following proposition, which applies to the general minimum cost flow problem.

Proposition 2.7: Every minimum cost flow problem with arc costs a_{ij} such that all simple forward cycles have nonnegative cost is equivalent to another minimum cost flow problem involving the same graph and nonnegative arc costs $\hat{a}_{ij}$ of the form

$$\hat{a}_{ij} = a_{ij} + d_i - d_j, \qquad \forall \ (i,j) \in \mathcal{A},$$

where the scalars d_i can be found by solving a single origin/all destinations shortest path problem. The two problems are equivalent in the sense that they have the same constraints, and the cost function of one is the same as the cost function of the other plus a constant.

Proof: Let $(\mathcal{N}, \mathcal{A})$ be the graph of the given problem. Introduce a new node 0 and an arc $(0, i)$ for each $i \in \mathcal{N}$, thereby obtaining a new graph $(\mathcal{N}', \mathcal{A}')$. Consider the shortest path problem involving this graph, with arc lengths a_{ij} for the arcs $(i, j) \in \mathcal{A}$ and 0 for the arcs $(0, i)$. Since all incident arcs of node 0 are outgoing, all simple forward cycles of $(\mathcal{N}', \mathcal{A}')$ are also simple forward cycles of $(\mathcal{N}, \mathcal{A})$ and, by assumption, have nonnegative length. Since any forward cycle can be decomposed into a collection of simple forward cycles (cf. Exercise 1.4 in Chapter 1), all forward cycles (not necessarily simple) of $(\mathcal{N}', \mathcal{A}')$ have nonnegative length. Furthermore, there is at least one path from node 0 to every other node i, namely the path consisting of arc $(0, i)$. Therefore, the shortest distances d_i from node 0 to all other nodes i can be found by a label correcting method, and by Prop. 2.2, we have

$$\hat{a}_{ij} = a_{ij} + d_i - d_j \geq 0, \qquad \forall \ (i,j) \in \mathcal{A}.$$

Let us now view $\sum_{(i,j) \in \mathcal{A}} \hat{a}_{ij} x_{ij}$ as the cost function of a minimum cost flow problem involving the graph $(\mathcal{N}, \mathcal{A})$ and the constraints of the original problem. We have

$$\sum_{(i,j) \in \mathcal{A}} \hat{a}_{ij} x_{ij} = \sum_{(i,j) \in \mathcal{A}} \left(a_{ij} + d_i - d_j \right) x_{ij}$$

$$= \sum_{(i,j) \in \mathcal{A}} a_{ij} x_{ij} + \sum_{i \in \mathcal{N}} d_i \left(\sum_{\{j | (i,j) \in \mathcal{A}\}} x_{ij} - \sum_{\{j | (j,i) \in \mathcal{A}\}} x_{ji} \right)$$

$$= \sum_{(i,j) \in \mathcal{A}} a_{ij} x_{ij} + \sum_{i \in \mathcal{N}} d_i s_i,$$

where s_i is the supply of node i. Thus, the two cost functions $\sum_{(i,j) \in \mathcal{A}} \hat{a}_{ij} x_{ij}$ and $\sum_{(i,j) \in \mathcal{A}} a_{ij} x_{ij}$ differ by the constant $\sum_{i \in \mathcal{N}} d_i s_i$.   **Q.E.D.**

It can be seen now that the all-pairs shortest path problem can be solved by using a label correcting method to solve the single origin/all destinations problem described in the above proof, thereby obtaining the scalars d_i and

$$\hat{a}_{ij} = a_{ij} + d_i - d_j, \qquad \forall \ (i,j) \in \mathcal{A},$$

and by then applying a label setting method N times to solve the all-pairs shortest path problem involving the nonnegative arc lengths $\hat{a}_{ij}$. The shortest distance D_{ij} from i to j is obtained by subtracting $d_i - d_j$ from the shortest distance from i to j found by the label setting method. To estimate the running time of this approach, note that the label correcting method requires $O(NA)$ computation using the Bellman-Ford method, and each of the N applications of the label setting method require less than $O(N^2)$ computation (the exact count depends on the method used). Thus the overall running time is less that the $O(N^3)$ required by the Floyd-Warshall algorithm, at least for sparse graphs.

Still another possibility for solving the all-pairs shortest path problem is to solve N separate single origin/all destinations problems but to also use the results of the computation for one origin to start the computation for the next origin; see our earlier discussion of initialization of label correcting methods and also the discussion at the end of Section 5.2.

2.8 NOTES, SOURCES, AND EXERCISES

The work on the shortest path problem is very extensive, so we will restrict ourselves to citing the references that relate most to the material presented. Literature surveys are given by Dreyfus [1969], Deo and Pang [1984], and Gallo and Pallottino [1988]. The latter reference also contains codes for the most popular shortest path methods, and extensive computational comparisons. A survey of applications in transportation networks is given in Pallottino and Scutellà [1997a]. Parallel computation aspects of shortest path algorithms, including asynchronous versions of some of the algorithms developed here, are discussed in Bertsekas and Tsitsiklis [1989], and Kumar, Grama, Gupta, and Karypis [1994].

The generic algorithm was proposed as a unifying framework of many of the existing shortest path algorithms in Pallottino [1984], and Gallo and Pallottino [1986]. The first label setting method was suggested in Dijkstra [1959], and also independently in Dantzig [1960], and Whitting and Hillier [1960]. The binary heap method was proposed by Johnson [1972]. Dial's algorithm (Dial [1969]) received considerable attention after the appearance of the paper by Dial, Glover, Karney, and Klingman [1979]; see also Denardo and Fox [1979].

The Bellman-Ford algorithm was proposed in Bellman [1957] and Ford [1956] in the form given in Exercise 2.6, where the labels of all nodes are iterated simultaneously. The D'Esopo-Pape algorithm appeared in Pape [1974] based on an earlier suggestion of D'Esopo. The SLF and SLF/LLL methods were proposed by Bertsekas [1993a], and by Bertsekas, Guerriero, and Musmanno [1996]. Chen and Powell [1997] gave a simple polynomial version of the SLF method (Exercise 2.9). The threshold algorithm was developed by Glover, Klingman, and Phillips [1985], Glover, Klingman, Phillips, and Schneider [1985], and Glover, Glover, and Klingman [1986].

Two-sided label setting methods for the single origin/single destination problem (Exercise 2.14) were proposed by Nicholson [1966]; see also Helgason, Kennington, and Stewart [1993], which contains extensive computational results. The idea of using underestimates of the shortest distance to the destination in label correcting methods originated with the A^* algorithm, a shortest path algorithm that is popular in artificial intelligence (see Nilsson [1971], [1980], and Pearl [1984]).

The Floyd-Warshall algorithm was given in Floyd [1962] and uses a theorem due to Warshall [1962]. Alternative algorithms for the all-pairs problem are given in Dantzig [1967] and Tabourier [1973]. Reoptimization approaches that use the results of a shortest path computation for one origin to initialize the computation for other origins are given by Gallo and Pallottino [1982], and Florian, Nguyen, and Pallottino [1981].

The auction algorithm for shortest paths is due to Bertsekas [1991b]. The idea of graph reduction was proposed by Pallottino and Scutellà [1991], and an $O(N^3)$ implementation of an auction algorithm with graph reduction was given by Bertsekas, Pallottino, and Scutellà [1995]. An analysis of a parallel asynchronous implementation is given by Polymenakos and Bertsekas [1994]. Some variants of the auction algorithm that use slightly different price updating schemes have been proposed in Cerulli, De Leone, and Piacente [1992], and Bertsekas [1992b] (see Exercise 2.33). A method that combines the auction algorithm with some dual price iterations was given by Pallottino and Scutellà [1997b].

EXERCISES

2.1

Consider the graph of Fig. 2.14. Find a shortest path from 1 to all nodes using the binary heap method, Dial's algorithm, the D'Esopo-Pape algorithm, the SLF method, and the SLF/LLL method.

2.2

Suppose that the only arcs that have negative lengths are outgoing from the origin node 1. Show how to adapt Dijkstra's algorithm so that it solves the all-destinations shortest path problem in at most $N - 1$ iterations.

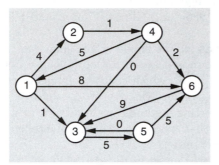

Figure 2.14: Graph for Exercise 2.1. The arc lengths are the numbers shown next to the arcs.

2.3

Give an example of a problem where the generic shortest path algorithm will reduce the label of node 1 to a negative value.

2.4 (Shortest Path Tree Construction)

Consider the single origin/all destinations shortest path problem and assume that all cycles have nonnegative length. Consider the generic algorithm of Section 2.2, and assume that each time a label d_j is decreased to $d_i + a_{ij}$ the arc (i,j) is stored in an array $PRED(j)$. Consider the subgraph of the arcs $PRED(j)$, $j \in \mathcal{N}$, $j \neq 1$. Show that at the end of each iteration this subgraph is a tree rooted at the origin, and that upon termination it is a tree of shortest paths.

2.5 (Uniqueness of Solution of Bellman's Equation)

Assume that all cycles have positive length. Show that if the scalars $d_1, d_2, \ldots, d_N$ satisfy

$$d_j = \min_{(i,j) \in \mathcal{A}} \{d_i + a_{ij}\}, \qquad \forall\, j \neq 1,$$

$$d_1 = 0,$$

then for all j, d_j is the shortest distance from 1 to j. Show by example that this need not be true if there is a cycle of length 0. *Hint:* Consider the arcs (i,j) attaining the minimum in the above equation and consider the paths formed by these arcs.

2.6 (The Original Bellman-Ford Method)

Consider the single origin/all destinations shortest path problem. The Bellman-Ford method, as originally proposed by Bellman and Ford, updates the labels of all nodes simultaneously in a single iteration. In particular, it starts with the initial conditions

$$d_1^0 = 0, \qquad d_j^0 = \infty, \qquad \forall\, j \neq 1,$$

and generates d_j^k, $k = 1, 2, \ldots$, according to

$$d_1^k = 0, \qquad d_j^k = \min_{(i,j) \in \mathcal{A}} \{d_i^{k-1} + a_{ij}\}, \qquad \forall \, j \neq 1.$$

(a) Show that for all $j \neq 1$ and $k \geq 1$, d_j^k is the shortest distance from 1 to j using paths with k arcs or less, where $d_j^k = \infty$ means that all the paths from 1 to j have more than k arcs.

(b) Assume that all cycles have nonnegative length. Show that the algorithm terminates after at most N iterations, in the sense that for some $k \leq N$ we have $d_j^k = d_j^{k-1}$ for all j. Conclude that the running time of the algorithm is $O(NA)$.

2.7 (The Bellman-Ford Method with Arbitrary Initialization)

Consider the single origin/all destinations shortest path problem and the following variant of the Bellman-Ford method of Exercise 2.6:

$$d_1^k = 0, \qquad d_j^k = \min_{(i,j) \in \mathcal{A}} \{d_i^{k-1} + a_{ij}\}, \qquad \forall \, j \neq 1,$$

where each of the initial iterates d_i^0 is an arbitrary scalar or ∞, except that $d_1^0 = 0$. We say that the algorithm *terminates after k iterations* if $d_i^k = d_i^{k-1}$ for all i.

(a) Given nodes $i \neq 1$ and $j \neq 1$, define

$$w_{ij}^k = \text{minimum path length over all paths starting at } i, \text{ ending at } j,$$
$$\text{and having } k \text{ arcs } (w_{ij}^k = \infty \text{ if there is no such path}).$$

For $i = 1$ and $j \neq 1$, define

$$w_{1j}^k = \text{minimum path length over all paths from 1 to } j \text{ having } k \text{ arcs or less}$$
$$(w_{1j}^k = \infty \text{ if there is no such path}).$$

Show by induction that

$$d_j^k = \min_{i=1,\ldots,N} \{d_i^0 + w_{ij}^k\}, \qquad \forall \, j = 2, \ldots, N, \text{ and } k \geq 1.$$

(b) Assume that there exists a path from 1 to every node i and that all cycles have positive length. Show that the method terminates at some iteration k, with d_i^k equal to the shortest distances d_i^*. *Hint:* For all $i \neq 1$ and $j \neq 1$, $\lim_{k \to \infty} w_{ij}^k = \infty$, while for all $j \neq 1$, $w_{1j}^k = d_j^*$ for all $k \geq N - 1$.

(c) Under the assumptions of part (b), show that if $d_i^0 \geq d_i^*$ for all $i \neq 1$, the method terminates after at most $m^* + 1$ iterations, where

$$m^* = \max_{i \neq 1} m_i \leq N - 1,$$

and m_i is the smallest number of arcs contained in a shortest path from 1 to i.

(d) Under the assumptions of part (b), let

$$\beta = \max_{i \neq 1}\{d_i^* - d_i^0\},$$

and assume that $\beta > 0$. Show that the method terminates after at most $\overline{k} + 1$ iterations, where $\overline{k} = N - 1$ if the graph is acyclic, and $\overline{k} = N - 2 - \lceil \beta/L \rceil$ if the graph has cycles, where

$$L = \min_{\text{All simple cycles}} \frac{\text{Length of the cycle}}{\text{Number of arcs on the cycle}},$$

is the, so called, *minimum cycle mean* of the graph. *Note:* See Section 4.1 of Bertsekas and Tsitsiklis [1989] for related analysis, and an example showing that the given upper bound on the number of iterations for termination is tight.

(e) (Finding the minimum cycle mean) Consider the following Bellman-Ford-like algorithm:

$$d^k(i) = \min_{(i,j) \in \mathcal{A}} \{a_{ij} + d^{k-1}(j)\}, \qquad \forall\ i = 1, \dots, N,$$

$$d^0(i) = 0, \qquad \forall\ i = 1, \dots, N.$$

We assume that there exists at least one cycle, but we do not assume that all cycles have positive length. Show that the minimum cycle mean L of part (d) is given by

$$L = \min_{i=1,\dots,N} \max_{k=0,\dots,N-1} \frac{d^N(i) - d^k(i)}{N - k}.$$

Hint: Show that $d^k(i)$ is equal to the minimum path length over all paths that start at i and have k arcs.

2.8 (Complexity of the Generic Algorithm)

Consider the generic algorithm, assuming that all arc lengths are nonnegative.

(a) Consider a node j satisfying at some time

$$d_j \leq d_i, \qquad \forall\ i \in V.$$

Show that this relation will be satisfied at all subsequent times and that j will never again enter V. Furthermore, d_j will remain unchanged.

(b) Suppose that the algorithm is structured so that it removes from V a node of minimum label at least once every k iterations (k is some integer). Show that the algorithm will terminate in at most kN iterations.

(c) Show that the running time of the threshold algorithm is $O(NA)$. *Hint:* Define a cycle to be a sequence of iterations between successive repartitionings of the candidate list V. In each cycle, the node of V with minimum label at the start of the cycle will be removed from V during the cycle.

2.9 (Complexity of the SLF Method)

The purpose of this exercise, due to Chen and Powell [1997], is to show one way to use the SLF method so that it has polynomial complexity. Suppose that the outgoing arcs of each node have been presorted in increasing order by length. The effect of this, in the context of the generic shortest path algorithm, is that when a node i is removed from the candidate list, we first examine the outgoing arc from i that has minimum length, then we examine the arc of second minimum length, etc. Show an $O(NA^2)$ complexity bound for the method.

2.10 (Label Correcting for Acyclic Graphs)

Consider the problem of finding shortest paths from the origin node 1 to all destinations, and assume that the graph does not contain any forward cycles. Let T_k be the set of nodes i such that every path from 1 to i has k arcs or more, and there exists a path from 1 to i with exactly k arcs. For each i, if $i \in T_k$ define $INDEX(i) = k$. Consider a label setting method that selects a node i from the candidate list that has minimum $INDEX(i)$.

(a) Show that the method terminates and that each node visits the candidate list at most once.

(b) Show that the sets T_k can be constructed in $O(A)$ time, and that the running time of the algorithm is also $O(A)$.

2.11

Consider the graph of Fig. 2.14. Find a shortest path from node 1 to node 6 using the generic single origin/single destination method of Section 2.5 with all distance underestimates equal to zero.

2.12

Consider the problem of finding a shortest path from the origin 1 to a single destination t, subject to the constraint that the path includes a given node s. Show how to solve this problem using the single origin/single destination algorithms of Section 2.5.

2.13 (Label Setting for Few Destinations)

Consider a label setting approach for finding shortest paths from the origin node 1 to a selected subset of destinations T. Let

$$\overline{a} = \min_{\{(i,t) \in \mathcal{A} \mid t \in T\}} a_{it},$$

and assume that $\overline{a} > 0$. Show that one may stop the method when the node of minimum label in V has a label d_{min} that satisfies

$$d_{min} + \overline{a} \geq \max_{t \in T} d_t.$$

2.14 (Two-Sided Label Setting)

Consider the shortest path problem from an origin node 1 to a destination node t, and assume that all arc lengths are nonnegative. This exercise considers an algorithm where label setting is applied simultaneously and independently from the origin and from the destination. In particular, the algorithm maintains a subset of nodes W, which are permanently labeled from the origin, and a subset of nodes V, which are permanently labeled from the destination. When W and V have a node i in common the algorithm terminates. The idea is that a shortest path from 1 to t cannot contain a node $j \notin W \cup V$; any such path must be longer than a shortest path from 1 to i followed by a shortest path from i to t (unless j and i are equally close to both 1 and to t).

Consider two subsets of nodes W and V with the following properties:

(1) $1 \in W$ and $t \in V$.

(2) W and V have nonempty intersection.

(3) If $i \in W$ and $j \notin W$, then the shortest distance from 1 to i is less than or equal to the shortest distance from 1 to j.

(4) If $i \in V$ and $j \notin V$, then the shortest distance from i to t is less than or equal to the shortest distance from j to t.

Let d_i^1 be the shortest distance from 1 to i using paths all the nodes of which, with the possible exception of i, lie in W ($d_i^1 = \infty$ if no such path exists), and let d_i^t be the shortest distance from i to t using paths all the nodes of which, with the possible exception of i, lie in V ($d_i^t = \infty$ if no such path exists).

(a) Show that such W, V, d_i^1, and d_i^t can be found by applying a label setting method simultaneously for the single origin problem with origin node 1 and for the single destination problem with destination node t.

(b) Show that the shortest distance D_{1t} from 1 to t is given by

$$D_{1t} = \min_{i \in W} \left\{ d_i^1 + d_i^t \right\} = \min_{i \in W \cup V} \left\{ d_i^1 + d_i^t \right\} = \min_{i \in V} \left\{ d_i^1 + d_i^t \right\}.$$

(c) Show that the nonempty intersection condition (2) can be replaced by the condition $\min_{i \in W} \left\{ d_i^1 + d_i^t \right\} \le \max_{i \in W} d_i^1 + \max_{i \in V} d_i^t$.

2.15

Apply the forward/reverse auction algorithm to the example of Fig. 2.13, and show that it terminates in a number of iterations that does not depend on the large arc length L. Construct a related example for which the number of iterations of the forward/reverse algorithm is not polynomially bounded.

2.16 (Finding an Initial Price Vector)

In order to initialize the auction algorithm, one needs a price vector p satisfying the condition

$$p_i \le a_{ij} + p_j, \qquad \forall\, (i,j) \in \mathcal{A}. \tag{2.19}$$

Such a vector may not be available if some arc lengths are negative. Furthermore, even if all arc lengths are nonnegative, there are many cases where it is important to use a favorable initial price vector in place of the default choice $p = 0$. This possibility arises in a reoptimization context with slightly different arc length data, or with a different origin and/or destination. This exercise gives an algorithm to obtain a vector p satisfying the condition (2.19), starting from another vector $\bar{p}$ satisfying the same condition for a different set of arc lengths $\bar{a}_{ij}$.

Suppose that we have a vector $\bar{p}$ and a set of arc lengths $\{\bar{a}_{ij}\}$, satisfying $\bar{p}_i \leq \bar{a}_{ij} + \bar{p}_j$ for all arcs (i,j), and we are given a new set of arc lengths $\{a_{ij}\}$. (For the case where some arc lengths a_{ij} are negative, this situation arises with $\bar{p} = 0$ and $\bar{a}_{ij} = \max\{0, a_{ij}\}$.) Consider the following algorithm that maintains a subset of arcs $\mathcal{E}$ and a price vector p, and terminates when $\mathcal{E}$ is empty. Initially

$$\mathcal{E} = \{(i,j) \in \mathcal{A} \mid a_{ij} < \bar{a}_{ij}, \ i \neq t\}, \qquad p = \bar{p}.$$

The typical iteration is as follows:

Step 1 (Select arc to scan): If $\mathcal{E}$ is empty, stop; otherwise, remove an arc (i,j) from $\mathcal{E}$ and go to Step 2.

Step 2 (Add affected arcs to $\mathcal{E}$): If $p_i > a_{ij} + p_j$, set

$$p_i := a_{ij} + p_j$$

and add to $\mathcal{E}$ every arc (k,i) with $k \neq t$ that does not already belong to $\mathcal{E}$.

Assuming that each node i is connected to the destination t with at least one path, and that all cycle lengths are positive, show that the algorithm terminates with a price vector p satisfying

$$p_i \leq a_{ij} + p_j, \qquad \forall \ (i,j) \in \mathcal{A} \text{ with } i \neq t.$$

2.17 (Extension for the Case of Zero Length Cycles)

Extend the auction algorithm for the case where all arcs have nonnegative length but some cycles may consist exclusively of zero length arcs. *Hint*: Any cycle of zero length arcs generated by the algorithm can be treated as a single node. An alternative is the idea of graph reduction discussed in Section 2.6.

2.18

Consider the two single origin/single destination shortest path problems shown in Fig. 2.15.

(a) Show that the number of iterations required by the forward auction algorithm is estimated accurately by

$$n_t - 1 + \sum_{i \in \mathcal{I}, \ i \neq t} (2n_i - 1),$$

where n_i is the number of nodes in a shortest path from 1 to i. Show also that the corresponding running times are $O(N^2)$.

(b) Show that for the problem of Fig. 2.15(a) the running time of the forward/reverse auction algorithm (with a suitable "reasonable" rule for switching between the forward and reverse algorithms) is $O(N^2)$ (the number of iterations is roughly half the corresponding number for the forward algorithm). Show also that for the problem of Fig. 2.15(b) the running time of the forward/reverse algorithm is $O(N)$.

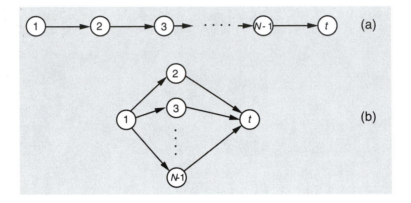

Figure 2.15: Shortest path problems for Exercise 2.18. In problem (a) the arc lengths are equal to 1. In problem (b), the length of each arc $(1,i)$ is i, and the length of each arc (i,t) is N.

2.19

In the auction algorithm of Section 2.6, let k_i be the first iteration at which node i becomes the terminal node of the path P. Show that if $k_i < k_j$, then the shortest distance from 1 to i is less or equal to the shortest distance from 1 to j.

2.20 (A Forward/Reverse Version of Dijkstra's Algorithm)

Consider the single origin/single destination shortest path problem and assume that all arc lengths are nonnegative. Let node 1 be the origin, let node t be the destination, and assume that there exists at least one path from 1 to t. This exercise provides a forward/reverse version of Dijkstra's algorithm, which is motivated by the balls-and-strings model analogy of Figs. 2.11 and 2.12. In particular, the algorithm may be interpreted as alternately lifting the model upward from the origin (the following Step 1), and pulling the model downward from the destination (the following Step 2). The algorithm maintains a price vector p and two node subsets W_1 and W_t. Initially, p satisfies the CS condition

$$p_i \le a_{ij} + p_j, \qquad \forall \, (i,j) \in \mathcal{A}, \tag{2.20}$$

$W_1 = \{1\}$, and $W_t = \{t\}$. One may view W_1 and W_t as the sets of permanently labeled nodes from the origin and from the destination, respectively. The algorithm terminates when W_1 and W_t have a node in common. The typical iteration is as follows:

Step 1 (Forward Step): Find

$$\gamma^+ = \min\{a_{ij} + p_j - p_i \mid (i,j) \in \mathcal{A}, \ i \in W_1, \ j \notin W_1\}$$

and let

$$V_1 = \{j \notin W_1 \mid \gamma^+ = a_{ij} + p_j - p_i \text{ for some } i \in W_1\}.$$

Set

$$p_i := \begin{cases} p_i + \gamma^+ & \text{if } i \in W_1, \\ p_i & \text{if } i \notin W_1. \end{cases}$$

Set

$$W_1 := W_1 \cup V_1.$$

If W_1 and W_t have a node in common, terminate the algorithm; otherwise, go to Step 2.

Step 2 (Backward Step): Find

$$\gamma^- = \min\{a_{ji} + p_i - p_j \mid (j,i) \in \mathcal{A}, \ i \in W_t, \ j \notin W_t\}$$

and let

$$V_t = \{j \notin W_t \mid \gamma^+ = a_{ji} + p_i - p_j \text{ for some } i \in W_t\}.$$

Set

$$p_i := \begin{cases} p_i - \gamma^- & \text{if } i \in W_t, \\ p_i & \text{if } i \notin W_t. \end{cases}$$

Set

$$W_t := W_t \cup V_t.$$

If W_1 and W_t have a node in common, terminate the algorithm; otherwise, go to Step 1.

(a) Show that throughout the algorithm, the condition (2.20) is maintained. Furthermore, for all $i \in W_1$, $p_1 - p_i$ is equal to the shortest distance from 1 to i. Similarly, for all $i \in W_t$, $p_i - p_t$ is equal to the shortest distance from i to t. *Hint*: Show that if $i \in W_1$, there exists a path from 1 to i such that $p_m = a_{mn} + p_n$ for all arcs (m, n) of the path.

(b) Show that the algorithm terminates and that upon termination, $p_1 - p_t$ is equal to the shortest distance from 1 to t.

(c) Show how the algorithm can be implemented so that its running time is $O(N^2)$. *Hint*: Let d_{mn} denote the shortest distance from m to n. Maintain the labels

$$v_j^+ = \min\{d_{1i} + a_{ij} \mid i \in W_1, \ (i,j) \in \mathcal{A}\}, \qquad \forall \ j \notin W_1,$$

$$v_j^- = \min\{a_{ji} + d_{it} \mid i \in W_t, \ (j,i) \in \mathcal{A}\}, \qquad \forall \ j \notin W_t.$$

Let p_j^0 be the initial price of node j. Show that

$$\gamma^+ = \min\left\{ \min_{j \notin W_1, j \notin W_t} \left(v_j^+ + p_j^0\right), \ p_t + \min_{j \notin W_1, j \in W_t} \left(v_j^+ + d_{jt}\right) \right\} - p_1, \quad (2.21)$$

$$\gamma^- = \min\left\{ \min_{j \notin W_1, j \notin W_t} \left(v_j^- - p_j^0\right), \ -p_1 + \min_{j \in W_1, j \notin W_t} \left(v_j^- + d_{1j}\right) \right\} + p_t.$$
$$(2.22)$$

Use these relations to calculate γ^+ and γ^- in $O(N)$ time.

(d) Show how the algorithm can be implemented using binary heaps so that its running time is $O(A \log N)$. *Hint:* One possibility is to use four heaps to implement the minimizations in Eqs. (2.21) and (2.22).

(e) Apply the two-sided version of Dijkstra's algorithm with arc lengths $a_{ij} + p_j - p_i$ of Exercise 2.14, and with the termination criterion of part (c) of that exercise. Show that the resulting algorithm is equivalent to the one of the present exercise.

2.21

Consider the all-pairs shortest path problem, and suppose that the minimum distances d_{ij}^* to go from any i to any j have been found. Suppose that a *single* arc length a_{mn} is reduced to a value $\bar{a}_{mn} < a_{mn}$. Show that if $d_{nm} + \bar{a}_{mn} \geq 0$, the new shortest distances can be obtained by

$$\bar{d}_{ij} = \min\{d_{ij}, \ d_{im} + \bar{a}_{mn} + d_{nj}\}.$$

What happens if $d_{nm} + \bar{a}_{mn} < 0$?

2.22 (The Doubling Algorithm)

The *doubling algorithm* for solving the all-pairs shortest path problem is given by

$$D_{ij}^1 = \begin{cases} a_{ij} & \text{if } (i,j) \in \mathcal{A}, \\ 0 & \text{if } i = j, \\ \infty & \text{otherwise,} \end{cases}$$

$$D_{ij}^{2k} = \begin{cases} \min_m\{D_{im}^k + D_{mj}^k\} & \text{if } i \neq j, \ k = 1, 2, \ldots, \lfloor \log(N-1) \rfloor, \\ 0 & \text{if } i = j, \ k = 1, 2, \ldots, \lfloor \log(N-1) \rfloor. \end{cases}$$

Show that for $i \neq j$, D_{ij}^k gives the shortest distance from i to j using paths with 2^{k-1} arcs or fewer. Show also that the running time is $O\left(N^3 \log m^*\right)$, where m^* is the maximum number of arcs in a shortest path.

2.23 (Dynamic Programming)

Consider the dynamic programming problem of Example 2.2. The standard dynamic programming algorithm is given by the recursion

$$J_k(x_k) = \min_{u_k}\big\{g_k(x_k, u_k) + J_{k+1}(x_{k+1})\big\}, \qquad k = 0, \ldots, N-1,$$

starting with

$$J_N(x_N) = G(x_N).$$

(a) In terms of the shortest path reformulation in Fig. 2.1, interpret $J_k(x_k)$ as the shortest distance from node x_k at stage k to the terminal node t.

(b) Show that the dynamic programming algorithm can be viewed as a special case of the generic label correcting algorithm with a special order for selecting nodes to exit the candidate list.

(c) Assume that $g_k(x_k, u_k) \geq 0$ for all x_k, u_k, and k. Suppose that by using some heuristic we can construct a "good" suboptimal control sequence $(u_0, u_1, \ldots, u_{N-1})$. Discuss how to use this sequence for initialization of a single origin/single destination label correcting algorithm (cf. the discussion of Section 2.5).

2.24 (Forward Dynamic Programming)

Given a problem of finding a shortest path from node s to node t, we can obtain an equivalent "reverse" shortest path problem, where we want to find a shortest path from t to s in a graph derived from the original by reversing the direction of all the arcs, while keeping their length unchanged. Apply this transformation to the dynamic programming problem of Example 2.2 and Exercise 2.23, and derive a dynamic programming algorithm that proceeds forwards rather than backwards in time.

2.25 (k Shortest Node-Disjoint Paths)

The purpose of this exercise, due to Castañon [1990], is to formulate a class of multiple shortest path problems and to indicate the method for their solution. Consider a graph with an origin 1, a destination t, and a length for each arc. We want to find k paths from 1 to t which share no node other 1 and t and which are such that the sum of the k path lengths is minimum. Formulate this problem as a minimum cost flow problem. (For an auction algorithm that solves this problem, see Bertsekas and Castañon [1993c].) *Hint:* Replace each node i other than 1 and t with two nodes i and i' and a connecting arc (i, i') with flow bounds $0 \leq x_{ii'} \leq 1$.

2.31 (Shortest Path Problems with Losses)

Consider a vehicle routing/shortest path-like problem where a vehicle wants to go on a forward path from an origin node 1 to a destination node t in a graph that has no forward cycles. For each arc (i,j) there is a given length a_{ij}, but there is also a given probability $p_{ij} \in [0,1]$ that the vehicle will be destroyed in crossing the arc. The length of a path is now a random variable, and is equal to the sum of the arc lengths on the path up to the time the vehicle reaches its destination or gets destroyed, whichever comes first. We want to find a forward path $P = (1, i_1, \ldots, i_k, t)$ whose expected length, given by

$$\bar{p}_{1i_1}\left(a_{1i_1} + \bar{p}_{i_1 i_2}\left(a_{i_1 i_2} + \bar{p}_{i_2 i_3}(\cdots + \bar{p}_{i_k t} a_{i_k t}) \cdots\right)\right),$$

is minimized, where $\bar{p}_{ij} = 1 - p_{ij}$ is the probability of survival in crossing the arc (i,j). Give an algorithm of the dynamic programming type for solving this problem (cf. Exercise 2.5). Does the problem always make sense when the graph has some forward cycles?

2.32

Consider the one origin-all destinations problem and the generic algorithm of Section 2.2. Assume that there exists a path that starts at node 1 and contains a cycle with negative length. Assume also that the generic algorithm is operated so that if a given node belongs to the candidate list for an infinite number of iterations, then it also exits the list an infinite number of times. Show that there exists at least one node j such that the sequence of labels d_j generated by the algorithm diverge to $-\infty$. *Hint:* Argue that if the limits $\bar{d}_j$ of all the label nodes are finite, then we have $\bar{d}_j \leq \bar{d}_i + a_{ij}$ for all arcs (i,j).

2.33 (A Modified Auction Algorithm for Shortest Paths)

Consider the problem of finding a shortest path from node 1 to a node t, assuming that there exists at least one such path and that all cycles have positive length. This exercise deals with a modified version of the auction algorithm, which was developed in Bertsekas [1992b], motivated by a similar earlier algorithm by Cerulli, De Leone, and Piacente [1994]. This modified version aims to use larger price increases than the original method. The algorithm maintains a price vector p and a simple path P that starts at the origin, and is initialized with $P = (1)$ and any price vector p satisfying

$$p_1 = \infty,$$

$$p_i \leq a_{ij} + p_j, \qquad \forall\, (i,j) \in \mathcal{A} \text{ with } i \neq 1.$$

The algorithm terminates when the destination t becomes the terminal node of P. To describe the algorithm, define

$$A(i) = \{j \mid (i,j) \in \mathcal{A}\} \cup \{i\}, \qquad \forall\, i \in \mathcal{N},$$

$$a_{ii} = 0, \qquad \forall\, i \in \mathcal{N}.$$

The typical iteration is as follows:

Let i be the terminal node of P, and let j_i be such that

$$j_i = \arg\min_{j \in A(i)} \big\{ a_{ij} + p_j \big\},$$

with the extra requirement that $j_i \neq i$ whenever possible; that is, we choose $j_i \neq i$ whenever the minimum above is attained for some $j \neq i$. Set

$$p_{j_i} := \min_{j \in A(i),\, j \neq j_i} \big\{ a_{ij} + p_j \big\} - a_{ij_i}.$$

If $j_i = i$ contract P; otherwise extend P by node j_i.

Note that if a contraction occurs, we have $j_i = i \neq 1$ and the price of the terminal node p_i is strictly increased. Note also that when an extension occurs from the terminal node i to a neighbor $j_i \neq i$, the price p_{j_i} *may be increased strictly*, while in the original auction algorithm there is no price change. Furthermore, the CS condition $p_i \leq a_{ij} + p_j$ for all (i, j) is *not* maintained. Show that:

(a) The algorithm maintains the conditions

$$\pi_i = a_{ij} + p_j, \qquad \forall\, (i, j) \in P,$$

$$\pi_i = p_i, \qquad \forall\, i \notin P,$$

where

$$\pi_i = \min \left\{ p_i, \min_{\{j \mid (i,j) \in \mathcal{A}\}} \big\{ a_{ij} + p_j \big\} \right\}, \qquad \forall\, i \in \mathcal{N}.$$

(b) Throughout the algorithm, P is a shortest path between its endnodes. *Hint:* Show that if $\tilde{P}$ is another path with the same endnodes, we have

$$\text{Length of } \tilde{P} - \text{Length of } P = \sum_{\{k \mid k \in \tilde{P},\, k \notin P\}} (\pi_k - p_k) - \sum_{\{k \mid k \in P,\, k \notin \tilde{P}\}} (\pi_k - p_k)$$

$$\geq 0.$$

(c) The algorithm terminates with a shortest path from 1 to t. *Note:* This is challenging. A proof is given in Bertsekas [1992b].

(d) Convert the shortest path problem to an equivalent assignment problem for which the conditions of part (a) are the complementary slackness conditions. Show that the algorithm is essentially equivalent to a naive auction algorithm applied to the equivalent assignment problem.

2.34 (Continuous Space Shortest Path Problems)

Consider a continuous-time dynamic system whose state $x(t) = \big(x_1(t), x_2(t)\big)$ evolves in two-dimensional space according to the differential equations

$$\dot{x}_1(t) = u_1(t), \qquad \dot{x}_2(t) = u_2(t)$$

where for each time t, $u(t) = \big(u_1(t), u_2(t)\big)$ is a two-dimensional control vector with unit norm. We want to find a state trajectory that starts at a given point $x(0)$, ends at another given point $x(T)$, and minimizes

$$\int_0^T r\big(x(t)\big)\,dt,$$

where $r(\cdot)$ is a given nonnegative and continuous function. The final time T and the control trajectory $\{u(t) \mid 0 \leq t \leq T\}$ are subject to optimization. Suppose we discretize the plane with a mesh of size δ that passes through $x(0)$ and $x(T)$, and we introduce a shortest path problem of going from $x(0)$ to $x(T)$ using moves of the following type: from each mesh point $\bar{x} = (\bar{x}_1, \bar{x}_2)$ we can go to each of the mesh points $(\bar{x}_1 + \delta, \bar{x}_2)$, $(\bar{x}_1 - \delta, \bar{x}_2)$, $(\bar{x}_1, \bar{x}_2 + \delta)$, and $(\bar{x}_1, \bar{x}_2 - \delta)$, at a cost $r(\bar{x})\delta$. Show by example that this is a bad discretization of the original problem in the sense that the shortest distance need not approach the optimal cost of the original problem as $\delta \to 0$. *Note:* This exercise illustrates a common pitfall. The difficulty is that the control constraint set (the surface of the unit sphere) should be finely discretized as well. For a proper treatment of the problem of discretization, see the original papers by Gonzalez and Rofman [1985], and Falcone [1987], the survey paper by Kushner [1990], the monograph by Kushner and Dupuis [1992], and the references cited there. For analogs of the label setting and label correcting algorithms of the present chapter, see the papers by Tsitsiklis [1995], and by Polymenakos, Bertsekas, and Tsitsiklis [1998].

3

The Max-Flow Problem

In this chapter, we focus on the max-flow problem introduced in Example 1.3 of Section 1.2. We have a graph $(\mathcal{N}, \mathcal{A})$ with flow bounds $x_{ij} \in [b_{ij}, c_{ij}]$ for each arc (i, j), and two special nodes s and t. We want to maximize the divergence out of s over all capacity-feasible flow vectors having zero divergence for all nodes except s and t.

The max-flow problem arises in a variety of practical contexts and also as a subproblem in the context of algorithms that solve other more complex problems. For example, it can be shown that checking the existence of a feasible solution of a minimum cost flow problem, and finding a feasible solution if one exists, is essentially equivalent to a max-flow problem (see Fig. 3.1, and Exercises 3.3 and 3.4). Furthermore, a number of interesting combinatorial problems can be posed as max-flow problems (see for example Exercises 3.8-3.10).

Like the shortest path problem, the max-flow problem embodies a number of methodological ideas that are central to the more general minimum cost flow problem. In fact, whereas the shortest path problem can be viewed as a minimum cost flow problem where arc capacities play no role, the max-flow problem can be viewed as a minimum cost flow problem where arc costs play no role. In this sense, the structures of the shortest path and max-flow problems are complementary, and together provide the foundation upon which much of the algorithmic methodology of the minimum cost flow problem is built.

Central to the max-flow problem is the *max-flow/min-cut theorem*, which is one of the most celebrated theorems of network optimization. In Section 3.1, we derive this result, and we discuss some of its applications. Later, in Chapter 4, we will interpret this result as a duality theorem (see Exercise 4.4). In Section 3.2, we introduce a central algorithm for solving the max-flow problem, the Ford-Fulkerson method. This is a fairly simple method, which however can behave in interesting and surprising ways. Much research has been devoted to developing clever and efficient implementations of the Ford-Fulkerson method. We describe some of these implementations in Sections 3.2 and 3.3, and in the exercises.

3.1 THE MAX-FLOW AND MIN-CUT PROBLEMS

The key idea in the max-flow problem is very simple: a feasible flow x can be improved if we can find a path from s to t that is *unblocked* with respect to x. Pushing a positive increment of flow along such a path results in larger divergence out of s, while maintaining flow feasibility. Most (though not all) of the available max-flow algorithms are based on iterative application of this idea.

We may also ask the reverse question. If we can't find an unblocked path from s to t, is the current flow maximal? The answer is positive,

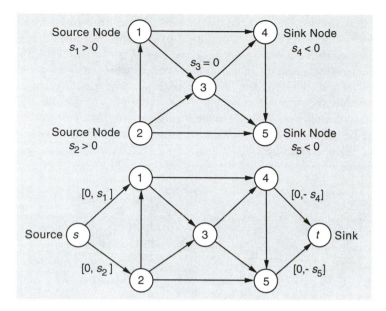

Figure 3.1: Essential equivalence of the problem of finding a feasible solution of a minimum cost flow problem and a max-flow problem. Given a set of divergences s_i satisfying $\sum_i s_i = 0$, and capacity intervals $[0, c_{ij}]$, consider the *feasibility problem* of finding a flow vector x satisfying

$$\sum_{\{j \mid (i,j) \in \mathcal{A}\}} x_{ij} - \sum_{\{j \mid (j,i) \in \mathcal{A}\}} x_{ji} = s_i, \qquad \forall\, i \in \mathcal{N}, \qquad (3.1)$$

$$0 \le x_{ij} \le c_{ij}, \qquad \forall\, (i,j) \in \mathcal{A}. \qquad (3.2)$$

Denote by $I^+ = \{i \mid s_i > 0\}$ the set of source nodes ($\{1,2\}$ in the figure) and by $I^- = \{i \mid s_i < 0\}$ the set of sink nodes ($\{4,5\}$ in the figure). If both these sets are empty, the zero vector is a feasible flow, and we are done. Otherwise, these sets are both nonempty (since $\sum_i s_i = 0$). We introduce a node s, and for all $i \in I^+$, the arcs (s,i) with flow range $[0, s_i]$. We also introduce a node t, and for all $i \in I^-$, the arcs (i,t) with flow range $[0, -s_i]$. Now consider the max-flow problem of maximizing the divergence out of s and into t, while observing the capacity constraints. Then there exists a solution to the feasibility problem of Eqs. (3.1) and (3.2), if and only if the maximum divergence out of s is equal to $\sum_{i \in I^+} s_i$. If this condition is satisfied, solutions of the feasibility problem are in one-to-one correspondence with optimal solutions of the max-flow problem.

If the capacity constraints involve lower bounds, $b_{ij} \le x_{ij} \le c_{ij}$, we may convert first the feasibility problem to one with zero lower flow bounds by a translation of variables, which replaces each variable x_{ij} with a variable $z_{ij} = x_{ij} - b_{ij}$.

Also, a max-flow problem can (in principle) be solved by an algorithm that solves the feasibility problem (we try to find a sequence of feasible flows with monotonically increasing divergence out of s, stopping with a maximum flow when no further improvement is possible). In fact, this is the main idea of the Ford-Fulkerson method, to be discussed in Section 3.2.

although the reason is not entirely obvious. For a brief justification, consider the minimum cost flow formulation of the max-flow problem, given in Example 1.3, which involves the artificial feedback arc (t, s) (see Fig. 3.2). Then, a cycle has negative cost if and only if it includes the arc (t, s), since this arc has cost -1 and is the only arc with nonzero cost. By Prop. 1.2, if a feasible flow vector x is not optimal, there must exist a simple cycle with negative cost that is unblocked with respect to x; this cycle must consist of the arc (t, s) and a path from s to t, which is unblocked with respect to x. Thus, if there is no path from s to t that is unblocked with respect to a given flow vector x, then there is no cycle of negative cost and x must be optimal.

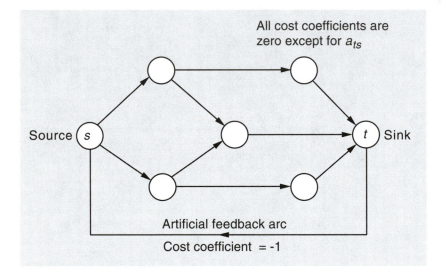

Figure 3.2: Minimum cost flow formulation of a max-flow problem, involving a feedback (t, s) arc with cost -1 and unconstrained arc flow $(-\infty < x_{ts} < \infty)$. For a nonoptimal flow x, there must exist a cycle that is unblocked with respect to x and has negative cost. Since all arcs other than the feedback arc have zero length, this cycle must contain the feedback arc. This implies that there must exist a path from s to t, which is unblocked with respect to x. Many max-flow algorithms push flow along such a path to iteratively improve an existing flow vector x.

The max-flow/min-cut theorem and the Ford-Fulkerson algorithm, to be described shortly, are based on the preceding ideas. However, rather than appealing to Prop. 1.2 (whose proof relies on the notion of a conformal decomposition), we couch the analysis of this chapter on first principles, taking advantage of the simplicity of the max-flow problem. This will also serve to develop some concepts that will be useful later. We first introduce some definitions.

3.1.1   Cuts in a Graph

A *cut* Q in a graph $(\mathcal{N}, \mathcal{A})$ is a partition of the node set $\mathcal{N}$ into two nonempty subsets, a set $\mathcal{S}$ and its complement $\mathcal{N} - \mathcal{S}$. We use the notation

$$Q = [\mathcal{S}, \mathcal{N} - \mathcal{S}].$$

Note that the partition is ordered in the sense that the cut $[\mathcal{S}, \mathcal{N} - \mathcal{S}]$ is distinct from the cut $[\mathcal{N} - \mathcal{S}, \mathcal{S}]$. For a cut $Q = [\mathcal{S}, \mathcal{N} - \mathcal{S}]$, we use the notation

$$Q^+ = \big\{ (i, j) \in \mathcal{A} \mid i \in \mathcal{S}, j \notin \mathcal{S} \big\},$$

$$Q^- = \big\{ (i, j) \in \mathcal{A} \mid i \notin \mathcal{S}, j \in \mathcal{S} \big\},$$

and we say that Q^+ and Q^- are the *sets of forward and backward arcs of the cut*, respectively. We say that the cut Q is *nonempty* if $Q^+ \cup Q^- \neq \emptyset$; otherwise we say that Q is *empty*. We say that the cut $[\mathcal{S}, \mathcal{N} - \mathcal{S}]$ *separates node s from node t* if $s \in \mathcal{S}$ and $t \notin \mathcal{S}$. These definitions are illustrated in Fig. 3.3.

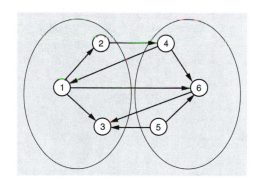

Figure 3.3: Illustration of a cut

$$Q = [\mathcal{S}, \mathcal{N} - \mathcal{S}],$$

where $\mathcal{S} = \{1, 2, 3\}$. We have

$$Q^+ = \{(2, 4), (1, 6)\},$$

$$Q^- = \{(4, 1), (6, 3), (5, 3)\}.$$

Given a flow vector x, the *flux across a nonempty cut* $Q = [\mathcal{S}, \mathcal{N} - \mathcal{S}]$ is defined to be the total net flow coming out of $\mathcal{S}$, i.e., the scalar

$$F(Q) = \sum_{(i,j) \in Q^+} x_{ij} - \sum_{(i,j) \in Q^-} x_{ij}.$$

Let us recall from Section 1.1.2 the definition of the divergence of a node i:

$$y_i = \sum_{\{j \mid (i,j) \in \mathcal{A}\}} x_{ij} - \sum_{\{j \mid (j,i) \in \mathcal{A}\}} x_{ji}, \qquad \forall \, i \in \mathcal{N}.$$

The following calculation shows that $F(Q)$ is also equal to the sum of the divergences y_i of the nodes in $\mathcal{S}$:

$$
\begin{aligned}
F(Q) &= \sum_{\{(i,j)\in\mathcal{A}\mid i\in\mathcal{S},\, j\notin\mathcal{S}\}} x_{ij} - \sum_{\{(i,j)\in\mathcal{A}\mid i\notin\mathcal{S},\, j\in\mathcal{S}\}} x_{ij} \\
&= \sum_{i\in\mathcal{S}} \left(\sum_{\{j\mid(i,j)\in\mathcal{A}\}} x_{ij} - \sum_{\{j\mid(j,i)\in\mathcal{A}\}} x_{ji} \right) \qquad (3.3) \\
&= \sum_{i\in\mathcal{S}} y_i.
\end{aligned}
$$

(The second equality holds because the flow of an arc with both end nodes in $\mathcal{S}$ cancels out within the parentheses; it appears twice, once with a positive and once with a negative sign.)

Given lower and upper flow bounds b_{ij} and c_{ij} for each arc (i, j), the *capacity of a nonempty cut Q* is

$$
C(Q) = \sum_{(i,j)\in Q^+} c_{ij} - \sum_{(i,j)\in Q^-} b_{ij}. \qquad (3.4)
$$

Clearly, for any capacity-feasible flow vector x, the flux $F(Q)$ across Q is no larger than the cut capacity $C(Q)$. If $F(Q) = C(Q)$, then Q is said to be a *saturated cut with respect to x*; the flow of each forward (backward) arc of such a cut must be at its upper (lower) bound. By convention, every empty cut is also said to be saturated. The following is a simple but useful result.

Proposition 3.1: Let x be a capacity-feasible flow vector, and let s and t be two nodes. Then exactly one of the following two alternatives holds:

(1) There exists a simple path from s to t that is unblocked with respect to x.

(2) There exists a saturated cut that separates s from t.

Proof: The proof is obtained by constructing an algorithm that terminates with either a path as in (1) or a cut as in (2). This algorithm is a special case of a general method, known as *breadth-first search*, and used to find a simple path between two nodes in a graph (see Exercise 3.2). The algorithm generates a sequence of node sets $\{T_k\}$, starting with $T_0 = \{s\}$; each set T_k represents the set of nodes that can be reached from s with an unblocked path of k arcs.

Unblocked Path Search Algorithm

For $k = 0, 1, \ldots$, given T_k, terminate if either T_k is empty or $t \in T_k$; otherwise, set

$$T_{k+1} = \{n \notin \cup_{i=0}^{k} T_i |\ \text{there is a node } m \in T_k, \text{ and either an arc } (m, n)$$
$$\text{with } x_{mn} < c_{mn}, \text{ or an arc } (n, m) \text{ with } b_{nm} < x_{nm}\}$$

and mark each node $n \in T_{k+1}$ with the label "(m, n)" or "(n, m)," where m is a node of T_k and (m, n) or (n, m) is an arc with the property stated in the above equation, respectively.

Figure 3.4 illustrates the preceding algorithm. Since the algorithm terminates if T_k is empty, and T_k must consist of nodes not previously included in $\cup_{i=0}^{k-1} T_i$, the algorithm must eventually terminate. Let $\mathcal{S}$ be the union of the sets T_i upon termination. There are two possibilities:

(a) The final set T_k contains t, in which case, by tracing labels backward from t, a simple unblocked path P from s to t can be constructed. The forward arcs of P are of the form (m, n) with $x_{mn} < c_{mn}$ and the label of n being "(m, n)"; the backward arcs of P are of the form (n, m) with $b_{nm} < x_{nm}$ and the label of n being "(n, m)." Any cut separating s from t must contain a forward arc (m, n) of P with $x_{mn} < c_{mn}$ or a backward arc (n, m) of P with $b_{nm} < x_{nm}$, and therefore cannot be saturated. Thus, the result is proved in this case.

(b) The final set T_k is empty, in which case from the equation defining T_k, it can be seen that the cut $Q = [\mathcal{S}, \mathcal{N} - \mathcal{S}]$ is saturated and separates s from t. To show that there is no simple unblocked path from s to t, note that any such path must have either an arc $(m, n) \in Q^+$ with $x_{mn} < c_{mn}$ or an arc $(n, m) \in Q^-$ with $b_{nm} < x_{nm}$, which is impossible, since Q is saturated.

Q.E.D.

Exercise 3.11 provides some variations of Prop. 3.1. In particular, in place of s and t, one may use two disjoint subsets of nodes $\mathcal{N}^+$ and $\mathcal{N}^-$. Furthermore, "simple path" in alternative (1) may be replaced by "path."

3.1.2 The Max-Flow/Min-Cut Theorem

Consider now the max-flow problem, where we want to maximize the divergence out of s over all capacity-feasible flow vectors having zero divergence for all nodes other than s and t. Given any such flow vector and any cut Q separating s from t, the divergence out of s is equal to the flux across Q [cf. Eq. (3.3)], which in turn is no larger than the capacity of Q. Thus, if

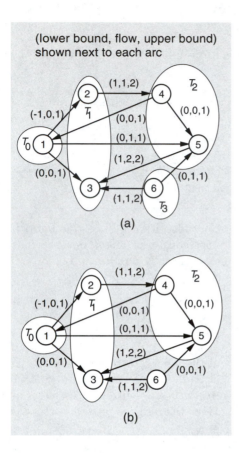

(lower bound, flow, upper bound) shown next to each arc

(a)

(b)

Figure 3.4: Illustration of the unblocked path search algorithm for finding an unblocked path from node 1 to node 6, or a saturated cut separating 1 from 6. The triplet (lower bound, flow, upper bound) is shown next to each arc. The figure shows the successive sets T_k generated by the algorithm. In case (a) there exists a unblocked path from 1 to 6, namely the path $(1, 3, 5, 6)$. In case (b), where the flow of arc $(6, 5)$ is at the lower bound rather than the upper bound, there is the saturated cut $[\mathcal{S}, \mathcal{N} - \mathcal{S}]$ separating 1 from 6, where $\mathcal{S} = \{1, 2, 3, 4, 5\}$ is the union of the sets T_k. Note that the algorithm works for any arc flows, and, in particular, does not require that the nodes other than the start node 1 and the end node 6 have zero divergence.

the max-flow problem is feasible, we have

$$\text{Maximum Flow} \leq \text{Capacity of } Q. \tag{3.5}$$

The following max-flow/min-cut theorem asserts that equality is attained for some Q. Part (a) of the theorem assumes the existence of an optimal solution to the max-flow problem. This assumption need not be satisfied; indeed it is possible that the max-flow problem has no feasible solution at all (consider a graph consisting of a single two-arc path from s to t, the arcs of which have disjoint feasible flow ranges). In Chapter 5, however, we will show using the theory of the simplex method (see Prop. 5.7), that the max-flow problem (and indeed every minimum cost flow problem) has an optimal solution if it has at least one feasible solution. [Alternatively, this can be shown using a fundamental result of mathematical analysis, the Weierstrass theorem, which states that a continuous function attains a maximum over a nonempty and compact set (see Appendix A and the sources given there).] If the lower flow bound is zero for every arc, the max-flow problem has at least one feasible solution, namely the zero flow vector.

Thus the theory of Chapter 5 (or the Weierstrass theorem) guarantees that the max-flow problem has an optimal solution in this case. This is stated as part (b) of the following theorem, even though its complete proof must await the developments of Chapter 5.

Proposition 3.2: (Max-Flow/Min-Cut Theorem)

(a) If x^* is an optimal solution of the max-flow problem, then the divergence out of s corresponding to x^* is equal to the minimum cut capacity over all cuts separating s from t.

(b) If all lower arc flow bounds are zero, the max-flow problem has an optimal solution, and the maximal divergence out of s is equal to the minimum cut capacity over all cuts separating s from t.

Proof: (a) Let F^* be the value of the maximum flow, that is, the divergence out of s corresponding to x^*. There cannot exist an unblocked path P from s to t with respect to x^*, since by increasing the flow of the forward arcs of P and by decreasing the flow of the backward arcs of P by a common positive increment, we would obtain a flow vector with a divergence out of s larger than F^*. Therefore, by Prop. 3.1, there must exist a cut Q, that is saturated with respect to x^* and separates s from t. The flux across Q is equal to F^* and is also equal to the capacity of Q [since Q is saturated; see Eqs. (3.3) and (3.4)]. Since we know that F^* is less or equal to the minimum cut capacity [cf. Eq. (3.5)], the result follows.

(b) See the discussion preceding the proposition.   **Q.E.D.**

3.1.3   The Maximal and Minimal Saturated Cuts

Given an optimal solution x^* of the max-flow problem, there may exist several saturated cuts $[\mathcal{S}, \mathcal{N} - \mathcal{S}]$ separating s and t. We will show that out of these cuts, there exists one, called *maximal*, corresponding to the union of the sets $\mathcal{S}$. Similarly, there is a *minimal* saturated cut, corresponding to the intersection of the sets $\mathcal{S}$. (The maximal and minimal cuts coincide if and only if there is a unique saturated cut.)

Indeed, let $\overline{\mathcal{S}}$ be the union of all node sets $\mathcal{S}$ such that $[\mathcal{S}, \mathcal{N} - \mathcal{S}]$ is a saturated cut separating s and t. Consider the cut

$$\overline{Q} = [\overline{\mathcal{S}}, \mathcal{N} - \overline{\mathcal{S}}].$$

Clearly $\overline{Q}$ separates s and t. If $(i, j) \in \overline{Q}^+$, then we have $x_{ij}^* = c_{ij}$ because i belongs to one of the sets $\mathcal{S}$ such that $[\mathcal{S}, \mathcal{N} - \mathcal{S}]$ is a saturated cut, and j does not belong to $\mathcal{S}$ since $j \notin \overline{\mathcal{S}}$. Thus we have $x_{ij}^* = c_{ij}$ for all $(i, j) \in \overline{Q}^+$.

Similarly, we obtain $x_{ij}^* = b_{ij}$ for all $(i,j) \in \overline{Q}^-$. Thus $\overline{Q}$ is a saturated cut separating s and t, and in view of its definition, it is the maximal such cut. By using set intersection in place of set union in the preceding argument, it is seen that we can similarly form the minimal saturated cut that separates s and t.

The maximal and minimal saturated cuts can be used to deal with infeasibility in the context of various network flow problems, as we discuss next.

3.1.4 Decomposition of Infeasible Network Problems

Consider the minimization of a separable cost function of the flow vector x,

$$\sum_{(i,j)\in\mathcal{A}} f_{ij}(x_{ij}),$$

subject to conservation of flow constraints

$$\sum_{\{j|(i,j)\in\mathcal{A}\}} x_{ij} - \sum_{\{j|(j,i)\in\mathcal{A}\}} x_{ji} = s_i, \qquad \forall\, i \in \mathcal{N},$$

and capacity constraints

$$0 \le x_{ij} \le c_{ij}, \qquad \forall\, (i,j) \in \mathcal{A}.$$

We assume that the scalars s_i are given and satisfy $\sum_{i\in\mathcal{N}} s_i = 0$, but that the problem is infeasible, because the capacities c_{ij} are not sufficiently large to carry all the supply from the set of supply nodes

$$I^+ = \{i \mid s_i > 0\}$$

to the set of demand nodes

$$I^- = \{i \mid s_i < 0\}.$$

Then it may make sense to minimize the cost function over the set of all *maximally feasible flows*, which is the set of flow vectors x whose divergences

$$y_i = \sum_{\{j|(i,j)\in\mathcal{A}\}} x_{ij} - \sum_{\{j|(j,i)\in\mathcal{A}\}} x_{ji}$$

satisfy

$$
\begin{aligned}
y_i &\ge 0 &&\text{if } i \in I^+, \\
y_i &\le 0 &&\text{if } i \in I^-, \\
y_i &= 0 &&\text{if } i \notin I^+ \cup I^-,
\end{aligned}
$$

and minimize

$$\sum_{i \in \mathcal{N}} |s_i - y_i|.$$

Thus, roughly, a flow vector is maximally feasible if it is capacity-feasible, and it satisfies as much of the given demand as possible by using as much of the given supply as possible.

Note that we can find a maximally feasible flow x^* by solving the max-flow problem given in Fig. 3.1. The vector x^* defines corresponding minimal and maximal saturated cuts

$$[\mathcal{S}_{min}, \mathcal{N} - \mathcal{S}_{min}], \qquad [\mathcal{S}_{max}, \mathcal{N} - \mathcal{S}_{max}],$$

respectively, separating the supply node set P from the demand node set D. Furthermore, the flows of all arcs (i, j) that belong to these cuts are equal to x_{ij}^* for *every* maximally feasible flow vector. It can now be seen that given x^*, we can decompose the problem of minimizing the cost function over the set of maximally feasible flows into two or three feasible and independent subproblems, depending on whether $\mathcal{S}_{min} = \mathcal{S}_{max}$ or not. The node sets of these problems are $\mathcal{S}_{min}$, $\mathcal{N} - \mathcal{S}_{max}$, and $\mathcal{S}_{max} - \mathcal{S}_{min}$, (if $\mathcal{S}_{max} \neq \mathcal{S}_{min}$). The supplies for these problems are appropriately adjusted to take into account the arc flows x_{ij}^* for the arcs (i, j) of the corresponding cuts, as illustrated in Fig. 3.5.

3.2   THE FORD-FULKERSON ALGORITHM

In this section, we focus on a fundamental algorithm for solving the max-flow problem. This algorithm is of the primal cost improvement type, because it improves the primal cost (the divergence out of s) at every iteration. The idea is that, given a feasible flow vector x (i.e., one that is capacity-feasible and has zero divergence out of every node other than s and t), and a path P from s to t, which is unblocked with respect to x, we can increase the flow of all forward arcs (i, j) of P and decrease the flow of all backward arcs (i, j) of P. The maximum increment of flow change is

$$\delta = \min\{\{c_{ij} - x_{ij} \mid (i, j) \in P^+\}, \{x_{ij} - b_{ij} \mid (i, j) \in P^-\}\},$$

where P^+ is the set of forward arcs of P and P^- is the set of backward arcs of P. The resulting flow vector $\bar{x}$, given by

$$\bar{x}_{ij} = \begin{cases} x_{ij} + \delta & \text{if } (i, j) \in P^+, \\ x_{ij} - \delta & \text{if } (i, j) \in P^-, \\ x_{ij} & \text{otherwise,} \end{cases}$$

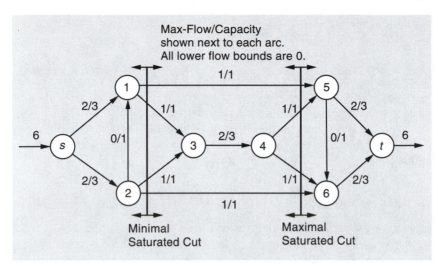

Figure 3.5: Decomposition of the problem of minimizing a separable cost function $\sum_{(i,j)\in\mathcal{A}} f_{ij}(x_{ij})$ over the set of maximally feasible flow vectors into three (feasible) optimization problems. The problem here is to send 6 units of flow from node s to node t, while satisfying capacity constraints $[0, c_{ij}]$ and minimizing a cost function $\sum_{(i,j)\in\mathcal{A}} f_{ij}(x_{ij})$. In this example, all arcs have capacity 1, except for arc $(3, 4)$ and the incident arcs to nodes s and t, which have capacity 3. The problem is infeasible, so we consider optimization over all maximally feasible solutions. We solve the max-flow problem from s to t, and we obtain the corresponding minimal and maximal saturated cuts, as shown in the figure. Note that the flows of the arcs across these cuts are unique, although the max-flow vector is not unique.

We can now decompose the original (infeasible) optimization problem into three (feasible) optimization problems, each with the cost function $\sum_{(i,j)} f_{ij}(x_{ij})$, where the summation is over the relevant set of arcs. These problems are:

(1) The problem involving the nodes s, 1, and 2, with conservation of flow constraints

$$x_{s1} + x_{s2} = 4, \qquad -x_{21} - x_{s1} = -2, \qquad x_{21} - x_{s2} = -2.$$

(2) The problem involving the nodes 3 and 4, with conservation of flow constraint (for both nodes) $x_{34} = 2$.

(3) The problem involving the nodes 5, 6, and t, with conservation of flow constraints

$$x_{5t} + x_{56} = 2, \qquad x_{6t} - x_{56} = 2, \qquad -x_{5t} - x_{6t} = -4.$$

Note that while in this example the 2nd problem is trivial (has only one feasible solution), the 1st and 3rd problems have multiple feasible solutions.

is feasible, and it has a divergence out of s that is larger by δ than the divergence out of s corresponding to x. We refer to P as an *augmenting path*, and we refer to the operation of replacing x by $\overline{x}$ as a flow *augmentation* along P. Such an operation may also be viewed as a modification of x along the negative cost cycle consisting of P and an artificial arc (t, s) that has cost -1; see the formulation of the max-flow problem as a minimum cost flow problem in Fig. 3.2, and the discussion at the beginning of Section 3.1.

The Ford-Fulkerson algorithm starts with a feasible flow vector. If the lower flow bound is zero for all arcs, the zero flow vector can be used as a starting vector; otherwise, a preliminary phase is needed to obtain a feasible starting flow vector. This involves solving an auxiliary max-flow problem with zero lower flow bounds starting from the zero flow vector and using the Ford-Fulkerson algorithm described below (cf. Fig. 3.1 and Exercise 3.4). At each iteration the algorithm has a feasible flow vector and uses the unblocked path search method, given in the proof of Prop. 3.1, to either generate a new feasible flow vector with larger divergence out of s or terminate with a maximum flow and a minimum capacity cut.

Iteration of Ford-Fulkerson Algorithm

Use the unblocked path search method to either

(1) find a saturated cut separating s from t or

(2) find an unblocked path P with respect to x starting from s and ending at t.

In case (1), terminate the algorithm; the current flow vector solves the max-flow problem. In case (2), perform an augmentation along P and go to the next iteration.

Figure 3.6 illustrates the Ford-Fulkerson algorithm. Based on the preceding discussion, we see that with each augmentation, the Ford-Fulkerson algorithm improves the primal cost (the divergence out of s) by the augmentation increment δ. Thus, if δ is bounded below by some positive number, the algorithm can execute only a finite number of iterations and must terminate with an optimal solution. In particular, if the arc flow bounds are integer and the initial flow vector is also integer, δ is a positive integer at each iteration, and the algorithm terminates. The same is true even if the arc flow bounds and the initial flow vector are rational; by multiplication with a suitably large integer, one can scale these numbers up to integer while leaving the problem essentially unaffected.

On the other hand, if the problem data are irrational, proving termination of the Ford-Fulkerson algorithm is nontrivial. The proof (outlined in Exercise 3.12) depends on the use of the specific unblocked path search

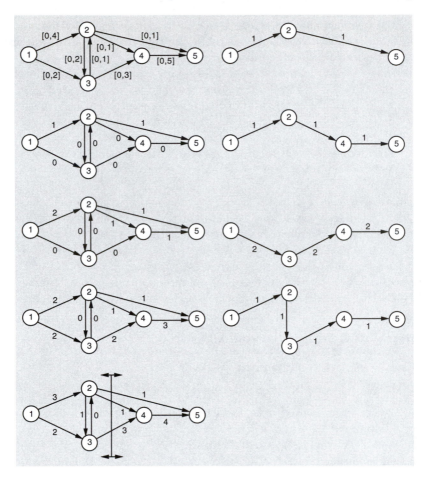

Figure 3.6: Illustration of the Ford-Fulkerson algorithm for finding a maximum flow from node $s = 1$ to node $t = 5$. The arc flow bounds are shown next to the arcs in the top left figure, and the starting flow is zero. The sequence of successive flow vectors is shown on the left, and the corresponding sequence of augmentations is shown on the right. The saturated cut obtained is $[\{1, 2, 3\}, \{4, 5\}]$. The capacity of this cut as well as the maximum flow is 5.

method of Prop. 3.1; this method (also referred to as *breadth-first search*, see Exercise 3.2) yields *augmenting paths with as few arcs as possible* (see Exercises 3.2 and 3.12). If unblocked paths are constructed using a different method, then, surprisingly, the Ford-Fulkerson algorithm need not terminate, and the generated sequence of divergences out of s may converge to a value strictly smaller than the maximum flow (for an example, see Exercise 3.7, and for a different example, see Ford and Fulkerson [1962], or Papadimitriou and Steiglitz [1982], p. 126, or Rockafellar [1984], p. 92). Even with integer problem data, if the augmenting paths are constructed using a different unblocked path search method, the Ford-Fulkerson algorithm may require a very large (pseudopolynomial) number of iterations to terminate; see Fig. 3.7.

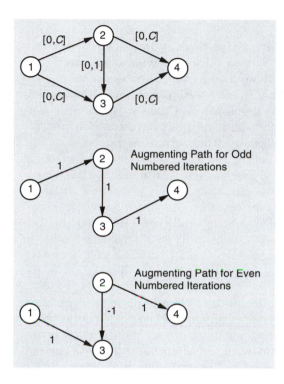

Figure 3.7: An example showing that if the augmenting paths used in the Ford-Fulkerson algorithm do not have a number of arcs that is as small as possible, the number of iterations may be very large. Here, C is a large integer. The maximum flow is $2C$, and can be produced after a sequence of $2C$ augmentations using the three-arc augmenting paths shown in the figure. Thus, the running time is pseudopolynomial (it is proportional to C).

If on the other hand the two-arc augmenting paths $(1, 2, 4)$ and $(1, 3, 4)$ are used, only two augmentations are needed.

Polynomial Max-Flow Algorithms

Using "shortest" augmenting paths (paths with as few arcs as possible) not only guarantees termination of the Ford-Fulkerson algorithm. It turns out that it also results in polynomial running time, as the example of Fig. 3.7 illustrates. In particular, the number of augmentations of the algorithm with shortest augmenting paths can be estimated as $O(NA)$; see Exercise 3.12. This yields an $O(NA^2)$ running time to solve the problem, since each augmentation requires $O(A)$ operations to execute the unblocked path search method and to carry out the subsequent flow update.

Much research has been devoted to developing max-flow algorithms with better than $O(NA^2)$ running time. The algorithms that we will discuss can be grouped into two main categories:

(a) Variants of the Ford-Fulkerson algorithm, which use special data structures and preprocessing calculations to generate augmenting paths efficiently. We will describe some algorithms of this type in what follows in this chapter.

(b) Algorithms that depart from the augmenting path approach, but instead move flow from the source to the sink in a less structured fashion than the Ford-Fulkerson algorithm. These algorithms, known as *preflow-push methods*, will be discussed in Section 7.3. Their underlying mechanism is related to the one of the auction algorithm described in Section 1.3.3.

The algorithms that have the best running times at present are the preflow-push methods. In particular, in Section 7.3 we will demonstrate an $O(N^3)$ running time for one of these methods, and we will describe another method with an $O(N^2A^{1/2})$ running time. Preflow-push algorithms with even better running times exist (see the discussion in Chapter 7). It is unclear, however, whether the best preflow-push methods outperform in practice the best of the Ford-Fulkerson-like algorithms of this chapter.

In the remainder of this chapter, we will discuss efficient variants of the Ford-Fulkerson algorithm. These variants are motivated by a clear inefficiency of the unblocked path search algorithm: *it discards all the labeling information collected from the construction of each augmenting path.* Since, in a large graph, an augmentation typically has a relatively small effect on the current flow vector, each augmenting path problem is similar to the next augmenting path problem. One would thus think that the search for an augmenting path could be organized to preserve information for use in subsequent augmentations.

A prime example of an algorithm that cleverly preserves such information is the historically important algorithm of Dinic [1970], illustrated in Figure 3.8. Let us assume for simplicity that each lower arc flow bound is zero. One possible implementation of the algorithm starts with the zero flow vector and operates in phases. At the start of each phase, we have a feasible flow vector x and we construct an acyclic network, called the *layered network*, which is partitioned in layers (subsets) of nodes as follows:

Construction of the Layered Network

Layer 0 consists of just the sink node t, and layer k consists of all nodes i such that the shortest unblocked path from i to t has k arcs. Let $k(i)$ be the layer number of each node i [$k(i) = \infty$ if i does not belong to any layer].

If the source node s does not belong to any layer, there must exist a saturated cut separating s from t, so the current flow is maximal and the algorithm terminates. Otherwise, we form the layered network as follows: we delete all nodes i such that $k(i) \geq k(s)$ and their incident arcs, and we delete all remaining arcs except the arcs (i, j) such that $k(i) = k(j) + 1$ and $x_{ij} < c_{ij}$, or $k(j) = k(i) + 1$ and $x_{ij} > 0$.

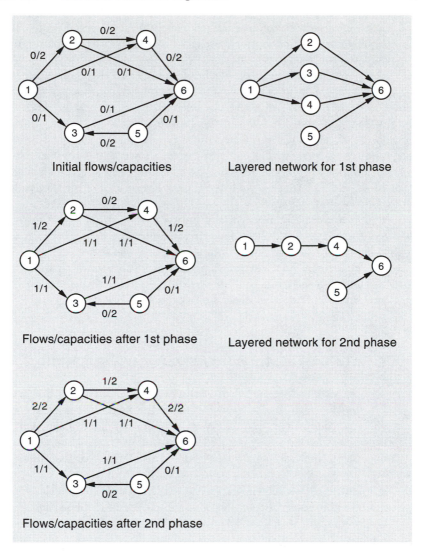

Figure 3.8: Illustration of Dinic's algorithm for the problem shown at the top left (node 1 is the source and node 6 is the sink).

In the first phase, there are three layers, as shown in the top right figure. There are three augmentations in the layered network ($1 \rightarrow 2 \rightarrow 6$, $1 \rightarrow 3 \rightarrow 6$, and $1 \rightarrow 4 \rightarrow 6$), and the resulting flows are shown in the middle left figure. In the second phase, there are four layers, as shown in the bottom right figure. There is only one augmenting path in the layered network ($1 \rightarrow 2 \rightarrow 4 \rightarrow 6$), and the resulting flows are shown in the bottom left figure. The algorithm then terminates because in constructing the layered network, no augmenting paths from 1 to 6 can be found.

Notice a key property of the algorithm: with each new phase, the layer number of the source node is strictly increased (from 2 to 3 in this example). This property shows that the number of phases is at most $N - 1$.

Each phase consists of successively performing augmentations using only arcs of the layered network constructed at the start of the phase, until no more augmentations can be performed.

It can be seen that with proper implementation, the layered network can be constructed in $O(A)$ time. Furthermore, the number of augmentations in each phase is at most A, since each augmentation makes at least one arc unusable for transferring flow from s to t. Given that the flow changes of each augmentation require $O(N)$ time, it follows that each phase requires $O(NA)$ time. Finally, it can be shown that with each phase, the layer number $k(s)$ of the source node s increases strictly, so that there can be at most $N-1$ phases (we leave this as Exercise 3.13 for the reader). It thus follows that the running time of the algorithm is $O(N^2 A)$.

We note that the Dinic algorithm motivated a number of other max-flow algorithms with improved complexity, including an algorithm of Karzanov [1974], which has a $O(N^3)$ running time (see the sources cited at the end of the chapter). The Karzanov algorithm in turn embodied some of the ideas that were instrumental for the development of the preflow-push algorithms for max-flow, which will be discussed in Section 7.3.

3.3 PRICE-BASED AUGMENTING PATH ALGORITHMS

In this section, we develop another type of Ford-Fulkerson algorithm, which reuses information from one augmentation to the next, but does not construct shortest augmenting paths. With proper implementation, this algorithm can be shown to have an $O(N^2 A)$ running time. However, there is evidence that in practice it outperforms the Dinic and the Karzanov algorithms, as well as the preflow-push algorithms of Section 7.3.

We mentioned earlier that constructing shortest augmenting paths provides some guarantee of computational efficiency in the Ford-Fulkerson algorithm. We can in fact view formally the problem of constructing such an augmenting path as a shortest path problem in a certain graph, which we will call the *reduced graph*. In particular, given a capacity-feasible flow vector x, this graph has a node set that is the same as the one of the original graph, and an arc set that is constructed from the one of the original graph by reversing the direction of some of the arcs and by duplicating some arcs and then reversing their direction. In particular, it contains:

(a) An arc (i, j) for each arc (i, j) of the original problem's graph with $x_{ij} < c_{ij}$.

(b) An arc (j, i) for each arc (i, j) of the original problem's graph with $b_{ij} < x_{ij}$.

Thus each incident arc of a node i (either outgoing or incoming) in the original graph along which flow can be pushed from i towards the opposite node, corresponds to an outgoing arc from i in the reduced graph. Furthermore, a path in the original graph is unblocked if it corresponds to a forward path of the reduced graph. Figure 3.9 illustrates the reduced graph.

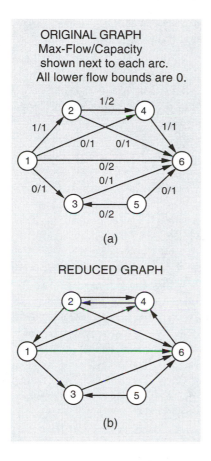

ORIGINAL GRAPH
Max-Flow/Capacity
shown next to each arc.
All lower flow bounds are 0.

(a)

REDUCED GRAPH

(b)

Figure 3.9: Illustration of the reduced graph corresponding to a given flow vector. Node 1 is the source, and node 6 is the sink.

Figure (a) shows the original graph, and the flow and upper flow bound next to each arc (all lower flow bounds are 0). Figure (b) shows the reduced graph. The arc (4,2) is added because the flow of arc (2,4) is strictly between the arc flow bounds. The arcs (1,2) and (4,6) are reversed because their flows are at the corresponding upper bounds.

Note that every forward path in the reduced graph, such as $(1, 4, 2, 6)$, corresponds to an unblocked path in the original graph.

It can now be seen that, given a capacity-feasible flow vector, the problem of finding an augmenting path from s to t with a minimum number of arcs is equivalent to the problem of finding a shortest path from s to t in the corresponding reduced graph, with each arc having length 1. This suggests the simple idea of embedding one of the shortest path algorithms of Chapter 2 within the Ford-Fulkerson method. The shortest path algorithm will be used to construct the sequence of augmenting paths from s to t. Ideally, the algorithm should reuse some information from one shortest path construction to the next; we mentioned earlier that this is a key to computational efficiency.

Reusing information for a shortest path method amounts to providing some form of advanced initialization, such as label information in the context of label correcting methods or price information in the context of auction algorithms. In particular, following a shortest path augmentation, and the attendant change of the reduced graph, one would like to be able to reuse at least some of the final data of the preceding shortest path construction, to provide an advanced start for the next shortest path construction. Unfortunately, label correcting methods do not seem well suited for this purpose, because it turns out that following a change of the reduced graph due to an augmentation, many of the corresponding node labels can become unusable.

On the other hand, the auction algorithm of Section 2.6 is much better suited. The reason is that the node prices in the auction algorithm are required to satisfy the CS condition

$$p_i \le p_j + 1 \tag{3.6}$$

for all arcs (i, j) of the reduced graph. Furthermore, upon discovery of a shortest augmenting path, there holds

$$p_i = p_j + 1$$

for all arcs (i, j) of the augmenting path. It can be seen that this equality guarantees that following a flow augmentation, the CS condition (3.6) will be satisfied for all newly created arcs of the reduced graph. As a result, following an augmentation along a shortest path found by the auction algorithm, *the node prices can be reused without modification* to start the auction algorithm for finding the next shortest augmenting path.

The preceding observations can be used to formally define a max-flow algorithm, where each augmenting path is found as a shortest path from s to t in the reduced graph using the auction algorithm as a shortest path subroutine. The initial node prices can be all equal to 0, and the prevailing prices upon discovery of a shortest augmenting path are used as the starting prices for searching for the next augmenting path. The auction algorithm maintains a path starting at s, which is contracted or extended at each iteration. The price of the terminal node of the path increases by at least 1 whenever there is a contraction. An augmentation occurs whenever the terminal node of the path is the sink node t. The overall algorithm is terminated when the price of the terminal node exceeds $N - 1$, indicating that there is no path starting at s and ending at t.

It is possible to show that, with proper implementation, the max-flow algorithm just described has an $O(N^2 A)$ running time. Unfortunately, however, the practical performance of the algorithm is not very satisfactory, because the computation required by the auction/shortest path algorithm is usually much larger than what is needed to find an augmenting path. The reason is that one needs *just a path* from s to t in the reduced graph and *insisting on obtaining a shortest path may involve a substantial additional computational cost.* In what follows, we will give a price-based method that constructs a (not necessarily shortest) path from s to t. This method is similar to the auction/shortest path algorithm, but when embedded within a sequential augmenting path construction scheme, it results in a max-flow algorithm that is much faster in practice.

3.3.1   A Price-Based Path Construction Algorithm

We will describe a special method for finding a simple forward path in a directed graph $(\mathcal{N}, \mathcal{A})$ that starts at a given node s and ends at a given node t. This method will be subsequently embedded within a max-flow context to construct augmenting paths. The algorithm maintains (except upon termination) a simple forward path $P = (s, n_1, \ldots, n_k)$ and a set of integer node prices p_i, $i \in \mathcal{N}$, satisfying

$$p_i \leq p_j + 1, \qquad \forall\ (i, j) \in \mathcal{A}, \tag{3.7}$$

$$p_s < N, \qquad p_t = 0, \tag{3.8}$$

$$p_i \geq p_j, \qquad \forall\ (i, j) \in P. \tag{3.9}$$

[Note the difference with the auction/shortest path algorithm of Section 2.6, where we require that $p_i = p_j + 1$ for all arcs (i, j) of the path P, rather than $p_i \geq p_j$.]

At the start of the algorithm, we require that $P = (s)$, and that p is such that Eqs. (3.7) and (3.8) hold. The path P is modified repeatedly using the following two operations:

(a) A *contraction* of P, which deletes the last arc of P, that is, replaces the path $P = (s, n_1, \ldots, n_k)$ by the path $P = (s, n_1, \ldots, n_{k-1})$. [In the degenerate case where $P = (s)$, a contraction leaves P unchanged.]

(b) An *extension* of P, which adds to P an arc outgoing from its end node, that is, replaces the path $P = (s, n_1, \ldots, n_k)$ by a path $P = (s, n_1, \ldots, n_k, n_{k+1})$, where (n_k, n_{k+1}) is an arc.

The prices p_i may also be increased in the course of the algorithm so that, together with P, they satisfy the conditions (3.7)-(3.9). A contraction always involves a price increase of the end node n_k. An extension may or may not involve such a price increase. An extension of P is always done to a neighbor node of n_k that has minimal price. The algorithm terminates if either node t becomes the end node of P (then P is the desired path), or else $p_s \geq N$ [in view of $p_t = 0$ and $p_i \leq p_j + 1$ for all arcs (i, j), as per Eqs. (3.7) and (3.8), this means that there is no forward path from s to t].

Path Construction Algorithm

Set $P = (s)$, and select p such that Eqs. (3.7) and (3.8) hold.

Step 1 (Check for contraction or extension): Let n_k be the end node of the current path P and if $n_k \neq s$, let $pred(n_k)$ be the predecessor node of n_k on P. If the set of downstream neighbors of n_k,

$$N(n_k) = \{j \mid (n_k, j) \in \mathcal{A}\},$$

is empty, set $p_{n_k} = N$ and go to Step 3. Otherwise, find a node in $N(n_k)$ with minimal price and denote it $succ(n_k)$,

$$succ(n_k) = \arg \min_{j \in N(n_k)} p_j. \tag{3.10}$$

Set

$$p_{n_k} = p_{succ(n_k)} + 1. \tag{3.11}$$

If $n_k = s$, or if

$$n_k \neq s \quad \text{and} \quad p_{pred(n_k)} > p_{succ(n_k)},$$

go to Step 2; otherwise go to Step 3.

Step 2 (Extend path): Extend P by node $succ(n_k)$ and the corresponding arc $\big(n_k, succ(n_k)\big)$. If $succ(n_k) = t$, terminate the algorithm; otherwise go to Step 1.

Step 3 (Contract path): If $P = (s)$ and $p_s \geq N$, terminate the algorithm; otherwise, contract P and go to Step 1.

Figure 3.10 illustrates the preceding path construction algorithm. In the special case where all initial prices are zero and there is a path from each node to t, by tracing the steps, it can be seen that the algorithm will work like depth-first search, raising to 1 the prices of the nodes of some path from s to t in a sequence of extensions with no intervening contractions. More generally, the algorithm terminates without performing any contractions if the initial prices satisfy $p_i \geq p_j$ for all arcs (i, j) and there is a path from each node to t.

Note that the algorithm does not necessarily generate a shortest path. Instead, it can be shown that it solves a special type of assignment problem by means of the auction algorithm of Section 1.3.3 (which will be further developed in Chapter 7); see Exercise 3.17.

We make the following observations:

(1) The prices remain integer throughout the algorithm [cf. Eq. (3.11)].

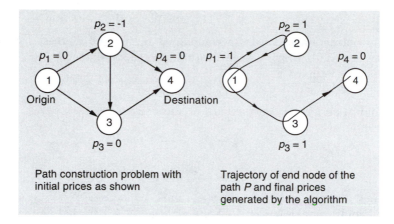

Path construction problem with initial prices as shown

Trajectory of end node of the path *P* and final prices generated by the algorithm

Iteration #	Path P prior to iteration	Type of action during iteration	Price vector p after the iteration
1	(1)	extension to 2	$(0, -1, 0, 0)$
2	$(1, 2)$	contraction at 2	$(0, 1, 0, 0)$
3	(1)	extension to 3	$(1, 1, 0, 0)$
4	$(1, 3)$	extension to 4	$(1, 1, 1, 0)$
5	$(1, 3, 4)$	stop	

Figure 3.10: An example illustrating the path construction algorithm from $s = 1$ to $t = 4$, where the initial price vector is $p = (0, -1, 0, 0)$.

(2) The conditions (3.7)-(3.9) are satisfied each time Step 1 is entered. The proof is by induction. These conditions hold initially by assumption. Condition (3.8) is maintained by the algorithm, since termination occurs as soon as $p_s \geq N$ or t becomes the end node of P. To verify conditions (3.7) and (3.9), we note that only the price of n_k can change in Step 1, and by Eqs. (3.10) and (3.11), this price change maintains condition (3.7) for all arcs, and condition (3.9) for all arcs of P, except possibly for the arc $\left(pred(n_k), n_k\right)$ in the case of an extension with the condition

$$p_{pred(n_k)} > p_{succ(n_k)}$$

holding. In the latter case, we must have

$$p_{pred(n_k)} \geq p_{succ(n_k)} + 1$$

because the prices are integer, so by Eq. (3.11), we have

$$p_{pred(n_k)} \geq p_{n_k}$$

at the next entry to Step 1. This completes the induction.

(3) A contraction is always accompanied by a price increase. Indeed by Eq. (3.9), which was just established, upon entering Step 1 with $n_k \neq s$, we have

$$p_{n_k} \leq p_{pred(n_k)},$$

and to perform a contraction, we must have

$$p_{pred(n_k)} \leq p_{succ(n_k)}.$$

Hence

$$p_{n_k} \leq p_{succ(n_k)},$$

implying by Eq. (3.11) that $p(n_k)$ must be increased to $p_{succ(n_k)} + 1$. It can be seen, however, by example (see Fig. 3.10), that an extension may or may not be accompanied by a price increase.

(4) Upon return to Step 1 following an extension, the end node n_k satisfies [cf. Eq. (3.11)]

$$p_{pred(n_k)} = p_{n_k} + 1.$$

This, together with the condition $p_i \geq p_j$ for all $(i,j) \in P$ [cf. Eq. (3.9)], implies that the path P will not be extended to a node that already belongs to P, thereby closing a cycle. Thus P remains a simple path throughout the algorithm.

The following proposition establishes the termination properties of the algorithm.

Proposition 3.3: If there exists a forward path from s to t, the path construction algorithm terminates via Step 2 with such a path. Otherwise, the algorithm terminates via Step 3 when $p_s \geq N$.

Proof: We first note that the prices of the nodes of P are upper bounded by N in view of Eqs. (3.8) and (3.9). Next we observe that there is a price change of at least one unit with each contraction, and since the prices of the nodes of P are upper bounded by N, there can be only a finite number of contractions. Since P never contains a cycle, there can be at most $N - 1$ successive extensions without a contraction, so the algorithm must terminate. Throughout the algorithm, we have $p_t = 0$ and $p_i \leq p_j + 1$ for all arcs (i,j). Hence, if a forward path from s to t exists, we must have $p_s < N$ throughout the algorithm, including at termination, and since termination via Step 3 requires that $p_s \geq N$, it follows that the algorithm must terminate via Step 2 with a path from s to t. If a forward path from s to t does not exist, termination can only occur via Step 3, in which case we must have $p_s \geq N$. **Q.E.D.**

3.3.2   A Price-Based Max-Flow Algorithm

Let us now return to the max-flow problem. We can construct an augmenting path algorithm of the Ford-Fulkerson type that uses the path construction algorithm just presented. The algorithm consists of a sequence of augmentations, each performed using the path construction algorithm to obtain a path of the reduced graph that starts at the source node s and ends at the sink node t. As starting price vector we can use the zero vector.

An important point here is that, *following an augmentation, the price vector of the path construction algorithm can remain unchanged.* The reason is that the node prices in the path construction algorithm are required to satisfy the condition

$$p_i \le p_j + 1 \tag{3.12}$$

for all arcs (i, j) of the reduced graph. Furthermore, upon discovery of an augmenting path P, there holds

$$p_i \ge p_j$$

for all arcs (i, j) of P. It follows that as the reduced graph changes due to the corresponding augmentation, for every newly created arc (j, i) of the reduced graph, the arc (i, j) must belong to P, so that $p_i \ge p_j$. Hence the newly created arc (j, i) of the reduced graph will also satisfy the required condition $p_j \le p_i + 1$ [cf. Eq. (3.12)].

For a practically efficient implementation of the max-flow algorithm just described, a number of fairly complex modifications may be needed. A description of these and a favorable computational comparison with other competing methods can be found in Bertsekas [1995c], where an $O(N^2 A)$ complexity bound is also shown for a suitable variant of the method.

3.4   NOTES, SOURCES, AND EXERCISES

The max-flow/min-cut theorem was independently given in Dantzig and Fulkerson [1956], Elias, Feinstein, and Shannon [1956], and Ford and Fulkerson [1956b]. The material of Section 3.1.4 on decomposition of infeasible problems is apparently new.

The proof that the Ford-Fulkerson algorithm with breadth-first search has polynomial complexity $O(NA^2)$ (Exercise 3.12) is due to Edmonds and Karp [1972]. Using the idea of a layered network, this bound was improved to $O(N^2 A)$ by Dinic [1970], whose work motivated a lot of research on max-flow algorithms with improved complexity. In particular, Dinic's complexity bound was improved to $O(N^3)$ by Karzanov [1974] and by Malhotra, Kumar, and Maheshwari [1978], to $O(N^2 A^{1/2})$ by Cherkasky [1977], to $O(N^{5/3} A^{2/3})$ by Galil [1980], and to $O(NA \log^2 N)$ by Galil and Naamad

[1980]. Dinic's algorithm when applied to the maximal matching problem
(Exercise 3.9) can be shown to have running time $O(N^{1/2}A)$ (see Hopcroft
and Karp [1973]). The survey paper by Ahuja, Magnanti, and Orlin [1989]
provides a complexity-oriented account of max-flow algorithms.

The max-flow algorithm of Section 3.3 is due to Bertsekas [1995c].
This reference contains several variants of the basic method, a discussion of
implementation issues, and extensive computational results that indicate
a superior practical performance over competing methods, including the
preflow-push algorithms of Chapter 7.

There are two important results in network optimization that deal
with the existence of feasible solutions for minimum cost flow problems.
The first is the *feasible distribution theorem*, due to Gale [1957] and Hoffman [1960], which is a consequence of the max-flow/min-cut theorem (Exercise 3.3). The second is the *feasible differential theorem*, due to Minty
[1960], which deals with the existence of a set of prices satisfying certain
constraints. This theorem is a consequence of the duality theory to be
fully developed in Chapter 5, and will be given in Exercise 5.11 (see also
Exercise 5.12).

EXERCISES

3.1

Consider the max-flow problem of Fig. 3.11, where $s = 1$ and $t = 5$.

(a) Enumerate all cuts of the form $[\mathcal{S}, \mathcal{N} - \mathcal{S}]$ such that $1 \in \mathcal{S}$ and $5 \notin \mathcal{S}$.
Calculate the capacity of each cut.

(b) Find the maximal and minimal saturated cuts.

(c) Apply the Ford-Fulkerson method to find the maximum flow and verify the
max-flow/min-cut equality.

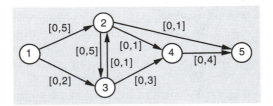

Figure 3.11: Max-flow problem
for Exercise 3.1. The arc capacities are shown next to the arcs.

3.2 (Breadth-First Search)

Let i and j be two nodes of a directed graph $(\mathcal{N}, \mathcal{A})$.

(a) Consider the following algorithm, known as *breadth-first search*, for finding a path from i to j. Let $T_0 = \{i\}$. For $k = 0, 1, \ldots$, let

$$T_{k+1} = \{n \notin \cup_{p=0}^{k} T_p \mid \text{for some node } m \in T_k, \, (m,n) \text{ or } (n,m) \text{ is an arc}\},$$

and mark each node $n \in T_{k+1}$ with the label "(m,n)" or "(n,m)," where m is a node of T_k such that (m,n) or (n,m) is an arc, respectively. The algorithm terminates if either (1) T_{k+1} is empty or (2) $j \in T_{k+1}$. Show that case (1) occurs if and only if there is no path from i to j. If case (2) occurs, how would you use the labels to construct a path from i to j?

(b) Show that a path found by breadth-first search has a minimum number of arcs over all paths from i to j.

(c) Modify the algorithm of part (a) so that it finds a *forward* path from i to j.

3.3 (Feasible Distribution Theorem)

Show that the minimum cost flow problem introduced in Section 1.2.1, has a feasible solution if and only if $\sum_{i \in \mathcal{N}} s_i = 0$ and for every cut $Q = [\mathcal{S}, \mathcal{N} - \mathcal{S}]$ we have

$$\text{Capacity of } Q \geq \sum_{i \in \mathcal{S}} s_i.$$

Show also that feasibility of the problem can be determined by solving a max-flow problem with zero lower flow bounds. *Hint*: Assume first that all lower flow bounds b_{ij} are zero. Use the conversion to a max-flow problem of Fig. 3.1, and apply the max-flow/min-cut theorem. In the general case, transform the problem to one with zero lower flow bounds.

3.4 (Finding a Feasible Flow Vector)

Describe an algorithm of the Ford-Fulkerson type for checking the feasibility and finding a feasible solution of a minimum cost flow problem (cf., Section 1.2.1). If the supplies s_i and the arc flow bounds b_{ij} and c_{ij} are integer, your algorithm should be guaranteed to find an integer feasible solution (assuming at least one feasible solution exists). *Hint*: Use the conversion to a max-flow problem of Fig. 3.1.

3.5 (Integer Approximations of Feasible Solutions)

Given a graph $(\mathcal{N}, \mathcal{A})$ and a flow vector x, show that there exists an integer flow vector $\bar{x}$ having the same divergence vector as x and satisfying

$$|x_{ij} - \bar{x}_{ij}| < 1, \qquad \forall \, (i,j) \in \mathcal{A}.$$

Hint: For each arc (i, j), define the integer flow bounds

$$b_{ij} = \lfloor x_{ij} \rfloor, \qquad c_{ij} = \lceil x_{ij} \rceil.$$

Use the result of Exercise 3.3.

3.6

Consider a graph with arc flow range $[0, c_{ij}]$ for each arc (i, j), and let x be a capacity-feasible flow vector.

(a) Consider any subset S of nodes all of which have nonpositive divergence and at least one of which has negative divergence. Show that there must exist at least one arc (i, j) with $i \notin S$ and $j \in S$ such that $x_{ij} > 0$.

(b) Show that for each node with negative divergence there is an augmenting path that starts at that node and ends at a node with positive divergence. *Hint:* Construct such a path using an algorithm that is based on part (a).

3.7 (Ford-Fulkerson Method Counterexample)

This counterexample (from Chvatal [1983]) illustrates how the version of the Ford-Fulkerson method where augmenting paths need not have as few arcs as possible may not terminate for a problem with irrational arc flow bounds. Consider the max-flow problem shown in Fig. 3.12.

(a) Verify that an infinite sequence of augmenting paths is characterized by the table of Fig. 3.12; each augmentation increases the divergence out of the source s but the sequence of divergences converges to a value, which can be arbitrarily smaller than the maximum flow.

(b) Solve the problem with the Ford-Fulkerson method (where the augmenting paths involve a minimum number of arcs, as given in Section 3.2).

3.8 (Graph Connectivity – Menger's Theorem)

Let s and t be two nodes in a directed graph. Use the max-flow/min-cut theorem to show that:

(a) The maximum number of forward paths from s to t that do not share any arcs is equal to the minimum number of arcs that when removed from the graph, eliminate all forward paths from s to t.

(b) The maximum number of forward paths from s to t that do not share any nodes (other than s and t) is equal to the minimum number of nodes that when removed from the graph, eliminate all forward paths from s to t.

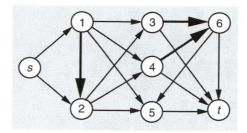

After Iter. #	Augm. Path	x_{12}	x_{36}	x_{46}	x_{65}
$6k+1$	$(s,1,2,3,6,t)$	σ	$1-\sigma^{3k+2}$	$\sigma-\sigma^{3k+1}$	0
$6k+2$	$(s,2,1,3,6,5,t)$	$\sigma-\sigma^{3k+2}$	1	$\sigma-\sigma^{3k+1}$	σ^{3k+2}
$6k+3$	$(s,1,2,4,6,t)$	σ	1	$\sigma-\sigma^{3k+3}$	σ^{3k+2}
$6k+4$	$(s,2,1,4,6,3,t)$	$\sigma-\sigma^{3k+3}$	$1-\sigma^{3k+3}$	σ	σ^{3k+2}
$6k+5$	$(s,1,2,5,6,t)$	σ	$1-\sigma^{3k+3}$	σ	σ^{3k+4}
$6k+6$	$(s,2,1,5,6,4,t)$	$\sigma-\sigma^{3k+4}$	$1-\sigma^{3k+3}$	$\sigma-\sigma^{3k+4}$	0
$6(k+1)+1$	$(s,1,2,3,6,t)$	σ	$1-\sigma^{3(k+1)+2}$	$\sigma-\sigma^{3(k+1)+1}$	0

Figure 3.12: Max-flow problem illustrating that if the augmenting paths in the Ford-Fulkerson method do not have a minimum number of arcs, then the method may not terminate. All lower arc flow bounds are zero. The upper flow bounds are larger than one, with the exception of the thick-line arcs; these are arc $(3,6)$ which has upper flow bound equal to one, and arcs $(1,2)$ and $(4,6)$ which have upper flow bound equal to $\sigma = \left(-1+\sqrt{5}\right)/2$. (Note a crucial property of σ; it satisfies $\sigma^{k+2} = \sigma^k - \sigma^{k+1}$ for all integer $k \geq 0$.) The table gives a sequence of augmentations.

3.9 (Max Matching/Min Cover Theorem (König-Egervary))

Consider a bipartite graph consisting of two sets of nodes $\mathcal{S}$ and $\mathcal{T}$ such that every arc has its start node in $\mathcal{S}$ and its end node in $\mathcal{T}$. A *matching* is a subset of arcs such that all the start nodes of the arcs are distinct and all the end nodes of the arcs are distinct. A maximal matching is a matching with a maximal number of arcs.

(a) Show that the problem of finding a maximal matching can be formulated as a max-flow problem.

(b) Define a *cover* $\mathcal{C}$ to be a subset of $\mathcal{S} \cup \mathcal{T}$ such that for each arc (i,j), either $i \in \mathcal{C}$ or $j \in \mathcal{C}$ (or both). A minimal cover is a cover with a minimal number of nodes. Show that the number of arcs in a maximal matching and the number of nodes in a minimal cover are equal. (Variants of this theorem were independently published by König [1931] and Egervary [1931].) *Hint:* Use the max-flow/min-cut theorem.

3.10 (Theorem of Distinct Representatives, Hall [1956])

Given finite sets $S_1, S_2, \ldots, S_k$, we say that the collection $\{s_1, s_2, \ldots, s_k\}$ is a system of distinct representatives if $s_i \in S_i$ for all i and $s_i \neq s_j$ for $i \neq j$. (For example, if $S_1 = \{a, b, c\}$, $S_2 = \{a, b\}$, $S_3 = \{a\}$, then $s_1 = c$, $s_2 = b$, $s_3 = a$ is a system of distinct representatives.) Show that there exists no system of distinct representatives if and only if there exists an index set $I \subset \{1, 2, \ldots, k\}$ such that the number of elements in $\cup_{i \in I} S_i$ is less than the number of elements in I. *Hint:* Consider a bipartite graph with each of the right side nodes representing an element of $\cup_{i \in I} S_i$, with each of the left side nodes representing one of the sets $S_1, S_2, \ldots S_k$, and with an arc from a left node S to a right node s if $s \in S$. Use the maximal matching/minimal cover theorem of Exercise 3.9. For additional material on this problem, see Hoffman and Kuhn [1956], and Mendelssohn and Dulmage [1958].

3.11

Prove the following generalizations of Prop. 3.1:

(a) Let x be a capacity-feasible flow vector, and let $\mathcal{N}^+$ and $\mathcal{N}^-$ be two disjoint subsets of nodes. Then exactly one of the following two alternatives holds:

    (1) There exists a simple path that starts at some node of $\mathcal{N}^+$, ends at some node of $\mathcal{N}^-$, and is unblocked with respect to x.

    (2) There exists a saturated cut $Q = [\mathcal{S}, \mathcal{N} - \mathcal{S}]$ such that $\mathcal{N}^+ \subset \mathcal{S}$ and $\mathcal{N}^- \subset \mathcal{N} - \mathcal{S}$.

(b) Show part (a) with "simple path" in alternative (1) replaced by "path". *Hint:* Use the path decomposition theorem of Exercise 1.4.

3.12 (Termination of the Ford-Fulkerson Algorithm)

Consider the Ford-Fulkerson algorithm as described in Section 3.2 (augmenting paths have as few arcs as possible). This exercise shows that the algorithm terminates and solves the max-flow problem in polynomial time, even when the problem data are irrational.

Let x^0 be the initial feasible flow vector; let x^k, $k = 1, 2, \ldots$, be the flow vector after the kth augmentation; and let P_k be the corresponding augmenting path. An arc (i, j) is said to be a k^+-*bottleneck* if (i, j) is a forward arc of P_k and $x_{ij}^k = c_{ij}$, and it is said to be a k^--*bottleneck* if (i, j) is a backward arc of P_k and $x_{ij}^k = b_{ij}$.

(a) Show that if $k < \bar{k}$ and an arc (i, j) is a k^+-bottleneck and a $\bar{k}^+$-bottleneck, then for some m with $k < m < \bar{k}$, the arc (i, j) is a backward arc of P_m. Similarly, if an arc (i, j) is a k^--bottleneck and a $\bar{k}^-$-bottleneck, then for some m with $k < m < \bar{k}$, the arc (i, j) is a forward arc of P_m.

(b) Show that P_k is a path with a minimal number of arcs over all augmenting paths with respect to x^{k-1}. (This property depends on the implementation of the unblocked path search as a breadth-first search.)

(c) For any path P that is unblocked with respect to x^k, let $n_k(P)$ be the number of arcs of P, let $a_k^+(i)$ be the minimum of $n_k(P)$ over all unblocked P from s to i, and let $a_k^-(i)$ be the minimum of $n_k(P)$ over all unblocked P from i to t. Show that for all i and k we have

$$a_k^+(i) \le a_{k+1}^+(i), \qquad a_k^-(i) \le a_{k+1}^-(i).$$

(d) Show that if $k < \overline{k}$ and arc (i,j) is both a k^+-bottleneck and a $\overline{k}^+$-bottleneck, or is both a k^--bottleneck and a $\overline{k}^-$-bottleneck, then $a_k^+(t) < a_{\overline{k}}^+(t)$.

(e) Show that the algorithm terminates after $O(NA)$ augmentations, for an $O(NA^2)$ running time.

3.13 (Layered Network Algorithm)

Consider the algorithm described near the end of Section 3.2, which uses phases and augmentations through a layered network.

(a) Provide an algorithm for constructing the layered network of each phase in $O(A)$ time.

(b) Show that the number of augmentations in each phase is at most A, and provide an implementation whereby these augmentations require $O(NA)$ total time.

(c) Show that with each phase, the layer number $k(s)$ of the source node s increases strictly, so that there can be at most $N - 1$ phases.

(d) Show that with the implementations of (a) and (b), the running time of the algorithm is $O(N^2A)$.

3.14 ($O(N^{2/3}A)$ Complexity for Unit Capacity Graphs)

Consider the max-flow problem in the special case where the arc flow range is $[0,1]$ for all arcs.

(a) Show that each path from the source to the sink that is unblocked with respect to the zero flow has at most $2N/\sqrt{M}$ arcs, where M is the value of the maximum flow. *Hint:* Let N_k be the number of nodes i such that the shortest unblocked path from s to i has k arcs. Argue that $k(k+1) \ge M$.

(b) Show that the running time of the layered network algorithm (cf. Fig. 3.8) is reduced to $O(N^{2/3}A)$. *Hint:* Argue that each arc of the layered network can be part of at most one augmenting path in a given phase, so the augmentations of each phase require $O(A)$ computation. Use part (a) to show that the number of phases is $O(N^{2/3})$.

3.15

(a) Solve the problem of Exercise 3.1 using the layered network algorithm (cf. Fig. 3.8).

(b) Construct an example of a max-flow problem where the layered network algorithm requires $N - 1$ phases.

3.16

Solve the problem of Exercise 3.1 using the max-flow algorithm of Section 3.3.2.

3.17 (Relation of Path Construction and Assignment)

The purpose of this exercise (from Bertsekas [1995c]) is to show the connection of the path construction algorithm of Section 3.3.1 with the assignment auction algorithm of Section 1.3.3.

(a) Show that the path construction problem can be converted into the problem of finding a solution of a certain assignment problem with all arc values equal to 0, as shown by example in Fig. 3.13. In particular, a forward path of a directed graph $\mathcal{G}$ that starts at node s and ends at node t corresponds to a feasible solution of the assignment problem, and conversely.

(b) Show how to relate the node prices in the path construction algorithm with the object prices of the assignment problem, so that if we apply the auction algorithm with $\epsilon = 1$, the sequence of generated prices and assignments corresponds to the sequence of generated prices and paths by the path construction algorithm.

3.18 (Decomposition of Infeasible Assignment Problems)

Apply the decomposition approach of Section 3.1.4 to an infeasible $n \times n$ assignment problem. Show that the set of persons can be partitioned in three disjoint subsets I_1, I_2, and I_3, and that the set of objects can be partitioned in three disjoint subsets J_1, J_2, and J_3 with the following properties (cf. Fig. 3.14):

(1) I_1, J_1, I_2, and J_2 are all nonempty, while I_3 and J_3 may be empty.

(2) There is no pair $(i, j) \in \mathcal{A}$ such that $i \notin I_1$ and $j \in J_1$, or $i \in I_2$ and $j \notin J_2$.

(3) If I_3 and J_3 are nonempty, then all pairs $(i, j) \in \mathcal{A}$ with $i \in I_3$ are such that $j \in J_3$.

Identify the three component problems of the decomposition in terms of the sets I_1, J_1, I_2, J_2, I_3, and J_3. Show that two of these problems are feasible asymmetric assignment problems (the numbers of persons and objects are unequal), while the third is a feasible symmetric assignment problem (the numbers of persons and objects are equal).

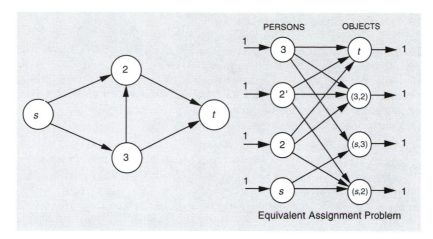

Equivalent Assignment Problem

Figure 3.13: Converting the path construction problem into an equivalent feasibility problem of assigning "persons" to "objects." Each arc (i, j) of the graph $\mathcal{G}$, with $i \neq t$, is replaced by an object labeled (i, j). Each node $i \neq t$ is replaced by $R(i)$ persons, where $R(i)$ is the number of arcs of $\mathcal{G}$ that are incoming to node i (for example node 2 is replaced by the two persons 2 and $2'$). Finally, there is one person corresponding to node s and one object corresponding to node t. For every arc (i, j) of $\mathcal{G}$, with $i \neq t$, there are $R(i) + R(j)$ incoming arcs from the persons corresponding to i and j. For every arc (i, t) of $\mathcal{G}$, there are $R(i)$ incoming arcs from the persons corresponding to i. Each path that starts at s and ends at t can be associated with a feasible assignment. Conversely, given a feasible assignment, one can construct an alternating path (a sequence of alternatively assigned and unassigned pairs) starting at s and ending at t, which defines a path from s to t.

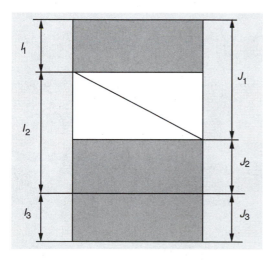

Figure 3.14: Decomposition of an infeasible assignment problem (cf. Exercise 3.18).

3.19 (Perfect Bipartite Matchings)

Consider the problem of matching n persons with n objects on a one-to-one basis (cf. Exercises 1.21 and 3.9). For each person i there is a given set of objects $A(i)$ that can be matched with i. A matching is a subset of pairs (i, j) with $j \in A(i)$, such that there is at most one pair for each person and each object. A perfect matching is one that consists of n pairs, i.e., one where every person is matched with a distinct object.

(a) Assume that there exists a perfect matching. Consider an imperfect matching $S = \{(i, j) \mid i \in I\}$, where I is a set of $m < n$ distinct persons, and let $J = \{j \mid \text{there exists } i \in I \text{ with } (i, j) \in S\}$. Show that given any $i \notin I$, there exists a sequence $\{i, j_1, i_1, j_2, i_2, \ldots, j_k, i_k, j\}$ such that $j \notin J$, the pairs $(i_1, j_1), \ldots, (i_k, j_k)$ belong to S, and $j_1 \in A(i)$, $j_2 \in A(i_1), \ldots, j_k \in A(i_{k-1})$, $j \in A(i_k)$. *Hint:* Try to find an augmenting path in a suitable graph.

(b) Show that there exists a perfect matching if and only if there is no subset $I \subset \{1, \ldots, n\}$ such that the set $\cup_{i \in I} A(i)$ has fewer elements than I.

(c) (König's Theorem on Perfect Matchings) Assume that all the sets $A(i)$, $i = 1, \ldots, n$, contain the same number of elements. Show that there exists a perfect matching.

3.20

Consider a feasible max-flow problem. Show that if the upper flow bound of each arc is increased by $\alpha > 0$, then the value of the maximum flow is increased by no more than αA, where A is the number of arcs.

3.21

A town has m dating agencies that match men and women. Agency i has a list of men and a list of women, and may match a maximum of c_i man/woman pairs from its lists. A person may be in the list of several agencies but may be matched with at most one other person. Formulate the problem of maximizing the number of matched pairs as a max-flow problem.

3.22

Consider an $n \times n$ chessboard and let A and B be two given squares.

(a) Consider the problem of finding the maximal number of knight paths that start at A, end at B, and do not overlap, in the sense that they do not share a square other than A and B. Formulate the problem as a max-flow problem.

(b) Solve the problem of part (a) using the max-flow algorithm of Section 3.3.2 for the case where $n = 8$, and the squares A and B are two opposite corners of the board.

3.23

Consider the problem of placing n queens on a chessboard of dimensions $n \times n$ so that there is no pair of queens that attack each other.

(a) Formulate the problem of finding a solution as a max-flow problem.

(b) Formulate the problem of counting the number of distinct solutions as a max-flow problem.

3.24 (Min-Flow Problem)

Consider the "opposite" to the max-flow problem, which is to minimize the divergence out of s over all capacity-feasible flow vectors having zero divergence for all nodes other than s and t.

(a) Show how to solve this problem by first finding a feasible solution, and by then using a max-flow algorithm.

(b) Derive an analog to the max-flow/min-cut theorem.

4

The Min-Cost Flow Problem

Contents

In this and the following three chapters, we focus on the minimum cost flow problem, introduced in Section 1.2:

$$\text{minimize} \quad \sum_{(i,j)\in\mathcal{A}} a_{ij}x_{ij}$$

$$\text{subject to} \quad \sum_{\{j|(i,j)\in\mathcal{A}\}} x_{ij} - \sum_{\{j|(j,i)\in\mathcal{A}\}} x_{ji} = s_i, \qquad \forall\, i \in \mathcal{N},$$

$$b_{ij} \leq x_{ij} \leq c_{ij}, \qquad \forall\, (i,j) \in \mathcal{A},$$

where a_{ij}, b_{ij}, c_{ij}, and s_i are given scalars.

We begin by discussing several equivalent ways to represent the problem. These are useful because different representations lend themselves better or worse for various analytical and algorithmic purposes. We then develop duality theory and the associated optimality conditions. This theory is fundamental for the algorithms of the following three chapters, and richly enhances our insight into the problem's structure.

4.1 TRANSFORMATIONS AND EQUIVALENCES

In this section, we describe how the minimum cost flow problem can be represented in several equivalent "standard" forms. This is often useful, because depending on the analytical or algorithmic context, a particular representation may be more convenient than the others.

4.1.1 Setting the Lower Flow Bounds to Zero

The lower flow bounds b_{ij} can be changed to zero by a translation of variables, that is, by replacing x_{ij} by $x_{ij} - b_{ij}$, and by adjusting the upper flow bounds and the supplies according to

$$c_{ij} := c_{ij} - b_{ij},$$

$$s_i := s_i - \sum_{\{j|(i,j)\in\mathcal{A}\}} b_{ij} + \sum_{\{j|(j,i)\in\mathcal{A}\}} b_{ji}.$$

Optimal flows and the optimal value of the original problem are obtained by adding b_{ij} to the optimal flow of each arc (i,j) and adding $\sum_{(i,j)\in\mathcal{A}} a_{ij}b_{ij}$ to the optimal value of the transformed problem, respectively. Working with the transformed problem saves computation time and storage, and for this reason most network flow codes assume that all lower flow bounds are zero.

4.1.2   Eliminating the Upper Flow Bounds

Once the lower flow bounds have been changed to zero, it is possible to eliminate the upper flow bounds, obtaining a problem with just a nonnegativity constraint on all the flows. This can be done by introducing an additional nonnegative variable z_{ij} that must satisfy the constraint

$$x_{ij} + z_{ij} = c_{ij}.$$

(In linear programming terminology, z_{ij} is known as a *slack variable*.) The resulting problem is a minimum cost flow problem involving for each arc (i, j), an extra node with supply c_{ij}, and two outgoing arcs, corresponding to the flows x_{ij} and z_{ij}; see Fig. 4.1.

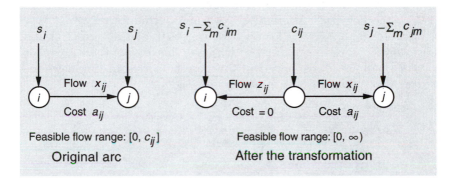

Figure 4.1: Eliminating the upper capacity bound by replacing each arc with a node and two outgoing arcs. Since for feasibility we must have $z_{ij} = c_{ij} - x_{ij}$, the upper bound constraint $x_{ij} \leq c_{ij}$ is equivalent to the lower bound constraint $0 \leq z_{ij}$. Furthermore, in view again of $x_{ij} = c_{ij} - z_{ij}$, the conservation of flow equation

$$-\sum_{j} z_{ij} - \sum_{j} x_{ji} = s_i - \sum_{j} c_{ij}$$

for the modified problem is equivalent to the conservation of flow equation

$$\sum_{j} x_{ij} - \sum_{j} x_{ji} = s_i$$

for the original problem. Using these facts, it can be seen that the feasible flow vectors (x, z) of the modified problem can be paired on a one-to-one basis with the feasible flow vectors x of the original problem, and that the corresponding costs are equal. Thus, the modified problem is equivalent to the original problem.

     Eliminating the upper flow bounds simplifies the statement of the problem, but complicates the use of some algorithms. The reason is that problems with upper (as well as lower) flow bounds are guaranteed to have at least one optimal solution if they have at least one feasible solution, as we will see in Chapter 5. However, a problem with just nonnegativity constraints may be *unbounded*, in the sense that it may have feasible solutions of arbitrarily small cost. This is one reason why most network flow codes require that upper and lower bound restrictions be placed on all the flow variables.

4.1.3   Reduction to a Circulation Format

The problem can be transformed into the *circulation format*, in which all node supplies are zero. One way to do this is to introduce an artificial "accumulation" node t and an arc (t, i) for each node i with nonzero supply s_i. We may then introduce the constraint $s_i \leq x_{ti} \leq s_i$ and an arbitrary cost for the flow x_{ti}. Alternatively, we may introduce an arc (t, i) and a constraint $0 \leq x_{ti} \leq s_i$ for all i with $s_i > 0$, and an arc (i, t) and a constraint $0 \leq x_{it} \leq -s_i$ for all i with $s_i < 0$. The cost of these arcs should be very small (i.e., large negative) to force the corresponding flows to be at their upper bound at the optimum; see Fig. 4.2.

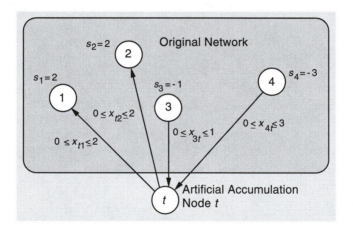

Figure 4.2: A transformation of the minimum cost flow problem into a circulation format by using an artificial "accumulation" node t and corresponding artificial arcs connecting t with all the nodes as shown. These arcs have very large negative cost, to force the corresponding flows to their upper bounds at the optimum.

4.1.4   Reduction to an Assignment Problem

Finally, the minimum cost flow problem may be transformed into a transportation problem of the form

$$\text{minimize} \quad \sum_{(i,j)\in\mathcal{A}} a_{ij}x_{ij}$$

$$\text{subject to} \quad \sum_{\{j|(i,j)\in\mathcal{A}\}} x_{ij} = \alpha_i, \qquad \forall\ i = 1,\dots,m,$$

$$\sum_{\{i|(i,j)\in\mathcal{A}\}} x_{ij} = \beta_j, \qquad \forall\ j = 1,\dots,n,$$

$$0 \le x_{ij} \le \min\{\alpha_i,\beta_j\}, \qquad \forall\ (i,j)\in\mathcal{A};$$

see Fig. 4.3. This transportation problem can itself be converted into an assignment problem by creating α_i unit supply sources (β_j unit demand sinks) for each transportation problem source i (sink j, respectively). For this reason, any algorithm that solves the assignment problem can be extended into an algorithm for the minimum cost flow problem. This motivates a useful way to develop and analyze new algorithmic ideas; apply them to the simpler assignment problem and generalize them using the construction just given to the minimum cost flow problem.

4.2   DUALITY

We have already introduced some preliminary duality ideas in the context of the assignment problem in Section 1.3.2. In this section, we consider the general minimum cost flow problem, and we obtain a dual problem using a procedure that is standard in duality theory. We introduce a Lagrange multiplier, also called a price p_i for the conservation of flow constraint for node i and we form the corresponding Lagrangian function

$$L(x,p) = \sum_{(i,j)\in\mathcal{A}} a_{ij}x_{ij} + \sum_{i\in\mathcal{N}} \left(s_i - \sum_{\{j|(i,j)\in\mathcal{A}\}} x_{ij} + \sum_{\{j|(j,i)\in\mathcal{A}\}} x_{ji} \right) p_i$$

$$= \sum_{(i,j)\in\mathcal{A}} (a_{ij} + p_j - p_i)x_{ij} + \sum_{i\in\mathcal{N}} s_i p_i. \tag{4.1}$$

Here, we use p to denote the vector whose components are the prices p_i.

Let us now fix p and consider minimizing $L(x,p)$ with respect to x *without the requirement to meet the conservation of flow constraints.* It is seen that p_i may be viewed as a penalty per unit violation of the conservation of flow constraint. If p_i is too small (or too large), there is an incentive for positive (or negative, respectively) violation of the constraint. This suggests that we should search for the correct values p_i for which,

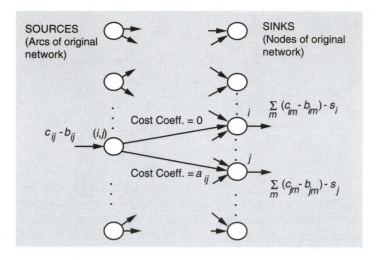

Figure 4.3: Transformation of a minimum cost flow problem into a transportation problem. The idea is to introduce a new node for each arc and introduce a slack variable for every arc flow; see Fig. 4.1. This not only eliminates the upper bound constraint on the arc flows, as in Fig. 4.1, but also creates a bipartite graph structure. In particular, we take as sources of the transportation problem the arcs of the original network, and as sinks of the transportation problem the nodes of the original network. Each transportation problem source has two outgoing arcs with cost coefficients as shown. The supply of each transportation problem source is the feasible flow range length of the corresponding original network arc. The demand of each transportation problem sink is the sum of the feasible flow range lengths of the outgoing arcs from the corresponding original network node minus the supply of that node, as shown. An arc flow x_{ij} in the minimum cost flow problem corresponds to flows equal to x_{ij} and $c_{ij} - b_{ij} - x_{ij}$ on the transportation problem arcs $\big((i,j),j\big)$ and $\big((i,j),i\big)$, respectively.

when $L(x,p)$ is minimized over all capacity-feasible x, there is no incentive for either positive or negative violation of all the constraints.

We are thus motivated to introduce the dual function value $q(p)$ at a vector p, defined by

$$q(p) = \min_x \{ L(x,p) \mid b_{ij} \le x_{ij} \le c_{ij}, (i,j) \in \mathcal{A} \}. \qquad (4.2)$$

Because the Lagrangian function $L(x,p)$ is separable in the arc flows x_{ij}, its minimization decomposes into a separate minimization for each arc (i,j). Each of these minimizations can be carried out in closed form, yielding

$$q(p) = \sum_{(i,j) \in \mathcal{A}} q_{ij}(p_i - p_j) + \sum_{i \in \mathcal{N}} s_i p_i, \qquad (4.3)$$

where

$$q_{ij}(p_i - p_j) = \min_{b_{ij} \leq x_{ij} \leq c_{ij}} (a_{ij} + p_j - p_i)x_{ij}$$

$$= \begin{cases} (a_{ij} + p_j - p_i)b_{ij} & \text{if } p_i \leq a_{ij} + p_j, \\ (a_{ij} + p_j - p_i)c_{ij} & \text{if } p_i > a_{ij} + p_j. \end{cases} \qquad (4.4)$$

Consider now the problem

maximize $q(p)$

subject to no constraint on p,

where q is the dual function given by Eqs. (4.3) and (4.4). We call this the
dual problem, and we refer to the original minimum cost flow problem as the
primal problem. We also refer to the dual function as the *dual cost function*
or *dual cost*, and we refer to the optimal value of the dual problem as the
optimal dual cost.† We will see that solving the dual problem provides the
correct values of the prices p_i, which will allow the optimal flows to be
obtained by minimizing $L(x, p)$.

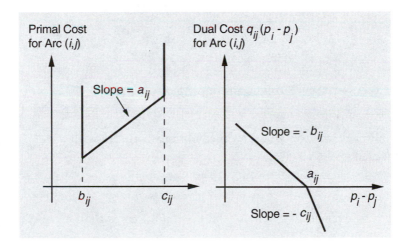

Figure 4.4: Form of the dual cost function q_{ij} for arc (i, j).

Figure 4.4 illustrates the form of the functions q_{ij}. Since each q_{ij} is
piecewise linear, the dual function q is also piecewise linear. The dual function also has some additional interesting structure. In particular, suppose

---

† There is a slight abuse of terminology here, since in a dual context we
are not minimizing a cost but rather maximizing a value, but there is some
uniformity advantage in referring to cost in both the primal and the dual context.
Besides, some problems such as the assignment problem in Section 1.3, are cast as
maximization problems and their duals become minimization problems, so using
the term "dual value" rather than "dual cost" would be inappropriate.

that all node prices are changed by the same amount. Then the values of the functions q_{ij} do not change, since these functions depend on the price differences $p_i - p_j$. If in addition we have $\sum_{i \in \mathcal{N}} s_i = 0$, as we must if the problem is feasible, we see that the term $\sum_{i \in \mathcal{N}} s_i p_i$ also does not change. Thus, the dual function value does not change when all node prices are changed by the same amount, implying that the equal cost surfaces of the dual cost function are unbounded. Figure 4.5 illustrates the dual function for a simple example.

We now turn to the development of the basic duality results for the minimum cost flow problem. To this end we appropriately generalize the notion of complementary slackness, introduced in Section 1.3 within the context of the assignment problem:

Definition 4.1: We say that a flow-price vector pair (x, p) satisfies *complementary slackness* (or CS for short) if x is capacity-feasible and

$$p_i - p_j \le a_{ij}, \qquad \forall \ (i, j) \in \mathcal{A} \text{ with } x_{ij} < c_{ij}, \qquad (4.5)$$

$$p_i - p_j \ge a_{ij}, \qquad \forall \ (i, j) \in \mathcal{A} \text{ with } b_{ij} < x_{ij}. \qquad (4.6)$$

Note that the CS conditions imply that

$$p_i = a_{ij} + p_j, \qquad \forall \ (i, j) \in \mathcal{A} \text{ with } b_{ij} < x_{ij} < c_{ij}.$$

An equivalent way to write the CS conditions is that, for all arcs (i, j), we have $b_{ij} \le x_{ij} \le c_{ij}$ and

$$x_{ij} = \begin{cases} c_{ij} & \text{if } p_i > a_{ij} + p_j, \\ b_{ij} & \text{if } p_i < a_{ij} + p_j. \end{cases}$$

Another equivalent way to state the CS conditions is that x_{ij} attains the minimum in the definition of q_{ij}

$$x_{ij} = \arg \min_{b_{ij} \le z_{ij} \le c_{ij}} (a_{ij} + p_j - p_i) z_{ij} \qquad (4.7)$$

for all arcs (i, j). Figure 4.6 provides a graphical interpretation of the CS conditions.

The following proposition is an important duality theorem, and will later form the basis for developing a more complete duality analysis with the aid of the simplex-related algorithmic developments of Chapter 5.

Proposition 4.1: A feasible flow vector x^* and a price vector p^* satisfy CS if and only if x^* and p^* are optimal primal and dual solutions, respectively, and the optimal primal and dual costs are equal.

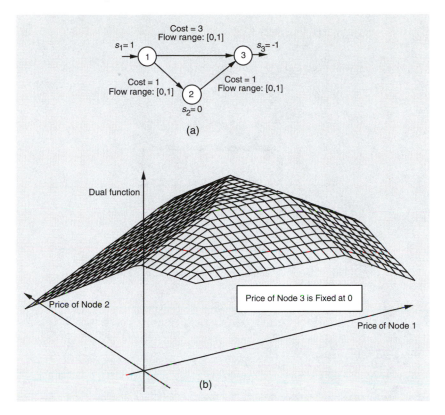

Figure 4.5: Form of the dual cost function q for the 3-node problem in (a). The optimal flow is $x_{12} = 1$, $x_{23} = 1$, $x_{13} = 0$. The dual function is

$$q(p_1, p_2, p_3) = \min\{0, 1 + p_2 - p_1\} + \min\{0, 1 + p_3 - p_2\}$$
$$+ \min\{0, 3 + p_3 - p_1\} + p_1 - p_3.$$

Diagram (b) shows the graph of the dual function in the space of p_1 and p_2, with p_3 fixed at 0. For a different value of p_3, say γ, the graph is "translated" by the vector (γ, γ); that is, we have $q(p_1, p_2, 0) = q(p_1 + \gamma, p_2 + \gamma, \gamma)$ for all (p_1, p_2). The dual function is maximized at the vectors p that satisfy CS together with the optimal x. These are the vectors of the form $(p_1 + \gamma, p_2 + \gamma, \gamma)$, where

$$1 \leq p_1 - p_2, \qquad p_1 \leq 3, \qquad 1 \leq p_2.$$

Proof: We first show that for any feasible flow vector x and any price vector p, the primal cost of x is no less than the dual cost of p. Indeed, we

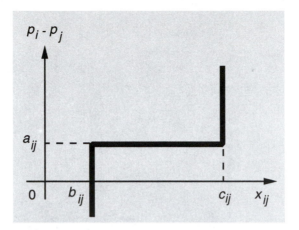

Figure 4.6: Illustration of CS for a flow-price pair (x, p). For each arc (i, j), the pair $(x_{ij}, p_i - p_j)$ should lie on the graph shown.

have from the definitions (4.1) and (4.2) of L and q, respectively,

$$
q(p) \leq L(x, p)
$$

$$
= \sum_{(i,j)\in\mathcal{A}} a_{ij}x_{ij} + \sum_{i\in\mathcal{N}} \left(s_i - \sum_{\{j|(i,j)\in\mathcal{A}\}} x_{ij} + \sum_{\{j|(j,i)\in\mathcal{A}\}} x_{ji} \right) p_i \qquad (4.8)
$$

$$
= \sum_{(i,j)\in\mathcal{A}} a_{ij}x_{ij},
$$

where the last equality follows from the feasibility of x.

If x^* is feasible and satisfies CS together with p^*, we have by the definition (4.2) of q

$$
q(p^*) = \min_{x}\{L(x, p^*) \mid b_{ij} \leq x_{ij} \leq c_{ij}, (i, j) \in \mathcal{A}\}
$$

$$
= L(x^*, p^*) \qquad (4.9)
$$

$$
= \sum_{(i,j)\in\mathcal{A}} a_{ij}x_{ij}^*,
$$

where the second equality is true because

(x^*, p^*) satisfies CS if and only if

$\quad x_{ij}^*$ minimizes $(a_{ij} + p_j^* - p_i^*)x_{ij}$ over all $x_{ij} \in [b_{ij}, c_{ij}], \ \forall \ (i, j) \in \mathcal{A}$,

[cf. Eq. (4.7)], and the last equality follows from the Lagrangian expression (4.1) and the feasibility of x^*. Therefore, Eq. (4.9) implies that x^* attains the minimum of the primal cost on the right-hand side of Eq. (4.8), and p^* attains the maximum of $q(p)$ on the left-hand side of Eq. (4.8), while the optimal primal and dual values are equal.

Conversely, suppose that x^* and p^* are optimal primal and dual solutions, respectively, and the two optimal costs are equal, that is,

$$q(p^*) = \sum_{(i,j)\in\mathcal{A}} a_{ij}x_{ij}^*.$$

We have by definition

$$q(p^*) = \min_x \left\{ L(x,p^*) \mid b_{ij} \leq x_{ij} \leq c_{ij}, (i,j) \in \mathcal{A} \right\},$$

and also, using the Lagrangian expression (4.1) and the feasibility of x^*,

$$\sum_{(i,j)\in\mathcal{A}} a_{ij}x_{ij}^* = L(x^*,p^*).$$

Combining the last three equations, we obtain

$$L(x^*,p^*) = \min_x \left\{ L(x,p^*) \mid b_{ij} \leq x_{ij} \leq c_{ij}, (i,j) \in \mathcal{A} \right\}.$$

Using the Lagrangian expression (4.1), it follows that for all arcs (i,j), we have

$$x_{ij}^* = \arg\min_{b_{ij}\leq x_{ij}\leq c_{ij}} (a_{ij} + p_j^* - p_i^*)x_{ij}.$$

This is equivalent to the pair (x^*,p^*) satisfying CS.   **Q.E.D.**

There are also several other important duality results. In particular, in Prop. 5.8 of Chapter 5 we will use a constructive algorithmic approach to show the following:

Proposition 4.2: If the minimum cost flow problem (with upper and lower bounds on the arc flows) is feasible, then there exist optimal primal and dual solutions, and the optimal primal and dual costs are equal.

Proof: See Prop. 5.8 of Chapter 5.   **Q.E.D.**

By combining Props. 4.1 and 4.2, we obtain the following variant of Prop. 4.1, which includes no statement on the equality of the optimal primal and dual costs:

Proposition 4.3: A feasible flow vector x^* and a price vector p^* satisfy CS if and only if x^* and p^* are optimal primal and dual solutions.

Proof: The forward statement is part of Prop. 4.1. The reverse statement, is obtained by using the equality of the optimal primal and dual costs (Prop. 4.2) and the reverse part of Prop. 4.1. **Q.E.D.**

4.2.1 Interpretation of CS and the Dual Problem

The CS conditions have a nice economic interpretation. In particular, think of each node i as choosing the flow x_{ij} of each of its outgoing arcs (i, j) from the range $[b_{ij}, c_{ij}]$, on the basis of the following economic considerations: For each unit of the flow x_{ij} that node i sends to node j along arc (i, j), node i must pay a transportation cost a_{ij} plus a storage cost p_j at node j; for each unit of the residual flow $c_{ij} - x_{ij}$ that node i does not send to j, node i must pay a storage cost p_i. Thus, the total cost to node j is $(a_{ij} + p_j)x_{ij} + (c_{ij} - x_{ij})p_i$, or

$$(a_{ij} + p_j - p_i)x_{ij} + c_{ij}p_i.$$

It can be seen that the CS conditions (4.5) and (4.6) are equivalent to requiring that node i act in its own best interest by selecting the flow that minimizes the corresponding costs for each of its outgoing arcs (i, j); that is,

(x, p) satisfies CS if and only if

$\quad x_{ij}$ minimizes $(a_{ij} + p_j - p_i)z_{ij}$ over all $z_{ij} \in [b_{ij}, c_{ij}], \ \forall \ (i, j) \in \mathcal{A},$

[cf. Eq. (4.7)].

To interpret the dual function $q(p)$, we continue to view a_{ij} and p_i as transportation and storage costs, respectively. Then, for a given price vector p and supply vector s, the dual function

$$q(p) = \min_{\substack{b_{ij} \leq x_{ij} \leq c_{ij} \\ (i,j) \in \mathcal{A}}} \left\{ \sum_{(i,j) \in \mathcal{A}} a_{ij}x_{ij} \right.$$

$$\left. + \sum_{i \in \mathcal{N}} \left(s_i - \sum_{\{j | (i,j) \in \mathcal{A}\}} x_{ij} + \sum_{\{j | (j,i) \in \mathcal{A}\}} x_{ji} \right) p_i \right\}$$

is the minimum total transportation and storage cost to be incurred by the nodes, by choosing flows that satisfy the capacity constraints.

Suppose now that we introduce an organization that sets the node prices, and collects the transportation and storage costs from the nodes. We see that if the organization wants to maximize its total revenue (given that the nodes will act in their own best interest), it must choose prices that solve the dual problem optimally.

4.2.2   Duality and CS for Nonnegativity Constraints

We finally note that there are variants of CS and Props. 4.1-4.3 for the versions of the minimum cost flow problem where $b_{ij} = -\infty$ and/or $c_{ij} = \infty$ for some arcs (i, j). In particular, in the case where in place of the capacity constraints $b_{ij} \leq x_{ij} \leq c_{ij}$, there are only nonnegativity constraints $0 \leq x_{ij}$, the CS conditions take the form

$$p_i - p_j \leq a_{ij}, \qquad \forall \, (i, j) \in \mathcal{A},$$

$$p_i - p_j = a_{ij}, \qquad \forall \, (i, j) \in \mathcal{A} \text{ with } 0 < x_{ij},$$

(see Fig. 4.7).

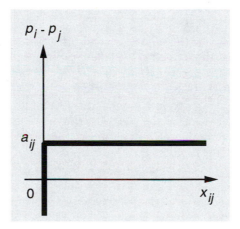

Figure 4.7: Illustration of CS for a flow-price pair (x, p) in the case of nonnegativity constraints $0 \leq x_{ij}$ for the flow of each arc (i, j). The pair $(x_{ij}, p_i - p_j)$ should lie on the graph shown.

Some of the modifications needed to prove counterparts of the duality results for nonnegativity constraints are outlined in Exercise 4.3. In particular, Prop. 4.1 holds for this case as stated. However, showing a counterpart of Prop. 4.2 involves a slight complication. In the case of nonnegativity constraints, it is possible that there exist feasible flow vectors of arbitrarily small cost; a problem where this happens will be called *unbounded* in Chapter 5. Barring this possibility, the existence of primal and dual optimal solutions with equal cost (cf. Prop. 4.2) will be shown in Prop. 5.6 of Section 5.2.

4.3 NOTES, SOURCES, AND EXERCISES

The minimum cost flow problem was formulated in the early days of linear programming. There has been extensive research on the algorithmic solution of the problem, much of which will be the subject of the following three chapters. This research has followed two fairly distinct directions. On one hand there has been intensive development of practically efficient algorithms. These algorithms were originally motivated by general linear programming methods such as the primal simplex, dual simplex, and primal-dual methods, but gradually other methods, such as auction algorithms, were proposed, which have no general linear programming counterparts. The focus of research in these algorithms was to establish their validity through a proof of guaranteed termination, to analyze their special properties, and to establish their practical computational efficiency through experimentation with "standard" test problems.

On the other hand there have been efforts to explore the worst-case complexity limits of the minimum cost flow problem using polynomial algorithms. Edmonds and Karp [1972] developed the first polynomial algorithm, using a version of the out-of-kilter method (a variant of the primal-dual method to be discussed in Chapter 6) that employed cost and capacity scaling. Subsequently, in the late 70s, polynomial algorithms for the general linear programming problem started appearing, and these were of course applicable to the minimum cost flow problem. All of these polynomial algorithms are not strongly polynomial because their running time depends not just on the number of nodes and arcs, but also on the arc costs and capacities. A strongly polynomial algorithm for the minimum cost flow problem was given by Tardos [1985]. The existence of a strongly polynomial algorithm distinguishes the minimum cost flow problem from the general linear programming problem, for which there is no known algorithm with running time that depends only on the number of variables and constraints. However, a point made earlier in Section 1.3.4 should be repeated: a polynomial running time does not guarantee good practical performance. For example, Tardos' algorithm has not been seriously considered for algorithmic solution of practical minimum cost flow problems. Thus, to select an algorithm for a practical problem one must typically rely on criteria other than worst-case complexity.

Duality theory is of central importance in linear programming, and is similarly important in network optimization. It has its origins in the work of von Neuman on zero sum games, and was first formalized by Gale, Kuhn, and Tucker [1951]. Similar to linear programming, there are several possible dual problems, depending on which of the constraints are "dualized" (assigned a Lagrange multiplier). The duality theory of this chapter, where the conservation of flow constraints are dualized, is the most common and useful for the minimum cost flow problem. We will develop alternative forms of duality when we discuss other types of network optimization problems in Chapters 8-10.

We finally note that one can illustrate the relation between the primal and the dual problems in terms of an intuitive geometric interpetation (see Fig. 4.8). This interpretation is directed toward the advanced reader and will not be needed later. It demonstrates why the cost of any feasible flow vector is no less than the dual cost of any price vector (later, in Chapter 8, this will be called the *weak duality theorem*), and why thanks to the linearity of the cost function and the constraints, the optimal primal and dual costs are equal.

EXERCISES

4.1 (Reduction to One Source/One Sink Format)

Show how the minimum cost flow problem can be transformed to an equivalent problem where all node supplies are zero except for one node that has positive supply and one node that has negative supply.

4.2 (Duality for Assignment Problems)

Consider the assignment problem of Example 1.2. Derive the dual problem and the CS conditions, and show that they are mathematically equivalent to the ones introduced in Section 1.3.2.

4.3 (Duality for Nonnegativity Constraints)

Consider the version of the minimum cost flow problem where there are nonnegativity constraints

$$\text{minimize} \quad \sum_{(i,j)\in\mathcal{A}} a_{ij}x_{ij}$$

$$\text{subject to} \quad \sum_{\{j|(i,j)\in\mathcal{A}\}} x_{ij} - \sum_{\{j|(j,i)\in\mathcal{A}\}} x_{ji} = s_i, \quad \forall\, i \in \mathcal{N},$$

$$0 \le x_{ij}, \quad \forall\, (i,j) \in \mathcal{A}.$$

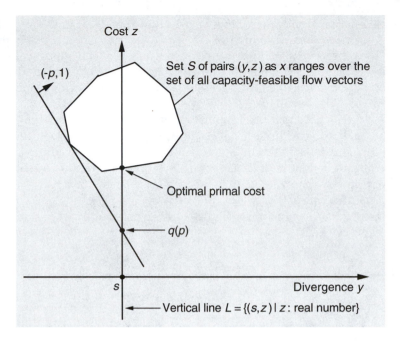

Figure 4.8: Geometric interpretation of duality for the reader who is familiar with the notion and the properties of hyperplanes in a vector space. Consider the (polyhedral) set S consisting of all pairs (y, z), where y is the divergence vector corresponding to x and z is the cost of x, as x ranges over all capacity-feasible flow vectors. Then feasible flow vectors correspond to common points of S and the vertical line

$$L = \{(s, z) \mid z : \text{ real number}\}.$$

The optimal primal cost corresponds to the lowest common point.

On the other hand, for a given price vector p, the dual cost $q(p)$ can be expressed as [cf. Eq. (4.2)]

$$q(p) = \min_{x: \text{ capacity feasible}} L(x, p) = \min_{(y,z) \in S} \left\{ z - \sum_{i \in \mathcal{N}} y_i p_i \right\} + \sum_{i \in \mathcal{N}} s_i p_i.$$

Based on this expression, it can be seen that $q(p)$ corresponds to the intersection point of the vertical line L with the hyperplane

$$\left\{ (y, z) \middle| z - \sum_{i \in \mathcal{N}} y_i p_i = q(p) - \sum_{i \in \mathcal{N}} s_i p_i \right\},$$

which supports from below the set S, and is normal to the vector $(-p, 1)$. The dual problem is to find a price vector p for which the intersection point is as high as possible. The figure illustrates the equality of the lowest common point of S and L (optimal primal cost), and the highest point of intersection of L by a hyperplane that supports S from below (optimal dual cost).

Show that a feasible flow vector x^* and a price vector p^* satisfy the following CS conditions

$$p_i^* - p_j^* \leq a_{ij}, \qquad \forall\ (i,j) \in \mathcal{A},$$

$$p_i^* - p_j^* = a_{ij}, \qquad \forall\ (i,j) \in \mathcal{A} \text{ with } 0 < x_{ij}^*,$$

if and only if x^* is primal optimal, p^* is an optimal solution of the following dual problem:

$$\text{maximize} \sum_{i \in \mathcal{N}} s_i p_i$$

$$\text{subject to} \quad p_i - p_j \leq a_{ij}, \qquad \forall\ (i,j) \in \mathcal{A},$$

and the optimal primal and dual costs are equal. *Hint*: Complete the details of the following argument. Define

$$q(p) = \begin{cases} \sum_{i \in \mathcal{N}} s_i p_i & \text{if } p_i - p_j \leq a_{ij}, \ \forall\ (i,j) \in \mathcal{A}, \\ -\infty & \text{otherwise}, \end{cases}$$

and note that

$$q(p) = \sum_{(i,j) \in \mathcal{A}} \min_{0 \leq x_{ij}} \left(a_{ij} + p_j - p_i \right) x_{ij} + \sum_{i \in \mathcal{N}} s_i p_i$$

$$= \min_{0 \leq x} \left\{ \sum_{(i,j) \in \mathcal{A}} a_{ij} x_{ij} + \sum_{i \in \mathcal{N}} \left(s_i - \sum_{\{j \mid (i,j) \in \mathcal{A}\}} x_{ij} + \sum_{\{j \mid (j,i) \in \mathcal{A}\}} x_{ji} \right) p_i \right\}.$$

Thus, for any feasible x and any p, we have

$$q(p) \leq \sum_{(i,j) \in \mathcal{A}} a_{ij} x_{ij} + \sum_{i \in \mathcal{N}} \left(s_i - \sum_{\{j \mid (i,j) \in \mathcal{A}\}} x_{ij} + \sum_{\{j \mid (j,i) \in \mathcal{A}\}} x_{ji} \right) p_i$$

$$\qquad\qquad\qquad\qquad\qquad\qquad\qquad\qquad\qquad\qquad\qquad\qquad\qquad (4.10)$$

$$= \sum_{(i,j) \in \mathcal{A}} a_{ij} x_{ij}.$$

On the other hand, we have

$$q(p^*) = \sum_{i \in \mathcal{N}} s_i p_i^* = \sum_{(i,j) \in \mathcal{A}} \left(a_{ij} + p_j^* - p_i^* \right) x_{ij}^* + \sum_{i \in \mathcal{N}} s_i p_i^* = \sum_{(i,j) \in \mathcal{A}} a_{ij} x_{ij}^*,$$

where the second equality holds because the CS conditions imply that $(a_{ij} + p_j^* - p_i^*) x_{ij}^* = 0$ for all $(i,j) \in \mathcal{A}$, and the last equality follows from the feasibility of x^*. Therefore, x^* attains the minimum of the primal cost on the right-hand side of Eq. (4.10). Furthermore, p^* attains the maximum of $q(p)$ on the left-hand side of Eq. (4.10), which means that p^* is an optimal solution of the dual problem.

4.4 (Duality and the Max-Flow/Min-Cut Theorem)

Consider a feasible max-flow problem and let $Q = [\mathcal{S}, \mathcal{N} - \mathcal{S}]$ be a minimum capacity cut separating s and t. Consider also the minimum cost flow problem formulation for the max-flow problem (see Example 1.3). Show that the price vector

$$p_i = \begin{cases} 1 & \text{if } i \in \mathcal{S}, \\ 0 & \text{if } i \notin \mathcal{S}, \end{cases}$$

is an optimal solution of the dual problem. Furthermore, show that the max-flow/min-cut theorem expresses the equality of the primal and dual optimal costs. *Hint*: Relate the capacity of Q with the dual function value corresponding to p.

4.5 (Min-Path/Max-Tension Theorem)

Consider a shortest path problem with arc lengths a_{ij}. For a price vector $p = (p_1, \ldots, p_N)$, define the *tension* of arc (i, j) as $t_{ij} = p_i - p_j$ and the tension of a forward path P as $T_P = \sum_{(i,j) \in P} t_{ij}$. Show that the shortest distance between two nodes i_1 and i_2 is equal to the maximal value of T_P over all forward paths P starting at i_1 and ending at i_2, and all price vectors p satisfying the constraint $t_{ij} \leq a_{ij}$ for all arcs (i, j). Interpret this as a duality result.

5

Simplex Methods

Primal cost improvement methods start with a feasible flow vector x and generate a sequence of other feasible flow vectors, each having a smaller primal cost than its predecessor. The main idea is that if the current flow vector is not optimal, an improved flow vector can be obtained by pushing flow along a simple cycle C with negative cost (see Prop. 1.2 and Exercise 1.33 in Chapter 1).

There are several methods for finding negative cost cycles, but the most successful in practice are specialized versions of the simplex method for linear programming. This chapter focuses on algorithms of this type.

Simplex methods are not only useful for algorithmic solution of the problem; they also provide constructive proofs of some important analytical results. Chief among these are duality theorems asserting the equality of the primal and the dual optimal values, and the existence of optimal primal and dual solutions, which are integer if the problem data are integer (see Prop. 5.6 in Section 5.2 and Prop. 5.8 in Section 5.3). There are alternative proofs that do not rely on the simplex method for the duality results (see e.g., Bertsimas and Tsitsiklis [1997], Rockafellar [1984]), and for the integrality results (see Exercise 1.34 in Chapter 1 and the discussion of unimodularity in Section 5.5). However, given our independent algorithmic interest in the simplex method, our approach to duality and the integrality of optimal solutions is simple and economical.

5.1 MAIN IDEAS IN SIMPLEX METHODS

In this section, we develop the basic concepts underlying simplex methods. To simplify the presentation, we first consider the version of the minimum cost flow problem with only nonnegativity constraints on the flows:

$$
\begin{aligned}
\text{minimize} \quad & \sum_{(i,j)\in\mathcal{A}} a_{ij}x_{ij} \\
\text{subject to} \quad & \sum_{\{j|(i,j)\in\mathcal{A}\}} x_{ij} - \sum_{\{j|(j,i)\in\mathcal{A}\}} x_{ji} = s_i, \qquad \forall\, i \in \mathcal{N}, \qquad (5.1) \\
& 0 \le x_{ij}, \qquad \forall\, (i,j) \in \mathcal{A},
\end{aligned}
$$

where a_{ij} and s_i are given scalars. We saw in Section 4.2 that the general minimum cost flow problem with upper and lower bounds on the arc flows can be converted to one with nonnegativity constraints. Thus, once we develop the main method for nonnegativity constraints, the extension to the more general problem will be straightforward (see Section 5.3).

The most important difference between the minimum cost flow problem with nonnegativity constraints and the one with upper and lower bounds is that the former can be *unbounded*. By this we mean that there exist feasible flows that take arbitrarily large values, while the corresponding cost takes arbitrarily small (i.e., large negative) values. In particular, *the problem is unbounded if it is feasible and there exists a simple forward cycle with negative cost*, since then we can reduce the cost to arbitrarily large negative values by adding arbitrarily large flow along the negative cost cycle to any feasible flow vector. The converse is also true: *if the problem is unbounded, there must exist a simple forward cycle with negative cost*. This follows from Prop. 2.7, which implies that if the cost of every simple forward cycle is nonnegative, then the cost function of the problem is bounded from below by some constant.

Spanning Trees and Basic Flow Vectors

The main idea in simplex methods is to generate negative cost cycles by using a *spanning tree* of the given graph. Recall from Section 1.1 that a tree is an acyclic connected graph, and that a spanning tree of a given graph is a subgraph that is a tree and includes all nodes of the given graph. A *leaf node* of a tree is defined to be a node with a single incident arc. Figure 5.1 illustrates a spanning tree and a leaf node. The following lemma collects some important properties of spanning trees that will be useful later.

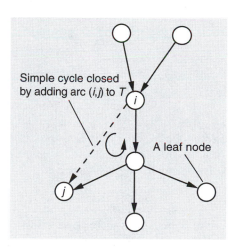

Figure 5.1: Illustration of a spanning tree T. Note that that there is a unique simple path of T connecting any pair of nodes. Furthermore, the addition of any arc to T [arc (i, j) in the figure] creates a unique simple cycle in which (i, j) is a forward arc.

Simple cycle closed by adding arc (i, j) to T

A leaf node

Lemma 1.1: Let T be a subgraph of a graph with N nodes.

(a) If T is acyclic and has at least one arc, then it must have at least one leaf node.

(b) T is a spanning tree if and only if it is connected and has N nodes and $N - 1$ arcs.

(c) If T is a tree, for any two nodes i and j of T there is a unique simple path of T starting at i and ending at j. Furthermore, any arc e that is not in T and has both of its end nodes in T, when added to T, creates a unique simple cycle in which e is a forward arc.

(d) If T is a tree and an arc (i, j) of T is deleted, the remaining arcs of T form two trees that are disjoint (share no nodes or arcs), one containing i and the other containing j.

Proof: (a) Choose a node n_1 of T with at least one incident arc e_1 and let n_2 be the opposite node of that arc. If n_2 is a leaf node, the result is proved; else choose an arc $e_2 \neq e_1$ that is incident to n_2, and let n_3 be the opposite end node. If n_3 is a leaf node, the result is proved; else continue similarly. Eventually a leaf node will be found, for otherwise some node will be repeated in the sequence, which is impossible since T is acyclic.

(b) Let T be a spanning tree. Then T has N nodes, and since it is connected and acyclic, it must have a leaf node n_1 by part (a). (We assume without loss of generality that $N \geq 2$.) Delete n_1 and its unique incident arc from T, thereby obtaining a connected graph T_1, which has $N - 1$ nodes and is acyclic. Repeat the process with T_1 in place of T, obtaining T_2, T_3, and so on. After $N - 1$ steps and $N - 1$ arc deletions, we will obtain T_{N-1}, which consists of a single node. This proves that T has $N - 1$ arcs.

Conversely, suppose that T is connected and has N nodes and $N - 1$ arcs. If T had a simple cycle, by deleting any arc of the cycle, we would obtain a graph T_1 that would have $N - 2$ arcs and would still be connected. Continuing similarly if necessary, we obtain for some $k \geq 1$ a graph T_k, which has $N - k - 1$ arcs, and is connected and acyclic (i.e., it is a spanning tree). This is a contradiction, because we proved earlier that a spanning tree has exactly $N - 1$ arcs. Hence, T has no simple cycle and must be a spanning tree.

(c) There is at least one simple path starting at a node i and ending at a node j because T is connected. If there were a second path starting at i and ending at j, by reversing this path so that it starts at j and ends at i, and by concatenating it to the first path, we would form a cycle. It can be seen that this cycle must contain a simple cycle, since otherwise the two paths from i to j would be identical. This contradicts the hypothesis that T is a tree.

If arc e is added to T, it will form a simple cycle together with any simple path that lies in T and connects its end nodes. There is only one such path, so together with this path, e forms a unique simple cycle in which e is a forward arc.

(d) It can be seen that removal of a single arc from any connected graph either leaves the graph connected or else creates exactly two connected components. The unique simple path of T connecting i to j consists of arc (i,j); with the removal of this arc, no path connecting i to j remains, and the graph cannot stay connected. Hence, removal of (i,j) must create exactly two connected components, which must be trees since, being subgraphs of T, they must be acyclic.   **Q.E.D.**

Suppose that we have a feasible problem and we are given a spanning tree T. A key property for our purposes is that there is a flow vector x, which satisfies the conservation of flow constraints, and is such that only arcs of T can have a nonzero flow. Such a flow vector is called *basic*† and is uniquely determined by T, as the following proposition shows.

Proposition 5.1: Consider the minimum cost flow problem with non-negativity constraints, and assume that $\sum_{i \in \mathcal{N}} s_i = 0$. Then, for any spanning tree T, there exists a unique flow vector x that satisfies the conservation of flow constraints

$$\sum_{\{j \mid (i,j) \in \mathcal{A}\}} x_{ij} - \sum_{\{j \mid (j,i) \in \mathcal{A}\}} x_{ji} = s_i, \qquad \forall\, i \in \mathcal{N},$$

and is such that all arcs not in T have zero flow. In particular, if an arc (i,j) of T separates T into two components T_i and T_j, containing i and j respectively, we have

$$x_{ij} = \sum_{n \in T_i} s_n.$$

Proof: To show uniqueness, note that for any flow vector x and arc $(i,j) \in T$ the flux across the cut $[T_i, \mathcal{N} - T_i]$ is equal to the sum of divergences of the nodes of T_i (cf. Section 3.1). Thus, if x satisfies the conservation of flow constraints, the flux across the cut must be $\sum_{n \in T_i} s_n$. If in addition all arcs of the cut carry zero flow except for (i,j), this flux is just x_{ij}, so

---

† The term "basic" comes from linear programming, where solutions of the constraint equations that have nonzero components only for suitably specified subsets of indices are called basic (see e.g., Dantzig [1963], Chvatal [1983], Bertsimas and Tsitsiklis [1997]). Our definition of basic flow vector is equivalent to the definition of a basic solution when the minimum cost flow problem of this section is viewed as a linear program.

we must have

$$x_{ij} = \begin{cases} \sum_{n \in T_i} s_n & \text{if } (i,j) \in T, \\ 0 & \text{if } (i,j) \notin T. \end{cases}$$

Thus, if a flow vector has the required properties, it must be equal to the vector x defined by the preceding formula.

To show existence, i.e. that the flow vector x, defined by the preceding formula, satisfies the conservation of flow constraints, we use a constructive proof based on the algorithm of Fig. 5.2. (An alternative algorithm is outlined in Exercise 5.4.) **Q.E.D.**

Note that a basic flow vector need not be feasible; some of the arc flows may be negative, violating the lower bound constraints (see the example of Fig. 5.2). A spanning tree is called (with slight abuse of terminology) a *feasible tree* if the corresponding basic flow vector is feasible.

Overview of Simplex Methods

Simplex methods start with a feasible tree and proceed in iterations, generating another feasible tree and a corresponding feasible basic flow vector at each iteration. The cost of each basic flow vector is no worse than the cost of its predecessor. Each iteration, also called a *pivot* in the standard terminology of linear programming, operates as follows:

(a) It adds a single arc to the tree such that the simple cycle created has negative cost.

(b) It pushes along the cycle as much flow as possible without violating feasibility.

(c) It discards one arc of the cycle, thereby obtaining another feasible tree to be used at the next iteration.

Any method that uses iterations of the type described above will be called *a simplex method*. There are several possible ways to add an arc to the tree and to discard an arc from the tree, so the above description defines a broad class of methods. However, in all cases the cost corresponding to the new tree is no larger than the cost corresponding to the preceding tree. In what follows, we will discuss and analyze various possibilities for arc selection, and we will delineate some methods that have sound theoretical properties.

Note that each tree $\overline{T}$ in the sequence generated by a simplex method differs from its predecessor T by two arcs: the *out-arc* e, which belongs to T but not to $\overline{T}$, and the *in-arc* $\overline{e}$, which belongs to $\overline{T}$ but not to T; see Fig. 5.3. We will use the notation

$$\overline{T} = T + \overline{e} - e$$

to express this relation. The arc $\overline{e}$ when added to T closes a unique simple cycle in which $\overline{e}$ is a forward arc. This is the cycle along which we try to

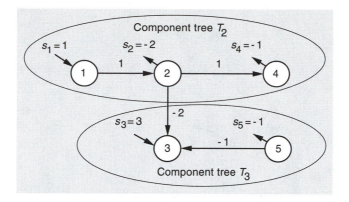

Iteration #	Leaf Node Selected	Arc Flow Computed
1	1	$x_{12} = 1$
2	5	$x_{53} = -1$
3	3	$x_{23} = -2$
4	2	$x_{24} = 1$

Figure 5.2: Method for constructing the flow vector corresponding to T, starting from the arc incident to some leaf node and proceeding "inward." The algorithm maintains a tree R, a flow vector x, and scalars $w_1, \ldots, w_N$. Upon termination, x is the desired flow vector. Initially, $R = T$, $x = 0$, and $w_i = s_i$ for all $i \in \mathcal{N}$.

Step 1: Choose a leaf node $i \in R$. If (i, j) is the unique incident arc of i, set

$$x_{ij} := w_i, \qquad w_j := w_j + w_i;$$

if (j, i) is the unique incident arc of i, set

$$x_{ji} := -w_i, \qquad w_j := w_j - w_i.$$

Step 2: Delete i and its incident arc from R. If R now consists of a single node, terminate; else, go to Step 1.

We now show that if $\sum_{n \in \mathcal{N}} s_n = 0$, the flow vector thus constructed satisfies the conservation of flow equations. Consider the typical iteration where the leaf node i of R is selected in Step 1. Suppose that (i, j) is the unique incident arc of R [the proof is similar if (j, i) is the incident arc]. Then just before this iteration, w_i is equal by construction to $s_i - \sum_{\{k \neq j \mid (i,k) \in \mathcal{A}\}} x_{ik} + \sum_{\{k \mid (k,i) \in \mathcal{A}\}} x_{ki}$, so by setting x_{ij} to w_i, the conservation of flow constraint is satisfied at node i. Upon termination, it is seen that for the last node i of R, w_i is equal to both $\sum_{n \in \mathcal{N}} s_n$ and $s_i - \sum_{\{k \mid (i,k) \in \mathcal{A}\}} x_{ik} + \sum_{\{k \mid (k,i) \in \mathcal{A}\}} x_{ki}$. Since $\sum_{n \in \mathcal{N}} s_n = 0$, the conservation of flow constraint is satisfied at this last node as well.

push flow. (By convention, we require that the orientation of the cycle is the same as the orientation of the arc $\bar{e}$.)

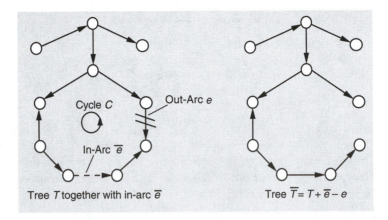

Figure above labels: Cycle C, Out-Arc e, In-Arc $\bar{e}$, Tree T together with in-arc $\bar{e}$, Tree $\overline{T} = T + \bar{e} - e$

Figure 5.3: Successive trees T and $\overline{T}$ generated by a simplex method.

Leaving aside for the moment the issue of how to select an initial feasible tree, the main questions now are:

(1) How to select the in-arc so as to close a cycle with negative cost or else detect that the current flow is optimal.

(2) How to select the out-arc so as to obtain a new feasible tree and associated flow vector.

(3) How to ensure that the method makes progress, eventually improving the primal cost. (The problem here is that even if a negative cost cycle is known, it may not be possible to push a positive amount of flow along the cycle because some backward arc on the cycle has zero flow. Thus, the flow vector may not change and the primal cost may not decrease strictly at any one pivot; in linear programming terminology, such a pivot is called *degenerate*. Having to deal with degeneracy is the price for simplifying the search for a negative cost cycle.)

We take up these questions in sequence.

5.1.1 Using Prices to Obtain the In-Arc

While simplex methods are primal cost improvement algorithms, they typically make essential use of price vectors and duality ideas. In particular, we will see how the complementary slackness (CS) conditions of Section 4.2.2,

$$p_i - p_j \leq a_{ij}, \qquad \forall\ (i,j) \in \mathcal{A}, \tag{5.2}$$

$$p_i - p_j = a_{ij}, \qquad \text{for all } (i,j) \in \mathcal{A} \text{ with } 0 < x_{ij}, \tag{5.3}$$

play an important role. Note here that if x is feasible and together with p satisfies these CS conditions, then x is an optimal solution of the problem and p is an optimal solution of its dual problem

$$\text{maximize} \sum_{i \in \mathcal{N}} s_i p_i$$

$$\text{subject to} \quad p_i - p_j \leq a_{ij}, \qquad \forall \, (i,j) \in \mathcal{A};$$

the proof of this closely parallels the proof of Prop. 4.1 and is outlined in Exercise 4.3 of Chapter 4.

Along with a feasible tree T, a simplex method typically maintains a *price vector* $p = (p_1, \ldots, p_N)$ such that

$$p_i - p_j = a_{ij}, \qquad \forall \, (i,j) \in T.$$

This price vector is obtained using the following steps:

(a) Fix a node r, called the *root of the tree*, and set p_r to some arbitrary scalar value.

(b) For each node i, let P_i be the unique simple path of T starting at the root node r and ending at i.

(c) Define p_i by

$$p_i = p_r - \sum_{(m,n) \in P_i^+} a_{mn} + \sum_{(m,n) \in P_i^-} a_{mn}, \qquad (5.4)$$

where P_i^+ and P_i^- are the sets of forward and backward arcs of P_i, respectively.

To see that with this definition of p_i we have $p_i - p_j = a_{ij}$ for all $(i,j) \in T$, write Eq. (5.4) for nodes i and j, subtract the two equations, and note that the paths P_i and P_j differ by just the arc (i,j).

For an equivalent construction method, select p_r arbitrarily, set the prices of the outward neighbors j of r with $(r,j) \in T$ to $p_j = p_r - a_{rj}$ and the prices of the inward neighbors j of r with $(j,r) \in T$ to $p_j = p_r + a_{jr}$, and then repeat the process with the neighbors j replacing r. Figure 5.4 gives an example.

It can be seen from Eq. (5.4), that *for each pair of nodes i and j, the price difference $(p_i - p_j)$ is independent of the arbitrarily chosen root node price p_r*; write Eq. (5.4) for node i and for node j, and subtract. Therefore, for each arc (i,j), the scalar

$$r_{ij} = a_{ij} + p_j - p_i, \qquad (5.5)$$

called the *reduced cost* of the arc, is uniquely defined by the spanning tree T. By the definition of p, we have

$$r_{ij} = 0, \qquad \forall \, (i,j) \in T,$$

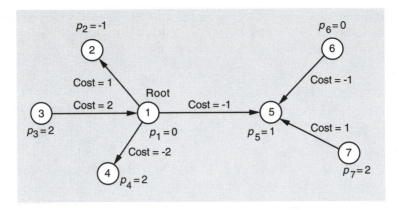

Figure 5.4: Illustration of the prices associated with a spanning tree. The root is chosen to be node 1, and its price is arbitrarily chosen to be 0. The other node prices are then uniquely determined by the requirement $p_i - p_j = a_{ij}$ for all arcs (i, j) of the spanning tree.

so if in addition we have

$$r_{ij} \geq 0, \qquad \forall \ (i, j) \notin T,$$

the pair (x, p) satisfies the CS conditions (5.2) and (5.3). It then follows from Prop. 4.1 of Section 4.3 (more precisely, from the version of that proposition, given in Exercise 4.3 of Chapter 4, that applies to the problem with only nonnegativity constraints) that x is an optimal primal solution and p is an optimal dual solution.

If on the other hand, we have

$$r_{\bar{i}\bar{j}} < 0 \tag{5.6}$$

for some arc $\bar{e} = (\bar{i}, \bar{j})$ not in T, then we claim that the unique simple cycle C formed by T and the arc $(\bar{i}, \bar{j})$ [cf. Lemma 1.1(c)] has negative cost. Indeed, the cost of C can be written in terms of the reduced costs of its arcs as

$$\sum_{(i,j) \in C^+} a_{ij} - \sum_{(i,j) \in C^-} a_{ij} = \sum_{(i,j) \in C^+} \left(a_{ij} + p_j - p_i\right) - \sum_{(i,j) \in C^-} \left(a_{ij} + p_j - p_i\right)$$

$$= \sum_{(i,j) \in C^+} r_{ij} - \sum_{(i,j) \in C^-} r_{ij}.$$

$$\tag{5.7}$$

Since $r_{ij} = 0$ for all $(i, j) \in T$ [see Eq. (5.5)], and $(\bar{i}, \bar{j})$ is a forward arc of C by convention, we have

$$\text{Cost of } C = r_{\bar{i}\bar{j}}$$

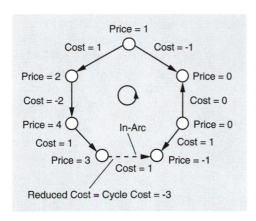

Figure 5.5: Obtaining a negative cost cycle in a simplex method. All the tree arcs of the cycle have zero reduced cost, so the reduced cost of the in-arc is also the cost of the cycle, based on the calculation of Eq. (5.7). Thus, if the in-arc is chosen to have negative reduced cost, the cost of the cycle is also negative.

which is negative by Eq. (5.6); see Fig. 5.5.

The role of the price vector p associated with a feasible tree now becomes clear. By checking the sign of the reduced cost

$$r_{ij} = a_{ij} + p_j - p_i$$

of all arcs (i, j) not in T, we will either verify optimality if r_{ij} is nonnegative for all (i, j), or else we will obtain a negative cost cycle by discovering an arc (i, j) for which r_{ij} is negative. The latter arc may be used as the in-arc to enter the tree of the next iteration.

There are a number of methods, also called *pivot rules*, for selecting the in-arc. For example, one may search for an in-arc with *most negative* reduced cost; this rule requires a lot of computation – a comparison of r_{ij} for all arcs (i, j) not in the current tree. A simpler alternative is to search the list of arcs not in the tree and to select the *first* arc with negative reduced cost. Most practical simplex codes use an intermediate strategy. They maintain a *candidate list of arcs*, and at each iteration they search through this list for an arc with most negative reduced cost; in the process, arcs with nonnegative reduced cost are deleted from the list. If no arc in the candidate list has a negative reduced cost, a new candidate list is constructed. One way to do this is to scan the full arc list and enter in the candidate list all arcs with negative reduced cost, up to the point where the candidate list reaches a maximum size, which is chosen heuristically. This procedure can also be used to construct the initial candidate list.

5.1.2   Obtaining the Out-Arc

Let T be a feasible tree generated by a simplex method with corresponding flow vector x and price vector p which are nonoptimal. Suppose that we have chosen the in-arc $\bar{e}$ and we have obtained the corresponding negative cost cycle C formed by T and $\bar{e}$. There are two possibilities:

(a) All arcs of C are oriented like $\bar{e}$, that is, C^- is empty. Then C is a forward cycle with negative cost, indicating that the problem is unbounded. Indeed, since C^- is empty, we can increase the flows of the arcs of C by an arbitrarily large common increment, while maintaining feasibility of x. The primal cost function changes by an amount that is equal to the cost of C for each unit flow change along C. Since C has negative cost, we see that the primal cost can be decreased to arbitrarily small (i.e. large negative) values.

(b) The set C^- of arcs of C with orientation opposite to that of $\bar{e}$ is nonempty. Then

$$\delta = \min_{(i,j)\in C^-} x_{ij} \qquad (5.8)$$

is the maximum increment by which the flow of all arcs of C^+ can be increased and the flow of all arcs of C^- can be decreased, while still maintaining feasibility. A simplex method computes δ and changes the flow vector from x to $\bar{x}$, where

$$\bar{x}_{ij} = \begin{cases} x_{ij} & \text{if } (i,j) \notin C, \\ x_{ij} + \delta & \text{if } (i,j) \in C^+, \\ x_{ij} - \delta & \text{if } (i,j) \in C^-. \end{cases} \qquad (5.9)$$

Any arc $e = (i,j) \in C^-$ that attains the minimum in the equation $\delta = \min_{(i,j)\in C^-} x_{ij}$ satisfies $\bar{x}_{ij} = 0$ and can serve as the out-arc; see Fig. 5.6. (A more specific rule for selecting the out-arc will be given later.) The new tree is

$$\overline{T} = T + \bar{e} - e \qquad (5.10)$$

and its associated basic flow vector is $\bar{x}$, given by Eq. (5.9).

Figures 5.7 and 5.8 illustrate the method for some simple examples.

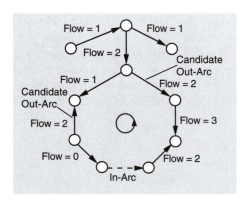

Figure 5.6: Choosing the out-arc in a simplex method. The in-arc, shown at the bottom, closes a cycle C. The orientation of C is in the direction of the in-arc. There are three arcs in C^-, and they define the flow increment

$$\delta = \min_{(i,j)\in C^-} x_{ij} = 2.$$

Out of these arcs, the two attaining the minimum are the candidates for out-arc, as shown.

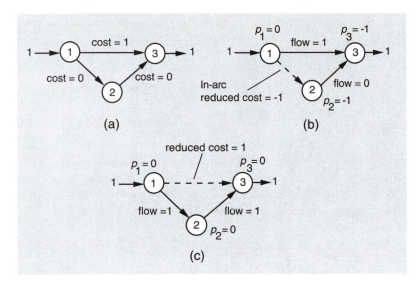

Figure 5.7: Illustration of a simplex method for the problem described in figure (a). The starting tree consists of arcs $(1,3)$ and $(2,3)$, and the corresponding flows and prices are as shown in figure (b). Arc $(1,2)$ has negative reduced cost and is thus eligible to be an in-arc. Arc $(1,3)$ is the only arc eligible to be the out-arc. The new tree is shown in figure (c). The corresponding flow is optimal because the reduced cost of arc $(1,3)$ is positive.

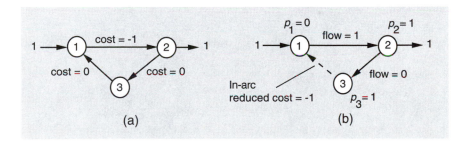

Figure 5.8: Illustration of a simplex method for the problem described in figure (a); this is an unbounded problem because the cycle $(1,2,3,1)$ has negative cost. The starting tree consists of arcs $(1,2)$ and $(2,3)$, and the corresponding flows and prices are as shown in figure (b). Arc $(3,1)$ has negative reduced cost and is thus eligible to be an in-arc. However, all the arcs of the corresponding cycle have the same orientation, so the problem is declared to be unbounded.

Note that the price vector $\bar{p}$ associated with the new tree $\overline{T}$ can be conveniently obtained from p as follows: Let $\bar{e} = (\bar{i}, \bar{j})$ be the in-arc and let e be the out-arc. If we remove e from T we obtain two trees, $T_{\bar{i}}$ and $T_{\bar{j}}$, containing the nodes $\bar{i}$ and $\bar{j}$, respectively; see Fig. 5.9. Then it is seen from the definition (5.4) that a price vector $\bar{p}$ associated with $\overline{T}$ is given by

$$\bar{p}_i = \begin{cases} p_i & \text{if } i \in T_{\bar{i}}, \\ p_i - r_{\bar{i}\bar{j}} & \text{if } i \in T_{\bar{j}}, \end{cases} \tag{5.11}$$

where

$$r_{\bar{i}\bar{j}} = a_{\bar{i}\bar{j}} + p_{\bar{j}} - p_{\bar{i}}$$

is the reduced cost of the in-arc $(\bar{i}, \bar{j})$. Thus, to update the price vector, one needs to increase the prices of the nodes in $T_{\bar{j}}$ by the common increment $(-r_{\bar{i}\bar{j}})$. We may also use any other price vector, obtained by adding the same constant to all the prices $\bar{p}_i$ defined above; it will simply correspond to a different price for the root node. The formula

$$\bar{p}_i = \begin{cases} p_i + r_{\bar{i}\bar{j}} & \text{if } i \in T_{\bar{i}}, \\ p_i & \text{if } i \in T_{\bar{j}}, \end{cases} \tag{5.12}$$

which involves a decrease of the prices of the nodes in $T_{\bar{i}}$, is useful in some implementations.

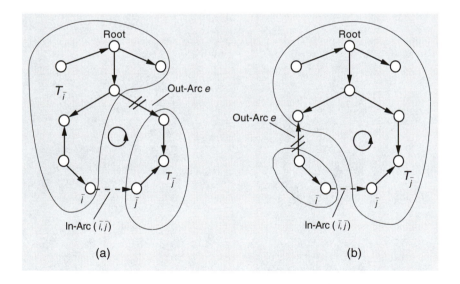

Figure 5.9: Component trees $T_{\bar{i}}$ and $T_{\bar{j}}$, obtained by deleting the out-arc e from T, where $\bar{e} = (\bar{i}, \bar{j})$ is the in-arc; these are the components that contain $\bar{i}$ and $\bar{j}$, respectively. Depending on the position of the out-arc e, the root node may be contained in $T_{\bar{i}}$ as in figure (a), or in $T_{\bar{j}}$ as in figure (b).

Note that if the flow increment $\delta = \min_{(i,j) \in C^-} x_{ij}$ [cf. Eq. (5.8)] is positive, then the cost corresponding to $\bar{x}$ will be strictly smaller than the cost corresponding to x (by δ times the cost of the cycle C). Thus, when

$\delta > 0$, a simplex method will never reproduce x and the corresponding tree T in future iterations.

On the other hand, if $\delta = 0$, then $\bar{x} = x$ and the pivot is degenerate. In this case there is no guarantee that the tree T will not be repeated after several degenerate iterations with no interim improvement in the primal cost. We thus need to provide a mechanism that precludes this from happening.

5.1.3   Dealing with Degeneracy

Suppose that the feasible trees generated by a simplex method are all distinct (which is true in particular when all pivots are nondegenerate). Then, since the number of distinct feasible trees is finite, the method will eventually terminate. Upon termination, there are two possibilities:

(a) The final flow and price vectors are primal and dual optimal, respectively.

(b) The problem is shown to be unbounded because at the final iteration, the cycle closed by the current tree and the in-arc $\bar{e}$ has no arc with orientation opposite to that of $\bar{e}$.

Unfortunately, if the tree sequence is not generated with some care, there is no guarantee that a tree will not be infinitely repeated. To rule out this possibility, thereby ensuring termination of the method, we will use feasible trees with a special property called *strong feasibility*. We will make sure that the initial tree has this property, and we will choose the out-arc in a way that the property is maintained by the algorithm.

Let us fix the root node r used to compute the price vectors associated with feasible trees. Given a feasible tree T, we say that arc $(i, j) \in T$ is *oriented away* from the root if the unique simple path of T from the root to j passes through i. A feasible tree T with corresponding flow vector x is said to be *strongly feasible* if every arc (i, j) of T with $x_{ij} = 0$ is oriented away from the root. Figure 5.10 illustrates strongly feasible trees. The following proposition motivates the use of strongly feasible trees.

Proposition 5.2: If the feasible trees generated by a simplex method are all strongly feasible, then these trees are distinct.

Proof: With each feasible tree T, with corresponding basic feasible vector x and price vector p, we associate the two scalars

$$c(T) = \sum_{(i,j)\in\mathcal{A}} a_{ij}x_{ij},$$

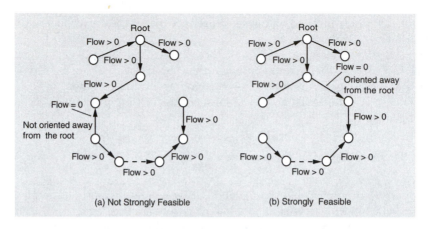

Figure 5.10: Illustration of a strongly feasible tree. The tree in (a) is not strongly feasible because the arc with zero flow on the tree is not oriented away from the root. The tree in (b) is strongly feasible. Note that these two trees are obtained from the strongly feasible tree in Fig. 5.6 by choosing a different out-arc.

$$w(T) = \sum_{i \in \mathcal{N}} (p_r - p_i),$$

where r is the root node. [The price differences $p_r - p_i$ are uniquely determined by T according to

$$p_r - p_i = \sum_{(m,n) \in P_i^+} a_{mn} - \sum_{(m,n) \in P_i^-} a_{mn}$$

[see Eq. (5.4)], so $w(T)$ is uniquely determined by T. Note that, $w(T)$ may be viewed as the "aggregate length" of T; it is the sum of the lengths of the paths P_i from the root to the nodes i along the tree T, where the length of an arc (m, n) is a_{mn} or $-a_{mn}$ depending on whether (m, n) is or is not oriented away from the root, respectively.]

We will show that if T and $\overline{T} = T + \overline{e} - e$ are two successive feasible trees generated by the simplex method, then either $c(\overline{T}) < c(T)$ or else $c(\overline{T}) = c(T)$ and $w(\overline{T}) < w(T)$. This proves that no tree can be repeated.

Indeed, if the pivot that generates $\overline{T}$ from T is nondegenerate, we have $c(\overline{T}) < c(T)$, and if it is degenerate we have $c(\overline{T}) = c(T)$. In the former case the result is proved, so assume the latter case holds, and let $\overline{e} = (\overline{i}, \overline{j})$ be the in-arc. Then after the pivot, $\overline{e}$ still has zero flow, and since $\overline{T}$ is strongly feasible, $\overline{e}$ must be oriented away from the root node r. This implies that r belongs to the subtree $T_{\overline{i}}$, and by Eq. (5.11) we have

$$w(\overline{T}) = w(T) + |T_{\overline{j}}| r_{\overline{i}\,\overline{j}},$$

where $r_{\overline{i}\,\overline{j}}$ is the reduced cost of $\overline{e}$, and $|T_{\overline{j}}|$ is the number of nodes in the subtree $T_{\overline{j}}$. Since $r_{\overline{i}\,\overline{j}} < 0$, it follows that $w(\overline{T}) < w(T)$.   **Q.E.D.**

The next proposition shows how to select the out-arc in a simplex iteration in order to maintain strong feasibility of the generated trees.

Proposition 5.3: Let T be a strongly feasible tree generated by a simplex method, let $\bar{e} = (\bar{i}, \bar{j})$ be the in-arc, let C be the cycle formed by T and $\bar{e}$, and suppose that C^- is nonempty. Let $\delta = \min_{(i,j) \in C^-} x_{ij}$, and let $\hat{C}$ be the set of candidate out-arcs, that is, the set

$$\hat{C} = \{(i,j) \in C^- \mid x_{ij} = \delta\}.$$

Define the *join of C* as the first node of C that lies on the unique simple path of T that starts from the root and ends at $\bar{i}$ (see Fig. 5.11). Suppose that the out-arc e is chosen to be the arc of $\hat{C}$ encountered first as C is traversed in the forward direction (the direction of $\bar{e}$) starting from the join node. Then the next tree $\overline{T} = T + \bar{e} - e$ generated by the method is strongly feasible.

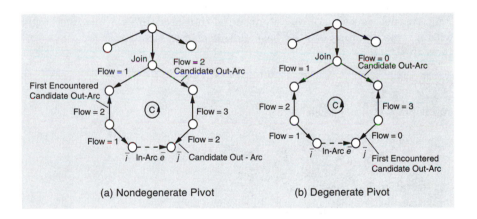

(a) Nondegenerate Pivot   (b) Degenerate Pivot

Figure 5.11: Maintaining a strongly feasible tree in a simplex method. Suppose that the in-arc $\bar{e} = (\bar{i}, \bar{j})$ is added to a strongly feasible T, closing the cycle C. Let $\hat{C}$ be the set of candidates for out-arc (the arcs of C^- attaining the minimum in $\delta = \min_{(i,j) \in C^-} x_{ij}$), and let e be the out-arc. The arcs of $\overline{T}$ with zero flow will be the arcs of $\hat{C} - e$ together with $\bar{e}$ if the pivot is degenerate. By choosing as out-arc the first encountered arc of $\hat{C}$ as C is traversed in the direction of $\bar{e}$ starting from the join, all of these arcs will be oriented away from the join and also from the root, so strong feasibility is maintained. Note that if the pivot is degenerate as in (b), then all arcs of $\hat{C}$ will be encountered after $\bar{e}$ (by strong feasibility of T), so the out-arc e must be encountered after $\bar{e}$. Thus, the in-arc $\bar{e}$ will be oriented away from the root in the case of a degenerate pivot, as required for strong feasibility of $\overline{T}$.

Proof: We first note that the flow or orientation relative to the root of the arcs of T which are not in C will not change during the simplex iteration. Therefore, to check strong feasibility of $\overline{T}$, we need only be concerned with the arcs of $C + \overline{e} - e$ for which $\overline{x}_{ij} = 0$. These will be the arcs of $\hat{C} - e$ and possibly arc $\overline{e}$ (in the case $\delta = 0$). By choosing e to be the first encountered arc of $\hat{C}$, all of the arcs of $\hat{C} - e$ will be encountered after e, and following the pivot, they will be oriented away from the join and therefore also from the root. If $\delta = 0$, the arcs (i, j) of $\hat{C}$ satisfy $x_{ij} = 0$, so by strong feasibility of T, all of them, including e, must be encountered *after* $\overline{e}$ as C is traversed in the direction of $\overline{e}$ starting from the join. Therefore, $\overline{e}$ will also be oriented away from the root following the pivot.   **Q.E.D.**

5.2   THE BASIC SIMPLEX ALGORITHM

In this section we will focus on a particular simplex algorithm based on the ideas of the preceding section. This algorithm may be viewed as the basic form of the simplex method for the minimum cost flow problem, and will be shown to have solid theoretical properties.

At the beginning of each iteration of the algorithm we have a strongly feasible tree T, an associated basic flow vector x such that

$$x_{ij} = 0, \qquad \forall \, (i, j) \notin T,$$

and a price vector p such that

$$r_{ij} = a_{ij} + p_j - p_i = 0, \qquad \forall \, (i, j) \in T.$$

The iteration has three possible outcomes:

(a) We will verify that x and p are primal and dual optimal, respectively.

(b) We will determine that the problem is unbounded.

(c) We will obtain by the method of Prop. 5.3 a strongly feasible tree $\overline{T} = T + \overline{e} - e$, differing from T by the in-arc $\overline{e}$ and the out-arc e.

Simplex Iteration

Select an in-arc $\overline{e} = (\overline{i}, \overline{j}) \notin T$ such that

$$r_{\overline{i}\overline{j}} = a_{\overline{i}\overline{j}} + p_{\overline{j}} - p_{\overline{i}} < 0.$$

(If no such arc can be found, terminate; x is primal optimal and p is dual optimal.) Consider the cycle C formed by T and $\bar{e}$. If C^- is empty, terminate (the problem is unbounded); else, obtain the out-arc $e \in C^-$ as described in Prop. 5.3.

5.2.1   Termination Properties of the Simplex Method

We now collect the facts already proved into a proposition that also deals with the integrality of the solutions obtained.

Proposition 5.4: Suppose that the simplex method just described is applied to the minimum cost flow problem with nonnegativity constraints, starting with a strongly feasible tree.

(a) If the problem is not unbounded, the method terminates with an optimal primal solution x and an optimal dual solution p, and the optimal primal cost is equal to the optimal dual cost. Furthermore, if the supplies s_i are all integer, the optimal primal solution x is integer. Also, if the starting price of the root node and the cost coefficients a_{ij} are all integer, the optimal dual solution p is integer.

(b) If the problem is unbounded, the method verifies this after a finite number of iterations.

Proof: (a) The trees generated by the method are strongly feasible, and by Prop. 5.2 these trees are all distinct, so the method terminates. Termination can only occur with either an optimal pair (x, p) or with the indication that the problem is unbounded. Thus, if the problem is not unbounded, the only possibility is termination with an optimal pair (x, p). Since upon termination x and p satisfy complementary slackness, the equality of the optimal primal and dual costs follows from Prop. 4.1 in Section 4.3. Also, if the supplies s_i are all integer, from Prop. 5.1 it follows that all basic flow vectors are integer, including the one obtained at termination. If the starting price of the root node and the cost coefficients a_{ij} are all integer, it can be checked that all operations of the algorithm maintain the integrality of p.

(b) If the problem is unbounded, there is no optimal solution, so the simplex method cannot terminate with an optimal pair (x, p). The only other possibility is that the method terminates with an indication that the problem is unbounded.   **Q.E.D.**

5.2.2   Initialization of the Simplex Method

In the absence of an apparent choice for an initial strongly feasible tree, one may use the so called *big-M method*. In this method, some artificial variables are introduced to simplify the choice of an initial basic solution, but the cost coefficient M for these variables is chosen large enough so that the optimal solutions of the problem are not affected. The big-M method is also useful in problems where the graph is not connected and therefore it has no spanning tree at all.

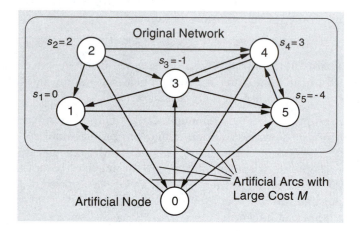

Figure 5.12: Artificial arcs used in the big-M method to modify the problem so as to facilitate the choice of an initial strongly feasible tree.

In the big-M method, we modify the problem by introducing an extra node, labeled 0 and having zero supply $s_0 = 0$, together with a set of artificial arcs $\overline{\mathcal{A}}$ consisting of an arc $(i, 0)$ for each node i with $s_i > 0$, and an arc $(0, i)$ for each node i with $s_i \leq 0$; see Fig. 5.12. The cost coefficient of all these arcs is taken to be a scalar M, and its choice will be discussed shortly. We thus arrive at the following problem, referred to as the *big-M version* of the original problem:

$$\text{minimize} \quad \sum_{(i,j)\in\mathcal{A}} a_{ij}x_{ij} + M \left(\sum_{(i,0)\in\overline{\mathcal{A}}} x_{i0} + \sum_{(0,i)\in\overline{\mathcal{A}}} x_{0i} \right)$$

$$\text{subject to} \quad \sum_{\{j|(i,j)\in\mathcal{A}\cup\overline{\mathcal{A}}\}} x_{ij} - \sum_{\{j|(j,i)\in\mathcal{A}\cup\overline{\mathcal{A}}\}} x_{ji} = s_i, \quad \forall\, i \in \mathcal{N} \cup \{0\},$$

$$0 \leq x_{ij}, \quad \forall\, (i,j) \in \mathcal{A} \cup \overline{\mathcal{A}}.$$

The artificial arcs constitute a readily available initial spanning tree for the big-M version; see Fig. 5.12. It can be seen that the corresponding basic flow vector is given by

$$x_{i0} = s_i, \qquad \forall \ i \text{ with } s_i > 0,$$

$$x_{0i} = -s_i, \qquad \forall \ i \text{ with } s_i \le 0,$$

$$x_{ij} = 0, \qquad \forall \ (i,j) \in \mathcal{A},$$

and is therefore feasible. Let us choose the root to be the artificial node 0. By construction, the artificial arcs that carry zero flow are then oriented away from the root, so the tree is strongly feasible.

The cost M of the artificial arcs should be taken to be large enough so that these arcs will carry zero flow at every optimal solution of the big-M version. In this case, the flows of the nonartificial arcs define an optimal solution of the original problem. The following proposition quantifies the appropriate level of M for this to happen, and collects a number of related facts.

Proposition 5.5: Consider the minimum cost flow problem with non-negativity constraints (referred to as the original problem), and consider also its big-M version. Suppose that

$$2M > \sum_{(i,j)\in P^+} a_{ij} - \sum_{(i,j)\in P^-} a_{ij} \tag{5.13}$$

for all simple paths P of the original problem graph, where P^+ and P^- are the sets of forward and backward arcs of P, respectively. Then:

(a) If the original problem is feasible but not unbounded, the big-M version has at least one optimal solution, and each of its solutions is of the form

$$\overline{x}_{ij} = \begin{cases} x_{ij} & \text{if } (i,j) \in \mathcal{A}, \\ 0 & \text{if } (i,j) \in \overline{\mathcal{A}}, \end{cases} \tag{5.14}$$

where x is an optimal solution of the original. Furthermore, every optimal solution x of the original problem gives rise to an optimal solution $\overline{x}$ of the big-M version via the preceding relation.

(b) If the original problem is unbounded, the big-M version is also unbounded.

(c) If the original problem is infeasible, then in every feasible solution of the big-M version some artificial arc carries positive flow.

Proof: (a) We first note that the big-M version cannot be unbounded unless the original problem is. To prove this, we argue by contradiction. If the big-M version is unbounded and the original problem is not, there would exist a simple forward cycle with negative cost in the big-M version. This cycle cannot consist of arcs of $\mathcal{A}$ exclusively, since the original is not unbounded. On the other hand, if the cycle consisted of the arcs $(m, 0)$ and $(0, n)$, and a simple path of the original graph, then by the condition (5.13) the cycle would have positive cost, arriving at a contradiction.

Having proved that the big-M version is not unbounded, we now note that, by Prop. 5.4(a), the simplex method starting with the strongly feasible tree of all the artificial arcs will terminate with optimal primal and dual solutions of the big-M version. Thus, optimal solutions of the big-M version exist, and for every optimal solution $\overline{x}$ of the form (5.14), the corresponding vector $x = \{x_{ij} \mid (i, j) \in \mathcal{A}\}$ with $x_{ij} = \overline{x}_{ij}$ for all $(i, j) \in \mathcal{A}$ is an optimal solution of the original problem.

To prove that all optimal solutions $\overline{x}$ of the big-M version are of the form (5.14), we argue by contradiction. Suppose that $\overline{x}$ is an optimal solution such that some artificial arcs carry positive flow. Let

$$\mathcal{N}^+ = \{m \mid s_m > 0, \ \overline{x}_{m0} > 0\},$$

$$\mathcal{N}^- = \{n \mid s_n \le 0, \ \overline{x}_{0n} > 0\}.$$

We observe that $\mathcal{N}^+$ and $\mathcal{N}^-$ must be nonempty and that there is no simple path P that starts at some $m \in \mathcal{N}^+$, ends at some $n \in \mathcal{N}^-$, and is unblocked with respect to $\overline{x}$; such a path, together with arcs $(m, 0)$ and $(0, n)$, would form an unblocked simple cycle, which would have negative cost in view of condition (5.13). Consider now the flow vector $x = \{x_{ij} \mid (i, j) \in \mathcal{A}\}$ with $x_{ij} = \overline{x}_{ij}$ for all $(i, j) \in \mathcal{A}$. Then, there is no path of the original problem graph $(\mathcal{N}, \mathcal{A})$ that starts at a node of $\mathcal{N}^+$, ends at a node of $\mathcal{N}^-$, and is unblocked with respect to x. By using a very similar argument as in the proof of Prop. 3.1, we can show (see Exercise 3.11 in Ch. 3) that there must exist a saturated cut $[\mathcal{S}, \mathcal{N} - \mathcal{S}]$ such that $\mathcal{N}^+ \subset \mathcal{S}$, $\mathcal{N}^- \subset \mathcal{N} - \mathcal{S}$. The capacity of this cut is equal to the sum of the divergences of the nodes $i \in \mathcal{S}$,

$$\sum_{i \in \mathcal{S}} y_i = \sum_{i \in \mathcal{S}} \left(\sum_{\{j \mid (i,j) \in \mathcal{A}\}} x_{ij} - \sum_{\{j \mid (j,i) \in \mathcal{A}\}} x_{ji} \right),$$

which is also equal to

$$\sum_{i \in \mathcal{S}} (s_i - \overline{x}_{i0}) = \sum_{i \in \mathcal{S}} s_i - \sum_{i \in \mathcal{N}^+} \overline{x}_{i0} < \sum_{i \in \mathcal{S}} s_i.$$

On the other hand, if the original problem is feasible, the capacity of any cut $[\mathcal{S}, \mathcal{N} - \mathcal{S}]$ cannot be less than $\sum_{i \in \mathcal{S}} s_i$, so we obtain a contradiction.

Finally, let x be an optimal solution of the original problem, and let $\overline{x}$ be given by Eq. (5.14). We will show that $\overline{x}$ is optimal for the big-M

version. Indeed, every simple cycle that is unblocked with respect to $\bar{x}$ in the big-M version either consists of arcs in $\mathcal{A}$ and is therefore unblocked with respect to x in the original, or else consists of the arcs $(m, 0)$ and $(0, n)$, and a simple path $\overline{P}$ that starts at n and ends at m. In the former case, the cost of the cycle is nonnegative, since x is optimal for the original problem; in the latter case, the cost of the cycle is positive by condition (5.13) (with the path P being the reverse of path $\overline{P}$). Hence, $\bar{x}$ is optimal for the big-M version.

(b) Note that every feasible solution x of the original problem defines a feasible solution $\bar{x}$ of equal cost in the big-M version via Eq. (5.14). Therefore, if the cost of the original is unbounded from below, the same is true of the big-M version.

(c) Observe that any feasible solution of the big-M version having zero flow on the artificial arcs defines a feasible solution x of the original via Eq. (5.14). **Q.E.D.**

Note that to satisfy the condition (5.13), it is sufficient to take

$$M > \frac{(N-1)C}{2},$$

where C is the arc cost range $C = \max_{(i,j) \in \mathcal{A}} |a_{ij}|$. Note also that if M does not satisfy the condition (5.13), then the big-M version may be unbounded, even if the original problem has an optimal solution (Exercise 5.7). Many practical simplex codes use an adaptive strategy for selecting M, whereby a moderate value of M is used initially, and this value is gradually increased if positive flows on the artificial arcs persist.

By combining the results of the preceding two propositions, we obtain the following:

Proposition 5.6: Assume that the minimum cost flow problem with nonnegativity constraints is feasible and is not unbounded. Then:

(a) There exists an optimal primal solution and an optimal dual solution, and the optimal primal cost is equal to the optimal dual cost.

(b) If the supplies s_i are all integer, there exists an optimal primal solution which is integer.

(c) If the cost coefficients a_{ij} are all integer, there exists an optimal dual solution which is integer.

Proof: Apply the simplex method to the big-M version with the initial strongly feasible tree of all the artificial arcs, and with M sufficiently large to satisfy condition (5.13). Then, by Prop. 5.5, the big-M version has optimal solutions, so by Prop. 5.4 the simplex method will provide an optimal pair $(\overline{x}, \overline{p})$, with $\overline{x}$ integer if the supplies are integer, and $\overline{p}$ integer if the cost coefficients are integer. By Prop. 5.5, the vector x defined by $x_{ij} = \overline{x}_{ij}$, for all $(i,j) \in \mathcal{A}$ will be an optimal solution of the original problem, while the price vector p defined by $p_i = \overline{p}_i$, for all $i \in \mathcal{N}$ will satisfy the CS conditions together with x. Hence, p will be an optimal dual solution. **Q.E.D.**

A Shortest Path Example

Consider a single origin/all destinations shortest path problem involving the graph of Fig. 5.13. We will use this example to illustrate the simplex method and some of its special properties when applied to shortest path problems. The corresponding minimum cost flow problem is

$$\text{minimize} \quad \sum_{(i,j)\in\mathcal{A}} a_{ij}x_{ij}$$

$$\text{subject to} \quad \sum_{\{j|(1,j)\in\mathcal{A}\}} x_{1j} - \sum_{\{j|(j,1)\in\mathcal{A}\}} x_{j1} = 3,$$

$$\sum_{\{j|(i,j)\in\mathcal{A}\}} x_{ij} - \sum_{\{j|(j,i)\in\mathcal{A}\}} x_{ji} = -1, \qquad i = 2,3,4,$$

$$0 \le x_{ij}, \qquad \forall\, (i,j) \in \mathcal{A}.$$

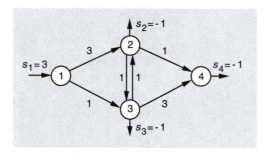

Figure 5.13: Example of a single origin/all destinations shortest path problem. Node 1 is the origin. The arc lengths are shown next to the arcs.

We select as root the origin node 1. To deal with the problem of the initial choice of a strongly feasible tree, we use a variant of the big-M method. We introduce artificial arcs connecting the origin with each node $i \neq 1$ with very large cost M, and we use as an initial tree the set of artificial arcs with root node the origin (with this choice, there will be two arcs connecting the origin with each of its neighbors, but this should not cause any confusion). In the corresponding flow vector, every artificial arc carries unit flow, so the initial tree is strongly feasible (all arcs are oriented away from the root).

The corresponding price vector is $(0, -M, -M, -M)$ and the associated reduced costs of the nonartificial arcs are

$$r_{1j} = a_{1j} - M, \qquad \forall\, (1, j) \in \mathcal{A},$$

$$r_{ij} = a_{ij}, \qquad \forall\, (i, j) \in \mathcal{A},\ i \neq 1,\ j \neq 1.$$

One possible outcome of the first iteration is to select some arc $(1, j) \in \mathcal{A}$ as in-arc, and to select the artificial arc connecting 1 and j as out-arc. The process will then be continued, first obtaining the flow and price vectors corresponding to the new tree, then obtaining the out-arc, then the in-arc, etc.

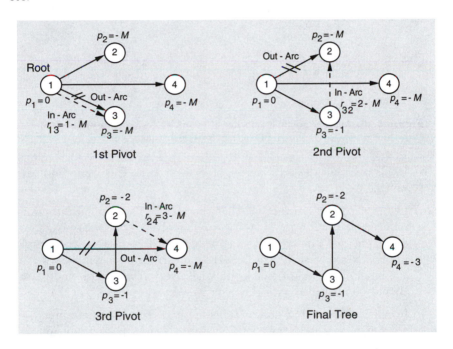

Figure 5.14: A possible sequence of pivots for the simplex method. The initial tree consists of the artificial arcs $(1, 2)$, $(1, 3)$, and $(1, 4)$, each carrying one unit of flow. The in-arc is selected to be the arc with minimum reduced cost and the method behaves like Dijkstra's algorithm, requiring only $N - 1$ $(= 3)$ pivots.

Figures 5.14 and 5.15 show two possible sequences of pivots. The following can be noted:

(a) Each artificial arc eventually becomes the out-arc but never becomes the in-arc.

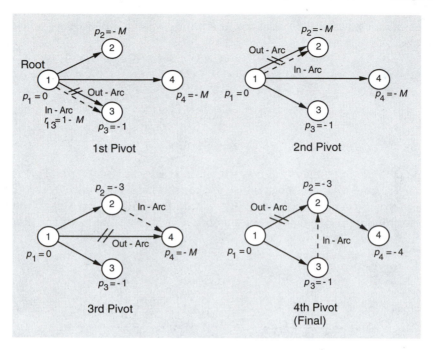

Figure 5.15: Another possible sequence of pivots for the simplex method. More than three pivots are required, in contrast with the sequence of Fig. 5.14.

(b) In all trees, all the arcs are oriented away from the origin and carry unit flow.

(c) In Fig. 5.14, we use the rule that the in-arc is an arc with minimum reduced cost. As a result, there are exactly $N - 1 (= 3)$ pivots, and each time the out-arc is an artificial arc. In this case the simplex method works exactly like Dijkstra's algorithm, permanently setting the label of one additional node with every pivot; here, node labels should be identified with the negative of node prices.

It can be shown that observations (a) and (b) above hold in general for the simplex method applied to feasible shortest path problems, and observation (c) also holds in general provided $a_{ij} \geq 0$ for all arcs (i, j). The proof of this is left as Exercise 5.13 for the reader.

The simplex method can also be used effectively to solve the all-pairs shortest path problem. In particular, one may first use the simplex method to solve the shortest path problem for a single origin, say node 1, and then modify the final tree T_1 to obtain an initial tree T_2 for applying the simplex method with another origin, say node 2. This can be done by deleting the unique arc of T_1 that is incoming to node 2, and replacing it with an artificial arc from 2 to 1 that has a very large length; see Fig. 5.16.

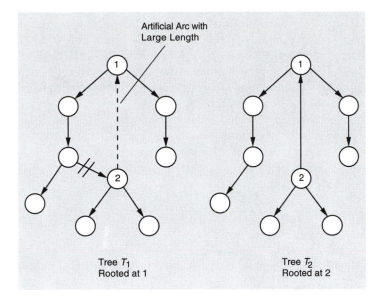

Figure 5.16: Obtaining an initial tree T_2 for the simplex method applied to the shortest path problem with origin 2, from the final tree T_1 of the simplex method applied for origin 1. We delete the unique arc of T_1 that is incoming to node 2, and replace it with an artificial arc from 2 to 1 that has a very large length.

5.3 EXTENSION TO PROBLEMS WITH UPPER AND LOWER BOUNDS

In this section, we consider the extension of the simplex method of the preceding section to the general minimum cost flow problem that involves upper and lower bounds

$$\text{minimize} \quad \sum_{(i,j)\in\mathcal{A}} a_{ij}x_{ij}$$

$$\text{subject to} \quad \sum_{\{j|(i,j)\in\mathcal{A}\}} x_{ij} - \sum_{\{j|(j,i)\in\mathcal{A}\}} x_{ji} = s_i, \qquad \forall\, i \in \mathcal{N}, \qquad (5.15)$$

$$b_{ij} \le x_{ij} \le c_{ij}, \qquad \forall\, (i,j) \in \mathcal{A}.$$

To simplify the presentation, we assume that $b_{ij} < c_{ij}$ for all arcs (i,j); any arc (i,j) with $b_{ij} = c_{ij}$ can be eliminated, and its flow, which is equal to the common bound, can be incorporated into the supplies s_i and s_j. A nice aspect of the problem is that we don't have to worry about unboundedness, since all arc flows are constrained to lie in a bounded interval.

The extension of the simplex method to the problem with upper and lower bounds is straightforward, and we will simply state the algorithm and the corresponding results without much elaboration. In fact, one may derive the simplex method for this problem by converting it to the minimum cost flow problem with nonnegativity constraints (cf. the discussion of Section 4.2), by applying the simplex method of the preceding section, and by appropriately streamlining the computations. We leave the verification of this as Exercise 5.15 for the reader.

The method uses at each iteration a spanning tree T. Only arcs of T can have flows that are neither at the upper bound nor at the lower bound. However, to uniquely associate a basic flow vector with T, we must also specify for each arc $(i, j) \notin T$ whether $x_{ij} = b_{ij}$ or $x_{ij} = c_{ij}$. Thus, the simplex method maintains a triplet

$$(T, L, U),$$

where

   T is a spanning tree,

   L is the set of arcs $(i, j) \notin T$ with $x_{ij} = b_{ij}$,

   U is the set of arcs $(i, j) \notin T$ with $x_{ij} = c_{ij}$.

Such a triplet will be called a *basis*. It uniquely specifies a flow vector x, called the *basic flow vector* corresponding to (T, L, U). In particular, if an arc (i, j) belongs to T and separates T into the subtrees T_i and T_j, we have

$$x_{ij} = \sum_{n \in T_i} s_n - \sum_{\{(m,n) \in L \mid m \in T_i, n \in T_j\}} b_{mn} - \sum_{\{(m,n) \in U \mid m \in T_i, n \in T_j\}} c_{mn}$$

$$+ \sum_{\{(m,n) \in L \mid m \in T_j, n \in T_i\}} b_{mn} + \sum_{\{(m,n) \in U \mid m \in T_j, n \in T_i\}} c_{mn}.$$

If x is feasible, then the basis (T, L, U) is called feasible.

Similar to the preceding section, we fix a root node r throughout the algorithm. A basis (T, L, U) specifies a price vector p using the same formula as in the preceding section:

$$p_i = p_r - \sum_{(m,n) \in P_i^+} a_{mn} + \sum_{(m,n) \in P_i^-} a_{mn}, \qquad \forall\, i \in \mathcal{N},$$

where P_i is the unique simple path of T starting at the root node r and ending at i, and P_i^+ and P_i^- are the sets of forward and backward arcs of P_i, respectively.

We say that the feasible basis (T, L, U) is *strongly feasible* if all arcs $(i, j) \in T$ with $x_{ij} = b_{ij}$ are oriented away from the root and if all arcs $(i, j) \in T$ with $x_{ij} = c_{ij}$ are oriented toward the root (that is, the unique simple path from the root to i passes through j).

Given the strongly feasible basis (T, L, U) with a corresponding flow vector x and price vector p, an iteration of the simplex method produces another strongly feasible basis $(\overline{T}, \overline{L}, \overline{U})$ as follows.

Simplex Iteration for Problems with Upper and Lower Bounds

Find an in-arc $\overline{e} = (\overline{i}, \overline{j}) \notin T$ such that either

$$r_{\overline{ij}} < 0 \qquad \text{if} \qquad \overline{e} \in L$$

or

$$r_{\overline{ij}} > 0 \qquad \text{if} \qquad \overline{e} \in U.$$

(If no such arc can be found, x is primal optimal and p is dual optimal.) Let C be the cycle closed by T and $\overline{e}$. Define the forward direction of C to be the same as the one of $\overline{e}$ if $\overline{e} \in L$ and opposite to $\overline{e}$ if $\overline{e} \in U$ (that is, $\overline{e} \in C^+$ if $\overline{e} \in L$ and $\overline{e} \in C^-$ if $\overline{e} \in U$). Also let

$$\delta = \min \left\{ \min_{(i,j) \in C^-} \{x_{ij} - b_{ij}\}, \min_{(i,j) \in C^+} \{c_{ij} - x_{ij}\} \right\},$$

and let $\hat{C}$ be the set of arcs where this minimum is obtained:

$$\hat{C} = \{(i,j) \in C^- \mid x_{ij} - b_{ij} = \delta\} \cup \{(i,j) \in C^+ \mid c_{ij} - x_{ij} = \delta\}.$$

Define the *join of C* as the first node of C that lies on the unique simple path of T that starts from the root and ends at $\overline{i}$. Select as out-arc the arc e of $\hat{C}$ that is encountered first as C is traversed in the forward direction starting from the join node. The new tree is $\overline{T} = T + \overline{e} - e$, and the corresponding flow vector $\overline{x}$ is obtained from x by

$$\overline{x}_{ij} = \begin{cases} x_{ij} & \text{if } (i,j) \notin C, \\ x_{ij} + \delta & \text{if } (i,j) \in C^+, \\ x_{ij} - \delta & \text{if } (i,j) \in C^-. \end{cases}$$

Note that it is possible that the in-arc is the same as the out-arc, in which case T is unchanged. In this case, the flow of this arc will simply move from one bound to the other, affecting the sets L and U, and thus affecting the basis. The proofs of the preceding section can be modified to show that the algorithm maintains a strongly feasible tree.

The following proposition deals with the validity of the method and the integrality of the optimal primal and dual solutions obtained. Its proof is very similar to the one of Prop. 5.4, and is omitted.

Proposition 5.7: Assume that the simplex method is applied to the minimum cost flow problem with upper and lower bounds, starting from a strongly feasible tree. Then:

(a) The method terminates with an optimal primal solution x and an optimal dual solution p.

(b) The optimal primal cost is equal to the optimal dual cost.

(c) If the supplies s_i and the flow bounds b_{ij}, c_{ij} are all integer, the optimal primal solution x is integer.

(d) If the starting price of the root node and the cost coefficients a_{ij} are all integer, the optimal dual solution p is integer.

If an initial strongly feasible tree is not readily available, we can solve instead a big-M version of the problem with suitably large value of M. This problem is

$$\text{minimize} \quad \sum_{(i,j)\in\mathcal{A}} a_{ij}x_{ij} + M\left(\sum_{(i,0)\in\overline{\mathcal{A}}} x_{i0} + \sum_{(0,i)\in\overline{\mathcal{A}}} x_{0i}\right)$$

$$\text{subject to} \quad \sum_{\{j|(i,j)\in\mathcal{A}\cup\overline{\mathcal{A}}\}} x_{ij} - \sum_{\{j|(j,i)\in\mathcal{A}\cup\overline{\mathcal{A}}\}} x_{ji} = s_i, \qquad \forall\, i \in \mathcal{N} \cup \{0\},$$

$$b_{ij} \le x_{ij} \le c_{ij}, \qquad \forall\, (i,j) \in \mathcal{A},$$

$$0 \le x_{i0} \le \overline{s}_i, \qquad \forall\, i \text{ with } s_i > 0,$$

$$0 \le x_{0i} \le \underline{s}_i, \qquad \forall\, i \text{ with } s_i \le 0,$$

where

$$\overline{s}_i = s_i - \sum_{\{j|(i,j)\in\mathcal{A}\}} b_{ij} + \sum_{\{j|(j,i)\in\mathcal{A}\}} b_{ji},$$

$$\underline{s}_i = -s_i + \sum_{\{j|(i,j)\in\mathcal{A}\}} b_{ij} - \sum_{\{j|(j,i)\in\mathcal{A}\}} b_{ji}.$$

The initial strongly feasible tree consists of the artificial arcs. The corresponding basic flow vector x is given by $x_{ij} = b_{ij}$ for all $(i,j) \in \mathcal{A}$, $x_{i0} = s_i$, for all i with $s_i > 0$, and $x_{0i} = -s_i$, for all i with $s_i \le 0$.

Similar to the case of the problem with nonnegativity constraints (cf. Prop. 5.6), we obtain the following.

Proposition 5.8: Assume that the minimum cost flow problem with upper and lower bounds is feasible. Then:

(a) There exists an optimal primal solution and an optimal dual solution, and the optimal primal cost is equal to the optimal dual cost.

(b) If the supplies s_i and the flow bounds b_{ij}, c_{ij} are all integer, there exists an optimal primal solution which is integer.

(c) If the cost coefficients a_{ij} are all integer, there exists an optimal dual solution which is integer.

5.4 IMPLEMENTATION ISSUES

To implement a network optimization algorithm efficiently it is essential to exploit the graph nature of the problem using appropriate data structures. There are two main issues here:

(a) Representing the problem in a way that facilitates the application of the algorithm.

(b) Using additional data structures that expedite the operations of the algorithm.

For simplex methods, the appropriate representations of the problem tend to be quite simple. However, additional fairly complex data structures are needed to implement efficiently the various operations related to flow and price computation, and tree manipulation. This is quite contrary to what happens in the methods to be discussed in the next two chapters, where the appropriate problem representations are quite complex but the additional data structures are simple.

Problem Representation for Simplex Methods

For concreteness, consider the following problem with zero lower arc flow bounds

$$
\begin{aligned}
\text{minimize} \quad & \sum_{(i,j)\in\mathcal{A}} a_{ij}x_{ij} \\
\text{subject to} \quad & \sum_{\{j|(i,j)\in\mathcal{A}\}} x_{ij} - \sum_{\{j|(j,i)\in\mathcal{A}\}} x_{ji} = s_i, \qquad \forall\, i \in \mathcal{N}, \\
& 0 \le x_{ij} \le c_{ij}, \qquad \forall\, (i,j) \in \mathcal{A}.
\end{aligned}
$$

This has become the standard form for commonly available minimum cost flow codes. As discussed in Section 4.2, a problem with nonzero lower arc flow bounds b_{ij} can be converted to one with nonnegativity constraints by using a flow translation (replacing each x_{ij} by $x_{ij} - b_{ij}$ and appropriately adjusting c_{ij}, s_i, and s_j).

One way to represent this problem, which is the most common in simplex codes, is to use the following four arrays of length A

$START(a)$: The start node of arc a,

$END(a)$: The end node of arc a,

$COST(a)$: The cost coefficient of arc a,

$CAPACITY(a)$: The upper flow bound of arc a,

and the following array of length N

$SUPPLY(i)$: The supply of node i.

Figure 5.17 gives an example of a problem represented in this way.

An alternative representation is to store the costs a_{ij} and the upper flow bounds c_{ij} in two-dimensional $N \times N$ arrays (or in one-dimensional arrays of length N^2, with the elements of each row stored contiguously). This wastes memory and requires a lot of extra overhead when the problem is sparse ($A << N^2$), but it may be a good choice for dense problems since it avoids the storage of the start and end nodes of each arc.

Data Structures for Tree Operations

Taking a closer look at the operations of the simplex method, we see that the main computational steps at each iteration are the following:

(a) Finding an in-arc with negative reduced cost.

(b) Identifying the cycle formed by the current tree and the in-arc.

(c) Modifying the flows along the cycle and obtaining the out-arc.

(d) Recalculating the node prices.

As mentioned in Section 5.1.1, most codes maintain a candidate list, i.e., a subset of arcs with negative reduced cost. The arc with most negative reduced cost from this list is selected as the in-arc at each iteration. The maximum size of the candidate list is set at some reasonable level (chosen heuristically), thereby avoiding a costly search and comparison of the reduced costs of all the arcs.

To identify the cycle and the associated flow increment at each iteration, simplex codes commonly use the following two arrays of length N:

(a) $PRED(i)$: The arc preceding node i on the unique path from the root to i on the current tree, together with an indication (such as a plus or a minus sign) of whether this is an incoming or outgoing arc of i.

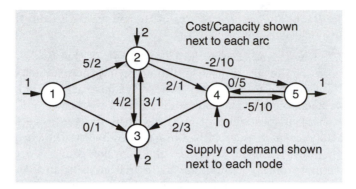

ARC	START	END	COST	CAPACITY
1	1	2	5	2
2	1	3	0	1
3	2	3	4	2
4	3	2	3	1
5	2	5	-2	10
6	2	4	2	1
7	3	4	2	3
8	5	4	0	5
9	4	5	-5	10

NODE	SUPPLY
1	1
2	2
3	-2
4	0
5	-1

Figure 5.17: Representation of a minimum cost flow problem in terms of the five arrays *START*, *END*, *COST*, *CAPACITY*, and *SUPPLY*.

(b) *DEPTH*(i): The number of arcs of the unique path from the root to i on the current tree.

The *PRED* array (together with the *START* and *END* arrays) is sufficient both to represent the current tree and to construct the unique path on the tree from any node i to any other node j. (Construct the paths from i to the root and from j to the root, and subtract out the common portion of these paths.) In particular, if (i,j) is the in-arc, the cycle formed by (i,j) and the current tree could be obtained by finding the path joining i and j in this way. By using the *DEPTH* array, however, the cycle can be constructed more quickly without having to go from i to j all the way to the root. In particular, one can start constructing the paths from i and j to the root simultaneously, adding a new node to the path whose current end node has greater *DEPTH* (ties are broken arbitrarily). The join of the cycle can then be identified as the first encountered common node in the two paths. The following procedure starting with the in-arc (i,j) accomplishes this. In this procedure, $\bar{i}$ and $\bar{j}$ represent successive nodes of the paths starting at i and j, respectively, and ending at the join of the cycle.

Identifying the Join of the Cycle Corresponding to the In-Arc (i,j)

Set $\bar{i} = i$, $\bar{j} = j$.

Step 1: If *DEPTH*$(\bar{i}) \geq$ *DEPTH*$(\bar{j})$, go to Step 2; else go to Step 3.

Step 2: Set $\bar{i} := START(PRED(\bar{i}))$ if $PRED(\bar{i})$ is an incoming arc to $\bar{i}$, and set $\bar{i} := END(PRED(\bar{i}))$ if $PRED(\bar{i})$ is an outgoing arc from $\bar{i}$. Go to Step 4.

Step 3: Set $\bar{j} := START(PRED(\bar{j}))$ if $PRED(\bar{j})$ is an incoming arc to $\bar{j}$, and set $\bar{i} := END(PRED(\bar{j}))$ if $PRED(\bar{j})$ is an outgoing arc from $\bar{j}$. Go to Step 4.

Step 4: If $\bar{i} = \bar{j}$, terminate; $\bar{i}$ is the join of the cycle corresponding to the in-arc (i,j). Else go to Step 1.

The cycle corresponding to the in-arc consists of the arcs $PRED(\bar{i})$ and $PRED(\bar{j})$ encountered during the above procedure. With a simple modification of the procedure, we can simultaneously obtain the out-arc and calculate the flow increment. With little additional work, we can also change the flow along the cycle, and update the *PRED* and *DEPTH* arrays consistently with the new tree.

We must still provide for a mechanism to calculate efficiently the prices corresponding to a given tree. This can be done iteratively, using the prices of the preceding tree as shown in Section 5.1; cf. Eqs. (5.11) and (5.12). To apply these equations, it is necessary to change the prices of

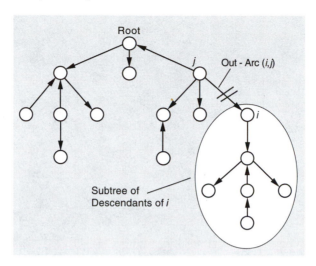

Figure 5.18: The two subtrees obtained when the out-arc is deleted from the current tree. The subtree containing the end node of the out-arc with larger $DEPTH$ (node i in the example of the figure) consists of all the descendants of that end node.

the descendants of one of the end nodes of the out-arc, whichever has the larger value of $DEPTH$; cf. Fig. 5.18. Thus, it is sufficient to be able to calculate the descendants of a given node i in the current tree (the nodes whose unique path to the root passes through i). For this it is convenient to use one more array, called $THREAD$. It defines a traversal order of the nodes of the tree in depth-first fashion. To understand this order, it is useful to think of the tree laid out in a plane, and to consider visiting all nodes starting from the root, and going "top to bottom" and "left to right." An example is given in Fig. 5.19. It can be seen that every node i appears in the traversal order immediately before all of its descendants. Hence the descendants of i are all the nodes immediately following node i in the traversal order up to the first node j with $DEPTH(j) \leq DEPTH(i)$. The array $THREAD$ encodes the traversal order by storing in $THREAD(i)$ the node following node i; cf. Fig. 5.19. An important fact is that when the tree changes, the $THREAD$ array can be updated quite efficiently [with $O(N)$ operations]. The details, however, are too tedious and complicated to be included here; for a clear presentation, see Chvatal [1983], p. 314.

5.5 NOTES, SOURCES, AND EXERCISES

The first specialized version of the simplex method for the transportation problem was given by Dantzig [1951]. This method was also described and extended to the minimum cost flow problem by Dantzig [1963]. A general

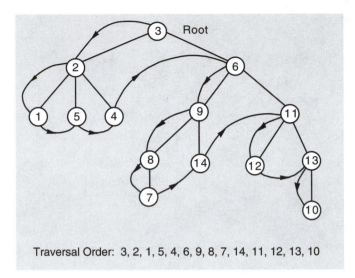

Traversal Order: 3, 2, 1, 5, 4, 6, 9, 8, 7, 14, 11, 12, 13, 10

i	1	2	3	4	5	6	7	8	9	10	11	12	13	14
$THREAD(i)$	5	1	2	6	4	9	14	7	8	0	12	13	10	11

Figure 5.19: Illustration of the $THREAD$ array, which defines a depth-first traversal order of the nodes in the tree. Given the set S of already traversed nodes, the next node traversed is an immediate descendant of one of the nodes in S, which has maximum value of $DEPTH$. For each node i, $THREAD(i)$ defines the successor of node i in this order (for the last node, $THREAD$ is equal to 0).

primal cost improvement algorithm involving flow changes along negative cost cycles was given by Klein [1967]. Strongly feasible trees and their use in resolving degeneracy were introduced by Cunningham [1976].

The subject of pivot selection has received considerable attention in the literature. Examples of poor performance of the simplex method are given by Zadeh [1973a], [1973b]. The performance of various pivot rules was studied empirically by Barr, Glover, and Klingman [1977], [1978], [1979], Bradley, Brown, and Graves [1977], Gavish, Schweitzer, and Shlifer [1977], Goldfarb and Reid [1977], Mulvey [1978a], [1978b], and Gibby, Glover, Klingman, and Mead [1983]. Generally, even with the use of strongly feasible trees, it is possible that the number of successive degenerate pivots is not polynomial. Pivot rules with guaranteed polynomial upper bounds on the lengths of sequences of degenerate pivots are given by Cunningham [1979], and Goldfarb, Hao, and Kai [1990a]. One of the simplest such rules maintains a strongly feasible tree and operates as follows: if the in-arc at some iteration has start node i, the in-arc at the next iteration must be the outgoing arc from node $(i+k)$ modulo N that has minimum reduced cost, where k is the smallest nonnegative integer such that node $(i+k)$ modulo N has at least one outgoing arc with negative reduced cost. For a textbook discussion of a variety of pivot rules, see Bazaraa, Jarvis, and Sherali [1990].

Specialized simplex methods have been developed for the assignment problem; see Barr, Glover, and Klingman [1977], Hung [1983], Balinski [1985], [1986], and Goldfarb [1985]. For analysis and application of simplex methods in shortest path and max-flow problems, see Fulkerson and Dantzig [1955], Florian, Nguyen, and Pallottino [1981], Glover, Klingman, Mote, and Whitman [1984], Goldfarb, Hao, and Kai [1990b], and Goldfarb and Hao [1990].

The existence of integer solutions of the minimum cost flow problem is a fundamental property that links linear network optimization with combinatorial optimization. This property can be generalized through the notion of unimodular matrices. In particular, a square matrix A with integer components is called *unimodular* if its determinant is 0, 1, or -1. Unimodularity can be used to assert the integrality of solutions of linear systems of equations. To see this, note that by Kramer's rule, it follows that if A is invertible and unimodular, then the inverse matrix A^{-1} has integer components. Therefore, the system $Ax = b$ has a unique solution x, which is integer for every integer vector b. A rectangular matrix with integer components is called *totally unimodular* if each of its square submatrices is unimodular. Using the property of unimodular matrices just described, we can show that all the extreme points (vertices) of polyhedra of the form $\{x \mid Ex = s,\ x \geq 0\}$, where E is totally unimodular and s is an integer vector, are integer. The constraint set of the minimum cost flow problem (with nonnegativity constraints) can be expressed as $\{x \mid Ex = s,\ x \geq 0\}$, where s is the vector of supplies, and E is the, so-called, arc incidence matrix of the graph. This matrix has a row for each node and a column for each arc. The component corresponding to the ith row and a given arc is a 1 if the arc is outgoing from i, is a -1 if the arc is incoming to i, and is a 0 otherwise. Basic flow vectors can be identified with extreme points of the polyhedron $\{x \mid Ex = s,\ x \geq 0\}$, while the matrix E can be shown to be totally unimodular (see Exercise 5.18). Thus the integrality property of solutions of the minimum cost flow problem is a special case of the result just mentioned about polyhedra involving unimodular matrices. For a development of the properties of unimodular matrices we refer to the literature (see e.g., Papadimitriou and Steiglitz [1982], Schrijver [1986], Nemhauser and Wolsey [1988], and Murty [1992]).

The development of good implementation techniques played a crucial role in the efficient use of the simplex method. Important contributions in this area include Johnson [1966], Srinivasan and Thompson [1973], Glover, Karney, and Klingman [1974], Glover, Karney, Klingman, and Napier [1974], Glover, Klingman, and Stutz [1974], Bradley, Brown, and

Graves [1977], and Mulvey [1978a], [1978b]. Presentations of these techniques that supplement ours are given by Kennington and Helgason [1980], Chvatal [1983], Bazaraa, Jarvis, and Sherali [1990], and Helgason and Kennington [1995]. The papers by Miller, Pekny, and Thompson [1990], Peters [1990], and Barr and Hickman [1994] describe implementations of the network simplex method in a parallel computing system. A code, called NETFLO, which implements the simplex method for the minimum cost flow problem is given by Kennington and Helgason [1980].

E X E R C I S E S

5.1

Consider the tree of Fig. 5.11(a).

(a) Suppose that the in-arc is $(\bar{j}, \bar{i})$ [instead of $(\bar{i}, \bar{j})$]. Which arc should be the out-arc?

(b) Suppose that the in-arc is the arc starting at the join and ending at $\bar{j}$ [instead of $(\bar{i}, \bar{j})$]. Which arc should be the out-arc in order to preserve strong feasibility of the tree?

5.2

Consider the minimum cost flow problem with nonnegativity constraints given in Fig. 5.20 (supplies and demands are shown next to the nodes, arc costs are immaterial). Find all basic flow vectors and their associated trees. Specify which of these are feasible and which are strongly feasible (the root node is node 1).

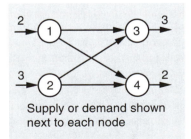

Figure 5.20: Graph for Exercise 5.2.

5.3 (From a Feasible to a Basic Feasible Flow Vector)

Consider a feasible minimum cost flow problem such that the corresponding graph is connected. Suppose we are given a feasible flow vector x. Construct an algorithm that suitably modifies x to obtain a basic feasible flow vector and an associated spanning tree. *Hint*: For a feasible flow vector x there are two possibilities: (1) The subgraph S consisting of the set of arcs

$$\mathcal{A}_x = \big\{(i,j) \in \mathcal{A} \mid x_{ij} > 0\big\}$$

and the corresponding set of incident nodes is acyclic, in which case show that x is basic. (2) The subgraph S is not acyclic, in which case show how to construct a feasible flow vector x' differing from x by a simple cycle flow, and for which the arc set $\mathcal{A}_{x'}$ has at least one arc less than the set $\mathcal{A}_x$.

5.4 (Alternative Construction of a Basic Feasible Flow Vector)

Consider the following algorithm that tries to construct a flow vector that has a given divergence vector s, and is zero on arcs which are not in a given spanning tree T. For any vector x, define the surplus of each node i by

$$g_i = \sum_{\{j \mid (j,i) \in \mathcal{A}\}} x_{ji} - \sum_{\{j \mid (i,j) \in \mathcal{A}\}} x_{ij} + s_i.$$

The algorithm is initialized with $x = 0$. The typical iteration starts with a flow vector x and produces another flow vector $\bar{x}$ that differs from x along a simple path consisting of arcs of T. It operates as follows: a node i with $g_i > 0$ and a node j with $g_j < 0$ are selected, and the unique path P_{ij} that starts at i, ends at j, and has arcs in T is constructed (if no such nodes i and j can be found the algorithm stops). Then the flow of the forward arcs of P_{ij} are increased by δ and the flow of the backward arcs of P_{ij} are decreased by δ, where $\delta = \min\{g_i, -g_j\}$. Show that the algorithm terminates in a finite number of iterations, and that upon termination, we have $g_i = 0$ for all i if and only if $\sum_{i \in \mathcal{N}} s_i = 0$. *Hint*: Show that all the nodes with zero surplus with respect to x also have zero surplus with respect to $\bar{x}$. Furthermore, at least one node with nonzero surplus with respect to x has zero surplus with respect to $\bar{x}$.

5.5

Consider a transportation problem involving the set of sources $\mathcal{S}$ and the set of sinks $\mathcal{T}$ (cf. Example 1.4 in Ch. 1). Suppose that there is no strict subset $\overline{\mathcal{S}}$ of $\mathcal{S}$ and strict subset $\overline{\mathcal{T}}$ of $\mathcal{T}$ such that

$$\sum_{i \in \overline{\mathcal{S}}} \alpha_i = \sum_{j \in \overline{\mathcal{T}}} \beta_j.$$

Show that for every feasible tree, the corresponding flow of every arc of the tree is positive. Conclude that for such a problem, starting from a feasible initial tree, degeneracy never arises in the simplex method.

5.6

Use the simplex method with the big-M initialization to solve the problem in Fig. 5.21.

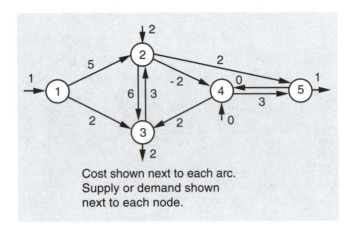

Cost shown next to each arc.
Supply or demand shown
next to each node.

Figure 5.21: Minimum cost flow problem with nonnegativity constraints for Exercise 5.6.

5.7

Construct an example where M does not satisfy the condition (5.13), and the original problem has an optimal solution, while the big-M version is unbounded. *Hint*: It is sufficient to consider a graph with two nodes.

5.8

Construct an example where M satisfies the condition (5.13), and the original problem is infeasible, while the big-M version is unbounded. *Hint*: Consider problems that are infeasible and also contain a simple forward cycle of negative cost.

5.9 (An Example of Cycling)

Consider an assignment problem with sources 1, 2, 3, 4 and sinks 5, 6, 7, 8. There is an arc between each source and each sink. The arc costs are as follows:

$$a_{16} = a_{17} = a_{25} = a_{27} = a_{35} = a_{36} = a_{48} = 1, \qquad a_{ij} = 0 \text{ otherwise.}$$

Let the initial feasible tree consist of arcs (1,5), (1,6), (2,6), (2,8), (4,8), (4,7), (3,7), with corresponding arc flows

$$x_{15} = x_{26} = x_{37} = x_{48} = 1, \qquad x_{ij} = 0 \text{ otherwise.}$$

Suppose that the simplex method is applied without restriction on the choice of
the out-arc (so the generated trees need not be strongly feasible). Verify that
one possible sequence of in-arc/out-arc pairs is given by

$$\big((1,8),(2,8)\big),\ \big((3,6),(1,6)\big),\ \big((4,6),(4,7)\big),$$

$$\big((3,5),(3,6)\big),\ \big((3,8),(1,8)\big),\ \big((2,5),(3,5)\big),$$

$$\big((4,5),(4,6)\big),\ \big((2,7),(2,5)\big),\ \big((2,8),(3,8)\big),$$

$$\big((1,7),(2,7)\big),\ \big((4,7),(4,5)\big),\ \big((1,6),(1,7)\big),$$

and that after these twelve pivots we obtain the initial tree again. (This example
comes from Chvatal [1983].)

5.10 (Rank of the Conservation of Flow Equations)

Let us say that the conservation of flow equations

$$\sum_{\{j\mid(i,j)\in\mathcal{A}\}} x_{ij} - \sum_{\{j\mid(j,i)\in\mathcal{A}\}} x_{ji} = s_i, \qquad \forall\, i \in \mathcal{N},$$

have *rank r* if one can find a subset $\overline{\mathcal{A}}$ of r arcs such that for every supply vector
$s = \{s_i \mid i \in \mathcal{N}\}$, the conservation of flow equations have a unique solution $x(s)$
with $x_{ij}(s) = 0$ for all $(i,j) \in \overline{\mathcal{A}}$. (This definition is consistent with the standard
definition of rank in linear algebra.)

(a) Show that if the graph is connected, the conservation of flow equations
have rank $N - 1$, where N is the number of nodes. *Hint*: Use a spanning
tree of the graph.

(b) Show that the conservation of flow equations have rank $N - r$ if the graph
is the union of r disconnected subgraphs, each of which is connected by
itself.

5.11 (Feasible Differential Theorem, Minty [1960])

Consider a directed graph $(\mathcal{N},\mathcal{A})$. For each arc $(i,j) \in \mathcal{A}$, we are given two
scalars $a_{ij}^- \in [-\infty,\infty)$ and $a_{ij}^+ \in (-\infty,\infty]$, with $a_{ij}^- \le a_{ij}^+$.

(a) Show that there exist scalar prices p_i, $i \in \mathcal{N}$, satisfying

$$a_{ij}^- \le p_i - p_j \le a_{ij}^+, \qquad \forall\,(i,j) \in \mathcal{A}, \tag{5.16}$$

if and only if for every cycle C, we have

$$0 \le \sum_{(i,j)\in C^+} a_{ij}^+ - \sum_{(i,j)\in C^-} a_{ij}^-. \tag{5.17}$$

Hint: Consider a minimum cost flow problem with arcs and cost coefficients constructed as follows:

(1) For each arc $(i,j) \in \mathcal{A}$ with $a_{ij}^+ < \infty$, introduce an arc (i,j) with cost coefficient a_{ij}^+ and feasible flow range $[0,1]$.

(2) For each arc $(i,j) \in \mathcal{A}$ with $a_{ij}^- > -\infty$, introduce an arc (j,i) with cost coefficient $-a_{ij}^-$ and feasible flow range $[0,1]$.

Show that a price vector p and the zero flow vector satisfy CS if and only if Eq. (5.16) holds. Use Prop. 1.2 to show that Eq. (5.17) is a necessary and sufficient condition for the zero flow vector to be optimal. Apply Props. 4.2 and 4.3, which rely on Prop. 5.8.

(b) For the case where $a_{ij}^- = a_{ij}^+ = a_{ij}$ for all (i,j), show the following version of the theorem: there exist p_i, $i \in \mathcal{N}$, such that

$$p_i = p_j + a_{ij}, \qquad \forall \, (i,j) \in \mathcal{A},$$

if and only if for every cycle C, we have

$$\sum_{(i,j) \in C^+} a_{ij} = \sum_{(i,j) \in C^-} a_{ij}.$$

Hint: Show that the condition (5.17) is equivalent to

$$\sum_{(i,j) \in C^+} a_{ij}^- - \sum_{(i,j) \in C^-} a_{ij}^+ \leq 0 \leq \sum_{(i,j) \in C^+} a_{ij}^+ - \sum_{(i,j) \in C^-} a_{ij}^-,$$

for all cycles C.

5.12 (Dual Feasibility Theorem)

Consider the minimum cost flow problem with nonnegativity constraints. Show that the dual problem is feasible, i.e., there exists a price vector p with

$$p_i - p_j \leq a_{ij}, \qquad \forall \, (i,j) \in \mathcal{A},$$

if and only if all forward cycles have nonnegative cost. *Hint*: Assume without loss of generality that the primal is feasible (take $s_i = 0$ if necessary), and note that all forward cycles have nonnegative cost if and only if the primal problem is not unbounded (see the discussion near the beginning of Section 5.1). Alternatively, apply the feasible differential theorem (Exercise 5.11) with $a_{ij}^+ = a_{ij}$ and $a_{ij}^- = -\infty$.

5.13 (Relation of Dijkstra and Simplex for Shortest Paths)

Consider the single origin/all destinations shortest path problem

$$\text{minimize} \quad \sum_{(i,j)\in\mathcal{A}} a_{ij}x_{ij}$$

$$\text{subject to} \quad \sum_{\{j|(1,j)\in\mathcal{A}\}} x_{1j} - \sum_{\{j|(j,1)\in\mathcal{A}\}} x_{j1} = N-1,$$

$$\sum_{\{j|(i,j)\in\mathcal{A}\}} x_{ij} - \sum_{\{j|(j,i)\in\mathcal{A}\}} x_{ji} = -1, \quad \forall\, i \neq 1,$$

$$0 \le x_{ij}, \quad \forall\, (i,j) \in \mathcal{A}.$$

Introduce an artificial arc $(1,i)$ for all $i \neq 1$ with very large cost M, and consider the simplex method starting with the strongly feasible tree of artificial arcs. Let the origin node 1 be the root node.

(a) Show that all the arcs of the trees generated by the simplex method are oriented away from the origin and carry unit flow.

(b) How can a negative length cycle be detected with the simplex method?

(c) Assume that $a_{ij} \ge 0$ for all $(i,j) \in \mathcal{A}$ and suppose that the in-arc is selected to have minimum reduced cost out of all arcs that are not in the tree. Use induction to show that after the kth pivot the tree consists of a shortest path tree from node 1 to the k closest nodes to node 1, together with the artificial arcs $(1,i)$ for all i that are not among the k closest nodes to node 1. Prove that this implementation of the simplex method is equivalent to Dijkstra's method.

5.14

Use the simplex method to solve the minimum cost flow problem with the data of Fig. 5.21, and with the arc flow bounds $0 \le x_{ij} \le 1$ for all $(i,j) \in \mathcal{A}$.

5.15

Suppose that the minimum cost flow problem with upper and lower bounds of Section 5.3 is transformed to a problem with nonnegativity constraints as in Section 4.2. Show that the simplex method of Section 5.2, when applied to the latter problem, is equivalent to the simplex method of Section 5.3. In particular, relate feasible trees, basic flow vectors, and price vectors generated by the two methods, and show that they are in one-to-one correspondence.

5.16 (Birkhoff's Theorem for Doubly Stochastic Matrices)

A *doubly stochastic* $n \times n$ matrix $X = \{x_{ij}\}$ is a matrix such that the elements of each of its rows and columns are nonnegative, and add to one, that is, $x_{ij} \geq 0$ for all i and j, $\sum_{j=1}^{n} x_{ij} = 1$ for all i, and $\sum_{i=1}^{n} x_{ij} = 1$ for all j. A *permutation matrix* is a doubly stochastic matrix whose elements are either one or zero. Furthermore, there is a single one in each row and each column, and all other elements are zero.

(a) Show that given a doubly stochastic matrix X, there exists a permutation matrix X^* such that, for all i and j, if $x_{ij}^* = 1$, then $x_{ij} > 0$. *Hint*: View X as a feasible solution of the minimum cost flow version of an assignment problem, and view X^* as a feasible assignment.

(b) Use part (a) to show constructively that every doubly stochastic matrix X can be written as $\sum_{i=1}^{k} \gamma_i X_i^*$, where X_i^* are permutation matrices and $\gamma_i \geq 0$, $\sum_{i=1}^{k} \gamma_i = 1$. *Hint*: Define a sequence of matrices $X_0, X_1, \ldots, X_k$, which are nonnegative multiples of doubly stochastic matrices, such that $X_0 = X$, $X_k = 0$, and for all i, $X_i - X_{i+1}$ is a positive multiple of a permutation matrix.

5.17 (Hall's Theorem for Perfect Matrices)

A *perfect* matrix is a matrix with nonnegative integer elements such that the elements of each of its rows and each of its columns add to the same integer k. Show that a perfect matrix can be written as the sum of k permutation matrices (defined in Exercise 5.16). *Hint*: Use the hints and constructions of Exercise 5.16.

5.18 (Total Unimodularity)

Consider the arc incidence matrix E of a graph. This matrix has a row for each node and a column for each arc. The component corresponding to the ith row and a given arc is a 1 if the arc is outgoing from i, is a -1 if the arc is incoming to i, and is a 0 otherwise. Show that E is totally unimodular (cf. the discussion in Section 5.5). *Hint*: We must show that the determinant of each square submatrix of E is 0, 1, or -1. Complete the details of the following argument, which uses induction on the dimension of the submatrix. The submatrices of dimension 1 of E are the scalar components of E, which are 0, 1, or -1. Suppose that the determinant of each square submatrix of dimension $n \geq 1$ is 0, 1, or -1. Consider a square submatrix of dimension $n + 1$. If this matrix has a column with all components 0, the matrix is singular, and its determinant is 0. If the matrix has a column with a single nonzero component (a 1 or a -1), by expanding its determinant along that component and using the induction hypothesis, we see that the determinant is 0, 1, or -1. Finally, if each column of the matrix has two components (a 1 and a -1), the sum of its rows is 0, so the matrix is singular, and its determinant is 0.

6

Dual Ascent Methods

Contents

In this chapter, we discuss our second major class of algorithms for the minimum cost flow problem. In Chapter 4 we introduced the dual problem, and in Chapter 5 we established, as a byproduct of our development of simplex methods, the full extent of the relationship between the primal and dual problems. We are now ready to develop iterative methods for solving the dual problem. These methods generate sequences of dual variables, that is, price vectors. Each new price vector has strictly improved dual cost over the preceding one, unless it is already optimal.

Together with price vectors, dual ascent methods generate corresponding capacity-feasible vectors that satisfy complementary slackness. These flow vectors violate the conservation of flow constraints, except upon termination of the method. We may view dual ascent methods as iterating on flow-price pairs, while maintaining complementary slackness and striving to satisfy flow feasibility, but we will not emphasize this viewpoint. Instead, in our development, we will focus on the dual ascent (cost improvement) property of the successive price vectors, and we will view the corresponding flow vectors merely as a convenient device for generating dual ascent directions.

We will concentrate on two main algorithms: the *primal-dual* method, developed in Section 6.2, and the *relaxation* method, developed in Section 6.3. These methods use different ascent directions, but admit fairly similar implementation.

6.1 DUAL ASCENT

In this section we develop the main ideas underlying the dual ascent approach. We focus on the minimum cost flow problem

$$\text{minimize} \quad \sum_{(i,j)\in\mathcal{A}} a_{ij}x_{ij}$$

subject to the constraints

$$\sum_{\{j|(i,j)\in\mathcal{A}\}} x_{ij} - \sum_{\{j|(j,i)\in\mathcal{A}\}} x_{ji} = s_i, \qquad \forall\, i \in \mathcal{N},$$

$$b_{ij} \le x_{ij} \le c_{ij}, \qquad \forall\, (i,j) \in \mathcal{A}.$$

Throughout the chapter we will assume that the scalars a_{ij}, b_{ij}, c_{ij}, and s_i are all integer. Usually, this is not an important practical restriction. However, there are extensions of the algorithms of this chapter that handle noninteger problem data, as will be discussed later.

The main idea of dual cost improvement (or dual ascent) algorithms is to start with a price vector and successively obtain new price vectors with improved dual cost, with the aim of solving the dual problem. Recall from Section 4.3 that this problem is

$$\text{maximize } q(p)$$
$$\text{subject to no constraint on } p, \tag{6.1}$$

where the dual function q is given by

$$q(p) = \sum_{(i,j) \in \mathcal{A}} q_{ij}(p_i - p_j) + \sum_{i \in \mathcal{N}} s_i p_i, \tag{6.2}$$

with

$$q_{ij}(p_i - p_j) = \min_{b_{ij} \le x_{ij} \le c_{ij}} \left\{ (a_{ij} + p_j - p_i) x_{ij} \right\}$$
$$= \begin{cases} (a_{ij} + p_j - p_i) b_{ij} & \text{if } p_i \le a_{ij} + p_j, \\ (a_{ij} + p_j - p_i) c_{ij} & \text{if } p_i > a_{ij} + p_j. \end{cases} \tag{6.3}$$

It is helpful here to introduce some terminology. For any price vector p, we say that an arc (i, j) is

$$\text{inactive if} \quad p_i < a_{ij} + p_j,$$

$$\text{balanced if} \quad p_i = a_{ij} + p_j,$$

$$\text{active if} \quad p_i > a_{ij} + p_j.$$

The *complementary slackness* (CS) conditions for a flow-price vector pair (x, p), introduced in Section 4.3, can be restated as follows:

$$x_{ij} = b_{ij}, \quad \text{for all inactive arcs } (i, j), \tag{6.4}$$

$$b_{ij} \le x_{ij} \le c_{ij}, \quad \text{for all balanced arcs } (i, j), \tag{6.5}$$

$$x_{ij} = c_{ij}, \quad \text{for all active arcs } (i, j), \tag{6.6}$$

(see Fig. 6.1).

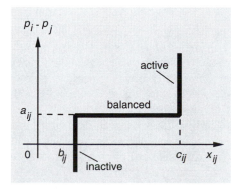

Figure 6.1: Illustration of the complementary slackness conditions. For each arc (i, j), the pair $(x_{ij}, p_i - p_j)$ should lie on the graph shown. The arc is inactive, active, or balanced in the regions shown.

We restate for convenience the following basic duality result, proved in Section 4.3 (cf. Prop. 4.1).

Proposition 6.1: If a feasible flow vector x^* and a price vector p^* satisfy the complementary slackness conditions (6.4)-(6.6), then x^* is an optimal solution of the minimum cost flow problem and p^* is an optimal solution of the dual problem (6.1).

The major dual ascent algorithms select at each iteration a connected subset of nodes $\mathcal{S}$, and change the prices of these nodes by equal amounts, while leaving the prices of all other nodes unchanged. In other words, each iteration involves a price vector change along a direction of the form $d_{\mathcal{S}} = (d_1, \ldots, d_N)$, where

$$d_i = \begin{cases} 1 & \text{if } i \in \mathcal{S}, \\ 0 & \text{if } i \notin \mathcal{S}, \end{cases}$$

and $\mathcal{S}$ is a connected subset of nodes. Such directions will be called *elementary*; see also Section 9.7.

To check whether $d_{\mathcal{S}}$ is a direction of dual ascent, we need to calculate the corresponding directional derivative of the dual cost along $d_{\mathcal{S}}$ and check whether it is positive. From the dual cost expression (6.2)-(6.3), it is seen that this directional derivative is

$$
\begin{aligned}
q'(p; d_{\mathcal{S}}) &= \lim_{\alpha \downarrow 0} \frac{q(p + \alpha d_{\mathcal{S}}) - q(p)}{\alpha} \\
&= \sum_{\substack{(j,i)\,:\,\text{active} \\ j \notin \mathcal{S},\, i \in \mathcal{S}}} c_{ji} + \sum_{\substack{(j,i)\,:\,\text{inactive or balanced} \\ j \notin \mathcal{S},\, i \in \mathcal{S}}} b_{ji} \\
&\quad - \sum_{\substack{(i,j)\,:\,\text{active or balanced} \\ i \in \mathcal{S},\, j \notin \mathcal{S}}} c_{ij} - \sum_{\substack{(i,j)\,:\,\text{inactive} \\ i \in \mathcal{S},\, j \notin \mathcal{S}}} b_{ij} \\
&\quad + \sum_{i \in \mathcal{S}} s_i.
\end{aligned}
\tag{6.7}
$$

In words, the directional derivative $q'(p; d_{\mathcal{S}})$ is the difference between inflow and outflow across the node set $\mathcal{S}$ when the flows of the inactive and active arcs are set at their lower and upper bounds, respectively, and the flow of each balanced arc incident to $\mathcal{S}$ is set to its lower or upper bound depending on whether the arc is incoming to $\mathcal{S}$ or outgoing from $\mathcal{S}$.

To obtain a suitable set $\mathcal{S}$, with positive directional derivative $q'(p, d_{\mathcal{S}})$, it is convenient to maintain a flow vector x satisfying CS together with p. This helps to organize the search for an ascent direction and to detect optimality, as we will now explain.

For a flow vector x, let us define the *surplus* g_i of node i as the difference between total inflow into i minus the total outflow from i, that is,

$$g_i = \sum_{\{j \mid (j,i) \in \mathcal{A}\}} x_{ji} - \sum_{\{j \mid (i,j) \in \mathcal{A}\}} x_{ij} + s_i. \tag{6.8}$$

We have

$$\sum_{i \in \mathcal{S}} g_i = \sum_{\{(j,i) \in \mathcal{A} \mid j \notin \mathcal{S}, i \in \mathcal{S}\}} x_{ji} - \sum_{\{(i,j) \in \mathcal{A} \mid i \in \mathcal{S}, j \notin \mathcal{S}\}} x_{ij} + \sum_{i \in \mathcal{S}} s_i, \tag{6.9}$$

and if x satisfies CS together with p [implying $x_{ij} = b_{ij}$ for all (i,j): inactive, and $x_{ij} = c_{ij}$ for all (i,j): active], we obtain using Eqs. (6.7) and (6.9)

$$\sum_{i \in \mathcal{S}} g_i = q'(p; d_{\mathcal{S}}) + \sum_{\substack{(j,i) \,:\, \text{balanced} \\ j \notin \mathcal{S}, i \in \mathcal{S}}} (x_{ji} - b_{ji})$$

$$+ \sum_{\substack{(i,j): \text{balanced} \\ i \in \mathcal{S}, j \notin \mathcal{S}}} (c_{ij} - x_{ij}) \tag{6.10}$$

$$\geq q'(p; d_{\mathcal{S}}).$$

We see, therefore, that only a node set $\mathcal{S}$ that has positive total surplus is a candidate for generating a direction $d_{\mathcal{S}}$ of dual ascent. In particular, if there is no balanced arc (i,j) with $i \in \mathcal{S}$, $j \notin \mathcal{S}$, and $x_{ij} < c_{ij}$, and no balanced arc (j,i) with $j \notin \mathcal{S}$, $i \in \mathcal{S}$, and $b_{ji} < x_{ji}$, then

$$\sum_{i \in \mathcal{S}} g_i = q'(p; d_{\mathcal{S}}). \tag{6.11}$$

Thus, if $\mathcal{S}$ has positive total surplus, then $d_{\mathcal{S}}$ is an ascent direction. The following lemma expresses this idea and provides the basis for the subsequent algorithms.

Lemma 6.1: Suppose that x and p satisfy the CS conditions, and let $\mathcal{S}$ be a subset of nodes. Let $d_{\mathcal{S}} = (d_1, d_2, \ldots, d_N)$ be the vector with $d_i = 1$ if $i \in \mathcal{S}$ and $d_i = 0$ otherwise, and assume that

$$\sum_{i \in \mathcal{S}} g_i > 0.$$

Then either $d_{\mathcal{S}}$ is a dual ascent direction, that is,

$$q'(p; d_{\mathcal{S}}) > 0,$$

or else there exist nodes $i \in \mathcal{S}$ and $j \notin \mathcal{S}$ such that either (i,j) is a balanced arc with $x_{ij} < c_{ij}$ or (j,i) is a balanced arc with $b_{ji} < x_{ji}$.

Proof: Follows from Eq. (6.10). **Q.E.D.**

Overview of Dual Ascent Algorithms

The algorithms of this chapter start with and maintain an integer flow-price vector pair (x, p), satisfying CS. They operate iteratively. At the beginning of each iteration, a subset of nodes $\mathcal{S}$ is selected such that

$$\sum_{i \in \mathcal{S}} g_i > 0.$$

Initially $\mathcal{S}$ consists of one or more nodes with positive surplus, which are chosen based on some rule that is algorithm-dependent. According to the preceding lemma, there are two possibilities (which are not mutually exclusive):

(a) *Dual ascent is possible*: $\mathcal{S}$ defines a dual ascent direction

$$d_{\mathcal{S}} = (d_1, d_2, \ldots, d_N),$$

where $d_i = 1$ if $i \in \mathcal{S}$, and $d_i = 0$ otherwise.

(b) *Enlargement of $\mathcal{S}$ is possible*: $\mathcal{S}$ can be enlarged by adding a node $j \notin \mathcal{S}$ with the property described in Lemma 6.1, that is, for some $i \in \mathcal{S}$, either (i, j) is a balanced arc with $x_{ij} < c_{ij}$, or (j, i) is a balanced arc with $b_{ji} < x_{ji}$.

In case (b), there are two possibilities:

(1) $g_j \geq 0$, in which case,

$$\sum_{i \in \mathcal{S} \cup \{j\}} g_i > 0,$$

and the process can be continued with

$$\mathcal{S} \cup \{j\}$$

replacing $\mathcal{S}$.

(2) $g_j < 0$, in which case, it can be seen that there is a path originating at some node i of the starting set $\mathcal{S}$ and ending at node j that is *unblocked*, that is, all its arcs have room for a flow increase in the direction from i to j (see Fig. 6.2). We refer to such a path as an *augmenting path*. By increasing the flow of the forward arcs (direction from i to j) of the path and by decreasing the flow of the backward arcs (direction from j to i) of the path, we can bring both surpluses g_i and g_j closer to zero by an integer amount while leaving the surplus of all other nodes unaffected and maintaining CS.

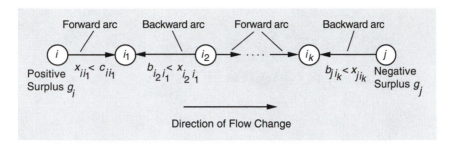

Figure 6.2: Illustration of an augmenting path. The initial node i and the final node j have positive and negative surplus, respectively. Furthermore, the path is unblocked, that is, each arc on the path has room for flow change in the direction from i to j. A flow change of magnitude $\delta > 0$ in this direction reduces the total absolute surplus $\sum_{m \in \mathcal{N}} |g_m|$ by 2δ provided $\delta \leq \min\{g_i, -g_j\}$.

Since the total absolute surplus $\sum_{i \in \mathcal{N}} |g_i|$ cannot be indefinitely reduced by integer amounts, it is seen that starting from an integer flow-price vector pair satisfying CS, after at most a finite number of iterations in which flow augmentations occur without finding an ascent direction, one of three things will happen:

(a) A dual ascent direction will be found; this direction can be used to improve the dual cost by an integer amount.

(b) $g_i = 0$ for all i; in this case the flow vector x is feasible, and since it satisfies CS together with p, by Prop. 6.1, x is primal-optimal and p is dual-optimal.

(c) $g_i \leq 0$ for all i but $g_i < 0$ for at least one i; since by adding Eq. (6.9) over all $i \in \mathcal{N}$ we have $\sum_{i \in \mathcal{N}} s_i = \sum_{i \in \mathcal{N}} g_i$ it follows that $\sum_{i \in \mathcal{N}} s_i < 0$, so the problem is infeasible.

Thus, for a feasible problem, the procedure just outlined can be used to find a dual ascent direction and improve the dual cost starting at any nonoptimal integer price vector. Figure 6.3 provides an illustration for a very simple problem.

In the next two sections, we discuss two different dual ascent methods. The first, known as *primal-dual*, in its classical form, tries at each iteration to use the *steepest ascent* direction, that is, the elementary direction with maximal directional derivative. We will show how this method can also be implemented by means of a shortest path computation. The second method, called *relaxation*, is usually faster in practice. It tries to use directions that are not necessarily steepest, but can be computed more quickly than the steepest ascent direction.

Another way to describe the difference between the primal-dual and the relaxation methods, is to consider the set $\mathcal{S}$ and the two possibilities described in Lemma 6.1:

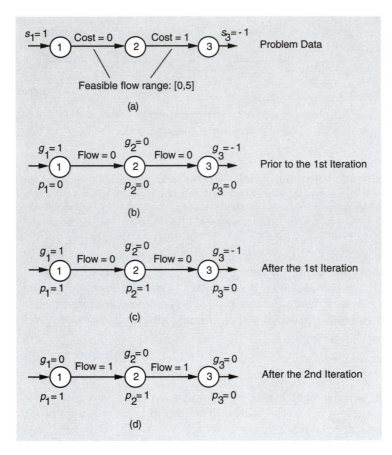

Figure 6.3: Illustration of a dual ascent method for the simple problem described in (a). Initially, we have $x = (0, 0)$ and $p = (0, 0, 0)$, as shown in (b).

The first iteration starts with $\mathcal{S} = \{1\}$. It can be seen using Eq. (6.10), that the directional derivative $q'(p; d_{\mathcal{S}})$ is -4 ($s_1 - c_{12} = 1 - 5 = -4$), so $d_{\mathcal{S}} = (1, 0, 0)$ is not a direction of ascent. We thus enlarge $\mathcal{S}$ by adding node 2 using the balanced arc $(1, 2)$. Since there is no incident balanced arc to $\mathcal{S} = \{1, 2\}$, the direction $d_{\mathcal{S}} = (1, 1, 0)$ is a direction of ascent [using Eq. (6.10), $q'(p; d_{\mathcal{S}}) = s_1 + s_2 = 1$]. We thus increase the prices of the nodes in $\mathcal{S}$ by a common increment γ, and we choose $\gamma = 1$ because this is the increment that maximizes the dual function along the direction $d_{\mathcal{S}}$ starting from p; this can be seen by checking the directional derivative of q at the price vector $(\gamma, \gamma, 0)$ along the direction $d_{\mathcal{S}}$ and finding that it switches from positive ($= 1$) to negative ($= -4$) at $\gamma = 1$ where the arc $(2, 3)$ becomes balanced.

The second iteration starts again with $\mathcal{S} = \{1\}$. As in the first iteration, $\mathcal{S}$ is enlarged to $\mathcal{S} = \{1, 2\}$. Since the corresponding direction $d_{\mathcal{S}} = (1, 1, 0)$ is not a direction of ascent [$q'(p; d_{\mathcal{S}}) = -4$], we explore the balanced incident arc $(2, 3)$ and we discover the negative surplus node 3. The augmenting path $(1, 2, 3)$ has now been obtained, and the corresponding augmentation sets the flows of the arcs $(1, 2)$ and $(2, 3)$ to 1. Since now all node surpluses become zero, the algorithm terminates; $x = (1, 1)$ is an optimal primal solution and $p = (1, 1, 0)$ is an optimal dual solution.

(a) Use $\mathcal{S}$ to define an ascent direction [if $q'(p; d_\mathcal{S}) > 0$] or

(b) Enlarge the set $\mathcal{S}$ with a node $j \notin \mathcal{S}$ such that either (i, j) is a balanced arc with $x_{ij} < c_{ij}$ or (j, i) is a balanced arc with $b_{ji} < x_{ji}$ (if such a node j exists).

The primal-dual and the relaxation methods operate identically when only one of the alternatives (a) and (b) is available. When, however, $\mathcal{S}$ and p are such that both alternatives are possible, the primal-dual method chooses alternative (b) while the relaxation method chooses alternative (a).

6.2 THE PRIMAL-DUAL (SEQUENTIAL SHORTEST PATH) METHOD

The primal-dual algorithm starts with any integer pair (x, p) satisfying CS. One possibility is to choose the integer vector p arbitrarily and to set $x_{ij} = b_{ij}$ if (i, j) is inactive or balanced, and $x_{ij} = c_{ij}$ otherwise. (Prior knowledge could be built into the initial choice of x and p using, for example, the results of an earlier optimization.) The algorithm preserves the integrality and CS property of the pair (x, p) throughout.

At the start of the typical iteration, we have an integer pair (x, p) satisfying CS. The iteration indicates that the primal problem is infeasible, or else indicates that (x, p) is optimal, or else transforms this pair into another pair satisfying CS.

In particular, if $g_i \leq 0$ for all i, then in view of the fact $\sum_{i \in \mathcal{N}} g_i = \sum_{i \in \mathcal{N}} s_i$ [see Eq. (6.9) with $\mathcal{S} = \mathcal{N}$], there are two possibilities:

(1) $g_i < 0$ for some i, in which case $\sum_{i \in \mathcal{N}} s_i < 0$ and the problem is infeasible.

(2) $g_i = 0$ for all i, in which case x is feasible and therefore also optimal, since it satisfies CS together with p.

In either case, the algorithm terminates.

If on the other hand we have $g_i > 0$ for at least one node i, the iteration starts by selecting a nonempty subset I of nodes i with $g_i > 0$. The iteration maintains two sets of nodes $\mathcal{S}$ and $\mathcal{L}$, with $\mathcal{S} \subset \mathcal{L}$. Initially, $\mathcal{S}$ is empty and $\mathcal{L}$ consists of the subset I. We use the following terminology.

$\mathcal{S}$: Set of *scanned* nodes (these are the nodes whose incident arcs have been "examined" during the iteration).

$\mathcal{L}$: Set of *labeled* nodes (these are the nodes that have either been scanned during the iteration or are current candidates for scanning).

In the course of the iteration we continue to add nodes to $\mathcal{L}$ and $\mathcal{S}$ until either an augmenting path is found or $\mathcal{L} = \mathcal{S}$, in which case $d_\mathcal{S}$ will be shown to be an ascent direction. The iteration also maintains a *label* for every node $i \in \mathcal{L} - I$, which is an incident arc of i. The labels are useful for constructing augmenting paths (see Step 3 of the following iteration).

Primal-Dual Iteration

Step 0 (Initialization): Select a set I of nodes i with $g_i > 0$. [If no such node can be found, terminate; the pair (x, p) is optimal if $g_i = 0$ for all i; otherwise the problem is infeasible.] Set $\mathcal{L} := I$ and $\mathcal{S} :=$ empty, and go to Step 1.

Step 1 (Choose a Node to Scan): If $\mathcal{S} = \mathcal{L}$, go to Step 4; else select a node $i \in \mathcal{L} - \mathcal{S}$, set $\mathcal{S} := \mathcal{S} \cup \{i\}$, and go to Step 2.

Step 2 (Label Neighbor Nodes of i): Add to $\mathcal{L}$ all nodes $j \notin \mathcal{L}$ such that either (j, i) is balanced and $b_{ji} < x_{ji}$ or (i, j) is balanced and $x_{ij} < c_{ij}$; also for every such j, give to j the label "(j, i)" if (j, i) is balanced and $b_{ji} < x_{ji}$, and otherwise give to j the label "(i, j)." If for all the nodes j just added to $\mathcal{L}$ we have $g_j \geq 0$, go to Step 1. Else select one of these nodes j with $g_j < 0$ and go to Step 3.

Step 3 (Flow Augmentation): An augmenting path P has been found that begins at a node i belonging to the initial set I and ends at the node j identified in Step 2. The path is constructed by tracing labels backward starting from j, and is such that we have

$$x_{mn} < c_{mn}, \quad \forall (m, n) \in P^+,$$

$$x_{mn} > b_{mn}, \quad \forall (m, n) \in P^-,$$

where P^+ and P^- are the sets of forward and backward arcs of P, respectively. Let

$$\delta = \min \{ g_i, -g_j, \{ c_{mn} - x_{mn} \mid (m, n) \in P^+ \},$$
$$\{ x_{mn} - b_{mn} \mid (m, n) \in P^- \} \}.$$

Increase by δ the flows of all arcs in P^+, decrease by δ the flows of all arcs in P^-, and go to the next iteration.

Step 4 (Price Change): Let

$$\gamma = \min \{ \{ p_j + a_{ij} - p_i \mid (i, j) \in \mathcal{A}, x_{ij} < c_{ij}, i \in \mathcal{S}, j \notin \mathcal{S} \}, \\ \{ p_j - a_{ji} - p_i \mid (j, i) \in \mathcal{A}, b_{ji} < x_{ji}, i \in \mathcal{S}, j \notin \mathcal{S} \} \}. \tag{6.12}$$

Set
$$p_i := \begin{cases} p_i + \gamma & \text{if } i \in \mathcal{S}, \\ p_i & \text{otherwise.} \end{cases}$$

Add to $\mathcal{L}$ all nodes j for which the minimum in Eq. (6.11) is attained by an arc (i, j) or an arc (j, i); also for every such j, give to j the label "(i, j)" if the minimum in Eq. (6.12) is attained by an arc (i, j), and otherwise give to j the label "(j, i)." If for all the nodes j just added to $\mathcal{L}$ we have $g_j \geq 0$, go to Step 1. Else select one of these nodes j with $g_j < 0$ and go to Step 3. [*Note:* If there is no arc (i, j) with $x_{ij} < c_{ij}$, $i \in \mathcal{S}$, and $j \notin \mathcal{S}$, or arc (j, i) with $b_{ji} < x_{ji}$, $i \in \mathcal{S}$, and $j \notin \mathcal{S}$, the problem is infeasible and the algorithm terminates; see Prop. 6.2 that follows.]

Note the following regarding the primal-dual iteration:

(a) All operations of the iteration preserve the integrality of the flow-price vector pair.

(b) The iteration maintains CS of the flow-price vector pair. To see this, note that arcs with both ends in $\mathcal{S}$, which are balanced just before a price change, continue to be balanced after a price change. This means that a flow augmentation step, even if it occurs following several executions of Step 4, changes only flows of balanced arcs, so it cannot destroy CS. Also, a price change in Step 4 maintains CS because no arc flow is modified in this step and the price increment γ of Eq. (6.12) is such that no arc changes status from active to inactive or vice versa.

(c) At all times we have $\mathcal{S} \subset \mathcal{L}$. Furthermore, when Step 4 is entered, we have $\mathcal{S} = \mathcal{L}$ and $\mathcal{L}$ contains no node with negative surplus. Therefore, based on the logic of Step 2, there is no balanced arc (i, j) with $x_{ij} < c_{ij}$, $i \in \mathcal{S}$, and $j \notin \mathcal{S}$, and no balanced arc (j, i) with $b_{ji} < x_{ji}$, $i \in \mathcal{S}$, and $j \notin \mathcal{S}$. It follows from the discussion preceding Lemma 6.1 [cf. Eq. (6.11)] that $d_{\mathcal{S}}$ is an ascent direction.

(d) Only a finite number of price changes occur at each iteration, so each iteration executes to completion, either terminating with a flow augmentation in Step 3, or with an indication of infeasibility in Step 4. To see this, note that between two price changes, the set $\mathcal{L}$ is enlarged by at least one node, so there can be no more than N price changes per iteration.

(e) Only a finite number of flow augmentation steps are executed by the algorithm, since each of these reduces the total absolute surplus $\sum_{i \in \mathcal{N}} |g_i|$ by an integer amount [by (a) above], while price changes do not affect the total absolute surplus.

(f) The algorithm terminates. The reason is that each iteration will execute to completion [by (d) above], and will involve exactly one augmentation, while there will be only a finite number of augmentations
[cf. (e) above].

The following proposition establishes the validity of the method.

Proposition 6.2: Consider the minimum cost flow problem and assume that a_{ij}, b_{ij}, c_{ij}, and s_i are all integer.

  (a) If the problem is feasible, then the primal-dual method terminates with an integer optimal flow vector x and an integer optimal price vector p.

  (b) If the problem is infeasible, then the primal-dual method terminates either because $g_i \leq 0$ for all i and $g_i < 0$ for at least one i
or because there is no arc (i, j) with $x_{ij} < c_{ij}$, $i \in \mathcal{S}$, and $j \notin \mathcal{S}$,
or arc (j, i) with $b_{ji} < x_{ji}$, $i \in \mathcal{S}$, and $j \notin \mathcal{S}$ in Step 4.

Proof: The algorithm terminates as argued earlier, and there are three
possibilities:

(1) The algorithm terminates because all nodes have zero surplus. In this
case the flow-price vector pair obtained upon termination is feasible
and satisfies CS, so it is optimal.

(2) The algorithm terminates because $g_i \leq 0$ for all i and $g_i < 0$ for at
least one i. In this case the problem is infeasible, since for a feasible
problem we must have $\sum_{i \in \mathcal{N}} g_i = 0$.

(3) The algorithm terminates because there is no arc (i, j) with $x_{ij} < c_{ij}$,
$i \in \mathcal{S}$, and $j \notin \mathcal{S}$, or arc (j, i) with $b_{ji} < x_{ji}$, $i \in \mathcal{S}$, and $j \notin \mathcal{S}$ in
Step 4. Then the flux across the cut $Q = [\mathcal{S}, \mathcal{N} - \mathcal{S}]$ is equal to the
capacity $C(Q)$ and is also equal to the sum of the divergences of the
nodes of $\mathcal{S}$, which is $\sum_{i \in \mathcal{S}}(s_i - g_i)$ [cf. Eq. (6.8)]. Since $g_i \geq 0$ for all
$i \in \mathcal{S}$, $g_i > 0$ for the nodes $i \in I$, and $I \subset \mathcal{S}$, we see that

$$C(Q) < \sum_{i \in \mathcal{S}} s_i.$$

This implies that the problem is infeasible, since for any feasible flow
vector we must have

$$\sum_{i \in \mathcal{S}} s_i = F(Q) \leq C(Q),$$

where $F(Q)$ is the corresponding flux across Q. [Another way to show
that the problem is infeasible in this case is to observe that $d_{\mathcal{S}}$ is a

dual ascent direction, and if no arc (i, j) with the property stated exists, the rate of increase of the dual function remains unchanged as we move indefinitely along d_S starting from p. This implies that the dual optimal value is infinite or equivalently (by Prop. 5.8) that the primal problem is infeasible.]

Since termination can occur only under the above circumstances, the desired conclusion follows.   **Q.E.D.**

There are a number of variations of the primal-dual method, using different choices of the initial set I of positive surplus nodes. The two most common possibilities are:

(1) I consists of a *single* node i with $g_i > 0$.

(2) I consists of *all* nodes i with $g_i > 0$.

The primal-dual method was originally proposed with the latter choice. In this case, whenever there is a price change, the set S contains all nodes with positive surplus, and from the directional derivative formulas (6.10) and (6.11), it follows that the ascent direction used in Step 4 has the *maximum* possible directional derivative among elementary directions. This leads to the interpretation of the primal-dual method as a steepest ascent method.

Figure 6.4 traces the steps of the primal-dual method for a simple example.

The Shortest Path Implementation

We will now provide an alternative implementation of the primal-dual method in terms of a shortest path computation. This is known as the *sequential shortest path method*; it will be seen to be mathematically equivalent with the primal-dual method given earlier in the sense that it produces the same sequence of flow-price vector pairs.

Given a pair (x, p) satisfying CS, define the *reduced cost* of an arc (i, j) by

$$r_{ij} = a_{ij} + p_j - p_i. \tag{6.13}$$

Recall that an unblocked path P with respect to x is a path such that $x_{ij} < c_{ij}$ for all forward arcs $(i, j) \in P^+$ and $b_{ij} < x_{ij}$ for all backward arcs $(i, j) \in P^-$. Furthermore, P is an augmenting path if its start and end nodes have positive and negative surplus, respectively. We define the *length* of an unblocked path P by

$$L_P = \sum_{(i,j)\in P^+} r_{ij} - \sum_{(i,j)\in P^-} r_{ij}. \tag{6.14}$$

Note that since (x, p) satisfies CS, all forward arcs of an unblocked path P must be inactive or balanced, while all backward arcs of P must be active

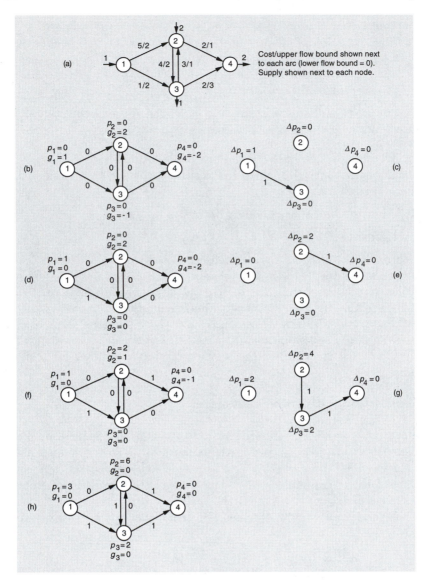

Figure 6.4: Example illustrating the primal-dual method, starting with zero prices.

(a) Problem data.

(b) Initial flows, prices, and surpluses.

(c) Augmenting path and price changes Δp_i of first iteration ($I = \{1\}$).

(d) Flows, prices, and surpluses after the first iteration.

(e) Augmenting path and price changes Δp_i of second iteration ($I = \{2\}$).

(f) Flows, prices, and surpluses after the second iteration.

(g) Augmenting path and price changes Δp_i of third iteration ($I = \{2\}$). There are two price changes here: first p_2 increases by 2, and then p_1, p_2, and p_3 increase by 2.

(h) Flows, prices, and surpluses after the third iteration. The algorithm terminates with an optimal flow-price pair, since all node surpluses are zero.

or balanced [cf. Eqs. (6.4)-(6.6)], so we have

$$r_{ij} \geq 0, \qquad \forall\ (i,j) \in P^+, \qquad\qquad (6.15)$$

$$r_{ij} \leq 0, \qquad \forall\ (i,j) \in P^-. \qquad\qquad (6.16)$$

Thus, the length of P is nonnegative.

The sequential shortest path method starts each iteration with an integer pair (x,p) satisfying CS and with a set I of nodes i with $g_i > 0$, and proceeds as follows.

Sequential Shortest Path Iteration

Construct an augmenting path P with respect to x that has minimum length over all augmenting paths with respect to x that start at some node $i \in I$. Then, carry out an augmentation along P (cf. Step 3 of the primal-dual iteration) and modify the node prices as follows:

Let $\bar{d}$ be the length of P and for each node $m \in \mathcal{N}$, let d_m be the minimum of the lengths of the unblocked paths with respect to x that start at some node in I and end at m ($d_m = \infty$ if no such path exists). The new price vector $\bar{p}$ is given by

$$\bar{p}_m = p_m + \max\{0, \bar{d} - d_m\}, \qquad \forall\ m \in \mathcal{N}. \qquad (6.17)$$

The method terminates under the following circumstances:

(a) All nodes i have zero surplus; in this case it will be seen that the current pair (x,p) is primal and dual optimal.

(b) $g_i \leq 0$ for all i and $g_i < 0$ for at least one i; in this case the problem is infeasible, since $\sum_{i \in \mathcal{N}} s_i = \sum_{i \in \mathcal{N}} g_i < 0$.

(c) There is no augmenting path with respect to x that starts at some node in I; in this case it will be seen that the problem is infeasible.

We will show shortly that the method preserves the integrality and the CS property of the pair (x,p), and that it terminates.

It is important to note that the shortest path computation can be executed using the standard shortest path algorithms described in Chapter 2. The idea is to use r_{ij} as the length of each forward arc (i,j) of an unblocked path, and to reverse the direction of each backward arc (i,j) of an unblocked path and to use $-r_{ij}$ as its length [cf. the unblocked path length formula (6.14)]. In particular, the iteration can be executed using the following procedure:

Consider the *residual graph*, which has the same node set $\mathcal{N}$ of the original problem graph, and has

an arc (i,j) with length r_{ij} for every arc $(i,j) \in \mathcal{A}$ with $x_{ij} < c_{ij}$, an arc (j, i) with length $-r_{ij}$ for every arc $(i, j) \in \mathcal{A}$ with $b_{ij} < x_{ij}$.

[If this creates two arcs in the same direction between two nodes, discard the arc with the larger length (in case of a tie, discard either arc).] Find a path P that is shortest among paths of the residual graph that start at some node in I and end at some node with negative surplus. Find also the shortest distances d_m from nodes of I to all other nodes m [or at least to those nodes m with d_m less than the length of P; cf. Eq. (6.17)].

Note here that by Eqs. (6.15) and (6.16), the arc lengths of the residual graph are nonnegative, so Dijkstra's method can be used for the shortest path computation. Since all forward paths in the residual graph correspond to unblocked paths in the original problem graph, and corresponding paths have the same length, it is seen that the shortest path P is an augmenting path as required and that the shortest distances d_m yield the vector $\overline{p}$ defined by Eq. (6.17).

Figure 6.5 illustrates the sequential shortest path method and shows the sequence of residual graphs for the example worked out earlier (cf. Fig. 6.4). We now prove the validity of the method.

Proposition 6.3: Consider the minimum cost flow problem and assume that a_{ij}, b_{ij}, c_{ij}, and s_i are all integer. Then, for the sequential shortest path method, the following hold:

(a) Each iteration maintains the integrality and the CS property of the pair (x, p).

(b) If the problem is feasible, then the method terminates with an integer optimal flow vector x and an integer optimal price vector p.

(c) If the problem is infeasible, then the method terminates either because $g_i \leq 0$ for all i and $g_i < 0$ for at least one i, or because there is no augmenting path starting at some node of the set I and ending at some node with negative surplus.

Proof: (a) We will show that if the starting pair (x, p) of an iteration is integer and satisfies CS, the same is true for a pair $(\overline{x}, \overline{p})$ produced by the iteration. Indeed, a flow augmentation maintains the integrality of the flows, since the upper and lower flow bounds are assumed integer. Furthermore, the arc lengths of the residual graph are integer, so by Eq. (6.17), $\overline{p}$ is integer.

To show that $(\overline{x}, \overline{p})$ satisfies CS, consider an arc (i, j) for which $\overline{x}_{ij} < c_{ij}$. We will show that $\overline{p}_i - \overline{p}_j \leq a_{ij}$. We distinguish two cases:

(1) $x_{ij} = c_{ij}$. In this case, we have $b_{ij} < x_{ij}$, the direction of (i, j) is reversed in the residual graph, and the reverse arc (j, i) lies on the

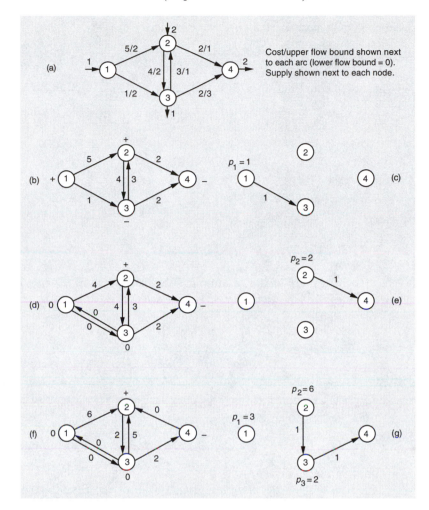

Figure 6.5: The sequential shortest path method applied to the problem of Fig. 6.4, starting with all zero prices. The sequences of flows, prices, and surpluses are the same as those generated by the primal-dual method.

(a) Problem data.

(b) Initial residual graph with the arc lengths shown next to the arcs. The nodes with positive, zero, and negative surplus are indicated by "+", "0", and "−", respectively.

(c) Shortest augmenting path and changed prices of first iteration ($I = \{1\}$).

(d) Residual graph with the arc lengths shown next to the arcs after the first iteration.

(e) Shortest augmenting path and changed prices of second iteration ($I = \{2\}$).

(f) Residual graph with the arc lengths shown next to the arcs after the second iteration.

(g) Shortest augmenting path and changed prices of third (and final) iteration ($I = \{2\}$).

shortest augmenting path P. Hence, we have

$$d_i \le \overline{d}, \qquad d_j \le \overline{d}, \qquad d_i = d_j - r_{ij}.$$

Using these equations, and Eqs. (6.13) and (6.17), we obtain

$$\begin{aligned}
\overline{p}_i - \overline{p}_j &= p_i - p_j + \max\{0, \overline{d} - d_i\} - \max\{0, \overline{d} - d_j\} \\
&= p_i - p_j - (d_i - d_j) \\
&= p_i - p_j + r_{ij} \\
&= a_{ij}.
\end{aligned}$$

(2) $x_{ij} < c_{ij}$. In this case we have

$$d_j \le d_i + r_{ij},$$

since (i, j) is an arc of the residual graph with length r_{ij}. Using this relation and the nonnegativity of r_{ij}, we see that

$$\begin{aligned}
\max\{0, \overline{d} - d_i\} &\le \max\{0, \overline{d} - d_j + r_{ij}\} \\
&\le \max\{r_{ij}, \overline{d} - d_j + r_{ij}\} \\
&= \max\{0, \overline{d} - d_j\} + r_{ij}.
\end{aligned}$$

Hence, we have

$$\overline{p}_i - \overline{p}_j = p_i - p_j + \max\{0, \overline{d} - d_i\} - \max\{0, \overline{d} - d_j\} \le p_i - p_j + r_{ij} = a_{ij}.$$

Thus, in both cases we have $\overline{p}_i - \overline{p}_j \le a_{ij}$. We can similarly show that if $b_{ij} < \overline{x}_{ij}$, then $\overline{p}_i - \overline{p}_j \ge a_{ij}$, completing the proof of the CS property of the pair $(\overline{x}, \overline{p})$.

(b) and (c) Every completed iteration in which a shortest augmenting path is found reduces the total absolute surplus $\sum_{i \in \mathcal{N}} |g_i|$ by an integer amount, so termination must occur. Part (a) shows that at the start of each iteration, the pair (x, p) satisfies CS. There are two possibilities:

(1) $g_i \le 0$ for all i. In this case, either $g_i = 0$ for all i in which case x is feasible, and x and p are primal and dual optimal, respectively, since they satisfy CS, or else $g_i < 0$ for some i, in which case the problem is infeasible.

(2) $g_i > 0$ for at least one i. In this case we can select a nonempty set I of nodes with positive surplus, form the residual graph, and attempt the corresponding shortest path computation. There are two possibilities: either a shortest augmenting path is found, in which case the iteration will be completed with an attendant reduction of the total absolute

surplus, or else there is no unblocked path with respect to x from a node of I to a node with negative surplus. In the latter case, we claim that the problem is infeasible. Indeed, by Prop. 3.1 (more accurately, the generalization given in Exercise 3.11 of Ch. 3), there exists a saturated cut $Q = [\mathcal{S}, \mathcal{N} - \mathcal{S}]$ such that all nodes of I belong to $\mathcal{S}$ and all nodes with negative surplus belong to $\mathcal{N} - \mathcal{S}$. The flux across Q is equal to the capacity $C(Q)$ of Q and is also equal to the sum of the divergences of the nodes of $\mathcal{S}$, which is $\sum_{i \in \mathcal{S}}(s_i - g_i)$ [cf. Eq. (6.8)]. Since $g_i \geq 0$ for all $i \in \mathcal{S}$, $g_i > 0$ for the nodes $i \in I$, and $I \subset \mathcal{S}$, we see that

$$C(Q) < \sum_{i \in \mathcal{S}} s_i.$$

This implies that the problem is infeasible, since for any feasible flow vector we must have $\sum_{i \in \mathcal{S}} s_i = F(Q) \leq C(Q)$, where $F(Q)$ is the corresponding flux across Q.

Thus, termination of the algorithm must occur in the manner stated in the proposition.   **Q.E.D.**

By appropriately adapting the shortest path algorithms of Chapter 2, one can obtain a variety of implementations of the sequential shortest path iteration. Here is an example, which adapts the generic single origin/single destination algorithm of Section 2.5.2 and supplements it with a labeling procedure that constructs the augmenting path. We introduce a candidate list V, a label d_i for each node i, a shortest distance estimate $\overline{d}$, and a node $\overline{j}$ whose initial choice is immaterial. Given a pair (x, p) satisfying CS and a set I of nodes with positive surplus, we set initially

$$V = I, \qquad \overline{d} = \infty,$$

$$d_i = \begin{cases} 0 & \text{if } i \in I, \\ \infty & \text{if } i \notin I. \end{cases}$$

The shortest path computation proceeds in steps and terminates when V is empty. The typical step (assuming V is nonempty) is as follows:

Shortest Path Step in a Sequential Shortest Path Iteration

Remove a node i from V. For each outgoing arc $(i, j) \in \mathcal{A}$, with $x_{ij} < c_{ij}$, if

$$d_i + r_{ij} < \min\{d_j, \overline{d}\},$$

give the label "(i, j)" to j, set

$$d_j := d_i + r_{ij},$$

add j to V if it does not already belong to V, and if $g_j < 0$, set $\overline{d} = d_i + r_{ij}$ and $\overline{j} = j$. Also, for each incoming arc $(j, i) \in \mathcal{A}$, with $b_{ji} < x_{ji}$, if

$$d_i - r_{ji} < \min\{d_j, \overline{d}\},$$

give the label "(j, i)" to j, set

$$d_j := d_i - r_{ji},$$

add j to V if it does not already belong to V, and if $g_j < 0$, set $\overline{d} = d_i - r_{ji}$ and $\overline{j} = j$.

When the shortest path computation terminates, an augmenting path of length $\overline{d}$ can be obtained by tracing labels backward from the node $\overline{j}$ to some node $i \in I$. The new price vector $\overline{p}$ is obtained via the equation $\overline{p}_m = p_m + \max\{0, \overline{d} - d_m\}$ for all $m \in \mathcal{N}$ [cf. Eq. (6.17)]. Note that if the node i removed from V has the minimum label property

$$d_i = \min_{j \in V} d_j,$$

the preceding algorithm corresponds to Dijkstra's method. However, other methods can also be used for selecting the node removed from V, including the SLF and threshold methods discussed in Section 2.4.

We finally note that the primal-dual method discussed earlier and the sequential shortest path method are mathematically equivalent in that they produce identical sequences of pairs (x, p), as shown by the following proposition (for an example, compare the calculations of Figs. 6.4 and 6.5). In fact with some thought, it can be seen that the primal-dual iteration amounts to the use of a form of Dijkstra's algorithm to calculate the shortest augmenting path and the corresponding distances.

Proposition 6.4: Suppose that a primal-dual iteration starts with a pair (x, p), and let I be the initial set of nodes i with $g_i > 0$. Then:

  (a) An augmenting path P may be generated in the augmentation Step 3 of the iteration (through some order of operations in Steps 1 and 2) if and only if P has minimum length over all augmenting paths with respect to x that start at some node in I.

  (b) If $\overline{p}$ is the price vector produced by the iteration, then

$$\overline{p}_m = p_m + \max\{0, \overline{d} - d_m\}, \qquad \forall\, m \in \mathcal{N}, \tag{6.18}$$

> where $\overline{d}$ is the length of the augmenting path P of the iteration and for each $m \in \mathcal{N}$, d_m is the minimum of the lengths of the unblocked paths with respect to x that start at some node in I and end at m.

Proof: Let $\overline{k} \geq 0$ be the number of price changes that occur in the given iteration. If $\overline{k} = 0$, i.e., no price change occurs, then any augmenting path P that can be produced by the iteration consists of balanced arcs, so its length is zero. Hence P has minimum length as stated in part (a). Furthermore, $\overline{p} = p$, which verifies Eq. (6.18).

Assume that $\overline{k} \geq 1$, let $\mathcal{S}_k$, $k = 1, \ldots, \overline{k}$, be the set of scanned nodes $\mathcal{S}$ when the kth price change occurs, and let γ_k, $k = 1, \ldots, \overline{k}$, be the corresponding price increment [cf. Eq. (6.12)]. Let also $\mathcal{S}_{\overline{k}+1}$ be the set $\mathcal{S}$ at the end of the iteration. We note that the sets $\mathcal{S}_k$ (and hence also γ_k) depend only on (x, p) and the set I, and are independent of the order of operations in Steps 1 and 2. In particular, $\mathcal{S}_1 - I$ is the set of all nodes j such that there exists an unblocked path of balanced arcs [with respect to (x, p)] that starts at some node $i \in I$ and ends at j. Thus, $\mathcal{S}_1$ and also γ_1, is uniquely defined by I and (x, p). Proceeding inductively, it is seen that $\mathcal{S}_{k+1} - \mathcal{S}_k$ is the set of all nodes j such that there exists an unblocked path of balanced arcs [with respect to (x, p^k), where p^k is the price vector after k price changes] that starts at some node $i \in \mathcal{S}_k$ and ends at j. Thus, $\mathcal{S}_{k+1}$ and γ_{k+1} are uniquely defined by I and (x, p) if $\mathcal{S}_1, \ldots, \mathcal{S}_k$ and $\gamma_1, \ldots, \gamma_k$ are.

It can be seen from Eq. (6.12) that for all k,

γ_k = minimum over the lengths of all (single arc) unblocked paths

starting at a node $i \in \mathcal{S}_k$ and ending at a node $j \notin \mathcal{S}_k$.

Using this property, and an induction argument (left for the reader), we can show that d_m, which is defined as the minimum over the lengths of all unblocked paths that start at some node $i \in I$ and end at node m, satisfies for all k,

$$d_m = \gamma_1 + \gamma_2 + \cdots + \gamma_k, \qquad \forall \, m \in \mathcal{S}_{k+1} - \mathcal{S}_k. \qquad (6.19)$$

Furthermore, the length of any unblocked path that starts at some node $i \in I$ and ends at a node $m \notin \mathcal{S}_{k+1}$ is larger than $\gamma_1 + \gamma_2 + \cdots + \gamma_k$. In particular, the length of any augmenting path produced by the iteration is

$$\gamma_1 + \gamma_2 + \cdots + \gamma_{\overline{k}},$$

so it has the property stated in part (a). Also, the price vector $\overline{p}$ produced by the primal-dual iteration is given by

$$\overline{p}_m = \begin{cases} p_m + \gamma_1 + \gamma_2 + \cdots + \gamma_k & \text{if } m \in \mathcal{S}_{k+1} - \mathcal{S}_k, \ k = 1, \ldots, \overline{k}, \\ p_m & \text{otherwise,} \end{cases}$$

which in view of Eq. (6.19), agrees with Eq. (6.18).   **Q.E.D.**

6.3   THE RELAXATION METHOD

The relaxation method admits a similar implementation to the one of the primal-dual method, but computes ascent directions much faster. In particular, while in the primal-dual method we continue to enlarge the scanned set $\mathcal{S}$ until it is equal to the labeled set $\mathcal{L}$ (in which case we are sure that $d_{\mathcal{S}}$ is an ascent direction), in the relaxation method we stop adding nodes to $\mathcal{S}$ immediately after $d_{\mathcal{S}}$ becomes an ascent direction [this is done by computing the directional derivative $q'(p; d_{\mathcal{S}})$ using an efficient incremental method and by checking its sign]. In practice, $\mathcal{S}$ often consists of a single node, in which case the ascent direction is a single price coordinate, leading to the interpretation of the method as a *coordinate ascent method*. Unlike the primal-dual method, the relaxation method cannot be implemented using a shortest path computation.

As in the primal-dual method, at the start of the typical iteration we have an integer pair (x, p) satisfying CS. The iteration indicates that the primal problem is infeasible, or else indicates that (x, p) is optimal, or else transforms this pair into another pair satisfying CS. In particular, if $g_i \leq 0$ for all i, then there are two possibilities: (1) $g_i < 0$ for some i, in which case $\sum_{i \in \mathcal{N}} s_i < 0$ and the problem is infeasible, or (2) $g_i = 0$ for all i, in which case x is feasible and therefore also optimal, since it satisfies CS together with p. In either case, the algorithm terminates.

If on the other hand we have $g_i > 0$ for at least one node i, the iteration starts by selecting a node $\bar{i}$ with $g_{\bar{i}} > 0$. As in the primal-dual method, the iteration maintains two sets of nodes $\mathcal{S}$ and $\mathcal{L}$, with $\mathcal{S} \subset \mathcal{L}$. At the start of the iteration, $\mathcal{S}$ is empty and $\mathcal{L}$ consists of the node $\bar{i}$ with $g_{\bar{i}} > 0$. The iteration also maintains a *label* for every node $i \in \mathcal{L}$ except for the starting node $\bar{i}$; the label is an incident arc of i.

Relaxation Iteration

Step 0 (Initialization): Select a node $\bar{i}$ with $g_{\bar{i}} > 0$. [If no such node can be found, terminate; the pair (x, p) is optimal if $g_i = 0$ for all i; otherwise the problem is infeasible.] Set $\mathcal{L} := \{\bar{i}\}$ and $\mathcal{S} :=$ empty, and go to Step 1.

Step 1 (Choose a Node to Scan): If $\mathcal{S} = \mathcal{L}$, go to Step 4; else select a node $i \in \mathcal{L} - \mathcal{S}$, set $\mathcal{S} := \mathcal{S} \cup \{i\}$, and go to Step 2.

Step 2 (Label Neighbor Nodes of i): If

$$q'(p; d_{\mathcal{S}}) > 0, \tag{6.20}$$

go to Step 4; else add to $\mathcal{L}$ all nodes $j \notin \mathcal{L}$ such that either (j, i) is balanced and $b_{ji} < x_{ji}$ or (i, j) is balanced and $x_{ij} < c_{ij}$; also for every

---

such j, give to j the label "(j,i)" if (j,i) is balanced and $b_{ji} < x_{ji}$, and otherwise give to j the label "(i,j)." If for every node j just added to $\mathcal{L}$, we have $g_j \geq 0$, go to Step 1; else select one of these nodes j with $g_j < 0$ and go to Step 3.

Step 3 (Flow Augmentation): An augmenting path P has been found that begins at the starting node $\bar{i}$ and ends at the node j identified in Step 2. The path is constructed by tracing labels backward starting from j, and is such that we have

$$x_{mn} < c_{mn}, \qquad \forall\, (m,n) \in P^+, \tag{6.21}$$

$$x_{mn} > b_{mn}, \qquad \forall\, (m,n) \in P^-, \tag{6.22}$$

where P^+ and P^- are the sets of forward and backward arcs of P, respectively. Let

$$\delta = \min\{g_i, -g_j, \{c_{mn} - x_{mn} \mid (m,n) \in P^+\},$$
$$\{x_{mn} - b_{mn} \mid (m,n) \in P^-\}\}.$$

Increase by δ the flows of all arcs in P^+, decrease by δ the flows of all arcs in P^-, and go to the next iteration.

Step 4 (Price Change): Set

$$x_{ij} = c_{ij}, \qquad \forall\ \text{balanced arcs } (i,j) \text{ with } i \in \mathcal{S},\ j \notin \mathcal{S}, \tag{6.23}$$

$$x_{ji} = b_{ji}, \qquad \forall\ \text{balanced arcs } (j,i) \text{ with } i \in \mathcal{S},\ j \notin \mathcal{S}. \tag{6.24}$$

Let

$$\gamma = \min\{\{p_j + a_{ij} - p_i \mid (i,j) \in \mathcal{A}, x_{ij} < c_{ij}, i \in \mathcal{S}, j \notin \mathcal{S}\},$$
$$\{p_j - a_{ji} - p_i \mid (j,i) \in \mathcal{A}, b_{ji} < x_{ji}, i \in \mathcal{S}, j \notin \mathcal{S}\}\}. \tag{6.25}$$

Set

$$p_i := \begin{cases} p_i + \gamma & \text{if } i \in \mathcal{S}, \\ p_i & \text{otherwise.} \end{cases} \tag{6.26}$$

Go to the next iteration. [*Note:* As in the case of the primal-dual iteration, if after the flow adjustments of Eqs. (6.23) and (6.24) there is no arc (i,j) with $x_{ij} < c_{ij}$, $i \in \mathcal{S}$, and $j \notin \mathcal{S}$, or arc (j,i) with $b_{ji} < x_{ji}$, $i \in \mathcal{S}$, and $j \notin \mathcal{S}$, the problem is infeasible and the algorithm terminates.]

It can be seen that the relaxation iteration is quite similar to the primal-dual iteration. However, there are two important differences. First, in the relaxation iteration, after a price change in Step 4, we do not return to Step 1 to continue the search for an augmenting path like we do in the primal-dual method. Thus, the relaxation iteration terminates with either an augmentation as in Step 3 or a price change as in Step 4, in contrast with the primal-dual iteration, which can only terminate with an augmentation. The second and more important difference is that in the relaxation iteration, a price change may be performed in Step 4 even if $\mathcal{S} \neq \mathcal{L}$ [cf. Eq. (6.20)]. It is because of this feature that the relaxation method identifies ascent directions faster than the primal-dual method. Note that in contrast with the primal-dual method, the total absolute surplus $\sum_{i \in \mathcal{N}} |g_i|$ may increase as a result of a relaxation iteration.

An important property of the method is that each time we enter Step 4, $d_{\mathcal{S}}$ is an ascent direction. To see this note that there are two possibilities: (1) we have $\mathcal{S} = \mathcal{L}$ (cf. Step 1) in which case $d_{\mathcal{S}}$ is an ascent direction similar to the corresponding situation in the primal-dual method, or (2) we have $\mathcal{S} \neq \mathcal{L}$ (cf. Step 2) in which case by Eq. (6.20) $d_{\mathcal{S}}$ is an ascent direction.

Note that it is possible to "combine" several iterations of the relaxation method into a single iteration in order to save computation time. This is done judiciously in the RELAX codes, which are publicly available implementations of the relaxation method (Bertsekas and Tseng [1988b], [1990], [1994]). Figure 6.6 traces the steps of the method for a simple example.

The following proposition establishes the validity of the method.

Proposition 6.5: Consider the minimum cost flow problem and assume that a_{ij}, b_{ij}, c_{ij}, and s_i are all integer. If the problem is feasible, then the relaxation method terminates with an integer optimal flow vector x and an integer optimal price vector p.

Proof: The proof is similar to the corresponding proof for the primal-dual method (cf. Prop. 6.2). We first note that all operations of the iteration preserve the integrality of the flow-price vector pair. To see that CS is also maintained, note that a flow augmentation step changes only flows of balanced arcs and therefore cannot destroy CS. Furthermore, the flow changes of Eqs. (6.23) and (6.24), and the price changes of Eqs. (6.25) and (6.26) maintain CS, because they set the flows of the balanced arcs that the price change renders active (or inactive) to the corresponding upper (or lower) bounds.

Every time there is a price change in Step 4, there is a strict improvement in the dual cost by the integer amount $\gamma q'(p; d_{\mathcal{S}})$ [using the CS property, it can be seen that $\gamma > 0$, and as argued earlier, $d_{\mathcal{S}}$ is an ascent direction so $q'(p; d_{\mathcal{S}}) > 0$]. Thus, for a feasible problem, we cannot have an infinite number of price changes. On the other hand, it is impossible to

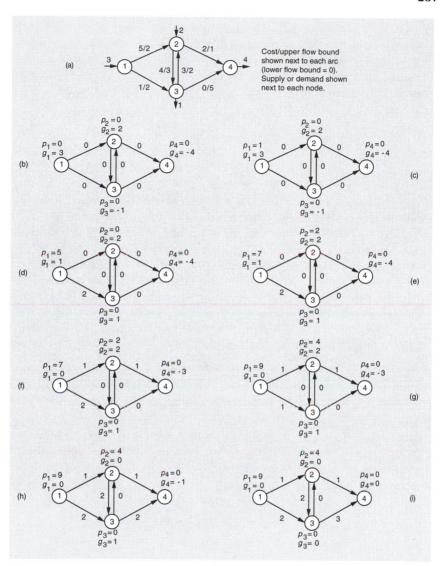

Figure 6.6   An illustration of the relaxation method, starting with all zero prices.
(a) Problem data.
(b) Initial flows, prices, and surpluses.
(c) After the first iteration, which consists of a price change of node 1.
(d) After the second iteration, which consists of another price change of node 1 [note the flow change of arc $(1,3)$; cf. Eq. (6.23)].
(e) After the third iteration, which consists of a price change of nodes 1 and 2.
(f) After the fourth iteration, which consists of an augmentation along the path $(1, 2, 4)$.
(g) After the fifth iteration, which consists of a price change of nodes 1 and 2.
(h) After the sixth iteration, which consists of an augmentation along the path $(2, 3, 4)$.
(i) After the seventh iteration, which consists of an augmentation along the path $(3, 4)$.

have an infinite number of flow augmentations between two successive price changes, since each of these reduces the total absolute surplus by an integer amount. It follows that the algorithm can execute only a finite number of iterations, and must terminate. Since upon termination x is feasible and satisfies CS together with p, it follows that x is primal-optimal and p is dual-optimal. **Q.E.D.**

If the problem is infeasible, the method may terminate because $g_i \leq 0$ for all i and $g_i < 0$ for at least one i, or because after the flow adjustments of Eqs. (6.23) and (6.24) in Step 4, there is no arc (i, j) with $x_{ij} < c_{ij}$, $i \in \mathcal{S}$, and $j \notin \mathcal{S}$, or arc (j, i) with $b_{ji} < x_{ji}$, $i \in \mathcal{S}$, and $j \notin \mathcal{S}$. However, there is also the possibility that the method will execute an infinite number of iterations and price changes, with the prices of some of the nodes increasing to ∞. Exercise 6.6 shows that, when the problem is feasible, the node prices stay below a certain precomputable bound in the course of the algorithm. This fact can be used as an additional test to detect infeasibility.

It is important to note that the directional derivative $q'(p; d_\mathcal{S})$ needed for the ascent test (6.20) in Step 2 can be calculated *incrementally* (as new nodes are added one-by-one to $\mathcal{S}$) using the equation

$$q'(p; d_\mathcal{S}) = \sum_{i \in \mathcal{S}} g_i - \sum_{\substack{(j,i):\ \text{balanced},\ j \notin \mathcal{S},\ i \in \mathcal{S}}} (x_{ji} - b_{ji})$$

$$- \sum_{\substack{(i,j):\ \text{balanced},\ i \in \mathcal{S},\ j \notin \mathcal{S}}} (c_{ij} - x_{ij});$$

cf. Eq. (6.10). Indeed, it follows from this equation that, given $q'(p; d_\mathcal{S})$ and a node $i \notin \mathcal{S}$, one can calculate the directional derivative corresponding to the enlarged set $\mathcal{S} \cup \{i\}$ using the formula

$$q'(p; d_{\mathcal{S} \cup \{i\}}) = q'(p; d_\mathcal{S}) + \sum_{\{j | (i,j):\ \text{balanced},\ j \in \mathcal{S}\}} (x_{ij} - b_{ij})$$

$$+ \sum_{\{j | (j,i):\ \text{balanced},\ j \in \mathcal{S}\}} (c_{ji} - x_{ji})$$

$$- \sum_{\{j | (j,i):\ \text{balanced},\ j \notin \mathcal{S}\}} (x_{ji} - b_{ji})$$

$$- \sum_{\{j | (i,j):\ \text{balanced},\ j \notin \mathcal{S}\}} (c_{ij} - x_{ij}).$$

This formula is convenient because it involves only the incident balanced arcs of the new node i, which must be examined anyway while executing Step 2.

In practice, the method is implemented using iterations that start from both positive and negative surplus nodes. This seems to improve substantially the performance of the method. It can be shown that for a feasible problem, the algorithm terminates properly under these circumstances (Exercise 6.6). Another important practical issue has to do with the initial choice of flows and prices. One possibility is to try to choose an initial price vector that is as close to optimal as possible (for example, using the results of some earlier optimization); one can then choose the arc flows to satisfy the CS conditions.

Line Search and Coordinate Ascent Iterations

The stepsize γ of Eq. (6.25) corresponds to the first break point of the piecewise linear dual function along the ascent direction d_S. It is also possible to calculate through a line search an optimal stepsize that maximizes the dual function along d_S. We leave it for the reader to verify that this computation can be done quite economically, using Eq. (6.7) or Eq. (6.10) to test the sign of the directional derivative of the dual function at successive break points along d_S. Computational experience shows that a line search is beneficial in practice. For this reason, it has been used in the RELAX codes mentioned earlier.

Consider now the case where there is a price change via Step 4 and the set S consists of just the starting node, say node i. This happens when the iteration scans the incident arcs of i at the first time Step 2 is entered and finds that the corresponding coordinate direction leads to a dual cost improvement $[q'(p; d_{\{i\}}) > 0]$. If a line search of the type just described is performed, the price p_i is changed to a break point where the right derivative is nonpositive and the left derivative is nonnegative (cf. Fig. 6.7).

A precise description of this single-node relaxation iteration with line search, starting from a pair (x, p) satisfying CS, is as follows:

Single-Node Relaxation Iteration

Choose a node i with $g_i > 0$. Let

$$B_i^+ = \{j \mid (i, j) : \text{ balanced, } x_{ij} < c_{ij}\}, \qquad (6.27)$$

$$B_i^- = \{j \mid (j, i) : \text{ balanced, } b_{ji} < x_{ji}\}. \qquad (6.28)$$

Step 1: If

$$g_i \geq \sum_{j \in B_i^+} (c_{ij} - x_{ij}) + \sum_{j \in B_i^-} (x_{ji} - b_{ji}),$$

go to Step 4. Otherwise, if $g_i > 0$, choose a node $j \in B_i^+$ with $g_j < 0$ and go to Step 2, or choose a node $j \in B_i^-$ with $g_j < 0$ and go to Step

---

3; if no such node can be found, or if $g_i = 0$, go to the next iteration.

Step 2 (Flow Adjustment on Outgoing Arc): Let

$$\delta = \min\{g_i, -g_j, c_{ij} - x_{ij}\}.$$

Set

$$x_{ij} := x_{ij} + \delta, \qquad g_i := g_i - \delta, \qquad g_j := g_j + \delta$$

and if $x_{ij} = c_{ij}$, delete j from B_i^+; go to Step 1.

Step 3 (Flow Adjustment on Incoming Arc): Let

$$\delta = \min\{g_i, -g_j, x_{ji} - b_{ji}\}.$$

Set

$$x_{ji} := x_{ji} - \delta, \qquad g_i := g_i - \delta, \qquad g_j := g_j + \delta$$

and if $x_{ji} = b_{ji}$, delete j from B_i^-; go to Step 1.

Step 4 (Increase Price of i): Set

$$g_i := g_i - \sum_{j \in B_i^+} (c_{ij} - x_{ij}) - \sum_{j \in B_i^-} (x_{ji} - b_{ji}), \tag{6.29}$$

$$x_{ij} = c_{ij}, \qquad \forall \, j \in B_i^+,$$
$$x_{ji} = b_{ji}, \qquad \forall \, j \in B_i^-,$$

$$p_i := \min\{\{p_j + a_{ij} \mid (i,j) \in \mathcal{A}, \, p_i < p_j + a_{ij}\}, \\ \{p_j - a_{ji} \mid (j,i) \in \mathcal{A}, \, p_i < p_j - a_{ji}\}\}. \tag{6.30}$$

If after these changes $g_i > 0$, recalculate the sets B_i^+ and B_i^+ using Eqs. (6.27) and (6.28), and go to Step 1; else, go to the next iteration. [*Note:* If the set of arcs over which the minimum in Eq. (6.30) is calculated is empty, there are two possibilities: (a) $g_i > 0$, in which case it can be shown that the dual cost increases without bound along p_i and the primal problem is infeasible, or (b) $g_i = 0$, in which case the cost stays constant along p_i; in this case we leave p unchanged and go to the next iteration.]

Note that the single-node iteration may be unsuccessful in that it may fail to change either x or p. In this case, it should be followed by a regular relaxation iteration that labels the appropriate neighbors of node i, etc. Experience has shown that the most efficient way to implement the relaxation iteration is to first attempt its single-node version; if this

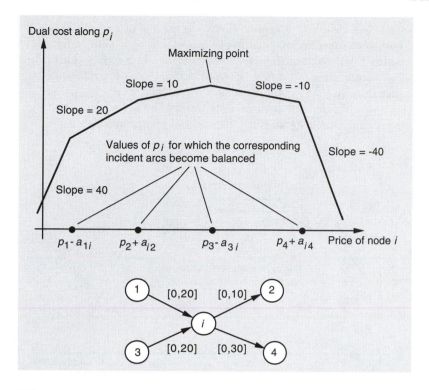

Figure 6.7: Illustration of single-node relaxation iteration. Here, node i has four incident arcs $(1, i)$, $(3, i)$, $(i, 2)$, and $(i, 4)$ with flow ranges $[0, 20]$, $[0, 20]$, $[0, 10]$, and $[0, 30]$, respectively, and supply $s_i = 0$. The arc costs and current prices are such that

$$p_1 - a_{1i} \leq p_2 + a_{i2} \leq p_3 - a_{3i} \leq p_4 + a_{i4},$$

as shown in the figure. The break points of the dual cost along the price p_i correspond to the values of p_i at which one or more incident arcs to node i become balanced. For values between two successive break points, there are no balanced arcs. For any price p_i to the left of the maximizing point, the surplus g_i must be positive to satisfy CS. A single-node iteration with line search increases p_i to the maximizing point.

fails to change x or p, then we proceed with the multiple node version, while salvaging whatever computation is possible from the single-node attempt. The RELAX codes make use of this idea. Experience shows that single-node iterations are very frequent in the early stages of the relaxation algorithm and account for most of the total dual cost improvement, but become much less frequent near the algorithm's termination.

A careful examination of the single-node iteration logic shows that in Step 4, after the surplus change of Eq. (6.29), the surplus g_i may be equal to zero; this will happen if $g_i = 0$ and simultaneously there is no balanced arc (i, j) with $x_{ij} < c_{ij}$, or balanced arc (j, i) with $b_{ji} < x_{ji}$. In this case, it can be shown (see also Fig. 6.7) that the price change of Eq. (6.30) leaves the dual cost unchanged, corresponding to movement of p_i along a flat segment to the next breakpoint of the dual cost, as shown in Fig. 6.8. This is known as a *degenerate ascent iteration*. Computational experience has shown that it is generally preferable to allow such iterations whenever possible. For special types of problems such as assignment, the use of degenerate ascent iterations can reduce significantly the overall computation time.

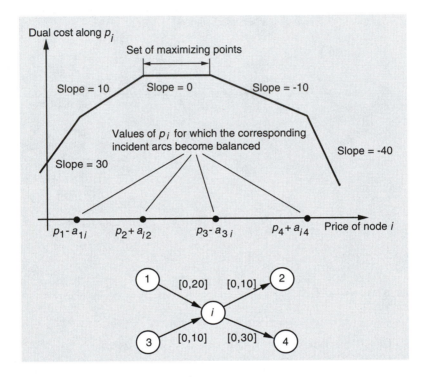

Figure 6.8: Illustration of a degenerate price increase. The difference between this example and the example of Fig. 6.8 is that the feasible flow range of arc $(3, i)$ is now $[0, 10]$ instead of $[0, 20]$. Here, there is a flat segment of the graph of the dual cost along p_i, corresponding to maximizing points. A degenerate price increase moves p_i from the extreme left maximizing point to the extreme right maximizing point.

We finally note that single-node relaxation iterations may be used to initialize the primal-dual method. In particular, one may start with several cycles of single-node iterations, where each node with nonzero surplus is taken up for relaxation once in each cycle. The resulting pair (x, p) is then used as a starting pair for the primal-dual method. Experience has shown that this initialization procedure is very effective.

6.4 SOLVING VARIANTS OF AN ALREADY SOLVED PROBLEM

In many practical situations, we need to solve not just one network problem, but a large number of similar problems. For example, we may want to perform *sensitivity analysis*, that is, change the problem data and observe the effect on the optimal solution. In particular, we may wish to check whether small changes in the data result in small changes in the optimal cost or the optimal solution structure. In other cases, some of the problem data may be under our control, and we may want to know if by changing them we can favorably influence the optimal solution. Still in other situations, the problem involves parameters whose values are estimates of some unknown true values, and we may want to evaluate the effect of the corresponding estimation errors.

In another context, prominently arising in the solution of integer-constrained problems (see Sections 10.2 and 10.3), we may have to solve many problems with slightly different cost function and/or constraints. For example, in the Lagrangian relaxation method, to be discussed in Section 10.3, the arc cost coefficients depend on values of Lagrange multipliers, which are modified as the method progresses.

In order to deal with such situations efficiently, it is important to be able to use the computed optimal solution of a problem as a starting point for solving slightly different problems. The dual ascent methods of the present chapter and the auction algorithms of the next chapter are generally better suited for this purpose than the simplex method.

For example, suppose we solve a problem and then modify it by changing a few arc capacities, and/or some node supplies. To solve the modified problem using the primal-dual or the relaxation method, we can use as starting node prices the prices obtained from the earlier solution, and set to the appropriate bounds the arc flows that violate the new arc flow bounds or the CS conditions. Typically, this starting flow-price pair is close to optimal, and the solution of the modified problem is extremely fast.

By contrast, to solve the modified problem using the simplex method one must provide a starting feasible tree. The optimal tree obtained from the previous problem will often be infeasible for the modified problem. As a result, a new starting tree must be constructed, and there are no simple ways to choose this tree to be nearly optimal.

6.5 IMPLEMENTATION ISSUES

To apply the methods of this chapter, one can represent the problem using the five arrays *START*, *END*, *COST*, *CAPACITY*, and *SUPPLY*, as in simplex methods (cf. Section 5.4). For an efficient implementation, however, it is essential to provide additional data structures that facilitate the labeling operations, the ascent steps of Step 4, and the shortest path computations. In particular, it is necessary to have easy access to the set of all incident arcs of each node. This can be done with the help of the following four additional arrays.

   FIRST_IN(i): The first arc incoming to node i ($= 0$ if i has no incoming arcs).

   FIRST_OUT(i): The first arc outgoing from node i ($= 0$ if i has no outgoing arcs).

   NEXT_IN(a): The arc following arc a with the same end node as a ($= 0$ if a is the last incoming arc of the end node of a).

   NEXT_OUT(a): The arc following arc a with the same start node as a ($= 0$ if a is the last outgoing arc of the start node of a).

Figure 6.9 illustrates these arrays. As an example of their use, suppose that we want to scan all the incoming arcs of node i. We first obtain the arc $a_1 = FIRST\_IN(i)$, then the arc $a_2 = NEXT\_IN(a_1)$, then the arc $a_3 = NEXT\_IN(a_2)$, etc., up to the arc a_k for which $NEXT\_IN(a_k) = 0$.

It is possible to forgo the use of the array *NEXT_OUT* if the arcs are stored in the order of their starting node, that is, the arcs outgoing from each node i are arcs $FIRST\_OUT(i)$ to $FIRST\_OUT(i+1) - 1$. Then the array *FIRST_OUT* is sufficient to generate all arcs outgoing from any one node. This saves storage of one array (and usually some computation as well). Unfortunately, this also complicates sensitivity analysis. In particular, when the problem data are changed to add or remove some arcs, the modification of the arrays describing the problem become more elaborate.

In the relaxation method, it is useful to employ an additional data structure that stores the *balanced* incident arcs of each node in order to facilitate the labeling step (Step 2). These arcs can be stored in two arrays of length N and two arrays of length A, much like the arrays *FIRST_IN*, *FIRST_OUT*, *NEXT_IN*, and *NEXT_OUT*. However, as the set of balanced arcs changes in the course of the algorithm, the arrays used to store this set must be updated. We will not go into further details, but the interested reader can study the publicly available source code of the RELAX implementation (Bertsekas and Tseng [1988b], [1990], [1994]) to see how this can be done efficiently.

Overall it can be seen that dual ascent methods require more arrays of length A than simplex methods, and therefore also more storage space (roughly twice as much).

6.6   NOTES, SOURCES, AND EXERCISES

An interesting dual ascent method that we have not discussed is the *dual simplex method*. This is a general linear programming method that has

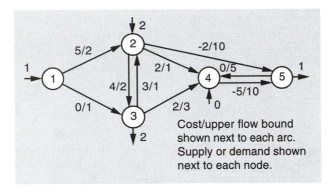

ARC	START	END	COST	CAPACITY	NEXT_IN	NEXT_OUT
1	1	2	5	2	4	2
2	1	3	0	1	3	0
3	2	3	4	2	0	5
4	3	2	3	1	0	7
5	2	5	-2	10	0	6
6	2	4	2	1	7	0
7	3	4	2	3	8	0
8	5	4	0	5	0	0
9	4	5	-5	10	5	0

NODE	SUPPLY	FIRST_IN	FIRST_OUT
1	1	0	1
2	2	1	3
3	-2	2	4
4	0	6	9
5	-1	9	8

Figure 6.9: Representation of the data of a minimum cost flow problem in terms of the nine arrays *START*, *END*, *COST*, *CAPACITY*, *SUPPLY*, *FIRST_IN*, *FIRST_OUT*, *NEXT_IN*, and *NEXT_OUT*.

been specialized to the minimum cost flow problem by several authors (see, for example, Helgason and Kennington [1977], and Jensen and Barnes [1980]). However, the method has not achieved much popularity because its practical performance has been mediocre.

The primal-dual method was first proposed by Kuhn [1955] for assignment problems under the name "Hungarian method." The method was generalized to the minimum cost flow problem by Ford and Fulkerson [1956a], [1957]. A further generalization, the *out-of-kilter* method, was proposed independently by Fulkerson [1961], Ford and Fulkerson [1962], and Minty [1960]; see Rockafellar [1984], Bazaraa, Jarvis, and Sherali [1990], and Murty [1992] for detailed discussions. The out-of-kilter method can be initialized with any flow-price vector pair, not necessarily one that satisfies CS. It appears, however, that there isn't much that can be gained in practice by this extra flexibility, since for any given flow-price vector pair one can modify very simply the arc flows to satisfy CS.

A method that is closely related to the primal-dual method and emphasizes the shortest path implementation was given by Busacker and Gowen [1961]. An extension of the primal-dual method to network problems with gains was given by Jewell [1962], and extensions of the primal-dual and out-of-kilter methods to network flow problems with separable convex cost functions are proposed by Rockafellar [1984]. Primal-dual methods for the assignment problem are discussed by Engquist [1982], McGinnis [1983], Derigs [1985], Carraresi and Sodini [1986], Glover, Glover, and Klingman [1986], and Carpaneto, Martello, and Toth [1988]. Combinations of naive auction and sequential shortest path methods are given by Bertsekas [1981], and Jonker and Volgenant [1986], [1987]. Variations of the Hungarian and the primal-dual methods that are well-suited for parallel asynchronous computation have been developed by Balas, Miller, Pekny, and Toth [1991], and by Bertsekas and Castañon [1993a], [1993b].

One can show a pseudopolynomial worst-case bound on the running time of the primal-dual method. The (practical) average running time of the method, however, is much better than the one suggested by this bound. It is possible to convert the algorithm to a polynomial one by using scaling procedures; see Edmonds and Karp [1972], and Bland and Jensen [1985]. Unfortunately, these procedures do not seem to improve the algorithm's performance in practice.

Despite the fundamentally different principles underlying the simplex and the primal-dual methods (primal cost versus dual cost improvement), these methods are surprisingly related. It can be shown that the big-M version of the simplex method with a particular pivot selection rule is equivalent to the steepest ascent version of the primal-dual method, where the starting set of nodes I consists of all i with $g_i > 0$ (Zadeh [1979]). This suggests that the simplex method with the empirically best pivot selection rule should be more efficient in practice than the primal-dual method. Computational experience tends to agree with this conjecture. However, as noted in Section 6.4, in many practical contexts, the primal-dual method has an advantage: it can easily use a good starting flow and price vector pair, obtained for example from the solution of a slightly different problem by modifying some of the arc flows to satisfy CS; this is true of all the methods of this chapter and the next. Simplex methods are generally less capable of exploiting such prior knowledge.

Primal-dual methods have a long history, yet it is not clear that their potential has been exhausted. Most of the implementations of the sequential shortest path approach use a version of Dijkstra's algorithm as a subroutine, which makes it hard to transfer price information from one iteration to the next. In particular, the labels d_i used in the shortest path step described in Section 6.2 are reinitialized following each augmentation. It would be more sensible to use an alternative shortest path method, which allows some information transfer between shortest path constructions. One such method, based on the auction/shortest path algorithm, is given in Section 7.5, but other possibilities, based for example on label correcting methods, have not been sufficiently explored.

The relaxation method was first proposed in the context of the assignment problem by Bertsekas [1981], and was extended to the general minimum cost flow problem by Bertsekas [1985]. An implementation of the method, the RELAX code, was given by Bertsekas and Tseng [1988b], [1990], [1994]. Extensions for problems with noninteger data, and for networks with gains are given in Tseng [1986], and Bertsekas and Tseng [1988a]. The method has also been extended to general linear programs (Tseng [1986], and Tseng and Bertsekas [1987]), to network flow problems with convex arc cost functions (Bertsekas, Hosein, and Tseng [1987]), to monotropic programming problems (Tseng and Bertsekas [1990]), and to large scale linear programs with a decomposable structure and side constraints (Tseng [1991]).

Extensive computational experience with randomly generated problems shows that the relaxation method typically outperforms primal-dual methods substantially for general minimum cost flow problems. In fact, primal-dual methods can often be speeded up considerably by initialization with a number of single-node relaxation iterations, although apparently not to the point of challenging the relaxation method.

The comparison between the relaxation method and simplex methods is less clear, although the relaxation method seems much faster for randomly generated problems. The relaxation method is also more capable of exploiting prior knowledge about an optimal solution; this advantage is shared with the primal-dual method. On the other hand, in contrast with the simplex method, the relaxation method requires that the problem data be integer (or rational, since by multiplication with a suitable integer, rational problem data can be turned to integer). Modified versions of the relaxation method that can handle irrational problem data are available (Tseng [1986], and Bertsekas and Tseng [1988a]). These methods, however, need not terminate, although they can be shown to yield optimal solutions asymptotically.

The preceding empirical comparisons between the simplex, primal-dual, and relaxation methods are only meant to provide a general guide, which, however, has many exceptions. A lot of the documented comparative computational tests use randomly generated problems that either have a randomly obtained graph or a highly artificial graph, such as a grid. On the other hand, special types of practical problems may have a structure that is not captured by random generators. As a result, two codes may compare quite differently for randomly generated problems and for specific types of practical problems. Practical experience has shown that an important structural characteristic of the problem's graph is its diameter (even though the diameter does not appear in any of the known complexity estimates for the minimum cost flow problem). Generally, the performance of all the algorithms discussed in this book tends to deteriorate as the graph diameter becomes relatively large (as for example in grid graphs). However, a relatively large graph diameter affects the performance of the primal-simplex method less than it affects the primal-dual and the relaxation methods. A plausible conjecture here is that when the graph diameter is large, the cycles that the simplex method constructs, as well the augmenting paths that the dual ascent methods use, tend to have many arcs. This has an adverse effect on the amount of computation needed by both types of methods, but the effect on the dual ascent methods seems to be more serious because of the special nature of the data structures that they use and the associated computations. A related phenomenon may be conjectured for the case of the auction algorithms of the next chapter. It may be said that there is no universally best method, so for challenging problems, it is advisable to try a variety of methods.

EXERCISES

6.1

Use the primal-dual method and the sequential shortest path method to solve the problem of Fig. 6.10. Verify that the two methods yield the same sequence of flows and prices (with identical initial data and appropriate choices of the initial sets I and augmenting paths).

6.2 (Relation of Primal-Dual and Ford-Fulkerson)

Consider the Ford-Fulkerson algorithm for the max-flow problem, where $b_{ij} = 0$ for all $(i, j) \in \mathcal{A}$. Show that the method can be interpreted as an application of the primal-dual method to the minimum cost flow formulation of the max-flow problem of Example 1.3 in Section 1.2, starting with $p = 0$ and $x = 0$ [except for

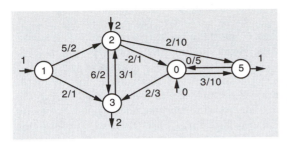

Figure 6.10: Minimum cost flow problem for Exercise 6.1. The cost/upper flow bound pair are shown next to each arc (the lower flow bound is 0). The supply or demand is shown next to each node.

the flow of the artificial arc (t, s), which must be at its upper bound to satisfy CS]. Show in particular that all iterations of the primal-dual method start at node s and terminate with an augmentation along a path ending at node t. Furthermore, the method executes only one price change, which occurs after a minimum cut is identified. The last iteration consists of an augmentation along the artificial arc (t, s).

6.3 (Relation of Primal-Dual and Dijkstra)

Consider the shortest path problem with node 1 being the origin and all other nodes being destinations. Formulate this problem as a minimum cost flow problem with the origin having supply $N - 1$ and all destinations having demand 1. Assume that all arc lengths are nonnegative. Start with all flows and prices equal to zero, and apply the primal-dual method. Show that the method is equivalent to Dijkstra's algorithm. In particular, each augmentation uses a shortest path from the origin to some destination, the augmentations are done in the order of the destinations' proximity to the origin, and upon termination, $p_1 - p_i$ gives the shortest distance from 1 to each destination i that can be reached from the origin via a forward path.

6.4 (Noninteger Problem Data)

Verify that the primal-dual method terminates even when the arc costs are noninteger. (Note, however, that the arc flow bounds must still be integer; the max-flow example of Exercise 3.7 in Chapter 3 applies to the primal-dual method as well, in view of the relation described in Exercise 6.2.) Modify the primal-dual method so that augmenting paths have as few arcs as possible. Show that with this modification, the arc flow bounds need not be integer for the method to terminate. How should the sequential shortest path method be modified so that it terminates even when the problem data are not integer?

6.5

Use the relaxation method to solve the problem of Fig. 6.10.

6.6 (An Infeasibility Test for the Relaxation Method)

Consider the relaxation method, let p_i^0 be the initial price of node i, and let $\mathcal{M}$ be the set of nodes that have negative surplus initially. For every simple path P that ends at a node $j \in \mathcal{M}$, let H_P be the sum of the costs of the forward arcs of the path minus the sum of the costs of the backward arcs of the path, and let $H = \max_P H_P$. Show that, if the problem is feasible, then during the course of the algorithm, the price of any positive surplus node cannot exceed its initial price by more than $H + \max_{j \in \mathcal{M}} p_j^0 - \min_{i \in \mathcal{N}} p_i^0$. Discuss how to use this bound to test for problem infeasibility in the relaxation method. *Hint*: Observe that at any point in the algorithm the prices of all nodes with negative surplus have not changed since the start of the algorithm. Show also that if i is a node with positive surplus, there must exist some node with negative surplus j and an unblocked path starting at i and ending at j.

6.7

Write the form of the relaxation iteration starting from *both* positive and negative surplus nodes. Show that the method terminates at an optimal flow-price vector pair if a feasible solution exists. *Hint*: Show that each price change improves the dual cost by an integer amount, while there can be only a finite number of flow augmentations between successive price changes.

7

Auction Algorithms

Contents

In this chapter we discuss the third major class of algorithms for minimum cost flow problems. These algorithms stem from and indeed are mathematically equivalent to the auction algorithm for the assignment problem, described in Section 1.3.3. The underlying reason is that the minimum cost flow problem can be transformed into an assignment problem, as shown in Section 4.2 and as will be discussed in more detail in Section 7.3.3.

Contrary to the algorithms of the preceding chapters, the algorithms of this chapter do not rely on cost improvement. At any one iteration, they may deteriorate both the primal and the dual cost. On the other hand, they can be interpreted as *approximate* coordinate ascent methods, as will be discussed in Section 7.1 for the case of an assignment problem, and in Section 7.4 for the general minimum cost flow problem.

Because all the major insights regarding auction algorithms can be obtained via the assignment problem, we pay particular attention to this problem, and we develop in detail the corresponding convergence and computational complexity theory in Section 7.1. In Section 7.2, we develop auction algorithms for special types of assignment problems. In Section 7.3, we analyze in some detail the preflow-push algorithm for max-flow, and we derive the computational complexity of some of its implementations. We also show that this algorithm is mathematically equivalent to applying auction to a special type of assignment problem. Finally, in Sections 7.4 and 7.5, we analyze in some detail two auction algorithms for the minimum cost flow problem, the ϵ-relaxation method and the auction/sequential shortest path algorithm, respectively.

Generally, auction algorithms perform well in practice, particularly for some simple types of minimum cost flow problems, such as assignment and max-flow. Furthermore, they have excellent computational complexity properties. Their running times are competitive and often superior to those of their primal and dual cost improvement competitors, as we will show in this chapter and in Chapter 9, in the context of the convex separable network flow problem.

7.1 THE AUCTION ALGORITHM FOR THE ASSIGNMENT PROBLEM

In this section we consider the assignment problem where we want to match n persons and n objects on a one-to-one basis. We are given a "value" or "benefit" a_{ij} for matching person i with object j, and we want to assign persons to objects so as to maximize the total benefit. The set of objects to which person i can be assigned is a nonempty set denoted $A(i)$. The set of all possible pairs that can be assigned is denoted by $\mathcal{A}$,

$$\mathcal{A} = \big\{(i,j) \mid j \in A(i),\ i = 1, \ldots, n\big\}.$$

Note that $\mathcal{A}$ is the set of arcs of the underlying assignment graph. The number of elements of $\mathcal{A}$ is denoted by A.

An *assignment* S is a (possibly empty) set of person-object pairs (i, j) such that $j \in A(i)$ for all $(i, j) \in S$; for each person i there can be at most one pair $(i, j) \in S$; and for every object j there can be at most one pair $(i, j) \in S$. Given an assignment S, we say that person i is *assigned* if there exists a pair $(i, j) \in S$; otherwise we say that i is *unassigned*. We use similar terminology for objects. An assignment is said to be *feasible* or *complete* if it contains n pairs, so that every person and every object is assigned; otherwise the assignment is called *partial*.

We call the problem just described the *symmetric* assignment problem, to distinguish it from the *asymmetric* assignment problem where the number of persons is smaller than the number of objects. We will discuss the asymmetric problem and associated auction algorithms later in Section 7.2.

7.1.1   The Main Auction Algorithm

We recall the auction algorithm, described somewhat loosely in Section 1.3.3. It was motivated by the simpler but flawed naive auction algorithm. A key notion, which made possible the correct operation of the algorithm was the notion of *ϵ-complementary slackness* (ϵ-CS for short) that relates a partial assignment S and a price vector $p = (p_1, \ldots, p_n)$. We say that S and p satisfy ϵ-CS if for every pair $(i, j) \in S$, object j is within ϵ of being the "best" object for person i, i.e.,

$$a_{ij} - p_j \geq \max_{k \in A(i)} \{a_{ik} - p_k\} - \epsilon, \qquad \forall \, (i, j) \in S. \tag{7.1}$$

The auction algorithm proceeds iteratively and terminates when a complete assignment is obtained. At the start of the generic iteration we have a partial assignment S and a price vector p that satisfy ϵ-CS. As an initial choice, we may use an arbitrary set of prices together with the empty assignment, which trivially satisfies ϵ-CS. We will show later that the iteration preserves the ϵ-CS condition. The iteration consists of two phases: the *bidding phase* and the *assignment phase*, which we now describe.

Bidding Phase of the Auction Iteration

Let I be a nonempty subset of persons i that are unassigned under the assignment S. For each person $i \in I$:

1. Find a "best" object j_i having maximum value, i.e.,

$$j_i = \arg \max_{j \in A(i)} \{a_{ij} - p_j\},$$

---

and the corresponding value

$$v_i = \max_{j \in A(i)} \{a_{ij} - p_j\}, \tag{7.2}$$

and find the best value offered by objects other than j_i

$$w_i = \max_{j \in A(i),\, j \neq j_i} \{a_{ij} - p_j\}. \tag{7.3}$$

[If j_i is the only object in $A(i)$, we define w_i to be $-\infty$, or for computational purposes, a number that is much smaller than v_i.]

2. Compute the "bid" of person i given by

$$b_{ij_i} = p_{j_i} + v_i - w_i + \epsilon = a_{ij_i} - w_i + \epsilon. \tag{7.4}$$

(Abusing terminology somewhat, we say that person i bid for object j_i, and that object j_i received a bid from person i.)

Assignment Phase of the Auction Iteration

For each object j, let $P(j)$ be the set of persons from which j received a bid in the bidding phase of the iteration. If $P(j)$ is nonempty, increase p_j to the highest bid,

$$p_j := \max_{i \in P(j)} b_{ij}, \tag{7.5}$$

remove from the assignment S any pair (i, j) (if j was assigned to some i under S), and add to S the pair (i_j, j), where i_j is a person in $P(j)$ attaining the maximum above.

Note that there is some freedom in choosing the subset of persons I that bid during an iteration. One possibility is to let I consist of a single unassigned person. This version is known as the *Gauss-Seidel version* because of its similarity with Gauss-Seidel methods for solving systems of nonlinear equations, and usually works best in a serial computing environment. The version where I consists of all unassigned persons is the one best suited for parallel computation; it is known as the *Jacobi version* because of its similarity with Jacobi methods for solving systems of nonlinear equations.

During an iteration, the objects whose prices are changed are the ones that received a bid during the iteration. Each price change involves an increase of at least ϵ. To see this, note that if person i bids for object

j_i, from Eqs. (7.2)-(7.4) the corresponding bid is

$$b_{ij_i} = a_{ij_i} - w_i + \epsilon \geq a_{ij_i} - v_i + \epsilon = p_{j_i} + \epsilon,$$

and exceeds the object's current price by at least ϵ. At the end of the iteration, we have a new assignment that differs from the preceding one in that each object that received a bid is now assigned to some person that was unassigned at the start of the iteration. However, the assignment at the end of the iteration need not have more pairs than the one at the start of the iteration, because it is possible that all objects that received a bid were assigned at the start of the iteration.

The choice of bidding increment [cf. Eq. (7.4)] is such that ϵ-CS is preserved by the algorithm, as shown by the following proposition (in fact, it can be seen that it is the largest bidding increment for which this is so).

Proposition 7.1: The auction algorithm preserves ϵ-CS throughout its execution; that is, if the assignment and the price vector available at the start of an iteration satisfy ϵ-CS, the same is true for the assignment and the price vector obtained at the end of the iteration.

Proof: Let p_j and p'_j be the object prices before and after a given iteration, respectively. Suppose that object j^* received a bid from person i and was assigned to i during the iteration. Then we have [see Eqs. (7.4) and (7.5)]

$$p'_{j^*} = a_{ij^*} - w_i + \epsilon.$$

Using this equation, we obtain

$$a_{ij^*} - p'_{j^*} = w_i - \epsilon = \max_{j \in A(i), j \neq j^*} \{a_{ij} - p_j\} - \epsilon.$$

Since $p'_j \geq p_j$ for all j, this equation implies that

$$a_{ij^*} - p'_{j^*} \geq \max_{j \in A(i)} \{a_{ij} - p'_j\} - \epsilon, \qquad (7.6)$$

which shows that the ϵ-CS condition (7.1) continues to hold after the assignment phase of an iteration for all pairs (i, j^*) that entered the assignment during the iteration.

Consider also any pair (i, j^*) that belonged to the assignment just before the iteration, and also belongs to the assignment after the iteration. Then, j^* must not have received a bid during the iteration, so $p'_{j^*} = p_{j^*}$. Therefore, Eq. (7.6) holds in view of the ϵ-CS condition that held prior to the iteration and the fact $p'_j \geq p_j$ for all j. Hence, the ϵ-CS condition (7.1) holds for all pairs (i, j^*) that belong to the assignment after the iteration, proving the result. **Q.E.D.**

The next result establishes the validity of the algorithm. The proof relies on the following observations:

(a) Once an object is assigned, it remains assigned throughout the remainder of the algorithm's duration. Furthermore, except at termination, there will always exist at least one object that has never been assigned, and has a price equal to its initial price. The reason is that a bidding and assignment phase can result in a reassignment of an already assigned object to a different person, but cannot result in the object becoming unassigned.

(b) Each time an object receives a bid, its price increases by at least ϵ [see Eqs. (7.4) and (7.5)]. Therefore, if the object receives a bid an infinite number of times, its price increases to ∞.

(c) Every $|A(i)|$ bids by person i, where $|A(i)|$ is the number of objects in the set $A(i)$, the scalar v_i defined by the equation

$$v_i = \max_{j \in A(i)} \{a_{ij} - p_j\} \tag{7.7}$$

decreases by at least ϵ. The reason is that a bid by person i either decreases v_i by at least ϵ, or else leaves v_i unchanged because there is more than one object j attaining the maximum in Eq. (7.7). However, in the latter case, the price of the object j_i receiving the bid will increase by at least ϵ, and object j_i will not receive another bid by person i until v_i decreases by at least ϵ. The conclusion is that if a person i bids an infinite number of times, v_i must decrease to $-\infty$.

> **Proposition 7.2:** If at least one feasible assignment exists, the auction algorithm terminates with a feasible assignment that is within $n\epsilon$ of being optimal (and is optimal if the problem data are integer and $\epsilon < 1/n$).

Proof: We argue by contradiction. If termination did not occur, the subset J^∞ of objects that received an infinite number of bids is nonempty. Also, the subset of persons I^∞ that bid an infinite number of times is nonempty. As argued in (b) above, the prices of the objects in J^∞ must tend to ∞, while as argued in (c) above, the scalars $v_i = \max_{j \in A(i)} \{a_{ij} - p_j\}$ must decrease to $-\infty$ for all persons $i \in I^\infty$. In view of ϵ-CS, this implies that

$$A(i) \subset J^\infty, \qquad \forall \, i \in I^\infty, \tag{7.8}$$

and that after a finite number of iterations, each object in J^∞ will be assigned to a person from I^∞. Since after a finite number of iterations at least one person from I^∞ will be unassigned at the start of each iteration, it follows that the number of persons in I^∞ is strictly larger than the number of objects in J^∞. This contradicts the existence of a feasible assignment, since by Eq. (7.8), persons in I^∞ can only be assigned to objects in J^∞. Therefore, the algorithm must terminate. The feasible assignment obtained upon termination satisfies ϵ-CS by Prop. 7.1, so by Prop. 1.4 of Section 1.3.3, this assignment is within $n\epsilon$ of being optimal.   **Q.E.D.**

7.1.2   Approximate Coordinate Descent Interpretation

The Gauss-Seidel version of the auction algorithm resembles coordinate descent algorithms, and the relaxation method of Chapter 6 in particular, because it involves the change of a single object price with all other prices held fixed. In contrast with the relaxation method, however, such a price change may worsen strictly the value of the dual function

$$q(p) = \sum_{i=1}^{n} \max_{j \in A(i)} \{a_{ij} - p_j\} + \sum_{j=1}^{n} p_j, \qquad (7.9)$$

which was introduced in Prop. 1.3 of Section 1.3.3.

Generally we can interpret the bidding and assignment phases as a simultaneous "approximate" coordinate descent step for all price coordinates that increase during the iteration. The coordinate steps are aimed at minimizing approximately the dual function. In particular, it can be shown that *the price p_j of each object j that receives a bid during the assignment phase is increased to either a value that minimizes $q(p)$ when all other prices are kept constant or else exceeds the largest such value by no more than ϵ.*

Figure 7.1 shows this property and suggests that the amount of deterioration of the dual cost is at most ϵ. Indeed, for the Gauss-Seidel version of the algorithm this can be deduced from the argument given in Fig. 7.1 and is left for the reader as Exercise 7.1.

7.1.3   Variants of the Auction Algorithm

There are several variants of the auction algorithm that differ from each other in small details. For example, as mentioned earlier, one or several persons may bid simultaneously with objects being awarded to the highest bidders, the price increment may be slightly different than the one of Eq. (7.5), etc. The important ingredients of the method are that for each iteration:

(a) ϵ-CS is maintained.

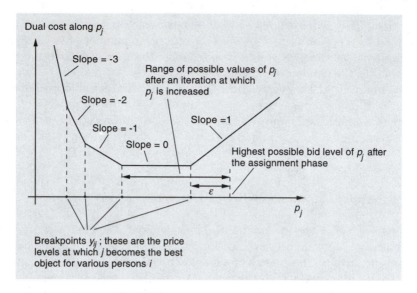

Figure 7.1: Form of the dual cost along the price coordinate p_j. From the definition (7.9) of the dual cost q, the right directional derivative of q along p_j is

$$d_j^+ = 1 - (\text{number of persons } i \text{ with } j \in A(i) \text{ and } p_j < y_{ij}),$$

where

$$y_{ij} = a_{ij} - \max_{k \in A(i), \, k \neq j} \{a_{ik} - p_k\}$$

is the level of p_j below which j is the best person for person i. The break points are y_{ij} for all i such that $j \in A(i)$. Let $\overline{y} = \max_{\{i \mid j \in A(i)\}} \{a_{ij} - p_j\}$, let $\overline{i}$ be a person such that $\overline{y} = y_{\overline{i}j}$, let $\hat{y} = \max_{\{i \mid j \in A(i), \, i \neq \overline{i}\}} \{a_{ij} - p_j\}$, let $\hat{i}$ be a person such that $\hat{i} \neq \overline{i}$ and $\hat{y} = y_{\hat{i}j}$. Note that the interval $[\hat{y}, \overline{y}]$ is the set of points that minimize q along the coordinate p_j.

Let p_j be the price of j just before an iteration at which j receives a bid and let p_j' be the price of j after the iteration. We claim that $\hat{y} \leq p_j' \leq \overline{y} + \epsilon$. Indeed, if i is the person that bids and wins j during the iteration, then $p_j' = y_{ij} + \epsilon$, implying that $p_j' \leq \overline{y} + \epsilon$. To prove that $p_j' \geq \hat{y}$, we note that if $p_j \geq \hat{y}$, we must also have $p_j' \geq \hat{y}$, since $p_j' \geq p_j$. On the other hand, if $p_j' < \hat{y}$, there are two possibilities:

(1) At the start of the iteration, $\overline{i}$ was not assigned to j. In this case, either $\overline{i}$ was unassigned in which case i will bid for j so that $p_j' = \overline{y} + \epsilon$, or else $\overline{i}$ was assigned to an object $\overline{j} \neq j$, in which case by ϵ-CS,

$$a_{\overline{i}j} - p_j - \epsilon \leq a_{\overline{i}\overline{j}} - p_{\overline{j}} \leq \max_{k \in A(\overline{i}), \, k \neq j} \{a_{\overline{i}k} - p_k\} = a_{\overline{i}j} - \overline{y}.$$

Thus, $p_j \geq \overline{y} - \epsilon$, implying that $p_j' \geq \overline{y}$ (since a bid increases a price by at least ϵ). In both cases we have $p_j' \geq \overline{y} \geq \hat{y}$.

(2) At the start of the iteration, $\overline{i}$ was assigned to j. In this case, $\hat{i}$ was not assigned to j, so by repeating the argument of the preceding paragraph with $\hat{i}$ and $\hat{y}$ replacing $\overline{i}$ and $\overline{y}$, respectively, we obtain $p_j' \geq \hat{y}$.

(b) At least one unassigned person gets assigned to some object, and the price of this object is increased by at least $\beta\epsilon$, where β is some fixed positive constant. Furthermore, the person previously assigned to an object that receives a bid during the iteration (if any) becomes unassigned.

(c) No price is decreased and every object that was assigned at the start of the iteration remains assigned at the end of the iteration (although the person assigned to it may change).

Any variant of the auction algorithm that obeys these three rules can be readily shown to have the termination property given in Prop. 7.2.

For example, in Section 7.2.3, we will focus on a special type of assignment problem, which involves groups of persons that are indistinguishable in the sense that they can be assigned to the same objects and with the same corresponding benefits. We will develop there a special variant of the auction algorithm that combines many bids into a "collective" bid for an entire group of similar persons. Not only this improves the efficiency of the method, but it also provides the vehicle for extending the auction algorithm to other problems, such as max-flow and minimum cost flow.

7.1.4   Computational Complexity – ϵ-Scaling

As discussed in Section 1.3.3, the running time of the auction algorithm can depend strongly on the value of ϵ as well as the maximum absolute object value

$$C = \max_{(i,j)\in\mathcal{A}} |a_{ij}|.$$

In practice, the dependence of the running time on ϵ and C can be significant, as can be seen in the examples of Section 1.3.3 (cf. Figs. 1.13 and 1.14).

The practical performance of the auction algorithm is often considerably improved by using the idea of ϵ-*scaling*, which was briefly discussed in Section 1.3.3. ϵ-scaling consists of applying the algorithm several times, starting with a large value of ϵ and successively reducing ϵ up to some final value $\bar{\epsilon}$ such that $n\bar{\epsilon}$ is deemed sufficiently small (cf. Prop. 7.2). Each application of the algorithm, called a *scaling phase*, provides good initial prices for the next application. The value of ϵ used for the $(k+1)$st scaling phase is denoted by ϵ^k. The sequence ϵ^k is generated by

$$\epsilon^{k+1} = \frac{\epsilon^k}{\theta}, \qquad k = 0, 1, \ldots, \tag{7.10}$$

where ϵ^0 is a suitably chosen starting value of ϵ, and θ is an integer with $\theta > 1$.†

In this section we derive an estimate of the worst-case running time of the auction algorithm with ϵ-scaling. This estimate is $O\big(nA\ln(\epsilon^0/\bar{\epsilon})\big)$, where A is the number of arcs in the underlying graph of the assignment problem, and ϵ^0 and $\bar{\epsilon}$ are the initial and final values of ϵ, respectively. Our analysis requires a few assumptions about the way the auction algorithm and the scaling process are implemented. In particular:

(a) We assume that a Gauss-Seidel implementation is used, where only one person submits a bid at each iteration.

(b) We require that each scaling phase begins with the empty assignment.

(c) We require that the initial prices for the first scaling phase are 0, and the initial prices for each subsequent phase are the final prices of the preceding phase. Furthermore, at each scaling phase, we introduce a modification of the scalars a_{ij}, which will be discussed later.

(d) We introduce a data structure, which ensures that the bid of a person is efficiently computed.

The above requirements are essential for obtaining a favorable worst-case estimate of the running time. It is doubtful, however, that strict adherence to these requirements is essential for good practical performance.

We first focus on the case where ϵ *is fixed*. For the data structure mentioned in (d) above to work properly, we must assume that the values $a_{ij} - p_j$ are integer multiples of ϵ throughout the auction algorithm. This will be so if the a_{ij} and the initial prices p_j are integer multiples of ϵ, since in this case it is seen that the bidding increment, as given by Eq. (7.4), will be an integer multiple of ϵ. (We will discuss later how to fulfill the requirement that ϵ evenly divides the a_{ij} and the initial p_j.) To motivate the data structure, suppose that each time a person i scans all the objects $j \in A(i)$ to calculate a bid for the best object j_i, he/she records in a list denoted $Cand(i)$ all the objects $j \neq j_i$ that are tied for offering the best

---

† In practice, if a_{ij} are integer, they are usually first multiplied by $n+1$ and the auction algorithm is applied with progressively lower values of ϵ, to the point where ϵ becomes 1 or smaller. In this case, typical values for sparse problems, where $A << n^2$, are

$$\frac{nC}{5} \leq \epsilon^0 \leq nC, \qquad 4 \leq \theta \leq 10.$$

For nonsparse problems, sometimes $\epsilon^0 = 1$, which in effect bypasses ϵ-scaling, works quite well. Note also that practical implementations of the auction algorithm sometimes use an *adaptive* form of ϵ-scaling, whereby, within the kth scaling phase, the value of ϵ is gradually *increased* to the value ϵ^k given above, starting from a relatively small value, based on the results of the computation.

value; that is, they attain the maximum in the relation [cf. Eq. (7.2)]

$$v_i = \max_{j \in A(i)} \{a_{ij} - p_j\}. \tag{7.11}$$

Along with each object $j \in Cand(i)$, the price p'_j of j that prevailed for j *at the time of the last scan of* j is also recorded. The list $Cand(i)$ is called the *candidate list* of i, and can be used to save some computation in iterations where there are ties in the best object calculation of Eq. (7.11). In particular, if node i is unassigned and its candidate list $Cand(i)$ contains an object j whose current price p_j is equal to the price p'_j, we know that j is the best object for i. Furthermore, the presence of a second object j in the list with $p_j = p'_j$ indicates that the bidding increment is exactly equal to ϵ. This suggests the following implementation for a bid of a person i, which will be assumed in the subsequent Prop. 7.3.

Bid Calculation

Step 1: Choose an unassigned person i.

Step 2: Examine the pairs (j, p'_j) corresponding to the candidate list $Cand(i)$, starting at the top. Discard any for which $p'_j < p_j$. Continue until reaching the end of the list, or the *second* element for which $p'_j = p_j$. If the end is reached, empty the candidate list and go to Step 4.

Step 3: Let j_i be the *first* element on the list for which $p'_j = p_j$. Discard the contents of the list up to, but not including, the *second* such element. Place a bid on j_i at price level $p_{j_i} + \epsilon$, assigning i to j_i and breaking any prior assignment of j_i.

Step 4: Scan the objects in $A(i)$, determining an object j_i of maximum value, the next best value w_i, as given by Eq. (7.3), and all objects (other than j_i) tied at value level w_i, and record these objects in the candidate list together with their current prices. Submit a bid for j_i at price level b_{ij_i}, as given by Eq. (7.4), assigning i to j_i and breaking any prior assignment of j_i.

We note that candidate lists are often used in the calculations of various auction algorithms to improve theoretical efficiency. For example they will also be used later in the algorithms of Sections 7.3 and 7.4.

The complexity analysis of the auction algorithm is based on the following proposition, which estimates the amount of computation needed to reduce the violation of CS by a given factor $r > 1$; that is, to obtain a feasible assignment and price vector satisfying ϵ-CS, starting from a feasible assignment and price pair satisfying $r\epsilon - CS$. Because each price increase is of size at least ϵ, the value

$$v_i = \max_{j \in A(i)} \{a_{ij} - p_j\}$$

decreases by at least ϵ each time the prices p_j of all the objects $j \in A(i)$ that attain the maximum above increase by at least ϵ. The significance of the preceding method for bid calculation is that for v_i to decrease by at least ϵ, it is sufficient to scan the objects in $A(i)$ in Step 4 *only once*. Assuming that the problem is feasible, we will provide in the following proposition an upper bound on the amount by which v_i can decrease, thereby bounding the number of bids that a person can submit in the course of the algorithm, and arriving at a running time estimate.

Proposition 7.3: Let the auction algorithm be applied to a feasible assignment problem, with a given $\epsilon > 0$ and with the bid calculation method just described. Assume that:

(1) All the scalars a_{ij} and all the initial object prices are integer multiples of ϵ.

(2) For some scalar $r \geq 1$, the initial object prices satisfy $r\epsilon$-CS together with some feasible assignment.

Then the running time of the algorithm is $O(rnA)$.

Proof: Let p^0 be the initial price vector and let S^0 be the feasible assignment together with which p^0 satisfies $r\epsilon$-CS. Let also (S, p) be an assignment-price pair generated by the algorithm *prior* to termination (so that S is infeasible). Define for all persons i

$$v_i = \max_{j \in A(i)} \{a_{ij} - p_j\}, \qquad v_i^0 = \max_{j \in A(i)} \{a_{ij} - p_j^0\}.$$

The values v_i are monotonically nonincreasing in the course of the algorithm. We will show that the differences $v_i^0 - v_i$ are upper bounded by $(r + 1)(n - 1)\epsilon$.

Let i be a person that is unassigned under S. We claim that there exists a path of the form

$$(i, j_1, i_1, \ldots, j_m, i_m, j_{m+1})$$

where $m \geq 0$ and:

(1) j_{m+1} is unassigned under S.

(2) If $m > 0$, then for $k = 1, \ldots, m$, i_k is assigned to j_k under S and is assigned to j_{k+1} under S^0.

This can be shown constructively using the following algorithm: Let j_1 be the object assigned to i under S^0. If j_1 is unassigned under S, stop; else let i_1 be the person assigned to j_1 under S, and note that $i_1 \neq i$. Let j_2 be the person assigned to i_1 under S^0, and note that $j_2 \neq j_1$ since j_1 is assigned to i under S^0 and $i_1 \neq i$. If j_2 is unassigned under S, stop; else continue similarly. This procedure cannot produce the same object twice, so it must terminate with the properties (1) and (2) satisfied after $m + 1$ steps, where $0 \leq m \leq n - 2$.

Since the pair (S^0, p^0) satisfies $r\epsilon$-CS, we have

$$v_i^0 = \max_{j \in A(i)} \{a_{ij} - p_j\} \leq a_{ij_1} - p_{j_1}^0 + r\epsilon,$$

$$a_{i_1 j_1} - p_{j_1}^0 \leq a_{i_1 j_2} - p_{j_2}^0 + r\epsilon,$$

$$\cdots$$

$$a_{i_m j_m} - p_{j_m}^0 \leq a_{i_m j_{m+1}} - p_{j_{m+1}}^0 + r\epsilon.$$

Since the pair (S, p) satisfies ϵ-CS, we have

$$v_i \geq a_{ij_1} - p_{j_1} - \epsilon,$$

$$a_{i_1 j_1} - p_{j_1} \geq a_{i_1 j_2} - p_{j_2} - \epsilon,$$

$$\cdots$$

$$a_{i_m j_m} - p_{j_m} \geq a_{i_m j_{m+1}} - p_{j_{m+1}} - \epsilon.$$

Since j_{m+1} is unassigned under S, we have $p_{j_{m+1}} = p_{j_{m+1}}^0$, so by adding the preceding inequalities, we obtain the desired relation

$$v_i^0 - v_i \leq (r+1)(m+1)\epsilon \leq (r+1)(n-1)\epsilon, \qquad \forall \, i. \qquad (7.12)$$

We finally note that because a_{ij} and p_j^0 are integer multiples of ϵ, all subsequent values of p_j, $a_{ij} - p_j$, and $v_i = \max_{j \in A(i)} \{a_{ij} - p_j\}$ will also be integer multiples of ϵ. Therefore, with the use of the candidate list $Cand(i)$, the typical bid calculation, as given earlier, scans only once the objects in $A(i)$ in Step 4 to induce a reduction of v_i by at least ϵ. It follows that the total number of computational operations for the bids of node i is proportional to $(r+1)(n-1)|A(i)|$, where $|A(i)|$ is the number of objects in $A(i)$. Thus, the algorithm's running time is $(r+1)(n-1)\sum_{i=1}^n |A(i)| = O(rnA)$, as claimed. **Q.E.D.**

Complexity with ϵ-Scaling

We will now estimate the running time of the auction algorithm with ϵ-scaling. A difficulty here is that in order to use the estimate of Prop. 7.3, the a_{ij} and p_j at each scaling phase must be integer multiples of the prevailing ϵ for that phase. We bypass this difficulty as follows:

(a) We start the first scaling phase with $p_j = 0$ for all j.

(b) We use the final prices of each scaling phase as the initial prices for the next scaling phase.

(c) We choose $\bar{\epsilon}$, the final value of ϵ, to divide evenly all the a_{ij}. [We assume that such a common divisor can be found. This will be true if the a_{ij} are rational. Otherwise, the a_{ij} may be approximated arbitrarily closely, say within some $\delta > 0$, by rational numbers, and the final assignment will be within $n(\bar{\epsilon} + \delta)$ of being optimal. If the a_{ij} are integer, we choose $\epsilon = 1/(n+1)$, which also guarantees optimality of the final assignment.] Furthermore, we choose ϵ^0 to be equal to a fraction of the range

$$C = \max_{(i,j)\in\mathcal{A}} |a_{ij}|,$$

which is fixed and independent of the problem data.

(d) We replace each a_{ij} at the beginning of the $(k+1)$st scaling phase with a corrected value a_{ij}^k that is divisible by ϵ^k. The correction is of size at most ϵ^k. In particular, we may use in place of a_{ij},

$$a_{ij}^k = \left\lceil \frac{a_{ij}}{\epsilon^k} \right\rceil \epsilon^k, \qquad \forall\ (i,j) \in \mathcal{A},\ k = 0,1,\dots$$

However, no correction is made in the last scaling phase, since each a_{ij} is divisible by $\bar{\epsilon}$ [cf. (c) above].

It can be seen that since the a_{ij}^0 and the initial (zero) p_j used in the first scaling phase are integer multiples of ϵ^0, the final prices of the first scaling phase are also integer multiples of ϵ^0, and thus also integer multiples of $\epsilon^1 = \epsilon^0/\theta$ (since θ is integer). Therefore, the a_{ij}^1 and initial p_j used in the second scaling phase are integer multiples of ϵ^1, which similarly guarantees that the final prices of the second scaling phase are also integer multiples of $\epsilon^2 = \epsilon^1/\theta$. Continuing in this manner (or using induction), we see that the object benefits and prices are integer multiples of the prevailing value of ϵ throughout the algorithm.

Thus, we can use Prop. 7.3 to estimate the complexity of the $(k+1)$st scaling phase as $O(r^k n A)$, where r^k is such that the initial prices p_j^k of the scaling phase satisfy $r^k \epsilon^k$-CS with some feasible assignment S^k, and with respect to the object benefits a_{ij}^k. Take S^k to be the final assignment of the preceding (the kth) scaling phase, which must satisfy ϵ^{k-1}-CS (or $\theta \epsilon^k$-CS) with respect to the object benefits a_{ij}^{k-1}. Since, for all $(i,j) \in \mathcal{A}$ and k, we have

$$|a_{ij}^k - a_{ij}^{k-1}| \leq |a_{ij}^k - a_{ij}| + |a_{ij} - a_{ij}^{k-1}| \leq \epsilon^k + \epsilon^{k-1} = (1+\theta)\epsilon^k,$$

it can be seen, using the definition of ϵ-CS, that S^k and p_j^k must satisfy $(\theta + 2(1+\theta))\epsilon^k$-CS. It follows that we can use $r^k = \theta + 2(1+\theta)$ in the complexity estimate $O(r^k n A)$ of the $(k+1)$st scaling phase. Thus the running time of all scaling phases except for the first is $O(nA)$. Because ϵ^0 is equal to a fixed fraction of the range C, the initial scaling phase will also have a running time $O(nA)$, since then the initial (zero) price vector will satisfy $r\epsilon^0$-CS with any feasible assignment, where r is some fixed constant. Since $\epsilon^k = \theta\epsilon^{k-1}$ for all $k = 0, 1, \ldots$, the total number of scaling phases is $O(\log(\epsilon^0/\bar{\epsilon}))$, and it follows that the running time of the auction algorithm with ϵ-scaling is $O(nA\log(\epsilon^0/\bar{\epsilon}))$.

Suppose now that the a_{ij} are integer, and that we use $\bar{\epsilon}$ equal to $1/(n+1)$ and ϵ^0 equal to a fixed fraction of the benefit range C. Then $\epsilon^0/\bar{\epsilon} = O(nC)$, and an optimal assignment will be found with $O(nA\log(nC))$ computation. This is a worst-case estimate. In practice, the average running time of the algorithm with ϵ-scaling seems to grow proportionally to something like $A\log n\log(nC)$; see also Exercise 7.3. Exercise 7.20 shows how to combine the auction algorithm with a primal-dual method to achieve an $O(n^{1/2}A\log(nC))$ worst-case running time. This is the best running time known at present for the assignment problem.

We note that the implementation using the candidate lists was important for the proof of Prop. 7.3 and the $O(nA\log(\epsilon^0/\bar{\epsilon}))$ running time of the method with ϵ-scaling. However, it is doubtful that the overhead for maintaining the candidate lists is justified. In practice, a simpler implementation is usually preferred, whereby each person scans all of its associated objects at each bid, instead of using candidate lists. Also the approach of modifying the a_{ij} to make them divisible by the prevailing value of ϵ, while important for the complexity analysis, is of questionable practical use. It is simpler and typically as effective in practice to forego this modification. An alternative approach to the complexity analysis, which uses a slightly different method for selecting the object that receives a bid, is described in Section 9.6, in the context of auction algorithms for separable convex problems.

7.1.5   Dealing with Infeasibility

Since termination of the auction algorithm can only occur with a feasible assignment, when the problem is infeasible, the auction algorithm will keep on iterating, as the user is wondering whether the problem is infeasible or just hard to solve. Thus for problems where existence of a feasible assignment is not known a priori, one must supplement the auction algorithm with a mechanism to detect infeasibility. There are several such mechanisms, which we will now discuss.

One criterion that can be used to detect infeasibility is based on the maximum values

$$v_i = \max_{j \in A(i)} \{a_{ij} - p_j\}.$$

It can be shown that if the problem is feasible, then in the course of the auction algorithm, all of these values will be bounded from below by a precomputable bound, but if the problem is infeasible, some of these values will be eventually reduced below this bound. In particular, suppose that the auction algorithm is applied to a symmetric assignment problem with initial object prices $\{p_j^0\}$. Then as shown in the proof of Prop. 7.3, if person i is unassigned with respect to the current assignment S and the problem is feasible, then there is an augmenting path with respect to S that starts at i. Furthermore, by adding the ϵ-CS condition along the augmenting path, as in the proof of Prop. 7.3, we obtain

$$v_i \geq -(2n-1)C - (n-1)\epsilon - \max_j\{p_j^0\}, \tag{7.13}$$

where $C = \max_{(i,j)\in\mathcal{A}} |a_{ij}|$. If the problem is feasible, then as discussed earlier, there exists at all times an augmenting path starting at each unassigned person, so the lower bound (7.13) on v_i will hold for all unassigned persons i throughout the auction algorithm. On the other hand, if the problem is infeasible, some persons i will be submitting bids infinitely often, and the corresponding values v_i will be decreasing towards $-\infty$. Thus, we can apply the auction algorithm and keep track of the values v_i as they decrease. Once some v_i gets below its lower bound, we know that the problem is infeasible.

Unfortunately, it may take many iterations for some v_i to reach its lower bound, so the preceding method may not work well in practice. An alternative method to detect infeasibility is to convert the problem to a feasible problem by adding a set of artificial pairs $\overline{\mathcal{A}}$ to the original set $\mathcal{A}$. The benefits a_{ij} of the artificial pairs (i, j) should be very small, so that none of these pairs participates in an optimal assignment unless the problem is infeasible. In particular, it can be shown that if the original problem is feasible, no pair $(i, j) \in \overline{\mathcal{A}}$ will participate in the optimal assignment, provided that

$$a_{ij} < -(2n-1)C, \qquad \forall\ (i, j) \in \overline{\mathcal{A}}, \tag{7.14}$$

where $C = \max_{(i,j)\in\mathcal{A}} |a_{ij}|$. To prove this by contradiction, assume that by adding to the set $\mathcal{A}$ the set of artificial pairs $\overline{\mathcal{A}}$ we create an optimal assignment S^* that contains a nonempty subset $\overline{S}$ of artificial pairs. Then, for every assignment S consisting exclusively of pairs from the original set $\mathcal{A}$ we must have

$$\sum_{(i,j)\in\overline{S}} a_{ij} + \sum_{(i,j)\in S^*-\overline{S}} a_{ij} \geq \sum_{(i,j)\in S} a_{ij},$$

from which

$$\sum_{(i,j)\in\overline{S}} a_{ij} \geq \sum_{(i,j)\in S} a_{ij} - \sum_{(i,j)\in S^*-\overline{S}} a_{ij} \geq -(2n-1)C.$$

This contradicts Eq. (7.14). Note that if $a_{ij} \geq 0$ for all $(i,j) \in \mathcal{A}$, the preceding argument can be modified to show that it is sufficient to have $a_{ij} < -(n-1)C$ for all artificial pairs (i,j).

On the other hand, the addition of artificial pairs with benefit $-(2n-1)C$ as per Eq. (7.14) expands the cost range of the problem by a factor of $(2n-1)$. In the context of ϵ-scaling, this necessitates a much larger starting value for ϵ and correspondingly large number of ϵ-scaling phases. If the problem is feasible, these extra scaling phases are wasted. Thus for problems which are normally expected to be feasible, it may be better to introduce artificial pairs with benefits that are of the order of $-C$, and then gradually scale downward these benefits towards the $-(2n-1)C$ threshold if artificial pairs persist in the assignments obtained by the auction algorithm. This procedure of scaling downward the benefits of the artificial pairs can be embedded in a number of ways within the ϵ-scaling procedure.

A third method to deal with infeasibility is based on the notion of maximally feasible flows and the decomposition method discussed in Section 3.1.4. It uses the property that even when the problem is infeasible, the auction algorithm will find an assignment of maximal cardinality in a finite number of iterations (this can be seen by a simple modification of the proof of Prop. 7.2). The idea now is to modify the auction algorithm so that during the first scaling phase we periodically check for the existence of an augmenting path from some unassigned person to some unassigned object (we can use a simple search of the breadth-first type, such as the one of Section 3.2). Once the cardinality of the current assignment becomes maximal while some person still remains unassigned, this check will establish that the problem is infeasible. With this modification, the auction algorithm will either find a feasible assignment and a set of prices satisfying ϵ-CS, or it will establish that the problem is infeasible and simultaneously obtain an assignment of maximal cardinality. In the former case, the algorithm will proceed with subsequent scaling phases of the algorithm, but with the breadth-first feature suppressed. In the latter case, we can use the maximal cardinality assignment obtained to decompose the problem into two or three component problems, as discussed in Section 3.1.4. Each of these problems is either a symmetric or an asymmetric assignment problem, which can be solved separately (see also Exercise 3.18).

Note a nice feature of the approach just described: In the case of a feasible problem, it involves little additional computation (the breadth-first searches of the first scaling phase) over the unmodified algorithm. In the case of an infeasible problem, the computation of the first scaling phase is not wasted, since it provides good starting prices for the subsequent scaling phases.

7.2 EXTENSIONS OF THE AUCTION ALGORITHM

The auction algorithm can be extended to deal effectively with the special features of modified versions of the assignment problem. In this section, we develop several such extensions.

7.2.1 Reverse Auction

In the auction algorithm, persons compete for objects by bidding and raising the price of their best object. It is possible to use an alternative form of the auction algorithm, called *reverse auction*, where, roughly, the *objects* compete for persons by essentially offering discounts.

To describe this algorithm, we introduce a *profit* variable π_i for each person i. Profits play for persons a role analogous to the role prices play for objects. We can describe reverse auction in two equivalent ways: one where unassigned objects lower their prices as much as possible to attract an unassigned person or to lure a person away from its currently held object without violating ϵ-CS, and another where unassigned objects select a best person and raise his or her profit as much as possible without violating ϵ-CS. For analytical convenience, we will adopt the second description rather than the first, leaving the proof of their equivalence as Exercise 7.8 for the reader.

Let us consider the following ϵ-CS condition for a (partial) assignment S and a profit vector π:

$$a_{ij} - \pi_i \geq \max_{k \in B(j)} \{a_{kj} - \pi_k\} - \epsilon, \qquad \forall\, (i,j) \in S, \qquad (7.15)$$

where $B(j)$ is the set of persons that can be assigned to object j,

$$B(j) = \{i \mid (i,j) \in \mathcal{A}\}.$$

We assume that this set is nonempty for all j, which is of course required for feasibility of the problem. Note the symmetry of this condition with the corresponding one for prices; cf. Eq. (7.1). The reverse auction algorithm starts with and maintains an assignment and a profit vector π satisfying the above ϵ-CS condition. It terminates when the assignment is feasible. At the beginning of each iteration, we have an assignment S and a profit vector π satisfying the ϵ-CS condition (7.15).

Iteration of Reverse Auction

Let J be a nonempty subset of objects j that are unassigned under the assignment S. For each object $j \in J$:

1. Find a "best" person i_j such that

$$i_j = \arg \max_{i \in B(j)} \{a_{ij} - \pi_i\},$$

and the corresponding value

$$\beta_j = \max_{i \in B(j)} \{a_{ij} - \pi_i\},$$

and find

$$\omega_j = \max_{i \in B(j), i \neq i_j} \{a_{ij} - \pi_i\}.$$

[If i_j is the only person in $B(j)$, we define ω_j to be $-\infty$ or, for computational purposes, a number that is much smaller than β_j.]

2. Each object $j \in J$ bids for person i_j an amount

$$b_{i_j j} = \pi_{i_j} + \beta_j - \omega_j + \epsilon = a_{i_j j} - \omega_j + \epsilon.$$

3. For each person i that received at least one bid, increase π_i to the highest bid,

$$\pi_i := \max_{j \in P(i)} b_{ij},$$

where $P(i)$ is the set of objects from which i received a bid; remove from the assignment S any pair (i, j) (if i was assigned to some j under S), and add to S the pair (i, j_i), where j_i is an object in $P(i)$ attaining the maximum above.

Note that reverse auction is identical to (forward) auction with the roles of persons and objects, and the roles of profits and prices interchanged. Thus, by using the corresponding (forward) auction result (cf. Prop. 7.2), we have the following proposition.

Proposition 7.4: If at least one feasible assignment exists, the reverse auction algorithm terminates with a feasible assignment that is within $n\epsilon$ of being optimal (and is optimal if the problem data are integer and $\epsilon < 1/n$).

Combined Forward and Reverse Auction

One of the reasons we are interested in reverse auction is to construct

algorithms that switch from forward to reverse auction and back. Such
algorithms must simultaneously maintain a price vector p satisfying the
ϵ-CS condition (7.1) and a profit vector π satisfying the ϵ-CS condition
(7.15). To this end we introduce an ϵ-CS condition for the *pair* (π, p),
which (as we will see) implies the other two. Maintaining this condition is
essential for switching gracefully between forward and reverse auction.

Definition 7.1: An assignment S and a pair (π, p) are said to satisfy
ϵ-CS if

$$\pi_i + p_j \geq a_{ij} - \epsilon, \qquad \forall\ (i,j) \in \mathcal{A}, \qquad (7.16)$$

$$\pi_i + p_j = a_{ij}, \qquad \forall\ (i,j) \in S. \qquad (7.17)$$

We have the following proposition.

Proposition 7.5: Suppose that an assignment S together with a
profit-price pair (π, p) satisfy ϵ-CS. Then:

(a) S and π satisfy the ϵ-CS condition

$$a_{ij} - \pi_i \geq \max_{k \in B(j)} \{a_{kj} - \pi_k\} - \epsilon, \qquad \forall\ (i,j) \in S. \qquad (7.18)$$

(b) S and p satisfy the ϵ-CS condition

$$a_{ij} - p_j \geq \max_{k \in A(i)} \{a_{ik} - p_k\} - \epsilon, \qquad \forall\ (i,j) \in S. \qquad (7.19)$$

(c) If S is feasible, then S is within $n\epsilon$ of being an optimal assignment.

Proof: (a) In view of Eq. (7.17), for all $(i,j) \in S$, we have $p_j = a_{ij} - \pi_i$,
so Eq. (7.16) implies that $a_{ij} - \pi_i \geq a_{kj} - \pi_k - \epsilon$ for all $k \in B(j)$. This
shows Eq. (7.18).

(b) The proof is similar to part (a), with the roles of π and p interchanged.

(c) Since by part (b) the ϵ-CS condition (7.19) is satisfied, Prop. 1.4 of
Section 1.3.3 implies that S is within $n\epsilon$ of being optimal. **Q.E.D.**

We now introduce a combined forward/reverse auction algorithm.
The algorithm starts with and maintains an assignment S and a profit-price
pair (π, p) satisfying the ϵ-CS conditions (7.16) and (7.17). It terminates

when the assignment is feasible.

Combined Forward/Reverse Auction Algorithm

Step 1 (Run forward auction): Execute a finite number of iterations of the forward auction algorithm (subject to the termination condition), and at the end of each iteration (after increasing the prices of the objects that received a bid) set

$$\pi_i = a_{ij_i} - p_{j_i} \tag{7.20}$$

for every person-object pair (i, j_i) that entered the assignment during the iteration. Go to Step 2.

Step 2 (Run reverse auction): Execute a finite number of iterations of the reverse auction algorithm (subject to the termination condition), and at the end of each iteration (after increasing the profits of the persons that received a bid) set

$$p_j = a_{i_j j} - \pi_{i_j} \tag{7.21}$$

for every person-object pair (i_j, j) that entered the assignment during the iteration. Go to Step 1.

Note that the additional overhead of the combined algorithm over the forward or the reverse algorithm is minimal; just one update of the form (7.20) or (7.21) is required per iteration for each object or person that received a bid during the iteration. An important property is that these updates maintain the ϵ-CS conditions (7.16) and (7.17) for the pair (π, p), and therefore, by Prop. 7.5, maintain the required ϵ-CS conditions (7.18) and (7.19) for π and p, respectively. This is shown in the following proposition.

Proposition 7.6: If the assignment and the profit-price pair available at the start of an iteration of either the forward or the reverse auction algorithm satisfy the ϵ-CS conditions (7.16) and (7.17), the same is true for the assignment and the profit-price pair obtained at the end of the iteration, provided Eq. (7.20) is used to update π (in the case of forward auction), and Eq. (7.21) is used to update p (in the case of reverse auction).

Proof: Assume for concreteness that forward auction is used, and let (π, p) and $(\overline{\pi}, \overline{p})$ be the profit-price pair before and after the iteration, respectively. Then, $\bar{p}_j \geq p_j$ for all j (with strict inequality if and only if j received a bid during the iteration). Therefore, we have $\bar{\pi}_i + \bar{p}_j \geq a_{ij} - \epsilon$ for all (i, j) such that $\pi_i = \bar{\pi}_i$. Furthermore, we have $\bar{\pi}_i + \bar{p}_j = \pi_i + p_j = a_{ij}$ for all (i, j) that belong to the assignment before as well as after the iteration. Also, in view of the update (7.20), we have $\bar{\pi}_i + \bar{p}_{j_i} = a_{ij_i}$ for all pairs (i, j_i) that entered the assignment during the iteration. What remains is to verify that the condition

$$\bar{\pi}_i + \bar{p}_j \geq a_{ij} - \epsilon, \qquad \forall\ j \in A(i), \tag{7.22}$$

holds for all persons i that submitted a bid and were assigned to an object, say j_i, during the iteration. Indeed, for such a person i, we have, by Eq. (7.4),

$$\bar{p}_{j_i} = a_{ij_i} - \max_{j \in A(i), j \neq j_i} \{a_{ij} - p_j\} + \epsilon,$$

which implies that

$$\bar{\pi}_i = a_{ij_i} - \bar{p}_{j_i} \geq a_{ij} - p_j - \epsilon \geq a_{ij} - \bar{p}_j - \epsilon, \qquad \forall\ j \in A(i).$$

This shows the desired relation (7.22). **Q.E.D.**

Note that during forward auction the object prices p_j increase while the profits π_i decrease, but exactly the opposite happens in reverse auction. For this reason, the termination proof that we used for forward and for reverse auction does not apply to the combined method. Indeed, it is possible to construct examples of feasible problems where the combined method never terminates if the switch between forward and reverse auctions is done arbitrarily. However, it is easy to provide a device guaranteeing that the combined algorithm terminates for a feasible problem; it is sufficient to ensure that some "irreversible progress" is made before switching between forward and reverse auction. One easily implementable possibility is to refrain from switching until the number of assigned person-object pairs increases by at least one.

The combined forward/reverse auction algorithm often works substantially faster than the forward version. It seems to be affected less by "price wars," that is, protracted sequences of small price rises by a number of persons bidding for a smaller number of objects. Price wars can still occur in the combined algorithm, but they arise through more complex and unlikely problem structures than in the forward algorithm. For this reason the combined forward/reverse auction algorithm depends less on ϵ-scaling for good performance than its forward counterpart; in fact, starting with $\epsilon = 1/(n+1)$, thus bypassing ϵ-scaling, is sometimes the best choice.

7.2.2 Auction Algorithms for Asymmetric Assignment

Reverse auction can be used in conjunction with forward auction to provide algorithms for solving the asymmetric assignment problem, where the number of objects n is larger than the number of persons m. Here we still require that each person be assigned to some object, but we allow objects to remain unassigned. As before, an assignment S is a (possibly empty) set of person-object pairs (i,j) such that $j \in A(i)$ for all $(i,j) \in S$; for each person i there can be at most one pair $(i,j) \in S$; and for every object j there can be at most one pair $(i,j) \in S$. The assignment S is said to be feasible if all persons are assigned under S.

The corresponding linear programming problem is

$$
\text{maximize} \quad \sum_{(i,j) \in \mathcal{A}} a_{ij} x_{ij}
$$

$$
\text{subject to} \quad \sum_{j \in A(i)} x_{ij} = 1, \quad \forall\, i = 1, \ldots, m,
$$

$$
\sum_{i \in B(j)} x_{ij} \leq 1, \quad \forall\, j = 1, \ldots, n,
$$

$$
0 \leq x_{ij}, \quad \forall\, (i,j) \in \mathcal{A}.
$$

We can convert this program to the minimum cost flow problem

$$
\text{minimize} \quad \sum_{(i,j) \in \mathcal{A}} (-a_{ij}) x_{ij}
$$

$$
\text{subject to} \quad \sum_{j \in A(i)} x_{ij} = 1, \quad \forall\, i = 1, \ldots, m,
$$

$$
\sum_{i \in B(j)} x_{ij} + x_{sj} = 1, \quad \forall\, j = 1, \ldots, n,
$$

$$
\sum_{j=1}^{n} x_{sj} = n - m,
$$

$$
0 \leq x_{ij}, \quad \forall\, (i,j) \in \mathcal{A},
$$

$$
0 \leq x_{sj}, \quad \forall\, j = 1, \ldots, n,
$$

by replacing maximization by minimization, by reversing the sign of a_{ij}, and by introducing a supersource node s, which is connected to each object node j by an arc (s,j) of zero cost and feasible flow range $[0, \infty)$ (see Fig. 7.2).

Using the duality theory of Section 4.2, it can be seen that the corresponding dual problem is

$$
\text{minimize} \quad \sum_{i=1}^{m} \pi_i + \sum_{j=1}^{n} p_j - (n - m)\lambda
$$

$$
\text{subject to} \quad \pi_i + p_j \geq a_{ij}, \quad \forall\, (i,j) \in \mathcal{A},
$$

$$
\lambda \leq p_j, \quad \forall\, j = 1, \ldots, n,
$$

(7.23)

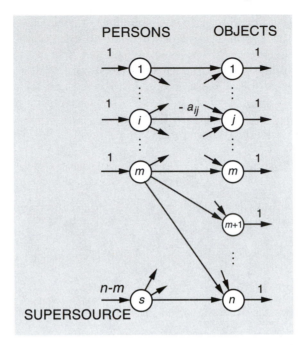

Figure 7.2: Converting an asymmetric assignment problem into a minimum cost flow problem involving a supersource node s and a zero cost artificial arc (s, j) with feasible flow range $[0, \infty)$ for each object j.

where we have converted maximization to minimization, we have used $-\pi_i$ in place of the price of each person node i, and we have denoted by λ the price of the supersource node s.

We now introduce an ϵ-CS condition for an assignment S and a pair (π, p).

Definition 7.2: An assignment S and a pair (π, p) are said to satisfy ϵ-CS if

$$\pi_i + p_j \geq a_{ij} - \epsilon, \qquad \forall \, (i, j) \in \mathcal{A}, \tag{7.24}$$

$$\pi_i + p_j = a_{ij}, \qquad \forall \, (i, j) \in S, \tag{7.25}$$

$$p_j \leq \min_{k:\ \text{assigned under } S} p_k, \qquad \forall \, j \text{ that are unassigned under } S. \tag{7.26}$$

The following proposition clarifies the significance of the preceding ϵ-CS condition.

Proposition 7.7: If a feasible assignment S satisfies the ϵ-CS conditions (7.24)-(7.26) together with a pair (π, p), then S is within $m\epsilon$ of being optimal for the asymmetric assignment problem. The triplet $(\hat{\pi}, \hat{p}, \lambda)$, where

$$\lambda = \min_{k:\ \text{assigned under } S} p_k, \tag{7.27}$$

$$\hat{\pi}_i = \pi_i + \epsilon, \qquad \forall\ i = 1, \ldots, m, \tag{7.28}$$

$$\hat{p}_j = \begin{cases} p_j & \text{if } j \text{ is assigned under } S, \\ \lambda & \text{if } j \text{ is unassigned under } S, \end{cases} \qquad \forall\ j = 1, \ldots, n, \tag{7.29}$$

is within $m\epsilon$ of being an optimal solution of the dual problem (7.23).

Proof: For any feasible assignment $\{(i, k_i) \mid i = 1, \ldots, m\}$ and for any triplet $(\overline{\pi}, \overline{p}, \lambda)$ satisfying the dual feasibility constraints $\overline{\pi}_i + \overline{p}_j \geq a_{ij}$ for all $(i, j) \in \mathcal{A}$ and $\lambda \leq \overline{p}_j$ for all j, we have

$$\sum_{i=1}^{m} a_{ik_i} \leq \sum_{i=1}^{m} \overline{\pi}_i + \sum_{i=1}^{m} \overline{p}_{k_i} \leq \sum_{i=1}^{m} \overline{\pi}_i + \sum_{j=1}^{n} \overline{p}_j - (n-m)\lambda.$$

By maximizing over all feasible assignments $\{(i, k_i) \mid i = 1, \ldots, m\}$ and by minimizing over all dual-feasible triplets $(\overline{\pi}, \overline{p}, \lambda)$, we see that

$$A^* \leq D^*,$$

where A^* is the optimal assignment value and D^* is the minimal dual cost.

Let now $S = \{(i, j_i) \mid i = 1, \ldots, m\}$ be the given assignment satisfying ϵ-CS together with (π, p), and consider the triplet $(\hat{\pi}, \hat{p}, \lambda)$ defined by Eqs. (7.27)-(7.29). Since for all i we have $\hat{\pi}_i + \hat{p}_{j_i} = a_{ij} + \epsilon$, we obtain

$$A^* \geq \sum_{i=1}^{m} a_{ij_i}$$

$$= \sum_{i=1}^{m} \hat{\pi}_i + \sum_{i=1}^{m} \hat{p}_{j_i} - m\epsilon$$

$$\geq \sum_{i=1}^{m} \hat{\pi}_i + \sum_{j=1}^{n} \hat{p}_j - (n-m)\lambda - m\epsilon$$

$$\geq D^* - m\epsilon,$$

where the last inequality holds because the triplet $(\hat{\pi}, \hat{p}, \lambda)$ is feasible for the dual problem. Since we showed earlier that $A^* \leq D^*$, the desired conclusion follows. **Q.E.D.**

Consider now trying to solve the asymmetric assignment problem by means of auction. We can start with any assignment S and pair (π, p) satisfying the first two ϵ-CS conditions (7.24) and (7.25), and perform a forward auction (as defined earlier for the symmetric assignment problem) up to the point where each person is assigned to a distinct object. For a feasible problem, by essentially repeating the proof of Prop. 7.2 for the symmetric case, it can be seen that this will yield, in a finite number of iterations, a feasible assignment S satisfying the first two conditions (7.24) and (7.25). However, this assignment may not be optimal, because the prices of the unassigned objects j are not minimal; that is, they do not satisfy the third ϵ-CS condition (7.26).

To remedy this situation, we introduce a modified form of reverse auction to lower the prices of the unassigned objects so that, after several iterations in which persons may be reassigned to other objects, the third condition, (7.26), is satisfied. We will show that the assignment thus obtained satisfies all the ϵ-CS conditions (7.24)-(7.26), and by Prop. 7.7, is optimal within $m\epsilon$ (and thus optimal if the problem data are integer and $\epsilon < 1/m$).

The modified reverse auction starts with a feasible assignment S and with a pair (π, p) satisfying the first two ϵ-CS conditions (7.24) and (7.25). [For a feasible problem, such an S and (π, p) can be obtained by regular forward or reverse auction, as discussed earlier.] Let us denote by λ the minimal assigned object price under the initial assignment,

$$\lambda = \min_{\substack{j:\ \text{assigned under the} \\ \text{initial assignment } S}} p_j.$$

The typical iteration of modified reverse auction is the same as the one of reverse auction, except that only unassigned objects j with $p_j > \lambda$ participate in the auction. In particular, the algorithm maintains a feasible assignment S and a pair (π, p) satisfying Eqs. (7.24) and (7.25), and terminates when all unassigned objects j satisfy $p_j \leq \lambda$, in which case it will be seen that the third ϵ-CS condition (7.26) is satisfied as well. The scalar λ is kept fixed throughout the algorithm.

Iteration of Reverse Auction for Asymmetric Assignment

Select an object j that is unassigned under the assignment S and satisfies $p_j > \lambda$ (if no such object can be found, the algorithm terminates). Find a "best" person i_j such that

$$i_j = \arg\max_{i \in B(j)} \{a_{ij} - \pi_i\},$$

and the corresponding value

$$\beta_j = \max_{i \in B(j)} \{a_{ij} - \pi_i\}, \tag{7.30}$$

and find

$$\omega_j = \max_{i \in B(j), \, i \neq i_j} \{a_{ij} - \pi_i\}. \tag{7.31}$$

[If i_j is the only person in $B(j)$, we define ω_j to be $-\infty$.] If $\lambda \geq \beta_j - \epsilon$, set $p_j := \lambda$ and go to the next iteration. Otherwise, let

$$\delta = \min\{\beta_j - \lambda, \beta_j - \omega_j + \epsilon\}. \tag{7.32}$$

Set

$$p_j := \beta_j - \delta, \tag{7.33}$$

$$\pi_{i_j} := \pi_{i_j} + \delta, \tag{7.34}$$

add to the assignment S the pair (i_j, j), and remove from S the pair (i_j, j'), where j' is the object that was assigned to i_j under S at the start of the iteration.

Note that the formula (7.32) for the bidding increment δ is such that the object j enters the assignment at a price which is no less that λ [and is equal to λ if and only if the minimum in Eq. (7.32) is attained by the first term]. Furthermore, when δ is calculated (that is, when $\lambda > \beta_j - \epsilon$) we have $\delta \geq \epsilon$, so it can be seen from Eqs. (7.33) and (7.34) that, throughout the algorithm, prices are monotonically decreasing and profits are monotonically increasing. The following proposition establishes the validity of the method.

Proposition 7.8: The preceding reverse auction algorithm for the asymmetric assignment problem terminates with an assignment that is within $m\epsilon$ of being optimal.

Proof: In view of Prop. 7.7, the result will follow once we prove the following:

(a) The modified reverse auction iteration preserves the first two ϵ-CS conditions (7.24) and (7.25), as well as the condition

$$\lambda \leq \min_{\substack{j: \text{ assigned under the} \\ \text{current assignment } S}} p_j, \tag{7.35}$$

so upon termination of the algorithm (necessarily with the prices of all unassigned objects less or equal to λ) the third ϵ-CS condition, (7.26), is satisfied.

(b) The algorithm terminates.

We will prove these facts in sequence.

We assume that the conditions (7.24), (7.25), and (7.35) are satisfied at the start of an iteration, and we will show that they are also satisfied at the end of the iteration. First consider the case where there is no change in the assignment, which happens when $\lambda \geq \beta_j - \epsilon$. Then Eqs. (7.25) and (7.35) are automatically satisfied at the end of the iteration; only p_j changes in the iteration according to

$$p_j := \lambda \geq \beta_j - \epsilon = \max_{i \in B(j)} \{a_{ij} - \pi_i\} - \epsilon,$$

so the condition (7.24) is also satisfied at the end of the iteration.

Next consider the case where there is a change in the assignment during the iteration. Let (π, p) and $(\overline{\pi}, \overline{p})$ be the profit-price pair before and after the iteration, respectively, and let j and i_j be the object and person involved in the iteration. By construction [cf. Eqs. (7.33) and (7.34)], we have $\overline{\pi}_{i_j} + \overline{p}_j = a_{i_j j}$, and since $\overline{\pi}_i = \pi_i$ and $\overline{p}_k = p_k$ for all $i \neq i_j$ and $k \neq j$, we see that the condition (7.25) $(\overline{\pi}_i + \overline{p}_k = a_{ik})$ is satisfied for all assigned pairs (i, k) at the end of the iteration.

To show that Eq. (7.24) holds at the end of the iteration, i.e.,

$$\overline{\pi}_i + \overline{p}_k \geq a_{ik} - \epsilon, \qquad \forall\ (i, k) \in \mathcal{A}, \tag{7.36}$$

consider first objects $k \neq j$. Then, $\overline{p}_k = p_k$ and since $\overline{\pi}_i \geq \pi_i$ for all i, the above condition holds, since our hypothesis is that at the start of the iteration we have $\pi_i + p_k \geq a_{ik} - \epsilon$ for all (i, k). Consider next the case $k = j$. Then condition (7.36) holds for $i = i_j$, since $\overline{\pi}_{i_j} + \overline{p}_j = a_{i_j j}$. Also using Eqs. (7.30)-(7.33) and the fact $\delta \geq \epsilon$, we have for all $i \neq i_j$

$$\begin{aligned}
\overline{\pi}_i + \overline{p}_j &= \pi_i + \overline{p}_j \\
&\geq \pi_i + \beta_j - (\beta_j - \omega_j + \epsilon) \\
&= \pi_i + \omega_j - \epsilon \\
&\geq \pi_i + (a_{ij} - \pi_i) - \epsilon \\
&= a_{ij} - \epsilon,
\end{aligned}$$

so condition (7.36) holds for $i \neq i_j$ and $k = j$, completing its proof. To see that condition (7.35) is maintained by the iteration, note that by Eqs. (7.30), (7.31), and (7.33), we have

$$\overline{p}_j = \beta_j - \delta \geq \beta_j - (\beta_j - \lambda) = \lambda.$$

Finally, to show that the algorithm terminates, we note that in the typical iteration involving object j and person i_j there are two possibilities:

(1) The price of object j is set to λ without the object entering the assignment; this occurs if $\lambda \geq \beta_j - \epsilon$.

(2) The profit of person i_j increases by at least ϵ [this is seen from the definition (7.32) of δ; we have $\lambda < \beta_j - \epsilon$ and $\beta_j \geq \omega_j$, so $\delta \geq \epsilon$].

Since only objects j with $p_j > \lambda$ can participate in the auction, possibility (1) can occur only a finite number of times. Thus, if the algorithm does not terminate, the profits of some persons will increase to ∞. This is impossible, since when person i is assigned to object j, we must have by Eqs. (7.25) and (7.35)

$$\pi_i = a_{ij} - p_j \leq a_{ij} - \lambda,$$

so the profits are bounded from above by $\max_{(i,j)\in\mathcal{A}} a_{ij} - \lambda$. Thus the algorithm must terminate.   **Q.E.D.**

Note that one may bypass the modified reverse auction algorithm by starting the forward auction with all object prices equal to zero. Upon termination of the forward auction, the prices of the unassigned objects will still be at zero, while the prices of the assigned objects will be nonnegative. Therefore the ϵ-CS condition (7.26) will be satisfied, and the modified reverse auction will be unnecessary (see Exercise 7.9).

Unfortunately the requirement of zero initial object prices is incompatible with ϵ-scaling. The principal advantage offered by the modified reverse auction algorithm is that it allows arbitrary initial object prices for the forward auction, thereby also allowing the use of ϵ-scaling. This can be shown to improve the theoretical worst-case complexity of the method, and is often beneficial in practice.

The method for asymmetric assignment problems just described operates principally as a forward algorithm and uses reverse auction only near the end, after the forward algorithm has terminated, to rectify violations of the ϵ-CS conditions. An alternative is to switch more frequently between forward and reverse auction, similar to the algorithm described earlier in this section for symmetric problems. We refer to Bertsekas and Castañon [1992] for methods of this type, together with computational results suggesting a more favorable practical performance over the asymmetric assignment method given earlier.

Reverse auction can also be used in the context of other types of network flow problems. One example is the variation of the asymmetric assignment problem where persons (as well as objects) need not be assigned if this degrades the assignment's value (see Exercise 7.11). Another assignment-like problem where reverse auction finds use is the multiassignment problem, discussed in Exercise 7.10.

7.2.3   Auction Algorithms with Similar Persons

In this section, we develop an auction algorithm to deal efficiently with assignment problems that involve groups of persons that are indistinguishable in the sense that they can be assigned to the same objects and with the same corresponding benefits. This algorithm provides a general approach to extend the auction algorithm to the minimum cost flow problem and some of its special cases, such as the max-flow and the transportation problems, as we will show in Section 7.3.3.

We introduce the following definition in the context of the asymmetric or the symmetric assignment problem:

Definition 7.3: We say that two persons i and i' are *similar*, if

$$A(i) = A(i'), \qquad \text{and} \qquad a_{ij} = a_{i'j} \ \ \forall \ j \in A(i).$$

For each person i, the set of all persons similar to i is called the *similarity class of i*.

When there are similar persons, the auction algorithm can get bogged down into a long sequence of bids (known as a "price war"), whereby a number of similar persons compete for a smaller number of objects by making small incremental price changes. An example is given in Fig. 7.3. It turns out that if one is aware of the presence of similar persons, one can "compress" a price war within a similarity class into a single iteration. It is important to note that the corresponding algorithm is still a special case of the auction algorithms of Section 7.1; the computations are merely streamlined by combining many bids into a "collective" bid by the persons of a similarity class.

The method to resolve a price war within a similarity class is to let the auction algorithm run its course, then look at the final results and see how they can be essentially reproduced with less calculation. In particular, suppose that we have an assignment-price pair (S, p) satisfying ϵ-CS, and that a similarity class M has m persons, only $q < m$ of which are assigned under S. Suppose that we restrict the auction algorithm to run within M; that is, we require the bidding person to be from M, until all persons in M are assigned. We call this the *M-restricted auction*.

The final results of an M-restricted auction are quite predictable. In particular, the set

$A_{new} =$ The m objects that are assigned to persons in M at the end
of the M-restricted auction

consists of the set

$A_{old} =$ The q objects that were assigned to persons in M at the beginning
of the M-restricted auction

plus $m - q$ extra objects that are not in A_{old}. These extra objects are those objects not in A_{old} that offered the best value $a_{ij} - p_j$ for the persons

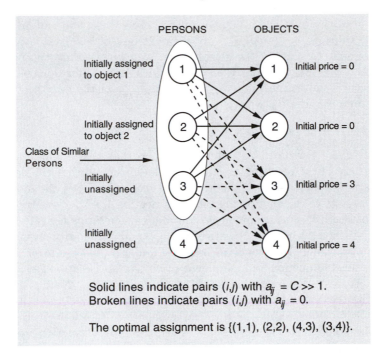

Figure 7.3: An example of an assignment problem with similar persons. Here the persons 1, 2, and 3 form a similarity class. This structure induces a price war in the auction algorithm. The persons 1, 2, and 3 will keep on bidding up the prices of objects 1 and 2 until the prices p_1 and p_2 reach a sufficiently high level (at least $C+3$), so that either object 3 or object 4 receives a bid from one of these persons. The price increments will be at most 2ϵ.

$i \in M$ (under the price vector p that prevailed at the start of the M-restricted auction). For a more precise description, let us label the set of objects not in A_{old} in order of decreasing value, that is,

$$\{j \mid j \notin A_{old}\} = \{j_1, \ldots, j_{m-q}, j_{m-q+1}, \ldots, j_{n-q}\}, \qquad (7.37)$$

where for all persons $i \in M$,

$$a_{ij_r} - p_{j_r} \ge a_{ij_{r+1}} - p_{j_{r+1}}, \qquad r = 1, \ldots, n - q - 1. \qquad (7.38)$$

Then

$$A_{new} = A_{old} \cup \{j_1, \ldots, j_{m-q}\}. \qquad (7.39)$$

The price changes of the objects as a result of the M-restricted auction can also be predicted to a great extent. In particular, the prices of the objects that are not in A_{new} will not change, since these objects do not receive any bid during the M-restricted auction. The ultimate prices of the objects $j \in A_{new}$ will be such that the corresponding values $a_{ij} - p_j$

for the persons $i \in M$ will all be within ϵ of each other, and will be no less than the value $a_{ij_{m-q+1}} - p_{j_{m-q+1}}$ of the next best object j_{m-q+1} minus ϵ. At this point, to simplify the calculations, we can just raise the prices of the objects $j \in A_{new}$ so that their final values $a_{ij} - p_j$ for persons $i \in M$ are exactly equal to the value $a_{ij_{m-q+1}} - p_{j_{m-q+1}}$ of the next best object j_{m-q+1} minus ϵ; that is, we set

$$p_j := a_{ij} - \left(a_{ij_{m-q+1}} - p_{j_{m-q+1}} \right) + \epsilon, \qquad \forall\, j \in A_{new}, \qquad (7.40)$$

where i is any person in M. It can be seen that this maintains the ϵ-CS property of the resulting assignment-price pair, and that the desirable termination properties of the algorithm are maintained (see the discussion of the variants of the auction algorithm in Section 7.1.3).

To establish some terminology, consider the operation that starts with an assignment-price pair (p, S) satisfying ϵ-CS and a similarity class M that has m persons, only q of which are assigned under S, and produces through an M-restricted auction an assignment-price pair specified by Eqs. (7.37)-(7.40). We call this operation an M-*auction iteration*. Note that when the similarity class M consists of a single person, an M-auction iteration produces the same results as the simpler auction iteration given earlier. Thus the algorithm that consists of a sequence of M-auction iterations generalizes the auction algorithm given earlier, and deals effectively with the presence of similarity classes. The table of Fig. 7.4 illustrates this algorithm.

Suppose now that this algorithm is started with an assignment-price pair for which the following property holds:

If A_M is the set of objects assigned to persons of a similarity class M, the values
$$a_{ij} - p_j, \qquad i \in M, \; j \in A_M,$$
are all equal, and no less than the values offered by all other objects $j \notin A_M$ minus ϵ.

Then it can seen from Eqs. (7.37)-(7.40) that throughout the algorithm this property is maintained. Thus, if in particular the benefits a_{ij} of the objects in a subset $A'_M \subset A_M$ are equal, the prices p_j, $j \in A'_M$ must all be equal. This property will be useful in Section 7.3.3, where we will develop the connection between the auction algorithm and some other price-based algorithms for the max-flow and the minimum cost flow problems.

7.3 THE PREFLOW-PUSH ALGORITHM FOR MAX-FLOW

In this section, we discuss the *preflow-push algorithm* for the max-flow problem. This algorithm was developed independently of the auction algorithm, and was motivated by the notion of a *preflow*, which is central in the

At Start of Iteration #	Object Prices	Assigned Pairs	Bidder Class M	Preferred Object(s)
1	0,0,3,4	(1,1),(2,2)	$\{1,2,3\}$	1,2,3
2	$C+4+\epsilon, C+4+\epsilon, 4+\epsilon, 4$	(1,1),(2,2),(3,3)	$\{4\}$	3
3	$C+4+\epsilon, C+4+\epsilon, C+4+\epsilon, 4$	(1,1),(2,2),(4,3)	$\{1,2,3\}$	1,2,4
Final	$2C+4+2\epsilon, 2C+4+2\epsilon$ $C+4+\epsilon, C+4+2\epsilon$	(1,1),(2,2) (4,3),(3,4)		

Figure 7.4: Illustration of the algorithm based on M-auction iterations for the problem of Fig. 7.3. In this example, the initial price vector is $(0,0,3,4)$ and the initial partial assignment consists of the pairs $(1,1)$ and $(2,2)$. We first perform an M-auction iteration for the similarity class $\{1,2,3\}$. We then perform an iteration for person 4, and then again an M-auction iteration for the similarity class $\{1,2,3\}$. The last iteration assigns the remaining object 4, and the algorithm terminates without a price war of the type discussed in Fig. 7.3.

max-flow algorithm of Karzanov [1974] (a preflow is a capacity-feasible flow vector, which has nonpositive divergence for each node except the source). In retrospect, however, it was found to be closely related to the auction algorithm. In particular, we will show in Section 7.3.3 that it is mathematically equivalent to a version of the auction algorithm applied to a special type of assignment problem.

We consider the max-flow problem of maximizing the flow out of the source node 1 (or the flow into the sink node N)

$$\sum_{\{j|(1,j)\in\mathcal{A}\}} x_{1j}$$

over all capacity-feasible flow vectors x such that the divergence of every node i except for the source node 1 and the sink node N is zero. We assume that the lower arc flow bounds are 0, so the capacity constraints are

$$0 \le x_{ij} \le c_{ij}, \qquad \forall\, (i,j) \in \mathcal{A}.$$

Furthermore, to avoid degenerate cases, we assume that each node has at least one incident arc and that the upper flow bound c_{ij} is positive for each arc (i,j).

The preflow-push algorithm shares some of the features of the price-based algorithm for the max-flow problem of Section 3.3. In particular, both algorithms use prices to guide flow changes, and maintain a valid flow-price pair that satisfies the same ϵ-CS condition. Let us introduce some definitions. Given a capacity-feasible flow vector x, the set of *eligible arcs* of i is

$$A(i, x) = \{(i, j) \mid x_{ij} < c_{ij}\} \cup \{(j, i) \mid 0 < x_{ji}\},$$

and the corresponding set of *eligible neighbors* of i is

$$N(i, x) = \{j \mid (i, j) \in A(i, x) \text{ or } (j, i) \in A(i, x)\}.$$

The *candidate list of a node i* is defined to be the (possibly empty) set of its eligible incident arcs (i, j) or (j, i) such that $p_i = p_j + 1$. A capacity-feasible flow vector x together with a price vector $p = \{p_i \mid i \in \mathcal{N}\}$ are said to be a *valid pair* if

$$p_i \leq p_j + 1, \qquad \forall\; j \text{ that are eligible neighbors of } i.$$

We will see in Section 7.3.3 that the above relation is a form of the ϵ-CS condition introduced in connection with the auction algorithm for the assignment problem. Finally, the opposite of the divergence of a node i,

$$g_i = \sum_{\{j \mid (j,i) \in A\}} x_{ji} - \sum_{\{j \mid (i,j) \in A\}} x_{ij},$$

is called the *surplus* of i.

The preflow-push algorithm starts with and maintains a valid flow-price pair (x, p) such that x is capacity-feasible, p has integer components, and

$$g_1 \leq 0, \qquad g_i \geq 0, \;\; \forall\; i \neq 1,$$

$$p_1 = N, \qquad p_N = 0, \qquad 0 \leq p_i < N, \;\; \forall\; i \neq 1. \tag{7.41}$$

A possible initial choice is the pair (x, p) given by

$$x_{ij} = \begin{cases} c_{1j} & \text{if } i = 1, \\ 0 & \text{if } i \neq 1, \end{cases} \tag{7.42}$$

$$p_i = \begin{cases} N & \text{if } i = 1, \\ 0 & \text{if } i \neq 1. \end{cases} \tag{7.43}$$

There are two types of operations in the preflow-push algorithm:

(1) A *flow change*, which modifies the flow of some arc belonging to the candidate list of some node. The flow change is always in the direction from the node of higher price to the node of lower price.

(2) A *price rise*, which increases the price of some node whose candidate list is empty. The increment of price increase is the largest that maintains the validity of the flow-price pair. With this price increment, the candidate list of the node becomes nonempty.

The idea of the algorithm is to direct flow from nodes of higher price to nodes of lower price. By setting the price of the source node to N and the price of the sink node to 0 [cf. Eq. (7.41)], the algorithm moves flow in the desired general direction from source to sink. This idea is shared with the price-based augmenting path algorithm of Section 3.3.

At the start of each iteration of the preflow-push algorithm, a node $i \neq N$ with $p_i < N$ and $g_i > 0$ is selected; if no such node can be found, the algorithm terminates. The typical iteration is as follows:

Iteration of the Preflow-Push Algorithm

Step 1: (Scan candidate arc) Select an arc (i,j) of the candidate list of i and go to Step 2, or an arc (j,i) of the candidate list of i and go to Step 3; if the candidate list is empty, go to Step 4.

Step 2: (Push flow forward along arc (i,j)) Increase x_{ij} by $\delta = \min\{g_i, c_{ij} - x_{ij}\}$. If now $g_i = 0$ and $x_{ij} < c_{ij}$, stop; else go to Step 1.

Step 3: (Push flow backward along arc (j,i)) Decrease x_{ji} by $\delta = \min\{g_i, x_{ji}\}$. If now $g_i = 0$ and $0 < x_{ji}$, stop; else go to Step 1.

Step 4: (Increase price of node i) Raise p_i to the level

$$\overline{p}_i = \min\{p_j + 1 \mid (i,j) \in \mathcal{A} \text{ and } x_{ij} < c_{ij}, \text{ or } (j,i) \in \mathcal{A} \text{ and } 0 < x_{ji}\}. \tag{7.44}$$

Go to Step 1.

Figure 7.5 illustrates the preflow-push algorithm. As this figure shows, and as we will demonstrate shortly, the algorithm terminates with a flow vector under which a minimum cut separating the source from the sink is saturated. This flow vector is not necessarily maximum or even feasible, because some nodes other than the source and the sink may have nonzero surplus. We will demonstrate later how, starting from this flow vector, we can construct a maximum flow.

7.3.1   Analysis and Complexity

We will now establish the validity of the preflow-push algorithm, and we will estimate its running time. For purposes of easy reference, let us call the operation of Step 4 a *price rise* at node i, and let us call the operation of Step 2 (or Step 3) a *flow push* on arc (i,j) [a flow push on arc (j,i), respectively]. A flow push on arc (i,j) [or arc (j,i)] is said to be *saturating* if it results in setting the flow x_{ij} to its upper bound c_{ij} (the flow x_{ji} to its lower bound 0, respectively); otherwise, the flow push is said to be *nonsaturating*.

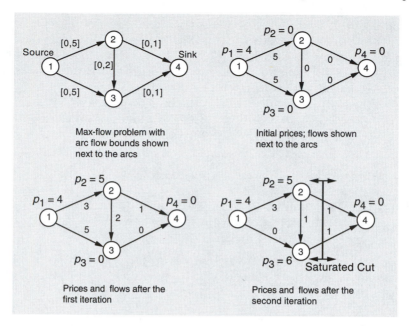

Figure 7.5: Preflow-push algorithm for the max-flow problem shown at the top left. The initialization of Eqs. (7.42) and (7.43) is shown at the top right.

1st Iteration: Node 2 is selected, its price is first raised to $p_2 = 1$, thereby creating the two candidate list arcs $(2,3)$ and $(2,4)$. Then 2 units of flow are pushed along $(2,3)$, and 1 unit of flow is pushed along $(2,4)$, thereby saturating these two arcs. The surplus of node 2 continues to be positive, so its price is again raised to $p_2 = 5$, thereby creating the candidate list arc $(1,2)$. Then 2 units of flow are pushed (backward) along this arc, to set the surplus of node 2 to 0. The resulting flow-price pair is shown at the bottom left.

2nd Iteration: Node 3 is selected, its price is first raised to $p_3 = 1$, thereby creating the candidate list arc $(3,4)$. Then 1 unit of flow is pushed along $(3,4)$. The surplus of node 3 continues to be positive, so its price is again raised to $p_3 = 5$, thereby creating the candidate list arc $(1,3)$. Then 5 units of flow are pushed (backward) along $(1,3)$. The surplus of node 3 continues to be positive, so its price is again raised to $p_3 = 6$, thereby creating the candidate list arc $(2,3)$. Then 1 unit of flow is pushed (backward) along this arc, to set the surplus of node 3 to 0. The resulting flow-price pair is shown at the bottom right.

    The algorithm terminates because all nodes other than the sink have prices that are no less than $N = 4$. Note that upon termination, the saturated cut obtained, $[\{1, 2, 3\}, \{4\}]$, is optimal. However, the flow obtained is not maximal or even feasible, because node 2 has positive surplus ($g_2 = 1$).

    For the purpose of calculating the running time of the algorithm, we assume that each time a price rise is performed at a node i, the candidate list of i is constructed and stored. At each iteration at node i, and up to the next price rise at i, arcs are selected from the top of the stored list at Step 1 of the iteration, and examined for eligibility. If an arc of the list is found not eligible or if the iteration results in a saturating push on that arc, the arc is removed from the list. In this way we are assured that between two successive price rises at a node, the incident arcs of the node are scanned only once in order to construct the candidate list.

The preflow-push algorithm leaves free the choice of the node i selected for iteration. It is possible to affect both the theoretical and the practical performance of the algorithm by proper choice of this node. We consider three particular choice rules:

(1) *Arbitrary Choice*: Here the node i chosen for iteration is arbitrary (subject to $i \neq N$, $p_i < N$, and $g_i > 0$).

(2) *First In-First Out Choice*: Here the nodes $i \neq N$ with $p_i < N$ and $g_i > 0$ are maintained in a first in-first out list and the node at the top of the list is chosen for iteration.

(3) *Highest Price Choice*: Here the node $i \neq N$ with $p_i < N$ and $g_i > 0$ whose price is maximum is chosen for iteration.

In all cases, we assume that the nodes $i \neq N$ with $p_i < N$ and $g_i > 0$ are kept in some list or data structure, which is such that the overhead for finding a node to iterate on is negligible in the sense that it does not affect the algorithm's complexity.

The following proposition shows that the algorithm terminates with an optimal saturated cut, and that with the first two methods for choice of node, the running time of the algorithm is $O(N^2A)$ and $O(N^3)$, respectively, where N is the number of nodes and A is the number of arcs. It turns out that the highest price choice method, with appropriate implementation, has a running time $O(N^2A^{1/2})$, which is faster than the running times of the other two methods. The proof of this is quite complex, however, so we refer to the original source, which is the paper by Cheriyan and Maheshwari [1989]. Based on the results of computational experimentation, the highest price choice method also appears to be the fastest in practice. For an example that provides some intuition for the reason, see Exercise 7.5. Following the proof of the proposition, we will show how a maximum flow can be constructed from the saturated cut by using a separate computation.

Proposition 7.9: The preflow-push algorithm terminates, and upon termination the flow vector x is such that there is a saturated cut $[\mathcal{N}^+, \mathcal{N}^-]$ with

$$1 \in \mathcal{N}^+, \qquad N \in \mathcal{N}^-, \tag{7.45}$$

$$g_i \geq 0, \qquad \forall\, i \neq 1 \text{ with } i \in \mathcal{N}^+, \tag{7.46}$$

$$g_i = 0, \qquad \forall\, i \neq N \text{ with } i \in \mathcal{N}^-. \tag{7.47}$$

This saturated cut is a minimum cut. Furthermore:

(a) With arbitrary choice of the node chosen for iteration, the running time is $O(N^2A)$.

(b) With first in-first out choice of the node chosen for iteration, the running time is $O(N^3)$.

Proof: We first make the following observations:

(1) All the flow-price pairs generated by the algorithm are valid.

(2) All the node prices are monotonically nondecreasing integers throughout the algorithm. Furthermore, a price rise at a node at Step 4 increases the price of the node by at least 1. This follows from Eq. (7.44) and the fact that a price rise at a node can be performed only if the candidate list of that node is empty.

(3) All the node prices range between 0 and $2N$, since all the initial prices are less or equal to N, a price rise at node i can set p_i to at most $1 + \max_{j \in \mathcal{N}} p_j$ and once p_i reaches or exceeds N, it remains constant.

(4) The surplus of every node other than node 1 is nonnegative throughout the algorithm. The reason is that a flow push from a node i cannot drive the surplus of i below zero, and cannot decrease the surplus of neighboring nodes.

Since by (2) above, a price rise at i increases p_i by at least 1 and once p_i exceeds $N-1$, it increases no further, it follows that there can be at most N price rises at each node. When iterating on node i and a saturating flow push occurs on an arc with end nodes i and j, we must have $p_i = p_j + 1$, so that one of the at most N increases of p_j must occur before this arc can become unsaturated and then saturated again in the direction from i to j. Thus the number of saturating flow pushes is at most $2N$ per arc, for a total of at most $2NA$.

We now argue by contradiction that the number of nonsaturating flow pushes is finite and therefore the algorithm terminates. Indeed, assume the contrary, i.e., that there is an infinite number of nonsaturating flow pushes. Since the number of price rises and saturating flow pushes is finite as argued earlier, it follows that there is an iteration after which the prices of all nodes remain constant at some final levels $\bar{p}_i$ while all flow pushes are nonsaturating. Since there is an infinite number of nonsaturating flow pushes, there must exist a pair of nodes i_2 and i_1 such that the number of flow pushes from i_2 to i_1 is infinite, implying that $\bar{p}_{i_2} = \bar{p}_{i_1} + 1$. Each of these nonsaturating flow pushes exhausts the surplus of i_2, so there must exist a node i_3 such that there is an infinite number of nonsaturating flow pushes from i_3 to i_2, implying that $\bar{p}_{i_3} = \bar{p}_{i_2} + 1$. Proceeding similarly, we can construct an infinite sequence of nodes i_k, $k = 1, 2, \ldots$, with corresponding prices satisfying $\overline{p}_{i_{k+1}} = \overline{p}_{i_k} + 1$ for all k. This is a contradiction since there is only a finite number of nodes.

Let us now show that upon termination of the algorithm, there is a saturated cut satisfying the conditions (7.45)-(7.47). Indeed, consider any node $i \neq N$ such that upon termination, we have $p_i \geq N$. We claim that there is no simple unblocked path from i to N upon termination. The reason is that if there exists such a path, and i_1 and i_2 are two successive nodes on this path, we must have $p_{i_1} \leq p_{i_2} + 1$, implying that p_i cannot exceed p_N (which is 0) by more than the number of arcs on the path, which is at most $N - 1$ – a contradiction. Thus, by Prop. 3.1, it follows that there must be a saturated cut $[\mathcal{N}^+, \mathcal{N}^-]$ separating node N from all the nodes i with $p_i \geq N$. The latter nodes include node 1 (by the algorithm's initialization), as well as the nodes i with $g_i > 0$ upon termination (by the rule for termination of the algorithm). This proves the conditions (7.45)-(7.47).

Consider a saturated cut $[\mathcal{N}^+, \mathcal{N}^-]$ obtained on termination and satisfying conditions (7.45)-(7.47). We will show that this cut is a minimum cut. To this end, we introduce a max-flow problem, referred to as the *modified problem*, which is the same as the original max-flow problem except that it contains an additional arc $(i, 1)$ with capacity g_i for each node $i \neq N$ with $g_i > 0$. We observe that each cut of the modified problem that separates the source 1 from the sink N has the same capacity as the same cut in the original problem, since the additional arcs $(i, 1)$ do not contribute to the cut's capacity. We will show that the cut $[\mathcal{N}^+, \mathcal{N}^-]$ is a minimum cut in the modified problem, and therefore also in the original max-flow problem. Indeed, consider a flow vector for the modified problem constructed as follows: the flow of each arc (i, j) of the original problem is the same as the flow obtained upon termination of the preflow-push algorithm, and the flow of each of the additional arcs $(i, 1)$ is g_i. It is seen that for this flow vector, the divergence of each node except 1 and N is 0. Furthermore, the cut $[\mathcal{N}^+, \mathcal{N}^-]$, which separates 1 and N, is saturated, and its capacity is equal to the divergence out of node 1. By the max-flow/min-cut theorem, this flow vector solves the modified max-flow problem, and the cut $[\mathcal{N}^+, \mathcal{N}^-]$ is a minimum cut.

To estimate the running time of the algorithm, we note that the dominant computational requirements are:

(1) The computation required for price rises and for constructing the candidate lists.

(2) The computation required for saturating flow pushes.

(3) The computation required for nonsaturating flow pushes.

Since there are $O(N)$ price rises per node and there is one candidate list construction between two successive price rises of a node, the total computation for (1) above is $O(NA)$. Since there are $O(N)$ saturating flow pushes per arc, and each saturating flow push requires $O(1)$ computation, the total computation for (2) above is also $O(NA)$. We will next estimate the number of nonsaturating flow pushes for each of the two methods for choosing a node for iteration.

(a) Assume an arbitrary choice of node. Denote

$$I = \{i \neq N \mid g_i > 0, \, p_i < N\},$$

$$M = \begin{cases} \sum_{i \in I} p_i & \text{if } I \text{ is nonempty,} \\ 0 & \text{if } I \text{ is empty,} \end{cases}$$

and note that M is an integer that in the course of the algorithm ranges between 0 and $2N^2$ (since $0 \leq p_i \leq 2N$, as noted earlier). Furthermore, we have $M = 0$ upon termination. We consider the effect of an iteration on M.

As a result of a price rise at node i in Step 4, M will increase by at most the corresponding price increment (in the case where $i \in I$ after the price rise). Since the total price increase per node is at most $2N$, it follows that the total increase of M as a result of price rises is at most $2N^2$.

As a result of a saturating flow push from a node i to a node j, M may increase by as much as the price p_j (if $g_j = 0$ and $p_j < N$ prior to the saturating flow push), so the total increase of M as a result of saturating flow pushes in Steps 2 and 3 is N times the number of saturating flow pushes, which as argued earlier is at most $2NA$. Thus the total increase of M as a result of price rises and saturating flow pushes is at most $2N^2 + 2N^2A$.

On the other hand, when a nonsaturating flow push occurs from a node i to a node j, M decreases by p_i (since the surplus g_i is set to 0 as a result of the nonsaturating flow push), while as a result of the surplus change of j, M increases by p_j or by 0 (depending on whether $g_j = 0$ and $p_j < N$ or not prior to the nonsaturating flow push). Since we must have $p_i = p_j + 1$ in order for (i, j) to be in the candidate list of i, it follows that M decreases by at least 1 with every nonsaturating flow push. This implies that the total number of nonsaturating flow pushes is at most $2N^2 + 2N^2A$. Each nonsaturating flow push requires $O(1)$ computation, so the total computation for nonsaturating flow pushes is $O(N^2A)$. Thus the overall running time of the preflow-push method with an arbitrary choice of node is $O(N^2A)$.

(b) Assume a first in-first out choice of node, and denote again

$$I = \{i \neq N \mid g_i > 0, \, p_i < N\}.$$

It can be seen that with this choice rule, the algorithm can be divided in cycles. The first cycle consists of a single iteration at each node i in the initial set I. The $(k+1)$st cycle consists of a single iteration at each node i in the set I obtained at the end of the kth cycle. We will first show that the total number of cycles is $O(N^2)$.

To this end, we define

$$M = \begin{cases} \max_{i \in I} p_i & \text{if } I \text{ is nonempty,} \\ 0 & \text{if } I \text{ is empty,} \end{cases}$$

and we consider the effect on M of a single cycle. There are two possibilities:

(1) M increases or stays constant during the cycle. Then there must be at least one price rise during the cycle, since otherwise the surplus of every node iterated on during the cycle would be shifted to a node with lower price and M would be decreased by at least 1. Since the total number of price rises is $O(N^2)$, it follows that the number of cycles where M increases or stays constant is $O(N^2)$. Furthermore, the sum of increases in M is bounded above by the sum of price increases of all the nodes, which was shown earlier to be $O(N^2)$.

(2) M decreases during the cycle. Since $M \geq 0$, the sum of decreases in M can exceed the sum of increases in M, which was shown above to be $O(N^2)$, by no more than the maximum initial price value, which is no more than N. Since M can decrease only in integer increments, we see that the number of cycles where M decreases is $O(N^2)$.

Thus the total number of cycles is $O(N^2)$. Since in each cycle there can be only one nonsaturating flow push per node, it follows that the total number of nonsaturating flow pushes is $O(N^3)$, resulting in an overall $O(N^3)$ running time.   **Q.E.D.**

The preceding proof suggests that the complexity bottleneck is the computation for nonsaturating flow pushes. Computational experience, however, indicates that, in practice, the $O(NA)$ operations associated with price rises is at least as much of a bottleneck.

The Second Phase: Constructing a Maximum Flow

Let us now discuss how to construct a maximum flow from the saturated cut and the flow vector obtained upon termination of the preflow-push algorithm. Suppose that the algorithm has terminated, and that we have obtained the saturated cut $[\mathcal{N}^+, \mathcal{N}^-]$ and the flow vector x such that

$$1 \in \mathcal{N}^+, \qquad N \in \mathcal{N}^-,$$

$$g_i \geq 0, \qquad \forall \ i \neq 1 \text{ with } i \in \mathcal{N}^+,$$

$$g_i = 0, \qquad \forall \ i \neq N \text{ with } i \in \mathcal{N}^-.$$

A maximum flow can be computed by solving a certain feasibility problem, which aims to return to the source the excess flow that has entered the graph from the source and has accumulated at the other nodes of $\mathcal{N}^+$. In particular, we delete all nodes in $\mathcal{N}^-$ and all arcs with at least one of their end nodes in $\mathcal{N}^-$, and for each node $i \neq 1$ with $i \in \mathcal{N}^+$ and

$$\sum_{\{(i,j)|j\in\mathcal{N}^-\}} c_{ij} > 0,$$

we introduce an arc $(i, 1)$ with flow and capacity

$$x_{i1} = c_{i1} = \sum_{\{(i,j)|j\in\mathcal{N}^-\}} c_{ij} \qquad (7.48)$$

[if the arc $(i, 1)$ already exists, we just change its capacity and flow to the above value]. In the resulting graph, we solve the feasibility problem of finding a capacity-feasible flow vector $\overline{x}$ such that the corresponding surpluses are all zero. Given a solution $\overline{x}$, the vector x^* defined by

$$x_{ij}^* = \begin{cases} \overline{x}_{ij} & \text{if } i \notin \mathcal{N}^-, \ j \notin \mathcal{N}^-, \\ x_{ij} & \text{otherwise,} \end{cases} \qquad (7.49)$$

can be shown to be a maximum flow. Indeed, it can be seen, using also the fact $g_i = 0$ for all $i \in \mathcal{N}^-$ with $i \neq N$, that x^* has surpluses g_i^* satisfying $g_i^* = 0$ for all $i \neq 1, N$, $g_1^* < 0$, $g_N^* > 0$, and saturates the cut $[\mathcal{N}^+, \mathcal{N}^-]$. Since $[\mathcal{N}^+, \mathcal{N}^-]$ was shown to be a minimum capacity cut, it follows that x^* is a maximum flow.

The feasibility problem just described can be solved with a suitably modified version of the preflow-push algorithm, illustrated in Fig. 7.6 (feasibility problems are essentially equivalent to max-flow problems as discussed in Section 3.1). It can be verified that the running time estimates of Prop. 7.9 apply to the second phase of the preflow-push algorithm, so that the estimates obtained for the first phase apply to the combined first and second phases as well.

We note that the two-phase implementation of the preflow-push algorithm that we have given is by far the most effective in practice, particularly when it is combined with a method for saturated cut detection, to be discussed shortly. The algorithm can be modified, however, so that it finds a maximum flow in a single phase. What is needed for this is to allow iterations at all nodes $i \neq N$ with $g_i > 0$, even if $p_i \geq N$. The termination and running time assertions of Prop. 7.9 can then be shown as stated, with a simple modification of the proof given above. Furthermore, the flow obtained upon termination is a maximum flow. We leave the verification of these facts as an exercise for the reader.

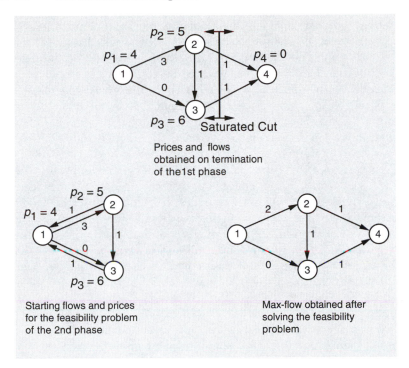

Figure 7.6: Illustration of the second phase of the preflow-push for the max-flow problem of Fig. 7.5. The final flows and prices of the first phase are shown at the top (cf. the bottom right graph of Fig. 7.5). The node 4 (which constitutes $\mathcal{N}^-$) is deleted, together with the connecting arcs $(2,4)$ and $(3,4)$. The arcs $(2,1)$ and $(3,1)$ are then added with flows and capacities equal to 1, and the feasibility problem of finding a circulation in the graph at the bottom left is considered. The solution of this problem is obtained by pushing (backward) to the source along arc $(1,2)$ the 1 unit of surplus of node 2. This yields the max-flow shown at the bottom right [cf. Eq. (7.49)].

7.3.2   Implementation Issues

In practice, it has been observed that for some problems (particularly those involving a sparse graph, where $A \ll N^2$), the preflow-push algorithm can create a saturated cut very quickly and may then spend a great deal of additional time to raise to the level N the prices of the nodes that are left with positive surplus. Computational studies have shown that for efficiency, it is extremely important to use a procedure that detects early the presence of a saturated cut. Several schemes are possible.

    One approach, called *global repricing*, uses breadth-first search from the sink to find periodically, in the course of the algorithm, the set

$$S = \{i \mid \text{there exists an unblocked path from } i \text{ to the sink}\}.$$

If all nodes in $\mathcal{S}$ have zero surplus, then $\mathcal{S}$ defines a minimum cut. Otherwise, the prices of the nodes in $\mathcal{S}$ are set to their shortest distances from the sink. Furthermore, all the nodes not in $\mathcal{S}$ can effectively be purged from the computation by setting their price equal to N. While global repricing can add substantial overhead to the algorithm, it has been generally shown to be beneficial in computational experiments. It is important to use an appropriate heuristic scheme that ensures that global repricing is not too frequent, in view of the associated overhead. In practice, repeating the test after a number of iterations, which is of the order of N, seems to work well.

Another approach (due to Derigs and Meier [1989] and called the *gap method*) is to maintain in a suitable data structure, for each integer k in the range $[1, N - 1]$, the number of nodes $m(k)$ whose price is equal to k. If for some k we have $m(k) = 0$ (this is called a *gap at price k*), then it can be shown (Exercise 7.22) that there is a saturated cut separating all nodes with price greater than k from all nodes whose price is less than k. All the nodes with price greater than k can effectively be purged from the computation by setting their price equal to N. Furthermore, if all nodes with price less than k have zero surplus, the separating saturated cut is a minimum cut.

Note a key advantage of the two saturated cut detection procedures given: they can purge from the computation a significant number of nodes before finding a minimum cut, thus saving the purposeless iterations that involve these nodes.

7.3.3   Relation to the Auction Algorithm

We will now develop the relationship between the preflow-push algorithm and the auction algorithm for the assignment problem, using the methodology for similar persons described in Section 7.2.3. This relationship provides insight into the convergence mechanism of the preflow-push method, but will not be used further in the sequel. Thus, the present section can be skipped without loss of continuity.

We start with a special type of feasibility problem, where we want to transfer a given amount of flow from a source node to a sink node in a given network. The benefit of the transfer is zero, but each arc has a capacity constraint on the flow that it can carry. In particular, we have a directed graph with set of nodes $\mathcal{N}$ and set of arcs $\mathcal{A}$. Node 1 is called the *source* and node N is called the *sink*. We assume that there are no incoming arcs to the source and no outgoing arcs from the sink. Each arc (i, j) carries a flow x_{ij}. We are given a positive integer s, and we consider the problem of finding a flow vector satisfying

$$\sum_{\{j \mid (i,j) \in \mathcal{A}\}} x_{ij} - \sum_{\{j \mid (j,i) \in \mathcal{A}\}} x_{ji} = 0, \qquad \forall\, i \in \mathcal{N},\, i \neq 1, N,$$

$$\sum_{\{j \mid (1,j) \in \mathcal{A}\}} x_{1j} = \sum_{\{j \mid (j,N) \in \mathcal{A}\}} x_{jN} = s,$$

$$0 \leq x_{ij} \leq c_{ij}, \qquad \forall \, (i,j) \in \mathcal{A},$$

where c_{ij} are given positive integers.

We call the above problem the *fixed-flow problem* to distinguish it from the *max-flow problem*, where s is an optimization variable that we try to maximize. The fixed-flow and max-flow problems are closely related, as we have shown in Chapter 3 (see Fig. 3.1). In particular, if s is equal to its (generally unknown) maximum value, the two problems coincide. Many max-flow algorithms solve in effect the fixed-flow problem for appropriate values of s. For example, the Ford-Fulkerson algorithm of Section 3.2 solves the fixed-flow problem for an increasing sequence of values of s until a saturated cut separating the source and the sink is constructed, in which case s cannot be increased further and the algorithm terminates. For convenience we will work with the fixed-flow problem, but the interpretations and conversions to be given have straightforward analogs for the max-flow case.

The fixed-flow problem can be converted to an equivalent feasibility/transportation problem by replacing each arc (i,j) that is not incident to the source or the sink ($i \neq 1$ or $j \neq N$) by a node labeled (i,j), and two arcs $\big(i,(i,j)\big)$ and $\big(j,(i,j)\big)$ that are incoming to that node as shown in Fig. 7.7. The flows of these arcs are denoted $y_{i(i,j)}$ and $z_{j(i,j)}$, and correspond to the arc flow x_{ij} via the transformation

$$y_{i(i,j)} = x_{ij}, \qquad z_{j(i,j)} = c_{ij} - x_{ij}.$$

All arc benefits are zero; see Fig. 7.8. This transportation problem can in turn be transformed to a feasibility/assignment problem with zero arc benefits and with similar persons by means of the following two devices (see Fig. 7.9):

(a) Create $\sum_{\{j \mid (j,i) \in \mathcal{A}\}} c_{ji}$ similar persons in place of each node/source $i \neq 1, N$ of the transportation problem, and s persons in place of the source node 1.

(b) Create c_{ij} duplicate objects in place of each arc/sink (i,j), $j \neq N$ of the transportation problem, and s duplicate objects in place of the sink node N.

We will now use this equivalence to transcribe the algorithm based on M-auction iterations of Section 7.2.3 into the fixed-flow context. The auction algorithm starts with all object prices being zero. The initial assignment corresponds to the zero flow vector $[x_{ij} = 0$ for all arcs $(i,j) \in \mathcal{A}]$, which implies that all the persons corresponding to the nodes $i \neq 1, N$ are assigned to the objects corresponding to the artificial arcs $[z_{j(i,j)} = c_{ij}$ for

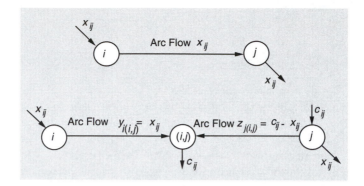

Figure 7.7: Transformation of a fixed-flow problem into a feasibility/transportation problem. Each arc (i, j) is replaced by a node labeled (i, j) and two incoming arcs $\big(i, (i, j)\big)$ and $\big(j, (i, j)\big)$ to that node.

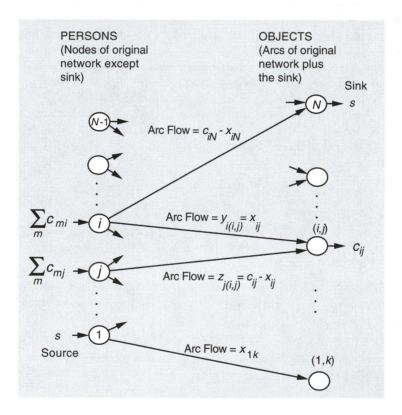

Figure 7.8: The equivalent feasibility/transportation problem. By viewing each arc (i, j) as c_{ij} duplicate objects and the sink as s duplicate objects, this problem can be viewed as an assignment problem with similar persons.

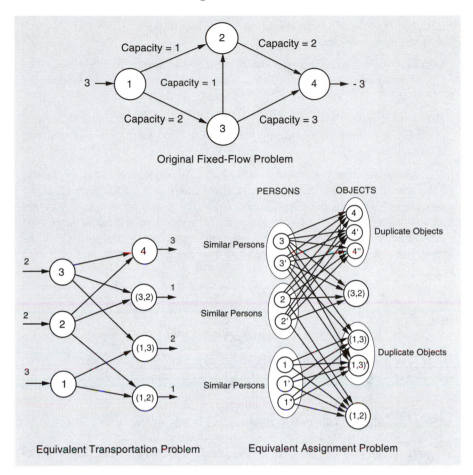

Figure 7.9: Example of a fixed-flow problem, and its corresponding equivalent feasibility/transportation and assignment problems. All arc benefits are zero.

all artificial arcs $\big(j, (i, j)\big)$]. Thus initially, only the s persons corresponding to the source and the s objects corresponding to the sink are unassigned.

As the auction algorithm executes, the objects corresponding to an arc (i, j) with $j \neq N$ are always assigned to some person and are divided in two classes (one of which may be empty):

(a) The objects assigned to some person of the similarity class of i. The number of these objects is x_{ij}, and their common price (see the remark at the end of Section 7.2.3) is denoted $\bar{p}_{ij}$.

(b) The objects assigned to some person of the similarity class of j. The number of these objects is $c_{ij} - x_{ij}$, and their common price (see the remark at the end of Section 7.2.3) is denoted $\underline{p}_{ij}$.

Similarly, the objects corresponding to an incoming arc (i, N) of the sink are divided in two classes:

(a) The objects assigned to some person of the similarity class of i. The number of these objects is x_{iN}, and their common price is denoted $\overline{p}_{iN}$.

(b) The objects that are unassigned. The number of these objects is $c_{iN} - x_{iN}$, and their common price is zero. For notational convenience, we define $\underline{p}_{iN} = 0$.

As remarked at the end of Section 7.2.3, all objects assigned to persons of the same similarity class must offer the same value for all persons of the class. Since the arc benefits for the underlying assignment problem are zero, it follows that *all objects assigned to persons of the same similarity class must have equal prices*. We see therefore that, in the course of the algorithm, for each node $i \neq 1$, there is a scalar p_i such that

$$p_i = \overline{p}_{ij}, \qquad \forall \ (i, j) \in \mathcal{A} \text{ such that } x_{ij} > 0, \qquad (7.50)$$

and

$$p_i = \underline{p}_{ji}, \qquad \forall \ (j, i) \in \mathcal{A} \text{ such that } x_{ji} < c_{ji}. \qquad (7.51)$$

Regarding the source 1, a slightly different definition of p_1 must be given because initially all outgoing arcs of 1 have zero flow. We define

$$p_1 = \begin{cases} 0 & \text{if } x_{1j} = 0 \text{ for all } (1, j) \in \mathcal{A}, \\ \overline{p}_{1j} & \text{otherwise, where } (1, j) \text{ is any arc with } x_{1j} > 0. \end{cases}$$

We call p_i the *implicit price* of i. Figure 7.10 illustrates the definition of the implicit prices.

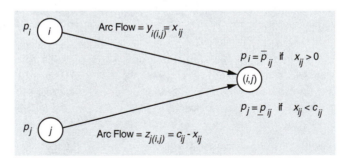

Figure 7.10: Definition of the implicit prices of the person/nodes in terms of the prices of the object/prices.

The assignment-price pairs generated by the auction algorithm satisfy ϵ-CS. Taking into account that all arc benefits are zero, the ϵ-CS condition for the transportation/assignment problem becomes

$$-\overline{p}_{ij} \geq \max \left\{ \max_{\{(i,k)|x_{ik}>0\}} -\overline{p}_{ik}, \quad \max_{\{(i,k)|x_{ik}<c_{ik}\}} -\underline{p}_{ik}, \right.$$

$$\left. \max_{\{(k,i)|x_{ki}>0\}} -\overline{p}_{ki}, \quad \max_{\{(k,i)|x_{ki}<c_{ki}\}} -\underline{p}_{ki} \right\} - \epsilon, \qquad \text{if } x_{ij} > 0, \tag{7.52}$$

$$-\underline{p}_{ji} \geq \max \left\{ \max_{\{(i,k)|x_{ik}>0\}} -\overline{p}_{ik}, \quad \max_{\{(i,k)|x_{ik}<c_{ik}\}} -\underline{p}_{ik}, \right.$$

$$\left. \max_{\{(k,i)|x_{ki}>0\}} -\overline{p}_{ki}, \quad \max_{\{(k,i)|x_{ki}<c_{ki}\}} -\underline{p}_{ki} \right\} - \epsilon, \qquad \text{if } x_{ji} < c_{ji}, \tag{7.53}$$

where in the above relations, and in similar relations in this section, we adopt the convention that the maximum and the minimum over the empty set is $-\infty$ and $+\infty$, respectively. By Eqs. (7.50) and (7.51), we have that if $x_{ij} > 0$, then

$$\overline{p}_{ij} = \overline{p}_{ik}, \quad \forall \, (i,k) \text{ with } x_{ik} > 0, \qquad \overline{p}_{ij} = \underline{p}_{ki}, \quad \forall \, (k,i) \text{ with } x_{ki} < c_{ki},$$

while if $x_{ji} < c_{ji}$, then

$$\underline{p}_{ji} = \overline{p}_{ik}, \quad \forall \, (i,k) \text{ with } x_{ik} > 0, \qquad \underline{p}_{ji} = \underline{p}_{ki}, \quad \forall \, (k,i) \text{ with } x_{ki} < c_{ki}.$$

Therefore, Eqs. (7.52) and (7.53) can be equivalently written as

$$\overline{p}_{ij} \leq \min \left\{ \min_{\{(i,k)|x_{ik}<c_{ik}\}} \underline{p}_{ik}, \quad \min_{\{(k,i)|x_{ki}>0\}} \overline{p}_{ki} \right\} + \epsilon, \qquad \text{if } x_{ij} > 0,$$

and

$$\underline{p}_{ji} \leq \min \left\{ \min_{\{(i,k)|x_{ik}<c_{ik}\}} \underline{p}_{ik}, \quad \min_{\{(k,i)|x_{ki}>0\}} \overline{p}_{ki} \right\} + \epsilon, \qquad \text{if } x_{ji} < c_{ji}.$$

When these relations are combined with the definition (7.50) and (7.51) of p_i, they can be written in the equivalent form

$$p_i \leq \min \left\{ \min_{\{(i,k)|x_{ik}<c_{ik}\}} \underline{p}_{ik}, \quad \min_{\{(k,i)|x_{ki}>0\}} \overline{p}_{ki} \right\} + \epsilon.$$

Using again Eqs. (7.50) and (7.51), we see that this condition is equivalent to

$$p_i \leq p_k + \epsilon \qquad \text{if } x_{ik} < c_{ik} \text{ or } x_{ki} > 0,$$

or alternatively

$$p_i \leq p_j + \epsilon \qquad \text{if } x_{ij} < c_{ij}, \tag{7.54}$$

$$p_j \leq p_i + \epsilon \qquad \text{if } x_{ij} > 0. \tag{7.55}$$

Note that here the value of ϵ does not matter, because all arc benefits are zero; as long as $\epsilon > 0$ the generated sequence of flows does not depend on ϵ, while the generated prices are just scaled by ϵ. We can thus select $\epsilon = 1$.

Consider now the condition under which the similarity class of a node i is eligible to bid at an iteration of the auction algorithm. For this, the similarity class of i must have some unassigned persons. From Fig. 7.8, it can be seen that this is equivalent to

$$\sum_{\{j|(j,i)\in\mathcal{A}\}} c_{ji} > \sum_{\{j|(i,j)\in\mathcal{A}\}} x_{ij} + \sum_{\{j|(j,i)\in\mathcal{A}\}} (c_{ji} - x_{ji}), \qquad \text{if } i \neq 1,$$

and

$$s > \sum_{\{j|(1,j)\in\mathcal{A}\}} x_{1j}, \qquad \text{if } i = 1.$$

Let us define the *surplus* of a node i by

$$g_i = \begin{cases} \sum_{\{j|(j,i)\in\mathcal{A}\}} x_{ji} - \sum_{\{j|(i,j)\in\mathcal{A}\}} x_{ij} & \text{if } i \neq 1, \\ s - \sum_{\{j|(1,j)\in\mathcal{A}\}} x_{1j} & \text{if } i = 1. \end{cases}$$

It is seen that *a similarity class is eligible to submit a bid in the auction algorithm at a given iteration if and only if the surplus of the corresponding node is positive.*

The table of Fig. 7.11 provides a list of the corresponding variables and relations between the fixed-flow problem and the preflow-push algorithm on one hand, and its equivalent transportation/assignment problem and the auction algorithm on the other.

Let us now transcribe the auction algorithm by using the correspondences of the table of Fig. 7.11. Initially all arc flows x_{ij} are zero and all implicit prices p_i are also zero. At the start of each iteration, a node $i \neq N$ with positive surplus g_i is chosen; if no such node can be found, the algorithm terminates.

Auction Iteration Applied to the Equivalent Assignment/Fixed-Flow Problem

Step 1: (Scan incident arc) Select an arc (i,j) such that $x_{ij} < c_{ij}$ and $p_i = p_j + 1$ and go to Step 2, or an arc (j,i) such that $0 < x_{ji}$ and $p_i = p_j + 1$ and go to Step 3. If no such arc can be found go to Step 4.

	Transportation/Assignment Problem	Fixed-Flow Problem
Flows	$y_{i(i,j)}, \quad z_{j(i,j)} = c_{ij} - y_{i(i,j)}$	$x_{ij} = y_{i(i,j)} = c_{ij} - z_{j(i,j)}$
Prices	$\overline{p}_{ij}, \qquad \underline{p}_{ij}$	$p_i = \begin{cases} \overline{p}_{ij} & \text{for all } (i,j) \text{ with } x_{ij} > 0 \\ \underline{p}_{ji} & \text{for all } (j,i) \text{ with } x_{ji} < c_{ji} \end{cases}$
ϵ-**CS** ($\epsilon = 1$)	$\overline{p}_{ij} \leq \min\Big\{\min_{x_{ik} < c_{ik}} \underline{p}_{ik},$ $\min_{x_{ki} > 0} \overline{p}_{ki}\Big\} + 1 \;$ if $x_{ij} > 0$ $\underline{p}_{ji} \leq \min\Big\{\min_{x_{ik} < c_{ik}} \underline{p}_{ik},$ $\min_{x_{ki} > 0} \overline{p}_{ki}\Big\} + 1 \;$ if $x_{ji} < c_{ji}$	$p_i \leq p_j + 1 \qquad \text{if} \qquad x_{ij} < c_{ij}$ $p_j \leq p_i + 1 \qquad \text{if} \qquad x_{ij} > 0$
	Select unassigned person	Select node with positive surplus
	Selected person finds best object	Selected node finds best incident arc
	Selected person gets assigned to best object and displaces current owner	Selected node pushes flow on best arc, opposite node retracts flow from the arc
	Selected person raises best object price by max increment maintaining 1-CS	Selected node raises its implicit price by max increment maintaining 1-CS

Figure 7.11: Correspondences between the fixed-flow problem and the preflow-push algorithm on one hand, and its transportation/assignment equivalent version and auction algorithm on the other. Here, $\epsilon = 1$.

Step 2: (Push flow forward along arc (i,j)) Increase x_{ij} by $\delta = \min\{g_i, c_{ij} - x_{ij}\}$. If now $g_i = 0$ and $x_{ij} < c_{ij}$, stop; else go to Step 1.

Step 3: (Push flow backward along arc (j,i)) Decrease x_{ji} by $\delta = \min\{g_i, x_{ji}\}$. If now $g_i = 0$ and $0 < x_{ji}$, stop; else go to Step 1.

Step 4: (Increase price of node i) Raise p_i to the level

$$\min\{p_j + 1 \mid (i,j) \in \mathcal{A} \text{ and } x_{ij} < c_{ij}, \text{ or } (j,i) \in \mathcal{A} \text{ and } 0 < x_{ji}\}. \tag{7.56}$$

Go to Step 1.

Note that Steps 2 and 3 correspond to changing the assignment by associating the persons in the similarity class of node i to their best objects corresponding to the incident arcs of i, up to the point where the surplus of i is exhausted. This modification of the assignment is done via perhaps multiple passes through Steps 2 and 3. When no suitable arc can be found in Step 1, this means that the price of the best objects for which the persons of i will bid will be strictly increased, and that the implicit price p_i will also be increased. Step 4 computes the appropriate level. It can be seen that the above algorithm is essentially equivalent to the preflow-push algorithm analyzed earlier in Section 7.3.1.

Interpretation of the Algorithm

For an intuitive interpretation of the fixed-flow algorithm as an auction, think of each node i as a city, and of each arc (i, j) as a transportation link of capacity c_{ij} between cities i and j. Suppose that the objective is to move s persons from city 1 to city N, while observing the capacity constraints of the transportation links [the number of forward person crossings minus the number of backward person crossings of each (i, j) must be no more than c_{ij} at all times]. The method for accomplishing the transfer is to *charge a rent p_i to each person in city i*. Persons will move from city i to city j along link (i, j) if $p_i > p_j$, to the extent that the capacity of link (i, j) allows. The rent of a city is successively raised to ϵ plus the minimum level at which all surplus population will move to a neighboring city. Assuming $\epsilon = 1$, this level is given by Eq. (7.56). With these rules, we obtain the fixed flow/auction algorithm of this section, which can thus be seen as an auction between the cities (except city N) to dispose of their surplus population by raising the corresponding rents.

Extension to the Min-Cost Flow Problem

Suppose that in the preceding interpretation there is a transportation cost a_{ij} for crossing link (i, j). Then persons will move from city i to city j if the current rent p_i is higher than the rent p_j plus the transportation cost a_{ij}. With this as a guide, we can modify in a straightforward way the preceding arguments for the case of the fixed flow problem and derive an auction algorithm for the minimum cost flow problem

$$\text{minimize} \quad \sum_{(i,j)\in\mathcal{A}} a_{ij} x_{ij}$$

$$\text{subject to} \quad \sum_{\{j|(i,j)\in\mathcal{A}\}} x_{ij} - \sum_{\{j|(j,i)\in\mathcal{A}\}} x_{ji} = 0, \qquad \forall\, i \in \mathcal{N},\ i \neq 1, N,$$

$$\sum_{\{j|(1,j)\in\mathcal{A}\}} x_{1j} = \sum_{\{j|(j,N)\in\mathcal{A}\}} x_{jN} = s,$$

$$0 \leq x_{ij} \leq c_{ij}, \qquad \forall \ (i,j) \in \mathcal{A},$$

where a_{ij} are given integers, and c_{ij} and s are given positive integers.

The above minimum cost flow problem is somewhat special because it involves a single source and a single sink, as well as a zero lower bound on the flow of each arc. However, more general versions can be converted to the problem above by introducing some artificial arcs and nodes (see Chapter 4), and the analysis of this section can be appropriately generalized. In fact this will be done implicitly in Section 7.4.

The equivalent transportation/assignment problem has the same graph as before (cf. Fig. 7.8). Taking into account the change from a maximization to a minimization problem, the benefits involved are $-a_{ij}$ for each of the arcs $\big(i, (i,j)\big)$, $j \neq N$, $-a_{iN}$ for each of the arcs (i, N), and zero for each of the other arcs.

The implicit prices are now defined by [cf. Eqs. (7.50) and (7.51)]

$$p_i = a_{ij} + \overline{p}_{ij}, \qquad \forall \ (i,j) \in \mathcal{A} \text{ such that } x_{ij} > 0,$$

and

$$p_i = \underline{p}_{ji}, \qquad \forall \ (j,i) \in \mathcal{A} \text{ such that } x_{ji} < c_{ji}.$$

The ϵ-CS condition becomes

$$p_i \leq a_{ij} + p_j + \epsilon \qquad \text{if } x_{ij} < c_{ij}, \tag{7.57}$$

$$a_{ij} + p_j \leq p_i + \epsilon \qquad \text{if } x_{ij} > 0. \tag{7.58}$$

[cf. Eqs. (7.54) and (7.55)]. Note that here the value of ϵ matters because the arc benefits are not all zero.

The auction algorithm when applied to the equivalent transportation/assignment problem can be transcribed similar to the one for the fixed flow problem. Initially the arc flows x_{ij} and the implicit prices p_i must satisfy ϵ-CS; for example, if a_{ij} are all nonnegative, we may use $x_{ij} = 0$ for all (i,j) and $p_i = 0$ for all i. At the start of each iteration, a node $i \neq N$ with positive surplus g_i is chosen; if no such node can be found the algorithm terminates.

Auction Iteration Applied to the Equivalent Assignment/Min Cost Flow Problem

Step 1: (Scan incident arc) Select an arc (i,j) such that $x_{ij} < c_{ij}$ and $p_i = a_{ij} + p_j + \epsilon$ and go to Step 2, or an arc (j,i) such that $0 < x_{ji}$ and $p_i = p_j - a_{ji} + \epsilon$ and go to Step 3. If no such arc can be found go to Step 4.

Step 2: (**Push flow forward along arc** (i,j)) Increase x_{ij} by $\delta = \min\{g_i, c_{ij} - x_{ij}\}$. If now $g_i = 0$ and $x_{ij} < c_{ij}$, stop; else go to Step 1.

Step 3: (**Push flow backward along arc** (j,i)) Decrease x_{ji} by $\delta = \min\{g_i, x_{ji}\}$. If now $g_i = 0$ and $0 < x_{ji}$, stop; else go to Step 1.

Step 4: (**Increase price of node** i) Raise p_i to the level

$$\overline{p}_i = \min\left\{\min_{\{(i,j)\in\mathcal{A}|x_{ij}<c_{ij}\}}\{a_{ij} + p_j + \epsilon\},\right.$$

$$\left.\min_{\{(j,i)\in\mathcal{A}|b_{ji}<x_{ji}\}}\{p_j - a_{ji} + \epsilon\}\right\}.$$

Go to Step 1.

The preceding algorithm is called ϵ-*relaxation method*, and is discussed in the next section for the slightly more general version of the minimum cost flow problem where there may be multiple source and sink nodes.

7.4 THE ϵ-RELAXATION METHOD

We now consider the minimum cost flow problem

$$\text{minimize} \quad \sum_{(i,j)\in\mathcal{A}} a_{ij}x_{ij}$$

$$\text{subject to} \quad \sum_{\{j|(i,j)\in\mathcal{A}\}} x_{ij} - \sum_{\{j|(j,i)\in\mathcal{A}\}} x_{ji} = s_i, \quad \forall\, i \in \mathcal{N},$$

$$b_{ij} \leq x_{ij} \leq c_{ij}, \quad \forall\, (i,j) \in \mathcal{A},$$

where the scalars a_{ij}, b_{ij}, c_{ij}, and s_i are given. In this section, we will introduce and analyze the ϵ-relaxation method for solving this problem. This is a slightly modified version of the method derived in Section 7.3.3 as a special case of the auction algorithm for the assignment problem.

Throughout this section, we assume that *all the scalars a_{ij}, b_{ij}, c_{ij}, and s_i are integer, and that the problem is feasible.* In practice, the method may be supplemented with additional mechanisms to detect infeasibility, as will be discussed later in the section. A version of the method that can deal with noninteger data will be developed in Section 9.6, in the context of the more general convex separable network problem.

Like all auction algorithms, the ϵ-relaxation method is based on the notion of ϵ-*complementary slackness* (ϵ-CS for short). We say that a capacity-feasible flow vector x and a price vector p satisfy ϵ-CS if

$$p_i - p_j \leq a_{ij} + \epsilon \qquad \text{for all } (i,j) \in \mathcal{A} \text{ with } x_{ij} < c_{ij}, \qquad (7.59)$$

$$p_i - p_j \geq a_{ij} - \epsilon \qquad \text{for all } (i,j) \in \mathcal{A} \text{ with } b_{ij} < x_{ij}, \qquad (7.60)$$

[compare with Eqs. (7.57) and (7.58) in Section 7.3.3; see Fig. 7.12]. The usefulness of ϵ-CS is due in large measure to the following proposition, which generalizes Prop. 7.2 for the assignment problem. The proposition relies on the integrality of the cost coefficients a_{ij} (see Exercise 7.13 for a generalization).

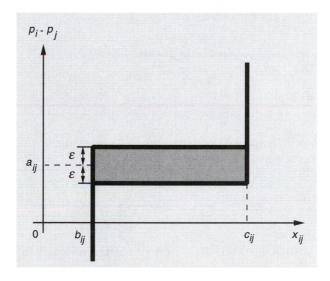

Figure 7.12: Illustration of ϵ-CS. All pairs of arc flows x_{ij} and price differences $p_i - p_j$ should either lie on the thick lines or in the shaded area between the thick lines.

Proposition 7.10: If $\epsilon < 1/N$, where N is the number of nodes, x is feasible, and x and p satisfy ϵ-CS, then x is optimal for the minimum cost flow problem.

Proof: If x is not optimal, then by Prop. 1.2 in Section 1.2, there exists a simple cycle Y that has negative cost, i.e.,

$$\sum_{(i,j)\in Y^+} a_{ij} - \sum_{(i,j)\in Y^-} a_{ij} < 0, \qquad (7.61)$$

and is unblocked with respect to x, i.e.,

$$x_{ij} < c_{ij}, \qquad \forall \ (i,j) \in Y^+,$$

$$b_{ij} < x_{ij}, \qquad \forall \ (i,j) \in Y^-.$$

By ϵ-CS [cf. Eqs. (7.59) and (7.60)], the preceding relations imply that

$$p_i \leq p_j + a_{ij} + \epsilon, \qquad \forall \ (i,j) \in Y^+,$$

$$p_j \leq p_i - a_{ij} + \epsilon, \qquad \forall \ (i,j) \in Y^-.$$

By adding these relations over all arcs of Y (whose number is no more than N), and by using the hypothesis $\epsilon < 1/N$, we obtain

$$\sum_{(i,j)\in Y^+} a_{ij} - \sum_{(i,j)\in Y^-} a_{ij} \geq -N\epsilon > -1.$$

Since the arc costs a_{ij} are integer, we obtain a contradiction of Eq. (7.61). **Q.E.D.**

Exercises 7.13 and 7.14 provide various improvements of the tolerance $\epsilon < 1/N$ in some specific contexts.

Let us denote by g_i the surplus of node i:

$$g_i = \sum_{\{j|(j,i)\in\mathcal{A}\}} x_{ji} - \sum_{\{j|(i,j)\in\mathcal{A}\}} x_{ij}.$$

In the ϵ-relaxation method, flows and prices are changed in a way that maintains ϵ-CS and tends to drive the nonzero node surpluses towards zero. Furthermore, flow is allowed to change along certain types of arcs, which we now introduce. Given a flow-price pair (x,p) satisfying ϵ-CS, we say that an arc (i,j) is ϵ^+-*unblocked* if

$$p_i = p_j + a_{ij} + \epsilon \qquad \text{and} \qquad x_{ij} < c_{ij}.$$

We say that an arc (j,i) is ϵ^--*unblocked* if

$$p_i = p_j - a_{ji} + \epsilon \qquad \text{and} \qquad b_{ji} < x_{ji}.$$

The *candidate list* of a node i is the (possibly empty) set of outgoing arcs (i,j) that are ϵ^+- unblocked, and incoming arcs (j,i) that are ϵ^--unblocked.

We use a fixed positive value of ϵ, and we start with a pair (x,p) satisfying ϵ-CS. Furthermore, the starting arc flows are integer, and it will be seen that the integrality of the arc flows is preserved thanks to the integrality of the node supplies and the arc flow bounds. Implementations that have good worst case complexity also require that all initial arc flows be at either their upper or their lower bound, as will be explained later. This can be easily enforced.

At the start of a typical iteration we have a flow-price vector pair (x, p) satisfying ϵ-CS and we select a node i with $g_i > 0$; if no such node can be found, the algorithm terminates.

Iteration of the ϵ-Relaxation Method

Step 1: (Scan incident arc) If the candidate list of node i is empty, go to Step 4; else select from the candidate list of i either an arc (i, j) and go to Step 2, or an arc (j, i) and go to Step 3.

Step 2: (Push flow forward along arc (i, j)) Increase x_{ij} by $\delta = \min\{g_i, c_{ij} - x_{ij}\}$. If now $g_i = 0$ and $x_{ij} < c_{ij}$, stop; else go to Step 1.

Step 3: (Push flow backward along arc (j, i)) Decrease x_{ji} by $\delta = \min\{g_i, x_{ji} - b_{ji}\}$. If now $g_i = 0$ and $b_{ji} < x_{ji}$, stop; else go to Step 1.

Step 4: (Increase price of node i) Raise p_i to the level

$$\overline{p}_i = \min \left\{ \min_{\{(i,j) \in \mathcal{A} \mid x_{ij} < c_{ij}\}} \{a_{ij} + p_j + \epsilon\}, \right.$$

$$\left. \min_{\{(j,i) \in \mathcal{A} \mid b_{ji} < x_{ji}\}} \{p_j - a_{ji} + \epsilon\} \right\}. \tag{7.62}$$

Go to Step 1.

There is an exceptional situation in Step 4, which requires special handling. This is the case where in Eq. (7.62) we have $x_{ij} = c_{ij}$ for all outgoing arcs (i, j) and $b_{ji} = x_{ji}$ for all incoming arcs (j, i); that is, the cut separating i from the remainder of the graph is saturated, while $g_i \geq 0$. This can arise under two circumstances: (1) $g_i > 0$, in which case, the problem must be infeasible, or (2) $g_i = 0$. To deal with the situation, we stop the algorithm in case (1), and we keep p_i at its current level and stop the iteration in case (2).

To see that the iteration is well-defined in the sense that it stops after a finite number of computational operations, observe the following:

(a) Integrality of the arc flows is maintained by the algorithm, since the starting arc flows, the node supplies, and the arc flow bounds are integer. In particular, the flow increments δ in Steps 2 and 3 are integer throughout the algorithm.

(b) At most one flow change per incident arc of node i is performed at each iteration since a flow change either sets the flow to one of its bounds, which causes the corresponding arc to drop out of the candidate list of i through the end of the iteration, or else results in $g_i = 0$, which leads the iteration to branch to Step 4 and subsequently stop. Therefore, the number of flow changes per iteration is finite. In addition we have $g_i > 0$ at the start and $g_i = 0$ at the end of an iteration, so at least one flow change must occur before an iteration can stop.

(c) After each price rise with $g_i > 0$ at least one flow change must be performed, so from (b) it follows that the number of price changes per iteration is finite.

Thus the method's iteration is guaranteed to stop after a finite number of operations.

Some insight into the ϵ-relaxation iteration can be obtained by noting that in the limit, as $\epsilon \to 0$, it yields the single node relaxation iteration of Section 6.3. Figure 7.13 illustrates the sequence of price rises in an ϵ-relaxation iteration; this figure should be compared with the corresponding Fig. 6.8 in Section 6.3 for the single node relaxation iteration. As Fig. 7.13 illustrates, the ϵ-relaxation iteration can be interpreted as an approximate coordinate ascent or Gauss-Seidel relaxation iteration. This interpretation parallels the approximate coordinate descent interpretation of the mathematically equivalent auction algorithm (cf. Fig. 7.1).

The following proposition establishes the validity of the ϵ-relaxation method.

Proposition 7.11: Assume that the minimum cost flow problem is feasible. Then the ϵ-relaxation method terminates with a pair (x, p) satisfying ϵ-CS. The flow vector x is feasible, and is optimal if $\epsilon < 1/N$.

Proof: We first make a few observations.

(a) The algorithm preserves ϵ-CS; this can be verified from the price change formula (7.62).

(b) The prices of all nodes are monotonically nondecreasing during the algorithm [this follows from the ϵ-CS property of (x, p) and Eq. (7.62)].

(c) Once a node has nonnegative surplus, its surplus stays nonnegative thereafter, since a flow change in Step 2 or 3 at a node i cannot drive the surplus of i below zero (since $\delta \le g_i$), and cannot decrease the surplus of neighboring nodes.

(d) If at some time a node has negative surplus, its price must have never been increased up to that time, and must be equal to its initial price. This is a consequence of (c) above and of the assumption that only nodes with nonnegative surplus can be chosen for iteration.

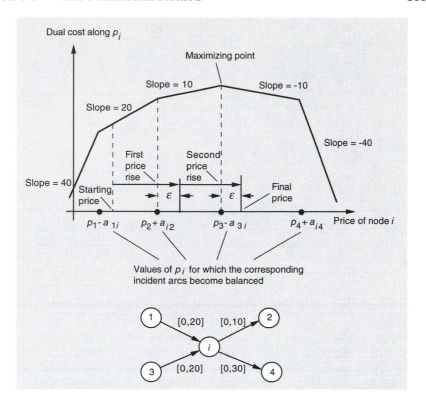

Figure 7.13: Illustration of the price rises of the ε-relaxation iteration. Here, node i has four incident arcs $(1, i)$, $(3, i)$, $(i, 2)$, and $(i, 4)$ with flow ranges $[0, 20]$, $[0, 20]$, $[0, 10]$, and $[0, 30]$, respectively, and supply $s_i = 0$. The arc costs and current prices are such that

$$p_1 - a_{1i} \le p_2 + a_{i2} \le p_3 - a_{3i} \le p_4 + a_{i4},$$

as shown in the figure. The break points of the dual cost along the price p_i correspond to the values of p_i at which one or more incident arcs to node i become balanced. For values between two successive break points, there are no balanced arcs. Each price rise of the ε-relaxation iteration increases p_i to the point which is ε to the right of the next break point larger than p_i, (assuming that the starting price of node i is to the left of the maximizing point by more than ε). In the example of the figure, there are two price rises, the second of which sets p_i at the point which is ε to the right of the maximizing point, leading to the approximate (within ε) coordinate ascent interpretation.

Suppose, to arrive at a contradiction, that the method does not terminate. Then, since there is at least one flow change per iteration, an infinite number of flow changes must be performed at some node i on some arc (i, j). Since for each flow change, the increment δ is integer, an infinite number of flow changes must also be performed at node j on the arc (i, j).

This means that arc (i, j) becomes alternately ϵ^+-unblocked with $g_i > 0$ and ϵ^--unblocked with $g_j > 0$ an infinite number of times, which implies that p_i and p_j must increase by amounts of at least 2ϵ an infinite number of times. Thus we have $p_i \to \infty$ and $p_j \to \infty$, while either $g_i > 0$ or $g_j > 0$ at the start of an infinite number of flow changes.

Let $\mathcal{N}^\infty$ be the set of nodes whose prices increase to ∞. To preserve ϵ-CS, we must have, after a sufficient number of iterations,

$$x_{ij} = c_{ij} \qquad \text{for all } (i, j) \in \mathcal{A} \text{ with } i \in \mathcal{N}^\infty, j \notin \mathcal{N}^\infty,$$

$$x_{ji} = b_{ji} \qquad \text{for all } (j, i) \in \mathcal{A} \text{ with } i \in \mathcal{N}^\infty, j \notin \mathcal{N}^\infty.$$

After some iteration, by (d) above, every node in $\mathcal{N}^\infty$ must have nonnegative surplus, so the sum of surpluses of the nodes in $\mathcal{N}^\infty$ must be positive at the start of the flow changes where either $g_i > 0$ or $g_j > 0$. It follows that

$$0 < \sum_{i \in \mathcal{N}^\infty} s_i - \sum_{\{(i,j) \in \mathcal{A} | i \in \mathcal{N}^\infty, j \notin \mathcal{N}^\infty\}} c_{ij} + \sum_{\{(j,i) \in \mathcal{A} | i \in \mathcal{N}^\infty, j \notin \mathcal{N}^\infty\}} b_{ji}.$$

For any feasible vector, the above relation implies that the sum of the divergences of nodes in $\mathcal{N}^\infty$ exceeds the capacity of the cut $[\mathcal{N}^\infty, \mathcal{N} - \mathcal{N}^\infty]$, which is impossible. It follows that there is no feasible flow vector, contradicting the hypothesis. Thus the algorithm must terminate. Since upon termination we have $g_i \leq 0$ for all i and the problem is assumed feasible, it follows that $g_i = 0$ for all i. Hence the final flow vector x is feasible and by (a) above it satisfies ϵ-CS together with the final p. By Prop. 7.10, if $\epsilon < 1/N$, x is optimal. **Q.E.D.**

7.4.1 Computational Complexity – ϵ-Scaling

We now discuss the running time of the ϵ-relaxation method. As in Section 7.1.4, we first focus on the case where ϵ is fixed, and we subsequently consider the ϵ-scaling case where ϵ is progressively reduced as in Section 7.1.4. We continue to assume that the problem data and the starting flows are integer. As in Section 7.1.4, *for the case where ϵ is fixed, we assume that the cost coefficients a_{ij}, and all the initial node prices are integer multiples of ϵ.* Under this assumption, it is seen from the price change operation (7.62) in Step 4 that all node prices will be integer multiples of ϵ throughout the algorithm, implying that *each price rise is of size at least ϵ.*

For purposes of easy reference, let us call the operation of Step 4 a *price rise* at node i, and let us call the operation of Step 2 (or Step 3) a *flow push* on arc (i, j) [a flow push on arc (j, i), respectively]. A flow push on arc (i, j) [or arc (j, i)] is said to be *saturating* if it results in setting the flow x_{ij} to its upper bound c_{ij} (the flow x_{ji} to its lower bound b_{ij}, respectively); otherwise, the flow push is said to be *nonsaturating*. The complexity analysis revolves around bounding the number of price rises, and saturating and nonsaturating flow pushes. We first bound the number of price rises.

Proposition 7.12: Assume that for some scalar $r \geq 1$, the initial price vector p^0 for the ϵ-relaxation method satisfies $r\epsilon$-CS together with some feasible flow vector x^0. Then, the ϵ-relaxation method performs at most $(r+1)(N-1)$ price rises per node.

Proof: Consider the pair (x, p) at the beginning of an ϵ-relaxation iteration. Since the surplus vector $g = (g_1, \ldots, g_N)$ is not zero, and the flow vector x^0 is feasible, we conclude that for each node s with $g_s > 0$ there exists a node t with $g_t < 0$ and a path H from t to s that contains no cycles and is such that:

$$b_{ij} \leq x_{ij}^0 < x_{ij} \leq c_{ij}, \qquad \forall \, (i,j) \in H^+, \tag{7.63}$$

$$b_{ij} \leq x_{ij} < x_{ij}^0 \leq c_{ij}, \qquad \forall \, (i,j) \in H^-, \tag{7.64}$$

where H^+ is the set of forward arcs of H and H^- is the set of backward arcs of H. [This can be seen from the conformal realization theorem (Prop. 1.1) as follows. For the flow vector $x - x^0$, the net outflow from node t is $-g_t > 0$ and the net outflow from node s is $-g_s < 0$ (here we ignore the flow supplies), so by the conformal realization theorem, there is a path H from t to s that contains no cycle and conforms to the flow $x - x^0$, that is, $x_{ij} - x_{ij}^0 > 0$ for all $(i,j) \in H^+$ and $x_{ij} - x_{ij}^0 < 0$ for all $(i,j) \in H^-$. Equations (7.63) and (7.64) then follow.]

Since the pair (x, p) satisfies ϵ-CS, we have using Eqs. (7.63) and (7.64),

$$p_i - p_j \leq a_{ij} + \epsilon, \qquad \forall \, (i,j) \in H^+, \tag{7.65}$$

$$p_i - p_j \geq a_{ij} - \epsilon, \qquad \forall \, (i,j) \in H^-. \tag{7.66}$$

Similarly, since the pair (x^0, p^0) satisfies $r\epsilon$-CS, we have

$$p_i^0 - p_j^0 \geq a_{ij} + r\epsilon, \qquad \forall \, (i,j) \in H^+, \tag{7.67}$$

$$p_i^0 - p_j^0 \leq a_{ij} - r\epsilon, \qquad \forall \, (i,j) \in H^-. \tag{7.68}$$

Combining Eqs. (7.65)-(7.68), we obtain

$$p_i - p_j \geq p_i^0 - p_j^0 - (r+1)\epsilon, \qquad \forall \, (i,j) \in H^+,$$

$$p_i - p_j \leq p_i^0 - p_j^0 + (r+1)\epsilon, \qquad \forall \, (i,j) \in H^-.$$

Applying the above inequalities for all arcs of the path H, we get

$$p_t - p_s \geq p_t^0 - p_s^0 - (r+1)|H|\epsilon, \tag{7.69}$$

where $|H|$ denotes the number of arcs of the path H. We observed earlier that if a node has negative surplus at some time, then its price is unchanged from the beginning of the method until that time. Thus $p_t = p_t^0$. Since the path contains no cycles, we also have that $|H| \leq N - 1$. Therefore, Eq. (7.69) yields

$$p_s - p_s^0 \leq (r+1)|H|\epsilon \leq (r+1)(N-1)\epsilon. \tag{7.70}$$

Since only nodes with positive surplus can increase their prices and each price rise increment is at least ϵ, we conclude from Eq. (7.70) that the total number of price rises that can be performed for node s is at most $(r+1)(N-1)$. **Q.E.D.**

The upper bound on the number of price rises given in Prop. 7.12 turns out to be tight, in the sense that examples can be found where rN price rises occur at a number of nodes that is proportional to N. Under these circumstances, the total number of price rises performed by the ϵ-relaxation method is no better than $O(rN^2)$. The following example, from Bertsekas and Tsitsiklis [1989], illustrates that the bound $O(rN^2)$ cannot be improved.

Example 7.2:

Consider an assignment problem with $2n$ nodes, nodes $s_1, ..., s_n$ being sinks (persons) and $t_1, ..., t_n$ being sources (objects). The arcs are (s_k, t_k) for $k = 1, ..., n$, and (s_k, t_{k+1}) for $k = 1, ..., n-1$. All arcs have unit capacity and zero cost. The problem may also be viewed as a max-flow problem by adjoining a "super source" node s and arcs (s, s_k), along with a "super sink" node t and arcs (t_k, t). Suppose that the ϵ-relaxation method is applied to the assignment version of this example, with $\epsilon = 1$, zero initial prices, and the rule that whenever it is possible to push flow away from a node on more than one arc, the one that is uppermost in Fig. 7.14(a) is selected. The nodes are chosen for iteration in the order $1, 2, ..., n$.

We claim that the ϵ-relaxation algorithm as applied to the example of Fig. 7.14(a) requires n^2 price rises. The final price of node s_k is $2k - 1$, and that of t_k is $2k - 2$. We prove this by induction. When $n = 1$, a single price rise at s_1 and the ensuing flow adjustment yield a solution in which s_1 has price 1, t_1 has price 0, and s_1 is assigned to t_1. This establishes the base case of the induction. Now assume the claim is true for the problem of size $n - 1$; we establish it for the problem of size n. After n price rises, the configuration of Fig. 7.14(b) will be attained. This leaves nodes $s_2, ..., s_n$ and $t_2, ..., t_n$ in precisely the same state as after $n - 1$ price rises in a problem of size $n - 1$. By induction, after another

$$(n-1)^2 - (n-1) = n^2 - 3n + 2$$

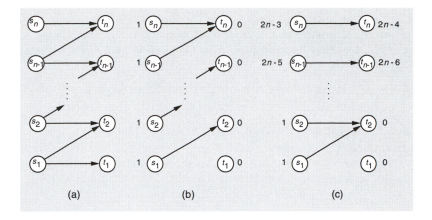

Figure 7.14: (a) An assignment example in which the number of price rises required by the ε-relaxation method is proportional to N^2. Note that the only feasible solution has each s_k assigned to the corresponding t_k. (b) The assignment example after n price rises, starting with zero prices. Prices are shown next to the corresponding node. Only arcs with positive flow are depicted. (c) The intermediate result after $(n-1)^2+1$ price rises.

price rises, the algorithm reaches the configuration of Fig. 7.14(c). Following the rules of ε-relaxation, the reader can confirm that the sequence of nodes now iterated on is $t_2, s_2, t_3, s_3, \ldots, t_n, s_n$, and the promised prices are obtained after $2(n-1)$ further price rises. Following this, the nodes are processed in the opposite order, and a primal feasible solution is obtained in $2n$ additional iterations (but no further price rises). The total number of price rises is

$$n + (n^2 - 3n + 2) + 2(n-1) = n^2.$$

This establishes the induction.

The total number of nodes here is $N = 2n$. Hence the number of price rises is $(N/2)^2 = N^2/4$, and increases with N at the same rate as its theoretical bound.

We now introduce the notion of the *admissible graph*, which will play an important role in the subsequent complexity analysis. For a given pair (x, p) satisfying ε-CS, consider an arc set $\mathcal{A}^*$ that contains all candidate list arcs oriented in the direction of flow change. In particular, for each arc (i, j) in the forward portion of the candidate list of a node i, we introduce an arc (i, j) in $\mathcal{A}^*$, and for each arc (j, i) in the backward portion of the candidate list of node i, we introduce an arc (i, j) in $\mathcal{A}^*$ (thus the direction of the latter arc is reversed). The set of nodes $\mathcal{N}$ and the set $\mathcal{A}^*$ define the *admissible graph* $\mathcal{G}^* = (\mathcal{N}, \mathcal{A}^*)$. Note that an arc can be in the candidate list of at most one node, so the admissible graph is well-defined.

For good performance of the ε-relaxation method, it may be important to start with a flow-price vector pair (x, p) satisfying ε-CS, and such that the corresponding admissible graph $\mathcal{G}^*$ is acyclic. One possibility is to select an initial price vector p and to set the initial arc flow x_{ij} for every arc $(i, j) \in \mathcal{A}$ so that the flow-price pair (x, p) satisfies 0-CS; for example

$$
x_{ij} = \begin{cases} b_{ij} & \text{if } p_i - p_j \leq a_{ij}, \\ c_{ij} & \text{if } p_i - p_j > a_{ij}, \end{cases} \qquad \forall \, (i, j) \in \mathcal{A}. \tag{7.71}
$$

It can be seen that with this choice, ϵ-CS is satisfied for every arc $(i, j) \in \mathcal{A}$, and that the initial admissible graph is empty and thus acyclic. Figure 7.15 provides an example illustrating the importance of starting with an acyclic admissible graph.

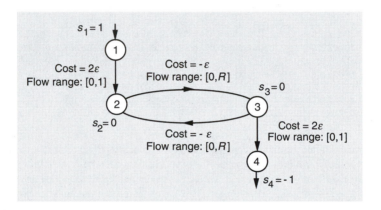

Figure 7.15: Example showing the importance of starting with an admissible graph that is acyclic. Initially, we choose $x = 0$ and $p = 0$, which do satisfy ϵ-CS. The initial admissible graph consists of arcs $(2, 3)$ and $(3, 2)$. The algorithm will start with a price rise of node 1 to $p_1 = 2\epsilon$, followed by a flow push of 1 unit from node 1 to node 2. Following this, node 2 will push 1 unit of flow to node 3, node 3 will push 1 unit of flow to node 2, and this will be repeated R times, until the arcs $(2, 3)$ and $(3, 2)$ become saturated. Thus the running time is proportional to the capacity R.

On the other hand, it turns out that if we choose the initial flow-price pair so that the admissible graph is initially acyclic, the algorithm cannot create cycles in this graph, and the type of poor performance illustrated in Fig. 7.15 cannot occur. This is shown in the following proposition.

Proposition 7.13: If the admissible graph is initially acyclic, it remains acyclic throughout the ϵ-relaxation method.

Proof: We use induction. Assume that the admissible graph $\mathcal{G}^*$ is acyclic up to the start of the mth iteration, for some $m \geq 1$. We will prove that following the mth iteration $\mathcal{G}^*$ remains acyclic. Clearly, after a flow push the admissible graph remains acyclic, since it either remains unchanged, or some arcs are deleted from it. Thus we only have to prove that after a price rise at a node i, no cycle involving i is created. We note that, after a price rise at node i, all incident arcs to i in the admissible graph at the start of the mth iteration are deleted and new arcs incident to i are added. We claim that i cannot have any incoming arcs which belong to the admissible graph. To see this, note that, just before a price rise at node i, we have

$$p_j - p_i \le a_{ji} + \epsilon, \qquad \forall \; (j, i) \in \mathcal{A},$$

and since each price rise is at least ϵ, we must have

$$p_j - p_i - a_{ji} \le 0, \qquad \forall \; (j, i) \in \mathcal{A},$$

after the price rise. Then, (j, i) cannot be in the candidate list of node j. By a similar argument, we have that (i, j) cannot be in the candidate list of j for all $(i, j) \in \mathcal{A}$. Thus, after a price rise at i, node i cannot have any incoming incident arcs belonging to the admissible graph, so no cycle involving i can be created.   **Q.E.D.**

In order to obtain a sharper complexity result, we introduce a special implementation of the ϵ-relaxation method, called the *sweep implementation*, whereby nodes are chosen for iteration in a way that enhances computational efficiency (for an illustration, see Fig. 7.16). We assume here that the initial admissible graph is acyclic. We introduce an order in which the nodes are chosen in iterations. All the nodes are kept in a list T, which is traversed from the first to the last element. The order of the nodes in the list is consistent with the successor order implied by the admissible graph, that is, if a node j is a successor of a node i, then j must appear after i in the list. If the initial admissible graph is empty, as is the case with the initialization of Eq. (7.71), the initial list is arbitrary. Otherwise, the initial list must be consistent with the successor order of the initial admissible graph. The list is updated in a way that maintains the consistency with the successor order. In particular, let i be a node on which we perform an ϵ-relaxation iteration, and let N_i be the subset of nodes of T that are after i in T. If the price of i changes, then node i is removed from its position in T and placed in the first position of T. The next node chosen for iteration, if N_i is nonempty, is the node $i' \in N_i$ with positive surplus which ranks highest in T. Otherwise, the positive surplus node ranking highest in T is picked. It can be seen that with this rule of repositioning nodes following a price rise, the list order is consistent with the successor order implied by the admissible graph throughout the method.

A *sweep cycle* is a set of iterations whereby all nodes are chosen once from the list T and an ϵ-relaxation iteration is performed on those nodes that have positive surplus. The idea of the sweep implementation is that

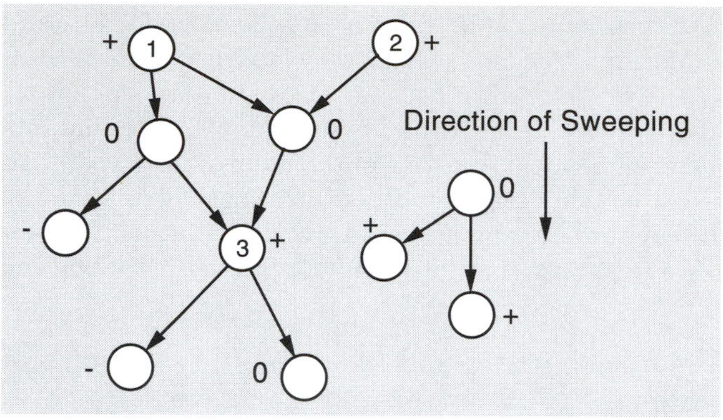

Figure 7.16: Illustration of the admissible graph consisting of the ϵ^+ - unblocked arcs and the ϵ^- - unblocked arcs with their directions reversed. These arcs specify the direction along which flow can be changed according to the rules of the algorithm. A "+" (or "-" or "0") indicates a node with positive (or negative or zero) surplus. The algorithm is operated so that the admissible graph is acyclic at all times. The sweep implementation requires that the high ranking nodes (e.g., nodes 1 and 2 in the graph) are chosen for iteration before the low ranking nodes (e.g., node 3 in the graph).

an ϵ-relaxation iteration at a node i that has predecessors with positive surplus may be wasteful, since the surplus of i will be set to zero and become positive again through a flow push at a predecessor node.

We have the following proposition that estimates the number of sweep cycles required for termination.

Proposition 7.14: Assume that for some scalar $r \geq 1$, the initial price vector for the sweep implementation of the ϵ-relaxation method satisfies $r\epsilon$-CS together with some feasible flow vector. Then, the number of sweep cycles up to termination is $O(rN^2)$.

Proof: Consider the start of any sweep cycle. Let $\mathcal{N}^+$ be the set of nodes with positive surplus that have no predecessor with positive surplus; let $\mathcal{N}^0$ be the set of nodes with nonpositive surplus that have no predecessor with positive surplus. Then, as long as no price rise takes place during the cycle, all nodes in $\mathcal{N}^0$ remain in $\mathcal{N}^0$, and an iteration on a node $i \in \mathcal{N}^+$ moves i from $\mathcal{N}^+$ to $\mathcal{N}^0$. So if no node changed price during the cycle, then all nodes in $\mathcal{N}^+$ will be moved to $\mathcal{N}^0$ and the method terminates. Therefore, there is a price rise in every cycle except possibly the last one. Since by Prop. 7.12 there are $O(rN^2)$ price rises, the result follows. **Q.E.D.**

We now bound the running time for the sweep implementation of the ϵ-relaxation method.

Proposition 7.15: Consider the ϵ-relaxation method with the sweep implementation, and assume that for some scalar $r \geq 1$ the initial price vector p^0 satisfies $r\epsilon$-CS together with some feasible flow vector x^0. Then, the method requires $O(rN^3)$ operations up to termination.

Proof: The dominant computational requirements are:

(1) The computation required for price rises.

(2) The computation required for saturating flow pushes.

(3) The computation required for nonsaturating flow pushes.

According to Prop. 7.12, there are $O(rN)$ price rises per node, so the requirements for (1) above are $O(rNA)$ operations. Furthermore, whenever a flow push at an arc is saturating, it takes at least one price rise at one of the end nodes of the arc before the arc's flow can be changed again. Thus the total requirement for (2) above is $O(rNA)$ operations also. Finally, for (3) above we note that for each sweep cycle there can be only one nonsaturating flow push per node. Thus an estimate for (3) is $O(N \cdot \text{total number of sweep cycles})$ which, by Prop. 7.12, is $O(rN^3)$ operations. Adding the computational requirements for (1), (2), and (3), and using the fact $A \leq N^2$, the result follows. **Q.E.D.**

ϵ-Scaling

Let us now apply the ϵ-scaling approach to the ϵ-relaxation method. Similar to the case of the auction algorithm (cf. Section 7.1.4), the idea is to use repeated applications of the method, called *scaling phases*, with progressively smaller values of ϵ. Each scaling phase uses price and flow information obtained from the preceding one. The kth scaling phase consists of applying the ϵ-relaxation method with $\epsilon = \epsilon^k$, where ϵ^k is updated by

$$\epsilon^{k+1} = \max\left\{\frac{\epsilon^k}{\theta}, \frac{1}{N+1}\right\}, \qquad k = 0, 1, \ldots,$$

where θ is an integer with $\theta > 1$. The first scaling phase is started with zero initial prices and an ϵ^0 that is a fixed fraction of the arc cost range $C = \max_{(i,j) \in \mathcal{A}} a_{ij}$. The total number of scaling phases is $\overline{k}$, which is the first positive integer k for which ϵ^{k-1} is equal to $1/(N+1)$. Thus the number of scaling phases is $O\big(\log(NC)\big)$.

Let p^k denote the initial price vector for the $(k+1)$st scaling phase. We have $p^0 = 0$, and we assume that for $k \geq 1$, p^k is the price vector obtained at the end of the kth scaling phase. As in Section 7.1.4, at the beginning of the $(k+1)$st scaling phase, we make a correction of size at most ϵ^k to each a_{ij} so that it is divisible by ϵ^k [no correction is made in the last phase since the a_{ij} are integer and the final value of ϵ is $1/(N+1)$]. Thus the arc cost coefficients in the $(k+1)$st scaling phase, denoted a_{ij}^k, are all divisible by ϵ^k, and satisfy

$$|a_{ij}^k - a_{ij}| \le \epsilon^k, \qquad \forall\,(i,j) \in \mathcal{A}.$$

The correction of the arc cost coefficients guarantees that all price rise increments and prices are integer multiples of the prevailing value of ϵ. The initial flow of each arc (i,j) for the $(k+1)$st scaling phase is

$$x_{ij} = \begin{cases} b_{ij} & \text{if } p_i^k - p_j^k \le a_{ij}^k, \\ c_{ij} & \text{if } p_i^k - p_j^k > a_{ij}^k. \end{cases}$$

With this choice, the initial admissible graph is empty and is therefore acyclic.

As in Section 7.1.4, we observe that in the $(k+1)$st scaling phase the initial price vector p^k satisfies $r\epsilon^k$-CS with some feasible flow vector (for $k \ge 1$, this is the flow vector obtained at the end of the kth scaling phase). Here r is a constant that depends on θ. Furthermore, p^k satisfies the other assumptions needed for Prop. 7.15 to apply. We conclude that the $(k+1)$st scaling phase has a running time of $O(N^3)$. Since the number of scaling phases is $O\big(\log(NC)\big)$, we obtain the following:

Proposition 7.16: The running time of the ϵ-relaxation method using the sweep implementation and ϵ-scaling as described above is $O\big(N^3 \log(NC)\big)$.

7.4.2   Implementation Issues

The efficient implementation of the ϵ-relaxation method requires a number of techniques that while not suggested by the complexity analysis, are essential for good practical performance.

Data Structures

The main operations of auction algorithms involve scanning the incident arcs of nodes; this is a shared feature with dual ascent methods. For this reason the data structures and implementation ideas discussed in connection with dual ascent methods, also apply to auction algorithms. In particular, for the max-flow and the minimum cost flow problems, using the

FIRST_IN, *FIRST_OUT*, *NEXT_IN*, and *NEXT_OUT* arrays, described in Section 6.5, is convenient. In addition, a similar set of arrays can be used to store the arcs of the candidate lists in the ϵ-relaxation method.

Contrary to what complexity analysis suggests, it is not clear whether the candidate list organization of the sweep implementation improves the practical performance, in view of the additional overhead it requires.

Surplus Scaling

When applying ϵ-scaling, except for the last scaling phase, it is not essential to reduce the surpluses of all nodes to zero; it is possible to terminate a scaling phase prematurely, and reduce ϵ further, in an effort to economize on computation. A technique that is typically quite effective is to iterate only on nodes whose surplus exceeds some threshold, which is gradually reduced to zero with each scaling phase. The threshold is usually set by some heuristic scheme.

Negative Surplus Node Iterations

It is possible to define a symmetric form of the ϵ-relaxation iteration that starts from a node with negative surplus and decreases (rather than increases) the price of that node. Furthermore, one can mix positive surplus and negative surplus iterations in the same algorithm; this is analogous to the combined forward/reverse auction algorithm for assignment and the forward/reverse auction algorithm for shortest paths. However, if the two types of iterations are mixed arbitrarily, the algorithm is not guaranteed to terminate even for a feasible problem; for an example, see Bertsekas and Tsitsiklis [1989], p. 373. For this reason, some care must be exercised in mixing the two types of iterations in order to guarantee that the algorithm eventually makes progress.

Dealing with Infeasibility

The issues and methods relating to infeasibility are similar to those discussed in Section 7.1.5, in connection with the assignment problem. One possibility is to monitor infeasibility by checking the price levels. If the problem is infeasible, the ϵ-relaxation method will either terminate with $g_i \leq 0$ for all i and $g_i < 0$ for at least one i, in which case infeasibility will be detected, or else it will perform an infinite number of iterations and, consequently, an infinite number of flow pushes and price rises. In the latter case, from the proof of Prop. 7.11 it can be seen that the prices of some of the nodes will diverge to infinity. This, together with a bound on the total price change of a node given in Exercise 7.15, can be used to detect infeasibility.

Alternatively, similar to the assignment problem, we can detect infeasibility by checking periodically for the presence of a saturated cut separating the set of nodes with positive surplus from the set of nodes with negative surplus. Such a cut will eventually be discovered if and only if the problem is infeasible. We may then try to optimize the cost function over the set of all maximally feasible flows, as discussed in Section 3.1. The flow obtained by the method upon detection of a saturated cut can be used to decompose the original problem into two or three component minimum cost flow problems, as discussed in Section 3.1, and each of these problems can be solved separately.

7.5 THE AUCTION/SEQUENTIAL SHORTEST PATH ALGORITHM

In this section, we develop an auction algorithm for the solution of the minimum cost flow problem, based on a sequential shortest path augmentation approach similar to the one discussed in Section 6.2. The main difference is that the shortest paths are constructed using the auction/shortest path algorithm of Section 2.6 rather than using a variant of Dijkstra's algorithm. An important feature of the auction approach is that it allows useful information to be passed from one shortest path construction to the next in the form of prices, similar to the max-flow algorithm of Section 3.3. This accounts for a better theoretical and practical performance of the algorithm of this section over the one of Section 6.2.

We recall that the primal-dual (or sequential shortest path) method of Section 6.2 maintains a pair (x, p) satisfying CS, and that at each iteration it constructs a shortest path from some node with positive surplus to the set of nodes with negative surplus, along which it performs an augmentation of the current flow vector. The shortest path computation is performed in the *reduced graph* $G_R = (\mathcal{N}, \mathcal{A_R})$ whose arc set $\mathcal{A_R}$ consists of an arc (i, j) for each arc $(i, j) \in \mathcal{A}$ with $x_{ij} < c_{ij}$, and an arc (j, i) for each arc $(i, j) \in \mathcal{A}$ with $b_{ij} < x_{ij}$. The arc lengths are $a_{ij} + p_j - p_i$ for the arcs $(i, j) \in \mathcal{A}$ with $x_{ij} < c_{ij}$, and $p_i - a_{ij} - p_j$ for the arcs (j, i) corresponding to arcs $(i, j) \in \mathcal{A}$ with $b_{ij} < x_{ij}$.

It is in principle possible to solve the shortest path problem using any shortest path method that requires nonnegative arc lengths, such as the Dijkstra-like method used in Section 6.2. The development of the auction/max-flow algorithm in Section 3.3 motivates using the auction algorithm for shortest paths because of its ability to transfer price information from one shortest path computation to the next. This method maintains a path, which is extended or contracted by a single arc at each iteration. Unfortunately, however, the method cannot be used conveniently in the context of the sequential shortest path method because it requires that all cycles have strictly positive length, while the reduced graph has cycles with zero length [each arc (i, j) with $b_{ij} < x_{ij} < c_{ij}$ gives rise to the zero length arcs (i, j) and (j, i) in the reduced graph]. Thus the path maintained by the method can "double up on itself" and close a cycle.

To overcome this difficulty, we use an approach that blends the auction/shortest path construction process with the remainder of the algorithm. In this approach, we use ϵ-perturbations of the arc lengths, related to ϵ-CS, which ensure that the path generated by the auction/shortest path method does not close a cycle through an extension. We first introduce some terminology.

We recall from Section 7.4 that given a flow-price pair (x, p) satisfying ϵ-CS, an arc (i, j) is said to be ϵ^+-*unblocked* if

$$p_i = p_j + a_{ij} + \epsilon \qquad \text{and} \qquad x_{ij} < c_{ij},$$

and an arc (j, i) is said to be ϵ^--*unblocked* if

$$p_i = p_j - a_{ji} + \epsilon \qquad \text{and} \qquad b_{ji} < x_{ji}.$$

The *admissible graph* corresponding to (x, p) is defined as $G^* = (\mathcal{N}, \mathcal{A}^*)$, where the arc set $\mathcal{A}^*$ consists of an arc (i, j) for each ϵ^+-unblocked arc $(i, j) \in \mathcal{A}$, and an arc (i, j) for each ϵ^--unblocked arc $(j, i) \in \mathcal{A}$.

We recall that a path P is a sequence of nodes $(n_1, n_2, \ldots, n_k)$ and a corresponding sequence of $k - 1$ arcs such that the ith arc in the sequence is either (n_i, n_{i+1}) or (n_{i+1}, n_i). For any path P, we denote by $s(P)$ and $t(P)$ the start and terminal nodes of P, respectively, and by P^+ and P^- the sets of forward and backward arcs of P, respectively. The path P is said to be ϵ-*unblocked* if all arcs of P^+ are ϵ^+-unblocked, and all arcs of P^- are ϵ^--unblocked. If P is ϵ-unblocked, and the start node $s(P)$ has positive surplus and the terminal node $t(P)$ has negative surplus, then P is an *augmenting path*. An augmentation along such a path consists of increasing the flow of all arcs in P^+ and reducing the flow of all arcs in P^- by the common increment

$$\delta = \min \left\{ g_{s(P)}, -g_{t(P)}, \min_{(i,j) \in P^+} \{c_{ij} - x_{ij}\}, \min_{(i,j) \in P^-} \{x_{ij} - b_{ij}\} \right\}.$$

Given a path $P = (n_1, n_2, \ldots, n_k)$, a *contraction* of P is the operation that deletes the terminal node of P together with the corresponding terminal arc. An *extension* of P by an arc (n_k, n_{k+1}) or an arc (n_{k+1}, n_k), replaces P by the path $(n_1, n_2, \ldots, n_k, n_{k+1})$ and adds to P the corresponding arc. For convenience, we allow a path P to consist of a single node i, in which case extension by an arc (i, j) or (j, i) gives a path with start node i and terminal node j.

The algorithm to be presented will be called *auction/sequential shortest path algorithm* (abbreviated ASSP). It uses a fixed $\epsilon > 0$, and maintains a flow-price pair (x, p) satisfying ϵ-CS and also a simple path P (possibly consisting of a single node). It terminates when all nodes have nonnegative surplus; then either all nodes have zero surplus and x is feasible, or else some node has negative surplus showing that the problem is infeasible. Throughout the algorithm, x is integer, and (x, p) and P satisfy:

(a) The admissible graph corresponding to (x, p) is acyclic.

(b) P belongs to the admissible graph, i.e., it is ϵ-unblocked. Furthermore, P starts at a node with positive surplus, and all its nodes have nonnegative surplus.

We assume that at the start of the algorithm we have a pair (x, p) satisfying ϵ-CS, as well as the above two properties. In particular, initially one may choose any price vector p, select x according to

$$
x_{ij} = \begin{cases} c_{ij} & \text{if } p_i \geq a_{ij} + p_j, \\ b_{ij} & \text{if } p_i < a_{ij} + p_j, \end{cases}
$$

and choose P to consist of a single node with positive surplus. For these choices, ϵ-CS is satisfied and the corresponding admissible graph is acyclic, since its arc set is empty.

At each iteration, the path P is either extended or contracted. In the case of a contraction, the price of the terminal node of P is strictly increased. In the case of an extension, no price rise occurs, but if the new terminal node has negative surplus, P becomes augmenting, and an augmentation along P is performed. Then the path P is replaced by the degenerate path that consists of a single node with positive surplus, and the process is repeated.

Iteration of the ASSP Algorithm

Let i be the terminal node of P. If

$$
p_i < \min \left\{ \min_{\{(i,j) \in \mathcal{A} \mid x_{ij} < c_{ij}\}} \{a_{ij} + p_j + \epsilon\}, \right.
$$
$$
\left. \min_{\{(j,i) \in \mathcal{A} \mid b_{ji} < x_{ji}\}} \{p_j - a_{ji} + \epsilon\} \right\} \tag{7.72}
$$

go to Step 1; else go to Step 2.

Step 1 (Contract path): Set

$$
p_i := \min \left\{ \min_{\{(i,j) \in \mathcal{A} \mid x_{ij} < c_{ij}\}} \{a_{ij} + p_j + \epsilon\}, \right.
$$
$$
\left. \min_{\{(j,i) \in \mathcal{A} \mid b_{ji} < x_{ji}\}} \{p_j - a_{ji} + \epsilon\} \right\} \tag{7.73}
$$

---

and if $i \neq s(P)$, contract P. Go to the next iteration.

Step 2 (Extend path): Extend P by an arc (i, j_i) or an arc (j_i, i) that attains the minimum in Eq. (7.72). If the surplus of j_i is negative go to Step 3; otherwise, go to the next iteration.

Step 3 (Augmentation): Perform an augmentation along P. If all nodes have nonpositive surplus, terminate the algorithm; otherwise, replace P by a path that consists of a single node with positive surplus and go to the next iteration.

The following proposition establishes that some basic properties are maintained by the algorithm.

Proposition 7.17: Suppose that at the start of an iteration of the ASSP algorithm the following two conditions hold:

(1) (x, p) satisfies ϵ-CS and the corresponding admissible graph is acyclic.

(2) P belongs to the admissible graph, starts at a node with positive surplus, and all its nodes have nonnegative surplus.

Then these two conditions hold at the start of the next iteration.

Proof: Suppose the iteration involves a contraction. Then it can be seen that the price increase (7.73) preserves ϵ-CS. Furthermore, since only the price of node i changes and no arc flow changes, the admissible graph remains unchanged except for the incident arcs of node i. In particular, all the incident arcs of i in the admissible graph at the start of the iteration are deleted and the arcs of the admissible graph corresponding to the arcs (i, j) and (j, i) that attain the minimum in Eq. (7.73) are added. Since all these arcs are outgoing from i in the admissible graph, a cycle cannot be closed. Finally, following a contraction, P does not contain the terminal node i, so it belongs to the admissible graph that we had before the iteration. Thus P consists of arcs that belong to the admissible graph that we obtain after the iteration.

Suppose the iteration involves an extension. Then by ϵ-CS, we must have

$$p_i = \min \left\{ \min_{\{(i,j) \in \mathcal{A} | x_{ij} < c_{ij}\}} \{a_{ij} + p_j + \epsilon\}, \min_{\{(j,i) \in \mathcal{A} | b_{ji} < x_{ji}\}} \{p_j - a_{ji} + \epsilon\} \right\},$$

at the start of the iteration. It follows that the path P obtained by extension is simple and ϵ-unblocked, since the extension arc (i, j_i) must belong to the admissible graph. Since no price or flow changes with an extension, the ϵ-CS conditions and the admissible graph stay unchanged following the extension. If there is a subsequent augmentation at Step 3 because the new terminal node j_i has negative surplus, the ϵ-CS conditions will not be affected, while the admissible graph will not gain any new arcs, so it will remain acyclic. **Q.E.D.**

Note that if we were to take $\epsilon = 0$ (rather than $\epsilon > 0$), the preceding proof would break down, because we would not be able to prove that the admissible graph remains acyclic following an augmentation. In particular, if following an augmentation, the flow of some arc (i, j) lies strictly between its lower and upper bound, the arcs (i, j) and (j, i) would both belong to the admissible graph, each with zero length, thereby closing a zero length cycle.

A sequence of iterations between two successive augmentations (or the sequence of iterations up to the first augmentation) will be called an *augmentation cycle*. Let us fix an augmentation cycle and let $\overline{p}$ be the price vector at the start of the cycle. The reduced graph $G_R = (\mathcal{N}, \mathcal{A}_\mathcal{R})$, defined earlier, will not change in the course of this augmentation cycle, since no arc flow will change during the cycle, except for the augmentation at the end. Suppose that we take as arc lengths of the reduced graph the reduced costs at the start of the cycle plus ϵ. In particular, during the cycle, the arc set $\mathcal{A}_\mathcal{R}$ consists of an arc (i, j) with length $a_{ij} + \overline{p}_j - \overline{p}_i + \epsilon$ for each arc $(i, j) \in \mathcal{A}$ with $x_{ij} < c_{ij}$, and an arc (j, i) with length $\overline{p}_i - a_{ij} - \overline{p}_j + \epsilon$ for each arc $(i, j) \in \mathcal{A}$ with $b_{ij} < x_{ij}$. Note that, because $(x, \overline{p})$ satisfies ϵ-CS, the arc lengths of the reduced graph are nonnegative. However, the reduced graph does not contain zero length cycles, since any such cycle must belong to the admissible graph, which is acyclic.

Using these observations, it can now be seen that the augmentation cycle is just the auction/shortest path algorithm of Section 2.6 applied to the problem of finding a shortest path from the starting node $s(P)$ to some node with negative surplus in the reduced graph G_R, using the preceding ϵ-perturbed arc lengths. To understand this, one should view $p_i - \overline{p}_i$ during the augmentation cycle as the price of node i that is maintained by the auction/shortest path algorithm. The price increments $p_i - \overline{p}_i$ obtained by the auction/shortest path algorithm are added in effect to the starting prices $\overline{p}_i$ at the end of the augmentation cycle to form the new prices that will be used for the shortest path construction of the next augmentation cycle.

By the theory of the auction/shortest path algorithm, a shortest path in the reduced graph will be found in a finite number of iterations if there exists at least one path from the starting node $s(P)$ to some node with negative surplus. Such a path is guaranteed to exist if the problem is feasible. Since the augmentation will change all the flows of the final path P by a positive integer amount, we see that each augmentation cycle reduces the total absolute surplus $\sum_{i \in \mathcal{N}} |g_i|$ by a positive integer. Therefore, there can be only a finite number of augmentation cycles, and we have shown the following proposition.

Proposition 7.18: Assume that the minimum cost flow problem is feasible. Then the ASSP algorithm terminates with a pair (x, p) satisfying ϵ-CS. The flow vector x is feasible and is optimal if $\epsilon < 1/N$.

It is interesting to try to relate the iterations of the algorithm with iterations of the ϵ-relaxation method. Each iteration of the algorithm involving a contraction can be viewed as an iteration of an ϵ-relaxation method, except that the iterating terminal node i may have zero surplus. Each iteration involving an extension without an augmentation changes neither the flow nor the price vectors; it merely extends the path P by a single arc. Finally, each iteration involving an augmentation can be viewed as a sequence of ϵ-relaxation iterations, each pushing the flow increment δ along the ϵ^+-unblocked forward arcs and the ϵ^--unblocked backward arcs of P. Thus we may view the algorithm as a variant of the ϵ-relaxation method.

ϵ-Scaling

As in all auction algorithms, the practical performance of the algorithm may be degraded by "price wars," that is, prolonged sequences of iterations involving small price increases. There is a built-in potential for price wars here because with a small ϵ, the reduced graph may contain cycles with small length, which slow down the underlying auction/shortest path algorithm. (There is a cycle of length 2ϵ for every arc whose flow lies strictly between the corresponding flow bounds.) This difficulty can be addressed by ϵ-scaling, that is, by applying the algorithm several times, each time decreasing ϵ by a constant factor, up to the threshold value of $1/(N+1)$, while using the final prices obtained for one value of ϵ as starting prices for the next value of ϵ. A polynomial complexity bound of $O\big(N^2 A \log(NC)\big)$, where C is the cost range

$$C = \max_{(i,j) \in \mathcal{A}} |a_{ij}|,$$

can be proved for the resulting method, after we introduce modifications similar to the ones of Section 7.4.1 for the ϵ-relaxation method. The unscaled version of the method, where ϵ is kept fixed at $1/(N+1)$, is pseudopolynomial. These complexity bounds can be derived using the lines of analysis of Section 7.4.1, and will not be proved here.

In addition to ϵ-scaling, there are several implementation techniques, which have been found to improve performance in practice. We refer to Bertsekas [1992c] for further details and computational results.

7.6 NOTES, SOURCES, AND EXERCISES

The auction algorithm, and the notions of ϵ-complementary slackness and ϵ-scaling were first proposed by the author (Bertsekas [1979a]; see also Bertsekas [1988]). The worst-case complexity of the algorithm was given by Bertsekas and Eckstein [1988], who used an alternative method of scaling whereby ϵ is kept constant and the a_{ij} are successively scaled to their final values; see also Bertsekas and Tsitsiklis [1989]. Exercise 7.3 that deals with the average complexity of the auction algorithm was inspired by Schwartz [1994], which derives related results for the Jacobi version of the algorithm and its potential for parallelism. Tutorial presentations of auction algorithms that supplement this chapter are given in Bertsekas [1990], [1992a].

Auction algorithms are particularly well-suited for parallel computation because both the bidding and the assignment phases are highly parallelizable. In particular, the bids can be computed simultaneously and in parallel for all persons participating in the auction. Similarly, the subsequent awards to the highest bidders can be computed in parallel by all objects that received a bid. In fact these operations maintain their validity in an asynchronous environment where the bidding phase is executed with price information that is outdated because of communication delays between the processors of the parallel computing system. The parallel computation aspects of the auction algorithm have been explored by Bertsekas and Tsitsiklis [1989], Bertsekas and Castañon [1991], Wein and Zenios [1991], Amini [1994], and Bertsekas, Castañon, Eckstein, and Zenios [1995].

The reverse auction algorithm and its application in asymmetric assignment problems is due to Bertsekas, Castañon, and Tsaknakis [1993]. This paper also discusses additional related algorithms, including the multiassignment algorithm of Exercise 7.10. An extensive computational study of forward and reverse auction algorithms is given in Castañon [1993]. Still another auction algorithm of the forward-reverse type for asymmetric assignment problems is given by Bertsekas and Castañon [1992]. An extension of the auction algorithm to transportation problems based on the notion of similar persons is given in Bertsekas and Castañon [1989].

Preflow-push methods for the max-flow problem originated with the work of Karzanov [1974], and Shiloah and Vishkin [1982]. They have been the subject of much development in the late eighties; see Goldberg and Tarjan [1986], Ahuja and Orlin [1989], Ahuja, Magnanti, and Orlin [1989], Cheriyan and Maheshvari [1989], Derigs and Meier [1989], and the references quoted therein. The $O(N^2 A^{1/2})$ estimate on the running time of the method that uses the highest price node for iteration is due to Cheriyan and Maheshvari [1989]. Slightly better estimates are possible through the use of sophisticated but somewhat impractical data structures (see the survey by Ahuja, Magnanti, and Orlin [1989]). The material of Section 7.3.3

is from Bertsekas [1993b], which also shows the mathematical equivalence of the auction algorithm and the ϵ-relaxation method.

The ϵ-relaxation method is due to the author; it was first published in Bertsekas [1986a], [1986b], although it was known much earlier (since the development of the mathematically equivalent auction algorithm). The sweep implementation was given in Bertsekas [1986b]. Various other implementations can be found in Bertsekas and Eckstein [1987], [1988], Bertsekas and Tsitsiklis [1989], Goldberg [1987], and Goldberg and Tarjan [1990]. The worst-case complexity of ϵ-scaling for the ϵ-relaxation method was first analyzed by Goldberg [1987]. The best known running time estimate for a scaled implementation of ϵ-relaxation is $O(NA \log(N) \log(NC))$; this implementation is due to Goldberg and Tarjan [1990], and uses *dynamic trees*, a complicated (and somewhat impractical) data structure. An efficient implementation of the ϵ-relaxation method, and a corresponding code named CS2 are given by Goldberg [1993]. The ϵ-relaxation method is better suited for parallel computation than the other minimum cost flow methods described in this book; see Bertsekas and Tsitsiklis [1989], Phillips and Zenios [1989], Bertsekas, Castañon, Eckstein, and Zenios [1995], Beraldi and Guerriero [1997], Beraldi, Guerriero, and Musmanno [1997], and Censor and Zenios [1997] for a discussion of various implementations and related issues. The auction/sequential shortest path algorithm is due to Bertsekas [1992c]. This algorithm is competitive to the ϵ-relaxation method in terms of practical performance. It has also found use as a preprocessor for other algorithms such as the relaxation method of Chapter 6, and the RELAX code of Bertsekas and Tseng [1994].

Generally, computational experience suggests that auction algorithms are competitive with the primal and dual cost improvement methods of Chapters 5 and 6. This is particularly so for the assignment and for the max-flow problems, for which good implementations of auction algorithms seem to outperform their competitors in practice. For general minimum cost flow problems, the situation is less clear, and much depends on the structure of the problem being solved.   Thus, in practice, one may want to experiment with several types of algorithms on a given problem.

EXERCISES

7.1

Consider the Gauss-Seidel version of the auction algorithm, where only one person can bid at each iteration. Show that, as a result of a bid, the dual cost can be degraded by at most ϵ.

7.2 (A Refinement of the Termination Tolerance)

Show that the assignment obtained upon termination of the auction algorithm is within $(n-1)\epsilon$ of being optimal (rather than $n\epsilon$). Also, for every $n \geq 2$, construct an example of an assignment problem with integer data such that the auction algorithm terminates with a nonoptimal assignment when $\epsilon = 1/(n-1)$. (Try first $n = 2$ and $n = 3$, and generalize.) *Hint*: Modify slightly the algorithm so that when the last object is assigned, its price is increased by $v_i - w_i$ (rather than $v_i - w_i + \epsilon$). Then the assignment obtained upon termination satisfies the ϵ-CS condition for $n-1$ objects and the CS condition ($\epsilon = 0$) for the last object. Modify the proof of Prop. 1.4 in Section 1.3.3.

7.3

This problem uses a rough (and flawed) argument to estimate the average complexity of the auction algorithm. We assume that at each iteration, only one person submits a bid (i.e., the Gauss-Seidel version of the algorithm is used). Furthermore, every object is the recipient of a bid with equal probability $(1/n)$, independently of the results of earlier bids. (This assumption clearly does not hold, but seems to capture somewhat the real situation where the problem is fairly dense and ϵ-scaling is used.)

(a) Show that when k objects are unassigned the average number of iterations needed to assign a new object is n/k.

(b) Show that, on the average, the number of iterations is $n(1+1/2+\cdots+1/n)$, which can be estimated as $O(n \log n)$.

(c) Assuming that the average number of bids submitted by each person is the same for all persons, show that the average running time is $O(A \log n)$.

7.4

Consider the auction algorithm applied to assignment problems with benefits in the range $[0, C]$, starting with zero prices.

(a) Show that for dense problems (every person can bid for every object) an object can receive a bid in at most $1 + C/\epsilon$ iterations.

(b) Use the example of Fig. 7.17 (due to D. Castañon) to show that, in general, some objects may receive a bid in a number of iterations that is proportional to nC/ϵ.

7.5

Consider the max-flow problem of Fig. 7.18.

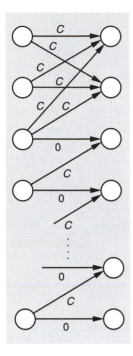

Figure 7.17: Assignment problem for which some objects receive a number of bids that is proportional to nC/ϵ. The arc values are shown next to the corresponding arcs.

(a) Apply the preflow-push algorithm with initial prices $p_1 = 0$, and $p_i = N - i$ for $i = 2, \ldots, N$. Use two different methods to choose the node for iteration: (1) Select the node with highest price, and (2) Select the node with lowest price. Explain why the first method works better, and speculate on the reason why this might be true in general.

(b) Write a computer program to solve the problem of Fig. 7.18 using the preflow-push algorithm with initial prices $p_1 = N$ and $p_i = 0$ for $i = 2, \ldots, N$. Use two different methods to choose the node for iteration: (1) Select the node with highest price, and (2) Select the node at random with equal probability among the possible choices. Plot the number of iterations required with the two methods as a function of N, starting with $N = 1000$ and up to some reasonable number. Can you make any experimental inferences about computational complexity.

7.6

Consider the following graph for an infeasible 7×7 assignment problem: persons 1, 2, and 3 can be assigned only to objects 1 and 2; persons 4 and 5 can be assigned only to objects 1,2, 3, 4, and 5; persons 6 and 7 can be assigned only to objects 6 and 7. Determine the problem's decomposition into feasible and independent components (cf. the discussion of Sections 7.1.5 and 3.1.4).

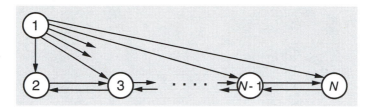

Figure 7.18: Graph for the max-flow problem of Exercise 7.5. The source is node 1 and the sink is node N. All arcs $(1, i)$, $i = 2, \ldots, N$ have capacity 1. All other arcs have capacity N.

7.7 (Using the Third Best Value in the Auction Algorithm)

Frequently in the auction algorithm the two best objects for a given person do not change between two successive bids of that person. This exercise develops an implementation idea that attempts to exploit this fact by using a test to check whether the two best objects from the preceding bid continue to be best. If the test is passed, the computation of the values $a_{ij} - p_j$ of the remaining objects is unnecessary.

Suppose that at a given iteration, when we calculate the bid of the person i on the basis of a price vector p we compute the best value $v_i = \max_{j \in A(i)} \{a_{ij} - p_j\}$, the best object $j_1 = \arg\max_{j \in A(i)} \{a_{ij} - p_j\}$, the second best value $w_i = \max_{j \in A(i), j \neq j_1} \{a_{ij} - p_j\}$, the second best object $j_2 = \arg\max_{j \in A(i), j \neq j_1} \{a_{ij} - p_j\}$, and the *third best value* $y_i = \max_{j \in A(i), j \neq j_1, j \neq j_2} \{a_{ij} - p_j\}$. Suppose that at a subsequent iteration when person i bids based on a price vector $\bar{p}$, we have $a_{ij_1} - \bar{p}_{j_1} \geq y_i$ and $a_{ij_2} - \bar{p}_{j_2} \geq y_i$. Show that j_1 and j_2 continue to be the two best objects for i (although j_1 need not be better than j_2).

7.8 (Equivalence of Two Forms of Reverse Auction)

Show that the iteration of the Gauss-Seidel version of the reverse auction algorithm for the (symmetric) assignment problem can equivalently be described by the following iteration, which maintains an assignment and a pair (π, p) satisfying the ϵ-CS condition of Section 7.2.1 (cf. Definition 7.1):

Step 1: Choose an unassigned object j.

Step 2: Decrease p_j to the highest level for which two or more persons will increase their profit by at least ϵ after assignment to j, that is, set p_j to the highest level for which $a_{ij} - p_j \geq \pi_i + \epsilon$ for at least two persons i, where π_i is the profit of i at the start of the iteration.

Step 3: From the persons in Step 2, assign to j a person i_j that experiences maximum profit increase after assignment to j, and cancel the prior assignment of i_j if he or she was assigned at the start of the iteration. Set the profit of i_j to $a_{i_j j} - p_j$.

7.9

Consider the asymmetric assignment problem and apply forward auction starting with the zero price vector and the empty assignment. Show that, for a feasible problem, the algorithm terminates with a feasible assignment that is within $m\epsilon$ of being optimal.

7.10 (Auction Algorithms for Multiassignment Problems)

Consider the following assignment problem, where it is possible to assign more than one object to a single person:

$$\text{maximize} \quad \sum_{(i,j)\in\mathcal{A}} a_{ij}x_{ij}$$

$$\text{subject to} \quad \sum_{j\in A(i)} x_{ij} \geq 1, \qquad \forall\, i = 1,\ldots,m,$$

$$\sum_{i\in B(j)} x_{ij} = 1, \qquad \forall\, j = 1,\ldots,n,$$

$$0 \leq x_{ij}, \qquad \forall\, (i,j) \in \mathcal{A}.$$

We assume that $m < n$.

(a) Show that a dual problem is given by

$$\text{minimize} \quad \sum_{i=1}^{m} \pi_i + \sum_{j=1}^{n} p_j + (n-m)\lambda$$

$$\text{subject to} \quad \pi_i + p_j \geq a_{ij}, \qquad \forall\, (i,j) \in \mathcal{A},$$

$$\lambda \geq \pi_i, \qquad \forall\, i = 1,\ldots,m.$$

(b) Define a *multiassignment* S to be a set of pairs $(i,j) \in \mathcal{A}$ such that for each object j, there is at most one pair (i,j) in S. A multiassignment S and a pair (π,p) are said to satisfy ϵ-CS if

$$\pi_i + p_j \geq a_{ij} - \epsilon, \qquad \forall\, (i,j) \in \mathcal{A},$$

$$\pi_i + p_j = a_{ij}, \qquad \forall\, (i,j) \in S,$$

$$\pi_i = \max_{k=1,\ldots,m} \pi_k, \qquad \text{if } i \text{ is multiassigned under } S.$$

Show that if a feasible multiassignment S satisfies ϵ-CS together with a pair (π,p), then S is within $n\epsilon$ of being optimal for the multiassignment problem. Furthermore, the triplet $(\hat{\pi},p,\hat{\lambda})$, where

$$\hat{\pi}_i = \pi_i + \epsilon, \qquad \forall\, i = 1,\ldots,m,$$

$$\hat{\lambda} = \max_{k=1,\ldots,m} \hat{\pi}_k,$$

is within $n\epsilon$ of being an optimal solution of the dual problem.

(c) Derive a forward-reverse auction algorithm that maintains ϵ-CS and terminates with a feasible multiassignment that is within $n\epsilon$ of being optimal.

7.11 (A Variation of the Asymmetric Assignment Problem)

Consider a problem which is the same as the asymmetric assignment problem with the exception that in a feasible assignment S there can be at most one incident arc for every person and at most one incident arc for every object (that is, there is no need for every person, as well as for every object, to be assigned). The corresponding linear program is

$$\text{maximize} \quad \sum_{(i,j)\in\mathcal{A}} a_{ij}x_{ij}$$

$$\text{subject to} \quad \sum_{j\in A(i)} x_{ij} \leq 1, \qquad \forall\, i = 1,\ldots,m,$$

$$\sum_{i\in B(j)} x_{ij} \leq 1, \qquad \forall\, j = 1,\ldots,n,$$

$$0 \leq x_{ij}, \qquad \forall\, (i,j) \in \mathcal{A}.$$

(a) Show that this problem can be converted to an asymmetric assignment problem where all persons must be assigned. *Hint*: For each person i introduce an artificial object i' and a zero cost arc (i, i').

(b) Adapt and streamline the auction algorithm for asymmetric assignment problems of Section 7.1 to solve the problem.

7.12 (A Refinement of the Optimality Conditions)

(a) Consider the asymmetric assignment problem with integer data, and suppose that we have a feasible assignment S and a pair (π, p) satisfying the first two ϵ-CS conditions (7.24) and (7.25) with $\epsilon < 1/m$. Show that in order for S to be optimal it is sufficient that

$$p_k \leq p_t$$

for all k and t such that k is unassigned under S, t is assigned under S, and there exists a path $(k, i_1, j_1, \ldots, i_q, j_q, i_{q+1}, t)$ such that $(i_r, j_r) \in S$ for $r = 1, \ldots, q$, and $(i_{q+1}, t) \in S$. *Hint*: Consider the existence of cycles with positive value along which S can be modified.

(b) Consider the multiassignment problem (cf. Exercise 7.10). Derive a result analogous to the one of part (a), with the condition $p_k \leq p_t$ replaced by the condition $\pi_k \geq \pi_t$, where k is any multiassigned person and t is any person for which there exists a path $(k, j_1, i_1, \ldots, j_q, i_q, j_{q+1}, t)$ such that $(k, j_1) \in S$ and $(i_r, j_{r+1}) \in S$ for $r = 1, \ldots, q$.

7.13 (Improved Optimality Condition)

Consider the minimum cost flow problem, without assuming that the problem data are integer. Show that if x is feasible, and x and p satisfy ϵ-CS, then x is optimal, provided

$$\epsilon < \min_{\text{All simple cycles } Y} \left\{ -\frac{\text{Cost of } Y}{\text{Number of arcs of } Y} \,\middle|\, \text{Cost of } Y < 0 \right\},$$

where

$$\text{Cost of } Y = \sum_{(i,j) \in Y^+} a_{ij} - \sum_{(i,j) \in Y^-} a_{ij}.$$

7.14 (Termination Tolerance for Transportation Problems)

Consider a transportation problem with m sources and n sinks, and integer data. Show that in order for a feasible x to be optimal it is sufficient that it satisfies ϵ-CS together with some p and that

$$\epsilon < \frac{1}{2 \min\{m, n\}}$$

[instead of $\epsilon < 1/(m+n)$]. *Hint*: Use the result of Exercise 7.13.

7.15 (Dealing with Infeasibility)

Consider the ϵ-relaxation algorithm applied to a minimum cost flow problem with initial prices p_i^0.

(a) Assume that the problem is feasible. Show that the total price increase $p_i - p_i^0$ of any node i prior to termination of the algorithm satisfies

$$p_i - p_i^0 \leq (N-1)(C+\epsilon) + \max_{j \in \mathcal{N}} p_j^0 - \min_{j \in \mathcal{N}} p_j^0,$$

where $C = \max_{(i,j) \in \mathcal{A}} |a_{ij}|$. *Hint*: Let x^0 be a feasible flow vector and let (x, p) be the flow-price vector pair generated by the algorithm prior to its termination. Show that there exist nodes t and s such that $g_t > 0$ and $g_s < 0$, and a simple path H starting at s and ending at t such that $x_{ij} - x_{ij}^0 > 0$ for all $(i,j) \in H^+$ and $x_{ij} - x_{ij}^0 < 0$ for all $(i,j) \in H^-$. Now use ϵ-CS to assert that

$$p_j + a_{ij} \leq p_i + \epsilon, \qquad \forall \, (i,j) \in H^+,$$

$$p_i \leq p_j + a_{ij} + \epsilon, \qquad \forall \, (i,j) \in H^-.$$

Add these conditions along H to obtain

$$p_t - p_s \leq (N-1)(C+\epsilon).$$

Use the fact $p_s = p_s^0$ to conclude that

$$p_t - p_t^0 \le (N-1)(C + \epsilon) + p_s - p_s^0 \le (N-1)(C + \epsilon) + \max_{j \in \mathcal{N}} p_j^0 - \min_{j \in \mathcal{N}} p_j^0.$$

(b) Discuss how the result of part (a) can be used to detect infeasibility.

(c) Suppose we introduce some artificial arcs to guarantee that the problem is feasible. Discuss how to select the cost coefficients of the artificial arcs so that optimal solutions are not affected in the case where the original problem is feasible.

7.16 (Suboptimality of a Feasible Flow Satisfying ϵ-CS)

Let x^* be an optimal flow vector for the minimum cost flow problem and let x be a feasible flow vector satisfying ϵ-CS together with a price vector p.

(a) Show that the cost of x is within $\epsilon \sum_{(i,j) \in \mathcal{A}} |x_{ij} - x_{ij}^*|$ from the optimal. *Hint*: Show that $(x - x^*)$ satisfies CS together with p for a minimum cost flow problem with arcs (i, j) having flow range $[b_{ij} - x_{ij}^*, c_{ij} - x_{ij}^*]$ and arc cost $\hat{a}_{ij}$ that differs from a_{ij} by no more than ϵ.

(b) Show by example that the suboptimality bound $\epsilon \sum_{(i,j) \in \mathcal{A}} |c_{ij} - b_{ij}|$ deduced from part (a) is tight. *Hint*: Consider a graph with two nodes and multiple arcs connecting these nodes. All the arcs have cost ϵ except for one that has cost $-\epsilon$.

7.17

Apply the ϵ-relaxation method to the problem of Fig. 6.4 of Section 6.2 with $\epsilon = 1$. Comment on the optimality of the solution obtained.

7.18 (Degenerate Price Rises)

In this exercise, we consider a variation of the ϵ-relaxation method that involves *degenerate price rises*. A degenerate price rise changes the price of a node that currently has zero surplus to the maximum possible value that does not violate ϵ-CS with respect to the current flow vector (compare with degenerate price rises in the context of the single-node relaxation iteration where $\epsilon = 0$, as illustrated in Fig. 6.8 of Section 6.5).

Consider a variation of the ϵ-relaxation method where there are two types of iterations: (1) *regular* iterations, which are of the form described in the present section, and (2) *degenerate* iterations, which consist of a single degenerate price rise.

(a) Show that if the problem is feasible and the number of degenerate iterations is bounded by a constant times the number of regular iterations, then the method terminates with a pair (x, p) satisfying ϵ-CS.

(b) Show that the assumption of part (a) is essential for the validity of the method.

7.19 (Deriving Auction from ϵ-Relaxation)

Consider the assignment problem formulated as a minimum cost flow problem (see Example 1.2 in Section 1.2). We say that source i is assigned to sink j if (i, j) has positive flow. We consider a version of the ϵ-relaxation algorithm in which ϵ-relaxation iterations are organized as follows: between iterations (and also at initialization), only source nodes i can have positive surplus. Each iteration finds any unassigned source i (i.e., one with positive surplus), and performs an ϵ-relaxation iteration at i, and then takes the sink j to which i was consequently assigned and performs an ϵ-relaxation iteration at j, even if j has zero surplus. (If j has zero surplus, such an iteration will consist of just a degenerate price rise; see Exercise 7.18.)

More specifically, an iteration by an unassigned source i works as follows:

(1) Source node i sets its price to $p_j + a_{ij} + \epsilon$, where j minimizes $p_k + a_{ik} + \epsilon$ over all k for which $(i, k) \in \mathcal{A}$. It then sets $x_{ij} = 1$, assigning itself to j.

(2) Node i then raises its price to $p_{j'} + a_{ij'} + \epsilon$, where j' minimizes $p_k + a_{ik} + \epsilon$ for $k \neq j$, $(i, k) \in \mathcal{A}$.

(3) If sink j had a previous assignment $x_{i'j} = 1$, it breaks the assignment by setting $x_{i'j} := 0$. (One can show inductively that if this occurs, $p_j = p_{i'} - a_{i'j} + \epsilon$.)

(4) Sink j then raises its price p_j to

$$p_i - a_{ij} + \epsilon = p_{j'} + a_{ij'} - a_{ij} + 2\epsilon.$$

Show that the corresponding algorithm is equivalent to the Gauss-Seidel version of the auction algorithm.

7.20 ($O\left(N^{1/2}A\log(NC)\right)$ Hybrid Auction Algorithm)

This exercise, due to Ahuja and Orlin [1987], shows how the auction algorithm can be combined with a more traditional primal-dual method to obtain an algorithm with an improved running time bound. The auction algorithm is used to assign the first $N - O\left(N^{1/2}\right)$ persons and the primal-dual method is used to assign the rest. Consider the solution of the assignment problem by the Gauss-Seidel variant of the scaled auction algorithm ($\epsilon = 1$ throughout).

(a) Extend the analysis of Section 7.1 to show that in any subproblem of the scaled auction algorithm we have $\sum_{i \in I}(\pi_i^0 - \pi_i) \leq 6\epsilon N$, where I is the set of unassigned persons, $\pi_i^0 = \max_{j \in A(i)}\left\{a_{ij} - p_j^0\right\}$, and p^0 is the vector of prices prevailing at the outset of the subproblem.

(b) Suppose that at the outset of each subproblem we use a modified Gauss-Seidel auction procedure in which only persons i with profit margins π_i greater than or equal to $\pi_i^0 - (6N)^{1/2}\epsilon$ are allowed to place bids. Show that this procedure can be implemented so that at most $(6N)^{1/2} + 1$ iterations are performed at each person node i, and that it terminates in $O(N^{1/2}A)$ time. Furthermore the number of unassigned persons after termination is at most $(6N)^{1/2}$.

(c) Assume that there exists some algorithm X which, given an incomplete assignment S and a price vector p obeying ϵ-CS, produces a new pair (S', p') obeying ϵ-CS in $O(A)$ time, with S' containing one more assignment than S (Exercise 7.21 indicates how such an algorithm may be constructed). Outline how one would construct an $O\left(N^{1/2} A \log(NC)\right)$ assignment algorithm.

7.21

Consider the primal-dual method of Chapter 6. Show that if the terms "balanced," "active," and "inactive" are replaced by "ϵ-balanced," "ϵ-active," and "ϵ-inactive," then the resulting method terminates in a finite number of iterations and that the final pairs (x, p) obtained satisfy ϵ-CS.

7.22 (Gap Method for Saturated Cut Detection)

Consider the gap method described at the end of Section 7.3.2. Suppose that in the course of the preflow-push algorithm the number $m(k)$ of nodes that have price equal to k is 0. Let S be the set of nodes with price less than k, and let $\overline{S}$ be the complementary set of nodes with price greater than k.

(a) Show that the cut $[\overline{S}, S]$ is saturated. *Hint*: The prices of the end nodes of the arcs of the cut differ by at least 2, so by 1-CS, their flows must be at the upper or lower bounds.

(b) Explain why the nodes in $\overline{S}$ can be purged from the computation by setting their prices to N. *Hint*: For every minimum cut $[\overline{S}', S']$, we must have $\overline{S} \subset \overline{S}'$.

8

Nonlinear Network Optimization

Contents

With this chapter, we begin our discussion of nonlinear network flow problems, which generalize the minimum cost flow problem discussed so far in two ways:

(a) The linear cost function is replaced by a general function $f(x)$ of the flow vector x.

(b) The capacity constraints are replaced by a general set X.

Thus the problem has the form

$$\text{minimize} \quad f(x)$$
$$\text{subject to} \quad x \in F,$$

where x is a flow vector in a given directed graph $(\mathcal{N}, \mathcal{A})$, the feasible set F is

$$F = \left\{ x \in X \ \Big| \ \sum_{\{j|(i,j)\in\mathcal{A}\}} x_{ij} - \sum_{\{j|(j,i)\in\mathcal{A}\}} x_{ji} = s_i, \ \forall \ i \in \mathcal{N} \right\},$$

and f is a given real-valued function that is defined on the space of flow vectors x. Here s_i are given supply scalars and X is a given subset of flow vectors.

We will focus on two main cases:

(a) The case where the feasible set F is convex and the function f is convex over F. For this case, we will provide natural extensions of some of the primal cost improvement, dual cost improvement, and auction algorithms of Chapters 2-7.

(b) The case where the feasible set F is not convex and involves integer constraints. For this case, we will derive some of the basic methodology for dealing with the integer constraints. We will also explain how some of the standard approaches to combinatorial optimization involve the solution of linear and convex network optimization problems.

In this chapter we discuss broad issues of structure and algorithmic methodology relating to nonlinear network problems, with an emphasis on the convex case. We defer some of the more detailed analysis to Chapters 9 and 10. In Sections 8.1-8.5 we focus on problem formulation. We delineate some important problem structures, involving separability, side constraints, multiple commodities, integer constraints, and arc gains, and we discuss their interplay with the analytical and algorithmic methodology. Our discussion in these sections covers a very broad spectrum of problems, including some discrete models (a more detailed discussion of discrete models will be given in Chapter 10). In Section 8.6, we discuss optimality conditions based on differentiability of the cost function f. In

Section 8.7, we develop some preliminary notions of duality (a deeper treatment of duality for separable problems is provided in Chapter 9). Finally, in Section 8.8, we describe some general techniques of nonlinear programming and we identify the network optimization contexts in which they are most applicable.

On Mathematical Background

In the remainder of the book, we will assume that the reader has some prior exposure to the basic notions of analysis and convexity in the n-dimensional Euclidean space $\Re^n$. We will be reviewing definitions and needed results as they arise (a summary is provided in Appendix A). We implicitly assume that all vectors are column vectors. A prime denotes transposition, so that if x and y are vectors, x' is a row vector, and $x'y$ denotes the inner product of x and y. The standard Euclidean norm of a vector x is denoted by $\|x\|$,

$$\|x\| = \sqrt{x'x}.$$

The reader may find the needed mathematical background in many standard texts. Some recommended sources are Hoffman and Kunze [1971], and Strang [1976] (linear algebra), Luenberger [1969], Ortega and Rheinboldt [1970], and Rudin [1976] (analysis), Hiriart-Urruty and Lemarechal [1993], and Rockafellar [1970] (convex analysis). The author's nonlinear programming text [1995b] contains two extensive optimization-oriented appendixes on analysis, linear algebra, and convexity, and uses the same notation as the one used here.

8.1 CONVEX AND SEPARABLE PROBLEMS

In this section, we consider convex network optimization problems and some of their special cases. We recall that a subset F of $\Re^n$ is called *convex* if it contains the line segment connecting any two of its points; that is, $\alpha x + (1 - \alpha)y$ belongs to F for all $x, y \in F$ and $\alpha \in [0, 1]$. A real-valued function f, defined on a subset of $\Re^n$ that contains a convex set F, is said to be *convex over* F if linear interpolation of the function based on its values at any two points of F provides an overestimate of the true function value; that is,

$$f\big(\alpha x + (1 - \alpha)y\big) \leq \alpha f(x) + (1 - \alpha)f(y), \qquad \forall\, x, y \in F,\ \alpha \in [0, 1].$$

The most general convex network optimization problem has the form

$$\begin{aligned} \text{minimize} \quad & f(x) \\ \text{subject to} \quad & x \in F, \end{aligned}$$

where:

x is a flow vector in a given graph, and

the feasible set F is

$$F = \left\{ x \in X \ \middle| \ \sum_{\{j | (i,j) \in \mathcal{A}\}} x_{ij} - \sum_{\{j | (j,i) \in \mathcal{A}\}} x_{ji} = s_i, \ \forall \ i \in \mathcal{N} \right\}, \quad (8.1)$$

where X is a given convex set and s_i are given supply scalars.

The cost function f is defined on the space of flow vectors and is assumed convex over F.

Important special cases of convex network problems involve constraints and/or a cost function with a structure that is separable with respect to arcs. In particular, we say that the problem is *constraint-separable* if the set X appearing in the feasible set F of Eq. (8.1) has the form

$$X = \left\{ x \mid x_{ij} \in X_{ij}, \ (i,j) \in \mathcal{A} \right\},$$

where each set X_{ij} is an interval of the real line (for example, X_{ij} is specified by arc flow bounds, $X_{ij} = [b_{ij}, c_{ij}]$).†

When, the problem is constraint-separable and in addition, the cost function f has the form

$$f(x) = \sum_{(i,j) \in \mathcal{A}} f_{ij}(x_{ij}),$$

where each function f_{ij} is convex over the corresponding interval X_{ij}, we say that the problem is *separable*. Note that the minimum cost flow problem is obtained as the special case of a separable problem where f is a linear function and each interval X_{ij} specifies upper and lower bounds on the corresponding arc flow x_{ij},

$$X_{ij} = [b_{ij}, c_{ij}].$$

Another interesting special case of the convex network optimization problem is the *convex network flow problem with side constraints*, to be discussed in Section 8.2. This is the special case where the set X appearing in the feasible set of Eq. (8.1) has the form

$$X = \left\{ x \mid x_{ij} \in X_{ij}, \ (i,j) \in \mathcal{A}, \ g_t(x) \leq 0, \ t = 1, \ldots, r \right\},$$

where X_{ij} are intervals of the real line and each g_t is a convex function of x. The constraints $g_t(x) \leq 0$ are called *side constraints*.

---

† An interval in our terminology is a nonempty and convex subset of the real line. It can be closed, or open, or neither closed nor open.

For purposes of easy reference, we list the definitions of the preceding network optimization problems. Generally, unless otherwise specified, when we refer to these problems we implicitly assume that they are convex.

Network Optimization Problem

$\quad$ minimize $\quad f(x)$

$\quad$ subject to $\quad x \in X,$

$$\sum_{\{j|(i,j)\in\mathcal{A}\}} x_{ij} - \sum_{\{j|(j,i)\in\mathcal{A}\}} x_{ji} = s_i, \quad \forall\, i \in \mathcal{N}.$$

Constraint-Separable Network Problem

$\quad$ minimize $\quad f(x)$

$\quad$ subject to $\quad x_{ij} \in X_{ij}, \quad \forall\, (i,j) \in \mathcal{A},$

$$\sum_{\{j|(i,j)\in\mathcal{A}\}} x_{ij} - \sum_{\{j|(j,i)\in\mathcal{A}\}} x_{ji} = s_i, \quad \forall\, i \in \mathcal{N}.$$

Separable Network Problem

$\quad$ minimize $\quad \displaystyle\sum_{(i,j)\in\mathcal{A}} f_{ij}(x_{ij})$

$\quad$ subject to $\quad x_{ij} \in X_{ij}, \quad \forall\, (i,j) \in \mathcal{A},$

$$\sum_{\{j|(i,j)\in\mathcal{A}\}} x_{ij} - \sum_{\{j|(j,i)\in\mathcal{A}\}} x_{ji} = s_i, \quad \forall\, i \in \mathcal{N}.$$

Network Problem with Side Constraints

$\quad$ minimize $\quad f(x)$

$\quad$ subject to $\quad x_{ij} \in X_{ij}, \quad \forall\, (i,j) \in \mathcal{A},$

$$\sum_{\{j|(i,j)\in\mathcal{A}\}} x_{ij} - \sum_{\{j|(j,i)\in\mathcal{A}\}} x_{ji} = s_i, \quad \forall\, i \in \mathcal{N},$$

$$g_t(x) \leq 0, \quad t = 1,\dots,r.$$

There are some additional convex optimization problems that will receive attention in the remainder of the book. One such problem is the *convex multicommodity flow problem*, which will be described in Section 8.3. This problem has in turn separable versions, where the cost function and/or the constraints are separable with respect to arcs, and there may or may not be some additional arc capacity constraints. In the case where there are capacity constraints, the problem can also be viewed as a special case of the convex network problem with side constraints, as we will see in Section 8.3. Another interesting problem is the *monotropic programming problem*, which generalizes the convex separable network problem described above, and is the most general type of convex program that exhibits the favorable combinatorial structure of linear programming; this problem will be described and analyzed in Section 9.7. Figure 8.1 lists the principal types of convex problems that we will discuss in this book and shows their interrelations.

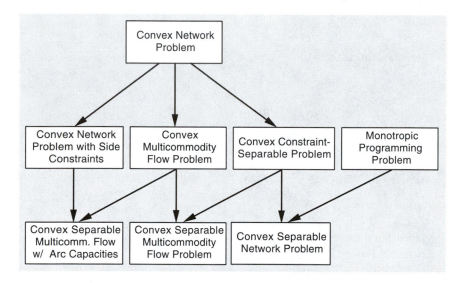

Figure 8.1: Some of the types of convex problems to be discussed in the remainder of the book and their interrelations.

Our development will suggest that separability is the most important structural characteristic of convex network problems. Generally, as the problem's structure deviates from the separable structure, its solution becomes more difficult. There are several reasons for this:

(a) A separable structure allows a sharper duality theory, as we will see in Section 8.7 and in Chapter 9.

(b) Some algorithms, such as certain types of relaxation methods, are most effective in the presence of a separable structure (see Chapter 9). Furthermore, other algorithms, such as auction and ϵ-relaxation, do not apply in the absence of a separable structure.

(c) Separable problems belong to the class of monotropic programming problems, which possess some special properties. As we will see in Chapter 9, for this class of problems, there exists a special *finite* set of directions, called *elementary*, among which a descent direction can be found at any nonoptimal vector. In the case of a convex separable network problem, these directions only depend on the problem's graph. For a primal minimum cost flow problem, these directions are associated with simple cycles (compare with Prop. 1.2), and for a dual minimum cost flow problem, these directions involve certain node subsets (compare with the discussion in Section 1.3). These nice properties do not generalize to nonseparable network problems, even in the presence of convexity.

Let us now describe some practical network models with a separable structure.

Example 8.1. Reservoir Control – Production Scheduling

Suppose that we want to construct an optimal schedule of water release from a reservoir over N time periods. Denote by:

x_k: The volume of water held by the reservoir at the start of the kth period (x_0 is assumed known, and x_k is constrained to lie within some given interval $[\underline{x}, \overline{x}]$).

u_k: The volume of water released by the reservoir during the kth period and used for some productive purpose (u_k is constrained to lie in a given interval $[0, c_k]$).

Thus, the volume x_k evolves according to

$$x_{k+1} = x_k - u_k, \qquad \forall \; k = 0, \ldots, N - 1.$$

There is a cost $G(x_N)$ for the terminal volume being x_N and there is a cost $g_k(u_k)$ for outflow u_k at period k. For example, when u_k is used for electric power generation, $g_k(u_k)$ may be equal to minus the value of power produced from u_k. We want to choose the outflows $u_0, \ldots, u_{N-1}$ to minimize

$$G(x_N) + \sum_{k=0}^{N-1} g_k(u_k),$$

while observing the constraints on the volume x_k and on the outflow u_k. It is natural to assume here that G and g_k are monotonically decreasing convex functions (increasing outflow has diminishing incremental returns).

We can formulate the problem as a convex separable network optimization problem. We represent each period $k = 0, \ldots, N - 1$ by a node k with an outgoing arc $(k, k + 1)$, whose flow is x_k (see Fig. 8.2). We introduce an artificial node A, which "accumulates" the outflow variables u_k. There is an arc from each node k to node A carrying flow u_k, there is an arc $(N - 1, A)$ carrying flow x_N, and an arc $(A, 0)$ carrying flow x_0. All of the arcs have capacity constraints [for the arc $(A, 0)$ the lower and upper bounds coincide with the given initial volume x_0], but only the arcs carrying the flows u_k and x_N have the nonzero cost function $g_k(u_k)$ and $G(x_N)$, respectively. Finally,

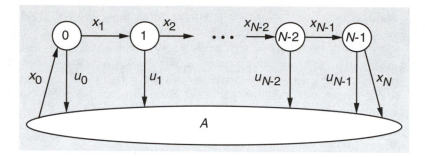

Figure 8.2: Formulation of the reservoir control problem as a convex separable cost network problem. This is a circulation problem; that is, the supply s_i of each node i in the conservation of flow equation is 0.

the flow vector must be a circulation; that is, the given supply s_i of each node i is 0.

There are several variants of the problem, which can also serve as models of other production planning contexts. We list some of the possibilities:

(a) There may be a known inflow v_k to the reservoir from the environment during period k, resulting in an equation of the form

$$x_{k+1} = x_k - u_k + v_k, \qquad \forall\ k = 0, \ldots, N-1.$$

This can be modeled with a known nonzero supply $s_k = v_k$ at the nodes $k = 0, \ldots, N-1$, and with a corresponding demand at the accumulation node A, which is $s_A = -\sum_{k=0}^{N-1} v_k$.

(b) There may be multiple reservoirs some of which are feeding into others with a delay of one or more time periods. For example, we may have two reservoirs in series, the first of which satisfies the equation

$$x_{k+1}^1 = x_k^1 - u_k^1 - y_k^{12}, \qquad \forall\ k = 0, \ldots, N-1,$$

while the second satisfies

$$x_{k+1}^2 = x_k^2 - u_k^2 + y_k^{12}, \qquad \forall\ k = 0, \ldots, N-1. \tag{8.2}$$

Here, x_k^1, x_k^2 and u_k^1, u_k^2 are the volumes and outflows of the two reservoirs at period k, respectively, and y_k^{12} is the water released from reservoir 1 to reservoir 2 during period k. [If there is a delay of d time periods for water to arrive from reservoir 1 to reservoir 2, we should replace y_k^{12} in Eq. (8.2) with y_{k-d}^{12}.] This problem and others like it, involving multiple reservoirs, can be similarly modeled as convex network problems. We need to introduce a node k_m for each period k and reservoir m, as well as corresponding arcs to an accumulation node and to the nodes of other reservoirs that carry the corresponding outflows. For example in the two-reservoir case, there should be an arc from node k_1 to node $(k+1)_2$ carrying flow y_k^{12}.

(c) There may be water losses that are proportional to the current volume, so that the relevant equation is

$$x_{k+1} = \beta_k x_k - u_k, \qquad \forall \, k = 0, \ldots, N-1,$$

where β_k are given scalars with $0 \le \beta_k < 1$. This type of model, together with its multireservoir version, is often encountered in general production planning systems. The resulting problem cannot be modeled as a convex separable network problem, but still involves an important structure, called *network with gains*, which will be discussed in Section 8.5.

The multireservoir problem of the preceding example is typical of *dynamic network flow* problems, which involve material flow between nodes of a network, but also a *time dimension*, whereby flows at a given time period affect the network's condition at future time periods. The mathematical formulation of the problem involves a *time-expanded network*, which includes a copy of the given network for each time period, and arcs that lead from given time periods to subsequent time periods (see Exercise 8.3).

Example 8.2. Least Squares Network Problems

Suppose that we are given a minimum cost flow problem including supplies s_i that do not necessarily add to 0 or that cannot be accommodated by the arc capacities. An interesting problem is then to obtain a capacity-feasible flow vector x whose divergences y_i are as close as possible to the given supplies s_i in a least squares sense. This is the problem

$$\text{minimize} \quad \sum_{i \in \mathcal{N}} w_i (y_i - s_i)^2$$

$$\text{subject to} \quad \sum_{\{j \mid (i,j) \in \mathcal{A}\}} x_{ij} - \sum_{\{j \mid (j,i) \in \mathcal{A}\}} x_{ji} = y_i, \qquad \forall \, i \in \mathcal{N},$$

$$b_{ij} \le x_{ij} \le c_{ij}, \qquad \forall \, (i,j) \in \mathcal{A},$$

where w_i are given positive weights, b_{ij}, c_{ij}, and s_i are given scalars, and the optimization variables are the flows x_{ij} and the divergences y_i.

We can formulate this problem as a convex separable network optimization problem by introducing an artificial node A, which "accumulates" the divergences y_i (see Fig. 8.3). There is an arc from each node i to node A, the flow of which is y_i and the cost of which is $w_i(y_i - s_i)^2$. In a variation of this problem, the "target supplies" s_i may be replaced by "target intervals" $[\underline{s}_i, \overline{s}_i]$, in which case the cost of each arc (i, A) is taken to be

$$w_i \big(\max\{0, y_i - \overline{s}_i\}\big)^2 + w_i \big(\max\{0, \underline{s}_i - y_i\}\big)^2.$$

Still another possibility is to use a nonquadratic cost function for each error $y_i - s_i$.

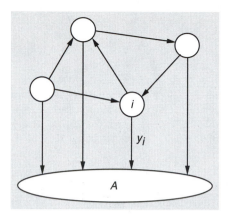

Figure 8.3: Formulation of the least squares network flow problem as a convex separable cost network problem. An artificial node A is introduced together with an arc (i, A) for each node i. The cost of the arc (i, A) is the square of the error between the divergence y_i of node i and the given target supply s_i of i.

In the preceding example, the divergences y_i are subject to optimization. In a different least squares setting, each y_i is required to be equal to a given supply s_i, and the cost function consists of the sum of squares

$$\sum_{(i,j)\in\mathcal{A}} w_{ij}(x_{ij} - m_{ij})^2,$$

where m_{ij} are the components of a given matrix and w_{ij} are given positive weights. The matrix balancing problem discussed in Example 1.5 of Chapter 1, is a special case of this model.

8.2 PROBLEMS WITH SIDE CONSTRAINTS

Many convex network flow problems (in addition to the conservation of flow constraints and interval constraints on the arc flows) have additional constraints of the form

$$g_t(x) \le 0, \qquad t = 1, \ldots, r,$$

which are called *side constraints*. The problem has the form

minimize $f(x)$

subject to $x_{ij} \in X_{ij}, \quad \forall \, (i,j) \in \mathcal{A},$

$$\sum_{\{j|(i,j)\in\mathcal{A}\}} x_{ij} - \sum_{\{j|(j,i)\in\mathcal{A}\}} x_{ji} = s_i, \quad \forall \, i \in \mathcal{N},$$

$$g_t(x) \le 0, \quad t = 1, \ldots, r,$$

where X_{ij} are intervals of the real line, and f and g_t, $t = 1, \ldots, r$, are convex functions of x. Here is an example:

Example 8.3. Inventory Control

Consider an inventory system that involves a single product type and operates over N time periods. Let us denote:

x_k: The amount of stock held by the system at the start of the kth period (x_0 is assumed known, and x_k may also take negative values, which represent back orders).

u_k: The amount of stock purchased (or produced) and immediately delivered at period k, at a cost of $c_k u_k$.

v_k: The amount of stock demanded at period k. This is given for all k.

Thus, the stock x_k evolves according to

$$x_{k+1} = x_k + u_k - v_k, \qquad \forall\ k = 0, \ldots, N-1.$$

There is a cost $h_k(x_k)$ for having stock x_k at period k. Generally, this involves a penalty for stock surplus ($x_k > 0$), as well as a penalty for stock shortage ($x_k < 0$). There is also a cost $H(x_N)$ for the terminal stock being x_N, and possibly a constraint that x_N should lie in a given interval. It is fairly natural to assume here that H and h_k are convex functions. We want to choose the purchases $u_0, \ldots, u_{N-1}$ to minimize

$$H(x_N) + \sum_{k=0}^{N-1} \Big(h_k(x_k) + c_k u_k \Big),$$

while observing the constraints on the volume x_k and on the outflow u_k.

We can formulate this as a convex separable network optimization problem, similar to the reservoir control example of Example 8.1. We represent each period $k = 0, \ldots, N-1$ by a node k with an outgoing arc $(k, k+1)$, whose flow is x_k. We introduce an artificial node A, which represents the "environment." There is an arc from node A to each node k, carrying flow u_k, there is an arc $(N-1, A)$ carrying flow x_N, and an arc $(A, 0)$ carrying flow x_0. There is also an arc from each node k to node A, carrying flow equal to the known demand v_k (see Fig. 8.4).

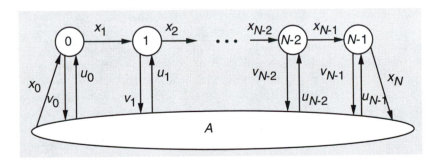

Figure 8.4: Formulation of the inventory control problem as a convex separable network problem. Once the "accumulation" node A is introduced, we obtain a circulation problem; that is, the supply s_i of each node i in the conservation of flow equation is 0.

If there were no other constraints, the problem would be separable. However, there may be several types of side constraints that couple the arc flows. An example is when there is a budget constraint whereby the total cost for inventory purchase may not exceed a given amount B,

$$\sum_{k=0}^{N-1} c_k u_k \leq B.$$

Another example is when there is a space constraint for the system, whereby the total inventory at the start of any period must not exceed a given constant S,

$$x_k + u_k \leq S, \qquad k = 0, \dots, N-1.$$

The preceding side constraints maintain convexity of the problem. However, in other variants of the inventory problem there may be additional integer constraints and couplings between the arc flows that destroy the convex character of the problem. For example, u_k may be subject to a positive fixed charge or startup cost that must be paid when u_k is positive, in addition to the purchase cost $c_k u_k$, i.e., the total purchase cost has the form

$$\begin{cases} C + c_k u_k & \text{if } u_k > 0, \\ 0 & \text{if } u_k = 0, \end{cases}$$

where $C > 0$ is the fixed charge. We will discuss cost structures of this type in Chapter 10.

Side constraints typically complicate the problem's solution because they represent a departure from a pure network structure. In fact, one should always consider the possibility of eliminating side constraints by dualization (see Section 8.7) or by some kind of approximation (see Section 8.8), in order to recover a more pure network structure.

Let us finally note that being able to formulate a given practical problem as a network problem with side constraints is not significant in itself. The reason is that *any convex programming problem can be formulated as a convex network problem with side constraints*, as can be seen from the construction of Fig. 8.5. Furthermore, it can be seen that any linear program can be reformulated as a linear network flow problem with linear side constraints. Thus the class of convex network problems with side constraints is very broad and unstructured. A similar statement can be made about network problems with side constraints and additional integer constraints. This suggests that a problem formulation as a network model with side constraints may be worth considering only if the side constraints "do not dominate" the problem. This notion is somewhat vague, but it roughly means that eliminating the side constraints leaves an "interesting" network structure intact, and does not change "radically" the character of the optimal solution. An example of a problem that is profitably viewed as a network model with side constraints is the multicommodity flow problem with arc capacity constraints, which will be discussed in the next section.

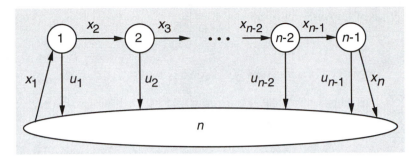

Figure 8.5: A convex network reformulation of a general convex optimization problem of the form

$$\text{minimize} \ \ f(x)$$

$$\text{subject to} \ \ x_k \in X_k, \ k = 1, \ldots, n, \quad g_t(x) \leq 0, \ t = 1, \ldots, r,$$

where $x_1, \ldots, x_n$ are the scalar components of the vector x. We assume that X_k is an interval of the real line for each k, and f and g_t are convex over $\Re^n$. We introduce additional artificial variables $u_1, \ldots, u_{n-1}$, and we construct the network depicted in the figure (the nodes are $1, \ldots, n$, the arcs are as shown, and the flows are shown next to the arcs). The cost function is $f(x)$, and in addition to the conservation of flow constraints

$$u_k = x_k - x_{k+1}, \qquad k = 1, \ldots, n-1,$$

we have the arc flow constraints $x_k \in X_k$, and the side constraints

$$g_t(x) \leq 0, \qquad t = 1, \ldots, r.$$

8.3 MULTICOMMODITY FLOW PROBLEMS

A multicommodity flow problem involves a collection of several networks whose flows must independently satisfy conservation of flow constraints, but are coupled through some other constraints or the cost function. As an example, consider a communication network that carries two different types of traffic, say telephone traffic from node A to node B, and video traffic from node C to node D. The telephone traffic and the video traffic must each satisfy its own conservation of flow constraints, but there may be coupling due to a communication capacity constraint of the network arcs, requiring that the *sum* of the two traffic flows on each arc be less than the capacity threshold of the arc. We formulate a general multicommodity flow problem as follows.

We have a directed graph $(\mathcal{N}, \mathcal{A})$, and we consider a finite collection of flow vectors $x(m)$, $m = 1, \ldots, M$, on the graph, where M is a given integer. We call $x(m)$ the *flow vector of commodity m*, and we denote the collection of all commodity flow vectors by

$$x = \big(x(1), \ldots, x(M)\big).$$

Each flow vector $x(m)$ must satisfy its own conservation of flow constraints

$$\sum_{\{j|(i,j)\in\mathcal{A}\}} x_{ij}(m) - \sum_{\{j|(j,i)\in\mathcal{A}\}} x_{ji}(m) = s_i(m), \qquad \forall\, i \in \mathcal{N},\, m = 1, \ldots, M,$$

(8.3)

where $s_i(m)$ are given supply scalars. Furthermore, the commodity flows must together satisfy

$$x = \big(x(1), \ldots, x(M)\big) \in X,$$ (8.4)

where X is a constraint set, which may encode special restrictions for the various commodities. For example, to force a commodity m to avoid some arc (i,j), we may introduce the constraint $x_{ij}(m) = 0$. In this way, we can model situations where each commodity is restricted to use only a subgraph of the given graph.

The feasible set is

$$F = \big\{x \in X \mid x \text{ satisfies the conservation of flow constraints (8.3)}\big\},$$

and the cost function is of the form

$$f(x) = f\big(x(1), \ldots, x(M)\big).$$ (8.5)

The general *convex multicommodity flow problem* is

$$\text{minimize} \quad f(x)$$
$$\text{subject to} \quad x \in F$$

where we assume that F is convex and f is convex over F.

Note that x may be viewed as a flow vector in an expanded graph consisting of M (disconnected) copies of the original graph $(\mathcal{N}, \mathcal{A})$. With this interpretation, it is seen that the only coupling between the commodities comes from the cost function (8.5) and from the constraint $x \in X$, cf. Eq. (8.4).

The version of the multicommodity problem that is most amenable to analysis and algorithmic solution is the *convex separable multicommodity flow problem*. In this problem the set X has the form

$$X = \big\{x \mid x_{ij}(m) \in X_{ij}(m),\, \forall\, (i,j) \in \mathcal{A},\, m = 1, \ldots, M\big\},$$ (8.6)

where $X_{ij}(m)$ are intervals of the real line, and the cost function has the form

$$f(x) = \sum_{(i,j)\in\mathcal{A}} f_{ij}(y_{ij}),$$ (8.7)

where y_{ij} is the *total flow* of arc (i,j)

$$y_{ij} = \sum_{m=1}^{M} x_{ij}(m),$$

and each $f_{ij} : \Re \mapsto \Re$ is a convex function of y_{ij}. Note here that the cost function is not separable with respect to the commodity flows $x_{ij}(m)$, only with respect to the total flows y_{ij}. There is also a *constraint-separable* version of the multicommodity flow problem, where the constraint set X has the form (8.6) but the cost function f does not have the separable form (8.7).

    In the separable multicommodity flow problem, commodities are coupled only through the total arc flows y_{ij} that appear in the separable cost function. Another type of commodity coupling in multicommodity problems arises when the set X includes additional upper bounds on the total flows of the arcs:

$$X = \big\{x \mid x_{ij}(m) \in X_{ij}(m),\ y_{ij} \le c_{ij},\ \forall\ (i,j) \in \mathcal{A},\ m = 1, \ldots, M\big\}, \quad (8.8)$$

where $X_{ij}(m)$ are given intervals of the real line, and c_{ij} are given scalars representing arc "capacities." The convex separable version of the resulting problem is referred to as a *convex separable multicommodity flow problem with arc capacities*. This problem may also be viewed as a special case of the convex network problem with side constraints, where the side constraints are the capacity constraints $y_{ij} \le c_{ij}$. For easy reference, we list the definitions of the various types of multicommodity network problems in the table of the following page:

    Multicommodity flow problems arise in several practical contexts. Here are some examples:

Example 8.4. Optimal Routing in a Data Network

We are given a directed graph $(\mathcal{N}, \mathcal{A})$, which is viewed as a model of a data communication network. We are also given a set of ordered node pairs (i_m, j_m), $m = 1, \ldots, M$, referred to as *origin-destination (OD) pairs*. The nodes i_m and j_m are referred to as the *origin* and the *destination* of the OD pair. For each OD pair (i_m, j_m), we are given a scalar r_m referred to as its *input rate*.

    In the context of routing of data in a communication network, r_m (measured in bits per unit time) is the arrival rate of traffic entering the network at node i_m and exiting at node j_m. (The traffic here is usually modeled by a stationary stochastic process, in which case r_m represents a stochastic average of the number of bit arrivals per unit time.) In a somewhat different context, r_m may represent the number of ongoing (phone or data) connections between i_m and j_m [within this context, the arc flows $x_{ij}(m)$ are integer, but they can be reasonably approximated with real numbers when a large number

Multicommodity Flow Problem

$$\text{minimize} \quad f(x)$$
$$\text{subject to} \quad x \in X,$$
$$\sum_{\{j|(i,j)\in\mathcal{A}\}} x_{ij}(m) - \sum_{\{j|(j,i)\in\mathcal{A}\}} x_{ji}(m) = s_i(m), \quad \forall\, i \in \mathcal{N},\, m = 1,\ldots,M.$$

Constraint-Separable Multicommodity Flow Problem

$$\text{minimize} \quad f(x)$$
$$\text{subject to} \quad x_{ij}(m) \in X_{ij}(m), \quad \forall\, (i,j) \in \mathcal{A},\, m = 1,\ldots,M,$$
$$\sum_{\{j|(i,j)\in\mathcal{A}\}} x_{ij}(m) - \sum_{\{j|(j,i)\in\mathcal{A}\}} x_{ji}(m) = s_i(m), \quad \forall\, i \in \mathcal{N},\, m = 1,\ldots,M.$$

Separable Multicommodity Flow Problem

$$\text{minimize} \quad \sum_{(i,j)\in\mathcal{A}} f_{ij}(y_{ij})$$
$$\text{subject to} \quad x_{ij}(m) \in X_{ij}(m), \quad \forall\, (i,j) \in \mathcal{A},\, m = 1,\ldots,M,$$
$$\sum_{\{j|(i,j)\in\mathcal{A}\}} x_{ij}(m) - \sum_{\{j|(j,i)\in\mathcal{A}\}} x_{ji}(m) = s_i(m), \quad \forall\, i \in \mathcal{N},\, m = 1,\ldots,M,$$
$$y_{ij} = \sum_{m=1}^{M} x_{ij}(m), \quad \forall\, (i,j) \in \mathcal{A}.$$

Separable Multicommodity Flow Problem with Arc Capacities

$$\text{minimize} \quad \sum_{(i,j)\in\mathcal{A}} f_{ij}(y_{ij})$$
$$\text{subject to} \quad x_{ij}(m) \in X_{ij}(m), \quad \forall\, (i,j) \in \mathcal{A},\, m = 1,\ldots,M,$$
$$\sum_{\{j|(i,j)\in\mathcal{A}\}} x_{ij}(m) - \sum_{\{j|(j,i)\in\mathcal{A}\}} x_{ji}(m) = s_i(m), \quad \forall\, i \in \mathcal{N},\, m = 1,\ldots,M,$$
$$y_{ij} = \sum_{m=1}^{M} x_{ij}(m), \quad \forall\, (i,j) \in \mathcal{A},$$
$$y_{ij} \leq c_{ij}, \quad \forall\, (i,j) \in \mathcal{A}.$$

of connections is involved]. The routing objective is to divide each r_m among the many paths from origin to destination in a way that the resulting total arc flow pattern minimizes a suitable cost function.

We view each OD pair (i_m, j_m) as a commodity, and we denote by $x(m)$ the corresponding flow vector. This vector must satisfy the conservation of flow equation for all $i \in \mathcal{N}$ and $m = 1, \ldots, M$,

$$\sum_{\{j|(i,j)\in\mathcal{A}\}} x_{ij}(m) - \sum_{\{j|(j,i)\in\mathcal{A}\}} x_{ji}(m) = \begin{cases} r_m & \text{if } i = i_m, \\ -r_m & \text{if } i = j_m, \\ 0 & \text{otherwise.} \end{cases}$$

Typically, there are also constraints of the form

$$0 \le x_{ij}(m), \quad y_{ij} \le c_{ij}, \qquad \forall \ (i,j) \in \mathcal{A}, \ m = 1, \ldots, M,$$

where

$$y_{ij} = \sum_{m=1}^{M} x_{ij}(m)$$

is the total flow of arc (i, j), and c_{ij} is its communication capacity. Frequently, the cost function has the separable form

$$\sum_{(i,j)\in\mathcal{A}} f_{ij}(y_{ij}),$$

where f_{ij} is a convex function that provides a measure of communication "delay" on arc (i, j). This delay depends on the flow of the arc and is usually based on some queueing model of the traffic flow on the arc (see e.g., the data network textbook by Bertsekas and Gallager [1992]). With the separable constraints and cost function above, the problem becomes a special case of the separable multicommodity flow problem with arc capacities.

There are some variations of the routing problem, which also arise in other practical applications of multicommodity flow models. For example:

(a) The capacity constraints $y_{ij} \le c_{ij}$ are not present, but instead they may appear implicitly in the cost functions f_{ij}. For example, the constraint $y_{ij} \le c_{ij}$ may be modeled with a function f_{ij} that rises steeply near c_{ij}. This is convenient because we then obtain a separable multicommodity flow problem, which turns out to be more amenable to algorithmic solution than the version involving arc capacities (see Section 8.8).

(b) The commodity input rates r_m may be subject to optimization within some given interval $[0, \overline{r}_m]$. In this case the cost function has the form

$$\sum_{(i,j)\in\mathcal{A}} f_{ij}(y_{ij}) + \sum_{m=1}^{m} g_m(r_m),$$

where g_m is a convex monotonically decreasing function within the given input range $[0, \overline{r}_m]$. This cost function captures the tradeoff between a

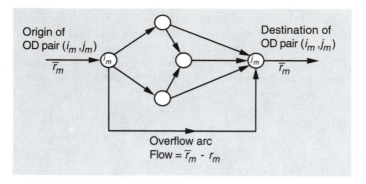

Figure 8.6: Converting a multicommodity problem with commodity input rates r_m that are subject to optimization, to a problem with fixed commodity input rates $\bar{r}_m$. For each commodity m, we introduce an overflow arc (i_m, j_m) that carries flow $x_{i_m j_m} = \bar{r}_m - r_m$.

cost for too much flow on the arcs, and a cost for too much throttling of input to the network. Note that the functions g_m may reflect different priorities for the different commodities. To convert this problem to a standard multicommodity problem, we introduce an "overflow" arc (i_m, j_m) for each commodity m, which carries flow $x_{i_m j_m} = \bar{r}_m - r_m$ and has arc cost function $\tilde{f}_{i_m j_m}(x_{i_m j_m}) = g_m(\bar{r}_m - x_{i_m j_m})$, and we use $\bar{r}_m$ as the fixed input of the OD pair (i_m, j_m) (see Fig. 8.6).

(c) The input rate of each commodity may be *indivisible*, that is, each commodity may be required to follow the same path through the network, rather than be divided among multiple paths. This is a major restriction that has a radical impact in the solution methodology. It changes the constraint set from convex to discrete, since one has to work with the integer-constrained variables

$$z_{ij}^m = \begin{cases} 1 & \text{if commodity } m \text{ is routed through arc } (i,j), \\ 0 & \text{otherwise.} \end{cases}$$

In the case where there is only one commodity, this is not a real complication: it can be seen that we can neglect the integer constraints and transform the problem to a single origin-single destination shortest path problem, which has an integer solution (see Chapter 5). However, it turns out that with two or more commodities, the corresponding problem may have a fractional solution, so the integer constraints cause genuine complications.

Example 8.5. Traffic Assignment

We are given a directed graph, which is viewed as a model of a transportation network. The arcs of the graph represent transportation links such as highways, rail lines, etc. The nodes of the graph represent junction points where traffic can exit from one transportation link and enter another. Similar to the preceding example, we are given a set of OD pairs (i_m, j_m), $m = 1, \ldots, M$. For OD pair (i_m, j_m), there is a known input r_m representing rate of traffic entering the network at the origin node i_m and exiting at the destination node j_m. The input r_m is to be divided among the paths that start at i_m and end at j_m.

For each arc (i, j), we are given a cost function $f_{ij}(y_{ij})$ of the total flow y_{ij} carried by the arc, and we want to minimize the separable cost

$$\sum_{(i,j) \in \mathcal{A}} f_{ij}(y_{ij}), \tag{8.9}$$

subject to the conservation of flow constraints and the constraints $x_{ij}(m) \geq 0$. Thus the mathematical formulation of this example is similar to the one of the preceding routing example. The only difference is that in the routing example there is often the constraint $y_{ij} \leq c_{ij}$ for some or all the arcs (i, j), while for the traffic assignment problem, some arcs may not have such a constraint. However, even this difference is somewhat artificial, since one can effectively model a constraint of the form $y_{ij} \leq c_{ij}$ by using a cost function that rises steeply as y_{ij} approaches c_{ij}.

We note that in some contexts, the separable cost function (8.9) is not quite appropriate because the traffic flow on a given arc may interact with the traffic flow on other arcs that share the same start or end node (this is familiar from everyday experience: a traffic jam in one road of an intersection often slows down the traffic on the other roads of the intersection). In such cases, it may be more appropriate for the cost functions f_{ij} to depend on the total flows of several arcs.

We finally mention that the modeling assumption that routes are optimally chosen by some central authority is unnatural in situations where travelers can choose independently their routes through the network. However, we will see later in this chapter (see Example 8.11) that problems of the latter type can be reduced to optimization problems of the type described in the present example.

8.4 INTEGER CONSTRAINTS

We have already discussed in Chapters 1-7 several combinatorial problems within the framework of the minimum cost flow problem, such as shortest path and assignment. These problems require that the arc flows be 0 or 1, but we have neglected these 0-1 constraints because even if we relax them and replace them with capacity intervals $[0, 1]$, we can obtain optimal flows that are 0 or 1 with the minimum cost flow algorithms that we have developed so far (e.g., the simplex methods of Chapter 5).

On the other hand, once we deviate from the minimum cost flow structure and we impose side constraints or use a nonlinear cost function, the integer character of optimal solutions is lost, and all additional integer constraints must be explicitly imposed. This often complicates dramatically the solution process. In particular, there is no known polynomial algorithm for solving an integer-constrained network problem that has side constraints.

The theory of computational complexity quantifies the difficulty of solving various classes of problems, and provides a useful guide for formulating combinatorial problems as network flow problems. We mention in particular the important class of *NP-complete problems*, for which no polynomial algorithm is known at present (and none exists according to a broadly held conjecture, commonly referred to as $P \neq NP$). An example of an NP-complete problem is the general linear network optimization problem with linear side constraints and 0-1 integer constraints on the arc flows. We refer to the books by Garey and Johnson [1979], and Papadimitriou and Steiglitz [1982] for detailed discussions of NP-completeness, and to the book by Bertsimas and Tsitsiklis [1997] for a lighter and more accessible introduction. An important point for our purposes is that, assuming $P \neq NP$ and given a problem that is NP-complete (or more generally, has nonpolynomial complexity), we should give up hope of formulating it as a minimum cost flow problem, which (as we know from Chapter 7) is solvable with polynomial algorithms. Furthermore, given a candidate algorithm for an NP-complete problem, we should give up hope of showing that it can solve the problem exactly if the algorithm is polynomial.

Given the inherent difficulty of solving integer-constrained problems with side constraints, one may prefer to settle for an approximate solution, obtained through some heuristic. Two of the simplest and most often used approaches are the following:

(a) Discard the integer constraints, solve the resulting problem as a "continuous" network flow problem (possibly having convex cost or side constraints), and use some ad hoc method to round the solution to integer.

(b) Discard the complicating side constraints, obtain an integer solution of the resulting network problem, and use some heuristic to correct this solution for feasibility of the violated side constraints. A variant of this approach is to compensate for the discarded side constraints by adding to the cost function a penalty for their violation. This tends to produce an integer solution that is closer to feasibility.

For an example of the first approach, based on rounding a fractional solution, consider a transportation problem with supply constraints $\sum_j x_{ij} = \alpha_i$ and demand constraints $\sum_i x_{ij} \leq \beta_j$. Suppose that there is an additional *indivisibility constraint*, which requires that the supply of each supply node cannot be divided between multiple demand nodes. Then a simple heuristic is to discard the latter constraint, solve the resulting problem using one of the algorithms of Chapters 5-7, and then round or shift on an ad hoc basis whatever divided node supplies are obtained to satisfy the indivisibility constraint. While this is a fairly crude heuristic, it may work well in the context of other more sophisticated procedures, such as the branch-and-bound and the rollout methods to be discussed in Chapter 10.

Let us also provide an example of the second approach, which is based on discarding the side constraints.

Example 8.6. Constrained Shortest Path Problem

Consider a shortest path problem where we want to find a simple path P from the origin node s to the destination node t that minimizes the path length

$$\sum_{(i,j)\in P} a_{ij}. \tag{8.10}$$

In some contexts, there may be additional requirements on P of the generic form

$$\sum_{(i,j)\in P} c_{ij}^k \le d^k, \qquad k = 1,\ldots,K. \tag{8.11}$$

For example, there may be a *timing constraint*, whereby the total time to traverse P should not exceed a given threshold T, i.e.,

$$\sum_{(i,j)\in P} \tau_{ij} \le T,$$

where τ_{ij} is the time required to traverse arc (i,j). Similarly, there could be a *safety constraint*, whereby the probability of being able to traverse the path P safely should be no less than a given threshold. Here, we assume that traversal of an arc (i,j) will be safe with a given probability p_{ij}. Assuming probabilistic independence of the safety of arc traversals, the probability that traversal of a path P will be safe is the product $\Pi_{(i,j)\in P}p_{ij}$. The requirement that this probability is no less than a given threshold β translates to the constraint

$$\sum_{(i,j)\in P} \ln(p_{ij}) \ge \ln(\beta).$$

We can formulate the shortest path problem with path length given by Eq. (8.10) and with the constraints (8.11) as the following network problem with side constraints and integer constraints:

$$\text{minimize} \quad \sum_{(i,j)\in\mathcal{A}} a_{ij}x_{ij}$$

$$\text{subject to} \quad \sum_{\{j|(i,j)\in\mathcal{A}\}} x_{ij} - \sum_{\{j|(j,i)\in\mathcal{A}\}} x_{ji} = \begin{cases} 1 & \text{if } i = s, \\ -1 & \text{if } i = t, \\ 0 & \text{otherwise,} \end{cases} \tag{8.12}$$

$$x_{ij} = 0 \text{ or } 1, \qquad \forall\, (i,j) \in \mathcal{A},$$

$$\sum_{(i,j)\in\mathcal{A}} c_{ij}^k x_{ij} \le d^k, \qquad \forall\, k = 1,\ldots,K.$$

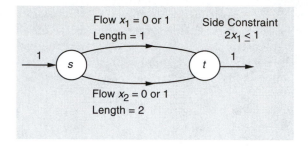

Figure 8.7: An example of a two-arc, single-constraint shortest path problem whose "relaxed" network optimization formulation (no integer constraints) has a fractional solution. There are two nodes, s and t, and two arcs/paths connecting s to t, denoted 1 and 2, with lengths 1 and 2, respectively. There is also the side constraint $2x_1 \leq 1$. Thus the only feasible solution is arc/path 2 and the shortest distance is the length 2 of the arc. Denoting by x_1 and x_2 the flows of arcs 1 and 2, respectively, the corresponding network optimization problem (8.12) is

$$\text{minimize} \quad x_1 + 2x_2$$
$$\text{subject to} \quad x_1 + x_2 = 1,$$
$$x_1 = 0 \text{ or } 1, \quad x_2 = 0 \text{ or } 1,$$
$$2x_1 \leq 1.$$

This problem yields the correct constrained shortest path solution, $x_1 = 0$ and $x_2 = 1$. If the integer constraints are relaxed and replaced by

$$0 \leq x_1 \leq 1, \qquad 0 \leq x_2 \leq 1,$$

the corresponding optimal solution is $x_1 = 0.5$ and $x_2 = 0.5$, and gives no information about the shortest path.

A path P from s to t is optimal if and only if the flow vector x defined by

$$x_{ij} = \begin{cases} 1 & \text{if } (i,j) \text{ belongs to } P, \\ 0 & \text{otherwise,} \end{cases}$$

is an optimal solution of the problem (8.12).

Note the 0-1 integer constraint on the arc flows x_{ij}. Without this constraint, the network optimization problem (8.12) may have a fractional solution from which recovery of a constrained shortest path may not be easy. This is illustrated in Fig. 8.7.

Let us now consider a few algorithms for solving the constrained shortest path problem (8.12).

(a) The first possibility is to discard the 0-1 arc flow constraints, replacing them with the flow bounds $0 \leq x_{ij} \leq 1$. The resulting problem is not a minimum cost flow problem because of the side constraints, but it can be solved as a linear program, using for example the simplex method for general linear programming. The (fractional) solution thus obtained can be decomposed using the conformal decomposition theorem (Prop. 1.1) into a finite collection of simple path flows that start at s and end at t (plus possibly some cycle flows). If $\mathcal{P}$ is the subset of the corresponding paths that are feasible with respect to the side constraints, one may select as an approximate solution the path in $\mathcal{P}$ that has minimum length. This approach will certainly work well for the example of Fig. 8.7, and is also likely to work well in problems with a single side constraint, because in such a problem, at least one path in $\mathcal{P}$ will satisfy the side constraint (why?). However, for problems involving multiple side constraints, this approach is not guaranteed to produce a feasible solution, even when the problem is feasible, in which case it needs to be supplemented with some additional heuristic.

(b) A second possibility is to discard the side constraints and to generate an enumeration of the sequence $\{P_1, P_2, \ldots\}$ of paths from s to t in order of increasing length, that is,

$$\sum_{(i,j)\in P_1} a_{ij} \le \sum_{(i,j)\in P_2} a_{ij} \le \cdots$$

Here P_1 is the best (shortest) path, P_2 is the 2nd best path, and more generally P_k is the kth best path. There are algorithms for producing this sequence of paths in order, starting with the shortest path P_1 (see Exercise 2.26 in Chapter 2), assuming there are no cycles of negative length. As we generate the paths P_k, we can test them for feasibility with respect to the side constraints. The first path that is found to be feasible is the (exactly) optimal solution of the original constrained shortest path problem.

(c) Unfortunately, the preceding method may generate a very large number of paths before finding an optimal solution. The reason is that the order in which paths are generated does not take into account at all the side constraints. To address this deficiency, one may compensate for the discarded side constraints $\sum_{(i,j)\in P} c_{ij}^k \le d^k$, by correcting the arc lengths to reflect a dependence on the cost coefficients c_{ij}^k. The corrected arc lengths have the form

$$\hat{a}_{ij} = a_{ij} + \sum_{k=1}^{K} \mu^k c_{ij}^k, \qquad (8.13)$$

where μ^k are some positive penalty coefficients, one per side constraint. We may view μ^k as a price or Lagrange multiplier for the constraint $\sum_{(i,j)\in P} c_{ij}^k \le d^k$, so a reasonable choice for μ^k is the corresponding Lagrange multiplier of the relaxed version of problem (8.12) with the 0-1 arc flow constraints replaced with the arc flow bounds $0 \le x_{ij} \le 1$. Thus, this approach can be combined with approach (a) above that is based on solving the relaxed version of the problem. One may also obtain suitable multipliers μ^k via the Lagrangian relaxation method to be discussed in Chapter 10. Now given the corrected arc lengths of Eq. (8.13), one can follow an approach similar to (b) above. In particular, one may generate the sequence $\{P_1, P_2, \ldots\}$ of paths from s to t in order of increasing length, using the *corrected* arc lengths $\hat{a}_{ij}$, check the paths for feasibility of the side constraints, and pick the first generated path that is feasible.

As the preceding example illustrates, there is a broad variety of heuristic procedures that are based on integer or side constraint relaxation. Some of these heuristics can be very sophisticated, and depending on the practical problem solved, may provide a satisfactory solution. In other cases, a heuristic may be inadequate and there may be a need for a more systematic procedure. In Chapter 10, we will discuss procedures of this type, such as the *branch-and-bound method*, which is capable in principle to obtain the optimal solution of an integer-constrained problem, albeit with a greatly increased computational effort.

We will also discuss in Chapter 10 *local search* methods, which move from one feasible solution to another improved "neighboring" feasible solution based on some scheme. Sometimes, local search methods are modified to allow excursions into the infeasible region, and/or relax the restriction of cost improvement at each iteration. *Genetic algorithms*, *tabu search*, and *simulated annealing* are some of the most popular local search methods, and will be briefly discussed in Chapter 10. A point that we want to emphasize here, however, is that heuristics often involve the solution of network problems without integer constraints, and that the minimum cost flow algorithms of Chapters 2-7 are frequently applicable.

8.5 NETWORKS WITH GAINS

Our entire discussion of networks so far was based on the conservation of flow assumption; that is, all the flow arriving at a node must exit the node, and the flow sent along an arc by the start node of the arc arrives in its entirety at its end node.

For some practical network models, however, it is useful to relax the conservation of flow assumption. In particular, for a given arc (j, i), we may consider introducing a positive multiplier g_{ji}, called the *gain* of (j, i), which models the factor by which the flow x_{ji} is diminished or amplified as it goes through the arc. Thus, flow x_{ji} sent by j arrives at i as $g_{ji}x_{ji}$, and the conservation of flow equation becomes

$$\sum_{\{j \mid (i,j) \in \mathcal{A}\}} x_{ij} - \sum_{\{j \mid (j,i) \in \mathcal{A}\}} g_{ji}x_{ji} = s_i, \qquad \forall\, i \in \mathcal{N}. \qquad (8.14)$$

The corresponding network optimization problem is to minimize a cost function $f(x)$ subject to the conservation of flow constraints (8.14), and some additional constraint of the generic form $x \in X$, expressing for example arc flow bounds, side constraints, integer constraints, etc. Problems of this type are referred to as *network problems with gains*, or *generalized network problems*. By distinction, network problems that do not involve gains are called *pure network problems*.

Two important examples of network problems with gains are characterized by:

(1) *A linear cost function, upper and lower flow bounds on the arc flows, and the conservation of flow constraints (8.14)*. This problem generalizes the minimum cost flow problem discussed in Chapters 1-7 to the case where there are arc gains. It turns out that all the major algorithms of Chapters 5-7 can be suitably modified to address this problem (see the sources cited at the end of the chapter).

(2) *A convex separable cost function, interval constraints on the arc flows, and the conservation of flow constraints (8.14)*. This problem generalizes the convex separable network problem of Section 8.1.

Generally, network problems with gains tend to be considerably more complex than their pure network counterparts. For example, one of the peculiarities of networks with gains is that *cycles can generate or absorb net flow*. In particular, let us define the *gain* of a cycle C as the product of the gains of positively traversed arcs of the cycle (the set of arcs C^+) divided by the product of the gains of the negatively traversed arcs of the cycle (the set of arcs C^-),

$$G_C = \frac{\Pi_{(i,j)\in C^+}g_{ij}}{\Pi_{(i,j)\in C^-}g_{ij}}.$$

If $G_C \neq 1$, the cycle C is said to be *active*, and otherwise it is called *passive*. An active cycle is said to be *flow generating* if $G_C > 1$, and it is said to be *flow absorbing* if $G_C < 1$. These definitions are illustrated in Fig. 8.8, where it is seen that the divergence out of a flow generating (or absorbing) cycle is greater (or smaller, respectively) than the divergence into the cycle.

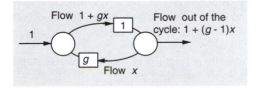

Figure 8.8: Illustration of flow generating and flow absorbing cycles. If the gain g of the cycle is larger than 1, the flow out of the cycle can be arbitrarily larger than the flow into the cycle. The value of x is restricted only by the capacity of the arcs of the cycle. Similarly, if $g < 1$, the flow out of the cycle can be smaller than the flow into the cycle.

A variation of network problems with gains arises when the divergences of some of the nodes are not fixed, but are instead required to lie between given bounds. The conservation of flow constraints of Eq. (8.14) then become

$$\underline{s}_i \le \sum_{\{j|(i,j)\in\mathcal{A}\}} x_{ij} - \sum_{\{j|(j,i)\in\mathcal{A}\}} g_{ji}x_{ji} \le \overline{s}_i, \qquad \forall\, i \in \mathcal{N}, \tag{8.15}$$

where the scalars $\underline{s}_i$ and $\overline{s}_i$ are given. Constraints of this type cause some difficulty because they cannot be converted to equality constrains as easily as they can in pure network counterparts. The device used in pure network problems involves the use of artificial accumulation nodes to convert the problem to the circulation format (cf. Exercise 1.6). However, when there are gains, this device does not work because the sum of the node supplies need not be zero. Figure 8.9 illustrates the difficulty and provides some ways for dealing with it.

Here are some examples of network problems with gains:

Example 8.7. Generalized Assignment Problems

Consider a problem of assigning m jobs to n machines. If job i is performed at machine j, it costs a_{ij} and requires t_{ij} time units. We want to find a minimum cost assignment of the jobs to the machines, given the total available time T_j at machine j.

We can formulate this as the following network optimization problem with gains:

$$\text{minimize} \quad \sum_{i=1}^{m}\sum_{j=1}^{n} a_{ij}x_{ij}$$

$$\text{subject to} \quad \sum_{j=1}^{n} x_{ij} = 1, \qquad i = 1,\ldots,m,$$

$$\sum_{i=1}^{m} t_{ij}x_{ij} \le T_j, \qquad j = 1,\ldots,n,$$

$$0 \le x_{ij} \le 1, \qquad i = 1,\ldots,m,\, j = 1,\ldots,n.$$

The constraints $0 \le x_{ij} \le 1$ embody the assumption that jobs can be partitioned and performed in multiple machines. The graph representation of the problem is shown in Fig. 8.10. This is an inequality constrained problem, since the total flow $\sum_{i=1}^{m} t_{ij}x_{ij}$ out of machine node j is required to lie in the interval $[0, T_j]$. Note that contrary to pure network problems, the total flow out of the entire set of machine nodes (i.e., the total time that the machines will be busy) is not known a priori, and depends on the flow vector x and the arc gains.

In the case where each job must be performed in its entirety at a single machine, the arc flow constraints must be changed to

$$x_{ij} = 0 \text{ or } 1, \qquad i = 1,\ldots,m,\, j = 1,\ldots,n,$$

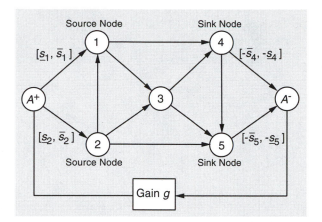

Figure 8.9: Illustration of the difficulty of converting a network problem with gains involving the inequality constraints

$$\underline{s}_i \leq \sum_{\{j|(i,j)\in\mathcal{A}\}} x_{ij} - \sum_{\{j|(j,i)\in\mathcal{A}\}} g_{ji}x_{ji} \leq \overline{s}_i, \qquad \forall\, i \in \mathcal{N},$$

to one involving equality constraints. For simplicity, suppose that there are two types of nodes i, *sources* for which $0 \leq \underline{s}_i \leq \overline{s}_i$, and *sinks* for which $\underline{s}_i \leq \overline{s}_i \leq 0$. Let us add a "supersource" node A^+ and a "supersink" node A^-, an arc (A^+, i) with feasible flow range $[\underline{s}_i, \overline{s}_i]$ to every source node i, and an arc (i, A^-) with feasible flow range $[-\overline{s}_i, -\underline{s}_i]$ from every sink node i. The difficulty now is that the flow going into the network from A^+ is not equal to the flow coming out of the network to A^-. It is possible, however, to reformulate the problem to one involving conservation of flow constraints of the equality type, and an arc (A^-, A^+) whose gain parameter g is unknown and is subject to optimization. An alternative possibility is to set the supply of node A^+ to $\sum_{\{i|\overline{s}_i>0\}} \overline{s}_i$ and the supply of node A^- to $\sum_{\{i|\underline{s}_i<0\}} \underline{s}_i$, and to also introduce an artificial cycle at each of the nodes A^+ and A^-, with gain that is less than 1. These two cycles involve two extra nodes $\overline{A}^+$ and $\overline{A}^-$, together with the arcs $(A^+, \overline{A}^+)$, $(\overline{A}^+, A^+)$, $(A^-, \overline{A}^-)$, and $(\overline{A}^-, A^-)$, each having a gain equal to some $\beta \in (0, 1)$.

thereby obtaining an integer-constrained problem. When there is only one machine, this problem is equivalent to a classical problem, called the *knapsack problem*. Here we want to place in a knapsack the most valuable subcollection out of a given collection of objects, subject to a total weight constraint

$$\sum_{i=1}^{m} w_i x_i \leq T,$$

where T is the total weight threshold, w_i is the weight of object i, and x_i is a variable which is 1 or 0 depending on whether the ith object is placed in the knapsack or not. The value to be maximized is $\sum_{i=1}^{m} v_i x_i$, where v_i is

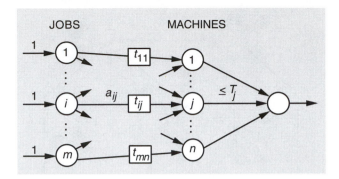

Figure 8.10: Illustration of the graph of a generalized assignment problem. Each arc (i, j) has gain t_{ij}. The divergence out of each machine node j is constrained to lie in the interval $[0, T_j]$.

the value of the ith object. We will discuss in more detail integer-constrained problems of this type in Chapter 10.

Example 8.8. Production Scheduling

Consider a system involving production of multiple types of products over N time periods. The system is similar to the one of Example 8.1, but is more general in that it allows product consumption and loss, as well as product conversion from one type to another. These new features introduce gains for the arc flows.

     The system is described by a set of equations

$$x_{k+1}^i = b_k^i x_k^i + \sum_{\{j|j\neq i\}} (c_k^{ji} y_k^{ji} - y_k^{ij}) - u_k^i, \quad i = 1, \ldots, m, \; k = 0, \ldots, N-1,$$

where

x_k^i: The amount of product of type i available at the start of the kth period.

y_k^{ji}: The amount of product of type j that is used for production of product of type i during the kth period.

u_k^i: The amount of product of type i that is consumed during the kth period.

The scalars b_k^i and c_k^{ji} are nonnegative and are known, and there are interval constraints on all the variables x_k^i, y_k^{ji}, and u_k^i. The cost function is

$$\sum_{i=1}^{m} \sum_{k=0}^{N-1} g_k^i(u_k^i),$$

where g_k^i are nonincreasing convex functions, and $-g_k^i(u_k^i)$ expresses the benefit corresponding to production of u_k^i units of product i at time k.

We can formulate the problem as a convex separable network problem with gains by introducing an artificial accumulation node, as shown in Fig. 8.11. The coefficients b_k^i and c_k^{ji} are the gains. The divergence from all nodes except the artificial node is constrained to be 0. The divergence from the artificial node is not constrained in any way, and is subject to optimization. This corresponds to Eq. (8.15) with the upper and lower bounds on the divergence being ∞ and $-\infty$, respectively.

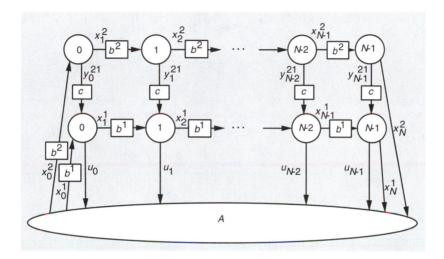

Figure 8.11: Illustration of the graph of a production scheduling problem for two products types, where the type 2 product is used to produce the type 1 product. The arcs have gains as shown. The divergence out of the artificial accumulation node A is unconstrained.

We finally note two transformations and equivalences that highlight the differences between networks with gains and pure networks. Figure 8.12 shows that *it is possible to transform a network problem with gains to a pure network problem, by introducing some side constraints.* Figure 8.13 shows that *a network problem with gains can be transformed to a pure network problem if all cycles are passive.*

8.6 OPTIMALITY CONDITIONS

In this section we develop some basic optimality conditions for convex network flow problems where the cost function f is continuously differentiable. By this we mean that for all flow vectors x, the partial derivatives $\partial f(x)/\partial x_{ij}$, $(i,j) \in \mathcal{A}$, exist and are continuous functions of x. The vector whose components are these partial derivatives is the gradient $\nabla f(x)$ of f at

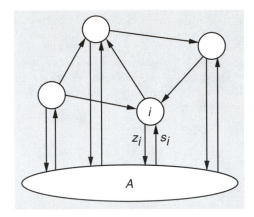

Figure 8.12: Transformation of a network problem with gains to a pure circulation problem with side constraints. We introduce a variable z_i for each node i, and we write the conservation of flow constraints

$$\underline{s}_i \le \sum_{\{j|(i,j)\in\mathcal{A}\}} x_{ij} - \sum_{\{j|(j,i)\in\mathcal{A}\}} g_{ji}x_{ji} \le \overline{s}_i$$

as

$$\underline{s}_i \le \sum_{\{j|(i,j)\in\mathcal{A}\}} x_{ij} - \sum_{\{j|(j,i)\in\mathcal{A}\}} x_{ji} + z_i \le \overline{s}_i,$$

while simultaneously requiring that the side constraints

$$z_i = \sum_{\{j|(j,i)\in\mathcal{A}\}} (1 - g_{ji})x_{ji}$$

be satisfied. We may interpret z_i as the flow of an arc from i to an artificial accumulation node A. With an additional arc (A, i) for each node i, with feasible flow range $[\underline{s}_i, \overline{s}_i]$, the problem is converted to a circulation problem without gains but with side constraints.

x (Appendix A summarizes definitions and results relating to differentiable functions).

Generally, for a differentiable function f defined on the Euclidean space $\Re^n$, the gradient is denoted by $\nabla f(x)$ and is considered to be a column vector. A prime denotes transposition, so that $\nabla f(x)'$ is a row vector, and $\nabla f(x)'y$ is the inner product of $\nabla f(x)$ with a vector y. A result that we will often use is that if f is continuously differentiable (over the entire space), then f is convex over a convex set F if and only if the first order approximation of f based on $f(x)$ and $\nabla f(x)$ underestimates f; that is, f is convex over F if and only if

$$f(y) \ge f(x) + \nabla f(x)'(y - x), \qquad \forall \ x, y \in F. \tag{8.16}$$

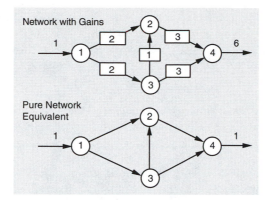

Figure 8.13: Illustration of the passivity condition under which a network problem with gains can be transformed to a pure network problem. Suppose that for each node i there exists a positive scalar γ_i such that

$$\gamma_i = g_{ji}\gamma_j, \qquad \forall \ (j,i) \in \mathcal{A}. \tag{*}$$

Then the conservation of flow equation

$$\sum_{\{j|(i,j)\in\mathcal{A}\}} x_{ij} - \sum_{\{j|(j,i)\in\mathcal{A}\}} g_{ji}x_{ji} = s_i, \qquad \forall \ i \in \mathcal{N},$$

can be written as

$$\sum_{\{j|(i,j)\in\mathcal{A}\}} x_{ij} - \sum_{\{j|(j,i)\in\mathcal{A}\}} \gamma_i\gamma_j^{-1}x_{ji} = s_i, \qquad \forall \ i \in \mathcal{N}.$$

By using the transformation of variables $x_{ij} = \gamma_i\xi_{ij}$, $s_i = \gamma_i\zeta_i$, we obtain

$$\sum_{\{j|(i,j)\in\mathcal{A}\}} \xi_{ij} - \sum_{\{j|(j,i)\in\mathcal{A}\}} \xi_{ji} = \zeta_i, \qquad \forall \ i \in \mathcal{N}.$$

Thus, the problem is equivalent to a pure network problem whose arc flows are ξ_{ij} (see the figure, where $\gamma_1 = 1$, $\gamma_2 = \gamma_3 = 2$, and $\gamma_4 = 6$). By denoting $p_i = -\ln\gamma_i$, we see that the condition (*) holds if and only if there exist scalars p_i such that

$$p_i = \ln g_{ij} + p_j, \qquad \forall \ (i,j) \in \mathcal{A}.$$

By the feasible differential theorem (Exercise 5.11 in Chapter 5), this is true if and only if for every cycle C, we have

$$\sum_{(i,j)\in C^+} \ln g_{ij} - \sum_{(i,j)\in C^-} \ln g_{ij} = 0,$$

which is equivalent to requiring that all cycles have gain equal to 1, i.e., that they be passive.

When the cost function f of an optimization problem is differentiable, an important analytical and algorithmic idea is *linearization*, which amounts to replacing f with its first order linear approximation around some vector $\bar{x}$

$$f(\bar{x}) + \nabla f(\bar{x})'(x - \bar{x}),$$

while leaving the constraint set unchanged. This idea underlies the following basic necessary and sufficient condition for optimality.

Proposition 8.1: Consider the minimization of a function $f : \Re^n \mapsto \Re$ over a convex subset F of the Euclidean space $\Re^n$. Assume that f is continuously differentiable and is convex over F. Then, a vector $x^* \in F$ is optimal if and only if

$$\nabla f(x^*)'(x - x^*) \geq 0, \qquad \forall\, x \in F. \tag{8.17}$$

Proof: Assume that x^* is an optimal solution. Then, for all $x \in F$ and all $\alpha \in (0, 1]$, we have $f(x^* + \alpha(x - x^*)) \geq f(x^*)$. Hence

$$\frac{f(x^* + \alpha(x - x^*)) - f(x^*)}{\alpha} \geq 0, \qquad \forall\, \alpha \in (0, 1].$$

By taking the limit as $\alpha \to 0$, we obtain $\nabla f(x^*)'(x - x^*) \geq 0$, which is Eq. (8.17).

Conversely, suppose that $x^* \in F$ and Eq. (8.17) holds. Since f is convex over F, we have by Eq. (8.16)

$$f(x) \geq f(x^*) + \nabla f(x^*)'(x - x^*), \qquad \forall\, x \in F.$$

Hence, using Eq. (8.17), we obtain $f(x) \geq f(x^*)$ for all $x \in F$. **Q.E.D.**

The optimality condition (8.17) is illustrated in Fig. 8.14. One way to interpret the condition is to note that it is equivalent to x^* being an optimal solution of the *linearized problem*

$$\text{minimize } \nabla f(x^*)'(x - x^*)$$
$$\text{subject to } x \in F.$$

Note that the optimality condition (8.17) holds at an optimal solution x^* even if f is nonconvex (the first part of the proof of Prop. 8.1 still applies as long as F is convex). However, in this case the condition is not sufficient to guarantee optimality of x^*.

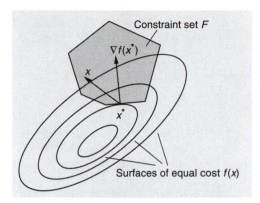

Figure 8.14: Geometric interpretation of the optimality condition of Prop. 8.1. A vector $x^* \in F$ is optimal if and only if the gradient $\nabla f(x^*)$ makes an angle less than or equal to 90 degrees with all feasible variations $x - x^*$, $x \in F$.

As a special case of Prop. 8.1, let us extend the nonnegative cycle condition of Prop. 1.2 for the minimum cost flow problem to the case of the constraint-separable convex network problem

$$
\begin{aligned}
\text{minimize} \quad & f(x) \\
\text{subject to} \quad & x_{ij} \in X_{ij}, \quad \forall \ (i,j) \in \mathcal{A}, \\
& \sum_{\{j \mid (i,j) \in \mathcal{A}\}} x_{ij} - \sum_{\{j \mid (j,i) \in \mathcal{A}\}} x_{ji} = s_i, \quad \forall \ i \in \mathcal{N},
\end{aligned}
\tag{8.18}
$$

where each X_{ij} is an interval of the real line (cf. Section 8.1). Similar to Section 1.1.2, we say that a cycle C is *unblocked* with respect to a flow vector x, if $x_{ij} \in X_{ij}$ for all arcs (i,j), and there exists a $\delta > 0$ such that $x_{ij} + \delta \in X_{ij}$ for all arcs (i,j) in C^+ (the set of forward arcs of C), and $x_{ij} - \delta \in X_{ij}$ for all arcs (i,j) in C^- (the set of backward arcs of C). We have the following proposition.

Proposition 8.2: (Nonnegative Cycle Condition) Consider the constraint-separable convex network flow problem (8.18), and assume that f is continuously differentiable over the entire space, and is convex over the feasible set. Then, a vector x^* is optimal if and only if x^* is feasible and for every simple cycle C that is unblocked with respect to x^* there holds

$$
\sum_{(i,j) \in C^+} \frac{\partial f(x^*)}{x_{ij}} - \sum_{(i,j) \in C^-} \frac{\partial f(x^*)}{x_{ij}} \geq 0.
\tag{8.19}
$$

Proof: By Prop. 8.1, x^* is optimal if and only if x^* is an optimal solution of the linearized problem, which is the minimum cost flow problem

$$\text{minimize} \quad \sum_{(i,j)\in\mathcal{A}} \frac{\partial f(x^*)}{\partial x_{ij}} x_{ij}$$

$$\text{subject to} \quad x_{ij} \in X_{ij}, \quad \forall\, (i,j) \in \mathcal{A},$$

$$\sum_{\{j|(i,j)\in\mathcal{A}\}} x_{ij} - \sum_{\{j|(j,i)\in\mathcal{A}\}} x_{ji} = s_i, \quad \forall\, i \in \mathcal{N}.$$

The result follows by applying Prop. 1.2 (even though this proposition is stated for the case where the X_{ij} are compact intervals, it is easily extended to the case where the X_{ij} are arbitrary intervals).   **Q.E.D.**

The idea of the preceding proposition is to use the linearized problem as a vehicle for generalizing results about linear network flow problems to nonlinear problems. This idea can be used in several different ways. For example, one can obtain analogs of the complementary slackness theorems of Section 4.2 for the constraint-separable convex network problem (see Exercise 8.7).

When the cost function is nondifferentiable at an optimal solution x^*, one may still use the argument of the proof of Prop. 8.1 to show that the directional derivative of f at x^* cannot be negative along any direction $x - x^*$ where x is feasible. We will use this approach for the case of a convex separable problem in Section 9.2, where we will generalize the nonnegative cycle condition of Prop. 8.2.

8.7 DUALITY

Duality theory for nonlinear network problems can be developed similar to the case of a minimum cost flow problem. We eliminate some of the constraints through the use of prices (or Lagrange multipliers). We then form a Lagrangian function, and we define a dual function by minimizing the Lagrangian subject to the remaining constraints. The dual problem is to maximize the dual function over the prices. We will focus on two important types of duality analysis in network optimization.

Convex Separable Network Problems

The first type of duality relates to the convex separable network problem of Section 8.1:

$$\text{minimize} \quad \sum_{(i,j)\in\mathcal{A}} f_{ij}(x_{ij})$$

$$\text{subject to} \quad x_{ij} \in X_{ij}, \quad \forall\, (i,j) \in \mathcal{A},$$

$$\sum_{\{j|(i,j)\in\mathcal{A}\}} x_{ij} - \sum_{\{j|(j,i)\in\mathcal{A}\}} x_{ji} = s_i, \quad \forall\, i \in \mathcal{N}.$$

Here, as in the development of duality for the minimum cost flow problem in Chapter 4, we use prices to eliminate the conservation of flow constraints. We introduce a price p_i for each node i and we form the Lagrangian function

$$L(x,p) = \sum_{(i,j)\in\mathcal{A}} f_{ij}(x_{ij}) + \sum_{i\in\mathcal{N}} p_i \left(\sum_{\{j|(j,i)\in\mathcal{A}\}} x_{ji} - \sum_{\{j|(i,j)\in\mathcal{A}\}} x_{ij} + s_i \right)$$

$$= \sum_{(i,j)\in\mathcal{A}} \big(f_{ij}(x_{ij}) - (p_i - p_j)x_{ij} \big) + \sum_{i\in\mathcal{N}} s_i p_i.$$

$$(8.20)$$

The dual function value $q(p)$ at a price vector p is obtained by minimizing $L(x,p)$ over all x satisfying the constraints $x_{ij} \in X_{ij}$. Thus, we have for every p

$$q(p) = \inf_{x_{ij}\in X_{ij},\,(i,j)\in\mathcal{A}} L(x,p) = \sum_{(i,j)\in\mathcal{A}} q_{ij}(p_i - p_j) + \sum_{i\in\mathcal{N}} s_i p_i,$$

where

$$q_{ij}(p_i - p_j) = \inf_{x_{ij}\in X_{ij}} \big\{ f_{ij}(x_{ij}) - (p_i - p_j)x_{ij} \big\}. \qquad (8.21)$$

(The reason for using inf, rather than min, in the above definition of q is that for a given p, it is not known whether the minimum over $x \in X$ is attained.) The dual problem is

$$\text{maximize}\quad q(p)$$

$$\text{subject to no constraint on } p.$$

There is a powerful and elegant theory around this problem, which is in many ways similar to the duality theory of Chapter 4. The theory involves a generalized notion of complementary slackness, and, in an algorithmic setting, a notion of ϵ-complementary slackness. Another interesting aspect of this theory is that if the functions f_{ij} are strictly convex over the intervals X_{ij} and the infimum is attained in Eq. (8.21) for all (i,j) and all p, then the dual function q is differentiable and its gradient can be calculated with a convenient formula, as will be shown in Section 9.4. We postpone further discussion of separable problem duality and algorithms for Chapter 9, where we will provide a detailed development.

Convex Network Problems with Side Constraints

The second type of duality relates to the convex network problem with side constraints, discussed in Section 8.2:

$$\text{minimize}\quad f(x)$$

$$\text{subject to}\quad x_{ij} \in X_{ij}, \quad \forall\, (i,j) \in \mathcal{A},$$

$$\sum_{\{j|(i,j)\in\mathcal{A}\}} x_{ij} - \sum_{\{j|(j,i)\in\mathcal{A}\}} x_{ji} = s_i, \quad \forall\, i \in \mathcal{N}, \qquad (8.22)$$

$$g_t(x) \le 0, \quad t = 1, \ldots, r,$$

where each set X_{ij} is an interval of the real line, and the functions f and g_t are assumed convex over the space of the flow vectors x.

Here, we use prices to eliminate some or all of the side constraints, thereby enhancing the problem's separable or other structure. The resulting theory is a special case of the general duality theory for convex programming programs, and does not have any distinctive features that can be attributed to the problem's network structure. Furthermore, we will not use this theory in a essential way in our subsequent development. For this reason, we will refer to the standard nonlinear programming literature for a deeper analysis, and for proofs of the results that we will state.

We introduce a Lagrange multiplier μ_t for each of the side constraints $g_t(x) \le 0$, and we form the corresponding Lagrangian function

$$L(x, \mu) = f(x) + \sum_{t=1}^{r} \mu_t g_t(x). \tag{8.23}$$

Let $\tilde{F}$ denote the set defined by the constraints of the problem except for the side constraints,

$$\tilde{F} = \left\{ x \ \middle| \ x_{ij} \in X_{ij}, \ \forall \ (i,j) \in \mathcal{A}, \right.$$

$$\left. \sum_{\{j \mid (i,j) \in \mathcal{A}\}} x_{ij} - \sum_{\{j \mid (j,i) \in \mathcal{A}\}} x_{ji} = s_i, \ \forall \ i \in \mathcal{N} \right\}.$$

The dual function is defined by

$$q(\mu) = \inf_{x \in \tilde{F}} L(x, \mu), \tag{8.24}$$

and the dual problem is

$$\begin{aligned} \text{maximize} \quad & q(p) \\ \text{subject to} \quad & \mu \ge 0. \end{aligned} \tag{8.25}$$

Note that q may not be real-valued because for some μ, the infimum in Eq. (8.24) can be $-\infty$. Thus the dual problem embodies the additional implicit constraint $\mu \in Q$, where Q is the "effective domain" of q given by

$$Q = \{\mu \mid q(\mu) > -\infty\}.$$

We refer to the optimal value attained in the primal and in the dual problems as the *optimal primal cost* and *optimal dual cost*, respectively. An important fact is that the optimal dual cost is always no greater than the optimal primal cost. This is known as the *weak duality theorem*. The proof is simple: for any $\mu \geq 0$, we have

$$
\begin{aligned}
q(\mu) = \inf_{x \in \tilde{F}} &\left\{ f(x) + \sum_{t=1}^{r} \mu_t g_t(x) \right\} \\
\leq \inf_{x \in \tilde{F},\, g_t(x) \leq 0,\, t=1,\ldots,r} &\left\{ f(x) + \sum_{t=1}^{r} \mu_t g_t(x) \right\} \\
\leq \inf_{x \in \tilde{F},\, g_t(x) \leq 0,\, t=1,\ldots,r} &\quad f(x),
\end{aligned}
$$

where the first inequality follows because the infimum of the Lagrangian is taken over a subset of $\tilde{F}$, and the last inequality follows using the nonnegativity of μ_t. Thus, by taking the supremum of the left-hand side over $\mu \geq 0$, we obtain

$$
\sup_{\mu \geq 0} q(\mu) \leq \inf_{x \in \tilde{F},\, g_t(x) \leq 0,\, t=1,\ldots,r} f(x). \tag{8.26}
$$

The two expressions on the left and the right above are recognized as the optimal dual cost and the optimal primal cost, respectively

     When the optimal dual cost is strictly smaller than the optimal primal cost, we say that there is a *duality gap*. In the convex case of problem (8.22), typically there is no duality gap. However, to guarantee this we need some technical assumptions, which are usually satisfied in practice. The following proposition makes this precise and also gives necessary and sufficient conditions for primal and dual optimality.

Proposition 8.3: Consider the convex network problem with side constraints (8.22).

(a) x^* is an optimal primal solution and μ^* is an optimal dual solution if and only if x^* is primal-feasible, $\mu^* \geq 0$, and

$$
x^* = \arg\min_{x \in \tilde{F}} L(x, \mu^*), \qquad \mu_t^* g_t(x^*) = 0, \quad t = 1, \ldots, r.
$$

(b) The optimal primal cost is equal to the optimal dual cost and there exists an optimal solution of the dual problem if one of the following two conditions holds:

> (1) The intervals X_{ij} are closed, and the functions g_t are linear.
>
> (2) There exists a feasible flow vector $\bar{x}$ such that $g_t(\bar{x}) < 0$ for all t and $\bar{x}_{ij}$ lies in the interior of the interval X_{ij} for all $(i,j) \in \mathcal{A}$ for which X_{ij} has nonempty interior.

The preceding proposition can be shown in a broader context that does not relate to network flows, so we refer to the literature for the proof. In particular, part (a) is shown in Prop. 5.1.5 of Bertsekas [1995b], while part (b) is shown in Props. 5.2.1 and 5.3.2 of the same reference.

In the two types of duality discussed so far in this section, either the conservation of flow constraints or the side constraints are dualized. There is also a third type of duality, where both of these constraints are dualized. Here, the Lagrangian function is given by [cf. Eqs. (8.20) and (8.23)]

$$L(x, p, \mu) = f(x) + \sum_{t=1}^{r} \mu_t g_t(x)$$

$$+ \sum_{i \in \mathcal{N}} p_i \left(\sum_{\{j | (j,i) \in \mathcal{A}\}} x_{ji} - \sum_{\{j | (i,j) \in \mathcal{A}\}} x_{ij} + s_i \right).$$

The dual function is defined by

$$q(p, \mu) = \inf_{x_{ij} \in X_{ij}, \, (i,j) \in \mathcal{A}} L(x, p, \mu), \tag{8.27}$$

and the dual problem is

$$\text{maximize} \quad q(p, \mu)$$
$$\text{subject to} \quad p \in \Re^N, \, \mu \geq 0.$$

It is also possible to derive a corresponding weak duality result and a proposition that is analogous to the one given above.

We finally mention that there are interesting nonconvex cases of problem (8.22), and their associated dual problems defined by Eqs. (8.25) and (8.27). In these cases, X_{ij} are not necessarily intervals and embody integer constraints, and the cost function f and the side constraint functions g_t are real-valued but not necessarily convex functions of x (for some examples, see Section 10.3). Then, there is usually a duality gap. However, the weak duality theorem [cf. Eq. (8.26)] still holds, because its derivation does not rely on convexity. We will see the utility of this fact when we discuss the Lagrangian relaxation method in Section 10.3.

8.8 ALGORITHMS AND APPROXIMATIONS

One of the most useful ideas in nonlinear optimization is to approximate the given problem with one or more simpler problems. We have already encountered the idea of linearization, whereby the nonlinear problem is replaced by a linear one. There are also other approximation approaches, where the simpler problems involve a parameter $\epsilon > 0$ that controls the quality of the approximation. As $\epsilon \to 0$, the approximation becomes more accurate. One then typically considers the solution of a sequence of approximate problems corresponding to a sequence $\{\epsilon^k\}$ of approximation parameters that tends to 0, thereby yielding solution of the original problem in the limit (under some appropriate continuity conditions). In this section we discuss some of the major approximation approaches and their associated algorithmic procedures.

8.8.1 Feasible Direction Methods

We have seen in Section 8.6 the value of the linearization approach for developing optimality conditions and for providing a link with the minimum cost flow analysis of Chapters 2-7. In this section, we discuss the use of the linearization idea for the development of a broad class of algorithms for convex problems.

Consider the generic problem of minimizing over a convex set F a function $f : \Re^n \mapsto \Re$ that is continuously differentiable and is convex over F. Given a feasible vector x, a *feasible direction* at x is a nonzero vector d such that $x + \alpha d$ is feasible for all α in some interval $[0, \overline{\alpha}]$, where $\overline{\alpha} > 0$ (see Fig. 8.15). We say that d is a *feasible descent direction* at x if there exists an $\overline{\alpha} > 0$ such that

$$x + \alpha d \in F, \qquad f(x + \alpha d) < f(x), \qquad \forall\, \alpha \in (0, \overline{\alpha}].$$

Since f is continuously differentiable, the inequality in the above relation is equivalent to $\nabla f(x)'d < 0$, as can be seen from the first order Taylor series expansion

$$f(x + \alpha d) = f(x) + \alpha \nabla f(x)'d + o(\alpha)$$

[for an α that is positive but sufficiently small, the term $\alpha \nabla f(x)'d$ dominates the term $o(\alpha)$, and its sign is the same as the sign of $f(x+\alpha d) - f(x)$]. The following proposition shows that at every feasible solution that is not optimal, there exists a feasible descent direction, and that by solving the linearized problem, we can obtain such a direction.

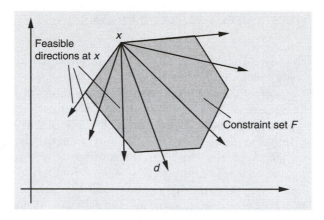

Figure 8.15: Feasible directions d at a feasible x. By definition, d is a feasible direction if changing x by a small amount in the direction d maintains feasibility.

Proposition 8.4: Consider the minimization over a convex set F of a function $f : \Re^n \mapsto \Re$ that is continuously differentiable and is convex over F. Let $\hat{x}$ be a feasible vector that is not optimal, and let $\bar{x}$ be an optimal solution of the linearized problem

$$\text{minimize} \ \ \nabla f(\hat{x})'(x - \hat{x})$$
$$\text{subject to} \ \ x \in F.$$

Then the vector $d = \bar{x} - \hat{x}$ is a feasible descent direction of f at $\hat{x}$.

Proof: Since $\hat{x}$ is not optimal, from Prop. 8.1 it follows that there exists a vector $\tilde{x} \in F$ such that $\nabla f(\hat{x})'(\tilde{x} - \hat{x}) < 0$, so $\tilde{x} - \hat{x}$ is a feasible descent direction of f at $\hat{x}$. If $\bar{x}$ solves the linearized problem, we have

$$\nabla f(\hat{x})'(\bar{x} - \hat{x}) \leq \nabla f(\hat{x})'(\tilde{x} - \hat{x}) < 0,$$

implying that $\bar{x} - \hat{x}$ is a feasible descent direction of f at $\hat{x}$.   **Q.E.D.**

The preceding proposition suggests an iterative primal cost improvement algorithm, whereby a sequence of flow vectors with decreasing cost is generated by making flow changes along feasible directions. For example, we may consider a method, which at each iteration solves the linearized problem at the current iterate, computes the corresponding feasible descent direction, and effects a correction along that direction (this is the conditional gradient method to be discussed shortly). More generally, we consider a *feasible direction method*, which starts with a feasible vector x^0

and aims to generate a sequence of feasible vectors $\{x^k\}$ according to

$$x^{k+1} = x^k + \alpha^k(\overline{x}^k - x^k),$$

where $\alpha^k \in (0, 1]$, and

$$\overline{x}^k \in F, \qquad \nabla f(x^k)'(\overline{x}^k - x^k) < 0.$$

For each x^k that is not optimal, there must exist such a vector $\overline{x}^k$, since otherwise we would have $\nabla f(x^k)'(x - x^k) \geq 0$ for all $x \in F$, contradicting the non-optimality of x^k (cf. Prop. 8.1). Figure 8.16 illustrates a feasible direction method.

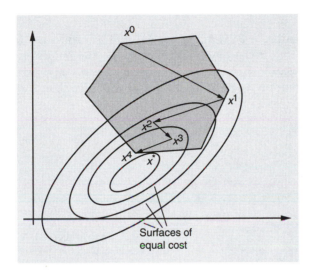

Figure 8.16: Sample path of a feasible direction method. At each iteration, we obtain a feasible point along a feasible descent direction.

There are several rules for choosing the stepsize α^k in feasible direction methods. Typically, α^k must be such that the cost is improved, that is,

$$f(x^{k+1}) < f(x^k).$$

For example, one may use the minimization rule, whereby α^k is chosen to minimize the cost along the feasible direction, that is,

$$f\big(x^k + \alpha^k(\overline{x}^k - x^k)\big) = \min_{\alpha \in [0,1]} f\big(x^k + \alpha(\overline{x}^k - x^k)\big). \qquad (8.28)$$

There are general results for feasible direction methods with the minimization rule, as well with other stepsize rules, which establish their validity by showing, under the convexity conditions of Prop. 8.4, that every limit point of the generated sequence $\{x^k\}$ is optimal. For a fairly extensive discussion, we refer to Bertsekas [1995b], Chapter 2.

Conditional Gradient Methods and Multicommodity Flows

We now consider a popular feasible direction method where the feasible descent direction is generated by solving the linearized problem

$$\text{minimize} \ \nabla f(x^k)'(x - x^k)$$
$$\text{subject to} \ x \in F, \tag{8.29}$$

(we assume here that an optimal solution of this problem exists for every k). Thus, $\overline{x}^k$ is given by

$$\overline{x}^k = \arg\min_{x \in F} \nabla f(x^k)'(x - x^k).$$

The corresponding feasible direction method is known as the *conditional gradient method*, or the *Frank-Wolfe method*. The process to obtain $\overline{x}^k$ is illustrated in Fig. 8.17. Note that in order for the method to make practical sense, the subproblem (8.29) must be much simpler than the original.

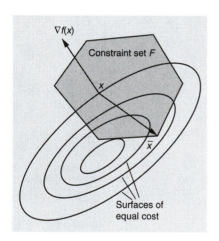

Figure 8.17: Finding the feasible descent direction $\overline{x} - x$ at a vector x in the conditional gradient method: $\overline{x}$ is a vector of F such that the inner product $\nabla f(x)'(\overline{x} - x)$ is most negative.

Let us describe the conditional gradient method in the context of the constraint-separable convex multicommodity flow problem introduced in Section 8.3:

$$\text{minimize} \ f(x)$$

$$\text{subject to} \ x_{ij}(m) \in X_{ij}(m), \quad \forall \ (i,j) \in \mathcal{A}, \ m = 1, \ldots, M,$$

$$\sum_{\{j|(i,j)\in\mathcal{A}\}} x_{ij}(m) - \sum_{\{j|(j,i)\in\mathcal{A}\}} x_{ji}(m) = s_i(m), \quad \forall \ i \in \mathcal{N}, \ m = 1, \ldots, M.$$

The linearized problem is to minimize

$$\nabla f(x^k)'(x - x^k)$$

over all x satisfying the conservation of flow constraints, and the interval constraints $x_{ij}(m) \in X_{ij}(m)$. This problem is easy to solve, because in view of the separability of the constraint set, it decomposes into a collection of subproblems, one per commodity. The subproblem for commodity m is a minimum cost flow problem with cost coefficient of arc (i, j) equal to $\partial f(x^k)/\partial x_{ij}(m)$, and can be solved with the efficient algorithms of Chapters 2-7.

A special case of the multicommodity flow problem is particularly interesting. This is the case where the constraints $x_{ij}(m) \in X_{ij}(m)$ have the form

$$0 \le x_{ij}(m), \qquad \forall \ (i, j) \in \mathcal{A}, \ m = 1, \ldots, M, \qquad (8.30)$$

and furthermore there is only one supply node per commodity m:

$$s_{i_m}(m) > 0, \qquad \text{for a unique origin node } i_m.$$

In this case, it can be seen that for each commodity m, the linearized problem becomes a *shortest path problem*, where the origin is node i_m and the length of each arc (i, j) is $\partial f(x^k)/\partial x_{ij}(m)$. Thus, the kth iteration of the conditional gradient method consists of the following steps:

(a) For each commodity m, obtain a shortest path from node i_m to each node i with $s_i(m) < 0$, where the length of arc (i, j) is $\partial f(x^k)/\partial x_{ij}(m)$.

(b) For each commodity m, route from node i_m to each node m with $s_i(m) < 0$ the corresponding amount of flow $-s_i(m)$ along the associated shortest path. Let $\bar{x}^k$ be the corresponding multicommodity flow vector.

(c) Obtain the new flow vector by

$$x^{k+1} = x^k + \alpha^k(\bar{x}^k - x^k),$$

where α^k is an appropriately chosen stepsize [e.g., using the minimization rule of Eq. (8.28)].

Unfortunately, the asymptotic rate of convergence of the conditional gradient method is not very fast. A partial explanation is that the vectors $\bar{x}^k$ used in the algorithm are typically extreme points (vertices) of F. Thus, the feasible direction used may tend to be orthogonal to the direction leading to the minimum (see Fig. 8.18). There are other feasible direction methods, which achieve a faster convergence rate, at the expense of greater overhead per iteration. For example, *gradient projection methods* obtain the feasible descent direction by using a quadratic cost approximation to f in place of the linear approximation used by the conditional gradient method. For a description and analysis of gradient projection and other feasible direction methods, we refer to the books by Bertsekas [1995b], and by Bertsekas and Gallager [1992], and to the survey by Florian and Hearn [1995]; see also Section 8.8.7.

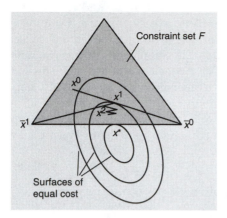

Figure 8.18: Illustration of the slow convergence rate of the conditional gradient method. The feasible direction used may tend to be orthogonal to the direction leading to the minimum.

8.8.2   Piecewise Linear Approximation

One possibility for dealing with a convex cost problem is to use efficient ways to reduce it to an essentially linear cost problem by piecewise linearization of the cost function. Then, if the constraint set is polyhedral, the resulting approximating problem can be solved using standard linear programming methods. This approach is often convenient and straightforward, although it may result in loss of insight, because generally, a nonlinear problem may have elegant features that are lost in a piecewise linear approximation.

A particularly interesting case is the convex separable network problem of Section 8.1:

$$\text{minimize} \quad \sum_{(i,j)\in\mathcal{A}} f_{ij}(x_{ij})$$

$$\text{subject to} \quad x_{ij} \in X_{ij}, \quad \forall\,(i,j)\in\mathcal{A},$$

$$\sum_{\{j|(i,j)\in\mathcal{A}\}} x_{ij} - \sum_{\{j|(j,i)\in\mathcal{A}\}} x_{ji} = s_i, \quad \forall\,i\in\mathcal{N}.$$

When piecewise linearization is applied to the arc cost functions f_{ij}, the resulting problem can be converted to a minimum cost flow problem with extra arcs, as discussed earlier (see Exercise 1.8). Note that one can use *inner linearization* [approximation from within using a discrete set of points, as in Fig. 8.19(a)], or *outer linearization* [approximation from without using a discrete set of tangent slopes, as in Fig. 8.19(b)].

It is possible to use a one-time piecewise linearization of the cost function. It is also possible to consider a sequential procedure, whereby the cost function is repeatedly approximated with ever-increasing approximation accuracy. In the most straightforward application of this idea, a number of breakpoints for inner linearization within each interval X_{ij} is

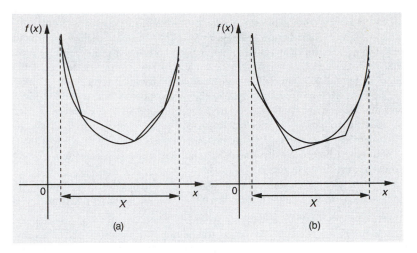

Figure 8.19: Inner and outer linearization of a convex function $f(x)$ of a single variable over an interval X.

chosen. These points are more or less regularly spaced and their number is gradually increased to improve the accuracy of the approximation. Usually, the solution obtained from each level of approximation is used as a starting point for the algorithm to solve the next (finer) level of approximation.

In a more sophisticated approach, one may use an *adaptive linearization* technique, whereby the selection of the breakpoints of the approximation is guided by the algorithmic progress. This approach aims to make the accuracy of the approximation better where it matters most, namely in the neighborhood of the optimal flows. Here is an important example of a method of this type.

Example 8.9. Cutting Plane Method

This is an iterative method, which will be discussed in more detail and in greater generality in Chapter 10. Given the initial flow vector x^0 and the flow vectors $x^1, \ldots, x^k$ obtained from the first k iterations, we form an outer linearization of each arc cost function f_{ij},

$$\hat{f}_{ij}^k(x_{ij}) = \max_{m=0,\ldots,k} \left\{ f_{ij}(x_{ij}^m) + \nabla f_{ij}(x_{ij}^m)(x_{ij} - x_{ij}^m) \right\}.$$

[We have used the gradient $\nabla f_{ij}(x_{ij}^m)$ here, but if f_{ij} is not differentiable at x_{ij}^m, a subgradient can be used; see Chapter 10.] We then obtain the next iterate x^{k+1} as an optimal solution of the approximate problem based on the outer linearization

$$x^{k+1} = \arg\min_{x \in F} \sum_{(i,j) \in \mathcal{A}} \hat{f}_{ij}^k(x_{ij}), \qquad k = 0, 1, \ldots$$

where F is the constraint set of the problem. Thus for each iteration $m = 1, 2, \ldots$, a line (linear approximation) $f_{ij}(x_{ij}^m) + \nabla f_{ij}(x_{ij}^m)(x_{ij} - x_{ij}^m)$ is added, and the maximum over all the lines is used to approximate $f_{ij}(x_{ij})$ (see Fig. 8.20). It must be assumed here that each of the approximate problems has an optimal solution, and this is guaranteed if each interval X_{ij} is compact.

The cutting plane method has the nice property that it tends to increase the approximation accuracy in the neighborhood of the iterates. In fact, it is possible to prove various convergence results, for which we refer to the literature cited at the end of the chapter. It is fairly easy to show that if the functions f_{ij} are piecewise linear to start with, the method finds an optimal solution in a finite number of iterations.

It is also possible to use a variant of the cutting plane method that is based on *inner linearization*. Here if $\hat{f}_{ij}^k$ is an inner approximation of f_{ij} based on $k+2$ breakpoints, and x^{k+1} minimizes $\sum_{(i,j) \in \mathcal{A}} \hat{f}_{ij}^k(x_{ij})$ over $x \in F$, a new breakpoint at x_{ij}^{k+1} is added to the approximation of f_{ij}. This method requires that each interval X_{ij} is compact so that its endpoints can be used as the two extreme breakpoints of $\hat{f}_{ij}^0(x_{ij})$.

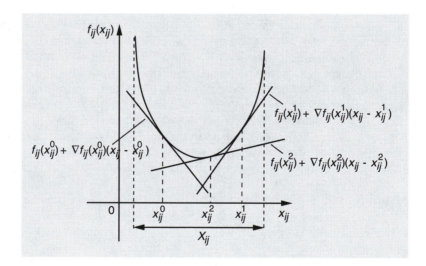

Figure 8.20: Illustration of the cutting plane method. At the kth iteration, the line

$$f_{ij}(x_{ij}^k) + \nabla f_{ij}(x_{ij}^k)(x_{ij} - x_{ij}^k),$$

corresponding to the optimal solution x^k of the current approximate problem, is added to the approximation.

8.8.3   Interior Point Methods

A standard nonlinear programming approach to deal with troublesome inequality constraints is to eliminate them by means of a barrier function. In particular, let us consider a convex network problem and let us assume that it can be written in the form

$$\text{minimize } f(x)$$

$$\text{subject to } x \in \overline{F}, \qquad g_t(x) \leq 0, \quad t = 1, \ldots, r,$$

where f and g_t are convex functions of the flow vector x, and $\overline{F}$ is a closed convex set. Here $\overline{F}$ includes the conservation of flow constraints and possibly some other constraints. Typically, the constraints $g_t(x) \leq 0$ include side constraints and possibly some arc flow bound constraints.

Consider the set

$$S = \left\{ x \in \overline{F} \mid g_t(x) < 0, \, t = 1, \ldots, r \right\},$$

and assume that it is nonempty. In barrier methods, we add to the cost a function $B(x)$, called the *barrier function*, which is defined in the interior set S. This function is continuous and tends to ∞ as any one of the constraints $g_t(x)$ approaches 0 from negative values. The two most common examples of barrier functions are:

$$B(x) = -\sum_{t=1}^{r} \ln\{-g_t(x)\}, \qquad \text{logarithmic},$$

$$B(x) = -\sum_{t=1}^{r} \frac{1}{g_t(x)}, \qquad \text{inverse}.$$

Note that both of these functions are convex, given the convexity of g_t.

The most common barrier method is defined by introducing a parameter sequence $\{\epsilon^k\}$ with

$$0 < \epsilon^{k+1} < \epsilon^k, \quad k = 0, 1, \ldots, \qquad \epsilon^k \to 0.$$

It consists of finding

$$x^k = \arg\min_{x \in S}\{f(x) + \epsilon^k B(x)\}, \qquad k = 0, 1, \ldots$$

Since the barrier function is defined only on the interior set S, the successive iterates of any method used for this minimization must be interior points. Note that the barrier term $\epsilon^k B(x)$ goes to zero for all interior points $x \in S$ as $\epsilon^k \to 0$. Thus the barrier term becomes increasingly inconsequential as far as interior points are concerned, while progressively allowing x^k to get closer to the boundary of S (as it should if the optimal solutions of the original constrained problem lie on the boundary of S). It can be shown, under our convexity assumptions, that every limit point of a sequence $\{x^k\}$ generated by a barrier method is an optimal solution of the original problem. For the proof we refer to Bertsekas [1995b], p. 314.

A major application of the logarithmic barrier method is to linear and quadratic programming problems. The corresponding methods belong to the general class of *interior point methods*, and have been the focus of much theoretical and applications-oriented research. As a result, there is a lot of accumulated experience with sophisticated implementations that can deal with very large problems. In particular, interior point methods have been applied to the dual minimum cost flow problem of maximizing over a price vector p the dual cost function

$$\sum_{(i,j)\in\mathcal{A}} \min\left[-b_{ij}(a_{ij}+p_j-p_i), -c_{ij}(a_{ij}+p_j-p_i)\right],$$

where a_{ij} are the arc cost coefficients, and b_{ij} and c_{ij} are the arc flow bounds (cf. the duality framework of Chapter 4). One may transform this problem to

$$\begin{aligned}
\text{minimize} \quad & \sum_{(i,j)\in\mathcal{A}} z_{ij} \\
\text{subject to} \quad & z_{ij} \geq b_{ij}(a_{ij}+p_j-p_i), && \forall\,(i,j)\in\mathcal{A}, \\
& z_{ij} \geq c_{ij}(a_{ij}+p_j-p_i), && \forall\,(i,j)\in\mathcal{A},
\end{aligned}$$

where z_{ij} is an auxiliary variable for each arc (i,j), and apply the logarithmic barrier method. We refer to the specialized literature cited at the end of the chapter.

8.8.4   Penalty and Augmented Lagrangian Methods

Another standard nonlinear programming approach to deal with troublesome constraints is to eliminate them by means of a penalty function. This is similar to the use of barrier functions, but penalty functions do not require that the region defined by the eliminated constraints has nonempty interior, so they can be used for equality constraints as well as for inequalities. Furthermore, their convergence and functionality can be improved through the use of Lagrange multiplier iterations, leading to *augmented Lagrangian methods*, which are among the most reliable and practically useful methods in nonlinear programming.

The theory of penalty and augmented Lagrangian methods is extensive and cannot be developed here in much detail. Thus we will just summarize the principal method and we will briefly discuss its properties.

We focus on the convex network problem with side constraints

$$\text{minimize} \quad f(x)$$
$$\text{subject to} \quad x_{ij} \in X_{ij}, \quad \forall \ (i,j) \in \mathcal{A},$$
$$\sum_{\{j|(i,j)\in\mathcal{A}\}} x_{ij} - \sum_{\{j|(j,i)\in\mathcal{A}\}} x_{ji} = s_i, \quad \forall \ i \in \mathcal{N},$$
$$g_t(x) \leq 0, \quad t = 1, \ldots, r.$$

Let us group together the constraints other than the side constraints in the set

$$\overline{F} = \Big\{ x \mid x_{ij} \in X_{ij}, \ \forall \ (i,j) \in \mathcal{A},$$
$$\sum_{\{j|(i,j)\in\mathcal{A}\}} x_{ij} - \sum_{\{j|(j,i)\in\mathcal{A}\}} x_{ji} = s_i, \ \forall \ i \in \mathcal{N} \Big\},$$

so that the problem is written as

$$\text{minimize} \quad f(x)$$
$$\text{subject to} \quad x \in \overline{F}, \qquad g(x) \leq 0,$$

where $g(x)$ is the column vector with components $g_1(x), \ldots, g_r(x)$.

Let $\mu = (\mu_1, \ldots, \mu_r)$ be a multiplier vector and let c be a positive scalar, which we call *penalty parameter*. Define

$$g_t^+(x, \mu, c) = \max\{g_t(x), -\mu_t/c\}, \qquad t = 1, \ldots, r,$$

and let $g^+(x, \mu, c)$ be the column vector with components $g_t^+(x, \mu, c)$. The augmented Lagrangian function is defined by

$$L_c(x, \mu) = f(x) + \mu' g^+(x, \mu, c) + \frac{c}{2} \|g^+(x, \mu, c)\|^2.$$

The augmented Lagrangian method consists of a sequence of minimizations

$$\text{minimize} \quad L_{c^k}(x, \mu^k)$$
$$\text{subject to} \quad x \in \overline{F},$$

where $\{c^k\}$ is some positive penalty parameter sequence and $\{\mu^k\}$ is generated by the iteration

$$\mu^{k+1} = \mu^k + c^k g^+(x^k, \mu^k, c^k).$$

As an example, consider the separable multicommodity network flow problem with arc capacities $y_{ij} \leq c_{ij}$ (cf. Section 8.3). It turns out that much of the algorithmic methodology for multicommodity problems applies only if the capacity constraints are absent (see also Sections 8.8.1 and 8.8.7).

It is thus often expedient to bring to bear this algorithmic methodology by eliminating the capacity constraints using the augmented Lagrangian method.

There is extensive convergence analysis and practical experience that supports the augmented Lagrangian approach, for which we refer to standard nonlinear programming textbooks. The book by Bertsekas [1982] is an extensive research monograph that focuses on augmented Lagrangian methods and their many variations. Generally, the main result for the convex problem discussed here is that if the penalty parameter sequence $\{c^k\}$ is nondecreasing and a dual optimal solution exists, then the multiplier sequence $\{\mu^k\}$ converges to some dual optimal solution. The convergence of $\{\mu^k\}$ is accelerated if $\{c^k\}$ is increased at a faster rate. On the other hand, there is a concern with ill-conditioning in the minimization of the augmented Lagrangian, if c^k is increased "too fast." Generally, the augmented Lagrangian approach provides a simple and reliable way to deal with troublesome constraints, and is strongly recommended in practice.

8.8.5 Proximal Minimization

Consider the convex network problem

$$
\begin{aligned}
&\text{minimize} \quad f(x) \\
&\text{subject to} \quad x \in F,
\end{aligned}
\tag{8.31}
$$

where F is convex and f is convex over F. An interesting special case is when f is strictly convex; that is, for all $x, y \in F$ with $x \neq y$, we have

$$
f\big(\alpha x + (1 - \alpha)y\big) < \alpha f(x) + (1 - \alpha)f(y), \qquad \forall\, \alpha \in (0, 1).
$$

In this case, one may show that the minimum of f is uniquely attained if it is attained at all. However, strict convexity of f has another and more far-reaching consequence, which will be shown in Chapter 9 in the context of separable problems (see also Danskin's theorem in Appendix A): under mild technical conditions, *strict convexity of f implies differentiability of the dual function*, and allows the use of gradient-based optimization algorithms that are considerably better-behaved than methods that can deal with nondifferentiable cost. This motivates an interesting approach, called *proximal minimization*, that artificially induces strict convexity by adding a quadratic term to the cost function f, and uses iterations that asymptotically eliminate the effect of this term.

Let us introduce an additional vector y, and consider the following optimization problem

$$
\begin{aligned}
&\text{minimize} \quad f(x) + \frac{1}{2c}\|x - y\|^2 \\
&\text{subject to} \quad x \in F, \ y \in F,
\end{aligned}
$$

where c is a positive scalar parameter. This problem is equivalent to the original problem (8.31) because any one of its optimal solutions (x^*, y^*) satisfies $x^* = y^*$, so that x^* must minimize f over F. The proximal minimization algorithm consists of a sequence of alternate minimizations, first with respect to x with y held fixed, and then with respect to y with x held fixed. Thus, with an iteration-dependent parameter c^k, the minimization with respect to x yields

$$x^{k+1} = \arg\min_{x \in F} \left\{ f(x) + \frac{1}{2c^k} \|x - y^k\|^2 \right\},$$

and the subsequent minimization with respect to y yields

$$y^{k+1} = x^{k+1} = \arg\min_{y \in F} \frac{1}{2c^k} \|x^{k+1} - y\|^2.$$

Equivalently,

$$x^{k+1} = \arg\min_{x \in F} \left\{ f(x) + \frac{1}{2c^k} \|x - x^k\|^2 \right\}.$$

It can be shown using the strict convexity of $\|x - x^k\|^2$ that if F is a closed set, the minimum above is uniquely attained for any x^k, and the method is well defined. Note an important property of the proximal minimization algorithm: it preserves separability of the problem when it is already present.

Figure 8.21 illustrates the convergence mechanism of the method. Generally, it can be shown that if the penalty parameter sequence $\{c^k\}$ is nondecreasing, the sequence $\{x^k\}$ converges to some optimal solution of the original problem, provided there is at least one optimal solution for this problem. As Fig. 8.21 indicates, it may be shown that if f is linear and F is polyhedral, the convergence of the algorithm is finite. The method of adjusting the parameter c^k has an important effect on the rate of convergence. The tradeoff here is similar to the one for the augmented Lagrangian approach: the convergence of $\{x^k\}$ is accelerated if c^k is increased at a faster rate. On the other hand, large values of c^k tend to diminish the effect of the proximal term $(1/2c^k)\|x - x^k\|^2$. In fact the proximal minimization algorithm is closely related to the augmented Lagrangian algorithm, and the convergence properties of these two algorithms are very similar. We refer to the sources cited at the end of the chapter for a detailed analysis.

8.8.6   Smoothing

Generally, the analytical and algorithmic methodology for differentiable problems is richer and more effective than the one for their nondifferentiable counterparts. Thus, it is usually advantageous when the cost function f is

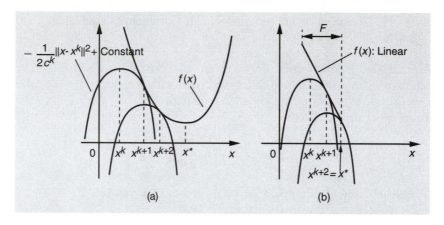

Figure 8.21: Graphical interpretation of the proximal minimization algorithm. Given the current iterate x^k, the graph of the function

$$-\frac{1}{2c^k}\|x - x^k\|^2$$

is vertically translated by a constant until it just touches the graph of f. The point of contact defines the new iterate x^{k+1}. It can be seen from figure (a) that as c^k increases, the convergence becomes faster. In the case of a linear problem, as in (b), the convergence is finite.

differentiable. On the other hand, in many problems, f is not differentiable but is instead *piecewise differentiable* of the form

$$f(x) = \max_{i \in I}\{f_i(x)\},$$

where I is a finite index set, and $f_i(x)$ is a differentiable convex function for each $i \in I$. In this case, it is possible to transform the convex cost network problem

$$\text{minimize} \quad f(x)$$
$$\text{subject to} \quad x \in F,$$

to the differentiable problem

$$\text{minimize} \quad z$$
$$\text{subject to} \quad x \in F,$$
$$f_i(x) \le z, \quad \forall\, i \in I,$$

where z is a new artificial variable. Unfortunately, this type of transformation may have an undesirable effect: by introducing additional side constraints, it may adversely affect the network structure of the problem.

An alternative possibility for dealing with the piecewise differentiable cost $f(x) = \max_{i \in I}\{f_i(x)\}$ is to approximate it with the exponential-like smooth cost

$$\frac{1}{c} \ln \left\{ \sum_{i \in I} \lambda_i e^{c f_i(x)} \right\}, \qquad (8.32)$$

where $c > 0$ and λ_i are positive numbers with $\sum_{i \in I} \lambda_i = 1$ (see Bertsekas [1982], Section 5.3). As c increases, the approximation becomes more accurate. It is also possible to improve the approximation by iterating on the multipliers λ_i (it turns out that this is related to the augmented Lagrangian approach, discussed earlier). Note that minimizing the smooth approximation above is equivalent to minimizing the function

$$\sum_{i \in I} \lambda_i e^{c f_i(x)},$$

which is separable with respect to the index i. The exponential smoothing approximation (8.32) is only one of many smoothing possibilities. We refer to the literature cited at the end of the chapter for further discussion.

The smoothing approach described above can also be extended to the case where f is the sum of several piecewise differentiable functions that can be smoothed individually. An example is a separable cost function of the form

$$f(x) = \sum_{(i,j) \in \mathcal{A}} f_{ij}(x_{ij}),$$

where each f_{ij} is a convex, piecewise differentiable function of x_{ij}. The nondifferentiability of this particular cost function can also be alternatively treated by introducing some extra arcs (see Exercise 8.4).

8.8.7   Transformations

In some network flow problems it is useful to consider a change of variables, thereby altering the problem's structure and making it more suitable for special methods. We discuss some possibilities, which are applicable, however, only in the presence of special structure, such as multiple commodities.

A useful type of transformation is possible when the cost function f depends on x through a vector y that is related to x by

$$y = \psi(x),$$

where $\psi(\cdot)$ is some known function; that is, for some function $\tilde{f}$, we have

$$f(x) = \tilde{f}(\psi(x)) = \tilde{f}(y).$$

The most common case is when ψ is linear, i.e.,

$$\psi(x) = Ax,$$

where A is a given matrix, but there are interesting cases where ψ is nonlinear.

As an example, in the multicommodity flow problems with commodities $m = 1, \ldots, M$, discussed in Section 8.3, we saw that the cost function often depends on the commodity flows $x_{ij}(m)$ through the total arc flows

$$y_{ij} = \sum_{m=1}^{M} x_{ij}(m), \qquad \forall \ (i,j) \in \mathcal{A}.$$

The above relation expresses the vector of total arc flows y in terms of a linear transformation of the vector of commodity flows x:

$$y = Ax,$$

where A is a suitable matrix. The problem of minimizing $f(x)$ over the feasible set F can be equivalently formulated in terms of y as

$$\text{minimize } \tilde{f}(y)$$
$$\text{subject to } y \in Y,$$

where the set Y is the image of F under the transformation A

$$Y = \{y \mid y = Ax, \ x \in F\}.$$

Even though Y is a complicated set that is given only implicitly through the above equation, in specially structured problems one may still apply particular types of algorithms in the space of the vector y (see the discussion of the conditional gradient method for multicommodity flow problems at the end of this section).

Another (nonlinear) transformation for multicommodity flow problems with nonnegativity constraints on the arc flows is based on expressing the flows of the outgoing arcs of each node as fractions of the total outgoing flow from the node. In particular, we introduce a variable $\phi_{ij}(m)$ for each arc (i,j) and commodity m, and we define a corresponding transformation by

$$\phi_{ij}(m) = \frac{x_{ij}(m)}{\sum_{\{k|(i,k)\in\mathcal{A}\}} x_{ik}(m)}, \qquad \forall \ (i,j) \in \mathcal{A}, \ m = 1, \ldots, M.$$

[This transformation is valid for nodes i and commodities m such that the outgoing flow $\sum_{\{k|(i,k)\in\mathcal{A}\}} x_{ik}(m)$ is positive; for i and m such that the outgoing flow is 0, the definition of $\phi_{ij}(m)$ does not matter.] A nice feature of this transformation is that the variables $\phi_{ij}(m)$ are subject to simple constraints:

$$\sum_{\{j|(i,j)\in\mathcal{A}\}} \phi_{ij}(m) = 1, \qquad \forall\, i \in \mathcal{N},\ m = 1, \ldots, M,$$

$$\phi_{ij}(m) \geq 0, \qquad \forall\, (i,j) \in \mathcal{A},\ m = 1, \ldots, M.$$

There are multicommodity flow algorithms that iterate on the arc flow fractions $\phi_{ij}(m)$ and offer some advantages in certain practical settings related to communications; see Gallager [1977], Bertsekas [1979b], Gafni [1979], Bertsekas, Gafni, and Gallager [1984], Ephremides [1986], Ephremides and Verdu [1989], and Powell, Berkkam, and Lustig [1993] for discussion, algorithms, and analysis.

The next example of transformation for multicommodity flow problems is based on expressing arc flows in terms of path flows, and will be discussed in some detail.

Path Flow Formulation for Multicommodity Flows

Our principal formulation of network flow problems so far has been in terms of the arc flow variables. On the other hand, from the conformal realization theorem (cf. Prop. 1.1), we know that every flow vector can be decomposed into a collection of conforming simple path and cycle flows, so we may consider using these path and cycle flows as the optimization variables. This viewpoint is well-suited to a multicommodity flow problem, where the mth commodity is associated with origin-destination (OD) pair (i_m, j_m) and supply r_m; that is, node i_m is the only source and node j_m is the only sink of commodity m, and the corresponding supply to be routed from i_m to j_m is a given positive scalar r_m.

For a path flow formulation to be applicable, we must introduce some assumptions guaranteeing that there is an optimal solution $x^* = \big(x^*(1), \ldots, x^*(M)\big)$ that does not involve any cycles; that is, for each commodity $m = 1, \ldots, M$, there is a conformal decomposition of $x^*(m)$ that consists only of simple path flows and no cycle flows. We thus assume that:

(a) The arc flows are constrained to be nonnegative.

(b) The cost function f is convex, continuously differentiable, and monotonically nondecreasing with respect to the arc flows $x_{ij}(m)$.

(c) Except for the conservation of flow and nonnegativity constraints, there are no other constraints (such as capacity constraints on the total arc flows or other side constraints).

The problem has the form

$$
\begin{aligned}
&\text{minimize} \quad f(x) \\
&\text{subject to} \quad x_{ij}(m) \geq 0, \qquad \forall \, (i,j) \in \mathcal{A}, \, m = 1, \ldots, M,
\end{aligned}
$$

$$
\sum_{\{j \mid (i,j) \in \mathcal{A}\}} x_{ij}(m) - \sum_{\{j \mid (j,i) \in \mathcal{A}\}} x_{ji}(m) =
\begin{cases}
r_m & \text{if } i = i_m, \\
-r_m & \text{if } i = j_m, \\
0 & \text{otherwise,}
\end{cases}
\qquad \forall \, i \in \mathcal{N}, \, m.
$$

It can be seen, using the monotonicity property of the cost function f, that an optimal flow vector can be constructed using only simple path flows. We can thus reformulate the problem in terms of path flows. Let us use the notation:

$\mathcal{P}_m$: The set of all simple forward paths that start at the origin i_m and end at the destination j_m of the OD pair (i_m, j_m).

h_p: The portion of the supply r_m assigned to a path $p \in \mathcal{P}_m$.

Then the constraints of the problem are equivalently written as the M simplex constraints

$$
\sum_{p \in \mathcal{P}_m} h_p = r_m, \qquad h_p \geq 0, \qquad \forall \, p \in \mathcal{P}_m, \, m = 1, \ldots, M. \tag{8.33}
$$

The arc flows can be expressed in terms of the path flows via the relation

$$
x_{ij}(m) = \sum_{\substack{\text{all paths } p \in \mathcal{P}_m \\ \text{containing } (i,j)}} h_p. \tag{8.34}
$$

Let us denote abstractly the above linear transformation as

$$
x = Ah, \tag{8.35}
$$

where h is the vector of path flows $\{h_p\}$, and let us consider the cost function in the transformed space of path flow vectors

$$
D(h) = f(Ah). \tag{8.36}
$$

The problem then is to find a path flow vector h that minimizes $D(h)$ subject to the constraints (8.33). Thus the problem is transformed from one with network constraints, to one with simplex constraints, which often results in some simplification.

For a feasible set of path flows

$$
h = \{h_p \mid p \in \mathcal{P}_m, \, m = 1, \ldots, M\},
$$

let

$$x = \big(x(1), \ldots, x(M)\big)$$

be the corresponding flow vector given by Eq. (8.34). Let us view the partial derivative

$$d_{ij}(x, m) = \frac{\partial f(x)}{\partial x_{ij}(m)}$$

as the *length of the arc* (i, j) *for commodity* m, and let us define the *first derivative length of a path* $p \in \mathcal{P}_m$ *with respect to* x to be the sum of the lengths of the arcs traversed by p:

$$d_p(x) = \sum_{\substack{\text{all arcs } (i,j) \\ \text{traversed by } p}} d_{ij}(x, m). \tag{8.37}$$

A key observation here is that, based on Eqs. (8.34)-(8.36), $d_p(x)$ is equal to the partial derivative of D with respect to h_p:

$$d_p(x) = \frac{\partial D(h)}{\partial h_p}. \tag{8.38}$$

The following proposition gives an important shortest path-based condition for optimality of a set of path flows.

Proposition 8.5: Under the preceding assumptions, a set of path flows $\{h_p^* \mid p \in \mathcal{P}_m, m = 1, \ldots, M\}$ and the corresponding arc flow vector x^* are optimal if and only if every path p with $h_p^* > 0$ has minimum first derivative length with respect to x^* over all paths of the same OD pair as p; that is, for all m and all paths $p \in \mathcal{P}_m$, we have

$$h_p^* > 0 \quad \Rightarrow \quad d_p(x^*) \leq d_{\bar{p}}(x^*), \qquad \forall\, \bar{p} \in \mathcal{P}_m. \tag{8.39}$$

The proof of the above proposition will be obtained by specializing the optimality conditions of Prop. 8.1 to the case of simplex constraints. This is done in the following proposition.

Proposition 8.6: (Optimization over a Simplex) Let $f : \Re^n \mapsto \Re$ be a continuously differentiable function of the vector $x = (x_1, \ldots, x_n)$, and let F be the simplex

$$F = \left\{ x \;\middle|\; x \geq 0, \; \sum_{i=1}^{n} x_i = r \right\},$$

where r is a given positive scalar. Assume that f is convex over F. Then, a vector $x^* \in F$ minimizes f over F if and only if

$$x_i^* > 0 \quad \Rightarrow \quad \frac{\partial f(x^*)}{\partial x_i} \le \frac{\partial f(x^*)}{\partial x_j}, \qquad \forall \; j. \qquad (8.40)$$

Proof: The optimality condition (8.17) of Prop. 8.1 becomes

$$\sum_{i=1}^{n} \frac{\partial f(x^*)}{\partial x_i} (x_i - x_i^*) \ge 0, \qquad \forall \; x_i \ge 0 \text{ with } \sum_{i=1}^{n} x_i = r. \qquad (8.41)$$

Let x^* be optimal, fix an index i for which $x_i^* > 0$ and let j be any other index. By using the feasible vector $x = (x_1, \ldots, x_n)$ with $x_i = 0$, $x_j = x_j^* + x_i^*$, and $x_m = x_m^*$ for all $m \ne i, j$ in Eq. (8.41), we obtain

$$\left(\frac{\partial f(x^*)}{\partial x_j} - \frac{\partial f(x^*)}{\partial x_i} \right) x_i^* \ge 0,$$

or equivalently

$$x_i^* > 0 \quad \Rightarrow \quad \frac{\partial f(x^*)}{\partial x_i} \le \frac{\partial f(x^*)}{\partial x_j}, \qquad \forall \; j.$$

Conversely, suppose that x^* belongs to F and satisfies Eq. (8.40). Let

$$\xi = \min_{i=1,\ldots,n} \frac{\partial f(x^*)}{\partial x_i}.$$

For every $x \in F$, we have $\sum_{i=1}^{n} (x_i - x_i^*) = 0$, so that

$$0 = \sum_{i=1}^{n} \xi (x_i - x_i^*) \le \sum_{\{i | x_i > x_i^*\}} \frac{\partial f(x^*)}{\partial x_i} (x_i - x_i^*) + \sum_{\{i | x_i < x_i^*\}} \xi (x_i - x_i^*).$$

If i is such that $x_i < x_i^*$, we must have $x_i^* > 0$ and, by condition (8.40), $\xi = \partial f(x^*)/\partial x_i$. Thus ξ can be replaced by $\partial f(x^*)/\partial x_i$ in the right-hand side of the preceding inequality, thereby yielding Eq. (8.41), which by Prop. 8.1, implies that x^* is optimal.   **Q.E.D.**

Proposition 8.6 admits a straightforward generalization to the case where F is a Cartesian product of several simplices. Then, there is a separate condition of the form (8.40) for each simplex; that is, the condition

$$\frac{\partial f(x^*)}{\partial x_i} \le \frac{\partial f(x^*)}{\partial x_j}$$

holds for all i with $x_i^* > 0$ and all j for which x_j is constrained by the same simplex as x_i. We now apply this condition to the path flow formulation of the multicommodity flow problem, i.e., the minimization of the cost function $D(h)$ of Eq. (8.36) subject to the simplex constraints of Eq. (8.33). By using the partial derivative expression (8.38), we obtain the condition (8.39) and the proof of Prop. 8.5.

Example 8.10. Routing in Data Networks Revisited

Let us consider the routing problem of Example 8.4 with OD pairs (i_m, j_m) and input flows r_m, $m = 1, \ldots, M$. Consider a separable cost function

$$f(x) = \sum_{(i,j)} f_{ij}(y_{ij}),$$

where each $f_{ij} : \Re \mapsto \Re$ is convex and continuously differentiable, and

$$y_{ij} = \sum_{m=1}^{M} x_{ij}(m)$$

is the total flow of arc (i, j). Assume also that there are no capacity constraints of the form $y_{ij} \leq c_{ij}$ (in practice, such constraints will always be present, but they may be introduced implicitly in the cost function through a barrier or a penalty function).

We can view the problem in terms of the path flow variables $\{h_p\}$, and we can apply Prop. 8.5. We see that optimal routing directs traffic exclusively along paths that are shortest with respect to arc lengths that depend on the flows carried by the arcs. In particular, a set of path flows is optimal if and only if, for each OD pair, path flow is positive only on paths with a minimum first derivative length.

Example 8.11. Traffic Assignment Revisited

Consider a path flow formulation of the traffic assignment problem of Example 8.5. The input r_m of OD pair (i_m, j_m) is to be divided among the set $\mathcal{P}_m$ of simple paths starting at the origin node i_m and ending at the destination node j_m. Let h_p denote the portion of r_m carried by a path $p \in \mathcal{P}_m$, and let h denote the vector of all path flows.

Suppose now that for each arc (i, j), we are given a function $t_{ij}(y_{ij})$ of the total arc flow y_{ij} of arc (i, j). This function models the time required for traffic to travel from the start node to the end node of the arc (i, j). An interesting problem is to find a path flow vector h^* that consists of path flows that are positive only on paths of minimum travel time. That is, for all paths $p \in \mathcal{P}_m$ and all m, we require that

$$h_p^* > 0 \quad \Rightarrow \quad t_p(h^*) \leq t_{p'}(h^*), \qquad \forall \, p' \in \mathcal{P}_m, \ m = 1, \ldots, M,$$

where $t_p(h)$, the travel time of path p, is defined as the sum of the travel times of the arcs of the path,

$$t_p(h) = \sum_{\substack{\text{all arcs } (i,j) \\ \text{on path } p}} t_{ij}(y_{ij}), \qquad \forall\, p \in \mathcal{P}_m,\ m = 1, \ldots, M.$$

The preceding problem draws its validity from a hypothesis, called the *user-optimization principle*, which asserts that traffic equilibrium is established when each user of the network chooses, among all available paths, a path of minimum travel time. Thus, assuming that the user-optimization principle holds, a path flow vector h^* that solves the problem also models accurately the distribution of traffic through the network, and can be used for traffic projections when planning modifications to the transportation network.

We now observe that the minimum travel time hypothesis is identical with the optimality condition of Prop. 8.5 if we introduce a separable cost function

$$f(x) = \sum_{(i,j)} f_{ij}(y_{ij}),$$

and we identify the travel time $t_{ij}(y_{ij})$ with the cost derivative $\partial f_{ij}(y_{ij})/\partial y_{ij}$. It follows that we can solve the transportation problem by converting it to the optimal routing problem of the preceding example using the identification

$$f_{ij}(y_{ij}) = \int_0^{y_{ij}} t_{ij}(\xi)d\xi.$$

If we assume that t_{ij} is continuous and monotonically nondecreasing, as is natural in a transportation context, it is straightforward to show that the function f_{ij} as defined above is convex with derivative equal to t_{ij}. It follows that a minimum first derivative length path is a path of minimum travel time.

Algorithms Based on the Path Flow Formulation

Aside from its analytical value, Prop. 8.5 provides the basis and a motivation for iterative feasible direction methods of the type discussed in Section 8.8.1. The idea is to calculate shortest paths corresponding to the current iterate and then shift flow from the nonshortest paths to the shortest paths, in an effort to reduce the violation of the optimality condition. Different methods for shifting flow define different feasible direction methods.

As an example, consider the conditional gradient method applied to the path flow formulation of minimizing the cost function $D(h)$ of Eq. (8.36) subject to the simplex constraints of Eq. (8.33). The typical iteration of the method is as follows: Given the current feasible set of path flows $\{h_p\}$, we find a shortest path (with respect to first derivative length) for each OD pair. Let $\{\overline{h}_p\}$ be the set of path flows that would result if all input r_m for each OD pair (i_m, j_m) is routed along the corresponding shortest path:

$$\overline{h}_p = \begin{cases} r_m & \text{if } p \text{ is the shortest path for OD pair } (i_m, j_m), \\ 0 & \text{if } p \text{ is not the shortest path for any OD pair.} \end{cases}$$

Let α^* be the stepsize that minimizes $D\big(h + \alpha(\overline{h} - h)\big)$ over all $\alpha \in [0, 1]$, where D is the cost function in the transformed space of path flows [cf. Eq. (8.36)]. The iteration defines the new set of path flows by

$$h_p := h_p + \alpha^*(\overline{h}_p - h_p), \quad \forall \, p \in \mathcal{P}_m, \, m = 1, \dots, M.$$

Note that for each nonshortest path p we have $\overline{h}_p = 0$, so for such a path the iteration takes the form

$$h_p := (1 - \alpha^*)h_p.$$

Thus, at each iteration of the method, a fraction α^* of the flow of each nonshortest path is shifted to the shortest path of the corresponding OD pair. The characteristic property here is that flow is shifted from the nonshortest paths in *equal* proportions. This distinguishes the conditional gradient method from other feasible direction methods, which also shift flow from the nonshortest paths to the shortest paths, however, they do so in generally unequal proportions.

Another interesting feasible direction method is the *gradient projection method* (Bertsekas [1980]; see also Bertsekas and Gafni [1982], [1983], Gafni and Bertsekas [1984]). This method uses the following iteration for the flows of the nonshortest paths (these flows also determine the flow on the shortest paths, since we have $\sum_{p \in \mathcal{P}_m} h_p = r_m$):

$$h_p := \max\big\{0, h_p + \alpha H_p^{-1}(d_{\overline{p}} - d_p)\big\}, \quad \forall \, p \in \mathcal{P}_m, \, p \neq \overline{p}, \, m = 1, \dots, M,$$

where

$\overline{p}$ is the shortest path in $\mathcal{P}_m$,

d_p is the first derivative length of path p [cf. Eq. (8.37)],

α is a constant positive stepsize,

H_p is a positive path-dependent scaling factor.

In the case of a twice differentiable separable cost function

$$f(x) = \sum_{(i,j) \in \mathcal{A}} f_{ij}(y_{ij}),$$

where y_{ij} is the total flow of arc (i, j),

$$y_{ij} = \sum_{m=1}^{M} x_{ij}(m),$$

there is an interesting definition of the scaling factor H_p based on the second derivatives of the functions f_{ij}. It is given by

$$H_p = \sum_{(i,j)\in L_p} \frac{\partial^2 f_{ij}(y_{ij})}{\partial y_{ij}^2}, \tag{8.42}$$

where L_p is the set of arcs that belong to either p or the shortest path of the OD pair corresponding to p, but not both.

When the scaling factor H_p is given by Eq. (8.42), it can be argued that the gradient projection method works as a diagonal approximation to a constrained form of Newton's method, and typically converges faster than the conditional gradient method. Some trial and error may be needed to choose the constant stepsize α, which determines the portion of the flow shifted from the nonshortest paths to the shortest paths (convergence results require that α should not exceed some unknown threshold). However, the use of the second derivatives of f_{ij} facilitates the stepsize selection process, and experience has shown that values of α near 1 typically work and result in convergence (for further discussion, analysis, and computational examples, see the book by Bertsekas and Gallager [1992], and the references given there).

8.9 NOTES, SOURCES, AND EXERCISES

Nonlinear network problems have been approached in the literature from two opposite ends: from the point of view of convex programming for problems with a continuous character, and from the point of view of combinatorial optimization and integer programming for problems with a discrete character. This is appropriate since the methodologies for continuous and discrete problems are quite different. However, there are important connections between the two types of problems, which we are trying to bring out in our presentation. In particular, discrete network problems are often solved by solving closely related continuous problems. Furthermore, convex separable problems have a distinct combinatorial character, as evidenced by the theory and algorithms of Chapters 2-7 for the single commodity-linear cost case, and as will also be seen in Chapter 9.

Convex separable problems have a number of special properties that do not readily generalize to nonseparable problems. We refer to Chapter 9 and to the references cited in that chapter.

There is a great variety of approaches for problems with side constraints. These include application of the simplex method for linear programming and decomposition techniques to be discussed in Section 10.3.4. The survey by Helgason and Kennington [1995] summarizes the simplex method as adapted to problems with side constraints and/or multiple commodities. The relaxation method of Chapter 6 has been extended to network problems with side constraints by Tseng [1991].

The algorithmic and applications literature on multicommodity flow problems is extensive. The surveys by Patricksson [1991], and by Florian and Hearn [1995] focus primarily on transportation problems, and give a large number of references. Applications in data communications, transportation, and economics are described in the books by Bertsekas and Gallager [1992], Sheffi [1985], and Nagurney [1993], respectively. These books give many additional references. There is also a substantial literature on the use of *variational inequality models* in the context of multicommodity flows; see the survey by Florian and Hearn [1995], and the book by Nagurney [1993]. Variational inequality problems cannot be transformed to optimization problems, but they can be addressed using optimization algorithms through the use of artificially constructed cost functions; see Hearn, Lawphongpanish, and Nguyen [1984], Marcotte and Dussault [1987], Marcotte and Guélat [1988], Auchmuty [1989], and Fukushima [1992].

For a broad discussion of models and applications of network problems with gains, we refer to Glover, Klingman, and Phillips [1992]. Simplex methods for these problems are described in Dantzig [1963], Kennington and Helgason [1980], Elam, Glover, and Klingman [1979], Jensen and Barnes [1980], Brown and McBride [1984], and Helgason and Kennington [1995]. The first specialized implementation of the simplex method for network problems with gains was given by Glover, Klingman, and Stutz [1973]. Analogs of the primal-dual method and the relaxation method for linear network problems with gains are given by Jewell [1962], and by Bertsekas and Tseng [1988a], respectively. The ϵ-relaxation method of Section 7.4 has been extended to linear and convex network problems with gains by Tseng and Bertsekas [1996].

For material on feasible direction, cutting plane methods, and penalty and augmented Lagrangians, see standard nonlinear programming textbooks, such as Bazaraa, Sherali, and Shetty [1993], Bertsekas [1995b], Gill, Murray, and Wright [1981], and Luenberger [1984]. The conditional gradient method was first applied to multicommodity flow problems by Fratta, Gerla, and Kleinrock [1973], and by Klessig [1974]. A related method that aims to remedy the slow convergence of the conditional gradient method is the, so-called, *simplicial decomposition method*; see Cantor and Gerla [1974], Holloway [1974], Lawphongpanich and Hearn [1984], [1986], Pang and Yu [1984], Hearn, Lawphongpanish, and Ventura [1985], [1987], Larsson and Patricksson [1992], and Ventura and Hearn [1993]. For applications of various types of feasible direction methods to network flow problems, see Dafermos and Sparrow [1969], Leventhal, Nemhauser, and Trotter [1973], Florian and Nguyen [1974], [1976], LeBlanc, Morlok, and Pierskalla [1974], [1975], Nguyen [1974], Dafermos [1980], [1982], Gartner [1980a], [1980b], Dembo and Klincewicz [1981], Bertsekas and Gafni [1982], [1983],

Fukushima [1984a], [1984b], Gafni and Bertsekas [1984], Pang [1984], Escudero [1985], LeBlanc, Helgason, and Boyce [1985], Marcotte [1985], Tsitsiklis and Bertsekas [1986], Dembo [1987], Florian, Guélat, and Spiess [1987], Dembo and Tulowitzki [1988], Nagurney [1988], Klincewitz [1989], Arezki and Van Vliet [1990], Hearn and Lawphongpanich [1990], Toint and Tuyttens [1990], Luo and Tseng [1994].

For algorithms for nonlinear network problems using piecewise linear approximations, see Meyer [1979], Rockafellar [1984], Minoux [1986b], and Hochbaum and Shantikumar [1990]. The literature on interior point methods is very extensive. Some representative works, which give many additional references, are Nesterov and Nemirovskii [1994], Wright [1997], and Ye [1997]. For applications of interior point methods to network optimization, see Resende and Veiga [1993], and Resende and Pardalos [1996]. The research monograph by Bertsekas [1982] focuses on penalty and augmented Lagrangian methods, and includes a description and analysis of smoothing methods (see also Bertsekas [1975a]). For recent work on smoothing, see Pinar and Zenios [1992], [1993], [1994]. The proximal minimization algorithm was proposed by Martinet [1970], and was extensively developed in a more general setting by Rockafellar [1976]. For analysis of the finite termination property for linear problems, see Bertsekas [1975b], Bertsekas and Tsitsiklis [1989], and Ferris [1991]. There has been much work on extensions of the algorithm to cases where the proximal term is nonquadratic; see Censor and Zenios [1992], Guler [1992], Teboulle [1992], Chen and Teboulle [1993], Tseng and Bertsekas [1993], Eckstein [1994], Iusem, Svaiter, and Teboulle [1994], and Kiwiel [1997a]. The book by Censor and Zenios [1997] discusses several nonlinear network optimization techniques and a variety of applications, with emphasis on parallel computation.

EXERCISES

8.1

Consider the convex separable problem of Fig. 8.22, where each arc cost function is $f_{ij}(x_{ij}) = x_{ij}^2$.

(a) Find the optimal solution and verify that it satisfies the optimality condition of Prop. 8.2.

(b) Derive and solve the dual problem based on the first formulation of Section 8.7.

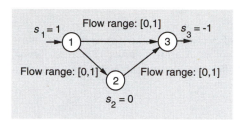

Figure 8.22: Problem for Exercise 8.1.

8.2

Consider a network with two nodes, 1 and 2, with supplies $s_1 = 1$ and $s_2 = -1$, and three arcs/paths connecting 1 and 2, whose flows are denoted by h_1, h_2, and h_3. The problem is

$$\text{minimize } (h_1^2) + 2(h_2^2) + (h_3^2)$$

$$\text{subject to } h_1 + h_2 + h_3 = 1$$

$$h_1, h_2, h_3 \geq 0$$

(a) Show that the optimal solution is $h_1^* = 2/3$, $h_2^* = 1/3$, and $h_3^* = 0$.

(b) Write a computer program to carry out several iterations of the conditional gradient method starting from $h^0 = (1/3, 1/3, 1/3)$. Do enough iterations to demonstrate a clear trend in rate of convergence. Plot the successive iterates on the simplex of feasible path flows.

8.3 (Dynamic Network Flows)

The arcs (i, j) of a graph carry flow $x_{ij}(t)$ in time period t, where $t = 1, \ldots, T$. Each arc requires one time unit for traversal; that is, flow $x_{ij}(t)$ sent from node i to node j along arc (i, j) at time t arrives at node j at time $t + 1$. The difference between the total flow departing and arriving at node i at time $t = 2, \ldots, T$ is a given scalar $s_i(t)$. The total flows departing from each node i at time 1 and arriving at each node i at time $T + 1$ are also given.

(a) Formulate the minimization of a cost function $f\big(x(1), \ldots, x(T)\big)$ subject to $x(t) \in X(t)$, $t = 1, \ldots, T$, where

$$x(t) = \big\{ x_{ij}(t) \mid (i, j) \in \mathcal{A} \big\}, \qquad t = 1, \ldots, T,$$

and $X(t)$ is a given set for each t, as a network optimization problem involving a suitable graph that consists of multiple copies of the given graph.

(b) Repeat part (a) for the more general case where traversal of an arc (i, j) requires a given integer number of periods τ_{ij}.

8.4 (Piecewise Differentiable Arc Costs)

Consider the convex separable problem of Section 8.1, where each arc cost function f_{ij} is differentiable everywhere except at a finite number of points. Show that the problem can be converted to a differentiable separable problem involving one extra arc for each point of nondifferentiability.

8.5 (Constrained Max-Flow Problem)

Consider the max-flow problem of Chapter 3 with the exception that there is a single side constraint of the form $\sum_{(i,j)} a_{ij}x_{ij} \leq b$, where a_{ij} and b are given scalars. Relate this problem to the min-cost flow problem of minimizing $\sum_{(i,j)} a_{ij}x_{ij}$ subject to the constraint that the divergence out of the source (and into the sink) is a given scalar r.

8.6 (Shortest Path Problems with Losses)

Consider the shortest path-like problem of Exercise 2.31 where a vehicle wants to go on a forward path from an origin node 1 to a destination node t in a graph with no forward cycles, and for each arc there is a given probability that the vehicle will be destroyed in crossing the arc. Formulate the problem as a network flow problem with gains. Provide conditions under which your formulation makes sense when the graph has some forward cycles and the arc lengths are nonnegative.

8.7 (Complementary Slackness – Constraint-Separable Problems)

Consider the constraint-separable convex network flow problem where

$$X = \left\{ x \mid b_{ij} \leq x_{ij} \leq c_{ij},\ (i,j) \in \mathcal{A} \right\},$$

and assume that f is continuously differentiable over the entire space and is convex over the feasible set. Show that a vector x^* is optimal if and only if there exists a price vector p^* such that

$$p_i^* - p_j^* \leq \frac{\partial f(x_{ij}^*)}{\partial x_{ij}}, \qquad \forall\ (i,j) \in \mathcal{A} \text{ with } x_{ij}^* < c_{ij},$$

$$p_i^* - p_j^* \geq \frac{\partial f(x_{ij}^*)}{\partial x_{ij}}, \qquad \forall\ (i,j) \in \mathcal{A} \text{ with } b_{ij} < x_{ij}^*.$$

Hint: Use Prop. 8.1 and the theory of Section 4.2.

8.8 (Complementary Slackness – Networks with Gains)

Consider a constraint-separable convex network flow problem with gains:

$$\text{minimize} \quad f(x)$$
$$\text{subject to} \quad b_{ij} \leq x_{ij} \leq c_{ij}, \quad \forall \, (i,j) \in \mathcal{A},$$
$$\sum_{\{j \mid (i,j) \in \mathcal{A}\}} x_{ij} - \sum_{\{j \mid (j,i) \in \mathcal{A}\}} g_{ji} x_{ji} = s_i, \quad \forall \, i \in \mathcal{N},$$

and assume that f is continuously differentiable over the entire space and is convex over the feasible set. Show that a vector x^* is optimal if and only if there exists a price vector p^* such that

$$p_i^* - g_{ij} p_j^* \leq \frac{\partial f(x_{ij}^*)}{\partial x_{ij}}, \qquad \forall \, (i,j) \in \mathcal{A} \text{ with } x_{ij}^* < c_{ij},$$

$$p_i^* - g_{ij} p_j^* \geq \frac{\partial f(x_{ij}^*)}{\partial x_{ij}}, \qquad \forall \, (i,j) \in \mathcal{A} \text{ with } b_{ij} < x_{ij}^*.$$

Hint: Use Prop. 8.1 and the theory of Section 8.7.

8.9 (Error Bounds in the Conditional Gradient Method)

Consider the conditional gradient method applied to the minimization of a continuously differentiable function $f : \Re^n \mapsto \Re$ over a convex and compact set F. Assume that f is convex over F. Show that at each iteration k, we have

$$f(x^k) + \min_{x \in F} \nabla f(x^k)'(x - x^k) \leq \min_{x \in F} f(x) \leq f(x^k).$$

Show also that if x^k converges to an optimal vector x^*, then the upper and lower bounds above converge to $f(x^*)$.

8.10

Consider the path flow formulation of the multicommodity flow problem of Section 8.8.7. Assume that for each OD pair (i_m, j_m) there is a "reverse" OD pair (j_m, i_m), and let $c_m > 0$ be the ratio of the supplies of these two OD pairs. Suppose that there is the restriction that the paths used by the OD pair (i_m, j_m) must be the reverse of the paths used by the OD pair (j_m, i_m) and the ratios of the corresponding flows must be c_m; that is, if h_p is the flow carried by a path p from i_m to j_m, then $c_m h_p$ must be the flow of the reverse path of p, from j_m to i_m. Derive an optimality condition like the one of Prop. 8.5, and the forms of the conditional gradient and gradient projection methods for this problem.

8.11

Consider the case of a separable cost function

$$f(x) = \sum_{(i,j)\in\mathcal{A}} f_{ij}(x_{ij}),$$

where each f_{ij} is convex over the real line, and except for the conservation of flow constraints, the only constraints are $x_{ij} \geq 0$ for all arcs (i,j). Suppose that $f_{ij}(x_{ij}) \geq 0$ for all x_{ij} and that $f_{ij}(0) = 0$. Provide and justify an equivalent path flow formulation of the problem.

8.12 (Convergence Proof of the Conditional Gradient Method)

Consider the minimization of a continuously differentiable function $f : \Re^n \mapsto \Re$ over a convex and compact set F. Assume that f is convex over F and the gradient of f satisfies

$$\left\| \nabla f(x) - \nabla f(y) \right\| \leq L \|x - y\|, \quad \forall\, x,y \in F,$$

where L is a positive constant.

(a) Show that if d is a descent direction at x, then

$$\min_{\alpha\in[0,1]} f(x + \alpha d) \leq f(x) + \delta,$$

where δ is the negative scalar given by

$$\delta = \begin{cases} \frac{1}{2}\nabla f(x)'d & \text{if } \nabla f(x)'d + L\|d\|^2 < 0, \\ -\frac{|\nabla f(x)'d|^2}{2LR^2} & \text{otherwise}, \end{cases}$$

where R is the diameter of F:

$$R = \max_{x,y\in F} \|x - y\|.$$

Hint: Let t be a scalar parameter and define $g(t) = f(x + td)$. Using the chain rule, we have $\partial g(t)/\partial t = d'\nabla f(x + td)$, and

$$f(x + d) - f(x) = g(1) - g(0)$$

$$= \int_0^1 \frac{\partial g(t)}{\partial t}\, dt$$

$$= \int_0^1 d'\nabla f(x + td)\, dt$$

$$\leq \int_0^1 d'\nabla f(x)\, dt + \left| \int_0^1 d'\left(\nabla f(x + td) - \nabla f(x)\right) dt \right|$$

$$\leq \int_0^1 d'\nabla f(x)\, dt + \int_0^1 \|d\| \cdot \|\nabla f(x + td) - \nabla f(x)\|\, dt$$

$$\leq d'\nabla f(x) + \|d\| \int_0^1 Lt\|d\|\, dt$$

$$= d'\nabla f(x) + \frac{L}{2}\|d\|^2.$$

Replace d with αd, and minimize over $\alpha \in [0, 1]$ both sides of this inequality.

(b) Consider the conditional gradient method

$$x^{k+1} = x^k + \alpha^k(\overline{x}^k - x^k),$$

where α^k minimizes $f\left(x^k + \alpha(\overline{x}^k - x^k)\right)$ over $\alpha \in [0, 1]$. Show that every limit of the sequence $\{x^k\}$ is optimal. *Hint*: Argue that, if $\{x^k\}$ has a limit point and δ^k corresponds to x^k as in part (a), then $\delta^k \to 0$, and, therefore, also $\nabla f(x^k)'(\overline{x}^k - x^k) \to 0$. Take the limit in the relation $\nabla f(x^k)'(\overline{x}^k - x^k) \leq \nabla f(x^k)'(x - x^k)$ for all $x \in F$.

8.13 (A Variant of the Conditional Gradient Method)

Consider the minimization of a continuously differentiable function $f : \Re^n \mapsto \Re$ over a closed and convex set F, and assume that f is convex over F and that the gradient of f satisfies

$$\left\|\nabla f(x) - \nabla f(y)\right\| \leq L\|x - y\|, \qquad \forall\ x, y \in F,$$

where L is a positive constant. Consider the conditional gradient method

$$x^{k+1} = x^k + \alpha^k(\overline{x}^k - x^k)$$

where α^k is given by

$$\alpha^k = \min\left\{1, \frac{\nabla f(x^k)'(x^k - \overline{x}^k)}{L\|x^k - \overline{x}^k\|^2}\right\}.$$

Show that every limit point of $\{x^k\}$ is optimal. *Hint*: Use the line of analysis of Exercise 8.12.

9

Convex Separable Network Problems

Contents

In this chapter, we focus on the convex separable problem introduced in Section 8.1. It has the form

$$\text{minimize} \quad \sum_{(i,j)\in\mathcal{A}} f_{ij}(x_{ij}) \tag{9.1}$$

$$\text{subject to} \quad \sum_{\{j|(i,j)\in\mathcal{A}\}} x_{ij} - \sum_{\{j|(j,i)\in\mathcal{A}\}} x_{ji} = s_i, \quad \forall\, i \in \mathcal{N}, \tag{9.2}$$

$$x_{ij} \in X_{ij}, \quad \forall\, (i,j) \in \mathcal{A}, \tag{9.3}$$

where x is a flow vector in a given directed graph $(\mathcal{N},\mathcal{A})$, s_i are given supply scalars, X_{ij} are nonempty intervals of scalars, and each function $f_{ij} : X_{ij} \mapsto \Re$ is convex.

We have already discussed this problem in Chapter 8, and we now provide a more extensive development of the associated optimality conditions, duality theory, and algorithmic solution. We begin with a development of the mathematical properties of convex functions of one variable, such as the ones appearing in the separable cost function (9.1). We then generalize, in Section 9.2, the optimality conditions of Section 8.6 so that they do not require differentiability of the cost function. In Section 9.3, we develop a duality theory that generalizes the one of Chapter 4 for the minimum cost flow problem. In Section 9.4, we show that under special circumstances (essentially, strict convexity of the primal cost function), the dual cost function is differentiable.

We then proceed with the development of algorithms for convex separable problems. In Section 9.5, we discuss gradient-based algorithms for solving the dual problem, when this problem is differentiable. In Section 9.6, we generalize and discuss in detail the auction algorithms of Chapter 7. These algorithms can deal with nondifferentiabilities in the dual problem and are also very efficient in practice. There is a solid theoretical basis for this efficiency, as we show with a computational complexity analysis.

We close this chapter with the development of a far-reaching generalization of the separable convex network problem: we replace the conservation of flow constraints with arbitrary linear equality constraints, obtaining a so-called *monotropic programming problem*. In this context, duality is symmetric, and the distinction between a primal and a dual problem disappear. Furthermore, the duality results are the sharpest possible. In fact, monotropic programming problems form the largest class of nonlinear programming problems with a duality theory that is as sharp as the one for linear programs.

9.1   CONVEX FUNCTIONS OF A SINGLE VARIABLE

In this section, we introduce some mathematical properties of convex functions of one variable, defined over an interval of the real line $\Re$. We recall that in our terminology, an interval is a nonempty and convex subset of the real line. The supremum (infimum) of an interval is called the *right endpoint* (the *left endpoint*, respectively). Thus, an interval is a set that has one of the forms (a, b), $(a, b]$, $[a, b)$, $[a, b]$, $(-\infty, b)$, $(-\infty, b]$, (a, ∞), $[a, \infty)$, $(-\infty, \infty)$, where a and b are scalars. The left endpoint is a (or $-\infty$) and the right endpoint is b (or ∞). The *interior* of an interval is the set (a, b) where a and b are the left and right endpoints, respectively.

Let $f : X \mapsto \Re$ be a convex function defined on an interval X.† The subset

$$\{(x, \gamma) \mid x \in X, \, f(x) \leq \gamma\}$$

of $\Re^2$ is called the *epigraph* of f, and is convex if and only if f is convex. It can be shown (as a consequence of convexity) that f is continuous at all points in the interior of X; that is, $\lim_{k \to \infty} f(x_k) = f(x)$ for all sequences $\{x_k\} \subset X$ converging to an interior point x of X. At an endpoint of X that is included in X, f may or may not be continuous. A condition that guarantees continuity of f over the entire interval X is that the epigraph of f is a closed subset of $\Re^2$. If this condition holds, we say that f is *closed*. *Throughout this chapter, we assume that the convex functions f_{ij} involved in the separable problem (9.1)-(9.3) are closed.* This assumption facilitates the analysis and is practically always satisfied.

The *right derivative* of f at a point $x \in X$ that is not the right endpoint of X is defined by

$$f^+(x) = \lim_{\alpha_k \to 0^+} \frac{f(x + \alpha_k) - f(x)}{\alpha_k},$$

where the limit is taken over any positive sequence $\{\alpha_k\}$ such that $x + \alpha_k \in X$ for all k. If X contains its right endpoint b, we define $f^+(b) = \infty$. Similarly, the *left derivative* of f at a point $x \in X$ that is not the left endpoint of X is defined by

$$f^-(x) = \lim_{\alpha_k \to 0^+} \frac{f(x - \alpha_k) - f(x)}{\alpha_k},$$

---

† Much of the literature of convex analysis treats convex functions as extended real-valued functions, which are defined over the entire real line but take the value ∞ outside their (effective) domain. In this format, a function $f : X \mapsto \Re$ that is convex over the convex interval X is represented by the function $\hat{f} : \Re \mapsto (-\infty, \infty]$ defined by

$$\hat{f}(x) = \begin{cases} f(x) & \text{if } x \in X, \\ \infty & \text{if } x \notin X. \end{cases}$$

There are notational advantages to this format, particularly for functions of several variables, as it is not necessary to keep track of the domains of various functions explicitly. It is simpler for our limited purposes, however, to maintain the more common framework of real-valued functions.

where the limit is taken over any positive sequence $\{\alpha_k\}$ such that $x - \alpha_k \in X$ for all k. If X contains its left endpoint a, we define $f^-(a) = -\infty$. In the degenerate case where X consists of a single point a, we define $f^-(a) = -\infty$ and $f^+(a) = \infty$. Note that the only point of X where f^+ may equal ∞ is the right endpoint (assuming it belongs to X), and the only point of X where f^- may equal $-\infty$ is the left endpoint (assuming it belongs to X).

It can be shown, as a consequence of convexity, that the right and left derivatives are monotonically nondecreasing and satisfy

$$f^-(x) \le f^+(x) \le f^-(y) \le f^+(y), \qquad \forall \ x, y \in X \text{ with } x < y. \qquad (9.4)$$

Furthermore, f^- is left continuous (f^+ is right continuous) over the interval where it is finite. If f is differentiable at a point $x \in X$, we have

$$f^-(x) = f^+(x) = \nabla f(x),$$

where $\nabla f(x)$ is the gradient of f at x. The right and left derivatives define the subset

$$\Gamma = \big\{ (x, t) \mid x \in X, \ f^-(x) \le t \le f^+(x) \big\}$$

of $\Re^2$, which is called the *characteristic curve* of f, and is illustrated in Fig. 9.1.

Directional Derivatives of Separable Convex Functions

Consider now a general convex set F in $\Re^n$, and a function $f : F \mapsto \Re$ that is convex. The *directional derivative* $f'(x; y)$ of f at a vector $x \in F$ in the direction y is defined to be the right derivative of the convex function $f(x + \alpha y)$ of the scalar α at $\alpha = 0$ (this function is defined over the interval of all α such that $x + \alpha y \in F$). In other words,

$$f'(x; y) = \lim_{\alpha \to 0^+} \frac{f(x + \alpha y) - f(x)}{\alpha}, \qquad (9.5)$$

where we use the convention $f(x + \alpha y) = \infty$ if $x + \alpha y \notin F$. Note that a vector $x^* \in F$ minimizes f over F if and only if

$$f'(x^*; y) \ge 0, \qquad \forall \ y. \qquad (9.6)$$

Let us consider the special case of a separable function of the flow vector x:

$$f(x) = \sum_{(i,j) \in \mathcal{A}} f_{ij}(x_{ij}),$$

where each f_{ij} is a closed convex function over an interval X_{ij}. Then, by applying the definition (9.5), we see that the directional derivative is given by

$$f'(x; y) = \sum_{\{(i,j) \in \mathcal{A} \mid y_{ij} > 0\}} f_{ij}^+(x_{ij}) y_{ij} + \sum_{\{(i,j) \in \mathcal{A} \mid y_{ij} < 0\}} f_{ij}^-(x_{ij}) y_{ij}, \qquad (9.7)$$

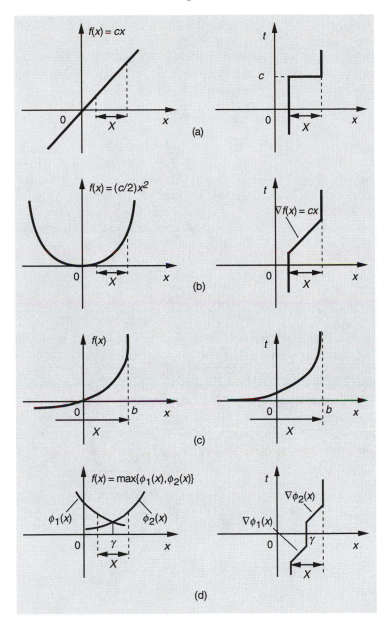

Figure 9.1: Illustration of various convex functions $f : X \mapsto \Re$ (on the left-hand side) and their right and left derivatives, and characteristic curves

$$\Gamma = \left\{ (x,t) \mid x \in X,\ f^-(x) \le t \le f^+(x) \right\}$$

(on the right-hand side). In example (c), X contains its right endpoint b, but we have $f^-(b) = f^+(b) = \infty$.

where $f_{ij}^-(x_{ij})$ and $f_{ij}^+(x_{ij})$ denote the left and the right derivative of f_{ij} at an arc flow $x_{ij} \in X_{ij}$. There is an ambiguity in the above equation when $f_{ij}^+(x_{ij}) = \infty$ for some (i,j) with $y_{ij} > 0$ and $f_{ij}^-(x_{ij}) = \infty$ for some (i,j) with $y_{ij} < 0$, in which case the sum $\infty - \infty$ appears. We resolve this ambiguity by adopting the convention

$$\infty - \infty = \infty.$$

It can be shown by using the definition (9.5) that with this convention, the directional derivative formula of Eq. (9.7) is correct even in cases where the ambiguity arises. To see this, note that if $f_{ij}^+(x_{ij}) = \infty$ for some (i,j), x_{ij} must be the right endpoint of the interval X_{ij}, so that if in addition $y_{ij} > 0$, it follows that $x_{ij} + \alpha y_{ij} \notin X_{ij}$ for all $\alpha > 0$. Thus $x + \alpha y$ is outside the domain of f for all $\alpha > 0$, so that, according to our convention, $f(x + \alpha y) = \infty$ for all $\alpha > 0$ and, from Eq. (9.5), $f'(x; y) = \infty$.

9.2 OPTIMALITY CONDITIONS

In this and the next two sections, we discuss the main analytical aspects of convex separable problems. The optimality conditions derived in Section 8.6 require differentiability of the cost function. However, the approach used there can be extended to a nondifferentiable separable convex cost by using directional differentiability. In particular, by arguing that the directional derivative of f cannot be negative along any feasible direction at x^* [cf. Eq. (9.6)], we obtain a generalization of the nonnegative cycle condition for optimality of Props. 1.2 and 8.2.

Proposition 9.1: (Nonnegative Cycle Condition) Consider the separable convex network problem. A vector x^* is optimal if and only if x^* is feasible and for every simple cycle C that is unblocked with respect to x^* there holds

$$\sum_{(i,j)\in C^+} f_{ij}^+(x_{ij}^*) - \sum_{(i,j)\in C^-} f_{ij}^-(x_{ij}^*) \geq 0. \qquad (9.8)$$

Proof: Let x^* be an optimal flow vector and let C be a simple cycle that is unblocked with respect to x^*. Consider the flow vector $d(C)$ with components

$$d_{ij}(C) = \begin{cases} 1 & \text{if } (i,j) \in C^+, \\ -1 & \text{if } (i,j) \in C^-, \\ 0 & \text{otherwise.} \end{cases} \qquad (9.9)$$

Then $d(C)$ is a feasible direction at x^* and using Eq. (9.7), it is seen that the directional derivative of f at x^* in the direction $d(C)$ is the left-hand side of Eq. (9.8). Since x^* is optimal, this directional derivative must be nonnegative [cf. Eq. (9.6)].

Conversely, suppose that x^* is feasible but not optimal. Let $\bar{x}$ be a feasible flow vector with cost smaller that the one of x^*. Consider a conformal decomposition of the circulation $\bar{x} - x^*$ into simple cycles $C_1, \ldots, C_M$, and the corresponding cycle flow vectors $d(C_1), \ldots, d(C_M)$ as per Eq. (9.9):

$$\bar{x} - x^* = \sum_{m=1}^{M} \gamma_m d(C_m), \qquad \gamma_m > 0, \ m = 1, \ldots, M. \tag{9.10}$$

Using Eqs. (9.7) and (9.10), we see that the directional derivative of f in the direction $\bar{x} - x^*$ is given by

$$f'(x^*; \bar{x} - x^*) = \sum_{\{(i,j)|\bar{x}_{ij} - x_{ij}^* > 0\}} f_{ij}^+(x_{ij}^*)(\bar{x}_{ij} - x_{ij}^*)$$

$$+ \sum_{\{(i,j)|\bar{x}_{ij} - x_{ij}^* < 0\}} f_{ij}^-(x_{ij}^*)(\bar{x}_{ij} - x_{ij}^*)$$

$$= \sum_{\{(i,j)|\bar{x}_{ij} - x_{ij}^* > 0\}} f_{ij}^+(x_{ij}^*) \sum_{m=1}^{M} \gamma_m d_{ij}(C_m)$$

$$+ \sum_{\{(i,j)|\bar{x}_{ij} - x_{ij}^* < 0\}} f_{ij}^-(x_{ij}^*) \sum_{m=1}^{M} \gamma_m d_{ij}(C_m)$$

$$= \sum_{m=1}^{M} \gamma_m \left(\sum_{\{(i,j)|d_{ij}(C_m) > 0\}} f_{ij}^+(x_{ij}^*) d_{ij}(C_m) \right.$$

$$\left. + \sum_{\{(i,j)|d_{ij}(C_m) < 0\}} f_{ij}^-(x_{ij}^*) d_{ij}(C_m) \right)$$

$$= \sum_{m=1}^{M} \gamma_m f'(x^*; d(C_m)).$$

[The last equality holds using the definition (9.7) of a directional derivative. The next-to-last inequality holds because for any arc (i, j) the sign of each nonzero arc flow $d_{ij}(C_m)$ is the same as the sign of $\bar{x}_{ij} - x_{ij}^*$, since the decomposition is conformal.] Since $f'(x^*; \bar{x} - x^*) < 0$ and $\gamma_m > 0$ for all m, we must have $f'(x^*; d(C_m)) < 0$ for at least one m, or

$$\sum_{(i,j) \in C_m^+} f_{ij}^+(x_{ij}^*) - \sum_{(i,j) \in C_m^-} f_{ij}^-(x_{ij}^*) < 0.$$

Thus if Eq. (9.8) holds, x^* must be optimal.   **Q.E.D.**

9.3 DUALITY

As in earlier developments of duality, we obtain a dual problem by introducing a price p_i for each node i and by forming the Lagrangian function

$$L(x,p) = \sum_{(i,j)\in\mathcal{A}} f_{ij}(x_{ij}) + \sum_{i\in\mathcal{N}} p_i \left(\sum_{\{j\mid(j,i)\in\mathcal{A}\}} x_{ji} - \sum_{\{j\mid(i,j)\in\mathcal{A}\}} x_{ij} + s_i \right)$$

$$= \sum_{(i,j)\in\mathcal{A}} \left(f_{ij}(x_{ij}) - (p_i - p_j)x_{ij} \right) + \sum_{i\in\mathcal{N}} s_i p_i.$$

$$(9.11)$$

The dual function value $q(p)$ at a price vector p is obtained by minimizing
$L(x,p)$ over all x satisfying the constraint $x_{ij} \in X_{ij}$. Thus,

$$q(p) = \inf_{x\in X} L(x,p) = \sum_{(i,j)\in\mathcal{A}} q_{ij}(p_i - p_j) + \sum_{i\in\mathcal{N}} s_i p_i,$$

where

$$q_{ij}(p_i - p_j) = \inf_{x_{ij}\in X_{ij}} \left\{ f_{ij}(x_{ij}) - (p_i - p_j)x_{ij} \right\}. \qquad (9.12)$$

The problem

$$\text{maximize} \quad q(p)$$

$$\text{subject to no constraint on } p,$$

is referred to as the *dual problem*, while the original problem of minimizing
f subject to the conservation of flow constraints and $x \in X$ is referred to
as the *primal problem*. The dual function is also referred to as the *dual
cost function* or *dual cost*, and the optimal value of the dual problem is
referred to as the *optimal dual cost*.

     Note that q_{ij} is concave since it is the pointwise infimum of linear
functions [the epigraph of $-q_{ij}$ is a convex set, since it is the intersection
of the epigraphs of the linear functions $(p_i - p_j)x_{ij} - f_{ij}(x_{ij})$ as x_{ij} ranges
over X_{ij}]. If X_{ij} is a compact set, then since f_{ij} is assumed closed and
hence continuous over X_{ij}, the infimum in the definition (9.12) of q_{ij} is
attained (by Weierstrass' theorem), and it follows that q_{ij} is real-valued;
that is, $q(p)$ is a real number for all p. If X_{ij} is not compact, it is possible
that q_{ij} is not real-valued. Thus the dual problem embodies the implicit
constraint $p \in Q$, where Q is the "effective domain" of q given by

$$Q = \{p \mid q(p) > -\infty\}.$$

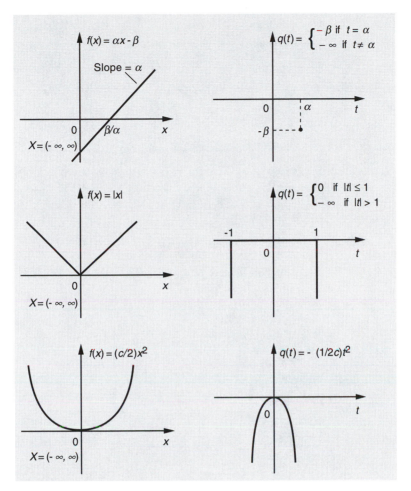

Figure 9.2: Illustration of primal and dual arc cost function pairs. Points where the primal function is nondifferentiable correspond to linear segments of the dual function.

We consequently say that a price vector p is *feasible* if $q(p) > -\infty$. The dual problem is said to be *infeasible* if there is no feasible price vector. The form of q_{ij} is illustrated in Fig. 9.2.†

Our objective is to generalize the duality theorems given in Chapter 4 for the minimum cost flow cost problem. For this, we must first generalize

---

† The relation between the primal and dual arc cost functions f_{ij} and q_{ij} is a special case of a conjugacy relation that is central in the theory of convex functions (see e.g., Rockafellar [1970], [1984]). There is a rich theory around this relation. Here, we will prove only those facts about conjugacy that we will need in our analysis.

the conditions for complementary slackness.

Definition 9.1: A flow-price vector pair (x, p) is said to satisfy *complementary slackness* (CS for short) if for all arcs (i, j), we have $x_{ij} \in X_{ij}$ and

$$f_{ij}^-(x_{ij}) \leq p_i - p_j \leq f_{ij}^+(x_{ij}).$$

Thus a pair (x, p) satisfies CS if for every arc (i, j), the pair $(x_{ij}, p_i - p_j)$ lies on the characteristic curve of the function f_{ij} (see Fig. 9.3). Note that an equivalent definition of CS is that x_{ij} attains the infimum in the definition of q_{ij} for all arcs (i, j):

$$f_{ij}(x_{ij}) - (p_i - p_j)x_{ij} = \min_{z_{ij} \in X_{ij}} \{f_{ij}(z_{ij}) - (p_i - p_j)z_{ij}\}.$$

It can be seen that these conditions generalize the corresponding CS conditions for the minimum cost flow problem.

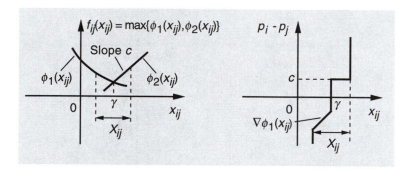

Figure 9.3: Illustration of CS. The pairs $(x_{ij}, p_i - p_j)$ must lie on the corresponding characteristic curves

$$\Gamma_{ij} = \{(x_{ij}, t_{ij}) \mid x_{ij} \in X_{ij}, \; f_{ij}^-(x_{ij}) \leq t_{ij} \leq f_{ij}^+(x_{ij})\},$$

shown in the right-hand side.

We are now ready to derive the basic duality results for separable problems.

Proposition 9.2: (Complementary Slackness Theorem) A feasible flow vector x^* and a price vector p^* satisfy CS if and only if x^* and p^* are optimal primal and dual solutions, respectively, and the optimal primal and dual costs are equal.

Proof: We first show that for any feasible flow vector x and any price vector p, the primal cost of x is no less than the dual cost of p. Indeed, using the definition of $q(p)$ and $L(x, p)$, we have

$$q(p) \leq L(x, p)$$

$$= \sum_{(i,j) \in \mathcal{A}} f_{ij}(x_{ij}) + \sum_{i \in \mathcal{N}} p_i \left(s_i - \sum_{\{j | (i,j) \in \mathcal{A}\}} x_{ij} + \sum_{\{j | (j,i) \in \mathcal{A}\}} x_{ji} \right)$$

$$= \sum_{(i,j) \in \mathcal{A}} f_{ij}(x_{ij}),$$

(9.13)

where the last equality follows from the feasibility of x.

If x^* is feasible and satisfies CS together with p^*, we have by the definition of q

$$q(p^*) = \inf_x \left\{ L(x, p^*) \mid x_{ij} \in X_{ij}, (i, j) \in \mathcal{A} \right\}$$

$$= L(x^*, p^*)$$

$$= \sum_{(i,j) \in \mathcal{A}} f_{ij}(x^*_{ij}) + \sum_{i \in \mathcal{N}} p^*_i \left(s_i - \sum_{\{j | (i,j) \in \mathcal{A}\}} x^*_{ij} + \sum_{\{j | (j,i) \in \mathcal{A}\}} x^*_{ji} \right)$$

$$= \sum_{(i,j) \in \mathcal{A}} f_{ij}(x^*_{ij}),$$

where the last equality follows from the feasibility of x^*, and the second equality holds because (x^*, p^*) satisfies CS if and only if

$$f_{ij}(x^*_{ij}) - (p^*_i - p^*_j)x^*_{ij} = \min_{x_{ij} \in X_{ij}} \left\{ f_{ij}(x_{ij}) - (p^*_i - p^*_j)x_{ij} \right\}, \quad \forall\, (i, j) \in \mathcal{A},$$

and $L(x^*, p^*)$ can be written as in Eq. (9.11). Therefore, x^* attains the minimum of the primal cost on the right-hand side of Eq. (9.13), and p^* attains the maximum of $q(p)$ on the left-hand side of Eq. (9.13), while the optimal primal and dual costs are equal.

Conversely, suppose that x^* and p^* are optimal flow and price vectors for the primal and dual problems, respectively, and the two optimal costs are equal; that is,

$$q(p^*) = \sum_{(i,j) \in \mathcal{A}} f_{ij}(x^*_{ij}).$$

We have by definition

$$q(p^*) = \inf_x \left\{ L(x, p^*) \mid x_{ij} \in X_{ij}, (i, j) \in \mathcal{A} \right\},$$

and also, using the Lagrangian expression (9.11) and the feasibility of x^*,

$$\sum_{(i,j) \in \mathcal{A}} f_{ij}(x^*_{ij}) = L(x^*, p^*).$$

Combining the last three equations, we obtain

$$L(x^*, p^*) = \min_x \{ L(x, p^*) \mid x_{ij} \in X_{ij}, (i,j) \in \mathcal{A} \}.$$

Using the Lagrangian expression (9.11), it follows that for all arcs (i,j), we have

$$f_{ij}(x_{ij}^*) - (p_i^* - p_j^*)x_{ij}^* = \min_{x_{ij} \in X_{ij}} \{ f_{ij}(x_{ij}) - (p_i^* - p_j^*)x_{ij} \}.$$

This is equivalent to the pair (x^*, p^*) satisfying CS.   **Q.E.D.**

An important question, which is left open by Prop. 9.2, is whether there exists a price vector that satisfies CS together with an optimal flow vector. For the minimum cost flow problem, this is always true, as we have seen in Chapter 4 (Prop. 4.2). However, answering this question for convex but nonlinear problems requires some qualifying condition of the type assumed in the duality results of Chapter 8 (cf. Prop. 8.3). We introduce such a condition in the following definition.

Definition 9.2: (Regularity) A flow vector x is called *regular* if for all arcs (i,j), we have

$$f_{ij}^-(x_{ij}) < \infty, \qquad -\infty < f_{ij}^+(x_{ij}).$$

It is quite unusual for a flow vector x *not* to be regular. For this to happen, there must exist an arc flow x_{ij} that lies at the right (left) endpoint of the corresponding constraint interval X_{ij} while both the left and the right slopes of f_{ij} at that endpoint are ∞ (or $-\infty$, respectively) [see Fig. 9.1(c) for an example]. In particular, if x_{ij} belongs to the interior of X_{ij} for all arcs (i,j), then x is regular. Furthermore, all flow vectors are regular if each f_{ij} is the restriction to the interval X_{ij} of some function that is convex over the entire real line, such as for example a linear function.

While nonregularity is unusual for a feasible flow vector, it is far more rare for an *optimal* flow vector. In particular, we claim that *if there exists at least one regular feasible solution, all optimal solutions must be regular.* To show this, note that if x^* is an optimal solution and $\bar{x}$ is another feasible solution, we have

$$x_{ij}^* < \bar{x}_{ij} \quad \Rightarrow \quad f_{ij}^+(x_{ij}^*) < \infty,$$

since if $x_{ij}^* < \bar{x}_{ij}$, then x_{ij}^* cannot be the right endpoint of the interval X_{ij}. Similarly, we have

$$\bar{x}_{ij} < x_{ij}^* \quad \Rightarrow \quad f_{ij}^-(x_{ij}^*) > -\infty.$$

It follows from the preceding two relations that

$$f_{ij}^+(x_{ij}^*)(\overline{x}_{ij} - x_{ij}^*) < \infty, \quad f_{ij}^-(x_{ij}^*)(\overline{x}_{ij} - x_{ij}^*) < \infty, \quad \forall\, (i,j) \in \mathcal{A}. \quad (9.14)$$

Now if $\overline{x}$ is regular and x^* is not regular but optimal, there must exist an arc (i,j) such that either (a) $f_{ij}^-(x_{ij}^*) = \infty$, or (b) $f_{ij}^+(x_{ij}^*) = -\infty$. In case (a), x_{ij}^* must be the right endpoint of X_{ij} and $\overline{x}_{ij} < x_{ij}^*$ (since $\overline{x}$ is regular). Hence the product $f_{ij}^-(x_{ij}^*)(\overline{x}_{ij} - x_{ij}^*)$ is $-\infty$, and in view of Eq. (9.14), we have

$$f'(x^*; \overline{x} - x^*) = -\infty,$$

contradicting the optimality of x^*. We similarly obtain a contradiction in case (b), completing the proof that regularity of at least one feasible flow vector implies regularity of every optimal flow vector. We use this to show the following proposition.

Proposition 9.3: Suppose that there exists at least one primal feasible solution that is regular. Then, if x^* is an optimal solution of the primal problem, there exists an optimal solution p^* of the dual problem that satisfies CS together with x^*.

Proof: By Prop. 9.1, for every simple cycle C that is unblocked with respect to x^* there holds

$$\sum_{(i,j)\in C^+} f_{ij}^+(x_{ij}^*) - \sum_{(i,j)\in C^-} f_{ij}^-(x_{ij}^*) \geq 0.$$

The discussion preceding the present proposition, implies that x^* must be regular. Using this fact, it is seen that the assumptions for the use of the feasible differential theorem (Exercise 5.11 in Chapter 5) are fulfilled with $a_{ij}^+ = f_{ij}^+(x_{ij}^*)$ and $a_{ij}^- = f_{ij}^-(x_{ij}^*)$. Using the conclusion of this theorem, we can assert that there exists a price vector p^* satisfying

$$f_{ij}^-(x_{ij}) \leq p_i^* - p_j^* \leq f_{ij}^+(x_{ij}),$$

for all arcs (i,j). Thus p^* satisfies CS together with x^*.   **Q.E.D.**

Figure 9.4 gives an example where the assertion of Prop. 9.3 does not hold in the absence of a regular feasible solution.

An important question, which is left open by Props. 9.2 and 9.3, relates to the equality of the optimal primal and dual costs in the absence of an optimal primal solution that is regular. Generally, for convex programs, it is possible that the optimal primal cost is strictly greater that the optimal dual cost, in which case we say that there is a *duality gap*. Using the

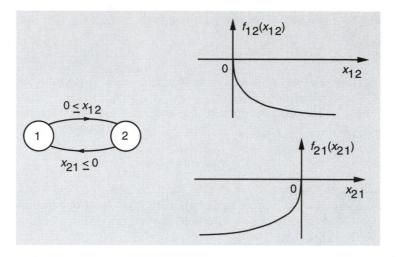

Figure 9.4: An example of a problem where there is no regular primal feasible solution, and the dual problem has no optimal solution (cf. Prop. 9.3). The primal problem is

$$\text{minimize} \ \ f_{12}(x_{12}) + f_{21}(x_{21})$$

$$\text{subject to} \ \ x_{12} = x_{21}, \qquad 0 \le x_{12} < \infty, \quad -\infty < x_{21} \le 0,$$

where

$$f_{12}(x_{12}) = -\sqrt{x_{12}}, \qquad x_{12} \in [0, \infty),$$

$$f_{21}(x_{21}) = -\sqrt{-x_{21}}, \qquad x_{21} \in (-\infty, 0].$$

The dual arc functions can be calculated to be

$$q_{12}(t_{12}) = \inf_{0 \le x_{12} < \infty} \left\{ -\sqrt{x_{12}} - t_{12}x_{12} \right\} = \begin{cases} \frac{1}{4t_{12}} & \text{if } t_{12} < 0, \\ -\infty & \text{otherwise,} \end{cases}$$

and

$$q_{21}(t_{21}) = \inf_{-\infty < x_{21} \le 0} \left\{ -\sqrt{-x_{21}} - t_{21}x_{21} \right\} = \begin{cases} -\frac{1}{4t_{21}} & \text{if } t > 0, \\ -\infty & \text{otherwise.} \end{cases}$$

The only primal feasible solution is the zero flow vector, which is nonregular. The optimal primal cost is 0. The dual problem is to maximize

$$\frac{1}{4(p_1 - p_2)} - \frac{1}{4(p_2 - p_1)}$$

over all (p_1, p_2) with $p_1 < p_2$, and has no optimal solution. The dual optimal cost is 0. Note that the optimal primal and dual costs are equal, consistently with the following Prop. 9.4.

machinery of the simplex method, we showed that for linear cost problems, this cannot happen (see Props. 4.2 and 5.8). However, the equality of the optimal primal and dual costs is a characteristic property of linear programs and the corresponding proof methods do not easily generalize to the case of a general convex cost function. It is thus somewhat unexpected that for the *separable* problem of this chapter the optimal primal and dual costs are equal under comparable assumptions to those for linear programs. This is a remarkable result due to Minty [1960] and Rockafellar ([1967] or [1970] or [1984]), and requires a fairly sophisticated proof, which will be given in Section 9.7. Exercise 9.1 outlines the proof of a weaker result, which states that if the primal problem is feasible and the intervals X_{ij} are compact, then the optimal primal and dual costs are equal, even though the optimal primal solutions may not be regular and the dual problem may not have an optimal solution.

Proposition 9.4: (Duality Theorem for Separable Problems)
If there exists at least one feasible solution to the primal problem, or at least one feasible solution to the dual problem, the optimal primal and dual costs are equal.

Note that part of the assertion of Prop. 9.4 is that if the primal problem is feasible but unbounded, then the dual problem is infeasible (the optimal costs of both problems are equal to $-\infty$), and that if the dual problem is feasible but unbounded, the primal problem is infeasible (the optimal costs of both problems are equal to ∞).

Duality and the Equilibrium Problem

We can use duality and CS to introduce a problem, which is referred to as the *equilibrium problem*. The name stems from the association with some classical problems of finding equilibrium solutions to various physical systems, as we will explain shortly.

Network Equilibrium Problem

Find a flow-price pair (x, p) such that x satisfies the conservation of flow equations, and for each arc (i, j), the pair $(x_{ij}, p_i - p_j)$ lies on the characteristic curve

$$\Gamma_{ij} = \left\{ (x_{ij}, t_{ij}) \mid x_{ij} \in X_{ij}, \; f_{ij}^-(x_{ij}) \le t_{ij} \le f_{ij}^+(x_{ij}) \right\}. \qquad (9.15)$$

Thus, the pair (x, p) is an equilibrium solution if and only if x is feasible and (x, p) satisfies CS. We have the following result:

Proposition 9.5: (Network Equilibrium Theorem) A flow-price pair (x^*, p^*) solves the equilibrium problem if and only if x^* and p^* are optimal primal and dual solutions, respectively

---

Proof: If (x^*, p^*) solve the equilibrium problem, then (x^*, p^*) satisfy CS, so by the forward part of Prop. 9.2, x^* is primal optimal and p^* is dual optimal. Conversely, if x^* is primal optimal and p^* is dual optimal, then x^* is primal feasible, so by Prop. 9.4, the optimal primal and dual costs are equal. It follows using the reverse part of Prop. 9.2 that x^* and p^* satisfy CS, and since x^* is feasible, they also solve the equilibrium problem. **Q.E.D.**

We provide some examples of network equilibrium problems and their connections to separable network optimization.

Example 9.1. Electrical Networks

Let us view the given graph as an electric circuit, where x_{ij} and p_i represent the current of arc (i, j) and the voltage of node i, respectively. Let us assume that all the supply scalars s_i are 0. Then, the conservation of flow equations become Kirchhoff's current law (all currents into a node add to 0). Each characteristic curve Γ_{ij} [cf. Eq. (9.15)] defines the locus for current-voltage differential pairs $(x_{ij}, p_i - p_j)$, so it corresponds to Ohm's law. Different types of curves Γ_{ij} define different type of electrical elements. For example a linear curve

$$\Gamma_{ij} = \left\{ (x_{ij}, p_i - p_j) \mid p_i - p_j = E_{ij} + R_{ij} x_{ij} \right\} \tag{9.16}$$

corresponds to an arc consisting of a linear resistor with resistance R_{ij} plus a voltage source of value E_{ij}. A curve

$$\Gamma_{ij} = \left\{ (x_{ij}, p_i - p_j) \mid x_{ij} = I \right\},$$

where I is a constant corresponds to a current source of value I. Nonlinear electric circuit branches, such as for example diodes, can similarly be represented, as long as the corresponding curves Γ_{ij} have the monotonicity properties that characterize the directional derivatives of convex functions of one variable.

Note that Prop. 9.5 asserts that the current-voltage pairs of the electric circuit that satisfy Kirchhoff's and Ohm's laws are exactly the optimal flow-price pairs of the corresponding optimization problem. In the special case of a linear resistive circuit with voltage sources, which has characteristic curves of the form (9.16), the corresponding optimization problem involves the quadratic cost function

$$\sum_{(i,j)\in\mathcal{A}}\left(E_{ij}x_{ij}+\frac{1}{2}R_{ij}x_{ij}^2\right).$$

This function has an electric energy interpretation. We thus obtain a result known since Maxwell's time, namely that the current-voltage pairs that solve a linear resistive circuit solve a minimum energy problem. Proposition 9.5 provides a generalization of this result that holds for nonlinear resistive circuits as well.

Example 9.2. Hydraulic Networks

Networks of pipes or other conduits carrying an incompressible fluid admit a very similar interpretation to the one given above for electric networks. Here x_{ij} correspond to the fluid flow rates through the pipes (i,j), which must satisfy a conservation of flow equation at each node. Also p_i corresponds to pressure head at node i, that is, to the level that the fluid would rise in an open pipe located at node i. The pressure differential $p_i - p_j$ of pipe (i,j) satisfies together with the flow x_{ij} a "resistance" relation, which is expressed by the curve Γ_{ij}.

Subnetworks as Black Boxes – Sensitivity

In many applications, it is convenient to be able to aggregate a subnetwork of the given graph into a single arc for the purpose of optimization of the remainder of the network. The subnetwork can then be treated as a "black box" whose impact on the problem depends only on the characteristics of the aggregate arc. In this way, a complicated subnetwork may be represented by its "input-output" behavior rather than by its detailed internal structure.

Mathematically, the simplest case of a black box representation can be obtained through the problem illustrated in Fig. 9.5(a). This is the special case of the convex separable problem where the divergences of all the nodes are required to be 0, except for two distinguished nodes A and B, whose divergences are required to be s and $-s$, respectively. Let us denote by $F(s)$ the feasible set of the problem, i.e., the set of flow vectors x such that

$$\sum_{\{j|(i,j)\in\mathcal{A}\}} x_{ij} - \sum_{\{j|(j,i)\in\mathcal{A}\}} x_{ji} = 0, \qquad \forall\ i \neq A, B,$$

$$\sum_{\{j|(A,j)\in\mathcal{A}\}} x_{Aj} - \sum_{\{j|(j,A)\in\mathcal{A}\}} x_{jA} = s,$$

$$\sum_{\{j|(B,j)\in\mathcal{A}\}} x_{Bj} - \sum_{\{j|(j,B)\in\mathcal{A}\}} x_{jB} = -s,$$

$$x_{ij} \in X_{ij}, \qquad \forall\ (i,j)\in\mathcal{A}.$$

Let us also denote by $V(s)$ the corresponding optimal cost,

$$V(s) = \inf_{x\in F(s)} \sum_{(i,j)\in\mathcal{A}} f_{ij}(x_{ij}). \tag{9.17}$$

A key fact, to be shown shortly, is that $V(s)$ is a convex function of s.

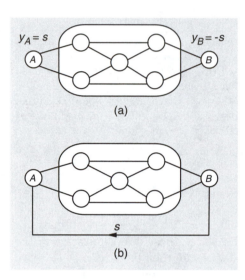

(a)

(b)

Figure 9.5: Problem framework for representation of a subnetwork as a black box. In (a), all nodes have divergence 0, except for A and B, which have divergence s and $-s$, respectively. In (b), an additional arc (B, A) with flow s has been connected to the network of (a), and all nodes have divergence 0.

Suppose now that we want to solve a variant of the problem where s is instead the flow through an arc with start node B and end node A, with a given flow range X_{BA}, and with a given cost function $G(s)$ [see Fig. 9.5(b)]. This is the problem

$$\text{minimize}\quad G(s) + \sum_{(i,j)\in\mathcal{A}} f_{ij}(x_{ij})$$

$$\text{subject to}\quad \sum_{\{j|(i,j)\in\mathcal{A}\}} x_{ij} - \sum_{\{j|(j,i)\in\mathcal{A}\}} x_{ji} = 0, \qquad \forall\ i\neq A,B,$$

$$\sum_{\{j|(A,j)\in\mathcal{A}\}} x_{Aj} - \sum_{\{j|(j,A)\in\mathcal{A}\}} x_{jA} = s,$$

$$\sum_{\{j|(B,j)\in\mathcal{A}\}} x_{Bj} - \sum_{\{j|(j,B)\in\mathcal{A}\}} x_{jB} = -s,$$

$$s \in X_{BA}, \qquad x_{ij}\in X_{ij}, \quad \forall\ (i,j)\in\mathcal{A}.$$

Then, knowing $V(s)$, the problem is reduced to the one-dimensional problem

$$\text{minimize}\ \ G(s) + V(s)$$
$$\text{subject to}\ \ s \in X_{BA}$$

and can be easily solved for practically any choice of cost function $G(s)$.

To see that the function V of Eq. (9.17) is convex, we note that for all s for which the above problem is feasible [i.e., $V(s) < \infty$], by Prop. 9.4, $V(s)$ is equal to the dual optimal cost

$$V(s) = \sup_p Q_p(s), \tag{9.18}$$

where for each fixed p, $Q_p(s)$ is the linear function given by

$$Q_p(s) = (p_A - p_B)s + \sum_{(i,j) \in \mathcal{A}} q_{ij}(p_i - p_j).$$

Thus, $V(s)$ is the pointwise supremum of a collection of linear functions, and must be convex (the epigraph of V is convex because it is the intersection of the epigraphs of Q_p, which are halfspaces). To be able to apply the theory of this chapter, it is also necessary that V be a closed function, which can also be easily shown (the epigraph of V is closed because the epigraphs of Q_p are closed).

Let us now use the preceding ideas to derive a famous theorem from electrical engineering.†

Example 9.3. Thevenin's Theorem

Thevenin's theorem is a classical result of electric circuit theory that often provides computational and conceptual simplification of the solution of electric network problems involving linear resistive elements. The theorem shows that, when viewed from two given terminals, a circuit can be described by a single branch involving just two electrical elements, a voltage source and a resistance (see Fig. 9.6). These elements can be viewed as sensitivity parameters, characterizing how the current across the given terminals varies as a function of the external load to the terminals.

Mathematically, Thevenin's theorem is an application of the black box representation derived above. In particular, the equilibrium problem for a linear resistive network involves the minimum energy problem with the arc cost functions

$$f_{ij}(x_{ij}) = E_{ij}x_{ij} + \frac{1}{2}R_{ij}x_{ij}^2,$$

---

† Leon Thevenin (1857-1926) was a French telegraph engineer. He formulated his theorem at the age of 26. His discovery met initially with skepticism and controversy within the engineering establishment of the time. Eventually the theorem was published in 1883. A brief biography of Thevenin together with an account of the development of his theorem is given by Suchet [1949].

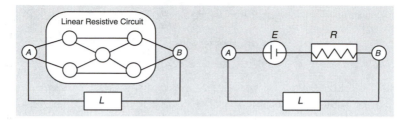

Figure 9.6: Illustration of Thevenin's theorem. A linear resistive circuit acts on a load connected to two of its terminals A and B like a series connection of a voltage source E and a resistance R. The parameters E and R depend only on the circuit and not on the load, so if in particular the load is a resistance L, the current drawn by the load is

$$I = \frac{E}{L + R}.$$

The parameters E and R can be obtained by solving the circuit for two different values of L.

(cf. Example 9.1). The corresponding dual function q_{ij} can be calculated to be

$$q_{ij}(p_i - p_j) = \min_{x_{ij}}\left\{ E_{ij}x_{ij} + \frac{1}{2}R_{ij}x_{ij}^2 - (p_i - p_j)x_{ij} \right\}$$

$$= -\frac{1}{2}R_{ij}^{-1}\left(E_{ij} - p_i + p_j \right)^2.$$

It can be shown [by explicitly carrying out the maximization in Eq. (9.18)] that the function $V(s)$ is quadratic and has the form

$$V(s) = Es + \frac{1}{2}Rs^2,$$

for suitable scalars E and R. These scalars represent the voltage source and the resistance of the Thevenin equivalent branch (cf. Fig. 9.6). For further analysis and algorithms relating to this example, see Bertsekas [1996].

9.4   DUAL FUNCTION DIFFERENTIABILITY

Generally, the dual function q is concave, but not necessarily differentiable, or even real-valued. However, q can be shown to be differentiable in the special case where the infimum in the definition of the dual arc cost function

$$q_{ij}(t_{ij}) = \inf_{x_{ij} \in X_{ij}} \left\{ f_{ij}(x_{ij}) - t_{ij}x_{ij} \right\}$$

is attained for all t_{ij} and f_{ij} is strictly convex over X_{ij}, that is,

$$f_{ij}(\alpha x_{ij} + (1-\alpha)y_{ij}) < \alpha f_{ij}(x_{ij}) + (1-\alpha)f_{ij}(y_{ij}), \qquad \forall\, \alpha \in (0,1),$$

for all $x_{ij}, y_{ij} \in X_{ij}$ with $x_{ij} \neq y_{ij}$. We will prove this property and derive the form of the gradient ∇q. We first need the following result, which establishes various relations between f_{ij} and q_{ij}. These relations are basic in the theory of conjugate functions (see e.g., Rockafellar [1970]).

Proposition 9.6: Let $f : X \mapsto \Re$ be a closed convex function over an interval X, and let

$$q(t) = \inf_{x \in X} \{f(x) - tx\}. \tag{9.19}$$

(a) We have

$$\sup_t \{q(t) + tx\} = \begin{cases} f(x) & \text{if } x \in X, \\ \infty & \text{otherwise,} \end{cases} \tag{9.20}$$

and the following statements are equivalent for any two scalars $x \in X$ and $t \in \Re$:

(1) $tx = f(x) - q(t)$.

(2) x attains the infimum in Eq. (9.19).

(3) t attains the supremum in Eq. (9.20).

(b) Assume that for each $t \in \Re$ the infimum in equation (9.19) is uniquely attained by a scalar denoted $x(t)$. Then q is real-valued and differentiable, and we have

$$\nabla q(t) = -x(t), \qquad \forall\, t \in \Re.$$

Proof: (a) Figure 9.7 proves Eq. (9.20). From Eqs. (9.19) and (9.20), we see that statements (2) and (3) are equivalent with statement (1). Therefore, (2) and (3) are also equivalent.

(b) Since the infimum in equation (9.19) is attained for each t, q is a real-valued concave function. Let us fix t, and let $q^+(t)$ and $q^-(t)$ be the right and left directional derivatives of q, respectively, at t. A scalar y satisfies

$$q^+(t) \leq y \leq q^-(t), \tag{9.21}$$

if and only if t maximizes $q(\xi) - \xi y$ over all ξ, which is true [by the equivalence of (2) and (3)] if and only if $-y$ attains the minimum in Eq. (9.19).

In view of our assumption that this minimum is (the unique) scalar $x(t)$, it follows that $-x(t)$ is the unique scalar y satisfying Eq. (9.21), and must be equal to the gradient $\nabla q(t)$. **Q.E.D.**

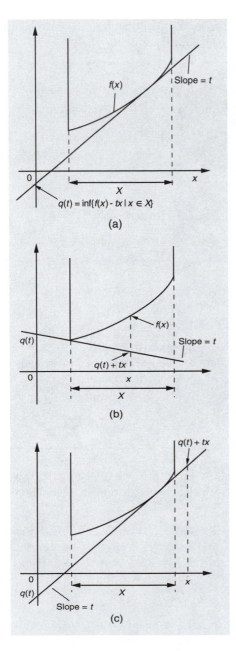

Figure 9.7: A geometrical proof that

$$\sup_t \left\{ q(t) + tx \right\}$$

is equal to $f(x)$ if $x \in X$ and is equal to ∞ otherwise [cf. Eq. (9.20)]. Our proof assumes that the reader is familiar with basic facts about hyperplanes and support properties of convex sets in two dimensions.

For any t, $q(t)$ is obtained by constructing a supporting line with slope t to the convex set

$$\left\{ (x,\gamma) \mid x \in X, \ f(x) \leq \gamma \right\},$$

(the epigraph of f), and by obtaining the point where this line intercepts the vertical axis.

For a given $x \in X$, $q(t) + tx$ is obtained by intercepting the vertical line passing through $\big(x, f(x)\big)$ with the line of slope t that supports the epigraph of f. This point of intercept cannot lie higher than $f(x)$, and with proper choice of t lies exactly at $f(x)$. This proves that

$$\sup_t \left\{ q(t) + tx \right\} = f(x)$$

for $x \in X$.

For $x \notin X$, the construction given shows that with proper choice of t, the value of $q(t) + tx$ can be made arbitrarily large. Hence

$$\sup_t \left\{ q(t) + tx \right\} = \infty.$$

The figure also illustrates the equivalence of statements (1)-(3) in Prop. 9.6.

Assume now that in the convex separable network problem, the functions f_{ij} and the intervals X_{ij} are such that the infimum in the equation

$$q_{ij}(t_{ij}) = \inf_{x_{ij} \in X_{ij}} \{ f_{ij}(x_{ij}) - t_{ij}x_{ij} \}$$

is uniquely attained for each scalar t_{ij}. This is true for example if each X_{ij} is compact and f_{ij} is strictly convex over X_{ij}. Let us derive the gradient of the dual function at a price vector p. We have for all $i \in \mathcal{N}$

$$
\begin{aligned}
\frac{\partial q(p)}{\partial p_i} &= \sum_{(m,n) \in \mathcal{A}} \frac{\partial q_{mn}(p_m - p_n)}{\partial p_i} + s_i \\
&= - \sum_{\{j | (j,i) \in \mathcal{A}\}} \nabla q_{ji}(p_j - p_i) + \sum_{\{j | (i,j) \in \mathcal{A}\}} \nabla q_{ij}(p_i - p_j) + s_i \quad (9.22) \\
&= \sum_{\{j | (j,i) \in \mathcal{A}\}} x_{ji}(p) - \sum_{\{j | (i,j) \in \mathcal{A}\}} x_{ij}(p) + s_i,
\end{aligned}
$$

where the last equality holds because by Prop. 9.6, the derivatives $\nabla q_{ij}(p_i - p_j)$ are equal to minus the unique arc flows $x_{ij}(p)$ satisfying CS together with p. The last expression in Eq. (9.22) can be recognized as the *surplus* of node i. Thus we obtain

$$\frac{\partial q(p)}{\partial p_i} = g_i(p),$$

where

$$
\begin{aligned}
g_i(p) &= \text{Surplus of node } i \text{ corresponding to the unique flow vector } x(p) \\
&\quad \text{satisfying CS together with } p \\
&= \sum_{\{j | (j,i) \in \mathcal{A}\}} x_{ji}(p) - \sum_{\{j | (i,j) \in \mathcal{A}\}} x_{ij}(p) + s_i.
\end{aligned}
$$

$$(9.23)$$

Example 9.4. Quadratic Cost Network Problems

Consider the case where each arc cost function f_{ij} is a positive definite quadratic and there are no arc flow bounds. This is the problem

$$\text{minimize} \quad \sum_{(i,j) \in \mathcal{A}} \left(a_{ij}x_{ij} + \frac{1}{2}w_{ij}x_{ij}^2 \right)$$

$$\text{subject to} \quad \sum_{\{j | (i,j) \in \mathcal{A}\}} x_{ij} - \sum_{\{j | (j,i) \in \mathcal{A}\}} x_{ji} = s_i, \qquad \forall \, i \in \mathcal{N},$$

where a_{ij}, w_{ij}, and s_i are given scalars, and $w_{ij} > 0$ for all arcs (i,j). The problem is interesting in its own right, but also arises as a subproblem in

Newton-like algorithms, which are based on quadratic approximations to a nonquadratic convex cost function.

The CS conditions here have the linear form

$$p_i - p_j = a_{ij} + w_{ij}x_{ij}, \qquad \forall\ (i,j) \in \mathcal{A},$$

so the unique flow vector $x(p)$ satisfying CS together with p is given by

$$x_{ij}(p) = \frac{p_i - p_j - a_{ij}}{w_{ij}}, \qquad \forall\ (i,j) \in \mathcal{A}.$$

As a result, the surplus/dual partial derivative $g_i(p)$ of Eq. (9.23) has the linear form

$$g_i(p) = \sum_{\{j|(j,i)\in\mathcal{A}\}} \frac{p_j - p_i - a_{ji}}{w_{ji}} - \sum_{\{j|(i,j)\in\mathcal{A}\}} \frac{p_i - p_j - a_{ij}}{w_{ij}} + s_i, \qquad (9.24)$$

which is particularly convenient for analytical and algorithmic purposes.

9.5 ALGORITHMS FOR DIFFERENTIABLE DUAL PROBLEMS

Dual problem differentiability has an important implication: it allows the use of standard iterative unconstrained minimization methods for solving the dual problem, such as steepest descent, and versions of the conjugate gradient method. As an example, for the strictly convex quadratic cost network problem (Example 9.4), the dual function is quadratic, so it can be maximized using the conjugate gradient method in a finite number of iterations (see nonlinear programming textbooks, such as Bertsekas [1995b]). For this, the dual function gradient is needed, and it can be calculated using the convenient expression (9.24).

Another interesting method that is well-suited to the special structure of the dual problem is the relaxation method, which is simply a coordinate ascent method applied to the maximization of the dual function. The relaxation method produces a sequence of price vectors each with a larger dual function value than the preceding one. Successive price vectors differ in only one coordinate/node price. At the start of the typical iteration of the relaxation method we have a price vector p. If the corresponding surplus/dual partial derivative $g_i(p)$ is zero for all nodes i, then p and the unique vector x satisfying CS together with p are dual and primal optimal, respectively, and the algorithm terminates. Otherwise the iteration proceeds as follows:

Relaxation Iteration

Choose any node i such that $g_i(p) \neq 0$ and change the ith coordinate of p, to obtain a vector $\bar{p}$ that maximizes q along that coordinate; that is,

$$g_i(\bar{p}) = 0.$$

There is a great deal of flexibility regarding the order in which nodes are taken up for relaxation. However, for the method to be valid, it is necessary to assume that every node is chosen as the node i in the relaxation iteration an infinite number of times.

An important point is that *when the primal problem is feasible*, the relaxation iteration is well defined, in the sense that *it is possible to adjust the price p_i as required, under very weak assumptions*. To see this, suppose that $g_i(p) > 0$ and that there does not exist a $\gamma > 0$ such that $g_i(p + \gamma e_i) = 0$, where e_i denotes the ith coordinate vector. Consider the price differentials $t_{ij}(\gamma)$, $(i,j) \in \mathcal{A}$ and $t_{ji}(\gamma)$, $(j,i) \in \mathcal{A}$, corresponding to the price vector $p + \gamma e_i$:

$$t_{ij}(\gamma) = p_i - p_j + \gamma, \qquad t_{ji}(\gamma) = p_j - p_i - \gamma.$$

We have $t_{ij}(\gamma) \to \infty$ and $t_{ji}(\gamma) \to -\infty$ as $\gamma \to \infty$. Therefore, the corresponding unique arc flows $x_{ij}(\gamma)$ and $x_{ji}(\gamma)$ satisfying CS together with $p + \gamma e_i$ tend to the corresponding endpoints

$$c_{ij} = \sup_{x_{ij} \in X_{ij}} x_{ij}, \qquad b_{ji} = \inf_{x_{ji} \in X_{ji}} x_{ji}$$

as $\gamma \to \infty$, and using the definition of $g_i(\cdot)$, it is seen that

$$\lim_{\gamma \to \infty} g_i(p + \gamma e_i) = \sum_{\{j \mid (j,i) \in \mathcal{A}\}} b_{ji} - \sum_{\{j \mid (i,j) \in \mathcal{A}\}} c_{ij} + s_i.$$

Let us assume now that either $-\infty < b_{mn}$ for all arcs $(m,n) \in \mathcal{A}$ or $c_{mn} < \infty$ for all arcs $(m,n) \in \mathcal{A}$, so that the sum $\infty - \infty$ does not arise in the above equation. Then, since $g_i(p + \gamma e_i) > 0$ for all $\gamma > 0$, we must have $b_{ji} > -\infty$ for all arcs (j,i) and $c_{ij} < \infty$ for all arcs (i,j). Therefore, there exists a finite value of γ such that $x_{ji}(\gamma) = b_{ji}$ for all arcs (j,i), and $x_{ij}(\gamma) = c_{ij}$ for all arcs (i,j). It follows that

$$\sum_{\{j \mid (j,i) \in \mathcal{A}\}} b_{ji} - \sum_{\{j \mid (i,j) \in \mathcal{A}\}} c_{ij} + s_i > 0,$$

which implies that the surplus of node i is positive for any feasible flow vector x, and contradicts the primal feasibility assumption. An analogous argument can be made for the case where $g_i(p) < 0$. Thus, for each pair (x, p) satisfying CS, the relaxation iteration produces a well-defined flow vector. For an example of what may happen if we have simultaneously $b_{ji} = -\infty$ for some arc (j, i) and $c_{ij} = \infty$ for some arc (i, j), the reader may wish to work out the relaxation iteration for the example of Fig. 9.4.

We mention also a generalization of the relaxation method, which allows the maximization along each coordinate to be inexact to some extent, and to be controlled by a given scalar $\delta \in [0, 1)$. Here the ith coordinate of p is changed to obtain a vector $\overline{p}$ such that

$$0 \leq g_i(\overline{p}) \leq \delta g_i(p) \qquad \text{if} \qquad g_i(p) > 0,$$

$$\delta g_i(p) \leq g_i(\overline{p}) \leq 0 \qquad \text{if} \qquad g_i(p) < 0.$$

With a judicious positive choice of δ, this variant of the relaxation method tends to be more efficient than the one where $\delta = 0$. Furthermore, it can seen that when $\delta > 0$ it is always possible to adjust the price p_i as required, without the assumption described in the preceding paragraph.

The relaxation method, with both exact and approximate maximization along each coordinate, has satisfactory convergence properties. Its convergence analysis is, however, quite intricate because of two complicating factors. The first is that the dual cost is differentiable and concave, but not necessarily strictly concave; general coordinate ascent methods require some form of strict concavity for showing convergence (see e.g., Bertsekas [1995b], Section 2.7). The second feature that complicates the analysis is that the level sets of the dual function are unbounded (if we change all prices by the same constant, the value of the dual function is unaffected). We thus omit this convergence analysis and we refer to the textbook by Bertsekas and Tsitsiklis [1989], which also contains a lot of material relating to the parallel implementation of the relaxation method. Another reference for the convergence analysis is the paper by Bertsekas, Hosein, and Tseng [1987], which in addition to the preceding relaxation method, develops another method that does not require dual function differentiability, and generalizes the relaxation method of Section 6.3 for the minimum cost flow problem.

Generally, experimentation has shown that the relaxation method has difficulty dealing with *ill-conditioning* in the dual cost function q, as manifested by a rate of change of the directional derivative of q along some directions that is much faster relative to other directions. Ill-conditioning is a well-known cause of slow convergence in (differentiable) nonlinear programming algorithms, and coordinate ascent methods are susceptible to it. The ϵ-relaxation method to be discussed in the next section, operates similar to the relaxation method, but has two advantages: it can be applied in the case of a nondifferentiable dual cost function, and (based on practical experience) it can deal much better with ill-conditioning.

9.6 AUCTION ALGORITHMS

In this section we develop auction algorithms for the separable convex network flow problem. Based on complexity analysis and experimentation, these algorithms are very efficient. With proper implementation, they appear to be minimally affected by ill-conditioning in the dual problem. We first develop an appropriate extension of the notion of ϵ-complementary slackness (ϵ-CS for short) that was introduced in Chapter 7. We then derive and analyze generalizations of the ϵ-relaxation and auction/sequential shortest path methods of Sections 7.4 and 7.5. Throughout this section, *we assume that the problem is feasible.*

Definition 9.3: Given $\epsilon \geq 0$, a flow-price vector pair (x, p) is said to satisfy ϵ-CS if for all arcs (i, j), we have $x_{ij} \in X_{ij}$ and

$$ f_{ij}^-(x_{ij}) - \epsilon \leq p_i - p_j \leq f_{ij}^+(x_{ij}) + \epsilon. $$

Figure 9.8 illustrates the definition of ϵ-CS. The intuition behind the ϵ-CS conditions is that a feasible flow-price pair is "approximately" primal and dual optimal if the ϵ-CS conditions are satisfied. This intuition is quantified in the following proposition:

Proposition 9.7: Let $\big(x(\epsilon), p(\epsilon)\big)$ be a flow-price pair satisfying ϵ-CS such that $x(\epsilon)$ is feasible, and let $\xi(\epsilon)$ be any flow vector satisfying CS together with $p(\epsilon)$ [note that $\xi(\epsilon)$ need not satisfy the conservation of flow constraints].

(a)
$$ 0 \leq f\big(x(\epsilon)\big) - q\big(p(\epsilon)\big) \leq \epsilon \sum_{(i,j) \in \mathcal{A}} |x_{ij}(\epsilon) - \xi_{ij}(\epsilon)|. \qquad (9.25) $$

(b) Assume that all the dual arc cost functions q_{ij} are real-valued. Then
$$ \lim_{\epsilon \to 0} \big(f\big(x(\epsilon)\big) - q\big(p(\epsilon)\big)\big) = 0. $$

Proof: (a) To simplify notation, let us replace $x(\epsilon)$, $p(\epsilon)$, and $\xi(\epsilon)$, by x, p, and ξ, respectively. Denote $t_{ij} = p_i - p_j$. Since ξ and p satisfy CS, we have

$$ f_{ij}(x_{ij}) = \xi_{ij} t_{ij} + q_{ij}(t_{ij}), \qquad \forall \ (i, j) \in \mathcal{A}. $$

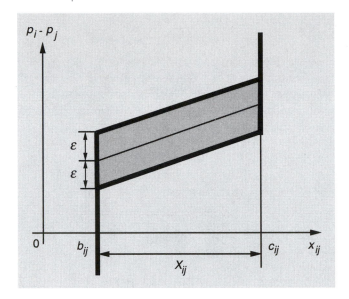

Figure 9.8: A visualization of the ϵ-CS conditions in terms of a "cylinder" around the characteristic curve. The shaded area represents flow-price differential pairs that satisfy the ϵ-CS conditions. In this figure, f_{ij} is a quadratic function whose curvature is the slope shown, and the arc flow range X_{ij} is the interval $[b_{ij}, c_{ij}]$ [cf. Fig. 9.1(b)].

Take an arc (i, j) such that $x_{ij} \geq \xi_{ij}$. Then

$$f_{ij}(x_{ij}) + (\xi_{ij} - x_{ij})f_{ij}^-(x_{ij}) \leq f_{ij}(\xi_{ij}) = \xi_{ij}t_{ij} + q_{ij}(t_{ij}).$$

Hence

$$f_{ij}(x_{ij}) - q_{ij}(t_{ij}) \leq (x_{ij} - \xi_{ij})\big(f_{ij}^-(x_{ij}) - t_{ij}\big) + x_{ij}t_{ij} \leq |x_{ij} - \xi_{ij}|\epsilon + x_{ij}t_{ij},$$

where the second inequality follows from ϵ-CS. This inequality is similarly obtained when $x_{ij} \leq \xi_{ij}$, so we have

$$f_{ij}(x_{ij}) - q_{ij}(t_{ij}) \leq |x_{ij} - \xi_{ij}|\epsilon + x_{ij}t_{ij}, \qquad \forall\, (i,j) \in \mathcal{A}.$$

From the definition of q_{ij}, we also have

$$x_{ij}t_{ij} \leq f_{ij}(x_{ij}) - q_{ij}(t_{ij}), \qquad \forall\, (i,j) \in \mathcal{A}.$$

By combining these two inequalities and adding over all arcs, we obtain

$$\sum_{(i,j)\in\mathcal{A}} x_{ij}t_{ij} \leq \sum_{(i,j)\in\mathcal{A}} \big(f_{ij}(x_{ij}) - q_{ij}(t_{ij})\big) \leq \epsilon \sum_{(i,j)\in\mathcal{A}} |x_{ij} - \xi_{ij}| + \sum_{(i,j)\in\mathcal{A}} x_{ij}t_{ij}.$$

Since x is feasible, we have

$$\sum_{(i,j)\in\mathcal{A}} x_{ij}t_{ij} = \sum_{i\in\mathcal{N}} p_i \left(\sum_{\{j|(i,j)\in\mathcal{A}\}} x_{ij} - \sum_{\{j|(j,i)\in\mathcal{A}\}} x_{ji} \right) = \sum_{i\in\mathcal{N}} p_i s_i.$$

Combining the last two relations, we obtain

$$0 \leq \sum_{(i,j)\in\mathcal{A}} \left(f_{ij}(x_{ij}) - q_{ij}(t_{ij}) \right) - \sum_{i\in\mathcal{N}} p_i s_i \leq \epsilon \sum_{(i,j)\in\mathcal{A}} |x_{ij} - \xi_{ij}|.$$

Using the definitions of $f(x)$ and $q(p)$, this relation is seen to be equivalent to the desired Eq. (9.25).

(b) We first argue by contradiction that $x(\epsilon)$ remains bounded as $\epsilon \to \infty$. Indeed, if this is not so, then since $x(\epsilon)$ is feasible for all ϵ, there exists a cycle C and a sequence ϵ_k converging to 0 such that $x_{ij}(\epsilon_k) \to \infty$ for all $(i,j) \in C^+$ and $x_{ij}(\epsilon_k) \to -\infty$ for all $(i,j) \in C^-$. Since all q_{ij} are assumed real-valued, we must have

$$\lim_{\xi\to\infty} f_{ij}^-(\xi) = \infty, \qquad \forall\, (i,j) \in C^+,$$

$$\lim_{\xi\to-\infty} f_{ij}^+(\xi) = -\infty, \qquad \forall\, (i,j) \in C^+.$$

This implies that for k sufficiently large,

$$t_{ij}(\epsilon_k) \geq f_{ij}^-\left(x_{ij}(\epsilon_k)\right) - \epsilon_k > t_{ij}(\epsilon_0), \qquad \forall\, (i,j) \in C^+, \tag{9.26}$$

$$t_{ij}(\epsilon_k) \leq f_{ij}^+\left(x_{ij}(\epsilon_k)\right) - \epsilon_k < t_{ij}(\epsilon_0), \qquad \forall\, (i,j) \in C^-. \tag{9.27}$$

On the other hand, since $t_{ij}(\epsilon_k) = p_i(\epsilon_k) - p_j(\epsilon_k)$, we have

$$\sum_{(i,j)\in C^+} t_{ij}(\epsilon_k) - \sum_{(i,j)\in C^-} t_{ij}(\epsilon_k) = 0, \qquad \forall\, k,$$

which contradicts Eqs. (9.26) and (9.27). Therefore $x(\epsilon)$ is bounded as $\epsilon \to 0$.

We will now show that $\xi_{ij}(\epsilon) - x_{ij}(\epsilon)$ is bounded for all arcs (i,j) as $\epsilon \to 0$, where $\xi(\epsilon)$ is any flow vector satisfying CS together with $p(\epsilon)$, i.e., for all arcs (i,j), we have

$$\xi_{ij}(\epsilon) \in X_{ij}, \qquad f_{ij}^-\left(\xi_{ij}(\epsilon)\right) \leq t_{ij}(\epsilon) \leq f_{ij}^+\left(\xi_{ij}(\epsilon)\right).$$

If the interval X_{ij} is unbounded above, we have $f_{ij}^-(\xi) \to \infty$ as $\xi \to \infty$. Since $x_{ij}(\epsilon)$ is bounded, we have that $t_{ij}(\epsilon)$ is bounded from above, which in turn implies that $\xi_{ij}(\epsilon)$ is bounded from above. Similarly, we can argue that $\xi_{ij}(\epsilon)$ is bounded from below. Therefore, $\xi_{ij}(\epsilon)$ is bounded for all arcs (i, j) as $\epsilon \to 0$, and it follows that $|x_{ij}(\epsilon) - \xi_{ij}(\epsilon)|$ is also bounded for all arcs (i, j) as $\epsilon \to 0$. This, together with Eq. (9.25), which was shown earlier, completes the proof.   **Q.E.D.**

Proposition 9.7 does not tell us how small ϵ must be to achieve a certain tolerance for the sum $f(x(\epsilon)) - q(p(\epsilon))$. On the other hand, if the the lengths of the intervals X_{ij} are bounded by some constant $L > 0$, then from Eq. (9.25), we obtain

$$f(x(\epsilon)) - q(p(\epsilon)) \leq \epsilon AL,$$

where A is the number of arcs.

For the remainder of this section, *we assume that the dual arc cost functions q_{ij} are real-valued*, as in Prop. 9.7(b). This is true in particular if the intervals X_{ij} are compact, or if $\lim_{x_{ij} \to \infty} f^+(x_{ij}) = \infty$ and $\lim_{x_{ij} \to -\infty} f^-(x_{ij}) = -\infty$ for all arcs (i, j).

We introduce a *generic auction algorithm*, whereby x and p are alternately adjusted so as to drive the surpluses

$$g_i = \sum_{\{j|(j,i)\in\mathcal{A}\}} x_{ji} - \sum_{\{j|(i,j)\in\mathcal{A}\}} x_{ij} + s_i$$

to zero while maintaining ϵ-CS at all iterations. The only additional requirements are that nodes with nonnegative surplus continue to have nonnegative surplus and that price changes are effected by increasing the price of a node with positive surplus by the maximum amount possible. We then consider two special cases of this generic algorithm. The first is the ϵ-relaxation method, which generalizes the method of Section 7.4; the second is the auction/sequential shortest path algorithm, which generalizes the method of Section 7.5.

Given a flow-price vector pair (x, p) satisfying ϵ-CS, an iteration of the generic auction algorithm updates (x, p) as follows:

Iteration of the Generic Auction Algorithm

If there is no node with positive surplus, terminate the algorithm. Otherwise, perform one of the following two operations:

(a) **(Flow change)** Adjust the flow vector x in a way that ϵ-CS is maintained and all nodes with nonnegative surplus continue to have nonnegative surplus. (Here p is unchanged.)

(b) **(Price rise)** Increase the price p_i of some node i with positive surplus by the maximum amount that maintains ϵ-CS. (Here x and all other coordinates of p are unchanged.)

Upon termination of the generic auction algorithm, the flow-price vector pair (x, p) satisfies ϵ-CS and all nodes have surplus that is non-positive (and is equal to 0 since the problem is assumed to be feasible). Thus, the validity of the method rests on whether it terminates finitely. The following proposition shows that the total number of price rises is finite under a suitable assumption.

Proposition 9.8: Let r be any nonnegative scalar such that the initial price vector p^0 for the generic auction algorithm satisfies $r\epsilon$-CS together with some feasible flow vector x^0. Also, assume that each price rise on a node increases the price of that node by at least $\beta\epsilon$, for some fixed $\beta \in (0, 1)$. Then, the method performs at most $(r + 1)(N - 1)/\beta$ price rises on each node.

Proof: Consider the pair (x, p) at the beginning of an iteration of the generic method. Since the surplus vector $g = (g_1, \ldots, g_N)$ is not zero, and the flow vector x^0 is feasible, we conclude that for each node s with $g_s > 0$ there exists a node t with $g_t < 0$ and a simple path P from t to s such that:

$$x_{ij} > x_{ij}^0, \qquad \forall \ (i, j) \in P^+, \tag{9.28}$$

$$x_{ij} < x_{ij}^0, \qquad \forall \ (i, j) \in P^-, \tag{9.29}$$

where P^+ is the set of forward arcs of P and P^- is the set of backward arcs of P. [This can be seen from the conformal realization theorem (Prop. 1.1) as follows. For the flow vector $x - x^0$, the divergence of node t is $-g_t > 0$ and the divergence of node s is $-g_s < 0$. Hence, by the conformal realization theorem, there is a simple path P from t to s that conforms to the flow $x - x^0$, that is, $x_{ij} - x_{ij}^0 > 0$ for all $(i, j) \in P^+$ and $x_{ij} - x_{ij}^0 < 0$ for all $(i, j) \in P^-$.]

From Eqs. (9.28) and (9.29), and the convexity of the functions f_{ij} for all $(i, j) \in \mathcal{A}$, we have

$$f_{ij}^-(x_{ij}) \geq f_{ij}^+(x_{ij}^0), \qquad \forall \ (i, j) \in P^+, \tag{9.30}$$

$$f_{ij}^+(x_{ij}) \leq f_{ij}^-(x_{ij}^0), \qquad \forall \ (i, j) \in P^-. \tag{9.31}$$

Since the pair (x, p) satisfies ϵ-CS, we also have that

$$p_i - p_j \in [f_{ij}^-(x_{ij}) - \epsilon, f_{ij}^+(x_{ij}) + \epsilon], \qquad \forall \ (i, j) \in \mathcal{A}. \tag{9.32}$$

Similarly, since the pair (x^0, p^0) satisfies $r\epsilon$-CS, we have

$$p_i^0 - p_j^0 \in [f_{ij}^-(x_{ij}^0) - r\epsilon, f_{ij}^+(x_{ij}^0) + r\epsilon], \qquad \forall \ (i, j) \in \mathcal{A}. \tag{9.33}$$

Combining Eqs. (9.30), (9.32), and (9.33), we obtain for all $(i,j) \in P^+$,

$$p_i - p_j \geq f_{ij}^-(x_{ij}) - \epsilon \geq f_{ij}^+(x_{ij}^0) - \epsilon \geq p_i^0 - p_j^0 - (r+1)\epsilon.$$

Similarly, combining Eqs. (9.31)-(9.33), we obtain for all $(i,j) \in P^-$,

$$p_i - p_j \leq p_i^0 - p_j^0 + (r+1)\epsilon.$$

Applying the above inequalities for all arcs of the path P, we get

$$p_t - p_s \geq p_t^0 - p_s^0 - (r+1)|P|\epsilon, \qquad (9.34)$$

where $|P|$ denotes the number of arcs of the path P. Since only nodes with positive surplus can change their prices and nodes with nonnegative surplus continue to have nonnegative surplus, it follows that if a node has negative surplus at some time, then its price is unchanged from the beginning of the method until that time. Thus $p_t = p_t^0$. Since the path is simple, we also have that $|P| \leq N - 1$. Therefore, Eq. (9.34) yields

$$p_s - p_s^0 \leq (r+1)|P|\epsilon \leq (r+1)(N-1)\epsilon. \qquad (9.35)$$

Since only nodes with positive surplus can increase their prices and, by assumption, each price rise increment is at least $\beta\epsilon$, we conclude from Eq. (9.35) that the total number of price rises that can be performed for node s is at most $(r+1)(N-1)/\beta$. **Q.E.D.**

The preceding proposition shows that the bound on the number of price rises is independent of the cost functions, but depends only on

$$r^0 = \min \big\{ r \in [0,\infty) \mid (x^0, p^0) \text{ satisfies } r\epsilon\text{-CS}$$
$$\text{for some feasible flow vector } x^0 \big\},$$

which is the minimum multiplicity of ϵ with which CS is violated by the initial price vector together with some feasible flow vector. Note that r^0 is well defined for any p^0 because, for all r sufficiently large, $r\epsilon$-CS is satisfied by p^0 and any feasible flow vector.

To ensure that the number of flow changes between successive price rises is finite and that each price rise is at least $\beta\epsilon$, we need to further specify how the price rises and flow changes should be effected. We thus proceed to introduce the key mechanisms for achieving this.

For any $\epsilon > 0$, any $\beta \in (0,1)$, and any flow-price vector pair (x,p) satisfying ϵ-CS, we define for each node $i \in \mathcal{N}$ its *candidate list* as the union of the following two sets of arcs

$$L^+(i) = \big\{ (i,j) \in \mathcal{A} \mid (1-\beta)\epsilon < p_i - p_j - f_{ij}^+(x_{ij}) \leq \epsilon \big\}, \qquad (9.36)$$

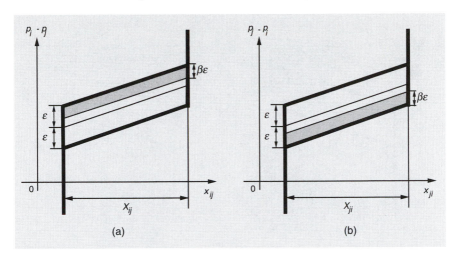

Figure 9.9: Visualization of the conditions satisfied by a candidate-list arc. The shaded area represents flow-price differential pairs corresponding to a candidate-list arc $(i, j) \in L^+(i)$ in figure (a), and to a candidate-list arc $(j, i) \in L^-(i)$ in figure (b). Note that at the right endpoint of X_{ij} the right derivative f_{ij}^+ is ∞, so at the right endpoint, $L^+(i)$ is empty. Similarly, at the left endpoint, $L^-(i)$ is empty.

$$L^-(i) = \left\{ (j, i) \in \mathcal{A} \mid -(1 - \beta)\epsilon > p_j - p_i - f_{ji}^-(x_{ji}) \geq -\epsilon \right\}. \qquad (9.37)$$

The arcs of the candidate list can be visualized in terms of the characteristic curves

$$\Gamma_{ij} = \left\{ (x_{ij}, t_{ij}) \in \Re^2 \mid f_{ij}^-(x_{ij}) \leq t_{ij} \leq f_{ij}^+(x_{ij}) \right\}.$$

Thus, (i, j) is in the candidate list of i (respectively, j) if $(x_{ij}, p_i - p_j)$ belongs to the "strip" at height between $(1 - \beta)\epsilon$ and ϵ above (respectively, below) Γ_{ij} (see Fig. 9.9).

For each arc (i, j) [respectively, (j, i)] in the candidate list of i, the supremum of δ for which

$$p_i - p_j \geq f_{ij}^+(x_{ij} + \delta)$$

[respectively, $p_j - p_i \leq f_{ji}^-(x_{ji} - \delta)$] is called the *flow margin* of the arc (see Fig. 9.10). An important fact, shown below, is that the flow margins of these arcs are always positive.

Proposition 9.9: All arcs in the candidate list of a node have positive flow margins.

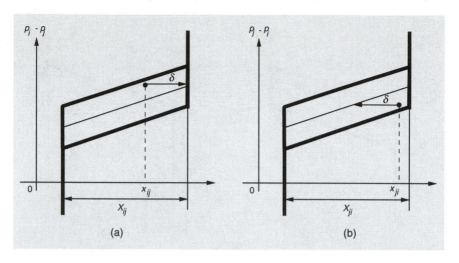

Figure 9.10: Illustration of the flow margin δ of a candidate-list arc $(i,j) \in L^+(i)$ in figure (a), and to a candidate-list arc $(j,i) \in L^-(i)$ in figure (b).

Proof: Assume that for an arc $(i,j) \in \mathcal{A}$ the flow margin is not positive; that is, we have

$$p_i - p_j < f^+_{ij}(x_{ij} + \delta), \quad \forall\, \delta > 0.$$

Since the function f^+_{ij} is right continuous, this yields

$$p_i - p_j \le \lim_{\delta \downarrow 0} f^+_{ij}(x_{ij} + \delta) = f^+_{ij}(x_{ij}),$$

and thus, based on the definition of Eq. (9.36), (i,j) cannot be in the candidate list of node i. A similar argument shows that an arc $(j,i) \in \mathcal{A}$ such that

$$p_j - p_i > f^-_{ji}(x_{ji} - \delta), \quad \forall\, \delta > 0,$$

cannot be in the candidate list of node i.   **Q.E.D.**

The method that we will use for flow changes is to decrease the surplus of a node with positive surplus by changing the flow of candidate-list arcs. This can be done either one arc at a time, as in the case of the ϵ-relaxation method of Section 7.4, or one path of arcs at a time, as in the case of the auction/sequential-shortest-path algorithm of Section 7.5. When the candidate list of the node is empty, we perform a price rise on the node. An important fact, shown below, is that the price rise increment for a node with empty candidate list is at least $\beta\epsilon$.

Proposition 9.10: If we perform a price rise on a node whose candidate list is empty, then the price of that node will increase by at least $\beta\epsilon$.

Proof: If the candidate list of a node i is empty, then for every arc $(i,j) \in \mathcal{A}$ we have $p_i - p_j - f_{ij}^+(x_{ij}) \le (1 - \beta)\epsilon$, and for every arc $(j,i) \in \mathcal{A}$ we have $p_j - p_i - f_{ji}^-(x_{ji}) \ge -(1 - \beta)\epsilon$. This implies that the numbers

$$p_j - p_i + f_{ij}^+(x_{ij}) + \epsilon, \qquad \forall\, (i,j) \in \mathcal{A},$$

$$p_j - p_i - f_{ji}^-(x_{ji}) + \epsilon, \qquad \forall\, (j,i) \in \mathcal{A},$$

are all greater than or equal to $\beta\epsilon$. Since a price rise on i adds to p_i the minimum of all these numbers, the result follows.   **Q.E.D.**

For any $\epsilon > 0$, any $\beta \in (0,1)$, and any flow-price vector pair (x,p) satisfying ϵ-CS, let us consider the arc set $\mathcal{A}^*$ that contains all candidate list arcs oriented in the direction of flow change. In particular, for each arc (i,j) in the forward portion $L^+(i)$ of the candidate list of a node i, we introduce an arc (i,j) in $\mathcal{A}^*$ and for each arc (j,i) in the backward portion $L^-(i)$ of the candidate list of node i, we introduce an arc (i,j) in $\mathcal{A}^*$ (thus the direction of the latter arc is reversed). The set of nodes $\mathcal{N}$ and the set $\mathcal{A}^*$ define the *admissible graph* $\mathcal{G}^* = (\mathcal{N}, \mathcal{A}^*)$. We will consider methods that keep $\mathcal{G}^*$ acyclic at all iterations. Intuitively, because we move flow in the direction of the arcs in $\mathcal{G}^*$, keeping $\mathcal{G}^*$ acyclic helps to limit the number of flow changes between price rises, as we have seen in Section 7.4. To ensure that initially the admissible graph is acyclic, one possibility is to choose, for any initial price vector p^0, the initial flow vector x^0 such that (x^0, p^0) satisfies 0-CS, that is,

$$f_{ij}^-(x_{ij}^0) \le p_i^0 - p_j^0 \le f_{ij}^+(x_{ij}^0), \qquad \forall\, (i,j) \in \mathcal{A}. \tag{9.38}$$

With this choice, ϵ-CS is satisfied by (x^0, p^0) for any $\epsilon > 0$, and the initial admissible graph is empty and thus acyclic.

In the next two sections, we will study two specializations of the generic auction algorithm. These methods perform flow changes by moving flow out of nodes with positive surplus along candidate-list arcs and they perform price rises only on nodes with empty candidate lists. In addition, they keep the admissible graph acyclic at all iterations and have favorable complexity bounds.

9.6.1   The ϵ-Relaxation Method

For fixed $\epsilon > 0$ and $\beta \in (0,1)$, and a given flow-price vector pair (x,p) satisfying ϵ-CS, an iteration of the ϵ-relaxation method updates (x,p) as follows:

Iteration of the ϵ-Relaxation Method

Step 1: Select a node i with positive surplus g_i; if no such node exists, terminate the method.

Step 2: (δ-**Flow push**) If the candidate list of i is empty, go to Step 3. Otherwise, choose an arc from the candidate list of i, and let

$$\delta = \min\{g_i, \text{flow margin of the chosen arc}\}.$$

Increase x_{ij} by δ if (i, j) is the arc, or decrease x_{ji} by δ if (j, i) is the arc. If as a result the surplus of i becomes zero, go to the next iteration; otherwise, go to Step 2.

Step 3: (**Price rise**) Increase the price p_i by the maximum amount that maintains ϵ-CS. Go to the next iteration.

To see that the ϵ-relaxation method is a specialization of the generic auction method of Section 2, note that Step 3 is a price rise on node i and that Step 2 adjusts the flows in such a way that ϵ-CS is maintained and nodes with nonnegative surplus continue to have nonnegative surplus for all subsequent iterations. The reason for the latter is that when iterating at a node i, a flow push cannot make the surplus of i negative (by the choice of δ in Step 2), and cannot decrease the surplus of neighboring nodes. Furthermore, the ϵ-relaxation method performs a price rise only on nodes with empty candidate list. Then, by Prop. 9.10, each price rise increment is at least $\beta\epsilon$ and, by Prop. 9.8, the number of price rises (i.e., Step 3) on each node is at most $(r + 1)(N - 1)/\beta$, where r is any nonnegative scalar such that the initial price vector satisfies $r\epsilon$-CS together with some feasible flow vector. Thus, to prove finite termination of the ϵ-relaxation method, it suffices to show that the number of flow pushes (i.e., Step 2) performed between successive price rises is finite. We show this by first showing that the method maintains the acyclicity of the admissible graph.

Proposition 9.11: If the admissible graph is initially acyclic, then it remains acyclic at all iterations of the ϵ-relaxation method.

Proof: We use induction. Initially, the admissible graph $\mathcal{G}^*$ is acyclic by assumption. Assume that $\mathcal{G}^*$ remains acyclic for all subsequent iterations up to the mth iteration for some m. We will prove that after the mth iteration $\mathcal{G}^*$ remains acyclic. Clearly, after a flow push in Step 2, the admissible graph remains acyclic, since it either remains unchanged, or some arcs are deleted from it. Thus we only have to prove that after a price rise on a node i, no cycle involving i is created. We note that, after a price rise on node i, all incident arcs to i in the admissible graph at the start of the mth iteration are deleted and new arcs incident to i are added. We claim that i cannot have any incoming arcs that belong to the admissible graph. To see this, note that just before a price rise on node i, we have

$$p_j - p_i - f_{ji}^+(x_{ji}) \le \epsilon, \qquad \forall \, (j, i) \in \mathcal{A},$$

and since each price rise increment is at least $\beta\epsilon$, we must have

$$p_j - p_i - f_{ji}^+(x_{ji}) \le (1 - \beta)\epsilon, \qquad \forall \, (j, i) \in \mathcal{A},$$

after the price rise. Then, by Eq. (9.36), (j, i) cannot be in the candidate list of node j. By a similar argument, we have that (i, j) cannot be in the candidate list of j for all $(i, j) \in \mathcal{A}$. Thus, after a price rise on node i, we see that i cannot have any incoming arcs belonging to the admissible graph, so no cycle involving i can be created. **Q.E.D.**

We say that a node i is a *predecessor* of a node j in the admissible graph $\mathcal{G}^*$ if a directed path (i.e., a path having no backward arc) from i to j exists in $\mathcal{G}^*$. Node j is then called a *successor* of i. Observe that, in the ϵ-relaxation method, flow is pushed towards the successors of a node and if $\mathcal{G}^*$ is acyclic, flow cannot be pushed from a node to any of its predecessors. A δ-flow push along an arc in $\mathcal{A}$ is said to be *saturating* if the flow increment δ is equal to the flow margin of the arc. By our choice of δ in the ϵ-relaxation method, a nonsaturating flow push always exhausts (i.e., sets to zero) the surplus of the starting node of the arc. Then, by using Prop. 9.11, we obtain the following result.

Proposition 9.12: If the admissible graph is initially acyclic, then the number of flow pushes between two successive price rises (not necessarily at the same node) performed by the ϵ-relaxation method is finite. Furthermore, the algorithm terminates with a flow-price pair satisfying ϵ-CS.

Proof: We observe that a saturating flow push along an arc removes the arc from the admissible graph, while a nonsaturating flow push does not add a new arc to the admissible graph. Thus the number of saturating flow pushes that can be performed between successive price rises is at most A. It will thus suffice to show that the number of nonsaturating flow pushes that can be performed between saturating flow pushes is finite. Assume the contrary, that is, there is an infinite sequence of successive nonsaturating flow pushes, with no intervening saturating flow push. Then the admissible graph remains fixed throughout this sequence. Furthermore, the surplus of some node i_0 must be exhausted infinitely often during this sequence. This can happen only if the surplus of some predecessor i_1 of i_0 is exhausted infinitely often during the sequence. Continuing in this manner, we construct an infinite sequence of predecessor nodes $\{i_k\}$. Thus, some node in this sequence must be repeated, which is a contradiction since the admissible graph is acyclic. Hence, the number of flow pushes between two successive price rises is finite. Since the number of price rises is finite (cf. Props. 9.8 and 9.10), termination of the algorithm follows.   **Q.E.D.**

By refining the proof of Prop. 9.12, we can further show that the number of flow pushes between successive price rises is at most $(N+1)A$, from which a complexity bound for the ϵ-relaxation method may be readily derived. However, we will focus on a special implementation of the method for which we will derive a more favorable running time.

Efficient Implementation

Let us consider a generalization of the sweep implementation, discussed in Section 7.4. This implementation defines the order in which nodes are selected for an ϵ-relaxation iteration. In particular, the nodes are maintained in a linked list T, which is traversed from the first to the last element. The order of the nodes in the list is consistent with the successor order implied by the admissible graph; that is, if a node j is a successor of a node i, then j must appear after i in the list. If the initial admissible graph is empty, as is the case with the initialization of Eq. (9.38), the initial list is arbitrary. Otherwise, the initial list must be consistent with the successor order of the initial admissible graph. The list is updated in a way that maintains the consistency with the successor order. In particular, let i be the node chosen in Step 1 of the iteration, and let N_i be the subset of nodes of T that are after i in T. If the price of i changes in this iteration, then node i is removed from its position in T and placed in the first position of T. The node chosen in the next iteration, if N_i is nonempty, is the node $i' \in N_i$ with positive surplus which ranks highest in T. Otherwise, the positive surplus node ranking highest in T is chosen. It can be seen as in Section 7.4 that, with this rule of repositioning the nodes following a price change, the list order is consistent with the successor order implied by the admissible graph at all iterations.

The next proposition gives a bound on the number of flow pushes made by the sweep implementation of the ϵ-relaxation method. This result is based on the observations that (a) between successive saturating flow pushes on an arc, there is at least one price rise performed on one of the end nodes of the arc, and (b) between successive price rises (not necessarily at the same node), the number of nonsaturating flow pushes is at most N. The proof parallels the one given in Section 7.4, and will be omitted.

Proposition 9.13: Let r be any nonnegative scalar such that the initial price vector for the sweep implementation of the ϵ-relaxation method satisfies $r\epsilon$-CS together with some feasible flow vector. Then, the number of price rises on each node, the number of saturating flow pushes, and the number of nonsaturating flow pushes up to termination of the method are $O(rN)$, $O(rNA)$, and $O(rN^3)$, respectively.

We now derive the running time for the sweep implementation of the ϵ-relaxation method. The dominant computational requirements are:

(1) The computation required for price rises.

(2) The computation required for saturating flow pushes.

(3) The computation required for nonsaturating flow pushes.

In contrast to the linear cost case, we cannot express the running time in terms of the size of the problem data since the latter is not well defined for convex cost functions. Instead, we introduce a set of simple operations performed by the ϵ-relaxation method, and we estimate the number of these operations. In particular, in addition to the usual arithmetic operations with real numbers, we consider the following operations:

(a) Given the flow x_{ij} of an arc (i, j), calculate the cost $f_{ij}(x_{ij})$, the left derivative $f_{ij}^-(x_{ij})$, and the right derivative $f_{ij}^+(x_{ij})$.

(b) Given the price differential $t_{ij} = p_i - p_j$ of an arc (i, j), calculate $\sup\{\xi \mid f_{ij}^+(\xi) \leq t_{ij}\}$ and $\inf\{\xi \mid f_{ij}^-(\xi) \geq t_{ij}\}$.

Operation (a) is needed to compute the candidate list of a node and a price increase increment; operation (b) is needed to compute the flow margin of an arc and the flow initialization of Eq. (9.38). Complexity will thus be measured in terms of the total number of operations performed by the method, as in the following proposition, which follows from Prop. 9.13.

Proposition 9.14: Let r be any nonnegative scalar such that the initial price vector for the sweep implementation of the ϵ-relaxation method satisfies $r\epsilon$-CS together with some feasible flow vector. Then, the method requires $O(rN^3)$ operations up to termination.

The theoretical and the practical performance of the ϵ-relaxation method can be further improved by ϵ-*scaling*, whereby we apply the ϵ-relaxation method several times, starting with a large value of ϵ, say ϵ^0, and successively reduce ϵ up to a final value, say $\bar{\epsilon}$, that will give the desirable degree of accuracy to our solution. Furthermore, the price and flow information from one application of the method is passed to the next. Similar to Section 7.4, it can be shown that if ϵ^0 is chosen sufficiently large so that the initial price vector satisfies ϵ^0-CS together with some feasible flow vector, then the running time of the ϵ-relaxation method using the sweep implementation and ϵ-scaling is $O\bigl(N^3 \ln(\epsilon^0/\bar{\epsilon})\bigr)$ operations.

9.6.2   Auction/Sequential Shortest Path Algorithm

We now consider the extension of the auction/sequential shortest path (ASSP) algorithm of Section 7.5. The algorithm is a special case of the generic auction method, and differs from the ϵ-relaxation method in that instead of pushing flow along a candidate-list arc to any node, it pushes flow along a path of candidate-list arcs ending at a node with negative surplus. In fact, whereas a flow push in the ϵ-relaxation method may increase the surplus of a node in absolute value (e.g., when flow is pushed to a neighboring node with nonnegative surplus), in the ASSP algorithm, the surplus of each node is nonincreasing in absolute value.

We first introduce some definitions. For a path P, we denote by $s(P)$ and $t(P)$ the starting node and the terminal node, respectively, of P. For any $\epsilon > 0$ and $\beta \in (0,1)$, and any flow-price vector pair (x,p) satisfying ϵ-CS, we say that a path P of a graph $(\mathcal{N}, \mathcal{A})$ is *augmenting* if each forward (respectively, backward) arc (i,j) of P is in the candidate list of i (respectively, j) and $s(P)$ is a *source* (i.e., has positive surplus) and $t(P)$ is a *sink* (i.e., has negative surplus). As in Section 7.5, we define two operations on a given path $P = (n_1, n_2, \ldots, n_k)$:

(a) A *contraction* of P, which deletes the terminal node of P and the arc incident to this node.

(b) An *extension* of P by an arc (n_k, n_{k+1}) or an arc (n_{k+1}, n_k), which replaces P by the path $(n_1, n_2, \ldots, n_k, n_{k+1})$ and adds to P the corresponding arc.

For a fixed $\epsilon > 0$ and $\beta \in (0,1)$, and a given flow-price vector pair (x,p) satisfying ϵ-CS, an iteration of the ASSP algorithm updates (x,p) as follows:

Iteration of the ASSP Algorithm

Step 1: Select a node i with positive surplus and let the path P consist of only this node; if no such node exists, terminate the algorithm.

Step 2: Let i be the terminal node of the path P. If the candidate list of i is empty, then go to Step 3; otherwise, go to Step 4.

Step 3: (Contract Path) Increase the price p_i by the maximum amount that maintains ϵ-CS. If $i \neq s(P)$, contract P. Go to Step 2.

Step 4: (Extend Path) Select an arc (i, j) [or (j, i)] from the candidate list of i and extend P by this arc. If the surplus of j is negative, go to Step 5; otherwise, go to Step 2.

Step 5: (Augmentation) Perform an *augmentation* along the path P by the amount

$$\delta = \min \left\{ g_{s(P)}, -g_{t(P)}, \text{minimum of flow margins of the arcs of } P \right\},$$

(i.e., increase the flow of all forward arcs of P and decrease the flow of all backward arcs of P by δ). Go to the next iteration.

Roughly speaking, at each iteration of the ASSP algorithm, the path P starts as a single source and is successively extended or contracted until the terminal node of P is a sink. Then an augmentation along P is performed so as to decrease (respectively, increase) the surplus of the starting node (respectively, terminal node), while leaving the surplus of the remaining nodes unchanged. In case of a contraction, the price of the terminal node of P is strictly increased.

We note that the ASSP algorithm is a special case of the generic auction algorithm. To see this, note that Step 2 is a price rise on node i and that Step 5 adjusts the flows in such a way that ϵ-CS is maintained and nodes with nonnegative surplus continue to have nonnegative surplus for all subsequent iterations. The reason for the latter is that an augmentation along P changes the surplus of only two nodes $s(P)$ and $t(P)$, and by our choice of δ, the surplus of the node $s(P)$ remains nonnegative after the augmentation.

We also note that the ASSP algorithm performs price rises only on nodes with empty candidate list. Thus, by Prop. 9.10, each price rise increment is at least $\beta \epsilon$ and, by Prop. 9.8, the number of price rises (i.e., path contractions) on each node is at most $(r + 1)(N - 1)/\beta$, where r is any nonnegative scalar such that the initial price vector satisfies $r\epsilon$-CS together with some feasible flow vector. It follows that to prove finite termination of the ASSP algorithm, it suffices to show that the number of path extensions (cf. Step 4) and the number of augmentations (cf. Step 5) performed between successive path contractions is finite. Similar to the case of the ϵ-relaxation method, we show this by first showing that the algorithm keeps the admissible graph acyclic and that the path P, when its backward arcs are reversed in direction, belongs to the admissible graph.

Proposition 9.15: If initially the admissible graph is acyclic, then the admissible graph remains acyclic at all iterations of the ASSP algorithm. Moreover, the path P maintained by the algorithm, when its backward arcs are reversed in direction, belongs to the admissible graph at all times.

Proof: The admissible graph can change either by a price rise (Step 3) or by an augmentation (Step 5). An augmentation keeps the admissible graph acyclic because, after an augmentation, the admissible graph either remains unchanged or some arcs are deleted from it. A price rise keeps the admissible graph acyclic, as was shown in the proof of Prop. 9.11.

To show that P, when its backward arcs are reversed in direction, belongs to the admissible graph at all times, we simply observe that a path extension maintains this property (since the arc added to P is in the candidate list of the terminal node of P) and that a path contraction also maintains this property (since a price rise on the terminal node of P changes the admissible graph only by adding/deleting arcs incident to this node and, after the contraction, this node and its incident arc in P are both deleted from P). **Q.E.D.**

We now use Prop. 9.15 to bound the number of augmentations and path extensions performed by the ASSP algorithm between successive path contractions. This shows that the algorithm terminates with a flow-price pair satisfying ϵ-CS.

Proposition 9.16: If initially the admissible graph is acyclic, then the number of augmentations and path extensions between two successive path contractions (not necessarily at the same node) performed by the ASSP algorithm is finite. Furthermore, the algorithm terminates with a flow-price pair satisfying ϵ-CS.

Proof: We observe that an augmentation does not increase the number of nodes with nonzero surplus and does not add any arc to the admissible graph. Moreover, after an augmentation, either an arc is removed from the admissible graph or a node has its surplus set to zero. Thus, the number of arcs in the admissible graph plus the number of nodes with nonzero surplus is decreased by at least one after each augmentation. It follows that the number of augmentations between successive path contractions is at most $A + N$.

By Prop. 9.15, the path P always belongs to the admissible graph which is acyclic, so P cannot have repeated nodes and hence the number of successive extensions of P (before a contraction or an augmentation is performed) is at most N. Thus, the number of path extensions between successive path contractions is at most $N \cdot$ (number of augmentations between successive path contractions) $\leq N(A + N)$. Since the number of contractions is finite (cf. Props. 9.8 and 9.10), termination of the algorithm follows. **Q.E.D.**

9.7 MONOTROPIC PROGRAMMING

In this section, we consider a substantial generalization of the convex separable network problem. In particular, we replace the conservation of flow constraint with a general subspace constraint. Specifically, the problem is

$$
\begin{aligned}
\text{minimize} \quad & \sum_{j=1}^{n} f_j(x_j) \\
\text{subject to} \quad & x \in S, \\
& x_j \in X_j, \qquad j = 1, \dots, n,
\end{aligned}
\tag{9.39}
$$

where x denotes a vector in $\Re^n$, consisting of the n scalar components $x_1, \dots, x_n$, and

X_j is a nonempty interval for each j,

$f_j : X_j \mapsto \Re$ is a closed convex function for each j,

S is a subspace of $\Re^n$.

We refer to this problem as a *monotropic programming problem.*†

When x is a flow vector and S is the *circulation subspace* of a graph $(\mathcal{N}, \mathcal{A})$,

$$
S = \left\{ x \ \Big| \ \sum_{\{j \mid (i,j) \in \mathcal{A}\}} x_{ij} - \sum_{\{j \mid (j,i) \in \mathcal{A}\}} x_{ji} = 0, \, \forall \, i \in \mathcal{N} \right\},
$$

we essentially recover the convex separable network problem. The only difference is that the constraint $x \in S$ implies that the node supplies are all 0, instead of being arbitrary scalars, but this is not a real restriction, because every separable network problem can be converted to the circulation format as indicated in Section 4.1.3.

Note that problems involving general linear constraints and a separable convex cost function can be converted to monotropic programming

---

† The name "monotropic" means "turning in a single direction" in Greek, and captures the characteristic monotonicity property of convex functions of a single variable such as f_j.

problems. In particular, the problem

$$
\text{minimize} \quad \sum_{j=1}^{n} f_j(x_j)
$$

$$
\text{subject to} \quad Ax = b, \qquad x_j \in X_j, \qquad j = 1, \ldots, n, \qquad (9.40)
$$

where A is a given matrix and b is a given vector, is equivalent to

$$
\text{minimize} \quad \sum_{j=1}^{n} f_j(x_j)
$$

$$
\text{subject to} \quad Ax - z = 0, \qquad z = b, \qquad x_j \in X_j, \quad j = 1, \ldots, n,
$$

where z is a vector of artificial variables. This is a monotropic programming problem with a constraint subspace $S = \{(x, z) \mid Ax - z = 0\}$. When the $f_j(x_j)$ are linear functions, problem (9.40) reduces to the general linear programming problem. When the $f_j(x_j)$ are positive semidefinite quadratic functions, problem (9.40) reduces to a convex separable quadratic programming problem. The general convex quadratic programming problem with cost function $x'C'Cx$, where C is a matrix, can be made separable by using the linear transformation $y = Cx$.

It can thus be seen that the monotropic programming problem contains as special cases broad classes of important optimization problems. These problems share the distinguishing structural characteristics of monotropic programming that we will develop in this section, including a powerful and symmetric duality theory, as well as extensions of many of the analytical and algorithmic ideas we developed earlier in this chapter.

Duality Theory

To develop the appropriate dual problem, we introduce an auxiliary vector $y \in \Re^n$ and we convert the monotropic programming problem (9.39) to the equivalent form

$$
\text{minimize} \quad \sum_{j=1}^{n} f_j(x_j)
$$

$$
\text{subject to} \quad x = y, \qquad y \in S,
$$

$$
x_j \in X_j, \qquad j = 1, \ldots, n.
$$

We then assign a Lagrange multiplier vector $t \in \Re^n$ to the equality constraint $x = y$, obtaining the Lagrangian function

$$
L(x, y, t) = \sum_{j=1}^{n} f_j(x_j) + t'(y - x),
$$

and the dual function

$$q(t) = \inf_{y \in S, \, x_j \in X_j, \, j=1,\ldots,n} L(x, y, t)$$

$$= \inf_{y \in S} t'y + \sum_{j=1}^{n} \inf_{x_j \in X_j} \{ f_j(x_j) - t_j x_j \}$$

$$= \begin{cases} \sum_{j=1}^{n} q_j(t_j) & \text{if } t \in S^{\perp}, \\ -\infty & \text{otherwise,} \end{cases}$$

where

$$q_j(t_j) = \inf_{x_j \in X_j} \{ f_j(x_j) - t_j x_j \}, \qquad j = 1, \ldots, n,$$

and $S^{\perp}$ is the orthogonal subspace of S,

$$S^{\perp} = \{ t \mid t'x = 0, \, \forall \, x \in S \}.$$

The properties of the functions q_j have been developed in Prop. 9.6. Furthermore, we have noted in Section 9.3 that $-q_j$ is a closed convex function whose domain is the interval

$$T_j = \{ t_j \mid q_j(t_j) > -\infty \}.$$

Thus the dual problem of maximizing q over $\Re^n$ can be written as

$$
\begin{aligned}
\text{maximize} \quad & \sum_{j=1}^{n} q_j(t_j) \\
\text{subject to} \quad & t \in S^{\perp}, \\
& t_j \in T_j, \qquad j = 1, \ldots, n.
\end{aligned}
\tag{9.41}
$$

It can be seen that with a change of sign to convert maximization to minimization, the dual problem has the same form as the primal. In fact, it can be verified using Prop. 9.6(a) [cf. Eq. (9.20)] that when the dual problem is dualized, it yields the primal problem. Thus the duality is fully symmetric, and any general algorithm that can solve the primal problem (without relying on any special structure of the subspace S) can be used to solve the dual problem and conversely.

Much of the analysis given in Sections 9.2-9.4 for the case where S is a circulation subspace can be generalized to the monotropic programming problem. In particular, a pair (x, t) is said to satisfy *complementary slackness* (CS for short) if it lies on the characteristic curve

$$\Gamma = \{ (x, t) \mid f_j^-(x_j) \leq t_j \leq f_j^+(x_j), \, j = 1, \ldots, n \},$$

or equivalently, if for all j, x_j attains the infimum in the equation

$$q_j(t_j) = \inf_{x \in X_j} \{ f_j(x) - t_j x \}.$$

By Prop. 9.6(a), this is also equivalent to t_j attaining the supremum in the equation

$$f_j(x_j) = \sup_{t \in T_j} \{ q_j(t) + t x_j \}.$$

This means that the characteristic curve can alternatively be defined by

$$\Gamma = \{ (x, t) \mid -q_j^-(t_j) \le x_j \le -q_j^+(t_j), \ j = 1, \ldots, n \},$$

where q_j^+ and q_j^- are the right and left derivatives of q_j, respectively.

Similar to Section 9.3, we call a vector x *regular* if

$$f_j^-(x_j) < \infty, \quad -\infty < f_j^+(x_j), \qquad \forall\, j = 1, \ldots, n.$$

We also consider a general *equilibrium problem*, which is to find a pair (x, t) on the curve Γ that satisfies

$$x \in S, \qquad t \in S^\perp.$$

The duality theorems of Section 9.3 generalize nearly verbatim. In particular, we have the following:

Proposition 9.17: (Complementary Slackness Theorem) A pair (x^*, t^*) such that $x^* \in S$ and $t^* \in S^\perp$ satisfies CS if and only if x^* and t^* are optimal primal and dual solutions, respectively, and the optimal primal and dual costs are equal.

Proposition 9.18: Suppose that there exists at least one primal feasible solution that is regular. Then, if x^* is an optimal solution of the primal problem, there exists an optimal solution p^* of the dual problem that satisfies CS together with x^*.

Proposition 9.19: (Duality Theorem) If there exists at least one feasible solution to the primal problem, or at least one feasible solution to the dual problem, the optimal primal and dual costs are equal.

Proposition 9.20: (Equilibrium Theorem) A pair (x^*, t^*) solves the equilibrium problem if and only if x^* and t^* are optimal primal and dual solutions, respectively.

The proofs of Props. 9.17, 9.18, and 9.20 are fairly straightforward, and are nearly identical to the proofs of Props. 9.2, 9.3, and 9.5, respectively. There remains to prove the duality theorem (Prop. 9.19 and its special case, Prop. 9.4). By repeating the proof of Prop. 9.2, we can show that weak duality holds; that is,

$$\sum_{j=1}^{n} q_j(t_j) \le \sum_{j=1}^{n} f_j(x_j), \qquad \forall\, x \in S,\, t \in S^\perp \text{ with } x_j \in X_j,\, t_j \in T_j,\, \forall\, j.$$
(9.42)

It will thus be sufficient to show the reverse inequality. Our proof is constructive and uses a conceptual descent algorithm, which we now introduce.

ϵ-Descent Algorithm

The feasible direction methods discussed in Section 8.8.1 operate on the principle of iterative cost improvement along feasible descent directions. These methods improve the cost function at a nonoptimal vector, but they do not guarantee a fixed amount of improvement. We will introduce a somewhat different method whereby if the current iterate is not within $\epsilon > 0$ of being optimal, there is a guarantee of an improvement of at least $\beta\epsilon$ at the next iteration, where $\beta > 0$ is a fixed scalar. We will derive this method for the separable case of a monotropic programming problem, although the idea can be extended to general convex programming.

For an $\epsilon > 0$, let us define for each $x_j \in X_j$, the ϵ-*subdifferential of the pair* (f_j, X_j) *at* x_j as the set

$$\partial_\epsilon f_j(x_j) = \{ t_j \mid f_j(z_j) \ge f_j(x_j) + t_j(z_j - x_j) - \epsilon,\, \forall\, z_j \in X_j \}. \qquad (9.43)$$

The elements of the ϵ-subdifferential are called ϵ-*subgradients*. It is easily seen that $\partial_\epsilon f_j(x_j)$ is a closed interval. In particular, its left endpoint is

$$f_{j,\epsilon}^-(x_j) = \begin{cases} \sup_{\delta < 0,\, x_j + \delta \in X_j} \dfrac{f_j(x_j + \delta) - f_j(x_j) + \epsilon}{\delta} & \text{if } \inf X_j < x_j, \\ -\infty & \text{if } \inf X_j = x_j, \end{cases} \qquad (9.44)$$

and its right endpoint is

$$f_{j,\epsilon}^+(x_j) = \begin{cases} \inf_{\delta > 0,\, x_j + \delta \in X_j} \dfrac{f_j(x_j + \delta) - f_j(x_j) + \epsilon}{\delta} & \text{if } x_j < \sup X_j, \\ \infty & \text{if } x_j = \sup X_j. \end{cases} \qquad (9.45)$$

Note that we have

$$f_{j,\epsilon}^-(x_j) \le f_j^-(x_j) \le f_j^+(x_j) \le f_{j,\epsilon}^+(x_j),$$

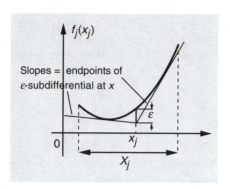

Figure 9.11: Illustration of the ϵ-subdifferential $\partial_\epsilon f_j(x_j)$. It corresponds to the set of slopes indicated in the figure. Note that $\partial_\epsilon f_j(x_j)$ is nonempty and includes the gradient of f_j at x_j if f_j is differentiable at x_j.

so the ϵ-subdifferential $\partial_\epsilon f_j(x_j)$ contains the left and right derivatives $f_j^-(x_j)$ and $f_j^+(x_j)$. We will also show shortly that $\partial_\epsilon f_j(x_j)$ is nonempty. Figure 9.11 illustrates the definition.

Let us derive some properties of ϵ-subgradients. We recall the definition

$$q_j(t_j) = \inf_{x \in X_j} \{f_j(x) - t_j x\}, \tag{9.46}$$

and the relation [cf. Prop. 9.6(a)]

$$f_j(x_j) = \sup_{t \in T_j} \{q_j(t) + t x_j\}, \tag{9.47}$$

where T_j is the effective domain of q_j

$$T_j = \{t_j \mid q_j(t_j) > -\infty\}.$$

Comparing these relations with the definition (9.43) of the ϵ-subdifferential, we see that

$$t_j \in \partial_\epsilon f_j(x_j) \quad \text{if and only if} \quad f_j(x_j) \le q_j(t_j) + t_j x_j + \epsilon. \tag{9.48}$$

Thus we have

$$t_j \in T_j, \qquad \forall \, t_j \in \partial_\epsilon f_j(x_j),$$

and furthermore t_j is an ϵ-subgradient at x_j if and only if t_j attains within ϵ the supremum in Eq. (9.47). From this it follows that the ϵ-subdifferential is nonempty at every $x_j \in X_j$.

Suppose now that x is a feasible solution such that

$$\sum_{j=1}^{n} f_j(x_j) > f^* + n\epsilon, \tag{9.49}$$

where f^* is the optimal primal cost. Then we claim that *the subspace $S^\perp$ does not intersect the set*

$$B_\epsilon(x) = \{(t_1, \ldots, t_n) \mid t_j \in \partial_\epsilon f_j(x_j), \, j = 1, \ldots, n\}.$$

Indeed, if this were not so, i.e., if there existed $t = (t_1, \ldots, t_n) \in S^\perp$ with $t_j \in \partial_\epsilon f_j(x_j)$ for all j, we would have by adding Eq. (9.48),

$$\sum_{j=1}^n f_j(x_j) \le \sum_{j=1}^n q_j(t_j) + \sum_{j=1}^n t_j x_j + n\epsilon \le f^* + n\epsilon,$$

where the last inequality holds because $\sum_{j=1}^n q_j(t_j) \le f^*$ (by weak duality) and $\sum_{j=1}^n t_j x_j = 0$ (since $x \in S$ and $t \in S^\perp$). We thus obtain a contradiction of Eq. (9.49).

Thus when Eq. (9.49) holds, we have

$$S^\perp \cap B_\epsilon(x) = \emptyset,$$

and it can be seen that there must exist a direction $d = (d_1, \ldots, d_n) \in S$ such that

$$t'd < 0, \qquad \forall\, t \in B_\epsilon(x);$$

see Fig. 9.12. We show in the following proposition that for such a vector d, we have

$$\inf_{\alpha > 0} \sum_{j=1}^n f_j(x_j + \alpha d_j) < \sum_{j=1}^n f_j(x_j) - \epsilon, \qquad (9.50)$$

so that it is possible to effect a cost improvement of more than ϵ by searching along the half line

$$x + \alpha d, \qquad \alpha > 0.$$

We refer to a vector d satisfying Eq. (9.50) as an *ϵ-descent direction at x*.

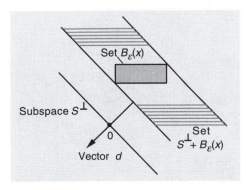

Figure 9.12: Illustration of the fact that if

$$S^\perp \cap B_\epsilon(x) = \emptyset,$$

there must exist a direction $d \in S$ such that

$$t'd < 0, \qquad \forall\, t \in B_\epsilon(x).$$

When $S^\perp \cap B_\epsilon(x) = \emptyset$, the set $S^\perp + B_\epsilon(x)$ does not contain the origin. The desired vector d is the opposite of the projection of the origin on the set $S^\perp + B_\epsilon(x)$.

Proposition 9.21: (ϵ-Descent Property) Suppose that x is a primal feasible solution satisfying

$$\sum_{j=1}^{n} f_j(x_j) > f^* + n\epsilon$$

for some $\epsilon > 0$. Then there exists a vector $d \in S$ such that

$$t'd < 0, \qquad \forall\, t \in B_\epsilon(x), \tag{9.51}$$

and this vector is an ϵ-descent direction at x.

Proof: The existence of a vector $d \in S$ satisfying Eq. (9.51) was shown in the preceding discussion, so we only need to prove the ϵ-descent property (9.50). The condition $\sum_{j=1}^{n} t_j d_j < 0$ is equivalent to

$$\sum_{\{j\,|\,d_j<0\}} f_{j,\epsilon}^-(x_j)d_j + \sum_{\{j\,|\,d_j>0\}} f_{j,\epsilon}^+(x_j)d_j < 0,$$

where $f_{j,\epsilon}^-(x_j)$ and $f_{j,\epsilon}^+(x_j)$ are the left and right endpoints of the ϵ-subdifferential $\partial_\epsilon f_j(x_j)$, respectively. Using the expressions Eqs. (9.44) and (9.45) for these endpoints, the preceding relation can equivalently be written as

$$\sum_{j=1}^{n} \inf_{\alpha>0} \frac{f_j(x_j + \alpha d_j) - f_j(x_j) + \epsilon}{\alpha} < 0.$$

Let $\alpha_1, \ldots, \alpha_n$ be positive scalars such that

$$\sum_{j=1}^{n} \frac{f_j(x_j + \alpha_j d_j) - f_j(x_j) + \epsilon}{\alpha_j} < 0. \tag{9.52}$$

Define

$$\overline{\alpha} = \frac{1}{\sum_{j=1}^{n} 1/\alpha_j}.$$

As a consequence of the convexity of f_j, it can be seen that the ratio $(f_j(x_j + \alpha d_j) - f_j(x_j))/\alpha$ is monotonically nondecreasing in α. Thus, since $\alpha_j \geq \overline{\alpha}$ for all j, we have

$$\frac{f_j(x_j + \alpha_j d_j) - f_j(x_j)}{\alpha_j} \geq \frac{f_j(x_j + \overline{\alpha} d_j) - f_j(x_j)}{\overline{\alpha}},$$

and Eq. (9.52) together with the definition of $\overline{\alpha}$ yields

$$0 > \sum_{j=1}^{n} \frac{f_j(x_j + \alpha_j d_j) - f_j(x_j) + \epsilon}{\alpha_j}$$

$$\geq \frac{\epsilon}{\overline{\alpha}} + \sum_{j=1}^{n} \frac{f_j(x_j + \overline{\alpha} d_j) - f_j(x_j)}{\overline{\alpha}}.$$

Thus, we have $\sum_{j=1}^{n} f_j(x_j + \overline{\alpha} d_j) < \sum_{j=1}^{n} f_j(x_j) - \epsilon$, and the result follows.
Q.E.D.

By using the preceding proposition, we define an algorithm, called the ϵ-*descent method*, whereby at each iterate x for which

$$S^{\perp} \cap B_\epsilon(x) = \emptyset,$$

we find a direction d satisfying Eq. (9.51), we perform a line search along that direction, and we reduce the primal cost by at least ϵ. In this form, the algorithm is not yet useful for solving the problem, because we have to specify the method for choosing and perhaps changing ϵ, and also the method by which we find the direction d and perform the line search. However, here we are not interested in a practical implementation of the algorithm but rather in its use for proving the duality theorem.

Proof of the Duality Theorem

Suppose that there exists a primal feasible solution. Start the ϵ-descent algorithm from this solution, and continue iterating up to the point where $S^{\perp}$ intersects the set $B_\epsilon(x)$. There are two possibilities:

(1) Termination never occurs, in which case the sequence of primal costs generated will diverge to $-\infty$, since by Prop. 9.21, there is a cost improvement of at least ϵ at each iteration. Thus the optimal dual cost must also be $-\infty$ by weak duality [cf. Eq. (9.42)].

(2) Termination occurs with some vector x and some vector $t \in S^{\perp} \cap B_\epsilon(x)$. In this case, by adding Eq. (9.48), we have

$$\sum_{j=1}^{n} f_j(x_j) \leq \sum_{j=1}^{n} q_j(t_j) + \sum_{j=1}^{n} t_j x_j + n\epsilon = \sum_{j=1}^{n} q_j(t_j) + n\epsilon,$$

where the last equation holds because $\sum_{j=1}^{n} t_j x_j = 0$, since $x \in S$ and $t \in S^{\perp}$. Thus, since $\sum_{j=1}^{n} q_j(t_j) \leq \sum_{j=1}^{n} f_j(x_j)$ (by weak duality), the optimal primal and dual costs differ by at most $n\epsilon$. Since ϵ can be taken arbitrarily small, it follows that the optimal primal and dual costs must be equal.

Thus, we have shown that if there exists a primal feasible solution, the optimal primal and dual costs are equal.

Finally, applying the preceding argument to the dual problem, and taking into account that the dual of the dual problem is the primal, we see that if there exists a dual feasible solution, the optimal primal and dual costs are equal. Thus the proof of the duality theorem is complete.

Additional Properties of Monotropic Programs

Monotropic programming problems have some interesting combinatorial properties. A complete analysis is beyond our scope, so we will only discuss some of the main ideas, and describe how they relate to network problems. These ideas revolve around the notion of the *support* of a vector z (i.e., the set of indices $\{j \mid z_j \neq 0\}$), and vectors that have minimal support, as in the following definition.

Definition 9.4: A nonzero vector z of a subspace S of $\Re^n$ is said to be *elementary* if there is no vector $\bar{z} \neq 0$ in S that has smaller support than z, i.e., for all nonzero $\bar{z} \in S$, $\{j \mid \bar{z}_j \neq 0\}$ is not a strict subset of $\{j \mid z_j \neq 0\}$.

It can be seen that if z and $\bar{z}$ are two elementary vectors with the same support, then z and $\bar{z}$ are scalar multiples of each other (if this were not so, the vector $z - \gamma\bar{z}$ would have smaller support than z and $\bar{z}$ for a suitable scalar γ). Thus, since the number of supports is finite, each subspace has only a finite number of elementary vectors, up to scalar multiplication. From the definition of elementary vector, it can also be seen that given any nonzero vector y, there exists an elementary vector z with support contained in the support of y (either y is elementary or else there exists a nonzero vector $\bar{z}$ with support strictly contained in the support of y; continue this argument until an elementary vector z is obtained).

For some examples that illustrate the definition, note that the elementary vectors of the entire space $\Re^n$ are the coordinate vectors that have a single nonzero component, while the elementary vectors of the subspace $\{(z_1, z_2, z_3) \mid z_1 + z_2 + z_3 = 0\}$ are the nonzero scalar multiples of the vectors $(1, -1, 0)$, $(1, 0, -1)$, $(0, 1, -1)$.

For another example that is particularly relevant to network optimization, one can verify that the elementary vectors of the circulation subspace S of a graph $(\mathcal{N}, \mathcal{A})$,

$$S = \left\{ x \ \bigg| \ \sum_{\{j \mid (i,j) \in \mathcal{A}\}} x_{ij} - \sum_{\{j \mid (j,i) \in \mathcal{A}\}} x_{ji} = 0, \ \forall \ i \in \mathcal{N} \right\},$$

are the simple cycle flows. Let us also consider the subspace that is orthogonal to the circulation subspace, given by

$$S^\perp = \big\{ t \mid \text{there exists a price vector } p \text{ with } t_{ij} = p_i - p_j, \ \forall \ (i,j) \in \mathcal{A} \big\}.$$

To characterize the elementary vectors of $S^\perp$, let us restrict attention to the case where the graph is connected, and let us consider cuts $Q = [\mathcal{S}, \mathcal{N} - \mathcal{S}]$, where $\mathcal{S}$ is a nonempty subset of nodes of the graph such that the deletion of all the arcs of Q leaves the graph with exactly two connected components. Such cuts are called *elementary*. We leave it as Exercise 9.7 for the reader to verify that the elementary vectors of $S^\perp$ have components of the form

$$t_{ij} = \begin{cases} \gamma & \text{if } (i,j) \in Q^+, \\ -\gamma & \text{if } (i,j) \in Q^-, \\ 0 & \text{otherwise}, \end{cases}$$

where Q is an elementary cut and γ is a nonzero scalar.

Finally, consider an $m \times n$ matrix A. It can be seen that the supports of the elementary vectors of the nullspace of A correspond to the minimal sets of linearly dependent columns of A. These are subsets of columns that are linearly dependent, but are such that any one of the columns in the set can be uniquely expressed as a linear combination of the remaining columns in the set. It turns out that this example bears an important relation with linear programming theory and basic solutions of systems of linear equations.

Several of the distinctive properties of network optimization involving simple cycles can be extended to monotropic programming using elementary vectors. For example, the notion of conformal decomposition can be generalized. In particular, let us say that a vector x *is in harmony* with a vector z if

$$x_j z_j \geq 0, \qquad \forall \ j = 1, \ldots, n.$$

We have the following generalization of the conformal realization theorem (Prop. 1.1).

Proposition 9.22: (Conformal Realization) Every nonzero vector x of a given subspace S can be written in the form

$$x = z^1 + \cdots + z^m,$$

where m is an integer with $m \leq n$, and each of the vectors $z^1, \ldots, z^m$ is an elementary vector of S that is in harmony with x, and has support that is contained in the support of x.

Proof: We first show that every nonzero vector $y \in S$ has the property that there exists an elementary vector of S that is in harmony with y and has support that is contained in the support of y.

We show this by induction on the number of nonzero components of y. Let V_k be the subset of nonzero vectors in S that have k or less nonzero components, and let $\overline{k}$ be the smallest k for which V_k is nonempty. Then the vectors in $V_{\overline{k}}$ must be elementary, so every $y \in V_{\overline{k}}$ has the desired property. Assume that all vectors in V_k have the desired property for some $k \geq \overline{k}$. We let y be a vector in V_{k+1} and we show that it also has the desired property. Let z be an elementary vector whose support is contained in the support of y. By using the negative of z if necessary, we can assume that $y_j z_j > 0$ for at least one index j. Then there exists a largest value of γ, call it $\overline{\gamma}$, such that

$$y_j - \gamma z_j \geq 0, \qquad \forall\, j \text{ with } y_j > 0,$$

$$y_j - \gamma z_j \leq 0, \qquad \forall\, j \text{ with } y_j < 0.$$

The vector $y - \overline{\gamma} z$ is in harmony with y and has support that is strictly contained in the support of y. Thus either $y - \overline{\gamma} z = 0$, in which case the elementary vector z is in harmony with y and has support equal to the support of y, or else $y - \overline{\gamma} z$ is nonzero. In the latter case, we have $y - \overline{\gamma} z \in V_k$, and by the induction hypothesis, there exists an elementary vector $\overline{z}$ that is in harmony with $y - \overline{\gamma} z$ and has support that is contained in the support of $y - \overline{\gamma} z$. The vector $\overline{z}$ is also in harmony with y and has support that is contained in the support of y. The induction is complete.

Consider now the given nonzero vector $x \in S$, and choose any elementary vector $\overline{z}^1$ of S that is in harmony with x and has support that is contained in the support of x (such a vector exists by the property just shown). By using the negative of $\overline{z}^1$ if necessary, we can assume that $x_j \overline{z}_j^1 > 0$ for at least one index j. Let $\overline{\gamma}$ be the largest value of γ such that

$$x_j - \gamma \overline{z}_j^1 \geq 0, \qquad \forall\, j \text{ with } x_j > 0,$$

$$x_j - \gamma \overline{z}_j^1 \leq 0, \qquad \forall\, j \text{ with } x_j < 0.$$

The vector $x - z^1$, where

$$z^1 = \overline{\gamma}\, \overline{z}^1,$$

is in harmony with x and has support that is strictly contained in the support of x. There are two cases: (1) $x = z^1$, in which case we are done, or (2) $x \neq z^1$, in which case we replace x by $x - z^1$ and we repeat the process. Eventually, after m steps where $m \leq n$ (since each step reduces the number of nonzero components by at least one), we will end up with the desired decomposition $x = z^1 + \cdots + z^m$. **Q.E.D.**

Using the preceding proposition, it is possible to derive a necessary and sufficient condition for the optimal solution set of a feasible monotropic programming problem to be nonempty and compact. This condition is that for all elementary vectors z of S, we have

$$\sum_{\{j \mid z_j > 0\}} \hat{f}_j^+ z_j + \sum_{\{j \mid z_j < 0\}} \hat{f}_j^- z_j > 0,$$

where

$$\hat{f}_j^+ = \begin{cases} \lim_{x_j \to \infty} f_j^+(x_j) & \text{if } X_j \text{ is unbounded above,} \\ \infty & \text{otherwise,} \end{cases}$$

and

$$\hat{f}_j^- = \begin{cases} \lim_{x_j \to \infty} f_j^-(x_j) & \text{if } X_j \text{ is unbounded below,} \\ -\infty & \text{otherwise.} \end{cases}$$

In the case of a linear network flow problem with nonnegativity constraints on the arc flows, this condition is equivalent to requiring that all simple forward cycles have positive cost (see the discussion in the beginning of Section 5.1).

As another consequence of Prop. 9.22, we derive an interesting algorithmic property of elementary vectors. To place this property in perspective, consider the subspace S and a convex set B, which is disjoint from $S^\perp$. According to an important theorem from convex analysis (see e.g., Rockafellar [1970], Luenberger [1984], Bertsekas [1995b]), there exists a hyperplane that "separates" $S^\perp$ from B in the sense that it contains $S^\perp$ and is disjoint from B; mathematically, this is expressed by saying that there exists a vector $z \in S$ such that $t'z < 0$ for all $t \in B$. The following proposition asserts that the vector z can be taken to be an *elementary* vector of S.

Proposition 9.23: (Combinatorial Separation Theorem) If S is a subspace and B is a Cartesian product of nonempty intervals, such that $B \cap S^\perp = \varnothing$, there exists an elementary vector z of S such that

$$t'z < 0, \qquad \forall \, t \in B.$$

Proof: For simplicity, assume that B is the Cartesian product of compact intervals, so that B has the form

$$B = \{t \mid \underline{b}_j \le t_j \le \overline{b}_j, \, j = 1, \ldots, n\},$$

where $\underline{b}_j$ and $\overline{b}_j$ are some scalars. The proof is easily modified for the case where B has a different form. As shown in Fig. 9.12, there exists a vector

$d \in S$ such that $t'd < 0$ for all $t \in B$, or equivalently

$$\sum_{\{j|d_j>0\}} \bar{b}_j d_j + \sum_{\{j|d_j<0\}} \underline{b}_j d_j < 0. \tag{9.53}$$

Let

$$d = z^1 + \cdots + z^m,$$

be a decomposition of d, where $z^1, \ldots, z^m$ are elementary vectors of S that are in harmony with x, and have supports that are contained in the support of d, as per Prop. 20.22. Then the condition (9.53) is equivalently written as

$$0 > \sum_{\{j|d_j>0\}} \bar{b}_j d_j + \sum_{\{j|d_j<0\}} \underline{b}_j d_j$$

$$= \sum_{\{j|d_j>0\}} \bar{b}_j \left(\sum_{i=1}^{m} z_j^i \right) + \sum_{\{j|d_j<0\}} \underline{b}_j \left(\sum_{i=1}^{m} z_j^i \right)$$

$$= \sum_{i=1}^{m} \left(\sum_{\{j|z_j^i>0\}} \bar{b}_j z_j^i + \sum_{\{j|z_j^i<0\}} \underline{b}_j z_j^i \right),$$

where the last equality holds because the vectors z^i are in harmony with d and their supports are contained in the support of d. From the preceding relation, we see that for at least one elementary vector z^i, we must have

$$0 > \sum_{\{j|z_j^i>0\}} \bar{b}_j z_j^i + \sum_{\{j|z_j^i<0\}} \underline{b}_j z_j^i,$$

or equivalently

$$0 > t'z^i, \qquad \forall\, t \in B.$$

Q.E.D.

From Prop. 9.23, we see that the directions used by the ϵ-descent algorithm can be selected from the finite set of elementary directions of S. By choosing a sufficiently small ϵ, we can also see that given a nonoptimal primal feasible vector x, it is possible to find a descent direction at x from among the finite set of elementary vectors of the subspace S. This generalizes a basic network optimization result that we have shown in Prop. 1.2 (see also Props. 8.2 and 9.1), i.e., that at a feasible nonoptimal flow vector there exists a simple unblocked cycle with nonnegative cost.

9.8   NOTES, SOURCES, AND EXERCISES

Our development of this chapter follows Rockafellar's work on monotropic programming, which was developed in his 1967 and 1969 papers. Rockafellar generalized and refined the important work of Minty [1960], which deals with the network case and includes most of the material we have presented in Sections 9.2 and 9.3. The relation between convex network optimization and equilibrium problems in electrical engineering goes back to the days of Maxwell for the quadratic cost case, which corresponds to a linear network. Prior to Minty, extensions to nonlinear networks were carried out by Duffin [1947], Birkhoff and Diaz [1956], and Dennis [1959]. Rockafellar's book on convex analysis [1970] contains detailed background for the material of the present chapter, including an extensive treatment of conjugate functions and duality theory for (nonseparable) convex programming problems.

The convergence of the relaxation method for strictly convex network problems was analyzed by Cottle and Pang [1982], and Bertsekas, Hosein, and Tseng [1987]. The method is particularly well suited for parallel implementation, which may also be asynchronous; see Zenios and Mulvey [1986], Bertsekas and El Baz [1987], Bertsekas and Tsitsiklis [1989], El Baz [1989], Tseng, Bertsekas, and Tsitsiklis [1990], and Chajakis and Zenios [1991]. An alternative dual ascent method is given by El Baz [1996]; see also El Baz, Spiteri, Miellou, and Gazen [1996].

The notion of ϵ-complementary slackness for convex network problems was introduced by Bertsekas, Hosein, and Tseng [1987], where it was used to generalize the relaxation method of Section 6.3 along lines similar to the ϵ-descent method of Section 9.7. The ϵ-relaxation and auction algorithms of Section 9.6, together with the associated complexity analysis, were developed in Bertsekas, Polymenakos, and Tseng [1997a], [1997b], and in the Ph.D. thesis by Polymenakos [1996]. The paper by Beraldi, Guerriero, and Musmanno [1996] discusses parallel computation aspects of the ϵ-relaxation method for separable convex problems. A closely related algorithm to the ϵ-relaxation method was given by De Leone, Meyer, and Zakarian [1996]. The paper by Tseng and Bertsekas [1996] extends the ϵ-relaxation method to convex separable network problems with gains. Karzanov and McCormick [1997] give another type of scaling algorithm for convex separable network problems.

The book of Rockafellar [1984] contains an extensive development of the theory of monotropic programming and its special cases in network optimization. The theory of elementary vectors was developed in Rockafellar [1969] (see also Rockafellar [1970], [1984]), where the connection with the theory of oriented matroids was also described. The proof of the duality theorem that we have presented in Section 9.7 is due to Rockafellar [1981] (see also Rockafellar [1984]). The ϵ-descent algorithm used in this proof is called *fortified descent algorithm* by Rockafellar. This algorithm, as well as the use of the ϵ-subdifferential in a descent algorithmic context, were first proposed by Bertsekas and Mitter [1971], [1973] for separable and for general convex programming problems. Generalizations of the simplex, primal-dual, and out-of-kilter methods to convex separable network problems and to monotropic programming problems are developed by Rockafellar [1984] using ϵ-descent ideas. Various implementations of the ϵ-descent algorithm have also been used for the numerical optimization of nondifferentiable convex functions in the context of the so-called *bundle methods*, introduced by Lemarechal [1974] (see e.g., Hiriart-Uruttu and Lemarechal [1993]). The relaxation method of Section 6.3 was extended to linear programs by Tseng and Bertsekas [1987], and to monotropic programming by Tseng and Bertsekas [1990]. There is no known generalization of auction algorithms to monotropic programming. However, the primal-dual and out-of-kilter methods were recently extended to monotropic programming by Tseng [1998], using the notion of ϵ-complementary slackness, and a complexity analysis was also given.

EXERCISES

9.1 (Proof of a Weaker Version of the Duality Theorem)

Show that if the primal problem is feasible and the intervals X_{ij} are compact, then the optimal primal and dual costs are equal (even though the dual problem may not have an optimal solution). *Hint*: Let x^* be a primal optimal solution. If x^* is regular, Prop. 9.3 applies and we are done. If x^* is not regular, there are arcs (i, j) where regularity is violated by some $x_{ij}^* \in X_{ij}$. For each such arc, approximate f_{ij} near the endpoint(s) where regularity is violated, using convex functions $\underline{f}_{ij} : X_{ij} \mapsto \Re$ and $\overline{f}_{ij} : X_{ij} \mapsto \Re$ such that

$$f_{ij}(x_{ij}) - \epsilon \le \underline{f}_{ij}(x_{ij}) \le f_{ij}(x_{ij}), \qquad \forall \; x_{ij} \in X_{ij},$$

$$f_{ij}(x_{ij}) \le \overline{f}_{ij}(x_{ij}) \le f_{ij}(x_{ij}) + \epsilon, \qquad \forall \; x_{ij} \in X_{ij}.$$

The functions $\underline{f}_{ij}$ and $\overline{f}_{ij}$ should be such that all flows $x_{ij} \in X_{ij}$ are regular. Now use Prop. 9.3.

9.2

Consider a problem with two nodes, 1 and 2, and two arcs $(1, 2)$ and $(2, 1)$. The node supplies are $s_1 = s_2 = 0$. The problem is

$$\text{minimize} \;\; f_{12}(x_{12}) + f_{21}(x_{21})$$

$$\text{subject to} \;\; x_{12} = x_{21}, \qquad 0 \le x_{12} < \infty, \quad 0 \le x_{21} < \infty,$$

where

$$f_{12}(x) = f_{21}(x) = -\sqrt{x}, \qquad x \in [0, \infty).$$

Calculate the dual function and verify that the optimal primal and dual costs are both equal to $-\infty$, consistently with Prop. 9.4.

9.3

Suppose that (x, p) and (x', p') are two solutions of the network equilibrium problem. Show that (x, p') and (x', p) are also solutions.

9.4 (Exact Penalty Functions)

Consider a problem where each function f_{ij} is convex over the entire real line, and there is a compact arc flow range $x_{ij} \in [b_{ij}, c_{ij}]$ for each arc (i, j). Suppose that we modify the problem by eliminating the bound constraints and by adding to the cost function the following penalty for their violation:

$$\frac{1}{\epsilon} \sum_{(i,j) \in \mathcal{A}} \left(\max\{0, b_{ij} - x_{ij}\} + \max\{0, x_{ij} - c_{ij}\} \right),$$

where ϵ is a positive scalar. Use Prop. 9.1 to show that there exists a threshold $\bar{\epsilon} > 0$ such that if $\epsilon \leq \bar{\epsilon}$, the optimal solutions of the problem remain unaffected by the modification.

9.5

Show that in the special case of a compact arc flow range,

$$X_{ij} = [b_{ij}, c_{ij}],$$

where b_{ij} and c_{ij} are scalars, the CS condition of Section 9.3 can be written in terms of the price differentials

$$t_{ij} = p_i - p_j,$$

as

$$t_{ij} \leq f_{ij}^+(b_{ij}) \qquad \Rightarrow \qquad x_{ij} = b_{ij},$$

$$t_{ij} \geq f_{ij}^-(c_{ij}) \qquad \Rightarrow \qquad x_{ij} = c_{ij},$$

$$f_{ij}^+(b_{ij}) < t_{ij} < f_{ij}^-(c_{ij}) \quad \Rightarrow \quad b_{ij} < x_{ij} < c_{ij} \text{ and } f_{ij}^-(x_{ij}) \leq t_{ij} \leq f_{ij}^+(x_{ij}).$$

9.6

Modify the example of Fig. 9.4 to show that the duality theorem (Prop. 9.4) need not hold if the functions f_{ij} are not closed.

9.7

Consider a connected graph $(\mathcal{N}, \mathcal{A})$, and the subspace

$$\big\{ t \mid \text{there exists a price vector } p \text{ with } t_{ij} = p_i - p_j, \ \forall \ (i,j) \in \mathcal{A} \big\}.$$

Show that the elementary vectors of the subspace have components of the form

$$
t_{ij} = \begin{cases} \gamma & \text{if } (i,j) \in Q^+, \\ -\gamma & \text{if } (i,j) \in Q^-, \\ 0 & \text{otherwise,} \end{cases}
$$

where Q is an elementary cut and γ is a nonzero scalar.

10

Network Problems with Integer Constraints

Contents

In this chapter, we focus again on the general nonlinear network problem of Chapter 8:

$$\text{minimize} \quad f(x)$$

$$\text{subject to} \quad x \in F,$$

where x is a flow vector in a given directed graph $(\mathcal{N}, \mathcal{A})$, the feasible set F is

$$F = \left\{ x \in X \;\middle|\; \sum_{\{j|(i,j)\in\mathcal{A}\}} x_{ij} - \sum_{\{j|(j,i)\in\mathcal{A}\}} x_{ji} = s_i, \; \forall \; i \in \mathcal{N} \right\},$$

and $f : F \mapsto \Re$ is a given real-valued function. Here s_i are given supply scalars and X is a given subset of flow vectors. We concentrate on the case where the feasible set F is discrete because the set X embodies some integer constraints and possibly some side constraints.

As we noted in Chapter 8, one may solve approximately problems with integer constraints and side constraints through some heuristic that neglects in one way or another the integer constraints. In particular, one may solve the problem as a "continuous" network flow problem and use some ad hoc method to round the fractional solution to integer. Alternatively, one may discard the complicating side constraints, obtain an integer solution of the resulting network problem, and use some heuristic to correct this solution for feasibility of the violated side constraints.

Unfortunately, there are many problems where heuristic methods of this type are inadequate, and they cannot be relied upon to produce a satisfactory solution. In such cases, one needs to strengthen the heuristics with more systematic procedures that can provide some assurance of an improved solution.

In this chapter we first describe a few examples of integer-constrained network problems, and we then focus on various systematic solution methods. In particular, in Section 10.2, we discuss the branch-and-bound method, which is in principle capable of producing an *exactly* optimal solution to an integer-constrained problem. This method relies on upper and lower bound estimates of the optimal cost of various problems that are derived from the given problem. Usually, the upper bounds are obtained with various heuristics, while the lower bounds are obtained through integer constraint relaxation or through the use of duality. A popular method for obtaining lower bounds, the Lagrangian relaxation method, is introduced in Section 10.3. This method requires the optimization of nondifferentiable functions, and two of the major algorithms that can be used for this purpose, subgradient and cutting plane methods, are discussed in Section 10.3.

Unfortunately, the branch-and-bound method is too time-consuming for exact optimal solution, so in many practical problems it can only be used as an approximation scheme. There are alternative possibilities, which do not offer the theoretical guarantees of branch-and-bound, but are much faster in practice. Two possibilities of this type, local search methods and rollout algorithms, are discussed in Sections 10.4 and 10.5, respectively.

10.1 FORMULATION OF INTEGER-CONSTRAINED PROBLEMS

There is a very large variety of integer-constrained network flow problems. Furthermore, small changes in the problem formulation can often make a significant difference in the character of the solution. As a result, it is not easy to provide a taxonomy of the major problems of interest. It is helpful, however, to study in some detail a few representative examples that can serve as paradigms when dealing with other problems that have similar structure. We have already discussed in Section 8.4 an example, the constrained shortest path problem. In this section, we provide some additional illustrative examples of broad classes of integer-constrained problems. In the exercises, we discuss several variants of these problems.

Example 10.1. Traveling Salesman Problem

An important model for scheduling a sequence of operations is the classical traveling salesman problem. This is perhaps the most studied of all combinatorial optimization problems. In addition to its use as a practical model, it has served as a testbed for a large variety of formal and heuristic approaches in discrete optimization.

In a colloquial description of the problem, a salesman wants to find a minimum mileage/cost tour that visits each of N given cities exactly once and returns to the city he started form. We associate a node with each city $i = 1, \ldots, N$, and we introduce an arc (i, j) with traversal cost a_{ij} for each ordered pair of nodes i and j. Note that we assume that the graph is *complete*; that is, there exists an arc for each ordered pair of nodes. There is no loss of generality in doing so because we can assign a very high cost a_{ij} to an arc (i, j) that is precluded from participation in the solution. We allow the possibility that $a_{ij} \neq a_{ji}$. Problems where $a_{ij} = a_{ji}$ for all i and j are sometimes called *symmetric* or *undirected* traveling salesman problems, because the direction of traversal of a given arc does not matter.

A *tour* (also called a *Hamiltonian cycle*; see Section 1.1) is defined to be a simple forward cycle that contains all the nodes of the graph. Equivalently, a tour is a connected subgraph that consists of N arcs, such that there is exactly one incoming and one outgoing arc for each node $i = 1, \ldots, N$. If we define the cost of a subgraph T to be the sum of the traversal costs of its arcs,

$$\sum_{(i,j)\in T} a_{ij},$$

the traveling salesman problem is to find a tour of minimum cost.

We formulate this problem as a network flow problem with node set $\mathcal{N} = \{1, \ldots, N\}$ and arc set $\mathcal{A} = \big\{(i,j) \mid i,j = 1, \ldots, N, \, i \neq j\big\}$, and with side constraints and 0-1 integer constraints:

$$\text{minimize} \quad \sum_{(i,j) \in \mathcal{A}} a_{ij} x_{ij}$$

$$\text{subject to} \quad \sum_{\substack{j=1,\ldots,N \\ j \neq i}} x_{ij} = 1, \qquad i = 1, \ldots, N,$$

$$\sum_{\substack{i=1,\ldots,N \\ i \neq j}} x_{ij} = 1, \qquad j = 1, \ldots, N,$$

$$x_{ij} = 0 \text{ or } 1, \qquad \forall \, (i,j) \in \mathcal{A},$$

the subgraph with node-arc set $\big(\mathcal{N}, \{(i,j) \mid x_{ij} = 1\}\big)$ is connected.   (10.1)

Note that, given the 0-1 constraints on the arc flows and the conservation of flow equations, the last constraint can be expressed through the set of side constraints

$$\sum_{i \in S, \, j \notin S} (x_{ij} + x_{ji}) \geq 2, \quad \forall \text{ nonempty proper subsets } S \text{ of nodes.}$$

If these constraints were not present, the problem would be an ordinary assignment problem. Unfortunately, however, these constraints are essential, since without them, there would be feasible solutions involving multiple disconnected cycles, as illustrated in Fig. 10.1.

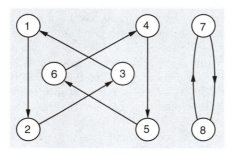

Figure 10.1: Example of an infeasible solution of a traveling salesman problem where all the constraints are satisfied except for the connectivity constraint (10.1). This solution may have been obtained by solving an $N \times N$ assignment problem and consists of multiple cycles [(1,2,3), (4,5,6), and (7,8) in the figure]. The arcs of the cycles correspond to the assigned pairs (i,j) in the assignment problem.

A simple approach for solving the traveling salesman problem is the *nearest neighbor* heuristic. We start from a path consisting of just a single node i_1 and at each iteration, we enlarge the path with a node that does not close a cycle and minimizes the cost of the enlargement. In particular, after k iterations, we have a forward path $\{i_1, \ldots, i_k\}$ consisting of distinct nodes, and at the next iteration, we add an arc (i_k, i_{k+1}) that minimizes $a_{i_k i}$ over all arcs (i_k, i) with $i \neq i_1, \ldots, i_k$. After $N - 1$ iterations, all nodes are included in the path, which is then converted to a tour by adding the final arc (i_N, i_1).

Given a tour, one may try to improve its cost by using some method that changes the tour incrementally. In particular, a popular method for the symmetric case ($a_{ij} = a_{ji}$ for all i and j) is the *k-OPT heuristic*, which creates a new tour by exchanging k arcs of the current tour with another k arcs that do not belong to the tour (see Fig. 10.2). The k arcs are chosen to optimize the cost of the new tour with $O(N^k)$ computation. The method stops when no improvement of the current tour is possible through a k-interchange.

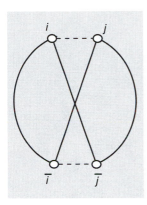

Figure 10.2: Illustration of the 2-OPT heuristic for improving a tour of the symmetric traveling salesman problem. The arcs (i, j) and $(\bar{i}, \bar{j})$ are interchanged with the arcs $(i, \bar{j})$ and $(\bar{i}, j)$. The choice of (i, j) and $(\bar{i}, \bar{j})$ is optimized over all pairs of nonadjacent arcs of the tour.

Another possibility for constructing an initial tour is the following two-step method:

(1) Discard the side constraints (10.1), and from the resulting assignment problem, obtain a solution consisting of a collection of subtours such as the ones shown in Fig. 10.1. More generally, use some method to obtain a "reasonable" collection of subtours such that each node lies on exactly one subtour.

(2) Use some heuristic to create a tour by combining subtours. For example, any two subtours T and $\bar{T}$ can be merged into a single subtour by selecting a node $i \in T$ and a node $\bar{i} \in \bar{T}$, adding the arc $(i, \bar{i})$, deleting the unique outgoing arc (i, j) of i on the subtour T and the unique incoming arc $(\bar{j}, \bar{i})$ of $\bar{j}$ on the subtour $\bar{T}$, and finally adding the arc $(\bar{j}, j)$, as shown in Fig. 10.3. The pair of nodes i and $\bar{i}$ can be chosen to minimize the cost of the created subtour. This optimization requires $O(mn)$ computation, where m and n are the numbers of nodes in T and $\bar{T}$, respectively.

Still another alternative for constructing an initial tour, is to start with some spanning tree and to gradually convert it into a tour. There are quite a few heuristics based on this idea; see e.g., the book by Nemhauser and Wolsey [1988], the survey by Junger, Reinelt, and Rinaldi [1995], and the references quoted there. Unfortunately, there are no heuristics with practically useful performance guarantees for the general traveling salesman problem (Sahni and Gonzalez [1976], and Johnson and Papadimitriou [1985] make this point precise). The situation is better, however, for some special types of symmetric

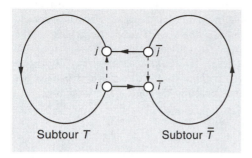

Figure 10.3: Merging two subtours T and $\overline{T}$ into a single subtour by selecting two nodes $i \in T$ and $\overline{i} \in \overline{T}$, and adding and deleting the appropriate arcs of T and $\overline{T}$.

problems where the arc costs satisfy the relation

$$a_{ij} \le a_{ik} + a_{kj}, \qquad \text{for all nodes } i, j, k.$$

known as the *triangle inequality* (see Exercises 10.7-10.8).

Example 10.2. Fixed Charge Problems

A fixed charge problem is a minimum cost flow problem where there is an extra cost b_{ij} for each arc flow x_{ij} that is positive (in addition to the usual cost $a_{ij}x_{ij}$). Thus b_{ij} may be viewed as a "purchase cost" for acquiring the arc (i,j) and using it to carry flow.

An example of a fixed charge problem is the *facility location problem*, where we must select a subset of locations from a given candidate set, and place in each of these locations a "facility" that will serve the needs of certain "clients." There is a 0-1 decision variable associated with selecting any given location for facility placement, at a given cost. Once these variables are chosen, an assignment (or transportation) problem must be solved to optimally match clients with facilities. Mathematically, we assume that there are m clients and n locations. By $x_{ij} = 1$ (or $x_{ij} = 0$) we indicate that client i is assigned to location j at a cost a_{ij} (or is not assigned, respectively). We also introduce a 0-1 integer variable y_j to indicate (with $y_j = 1$) that a facility is placed at location j at a cost b_j. The problem is

$$\text{minimize} \quad \sum_{(i,j)\in\mathcal{A}} a_{ij}x_{ij} + \sum_{j=1}^{n} b_j y_j$$

$$\text{subject to} \quad \sum_{\{j|(i,j)\in\mathcal{A}\}} x_{ij} = 1, \qquad i = 1, \ldots, m,$$

$$\sum_{\{i|(i,j)\in\mathcal{A}\}} x_{ij} \le y_j c_j, \qquad j = 1, \ldots, n,$$

$$x_{ij} = 0 \text{ or } 1, \qquad \forall\, (i,j) \in \mathcal{A},$$

$$y_j = 0 \text{ or } 1, \qquad j = 1, \ldots, n,$$

where c_j is the maximum number of customers that can be served by a facility at location j.

We can formulate this problem as a network flow problem with side constraints and integer constraints. In particular, we can view x_{ij} as the arc flows of the graph of a transportation problem (with inequality constraints). We can also view y_j as the arc flows of an artificial graph that is disconnected from the transportation graph, but is coupled to it through the side constraints $\sum_i x_{ij} \leq y_j c_j$ (see Fig. 10.4). This formulation does not necessarily facilitate the algorithmic solution of the problem, but serves to illustrate the generality of our framework for network problems with side constraints.

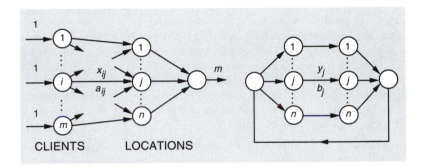

Figure 10.4: Formulation of the facility location problem as a network flow problem with side constraints and 0-1 integer constraints. There are two disconnected subgraphs: the first is a transportation-like graph that involves the flow variables x_{ij} and the second is an artificial graph that involves the flow variables y_j. The arc flows of the two subgraphs are coupled through the side constraints $\sum_i x_{ij} \leq y_j c_j$.

Example 10.3. Optimal Tree Problems

There are many network applications where one needs to construct an optimal tree subject to some constraints. For example, in data networks, a spanning tree is often used to broadcast information from some central source to all the nodes. In this context, it makes sense to assign a cost or weight a_{ij} to each arc (communication link) (i, j) and try to find a spanning tree that has minimum total weight (minimum sum of arc weights). This is the *minimum weight spanning tree problem*, which we have briefly discussed in Chapter 2 (see Exercise 2.30).

We can formulate this problem as an integer-constrained problem in several ways. For example, let x_{ij} be a 0-1 integer variable indicating whether arc (i, j) belongs to the spanning tree. Then the problem can be written as

$$\text{minimize} \quad \sum_{(i,j) \in \mathcal{A}} a_{ij} x_{ij}$$

$$\text{subject to} \quad \sum_{(i,j) \in \mathcal{A}} x_{ij} = N - 1,$$

$$\sum_{i \in S, j \notin S} (x_{ij} + x_{ji}) \geq 1, \quad \forall \text{ nonempty proper subsets } S \text{ of nodes,}$$

$$x_{ij} = 0 \text{ or } 1, \qquad \forall \; (i, j) \in \mathcal{A}.$$

The first two constraints guarantee that the graph defined by the set $\{(i, j) \mid x_{ij} = 1\}$ has $N - 1$ arcs and is connected, so it is a spanning tree.

In Exercise 2.30, we discussed how the minimum weight spanning tree problem can be solved with a *greedy* algorithm. An example is the *Prim-Dijkstra algorithm*, which builds an optimal spanning tree by generating a sequence of subtrees. It starts with a subtree consisting of a single node and it iteratively adds to the current subtree an incident arc that has minimum weight over all incident arcs that do not close a cycle. We indicated in Exercise 2.30 that this algorithm can be implemented so that it has an $O(N^2)$ running time. This is remarkable, because except for the minimum cost flow problems discussed in Chapters 2-7, very few other types of network optimization problems can be solved with a polynomial-time algorithm.

There are a number of variations of the minimum weight spanning tree problem. Here are some examples:

(a) There is a constraint on the number of tree arcs that are incident to a single given node. This is known as the *degree constrained minimum weight spanning tree problem*. It is possible to solve this problem using a polynomial version of the greedy algorithm (see Exercise 10.10). On the other hand, if there is a degree constraint on *every* node, the problem turns out to be much harder. For example, suppose that the degree of each node is constrained to be at most 2. Then a spanning tree subject to this constraint must be a path that goes through each node exactly once, so the problem is essentially equivalent to a symmetric traveling salesman problem (see Exercise 10.6).

(b) The *capacitated spanning tree problem*. Here the arcs of the tree are to be used for routing specified supplies from given supply nodes to given demand nodes. The tree specifies the routes that will carry the flow from the supply points to the demand points, and hence also specifies the corresponding arc flows. We require that the tree is selected so that the flow of each arc does not exceed a given capacity constraint. This is an integer-constrained problem, which is not polynomially solvable. However, there are some practical heuristic algorithms, such as an algorithm due to Esau and Williams [1966] (see Fig. 10.5).

(c) The *Steiner tree problem*, where the requirement that all nodes must be included in the tree is relaxed. Instead, we are given a subset S of the nodes, and we want to find a tree that includes the subset S and has minimum total weight. [J. Steiner (1796-1863), "the greatest geometer since Apollonius," posed the problem of finding the shortest tree spanning a given set of points on the plane.] An important application of the Steiner tree problem arises in broadcasting information over a communication network from a special node to a selected subset S of nodes. This broadcasting is most efficiently done over a Steiner tree, where the cost of each arc corresponds to the cost of communication over that arc. The Steiner tree problem also turns out to be a difficult

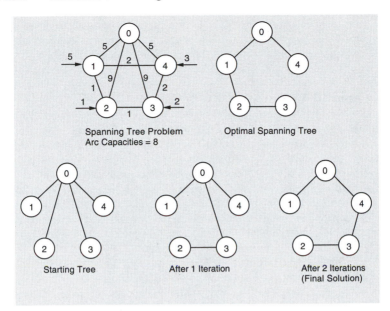

Figure 10.5: The Esau-Williams heuristic for solving a capacitated minimum weight spanning tree problem. Each arc (i, j) has a cost (or weight) a_{ij} and a capacity c_{ij}. The problem is symmetric, so that $a_{ij} = a_{ji}$ and $c_{ij} = c_{ji}$. We assume that the graph is complete [if some arcs (i, j) do not exist, we introduce them artificially with a very large cost and infinite capacity]. There is a special concentrator node 0, and for every other node $i = 1, \ldots, N$, there is a supply $s_i \geq 0$ that must be transferred to node 0 along the arcs of the spanning tree without violating the arc capacity constraints. The Esau-Williams algorithm generates a sequence of feasible spanning trees, each having a lower cost than its predecessor, by using an arc exchange heuristic. In particular, we start with a spanning tree where the concentrator node 0 is directly connected with each of the N other nodes, as in the bottom left figure [we assume that the arcs $(i, 0)$ can carry at least the supply of node i, that is, $c_{i0} \geq s_i$]. At each successive iteration, an arc $(i, 0)$ is deleted from the current spanning tree, and another arc (i, j) is added, so that:

(1) No cycle is formed.

(2) The capacity constraints of all the arcs of the new spanning tree are satisfied.

(3) The saving $a_{i0} - a_{ij}$ in cost obtained by exchanging arcs $(i, 0)$ and (i, j) is positive and is maximized over all nodes i and and j for which (1) and (2) above are satisfied.

The figure illustrates the algorithm, for the problem shown at the top left, where the cost of each arc is shown next to each arc, the capacity of each arc is 8, and the supplies of the nodes $i > 0$ are shown next to the arrows. The algorithm terminates after two iterations with the tree shown, which has a total cost of 13. Termination occurs because when arc $(1, 0)$ or $(4, 0)$ is removed and an arc that is not incident to node 0 is added, some arc capacity is violated. The optimal spanning tree has cost equal to 12.

integer-constrained problem, for which, however, effective heuristics are available (see Exercise 10.11). Note that there are degree-constrained and capacitated versions of the problem, as in (a) and (b) above.

Example 10.4. Matching Problems

A matching problem involves dividing a collection of objects into pairs. There may be some constraints regarding the objects that can be paired, and there is a benefit or value associated with matching each of the eligible pairs. The objective is to find a matching of maximal total value. We have already studied extensively special cases of matching, namely the assignment problems of Chapter 7, which are also called *bipartite matching problems*. These are matching problems where the objects are partitioned in two groups, and pairs must involve only one element from each group. Matching problems where there is no such partition are called *nonbipartite*.

To pose a matching problem as a network flow problem, we introduce a graph $(\mathcal{N}, \mathcal{A})$ that has a node for each object, and an arc (i, j) of value a_{ij} connecting any two objects i and j that can be paired. The orientation of this arc does not matter [alternatively, we may introduce both arcs (i, j) and (j, i), and assign to them equal values]. We consider a flow variable x_{ij} for each arc (i, j), where x_{ij} is 1 or 0 depending on whether objects i and j are matched or not, respectively. The objective is to maximize

$$\sum_{(i,j)\in\mathcal{A}} a_{ij} x_{ij}$$

subject to the constraints

$$\sum_{\{j|(i,j)\in\mathcal{A}\}} x_{ij} + \sum_{\{j|(j,i)\in\mathcal{A}\}} x_{ji} \le 1, \qquad \forall\, i \in \mathcal{N}, \tag{10.2}$$

$$x_{ij} = 0 \text{ or } 1, \qquad \forall\, (i, j) \in \mathcal{A}.$$

The constraint (10.2) expresses the requirement that an object can be matched with at most one other object. In a variant of the problem, it is specified that the matching should be *perfect*; that is, every object should be matched with some other object. In this case, the constraint (10.2) should be changed to

$$\sum_{\{j|(i,j)\in\mathcal{A}\}} x_{ij} + \sum_{\{j|(j,i)\in\mathcal{A}\}} x_{ji} = 1, \qquad \forall\, i \in \mathcal{N}. \tag{10.3}$$

The special case where $a_{ij} = 1$ for all arcs (i, j) is the *maximum cardinality matching problem*, i.e., finding a matching with a maximum number of matched pairs.

It is possible to view nonbipartite matching as an optimal network flow problem of the assignment type with integer constraints and with the side constraints defined by Eq. (10.2) or Eq. (10.3) (see Exercise 10.15). We would thus expect that the problem is a difficult one, and that it is not polynomially solvable (cf. the discussion of Section 8.4). However, this is not so. It turns out that nonbipartite matching has an interesting and intricate structure, which is quite unique among combinatorial and network optimization problems. In particular, nonbipartite matching problems can be solved with polynomial-time algorithms. These algorithms share some key structures with their bipartite counterparts, such as augmenting paths, but they generally become simpler and run faster when specialized to bipartite matching. One such algorithm, due to Edmonds [1965] can be implemented so that it has $O(N^3)$ running time. Furthermore, nonbipartite matching can be formulated as a linear program *without* integer constraints, and admits an analysis based on linear programming duality. We refer to the literature cited at the end of the chapter for an account.

Example 10.5. Vehicle Routing Problems

In vehicle routing problems, there is a fleet of vehicles that must pick up a number of "customers" (e.g., persons, packages, objects, etc.) from various nodes in a transportation network and deliver them at some other nodes using the network arcs. The objective is to minimize total cost subject to a variety of constraints. The cost here may include, among other things, transportation cost, and penalties for tardiness of pickup and delivery. The constraints may include vehicle capacity, and pickup and delivery time restrictions.

Vehicle routing problems are among the hardest integer programming problems because they tend to have a large number of integer variables, and also because they involve both a resource allocation and a scheduling aspect. In particular, they combine the difficult combinatorial aspects of two problems that we have already discussed:

(a) The generalized assignment problem discussed in Section 8.5 (determine which vehicles will service which customers).

(b) The traveling salesman problem discussed in Example 10.1 (determine the sequence of customer pickups and deliveries by a given vehicle). In fact, the traveling salesman problem may itself be viewed as a simple version of the vehicle routing problem, involving a single vehicle of unlimited capacity, N customers that must be picked up in some unspecified order, and a travel cost a_{ij} from customer i to customer j.

For a common type of vehicle routing problem, suppose that there are K vehicles (denoted $1, \ldots, K$) with corresponding capacities $c_1, \ldots, c_K$, which make deliveries to N customers (nodes $1, \ldots, N$) starting from a central depot (node 0). The delivery to customer i is of given size d_i, and the cost of traveling from node i to node j is denoted by a_{ij}. The problem is to find the route of each vehicle (a cycle of nodes starting from node 0 and returning to 0), that satisfies the customer delivery constraints, and the vehicle capacity constraints.

There are several heuristic approaches for solving this problem, some of which bear similarity to the heuristic approaches for solving the traveling salesman problem. For example, one may start with some set of routes, which may be infeasible because their number may exceed the number of vehicles K. One may then try to work towards feasibility by combining routes in a way that satisfies the vehicle capacity constraints, while keeping the cost as small as possible. Alternatively, one may start with a solution of a K-traveling salesmen problem (see Exercise 10.9), corresponding to the K vehicles, and then try to improve on this solution by interchanging customers between routes, while trying to satisfy the capacity constraints. These heuristics often work well, but generally they offer no guarantee of good performance, and may occasionally result in a solution that is far from optimal.

An alternative possibility, which is ultimately also based on heuristics, is to formulate the problem mathematically in a way that emphasizes its connections to both the generalized assignment problem and the traveling salesman problem. In particular, we introduce the integer variables

$$y_{ik} = \begin{cases} 1 & \text{if node } i \text{ is visited by vehicle } k, \\ 0 & \text{otherwise,} \end{cases}$$

and the vectors $y_k = (y_{1k}, \ldots, y_{Nk})$. For each $k = 1, \ldots, K$, let $f_k(y_k)$ denote the optimal cost of a traveling salesman problem involving the set of nodes

$$N_k(y_k) = \{i \mid y_{ik} = 1\}.$$

We can pose the problem as

$$\text{minimize} \quad \sum_{k=1}^{K} f_k(y_k)$$

$$\text{subject to} \quad \sum_{k=1}^{K} y_{ik} = \begin{cases} K & \text{if } i = 0, \\ 1 & \text{if } i = 1, \ldots, N, \end{cases}$$

$$\sum_{i=0}^{N} d_i y_{ik} \le c_k, \qquad k = 1, \ldots, K,$$

$$y_{ik} = 0 \text{ or } 1, \qquad i = 0, \ldots, N, \ k = 1, \ldots, N,$$

which is a generalized assignment problem (see Section 8.5).

The difficulty with the generalized assignment formulation is that the functions f_k are generally unknown. It is possible, however, to try to approximate heuristically these functions with some linear functions of the form

$$\tilde{f}_k(y_k) = \sum_{i=0}^{N} w_{ik} y_{ik},$$

solve the corresponding generalized assignment problems for the vectors y_k, and then solve the corresponding traveling salesman problems. The weights w_{ik} can be determined in some heuristic way. For example, first specify a "seed" customer i_k to be picked up by vehicle k, and then set

$$w_{ik} = a_{0i} + a_{ii_k} - a_{0i_k},$$

which is the incremental cost of inserting customer i into the route $0 \mapsto i_k \mapsto 0$. The seed customers specify the general direction of the route taken by vehicle k, and the weight w_{ik} represents the approximate cost for picking up customer i along the way. One may select the seed customers using one of a number of heuristics, for which we refer to the literature cited at the end of the chapter.

There are several extensions and more complex variants of the preceding vehicle routing problems. For example:

(a) Some of the customers may have a "time window," in the sense that they may be served only within a given time interval. Furthermore, the total time duration of a route may be constrained.

(b) There may be multiple depots, and each vehicle may be restricted to start from a given subset of the depots.

(c) Delivery to some of the customers may not be required. Instead there may be a penalty for nondelivery or for tardiness of delivery (in the case where there are time windows).

(d) There may be precedence constraints, requiring that some of the customers be served before some others.

With additional side constraints of the type described above, the problem can become very complex. Nonetheless, with a combination of heuristics and the more formal approaches to be described in this chapter, some measure of success has been obtained in solving practical vehicle routing problems.

Example 10.6. Arc Routing Problems

Arc routing problems are similar to vehicle routing problems, except that the emphasis regarding cost and constraints is placed on arc traversals rather than node visits. Here each arc (i, j) has a cost a_{ij}, and we want to find a set of arcs that satisfy certain constraints and have minimum sum of costs. For example, a classical arc routing problem is the *Chinese postman problem*, where we want to find a cycle that traverses every arc of a graph, and has minimum sum of arc costs; here traversals in either direction and multiple traversals are allowed.† The costs of all arcs must be assumed nonnegative here in order to guarantee that the problem has an optimal solution (otherwise cycles of arbitrarily small cost would be possible by crossing back and forth an arc of negative cost).

An interesting related question is whether there exists an *Euler cycle* in the given graph, i.e., a cycle that contains every arc exactly once, with arc traversals in either direction allowed (such a cycle, if it exists, solves the Chinese postman problem since the arc costs are assumed nonnegative). This

---

† An analogy here is made with a postman who must traverse each arc of the road network of some town (in at least one direction), while walking the minimum possible distance. The problem was first posed by the Chinese mathematician Kwan Mei-Ko [1962].

question was posed by Euler in connection with the famous Königsberg bridge problem (see Fig. 10.6). The solution is simple: *there exists an Euler cycle if and only if the graph is connected and every node has even degree* (in an Euler cycle, the number of entrances to a node must be equal to the number of exits, so the number of incident arcs to each node must be even; for a proof of the converse, see Exercise 1.5). It turns out that even when there are nodes of odd degree, a solution to the Chinese postman problem can be obtained by constructing an Euler cycle in an expanded graph that involves some additional arcs. These arcs can be obtained by solving a nonbipartite matching problem involving the nodes of odd degree (see Exercise 10.17). Thus, since the matching problem can be solved in polynomial time as noted in Example 10.4, the Chinese postman problem can also be solved in polynomial time (see also Edmonds and Johnson [1973], who explored the relation between matching and the Chinese postman problem).

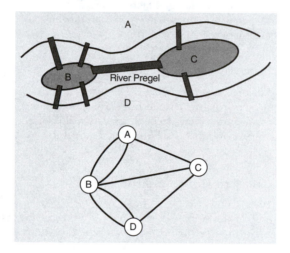

Figure 10.6: The Königsberg bridge problem, generally considered to mark the origin of graph theory. Euler attributed this problem to the citizens of Königsberg, an old port town that lies north of Warsaw on the Baltic sea (it is now called Kaliningrad). The problem, addressed by Euler in 1736, is whether it is possible to cross each of the seven bridges of the river Pregel in Königsberg exactly once, and return to the starting point. In the graph representation of the problem, shown in the figure, each bridge is associated with an arc, and each node is associated with a land area that is incident to several bridges. The question amounts to asking whether an Euler cycle exists. The answer is negative since there are nodes with odd degree.

There is also a "directed" version of the Chinese postman problem, where we want to find a *forward* cycle that traverses every arc of a graph (possibly multiple times), and has minimum sum of arc costs. It can be seen that this problem has a feasible solution if and only if the graph is strongly connected, and that it has an optimal solution if in addition all forward cycles have nonnegative cost. The problem is related to the construction of *forward* Euler cycles, in roughly the same way as the undirected Chinese postman problem was related above to the construction of an (undirected) Euler cycle. Exercise 1.8 states the basic result about the existence of a forward Euler cycle: such a cycle exists if and only if the number of incoming arcs to each node is equal to the number of its outgoing arcs. A forward Euler cycle, if it exists, is also a solution to the directed Chinese postman problem. More generally, it turns out that a solution to the directed Chinese postman problem (assuming one exists) can be obtained by finding a directed Euler cycle in an associated graph obtained by solving a certain minimum cost flow problem (see Exercise 10.17).

By introducing different constraints, one may obtain a large variety of arc routing problems. For example, a variant of the Chinese postman problem is to find a cycle of minimum cost that traverses only a given subset of the arcs. This is known as the *rural postman problem*. Other variants are characterized by arc time-windows and arc precedence constraints, similar to vehicle routing problem variants discussed earlier. In fact, it is always possible to convert an arc routing problem to a "node routing problem," where the constraints are placed on some of the nodes rather than on the arcs. This can be done by replacing each arc (i, j) with two arcs (i, k_{ij}) and (k_{ij}, j) separated by an artificial middle node k_{ij}. Traversal of an arc (i, j) then becomes equivalent to visiting the artificial node k_{ij}. However, this transformation often masks important characteristics of the problem. For example it would be awkward to pose the question of existence of an Euler cycle as a node routing problem.

Example 10.7. Multidimensional Assignment Problems

In the assignment problems we have considered so far, we group the nodes of the graph in pairs. Multidimensional assignment problems involve the grouping of the nodes in subsets with more than two elements, such as triplets or quadruplets of nodes. For an example of a 3-dimensional assignment problem, suppose that the performance of a job j requires a machine m and a worker w, and that there is a given value a_{jmw} corresponding to the triplet (j, m, w). Given a set of jobs J, a set of machines M, and a set of workers W, we want to find a collection of job/machine/worker triplets that has maximum total value.

To pose this problem mathematically, we introduce 0-1 integer variables

$$x_{jmw} = \begin{cases} 1 & \text{if job } j \text{ is performed at machine } m \text{ by worker } w, \\ 0 & \text{otherwise,} \end{cases}$$

and we maximize

$$\sum_{j \in J} \sum_{m \in M} \sum_{w \in W} a_{jmw} x_{jmw}$$

subject to standard assignment constraints. In particular, if the numbers of jobs, machines, and workers are all equal, and all jobs must be assigned, we have the constraints

$$\sum_{m \in M} \sum_{w \in W} x_{jmw} = 1, \qquad \forall \, j \in J,$$

$$\sum_{j \in J} \sum_{w \in W} x_{jmw} = 1, \qquad \forall\; m \in M,$$

$$\sum_{j \in J} \sum_{m \in M} x_{jmw} = 1, \qquad \forall\; w \in W.$$

In alternative formulations, some of these constraints may involve inequalities.

An important and particularly favorable special case of the problem arises when the values a_{jmw} have the *separable* form

$$a_{jmw} = \beta_{jm} + \gamma_{mw},$$

where β_{jm} and γ_{mw} are given scalars. In this case, there is no coupling between jobs and workers, and the problem can be solved by solving two decoupled (2-dimensional) assignment problems: one involving the pairing of jobs and machines, with the β_{jm} as values, and the other involving the pairing of machines and workers, with the γ_{mw} as values. In general, however, the 3-dimensional assignment problem is a difficult integer programming problem, for which there is no known polynomial algorithm.

A simple heuristic approach is based on relaxing each of the constraints in turn. In particular, suppose that the constraint on the workers is neglected first. It can then be seen that the problem takes the 2-dimensional assignment form

$$\text{maximize} \quad \sum_{j \in J} \sum_{m \in M} b_{jm} y_{jm}$$

$$\text{subject to} \quad \sum_{m \in M} y_{jm} = 1, \qquad \forall\; j \in J,$$

$$\sum_{j \in J} y_{jm} = 1, \qquad \forall\; m \in M,$$

$$y_{jm} = 0 \text{ or } 1, \qquad \forall\; j \in J,\, m \in M,$$

where

$$b_{jm} = \max_{w \in W} a_{jmw}, \tag{10.4}$$

and $y_{jm} = 1$ indicates that job j must be performed at machine m. For each $j \in J$, let j_m be the job assigned to machine m, according to the solution of this problem. We can now optimally assign machines m to workers w, using as assignment values

$$c_{mw} = a_{j_m mw},$$

and obtain a 3-dimensional assignment $\{(j_m, m, w_m) \mid m \in M\}$. It can be seen that this approach amounts to *enforced separation*, whereby we replace the values a_{jmw} with the separable approximations $b_{jm} + c_{mw}$. In fact, it can be shown that if the problem is ϵ-*separable*, in the sense that for some (possibly unknown) $\overline{\beta}_{jm}$ and $\overline{\gamma}_{mw}$, and some $\epsilon \geq 0$, we have

$$|\overline{\beta}_{jm} + \overline{\gamma}_{mw} - a_{jmw}| \leq \epsilon, \qquad \forall\; j \in J,\, m \in M,\, w \in W,$$

then the assignment $\{(j_m, m, w_m) \mid m \in M\}$ obtained using the preceding enforced separation approach achieves the optimal value of the problem within $4n\epsilon$, where n is the cardinality of the sets J, M, and W (see Exercise 10.31).

The enforced separation approach is simple and can be generalized to multidimensional assignment problems of dimension more than 3. However, it often results in significant loss of optimality. A potential improvement is to introduce some corrections to the values b_{jm} that reflect some dependence on the values of workers. For example, we can use instead of the values b_{jm} of Eq. (10.4), the modified values

$$\hat{b}_{jm} = \max_{w \in W}\{a_{jmw} - \mu_w\},$$

where μ_w is a nonnegative scalar that can be viewed as a *wage* to be paid to worker w. This allows the possibility of adjusting the scalars μ_w to some "optimal" values. Methods for doing this will be discussed in Section 10.3 in the context of the Lagrangian relaxation method, where we will view μ_w as a Lagrange multiplier corresponding to the constraint $\sum_{j \in J} \sum_{m \in M} x_{jmw} = 1$.

There are several extensions of the multidimensional assignment problem. For example, we may have transportation constraints, where multiple jobs can be performed on the same machine, and/or multiple machines can be operated by a single worker. In this case, our preceding discussion of the enforced separation heuristic applies similarly. We may also have generalized assignment constraints such as

$$\sum_{j \in J} \sum_{w \in W} g_{jmw} x_{jmw} \leq 1, \qquad \forall\ m \in M,$$

where g_{jmw} represents the portion of machine m needed to perform job j by worker w. In this case, the enforced separation heuristic results in difficult integer-constrained generalized assignment problems, which we may have to solve heuristically. Alternatively, we may use the more formal methodology of the next two sections.

10.2 BRANCH-AND-BOUND

The branch-and-bound method implicitly enumerates all the feasible solutions, using calculations where the integer constraints of the problem are relaxed. The method can be very time-consuming, but is in principle capable of yielding an exactly optimal solution.

To describe the branch-and-bound method, consider the general discrete optimization problem

$$\text{minimize}\quad f(x)$$
$$\text{subject to}\quad x \in F,$$

where the feasible set F is a *finite* set. The branch-and-bound algorithm uses an acyclic graph known as the *branch-and-bound tree*, which corresponds to a progressively finer partition of F. In particular, the nodes of this graph correspond to a collection $\mathcal{F}$ of subsets of F, which is such that:

1. $F \in \mathcal{F}$ (i.e., the set of all solutions is a node).

2. If x is a feasible solution, then $\{x\} \in \mathcal{F}$ (i.e., each solution viewed as a singleton set is a node).

3. If a set $Y \in \mathcal{F}$ contains more than one solution $x \in F$, then there exist disjoint sets $Y_1, \ldots, Y_n \in \mathcal{F}$ such that

$$\bigcup_{i=1}^{n} Y_i = Y.$$

   The set Y is called the *parent* of $Y_1, \ldots, Y_n$, and the sets $Y_1, \ldots, Y_n$ are called the *children* or *descendants* of Y.

4. Each set in $\mathcal{F}$ other than F has a parent.

The collection of sets $\mathcal{F}$ defines the branch-and-bound tree as in Fig. 10.7. In particular, this tree has the set of all feasible solutions F as its root node and the singleton solutions $\{x\}$, $x \in F$, as terminal nodes. The arcs of the graph are those that connect parents Y and their children Y_i.

   The key assumption in the branch-and-bound method is that for every nonterminal node Y, there is an algorithm that calculates:

(a) A lower bound $\underline{f}_Y$ to the minimum cost over Y

$$\underline{f}_Y \leq \min_{x \in Y} f(x).$$

(b) A feasible solution $\overline{x} \in Y$, whose cost $f(\overline{x})$ can serve as an upper bound to the optimal cost of the original problem $\min_{x \in F} f(x)$.

The main idea of the branch-and-bound algorithm is to save computation by discarding the nodes/subsets of the tree that have no chance of containing an optimal solution. In particular, the algorithm selects nodes Y from the branch-and-bound tree, and checks whether the lower bound $\underline{f}_Y$ exceeds the best available upper bound [the minimal cost $f(\overline{x})$ over all feasible solutions $\overline{x}$ found so far]. If this is so, we know that Y cannot contain an optimal solution, so all its descendant nodes in the tree need not be considered further.

   To organize the search through the tree, the algorithm maintains a node list called OPEN, and also maintains a scalar called UPPER, which is equal to the minimal cost over feasible solutions found so far. Initially, OPEN contains just F, and UPPER is equal to ∞ or to the cost $f(\overline{x})$ of some feasible solution $\overline{x} \in F$.

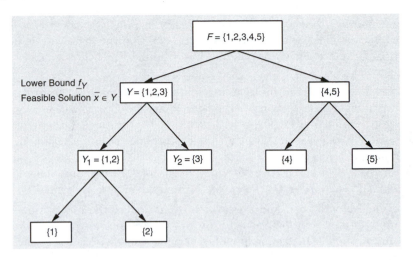

Figure 10.7: Illustration of a branch-and-bound tree. Each node Y (a subset of the feasible set F), except those consisting of a single solution, is partitioned into several other nodes (subsets) $Y_1, \ldots, Y_n$. The original feasible set is divided repeatedly into subsets until no more division is possible. For each node/subset Y of the tree, one may compute a lower bound $\underline{f}_Y$ to the optimal cost of the corresponding restricted subproblem $\min_{x \in Y} f(x)$, and a feasible solution $\overline{x} \in Y$, whose cost can serve as an upper bound to the optimal cost $\min_{x \in F} f(x)$ of the original problem. The idea is to use these bounds to economize computation by eliminating nodes of the tree that cannot contain an optimal solution.

Branch-and-Bound Algorithm

Step 1: Remove a node Y from OPEN. For each child Y_j of Y, do the following: Find the lower bound $\underline{f}_{Y_j}$ and a feasible solution $\overline{x} \in Y_j$. If

$$\underline{f}_{Y_j} < \text{UPPER},$$

place Y_j in OPEN. If in addition

$$f(\overline{x}) < \text{UPPER},$$

set

$$\text{UPPER} = f(\overline{x})$$

and mark $\overline{x}$ as the best solution found so far.

Step 2: (Termination Test) If OPEN is nonempty, go to step 1. Otherwise, terminate; the best solution found so far is optimal.

A node Y_j that is not placed in OPEN in Step 1 is said to be *fathomed*. Such a node cannot contain a better solution than the best solution found so far, since the corresponding lower bound $\underline{f}_{Y_j}$ is not smaller than UPPER. Therefore nothing is lost when we drop this node from further consideration and forego the examination of its descendants. Regardless of how many nodes are fathomed, the branch-and-bound algorithm is guaranteed to examine either explicitly or implicitly (through fathoming) all the terminal nodes, which are the singleton solutions. As a result, it will terminate with an optimal solution.

Note that a small (near-optimal) value of UPPER and tight lower bounds $\underline{f}_{Y_j}$ contribute to the quick fathoming of large portions of the branch-and-bound tree, and an early termination of the algorithm, with either an optimal solution or a solution that is within some given tolerance of being optimal. In fact, a popular variant, aimed at accelerating the branch-and-bound algorithm, is to fix an $\epsilon > 0$, and replace the test

$$\underline{f}_{Yj} < \text{UPPER}$$

with

$$\underline{f}_{Yj} < \text{UPPER} - \epsilon$$

in Step 1. This variant may terminate much faster, while the best solution obtained upon termination is guaranteed to be within ϵ of optimality.

Other variations of branch-and-bound relate to the method for selecting a node from OPEN in Step 1. For example, a possible strategy is to choose the node with minimal lower bound; alternatively, one may choose the node containing the best solution found so far. In fact it is neither practical nor necessary to generate a priori the branch-and-bound tree. Instead, one may adaptively decide on the order and the manner in which the nodes are partitioned into descendants based on the progress of the algorithm.

Branch-and-bound typically uses "continuous" network optimization problems (without integer constraints) to obtain lower bounds to the optimal costs of the restricted problems $\min_{x \in Y} f(x)$ and to construct corresponding feasible solutions. For example, suppose that our original problem has a convex cost function, and a feasible set F that consists of convex set constraints and side constraints, *plus the additional constraint that all the arc flows must be 0 or 1*. Then a restricted subset Y may specify that the flows of some given subset of arcs are fixed at 0 or at 1, while the remaining arc flows may take either the value 0 or the value 1. A lower bound to the restricted optimal cost $\min_{x \in Y} f(x)$ is then obtained by relaxing the 0-1 constraint on the latter arc flows, thereby allowing them to take any value in the interval $[0, 1]$ and resulting in a convex network problem with side constraints. Thus the solution by branch-and-bound of a network problem with convex cost and side constraints *plus* additional integer constraints requires the solution of many convex network problems with side constraints but *without* integer constraints.

Example 10.8. Facility Location Problems

Let us consider the facility location problem introduced in Example 10.2, which involves m clients and n locations. By $x_{ij} = 1$ (or $x_{ij} = 0$) we indicate that client i is assigned to location j at a cost a_{ij} (or is not assigned, respectively). We also introduce a 0-1 integer variable y_j to indicate (with $y_j = 1$) that a facility is placed at location j at a cost b_j. The problem is

$$\text{minimize} \quad \sum_{(i,j)\in\mathcal{A}} a_{ij}x_{ij} + \sum_{j=1}^{n} b_j y_j$$

$$\text{subject to} \quad \sum_{\{j|(i,j)\in\mathcal{A}\}} x_{ij} = 1, \qquad i = 1,\ldots,m,$$

$$\sum_{\{i|(i,j)\in\mathcal{A}\}} x_{ij} \le y_j c_j, \qquad j = 1,\ldots,n,$$

$$x_{ij} = 0 \text{ or } 1, \qquad \forall\, (i,j) \in \mathcal{A},$$

$$y_j = 0 \text{ or } 1, \qquad j = 1,\ldots,n,$$

where c_j is the maximum number of customers that can be served by a facility at location j.

The solution of the problem by branch-and-bound involves the partition of the feasible set F into subsets. The choice of subsets is somewhat arbitrary, but it is convenient to select subsets of the form

$$F(J_0, J_1) = \big\{ (x,y) \in F \mid y_j = 0,\, \forall\, j \in J_0,\; y_j = 1,\, \forall\, j \in J_1 \big\},$$

where J_0 and J_1 are disjoint subsets of the index set $\{1,\ldots,n\}$ of facility locations. Thus, $F(J_0, J_1)$ is the subset of feasible solutions such that:

a facility is placed at the locations in J_1,

no facility is placed at the locations in J_0,

a facility may or may not be placed at the remaining locations.

For each node/subset $F(J_0, J_1)$, we may obtain a lower bound and a feasible solution by solving the linear program where all integer constraints are relaxed except for the variables y_j, $j \in J_0 \cup J_1$, which have been fixed at either 0 or 1:

$$\text{minimize} \quad \sum_{(i,j)\in\mathcal{A}} a_{ij}x_{ij} + \sum_{j=1}^{n} b_j y_j$$

$$\text{subject to} \quad \sum_{\{j|(i,j)\in\mathcal{A}\}} x_{ij} = 1, \qquad i = 1,\ldots,m,$$

$$\sum_{\{i|(i,j)\in\mathcal{A}\}} x_{ij} \le y_j c_j, \qquad j = 1,\ldots,n,$$

$$x_{ij} \in [0,1], \qquad \forall\, (i,j) \in \mathcal{A},$$

$$y_j \in [0,1], \qquad \forall\, j \notin J_0 \cup J_1,$$

$$y_j = 0, \quad \forall\, j \in J_0, \qquad y_j = 1, \quad \forall\, j \in J_1.$$

As an illustration, let us work out the example shown in Figure 10.8, which involves 3 clients and 2 locations. The facility capacities at the two locations are $c_1 = c_2 = 3$. The cost coefficients a_{ij} and b_j are shown next to the corresponding arcs. The optimal solution corresponds to $y_1 = 0$ and $y_2 = 1$, that is, placing a facility only in location 2 and serving all the clients at that facility. The corresponding optimal cost is

$$f^* = 5.$$

Let us apply the branch-and-bound algorithm using the tree shown in Fig. 10.8. We first consider the top node $\big(J_0 = \emptyset, J_1 = \emptyset\big)$, where neither y_1 nor y_2 is fixed at 0 or 1. The lower bound $\underline{f}_Y$ is obtained by solving the (relaxed) linear program

minimize $(2x_{11} + x_{12}) + (2x_{21} + x_{22}) + (x_{31} + 2x_{32}) + 3y_1 + y_2$

subject to $x_{11} + x_{12} = 1, \qquad x_{21} + x_{22} = 1, \qquad x_{31} + x_{32} = 1,$

$\qquad\qquad x_{11} + x_{21} + x_{31} \le 3y_1, \qquad x_{12} + x_{22} + x_{32} \le 3y_2,$

$\qquad\qquad 0 \le x_{ij} \le 1, \qquad \forall\, (i,j) \in \mathcal{A},$

$\qquad\qquad 0 \le y_1 \le 1, \qquad 0 \le y_2 \le 1.$

The optimal solution of this program is

$$x_{ij} = \begin{cases} 1 & \text{if } (i,j) = (1,2),(2,2),(3,1), \\ 0 & \text{otherwise}, \end{cases}$$

$$y_1 = 1/3, \qquad y_2 = 2/3,$$

and the corresponding optimal cost (lower bound) is

$$\underline{f}_Y = 4.66.$$

A feasible solution of the original problem is obtained by rounding the fractional values of y_1 and y_2 to

$$\bar{y}_1 = 1, \qquad \bar{y}_2 = 1,$$

and the associated cost is 7. Thus, we set

$$\text{UPPER} = 7,$$

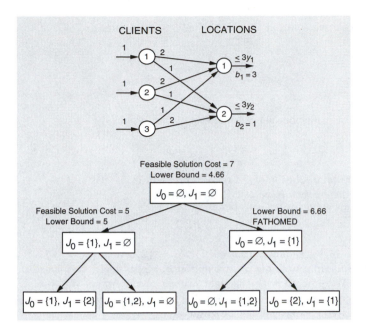

Figure 10.8: Branch-and-bound solution of a facility location problem with 3 clients and 2 locations. The facility capacities at the two locations are $c_1 = c_2 = 3$. The cost coefficients a_{ij} and b_j are shown next to the corresponding arcs. The relaxed problem for the top node $\left(J_0 = \varnothing, J_1 = \varnothing\right)$, corresponding to relaxing all the integer constraints, is solved first, obtaining the lower and upper bounds shown. Then the relaxed problem corresponding to the left node $\left(J_0 = \{1\}, J_1 = \varnothing\right)$ is solved, obtaining the lower and upper bounds shown. Finally, the relaxed problem corresponding to the right node $\left(J_0 = \varnothing, J_1 = \{1\}\right)$ is solved, obtaining a lower bound that is higher than the current value of UPPER. As a result this node can be fathomed, and its descendants need not be considered further.

and we place in OPEN the two descendants $\left(J_0 = \{1\}, J_1 = \varnothing\right)$ and $\left(J_0 = \varnothing, J_1 = \{1\}\right)$, corresponding to fixing y_1 at 0 and at 1, respectively.

We proceed with the left branch of the branch-and-bound tree, and consider the node $\left(J_0 = \{1\}, J_1 = \varnothing\right)$, corresponding to fixing y_1 as well as the corresponding flows x_{11}, x_{21}, and x_{31} to 0. The associated (relaxed) linear program is

$$
\begin{aligned}
\text{minimize} \quad & x_{12} + x_{22} + 2x_{32} + y_2 \\
\text{subject to} \quad & x_{12} = 1, \qquad x_{22} = 1, \qquad x_{32} = 1, \\
& x_{12} + x_{22} + x_{32} \leq 3y_2, \\
& 0 \leq x_{12} \leq 1, \quad 0 \leq x_{22} \leq 1, \quad 0 \leq x_{32} \leq 1, \\
& 0 \leq y_2 \leq 1.
\end{aligned}
$$

The optimal solution (in fact the only feasible solution) of this program is

$$x_{ij} = \begin{cases} 1 & \text{if } (i,j) = (1,2), (2,2), (3,2), \\ 0 & \text{otherwise,} \end{cases}$$

$$y_2 = 1,$$

and the corresponding optimal cost (lower bound) is

$$\underline{f}_Y = 5.$$

The optimal solution of the relaxed problem is integer, and its cost, 5, is lower than the current value of UPPER, so we set

$$\text{UPPER} = 5.$$

The two descendants, $\big(J_0 = \{1\}, J_1 = \{2\}\big)$ and $\big(J_0 = \{1, 2\}, J_1 = \varnothing\big)$, corresponding to fixing y_2 at 1 and at 0, respectively, are placed in OPEN.

We proceed with the right branch of the branch-and-bound tree, and consider the node $\big(J_0 = \varnothing, J_1 = \{1\}\big)$, corresponding to fixing y_1 to 1. The associated (relaxed) linear program is

$$\text{minimize} \quad (2x_{11} + x_{12}) + (2x_{21} + x_{22}) + (x_{31} + 2x_{32}) + 3 + y_2$$
$$\text{subject to} \quad x_{11} + x_{12} = 1, \qquad x_{21} + x_{22} = 1, \qquad x_{31} + x_{32} = 1,$$
$$x_{11} + x_{21} + x_{31} \le 3, \qquad x_{12} + x_{22} + x_{32} \le 3y_2,$$
$$0 \le x_{ij} \le 1, \qquad \forall\, (i,j) \in \mathcal{A},$$
$$0 \le y_2 \le 1.$$

The optimal solution of this program is

$$x_{ij} = \begin{cases} 1 & \text{if } (i,j) = (1,2), (2,2), (3,1), \\ 0 & \text{otherwise,} \end{cases}$$

$$y_2 = 2/3,$$

and the corresponding optimal cost (lower bound) is

$$\underline{f}_Y = 6.66.$$

This is larger than the current value of UPPER, so the node can be fathomed, and its two descendants are not placed in OPEN.

We conclude that one of the two descendants of the left node, $\big(J_0 = \{1\}, J_1 = \{2\}\big)$ and $\big(J_0 = \{1, 2\}, J_1 = \varnothing\big)$ (the only nodes in OPEN), contains the optimal solution. We can proceed to solve the relaxed linear programs corresponding to these two nodes, and obtain the optimal solution. However, there is also a shortcut here: since these are the only two remaining nodes and the upper bound corresponding to these nodes coincides with the lower bound, we can conclude that the lower bound is equal to the optimal cost and the corresponding integer solution ($y_1 = 0$, $y_2 = 1$) is optimal.

Generally, for the success of the branch-and-bound approach it is important that the lower bounds are as tight as possible, because this facilitates the fathoming of nodes, and leads to fewer restricted problem solutions. On the other hand, the tightness of the bounds strongly depends on how the problem is formulated as an integer programming problem. There may be several possible formulations, some of which are "stronger" than others in the sense that they provide better bounds within the branch-and-bound context. As an illustration, consider the following example.

Example 10.9. Facility Location – Alternative Formulation

Consider the following alternative formulation of the preceding facility location problem

$$\text{minimize} \quad \sum_{(i,j)\in\mathcal{A}} a_{ij}x_{ij} + \sum_{j=1}^{n} b_j y_j$$

$$\text{subject to} \quad \sum_{\{j|(i,j)\in\mathcal{A}\}} x_{ij} = 1, \qquad i = 1,\ldots,m,$$

$$\sum_{\{i|(i,j)\in\mathcal{A}\}} x_{ij} \leq c_j, \qquad j = 1,\ldots,n,$$

$$x_{ij} \leq y_j, \qquad \forall\, (i,j) \in \mathcal{A},$$

$$x_{ij} = 0 \text{ or } 1, \qquad \forall\, (i,j) \in \mathcal{A},$$

$$y_j = 0 \text{ or } 1, \qquad j = 1,\ldots,n.$$

This formulation involves a lot more constraints, but is in fact superior to the one given earlier (cf. Example 10.8). The reason is that, if we relax the 0-1 constraints on x_{ij} and y_j, the side constraints $\sum_{i=1}^{m} x_{ij} \leq y_j c_j$ of Example 10.8 are implied by the constraints $\sum_{i=1}^{m} x_{ij} \leq c_j$ and $x_{ij} \leq y_j$ of the present example. As a result, the lower bounds obtained by relaxing some of the 0-1 constraints are tighter in the alternative formulation just given, thereby enhancing the effectiveness of the branch-and-bound method. In fact, it can be verified that for the example of Fig. 10.8, by relaxing the 0-1 constraints in the stronger formulation of the present example, we obtain the correct optimal integer solution at the very first node of the branch-and-bound tree.

An important conclusion from the preceding example is that *it is possible to accelerate the branch-and-bound solution of a problem by adding more side constraints*. Even if these constraints do not affect the set of feasible integer solutions, they can improve the lower bounds obtained by relaxing the 0-1 constraints. Basically, when the integer constraints are relaxed, one obtains a superset of the feasible set of integer solutions, so with more side constraints, the corresponding superset becomes smaller and approximates better the true feasible set (see Fig. 10.9). It is thus very important to select a problem formulation such that when the integer constraints are relaxed, the feasible set is as small as possible.

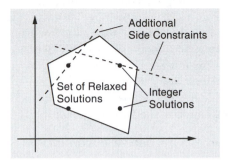

Figure 10.9: Illustration of the effect of additional side constraints. They do not affect the set of feasible integer solutions, but they reduce the set of "relaxed solutions," that is, those x that satisfy all the constraints except for the integer constraints. This results in improved lower bounds and a faster branch-and-bound solution.

We note that the subject of characterizing the feasible set of an integer programming problem, and approximating it tightly with a polyhedral set has received extensive attention. In particular, there is a lot of theory and accumulated practical knowledge on characterizing the feasible set in specific problem contexts; see the references cited at the end of the chapter. A further discussion of branch-and-bound is beyond our scope. We refer to sources on linear and combinatorial optimization, such as Zoutendijk [1976], Papadimitriou and Steiglitz [1982], Schrijver [1986], Nemhauser and Wolsey [1988], Bertsimas and Tsitsiklis [1997], Cook, Cunningham, Pulleyblank, and Schrijver [1998], which also describe many applications.

10.3 LAGRANGIAN RELAXATION

In this section, we consider an important approach for obtaining lower bounds to use in the branch-and-bound method. Let us consider the case of the network optimization problem with linear cost function, linear side constraints, and integer constraints on the arc flows:

$$
\begin{aligned}
\text{minimize} \quad & a'x \\
\text{subject to} \quad & \sum_{\{j|(i,j)\in\mathcal{A}\}} x_{ij} - \sum_{\{j|(j,i)\in\mathcal{A}\}} x_{ji} = s_i, \quad \forall\, i \in \mathcal{N}, \\
& c_t'x \le d_t, \quad t = 1,\ldots,r, \\
& x_{ij} \in X_{ij}, \quad \forall\, (i,j) \in \mathcal{A},
\end{aligned}
$$

where a and c_t are given vectors, d_t are given scalars, and each X_{ij} is a *finite* subset of contiguous integers (i.e., the convex hull of X_{ij} contains all the integers in X_{ij}, as for example in the cases $X_{ij} = \{0,1\}$ or $X_{ij} = \{1,2,3,4\}$). We assume that *the supplies s_i are integer*, so that if the side constraints $c_t'x \le d_t$ were not present, the problem would become a minimum cost flow problem that has integer optimal solutions, according to the theory developed in Chapter 5. Note that for this it is not necessary that the arc cost coefficients a_{ij} (the components of the vectors a) be integer.

In the Lagrangian relaxation approach, we eliminate the side constraints $c_t' x \le d_t$ by adding to the cost function the terms $\mu_t(c_t' x - d_t)$, thereby forming the Lagrangian function

$$L(x, \mu) = a'x + \sum_{t=1}^{r} \mu_t(c_t' x - d_t),$$

where $\mu = (\mu_1, \ldots, \mu_r)$ is a vector of nonnegative scalars. Each μ_t may be viewed as a penalty per unit violation of the corresponding side constraint $c_t' x \le d_t$, and may also be viewed as a Lagrange multiplier.

A key idea of Lagrangian relaxation is that regardless of the choice of μ, *the minimization of the Lagrangian $L(x, \mu)$ over the set of remaining constraints*

$$\tilde{F} = \{x \mid x_{ij} \in X_{ij}, \ x \text{ satisfies the conservation of flow constraints}\},$$

yields a lower bound to the optimal cost of the original problem (cf. the weak duality property, discussed in Section 8.7). To see this, note that we have

$$
\begin{aligned}
\min_{x \in \tilde{F}} L(x, \mu) &= \min_{x \in \tilde{F}} \left\{ a'x + \sum_{t=1}^{r} \mu_t(c_t' x - d_t) \right\} \\
&\le \min_{x \in \tilde{F}, \ c_t' x - d_t \le 0, \ t=1,\ldots,r} \left\{ a'x + \sum_{t=1}^{r} \mu_t(c_t' x - d_t) \right\} \\
&\le \min_{x \in \tilde{F}, \ c_t' x - d_t \le 0, \ t=1,\ldots,r} a'x,
\end{aligned}
$$

where the first inequality follows because the minimum of the Lagrangian in the next-to-last expression is taken over a subset of $\tilde{F}$, and the last inequality follows using the nonnegativity of μ_t. The lower bound $\min_{x \in \tilde{F}} L(x, \mu)$ can in turn be used in the branch-and-bound procedure discussed earlier.

Since in the context of branch-and-bound, it is important to use as tight a lower bound as possible, we are motivated to search for an optimal lower bound through adjustment of the vector μ. To this end, we form the following dual function (cf. Section 8.7)

$$q(\mu) = \min_{x \in \tilde{F}} L(x, \mu),$$

and we consider the dual problem

$$\text{maximize} \ \ q(\mu)$$
$$\text{subject to} \ \ \mu_t \ge 0, \quad t = 1, \ldots, r.$$

Solution of this problem yields the tightest lower bound to the optimal cost of the original problem.

Example 10.10. Constrained Shortest Path Problem

As an example of the use of Lagrangian relaxation, consider the constrained shortest path problem discussed in Example 8.6 of Section 8.4. Here, we want to find a simple forward path P from an origin node s to a destination node t that minimizes the path length

$$\sum_{(i,j)\in P} a_{ij},$$

subject to the following side constraints on P:

$$\sum_{(i,j)\in P} c_{ij}^k \le d^k, \qquad k = 1,\ldots,K.$$

As discussed in Section 8.4, we can formulate this as the following network flow problem with integer constraints and side constraints:

$$\text{minimize} \quad \sum_{(i,j)\in\mathcal{A}} a_{ij}x_{ij}$$

$$\text{subject to} \quad \sum_{\{j\mid(i,j)\in\mathcal{A}\}} x_{ij} - \sum_{\{j\mid(j,i)\in\mathcal{A}\}} x_{ji} = \begin{cases} 1 & \text{if } i = s, \\ -1 & \text{if } i = t, \\ 0 & \text{otherwise}, \end{cases} \quad (10.7)$$

$$x_{ij} = 0 \text{ or } 1, \qquad \forall\, (i,j) \in \mathcal{A},$$

$$\sum_{(i,j)\in\mathcal{A}} c_{ij}^k x_{ij} \le d^k, \qquad k = 1,\ldots,K.$$

Here, a path P from s to t is optimal if and only if the flow vector x defined by

$$x_{ij} = \begin{cases} 1 & \text{if } (i,j) \text{ belongs to } P, \\ 0 & \text{otherwise}, \end{cases}$$

is an optimal solution of the problem (10.7).

     To apply Lagrangian relaxation, we eliminate the side constraints, and we form the corresponding Lagrangian function assigning a nonnegative multiplier μ^k to the kth constraint. Minimization of the Lagrangian now becomes a shortest path problem with respect to corrected arc lengths $\hat{a}_{ij}$ given by

$$\hat{a}_{ij} = a_{ij} + \sum_{k=1}^{K} \mu^k c_{ij}^k.$$

(We assume here that there are no negative length cycles with respect to the arc lengths $\hat{a}_{ij}$; this will be so if all the a_{ij} and c_{ij}^k are nonnegative.) We then obtain μ^* that solves the dual problem $\max_{\mu\ge 0} q(\mu)$ and we obtain a corresponding optimal cost/lower bound. We can then use μ^* to obtain a feasible solution (a path that satisfies the side constraints) as discussed in Example 8.6.

The preceding example illustrates an important advantage of Lagrangian relaxation, as applied to integer-constrained network problems: it eliminates the side constraints *simultaneously* with the integer constraints. In particular, *minimizing $L(x, \mu)$ over the set*

$$\tilde{F} = \{x \mid x_{ij} \in X_{ij}, \ x \text{ satisfies the conservation of flow constraints}\}$$

is a (linear) minimum cost flow problem that can be solved using the methodology of Chapters 2-7: the Lagrangian $L(x, \mu)$ is linear in x and the integer constraints do not matter, and can be replaced by the interval constraints $x_{ij} \in \hat{X}_{ij}$, where $\hat{X}_{ij}$ is the convex hull of the set X_{ij}. This should be contrasted with the integer constraint relaxation approach, where we eliminate just the integer constraints, while leaving the side constraints unaffected (see the facility location problem that we solved using branch-and-bound in Example 10.8). As a result, the minimum cost flow methodology of Chapters 2-7 does not apply when there are side constraints and the integer constraint relaxation approach is used. This is the main reason for the widespread use of Lagrangian relaxation in combination with branch-and-bound.

Actually, in Lagrangian relaxation it is not mandatory to eliminate just the side constraints. One may eliminate the conservation of flow constraints, in addition to or in place of the side constraints. (The multipliers corresponding to the conservation of flow constraints should be unconstrained in the dual problem, because the conservation of flow is expressed in terms of equality constraints; cf. the discussion in Section 8.7.) One still obtains a lower bound to the optimal cost of the original problem, because of the weak duality property (cf. Section 8.7). However, the minimization of the Lagrangian is not a minimum cost flow problem anymore. Nonetheless, by choosing properly the constraints to eliminate and by taking advantage of the special structure of the problem, the minimization of the Lagrangian over the remaining set of constraints may be relatively simple. The following is an illustrative example.

Example 10.11. Traveling Salesman Problem

Consider the traveling salesman problem of Example 10.1. Here, we want to find a minimum cost tour in a complete graph where the cost of arc (i, j) is denoted a_{ij}. We formulate this as the following network problem with side constraints and 0-1 integer constraints:

$$\text{minimize} \quad \sum_{(i,j) \in \mathcal{A}} a_{ij} x_{ij}$$

$$\text{subject to} \quad \sum_{\substack{j=1,\ldots,N \\ j \neq i}} x_{ij} = 1, \qquad i = 1, \ldots, N, \tag{10.8}$$

$$\sum_{\substack{i=1,\dots,N \\ i\neq j}} x_{ij} = 1, \qquad j = 1,\dots,N, \tag{10.9}$$

$$x_{ij} = 0 \text{ or } 1, \qquad \forall \, (i,j) \in \mathcal{A}, \tag{10.10}$$

the subgraph with node-arc set $\big(\mathcal{N}, \{(i,j) \mid x_{ij} = 1\}\big)$ is connected. (10.11)

We may express the connectivity constraint (10.11) in several different ways, leading to different Lagrangian relaxation and branch-and-bound algorithms. One of the most successful formulations is based on the notion of a *1-tree*, which consists of a tree that spans nodes $2,\dots,N$, *plus* two arcs that are incident to node 1. Equivalently, a 1-tree is a connected subgraph that contains a single cycle passing through node 1 (see Fig. 10.10). Note that if the conservation of flow constraints (10.8) and (10.9), and the integer constraints (10.10) are satisfied, then the connectivity constraint (10.11) is equivalent to the constraint that the subgraph $\big(\mathcal{N}, \{(i,j) \mid x_{ij} = 1\}\big)$ is a 1-tree.

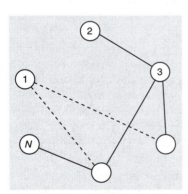

Figure 10.10: Illustration of a 1-tree. It consists of a tree that spans nodes $2,\dots,N$, *plus* two arcs that are incident to node 1.

Let X_1 be the set of all x with $0 - 1$ components, and such that the subgraph $\big(\mathcal{N}, \{(i,j) \mid x_{ij} = 1\}\big)$ is a 1-tree. Let us consider a Lagrangian relaxation approach based on elimination of the conservation of flow equations. Assigning multipliers u_i and v_j to the constraints (10.8) and (10.9), respectively, the Lagrangian function is

$$L(x, u, v) = \sum_{i,j,i\neq j} (a_{ij} + u_i + v_j)x_{ij} - \sum_{i=1}^{N} u_i - \sum_{j=1}^{N} v_j.$$

The minimization of the Lagrangian is over all 1-trees, leading to the problem

$$\min_{x \in X_1} \left\{ \sum_{i,j,i\neq j} (a_{ij} + u_i + v_j)x_{ij} \right\}.$$

If we view $a_{ij} + u_i + v_j$ as a *modified cost* of arc (i,j), this minimization is quite easy. It is equivalent to obtaining a tree of minimum modified cost that spans the nodes $2, \ldots, N$, and then adding two arcs that are incident to node 1 and have minimum modified cost. The minimum cost spanning tree problem can be easily solved using the Prim-Dijkstra algorithm (see Exercise 2.30).

Unfortunately, the Lagrangian relaxation method has several weaknesses:

(a) Even if we find an optimal μ, we still have only a lower bound to the optimal cost of the original problem.

(b) The minimization of $L(x, \mu)$ over the set

$$\tilde{F} = \{x \mid x_{ij} \in X_{ij}, \ x \text{ satisfies the conservation of flow constraints}\},$$

may yield an x that violates some of the side constraints $c_t'x - d_t \leq 0$, so it may be necessary to adjust this x for feasibility using some heuristic.

(c) The maximization of $q(\mu)$ over $\mu \geq 0$ may be quite nontrivial for a number of reasons, including the fact that q is typically nondifferentiable.

In what follows in this section, we will discuss the algorithmic methodology for solving the dual problem, including the subgradient and cutting plane methods, which have enjoyed a great deal of popularity. These methods have also been used widely in connection with various decomposition schemes for large-scale problems with special structure. For further discussion, we refer to the nonlinear programming literature (see for example Lasdon [1970], Auslender [1976], Shapiro [1979], Shor [1985], Poljak [1987], Hiriart-Urruty and Lemarechal [1993], and Bertsekas [1995b]).

10.3.1   Subgradients of the Dual Function

Let us consider the algorithmic solution of the dual problem

$$\text{maximize} \quad q(\mu)$$
$$\text{subject to} \quad \mu_t \geq 0, \ t = 1, \ldots, r.$$

The dual function is

$$q(\mu) = \min_{x \in \tilde{F}} L(x, \mu),$$

where

$$\tilde{F} = \{x \mid x_{ij} \in X_{ij}, \ x \text{ satisfies the conservation of flow constraints}\},$$

and $L(x, \mu)$ is the Lagrangian function

$$L(x, \mu) = a'x + \sum_{t=1}^{r} \mu_t(c_t'x - d_t).$$

Recall here that the set $\tilde{F}$ is finite, because we have assumed that each X_{ij} is a finite set of contiguous integers.

We note that for a fixed $x \in \tilde{F}$, the Lagrangian $L(x, \mu)$ is a linear function of μ. Thus, because the set $\tilde{F}$ is finite, the dual function q is the minimum of a finite number of linear functions of μ – there is one such function for each $x \in \tilde{F}$. For conceptual simplification, we may write q in the following generic form:

$$q(\mu) = \min_{i \in I}\{\alpha'_i \mu + \beta_i\}, \qquad (10.12)$$

where I is some finite index set, and α_i and β_i are suitable vectors and scalars, respectively (see Fig. 10.11).

Of particular interest for our purposes are the "slopes" of q at various vectors μ, i.e., the vectors α_{i_μ}, where $i_\mu \in I$ is an index attaining the minimum of $\alpha'_i \mu + \beta_i$ over $i \in I$ [cf. Eq. (10.12)]. If i_μ is the *unique* index attaining the minimum, then q is differentiable (in fact linear) at μ, and its gradient is a_{i_μ}. If there are multiple indices i attaining the minimum, then q is nondifferentiable at μ (see Fig. 10.11). To deal with such differentiabilities, we generalize the notion of a gradient. In particular, we define a *subgradient* of q at a given $\mu \geq 0$ to be any vector g such that

$$q(\nu) \leq q(\mu) + (\nu - \mu)'g, \qquad \forall \, \nu \geq 0, \qquad (10.13)$$

(see Fig. 10.11). The right-hand side of the above inequality provides a linear approximation to the dual function q using the function value $q(\mu)$ at the given μ and the corresponding subgradient g. The approximation is exact at the vector μ, and is an overestimate at other vectors ν. Some further properties of subgradients are summarized in Appendix A.

We now consider the calculation of subgradients of the dual function. For any μ, let x_μ minimize the Lagrangian $L(x, \mu)$ over $x \in \tilde{F}$,

$$x_\mu = \arg \min_{x \in \tilde{F}} L(x, \mu).$$

Let us show that *the vector $g(x_\mu)$ that has components*

$$g_t(x_\mu) = c'_t x_\mu - d_t, \qquad t = 1, \ldots, r,$$

is a subgradient of q at μ. To see this, we use the definition of L, q, and x_μ to write for all $\nu \geq 0$,

$$\begin{aligned}
q(\nu) &= \min_{x \in \tilde{F}} L(x, \nu) \\
&\leq L(x_\mu, \nu) \\
&= a'x_\mu + \nu'g(x_\mu) \\
&= a'x_\mu + \mu'g(x_\mu) + (\nu - \mu)'g(x_\mu) \\
&= q(\mu) + (\nu - \mu)'g(x_\mu),
\end{aligned}$$

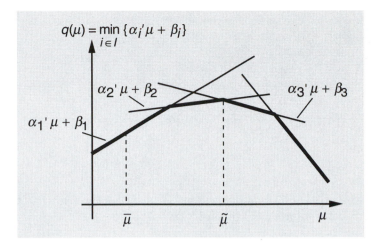

Figure 10.11: Illustration of the dual function q and its subgradients. The generic form of q is

$$q(\mu) = \min_{i \in I} \{\alpha_i'\mu + \beta_i\},$$

where I is some finite index set, and α_i and β_i are suitable vectors and scalars, respectively. Given μ, and an index $i_\mu \in I$ attaining the minimum in the above equation, the vector α_{i_μ} is a subgradient at μ. Furthermore, any subgradient at μ is a convex combination of vectors a_{i_μ} such that $i_\mu \in I$ and i_μ attains the minimum of $\alpha_i'\mu + \beta_i$ over $i \in I$. For example, at the vector $\overline{\mu}$ shown in the figure, there is a unique subgradient, the vector α_1. At the vector $\tilde{\mu}$ shown in the figure, the set of subgradients is the line segment connecting the vectors α_2 and α_3.

so the subgradient inequality (10.13) is satisfied for $g = g(x_\mu)$. Thus, for a given μ, *the evaluation of* $q(\mu)$, *which requires finding a minimizer* x_μ *of* $L(x, \mu)$ *over* $\tilde{F}$, *yields as a byproduct the subgradient* $g(x_\mu)$. This convenience in calculating subgradients is particularly important for the algorithms that we discuss in what follows in this section.

10.3.2 Subgradient Methods

We now turn to algorithms that use subgradients for solving the dual problem. The *subgradient method* consists of the iteration

$$\mu^{k+1} = \left[\mu^k + s^k g^k\right]^+, \qquad (10.14)$$

where g^k is any subgradient of q at μ^k, s^k is a positive scalar stepsize, and $[y]^+$ is the operation that sets to 0 all the negative components of the vector y. Thus the iteration (10.14) can be written as

$$\mu_t^{k+1} = \max\{0, \mu_t^k + s^k g_t^k\}, \qquad t = 1, \ldots, r.$$

The simplest way to calculate the subgradient g^k is to find an x_{μ^k} that minimizes $L(x, \mu^k)$ over $x \in \tilde{F}$, and to set

$$g^k = g(x_{\mu^k}),$$

where for every x, $g(x)$ is the r-dimensional vector with components

$$g_t(x) = c_t' x - d_t, \qquad t = 1, \ldots, r.$$

An important fact about the subgradient method is that the new iterate may not improve the dual cost for all values of the stepsize s^k; that is, we may have

$$q\big([\mu^k + s^k g^k]^+\big) < q(\mu^k), \qquad \forall \, s^k > 0$$

(see Fig. 10.12). What makes the subgradient method work is that for sufficiently small stepsize s^k, *the distance of the current iterate to the optimal solution set is reduced*, as illustrated in Fig. 10.12, and as shown in the following proposition.

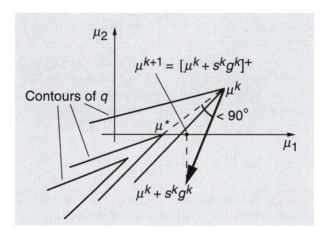

Figure 10.12: Illustration of how it may not be possible to improve the dual function by using the subgradient iteration $\mu^{k+1} = [\mu^k + s^k g^k]^+$, regardless of the value of the stepsize s^k. However, the distance to any optimal solution μ^* is reduced using a subgradient iteration with a sufficiently small stepsize. The crucial fact, which follows from the definition of a subgradient, is that the angle between the subgradient g^k and the vector $\mu^* - \mu^k$ is less than 90 degrees. As a result, for s^k small enough, the vector $\mu^k + s^k g^k$ is closer to μ^* than μ^k. Furthermore, the vector $[\mu^k + s^k g^k]^+$ is closer to μ^* than $\mu^k + s^k g^k$ is.

Proposition 10.1: If μ^k is not optimal, then for any dual optimal solution μ^*, we have

$$\|\mu^{k+1} - \mu^*\| < \|\mu^k - \mu^*\|,$$

for all stepsizes s^k such that

$$0 < s^k < \frac{2\bigl(q(\mu^*) - q(\mu^k)\bigr)}{\|g^k\|^2}. \qquad (10.15)$$

Proof: We have

$$\|\mu^k + s^k g^k - \mu^*\|^2 = \|\mu^k - \mu^*\|^2 - 2s^k(\mu^* - \mu^k)'g^k + (s^k)^2\|g^k\|^2,$$

and by using the subgradient inequality (10.13),

$$(\mu^* - \mu^k)'g^k \geq q(\mu^*) - q(\mu^k).$$

Combining the last two relations, we obtain

$$\|\mu^k + s^k g^k - \mu^*\|^2 \leq \|\mu^k - \mu^*\|^2 - 2s^k\bigl(q(\mu^*) - q(\mu^k)\bigr) + (s^k)^2\|g^k\|^2.$$

We can now verify that for the range of stepsizes of Eq. (10.15) the sum of the last two terms in the above relation is negative. In particular, with a straightforward calculation, we can write this relation as

$$\|\mu^k + s^k g^k - \mu^*\|^2 \leq \|\mu^k - \mu^*\|^2 - \frac{\gamma^k(2 - \gamma^k)\bigl(q(\mu^*) - q(\mu^k)\bigr)^2}{\|g^k\|^2}, \qquad (10.16)$$

where

$$\gamma^k = \frac{s^k\|g^k\|^2}{q(\mu^*) - q(\mu^k)}.$$

If the stepsize s^k satisfies Eq. (10.15), then $0 < \gamma^k < 2$, so Eq. (10.16) yields

$$\|\mu^k + s^k g^k - \mu^*\| < \|\mu^k - \mu^*\|.$$

We now observe that since $\mu^* \geq 0$, we have

$$\bigl\|\bigl[\mu^k + s^k g^k\bigr]^+ - \mu^*\bigr\| \leq \|\mu^k + s^k g^k - \mu^*\|,$$

and from the last two inequalities, we obtain $\|\mu^{k+1} - \mu^*\| < \|\mu^k - \mu^*\|$.
Q.E.D.

The inequality (10.16) can also be used to establish convergence and rate of convergence results for the subgradient method with stepsize rules satisfying

$$0 < s^k < \frac{2\big(q(\mu^*) - q(\mu^k)\big)}{\|g^k\|^2}$$

[cf. Eq. (10.15)]. Unfortunately, however, unless we know the dual optimal cost $q(\mu^*)$, which is rare, the range of stepsizes (10.15) is unknown. In practice, a frequently used stepsize formula is

$$s^k = \frac{\alpha^k\big(q^k - q(\mu^k)\big)}{\|g^k\|^2}, \tag{10.17}$$

where q^k is an approximation to the optimal dual cost and

$$0 < \alpha^k < 2.$$

Note that we can estimate the optimal dual cost from below with the best current dual cost

$$\hat{q}^k = \max_{0 \le i \le k} q(\mu^i).$$

As an overestimate of the optimal dual cost, we can use the cost $f(\bar{x})$ of any primal feasible solution $\bar{x}$; in many circumstances, primal feasible solutions are naturally obtained in the course of the algorithm. Finally, the special structure of many problems can be exploited to yield improved bounds to the optimal dual cost.

Here are two common ways to choose α^k and q^k in the stepsize formula (10.17):

(a) q^k is the best known upper bound to the optimal dual cost at the kth iteration and α^k is a number, which is initially equal to one and is decreased by a certain factor (say, two) every few (say, five or ten) iterations. An alternative formula for α^k is

$$\alpha^k = \frac{m}{k + m},$$

where m is a positive integer.

(b) $\alpha^k = 1$ for all k and q^k is given by

$$q^k = \big(1 + \beta(k)\big)\hat{q}^k, \tag{10.18}$$

where $\hat{q}^k$ is the best current dual cost $\hat{q}^k = \max_{0 \le i \le k} q(\mu^i)$. Furthermore, $\beta(k)$ is a number greater than zero, which is increased by a certain factor if the previous iteration was a "success," that is, if it improved the best current dual cost, and is decreased by some other factor otherwise. This method requires that $\hat{q}^k > 0$. Also, if upper bounds $\tilde{q}^k$ to the optimal dual cost are available as discussed earlier, then a natural improvement to Eq. (10.18) is

$$q^k = \min\{\tilde{q}^k, (1 + \beta(k))\hat{q}^k\}.$$

For a convergence analysis of the subgradient method and its variants, we refer to the literature cited at the end of the chapter (see also Exercises 10.36-10.38). However, the convergence properties of the schemes most often preferred in practice, including the ones given above, are neither solid nor well understood. It is easy to find problems where the subgradient method works very poorly. On the other hand, the method is simple and works well for many types of problems, yielding good approximate solutions within a few tens or hundreds of iterations. Also, frequently a good primal feasible solution can be obtained using effective heuristics, even with a fairly poor dual solution.

10.3.3   Cutting Plane Methods

Consider again the dual problem

$$\text{maximize} \quad q(\mu)$$
$$\text{subject to} \quad \mu \geq 0.$$

The cutting plane method, at the kth iteration, replaces the dual function q by a polyhedral approximation Q^k, constructed using the vectors μ^i and corresponding subgradients g^i, $i = 0, 1, \ldots, k - 1$, obtained so far. It then solves the problem

$$\text{maximize} \quad Q^k(\mu)$$
$$\text{subject to} \quad \mu \geq 0.$$

In particular, for $k = 1, 2, \ldots$, Q^k is given by

$$Q^k(\mu) = \min_{i=0,\ldots,k-1}\{q(\mu^i) + (\mu - \mu^i)'g^i\}, \qquad (10.19)$$

and the kth iterate is generated by

$$\mu^k = \arg\max_{\mu \geq 0} Q^k(\mu). \qquad (10.20)$$

As in the case of subgradient methods, the simplest way to calculate the subgradient g^i is to find an x_{μ^i} that minimizes $L(x, \mu^i)$ over $x \in \tilde{F}$, and to set

$$g^i = g(x_\mu^i),$$

where for every x, $g(x)$ is the r-dimensional vector with components

$$g_t(x) = c_t'x - d_t, \qquad t = 1, \ldots, r.$$

Note that the approximation $Q^k(\mu)$ is an *overestimate* of the dual function q,

$$q(\mu) \leq Q^k(\mu), \qquad \mu \geq 0, \tag{10.21}$$

since, in view of the definition of a subgradient [cf. Eq. (10.13)], each of the linear terms in the right-hand side of Eq. (10.19) is an overestimate of $q(\mu)$.

We assume that, for all k, it is possible to find a maximum μ^k of Q^k over $\mu \geq 0$. To ensure this, the method has to be suitably initialized; for example by selecting a sufficiently large number of vectors μ, and by computing corresponding subgradients, to form an initial approximation that is bounded from above over the set $\{\mu \mid \mu \geq 0\}$. Thus, in this variant, we start the method at some iteration $\bar{k} > 0$, with the vectors $\mu^0, \ldots, \mu^{\bar{k}-1}$ suitably selected so that $Q^{\bar{k}}(\mu)$ is bounded from above over $\mu \geq 0$. Alternatively, we may maximize Q^k over a suitable bounded polyhedral set that is known to contain an optimal dual solution, instead of maximizing over $\mu \geq 0$. We note that given the iterate μ^k, the method produces both the exact and the approximate dual values $q(\mu^k)$ and $Q^k(\mu^k)$. It can be seen, using Eqs. (10.20) and (10.21), that the optimal dual cost is bracketed between these two values:

$$q(\mu^k) \leq \max_{\mu \geq 0} q(\mu) \leq Q^k(\mu^k). \tag{10.22}$$

Thus, in particular, the equality

$$q(\mu^k) = Q^k(\mu^k) \tag{10.23}$$

guarantees the optimality of the vector μ^k. It turns out that because the dual function is piecewise linear, and consequently only a finite number of subgradients can be generated, the optimality criterion (10.23) is satisfied in a finite number of iterations, and the method terminates. This is shown in the following proposition and is illustrated in Fig. 10.13.

Proposition 10.2: The cutting plane method terminates finitely; that is, for some k, μ^k is a dual optimal solution and the termination criterion (10.23) is satisfied.

Proof: For notational convenience, let us write the dual function in the polyhedral form

$$q(\mu) = \min_{i \in I} \{\alpha_i' \mu + \beta_i\},$$

where I is some finite index set and α_i, β_i, $i \in I$, are suitable vectors and scalars, respectively. Let i^k be an index attaining the minimum in the equation

$$q(\mu^k) = \min_{i \in I} \{\alpha_i' \mu^k + \beta_i\},$$

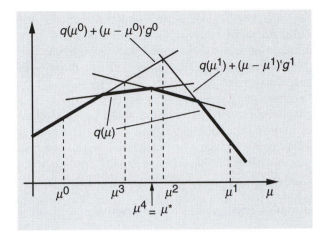

Figure 10.13: Illustration of the cutting plane method. With each new iterate μ^i, a new hyperplane $q(\mu^i) + (\mu - \mu^i)'g^i$ is added to the polyhedral approximation of the dual function. The method converges finitely, since if μ^k is not optimal, a new cutting plane will be added at the corresponding iteration, and there can be only a finite number of cutting planes.

so that α_{ik} is a subgradient at μ^k. If the termination criterion (10.23) is not satisfied at μ^k, we must have

$$\alpha'_{ik}\mu^k + \beta_{ik} = q(\mu^k) < Q^k(\mu^k).$$

Since

$$Q^k(\mu^k) = \min_{0 \le m \le k-1}\{\alpha'_{im}\mu^k + \beta_{im}\},$$

it follows that the pair $(\alpha_{ik}, \beta_{ik})$ is not equal to any of the preceding pairs $(\alpha_{i0}, \beta_{i0}), \ldots, (\alpha_{ik-1}, \beta_{ik-1})$. Since the index set I is finite, it follows that there can be only a finite number of iterations for which the termination criterion (10.23) is not satisfied. **Q.E.D.**

Despite its finite convergence property, the cutting plane method may converge slowly, and in practice one may have to stop it short of finding an optimal solution [the error bounds (10.22) may be used for this purpose]. An additional drawback of the method is that it can take large steps away from the optimum even when it is close to (or even at) the optimum. This phenomenon is referred to as *instability*, and has another undesirable effect, namely, that μ^{k-1} may not be a good starting point for the algorithm that minimizes $Q^k(\mu)$. A way to limit the effects of this phenomenon is to add to the polyhedral function approximation a quadratic term that penalizes large deviations from the current point. In this method, μ^k is obtained as

$$\mu^k = \arg\max_{\mu \ge 0}\left\{Q^k(\mu) - \frac{1}{2c^k}\|\mu - \mu^{k-1}\|^2\right\},$$

where $\{c^k\}$ is a positive nondecreasing scalar parameter sequence. This is known as the *proximal cutting plane algorithm*, and is related to the proximal minimization method discussed in Section 8.8.5. It can be shown that this variant of the cutting plane method also terminates finitely thanks to the polyhedral nature of q.

Another interesting variant of the cutting plane method, known as the *central cutting plane method*, maintains the polyhedral approximation $Q^k(\mu)$ to the dual function q, but generates the next vector μ^k by using a somewhat different mechanism. In particular, instead of maximizing Q^k, the method obtains μ^k by finding a "central pair" (μ^k, z^k) within the subset

$$S^k = \big\{(\mu, z) \mid \mu \geq 0,\ \hat{q}^k \leq q(\mu),\ \hat{q}^k \leq z \leq Q^k(\mu)\big\},$$

where $\hat{q}^k$ is the best lower bound to the optimal dual cost that has been found so far,

$$\hat{q}^k = \max_{i=0,\ldots,k-1} q(\mu^i).$$

The set S^k is illustrated in Fig. 10.14.

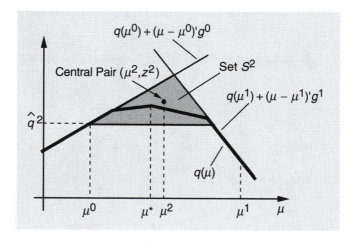

Figure 10.14: Illustration of the set

$$S^k = \big\{(\mu, z) \mid \mu \geq 0,\ \hat{q}^k \leq q(\mu),\ \hat{q}^k \leq z \leq Q^k(\mu)\big\},$$

for $k = 2$, in the central cutting plane method.

There are several possible methods for finding the central pair (μ^k, z^k). Roughly, the idea is that the central pair should be "somewhere in the middle" of S^k. For example, consider the case where S^k is polyhedral with nonempty interior. Then (μ^k, z^k) could be the *analytic center* of S^k, where for any polyhedron

$$P = \{y \mid a_p' y \leq c_p,\ p = 1, \ldots, m\}$$

with nonempty interior, its analytic center is the unique maximizer of $\sum_{p=1}^{m} \ln(c_p - a_p' y)$ over $y \in P$. Another possibility is the *ball center* of S, that is, the center of the largest inscribed sphere in S. Assuming that the polyhedron P given above has nonempty interior, its ball center can be obtained by solving the following problem with optimization variables (y, σ):

$$\text{maximize } \sigma$$
$$\text{subject to } a_p'(y + d) \le c_p, \quad \forall \ \|d\| \le \sigma, \ p = 1, \dots, m.$$

It can be seen that this problem is equivalent to the linear program

$$\text{maximize } \sigma$$
$$\text{subject to } a_p' y + \|a_p\| \sigma \le c_p, \quad p = 1, \dots, m.$$

While the central cutting plane methods are not guaranteed to terminate finitely, their convergence properties are satisfactory. Furthermore, the methods have benefited from advances in the implementation of interior point methods; see the references cited at the end of the chapter.

10.3.4   Decomposition and Multicommodity Flows

Lagrangian relaxation is particularly convenient when by eliminating the side constraints, we obtain a network problem that decomposes into several independent subproblems. A typical example arises in multicommodity flow problems where we want to minimize

$$\sum_{m=1}^{M} \sum_{(i,j) \in \mathcal{A}} a_{ij}(m) x_{ij}(m) \tag{10.24}$$

subject to the conservation of flow constraints

$$\sum_{\{j | (i,j) \in \mathcal{A}\}} x_{ij}(m) - \sum_{\{j | (j,i) \in \mathcal{A}\}} x_{ji}(m) = s_i(m), \qquad \forall \ i \in \mathcal{N}, \ m = 1, \dots, M, \tag{10.25}$$

the set constraints

$$x_{ij}(m) \in X_{ij}(m), \qquad \forall \ m = 1, \dots, M, \ (i,j) \in \mathcal{A}, \tag{10.26}$$

and the side constraints

$$\sum_{m=1}^{M} A(m) x(m) \le b. \tag{10.27}$$

Here $s_i(m)$ are given supply integers for the mth commodity, $A(m)$ are given matrices, b is a given vector, and $x(m)$ is the flow vector of the mth commodity, with components $x_{ij}(m)$, $(i, j) \in \mathcal{A}$. Furthermore, each $X_{ij}(m)$ is a *finite* subset of contiguous integers.

The dual function is obtained by relaxing the side constraints (10.27), and by minimizing the corresponding Lagrangian function. This minimization separates into m independent minimizations, one per commodity:

$$q(\mu) = -\mu'b + \sum_{m=1}^{M} \min_{x(m) \in F(m)} \left(a(m) + A(m)'\mu\right)' x(m), \qquad (10.28)$$

where $a(m)$ is the vector with components $a_{ij}(m)$, $(i, j) \in \mathcal{A}$, and

$$F(m) = \left\{x(m) \text{ satisfying Eq. (10.25)} \mid x_{ij}(m) \in X_{ij}(m), \forall \ (i, j) \in \mathcal{A}\right\}.$$

An important observation here is that each of the minimization subproblems above is a minimum cost flow problem that can be solved using the methods of Chapters 2-7. Furthermore, if $x^\mu(m)$ solves the mth subproblem, the vector

$$g^\mu = \sum_{m=1}^{M} A(m)x^\mu(m) - b \qquad (10.29)$$

is a subgradient of q at μ.

Let us now discuss the computational solution of the dual problem $\max_{\mu \geq 0} q(\mu)$. The application of the subgradient method is straightforward, so we concentrate on the cutting plane method, which leads to a method known as *Dantzig-Wolfe decomposition*. This method consists of the iteration

$$\mu^k = \arg\max_{\mu \geq 0} Q^k(\mu),$$

where $Q^k(\mu)$ is the piecewise linear approximation of the dual function based on the preceding function values $q(\mu^0), \ldots, q(\mu^{k-1})$, and the corresponding subgradients $g^0, \ldots, g^{k-1}$:

$$Q^k(\mu) = \min\left\{q(\mu^0) + (\mu - \mu^0)'g^0, \ldots, q(\mu^{k-1}) + (\mu - \mu^{k-1})'g^{k-1}\right\}.$$

Consider now the cutting plane subproblem $\max_{\mu \geq 0} Q^k(\mu)$. By introducing an auxiliary variable v, we can write this problem as

maximize v

subject to $q(\mu^i) + (\mu - \mu^i)'g^i \geq v, \quad i = 0, \ldots, k-1, \qquad (10.30)$

$\mu \geq 0.$

This is a linear program in the variables v and μ. We can form its dual problem by assigning a Lagrange multiplier ξ^i to each of the constraints

$q(\mu^i) + (\mu - \mu^i)'g^i \geq v$. After some calculation, this dual problem can be verified to have the form

$$\text{minimize} \quad \sum_{i=0}^{k-1} \xi^i \left(q(\mu^i) - \mu^{i'}g^i \right)$$

$$\text{subject to} \quad \sum_{i=0}^{k-1} \xi^i = 1, \quad \sum_{i=0}^{k-1} \xi^i g^i \leq 0, \tag{10.31}$$

$$\xi^i \geq 0, \quad i = 0, \ldots, k-1.$$

Using Eqs. (10.28) and (10.29), we have

$$q(\mu^i) = -\mu^{i'}b + \sum_{m=1}^{M} \left(a(m) + A(m)'\mu^i \right)' x^{\mu^i}(m),$$

$$g^i = \sum_{m=1}^{M} A(m)x^{\mu^i}(m) - b,$$

so the problem (10.31) can be written as

$$\text{minimize} \quad \sum_{m=1}^{M} a(m)' \sum_{i=0}^{k-1} \xi^i x^{\mu^i}(m)$$

$$\text{subject to} \quad \sum_{i=0}^{k-1} \xi^i = 1, \quad \sum_{m=1}^{M} A(m) \sum_{i=0}^{k-1} \xi^i x^{\mu^i}(m) \leq b, \tag{10.32}$$

$$\xi^i \geq 0, \quad i = 0, \ldots, k-1.$$

The preceding problem is called the *master problem*. It is the dual of the cutting plane subproblem $\max_{\mu \geq 0} Q^k(\mu)$, which in turn approximates the dual problem $\max_{\mu \geq 0} q(\mu)$; in short, it is the *dual of the approximate dual*. We may view this problem as an approximate version of the primal problem where the commodity flow vectors $x(m)$ are constrained to lie in the convex hull of the already generated vectors $x^{\mu^i}(m)$, $i = 0, \ldots, k-1$, rather than in their original constraint set. It can be shown, using linear programming theory, that if the problem (10.30) has an optimal solution [i.e., enough vectors μ^i are available so that the maximum of $Q^k(\mu)$ over $\mu \geq 0$ is attained], then the master problem also has an optimal solution.

Suppose now that we solve the master problem (10.32) using a method that yields a Lagrange multiplier vector, call it μ^k, corresponding to the constraints

$$\sum_{m=1}^{M} A(m) \sum_{i=0}^{k-1} \xi^i x^{\mu^i}(m) \leq b.$$

(Standard linear programming methods, such as the simplex method, can be used for this.) Then, the dual of the master problem [which is the cutting plane subproblem $\max_{\mu \geq 0} Q^k(\mu)$] is solved by the Lagrange multiplier μ^k. Therefore, μ^k is the next iterate of the cutting plane method.

We can now piece together the typical cutting plane iteration.

Cutting Plane – Dantzig-Wolfe Decomposition Iteration

Step 1: Given $\mu^0, \ldots, \mu^{k-1}$, and the commodity flow vectors $x^{\mu^i}(m)$ for $m = 1, \ldots, M$ and $i = 0, \ldots, k-1$, solve the master problem

$$\text{minimize} \quad \sum_{m=1}^{M} a(m)' \sum_{i=0}^{k-1} \xi^i x^{\mu^i}(m)$$

$$\text{subject to} \quad \sum_{i=0}^{k-1} \xi^i = 1, \qquad \sum_{m=1}^{M} A(m) \sum_{i=0}^{k-1} \xi^i x^{\mu^i}(m) \leq b,$$

$$\xi^i \geq 0, \quad i = 0, \ldots, k-1.$$

and obtain μ^k, which is a Lagrange multiplier vector of the constraints

$$\sum_{m=1}^{M} A(m) \sum_{i=0}^{k-1} \xi^i x^{\mu^i}(m) \leq b.$$

Step 2: For each $m = 1, \ldots, M$, obtain a solution $x^{\mu^k}(m)$ of the minimum cost flow problem

$$\min_{x(m) \in F(m)} \left(a(m) + A(m)' \mu^k \right)' x(m).$$

Step 3: Use $x^{\mu^k}(m)$ to modify the master problem by adding one more variable ξ^k and go to the next iteration.

Decomposition by Right-Hand Side Allocation

There is an alternative decomposition approach for solving the multicommodity flow problem with side constraints (10.24)-(10.27). In this approach, we introduce auxiliary variables $y(m)$, $m = 1, \ldots, M$, and we write the problem as

$$\text{minimize} \quad \sum_{m=1}^{M} a(m)'x(m)$$

$$\text{subject to} \quad x(m) \in F(m), \qquad m = 1, \ldots, M,$$

$$\sum_{m=1}^{M} y(m) = b, \qquad A(m)x(m) \le y(m), \quad m = 1, \ldots, M.$$

Equivalently, we can write the problem as

$$\text{minimize} \quad \sum_{m=1}^{M} \min_{\substack{x(m) \in F(m) \\ A(m)x(m)=y(m)}} a(m)'x(m) \tag{10.33}$$

$$\text{subject to} \quad \sum_{m=1}^{M} y(m) = b, \qquad y(m) \in Y(m), \quad m = 1, \ldots, M,$$

where $Y(m)$ is the set of all vectors $y(m)$ for which the inner minimization problem

$$\text{minimize} \quad a(m)'x(m)$$
$$\text{subject to} \quad x(m) \in F(m), \qquad A(m)x(m) \le y(m) \tag{10.34}$$

has at least one feasible solution.
    Let us define

$$p_m\big(y(m)\big) = \min_{\substack{x(m) \in F(m) \\ A(m)x(m) \le y(m)}} a(m)'x(m).$$

Then, problem (10.33) can be written as

$$\text{minimize} \quad \sum_{m=1}^{M} p_m\big(y(m)\big)$$

$$\text{subject to} \quad \sum_{m=1}^{M} y(m) = b, \qquad y(m) \in Y(m), \quad m = 1, \ldots, M.$$

This problem, called the *master problem*, may be solved with nondifferentiable optimization methods, and in particular with the subgradient and the cutting plane methods. Note, however, that the commodity problems (10.34) involve the side constraints $A(m)x(m) \le y(m)$, and need not be of the minimum cost flow type, except in special cases. We refer to the literature cited at the end of the chapter for further details.

10.4 LOCAL SEARCH METHODS

Local search methods are a broad and important class of heuristics for discrete optimization. They apply to the general problem of minimizing a function $f(x)$ over a *finite* set F of (feasible) solutions. In principle, one may solve the problem by *global enumeration* of the entire set F of solutions (this is what branch-and-bound does). A local search method tries to economize on computation by using *local enumeration*, based on the notion of a *neighborhood* $N(x)$ of a solution x, which is a (usually very small) subset of F, containing solutions that are "close" to x in some sense.

In particular, given a solution x, the method selects among the solutions in the neighborhood $N(x)$ a successor solution $\bar{x}$, according to some rule. The process is then repeated with $\bar{x}$ replacing x (or stops when some termination criterion is met). Thus a local search method is characterized by:

(a) The method for choosing a starting solution.

(b) The definition of the neighborhood $N(x)$ of a solution x.

(c) The rule for selecting a successor solution from within $N(x)$.

(d) The termination criterion.

For an example of a local search method, consider the k-OPT heuristic for the traveling salesman problem that we discussed in Example 10.1. Here the starting tour is obtained by using some method, based for example on subtour elimination or a minimum weight spanning tree, as discussed in Example 10.1. The neighborhood of a tour T is defined as the set $N(T)$ of all tours obtained from T by exchanging k arcs that belong to T with another k arcs that do not belong to T. The rule for selecting a successor tour is based on cost improvement; that is, the tour selected from $N(T)$ has minimum cost over all tours in $N(T)$ that have smaller cost than T. Finally, the algorithm terminates when no tour in $N(T)$ has smaller cost than T. Another example of a local search method is provided by the Esau-Williams heuristic of Fig. 10.5.

The definition of a neighborhood often involves intricate calculations and suboptimizations that aim to bring to consideration promising neighbors. Here is an example, due to Kernighan and Lin [1970]:

Example 10.12. (Uniform Graph Partitioning)

Consider a graph $(\mathcal{N}, \mathcal{A})$ with $2n$ nodes, and a cost a_{ij} for each arc (i, j). We want to find a partition of $\mathcal{N}$ into two subsets $\mathcal{N}_1$ and $\mathcal{N}_2$, each with n nodes, so that the total cost of the arcs connecting $\mathcal{N}_1$ and $\mathcal{N}_2$,

$$\sum_{(i,j),\, i\in\mathcal{N}_1, j\in\mathcal{N}_2} a_{ij} + \sum_{(i,j),\, i\in\mathcal{N}_2, j\in\mathcal{N}_1} a_{ij},$$

is minimized.

Here a natural neighborhood of a partition $(\mathcal{N}_1, \mathcal{N}_2)$ is the *k-exchange neighborhood*. This is the set of all partitions obtained by selecting a fixed number k of pairs of nodes (i, j) with $i \in \mathcal{N}_1$ and $j \in \mathcal{N}_2$, and interchanging them, that is, moving i into $\mathcal{N}_2$ and j into $\mathcal{N}_1$. The corresponding local search algorithm moves from a given solution to its minimum cost neighbor, and terminates when no neighbor with smaller cost can be obtained. Unfortunately, the amount of work needed to generate a k-exchange neighborhood increases exponentially with k [there are $\binom{m}{k}$ different ways to select k objects out of m]. One may thus consider a *variable depth neighborhood* that involves multiple successive k-exchanges with small k. As an example, for $k = 1$ we obtain the following algorithm:

Given the starting partition $(\mathcal{N}_1, \mathcal{N}_2)$, consider all pairs (i, j) with $i \in \mathcal{N}_1$ and $j \in \mathcal{N}_2$, and let $c(i, j)$ be the cost change that results from moving i into $\mathcal{N}_2$ and j into $\mathcal{N}_1$. If $(\bar{i}, \bar{j})$ is the pair that minimizes $c(i, j)$, move $\bar{i}$ into $\mathcal{N}_1$ and $\bar{j}$ into $\mathcal{N}_2$, and let $c_1 = c(\bar{i}, \bar{j})$. Repeat this process a fixed number M of times, obtaining a sequence $c_2, c_3, \ldots, c_M$ of minimal cost changes resulting from the sequence of exchanges. Then find

$$\overline{m} = \arg \min_{m=1,\ldots,M} \sum_{l=1}^{m} c_l,$$

and accept as the next partition the one involving the first $\overline{m}$ exchanges.

This type of algorithm avoids the exponential running time of k-exchange neighborhoods, while still considering neighbors differing by as many as M node pairs.

While the definition of neighborhood is often problem-dependent, some general classes of procedures for generating neighborhoods have been developed. One such class is *genetic algorithms*, to be discussed shortly. In some cases, neighborhoods are dynamically changing, and they may depend not only on the current solution, but also on several past solutions. The method of *tabu search*, to be discussed shortly, falls in this category.

The criterion for selecting a solution from within a neighborhood is usually the cost of the solution, but sometimes a more complex criterion based on various problem characteristics and/or constraint violation considerations is adopted. An important possibility, which is the basis for the *simulated annealing method*, to be discussed shortly, is to use a random mechanism for selecting the successor solution within a neighborhood.

Finally, regarding the termination criterion, many local search methods are *cost improving*, and stop when an improved solution cannot be found within the current neighborhood. This means that these methods stop at a *local minimum*, that is, a solution that is no worse than all other solutions within its neighborhood. Unfortunately, for many problems, a local minimum may be far from optimal, particularly if the neighborhood used is relatively small. Thus, for a cost improving method, there is a basic tradeoff between using a large neighborhood to diminish the difficulty with local minima, and paying the cost of increased computation per iteration. Note that there is an important advantage to a cost improving method: *it can never repeat the same solution*, so that in view of the finiteness of the feasible set F, it will always terminate with a local minimum.

An alternative type of neighbor selection and termination criterion, used by simulated annealing and tabu search, is to allow successor solutions to have worse cost than their predecessors, but to also provide mechanisms that ensure the future generation of improved solutions with substantial likelihood. The advantage of accepting solutions of worse cost is that stopping at a local minimum becomes less of a difficulty. For example, the method of simulated annealing, cannot be trapped at a local minimum, as we will see shortly. Unfortunately, methods that do not enforce cost improvement run the danger of cycling through repetition of the same solution. It is therefore essential in these methods to provide a mechanism by virtue of which cycling is either precluded, or becomes highly unlikely.

As a final remark, we note an important advantage of local search methods. While they offer no solid guarantee of finding an optimal or near-optimal solution, they offer the promise of substantial improvement over any heuristic that can be used to generate the starting solution. Unfortunately, however, one can seldom be sure that this promise will be fulfilled in a given practical problem.

10.4.1   Genetic Algorithms

These are local search methods where the neighborhood generation mechanism is inspired by real-life processes of genetics and evolution. In particular, the current solution is modified by "splicing" and "mutation" to obtain neighboring solutions. A typical example is provided by problems of scheduling, such as the traveling salesman problem. The neighborhood of a schedule T may be a collection of other schedules obtained by modifying some contiguous portion of T in some way, while keeping the remainder of the schedule T intact. Alternatively, the neighborhood of a schedule may be obtained by interchanging the position of a few tasks, as in the k-OPT traveling salesman heuristic.

In a variation of this approach, a pool of solutions may be maintained. Some of these solutions may be modified, while some pairs of these solutions may be combined to form new solutions. These solutions, are added to the pool if some criterion, typically based on cost improvement, is met, and some of the solutions of the existing pool may be dropped. In this way, it is argued, the pool is "evolving" in a Darwinian way through a "survival of the fittest" process.

A specific example implementation of this approach operates in phases. At the beginning of a phase, we have a *population X* consisting of n feasible solutions $x_1, \ldots, x_n$. The phase proceeds as follows:

Typical Phase of a Genetic Algorithm

Step 1: (Local Search) Starting from each solution x_i of the current population X, apply a local search algorithm up to obtaining a local minimum $\overline{x}_i$. Let $\overline{X} = \{\overline{x}_1, \ldots, \overline{x}_n\}$.

Step 2: (Mutation) Select at random a subset of elements of $\overline{X}$, and modify each element according to some (problem dependent) mechanism, to obtain another feasible solution.

Step 3: (Recombination) Select at random a subset of pairs of elements of $\overline{X}$, and produce from each pair a feasible solution according to some (problem dependent) mechanism.

Step 4: (Survivor Selection) Let $\tilde{X}$ be the set of feasible solutions obtained from the mutation and recombination Steps 3 and 4. Out of the population $\overline{X} \cup \tilde{X}$, select a subset of n elements according to some criterion. Use this subset to start the next phase.

Mutation allows speculative variations of the local minima at hand, while recombination (also called *crossover*) aims to combine attributes of a pair of local minima. The processes of mutation and recombination are usually performed with the aid of some data structure that is used to represent a solution, such as for example a string of bits. There is a very large number of variants of genetic algorithm approaches. Typically, these approaches are problem-dependent and require a lot of trial-and-error. However, genetic algorithms are quite easy to implement, and have achieved considerable popularity. We refer to the literature cited at the end of the chapter for more details.

10.4.2   Tabu Search

Tabu search aims to avoid getting trapped at a poor local minimum, by accepting on occasion a worse or even infeasible solution from within the current neighborhood. Since cost improvement is not enforced, tabu search runs the danger of cycling, i.e., repeating the same sequence of solutions indefinitely. To alleviate this problem, tabu search keeps track of recently obtained solutions in a "forbidden" (tabu) list. Solutions in the tabu list cannot be regenerated, thereby avoiding cycling, at least in the short run. In a more sophisticated variation of this strategy, the tabu list contains attributes of recently obtained solutions rather than the solutions themselves. Solutions with attributes in the tabu list are forbidden from being generated (except under particularly favorable circumstances, under which the tabu list is overridden).

Tabu search is also based on an elaborate web of implementation heuristics that have been developed through experience with a large number of practical problems. These heuristics regulate the size of the current neighborhood, the criterion of selecting a new solution from the current neighborhood, the criterion for termination, etc. These heuristics may also involve selective memory storage of previously generated solutions or their attributes, penalization of the constraints with (possibly time-varying) penalty parameters, and multiple tabu lists. We refer to the literature cited at the end of the chapter for further details.

10.4.3   Simulated Annealing

Simulated annealing is similar to tabu search in that it occasionally allows solutions of inferior cost to be generated. It differs from tabu search in the manner in which it avoids cycling. Instead of checking deterministically the preceding solutions for cycling, it simply randomizes its selection of the next solution. In doing so, it not only avoids cycling, but also provides some theoretical guarantee of escaping from local minima and eventually finding a *global* minimum.

Being able to find a global minimum is not really exciting in itself. For example, under fairly general conditions, one can do so by using unsophisticated *random search* methods, such as for example a method where feasible solutions are sampled at random. However, simulated annealing randomizes the choice of the successor solution from within the current neighborhood in a way that gives preference to solutions of smaller cost, and in doing so, it aims to find a global minimum faster than simple-minded random search methods.

In particular, given a solution x, we select by random sampling a candidate solution $\bar{x}$ from the neighborhood $N(x)$. The sampling probabilities are positive for all members of $N(x)$, but are otherwise unspecified. The solution $\bar{x}$ is accepted if it is cost improving, that is

$$f(\bar{x}) < f(x).$$

Otherwise, $\bar{x}$ is accepted with probability

$$e^{-\left(f(\bar{x})-f(x)\right)/T},$$

where T is some positive constant, and is rejected with the complementary probability.

The constant T regulates the likelihood of accepting solutions of worse cost. It is called the *temperature* of the process (the name is inspired by a certain physical analogy that will not be discussed here). The likelihood of accepting a solution $\bar{x}$ of worse cost than x decreases as its cost increases. Furthermore, when T is large (or small), the probability of accepting a worse solution is close to 1 (or close to 0, respectively). In practice, it is typical to start with a large T, allowing a better chance of escaping from local minima, and then to reduce T gradually to enhance the selectivity of the method towards improved solutions.

Contrary to genetic algorithms and tabu search, which offer no general theoretical guarantees of good performance, simulated annealing is supported by solid theory. In particular, under fairly general conditions, it can be shown that a global minimum will be eventually visited (with probability 1), and that with gradual reduction of the temperature T, the search process will be confined with high likelihood to solutions that are globally optimal.

For an illustrative analysis, assume that T is kept constant and let p_{xy} be the probability that when the current solution is x, the next solution sampled is y. Consider the special case where $p_{xy} = p_{yx}$ for all feasible solutions x and y, and assume that the Markov chain defined by the probabilities p_{xy} is *irreducible*, in the sense that there is positive probability to go from any x to any y, with one or more samples. Then it can be shown (see Exercise 10.20) that the steady-state probability of a solution $\bar{x}$ is

$$\frac{e^{-f(\bar{x})/T}}{\sum_{x \in F} e^{-f(x)/T}}.$$

Essentially, this says that for very small T and far into the future, the current solution is almost always optimal.

When the condition $p_{xy} = p_{yx}$ does not hold, one cannot obtain a closed-form expression for the steady-state probabilities of the various solutions. However, as long as the underlying Markov chain is irreducible, the behavior is qualitatively similar: the steady-state probability of nonoptimal solutions diminishes to 0 as T approaches 0. There is also related analysis for the case where the temperature parameter T is time-varying and converges to 0; see the references cited at the end of the chapter.

The results outlined above should be viewed with a grain of salt. In practice, *speed of convergence* is as important as eventual convergence to the optimum, and solving a given problem by simulated annealing can be very slow. A nice aspect of the method is that it depends very little on the structure of the problem being solved, and this enhances its value for relatively unstructured problems that are not well-understood. For other problems, where there exists a lot of accumulated insight and experience, simulated annealing is usually inferior to other local search approaches.

10.5 ROLLOUT ALGORITHMS

The branch-and-bound algorithm is guaranteed to find an optimal flow vector, but it may require the solution of a very large number of subproblems. Basically, the algorithm amounts to an exhaustive search of the entire branch-and-bound tree. An alternative is to consider faster methods that are based on intelligent but nonexhaustive search of the tree. In this section, we develop one such method, the *rollout algorithm*, which, in its simplest version, sequentially constructs a suboptimal flow vector by fixing the arc flows, a few arcs at a time. The rollout algorithm can be combined with most heuristics, including the local search methods of the preceding section, and is capable of magnifying their effectiveness.

Let us consider the minimization of a function f of a flow vector x over a feasible set F, and let us assume that F is *finite* (presumably because of some integer constraints on the arc flows). Define a *partial solution* to be a collection of arc flows $\{x_{ij} \mid (i,j) \in S\}$, corresponding to some proper subset of arcs $S \subset \mathcal{A}$. Such a collection is distinguished from a flow vector $(S = \mathcal{A})$, which is also referred to as a *complete solution*.

The rollout algorithm generates a sequence of partial solutions, culminating with a complete solution. For this purpose, it employs some problem-dependent heuristic algorithm, called the *base heuristic*. This algorithm, given a partial solution

$$P = \{x_{ij} \mid (i,j) \in S\},$$

produces a *complementary solution*

$$\overline{P} = \{x_{ij} \mid (i,j) \notin S\},$$

and a corresponding (complete) flow vector

$$x = \{x_{ij} \mid (i,j) \in \mathcal{A}\} = P \cup \overline{P}.$$

The cost of this flow vector is denoted by

$$H(P) = \begin{cases} f(x) & \text{if } x \in F, \\ \infty & \text{otherwise,} \end{cases}$$

and is called the *heuristic cost of the partial solution P*. If P is a complete solution, which is feasible, i.e., a flow vector $x \in F$, by convention the heuristic cost of P is the true cost $f(x)$. There are no restrictions on the nature of the base heuristic; a typical example is an integer rounding heuristic applied to the solution of some related linear or convex network problem, which may be obtained by relaxing/neglecting the integer constraints.

The rollout algorithm starts with some partial solution, or with the empty set of arcs, $S = \emptyset$. It enlarges a partial solution iteratively, with a few arc flows at a time. The algorithm terminates when a complete solution is obtained. At the start of the typical iteration, we have a current partial solution

$$P = \{x_{ij} \mid (i,j) \in S\},$$

and at the end of the iteration, we augment this solution with some more arc flows. The steps of the iteration are as follows:

Iteration of the Rollout Algorithm

Step 1: Select a subset T of arcs that are not in S according to some criterion. (The arc selection method is usually based on some heuristic preliminary optimization, and is problem-dependent.)

Step 2: Consider the collection F_T of all possible values of the arc flows $y = \{y_{ij} \mid (i,j) \in T\}$, and apply the base heuristic to compute the heuristic cost $H(P_y^+)$ of the augmented partial solution

$$P_y^+ = \{\{x_{ij} \mid (i,j) \in S\}, \{y_{ij} \mid (i,j) \in T\}\}$$

for each $y \in F_T$.

Step 3: Choose from the set F_T the arc flows $\overline{y} = \{\overline{y}_{ij} \mid (i,j) \in T\}$ that minimize the heuristic cost $H(P_y^+)$; that is, find

$$\overline{y} = \arg \min_{y \in F_T} H(P_y^+). \tag{10.35}$$

Step 4: Augment the current partial solution $\{x_{ij} \mid (i,j) \in S\}$ with the arc flows $\{\overline{y}_{ij} \mid (i,j) \in T\}$ thus obtained, and proceed with the next iteration.

As an example of this algorithm, let us consider the traveling salesman problem, and let us use as base heuristic the nearest neighbor method, whereby we start from some simple path and at each iteration, we add a node that does not close a cycle and minimizes the cost of the enlarged path. The rollout algorithm operates as follows: After k iterations, we have a path $\{i_1, \ldots, i_k\}$ consisting of distinct nodes. At the next iteration, we run the nearest neighbor heuristic starting from each of the paths $\{i_1, \ldots, i_k, i\}$ with $i \neq i_1, \ldots, i_k$, and obtain a corresponding tour. We then select as next node i_{k+1} of the path the node i that corresponds to the best tour thus obtained. Here, the set of arcs used to augment the current partial solution in the rollout algorithm is

$$T = \{(i_k, i) \mid i \neq i_1, \ldots, i_k\},$$

and at the kth iteration the flows of all of these arcs are set to 0, except for arc (i_k, i_{k+1}) whose flow is set to 1.

Note that a rollout algorithm requires considerably more computation than the base heuristic. For example, in the case where the subset T in Step

1 consists of a single arc, the rollout algorithm requires $O(mn)$ applications of the base heuristic, where

m is the number of arcs, and

n is a bound on the number of possible values of each arc flow.

Nonetheless the computational requirements of the rollout algorithm may be quite manageable. In particular, if the arc flows are restricted to be 0 or 1, and the base heuristic has polynomial running time, so does the corresponding rollout algorithm.

An important question is whether, given an initial partial solution, the rollout algorithm performs at least as well as its base heuristic when started from that solution. This can be guaranteed if the base heuristic is *sequentially consistent*. By this we mean that the heuristic has the following property:

Suppose that starting from a partial solution

$$P = \{x_{ij} \mid (i,j) \in S\},$$

the heuristic produces the complementary solution

$$\overline{P} = \{x_{ij} \mid (i,j) \notin S\}.$$

Then starting from the partial solution

$$P^+ = \{x_{ij} \mid (i,j) \in S \cup T\},$$

the heuristic produces a complementary solution

$$\overline{P}^+ = \{x_{ij} \mid (i,j) \notin S \cup T\},$$

which coincides with $\overline{P}$ on the arcs $(i,j) \notin S \cup T$.

As an example, it can be seen that the nearest neighbor heuristic for the traveling salesman problem, discussed earlier, is sequentially consistent. This is a manifestation of a more general property: many common base heuristics of the greedy type are by nature sequentially consistent (see Exercise 10.21). It may be verified, based on Eq. (10.35), that a sequentially consistent rollout algorithm keeps generating the same solution $P \cup \overline{P}$, up to the point where by examining the alternatives in Eq. (10.35) and by calculating their heuristic costs, it discovers a better solution. As a result, sequential consistency guarantees that the costs of the successive solutions $P \cup \overline{P}$ produced by the rollout algorithm are monotonically nonincreasing; that is, we have

$$H(P^+) \leq H(P)$$

at every iteration. Thus, the cost $f(x_t)$ of the solution x_t produced upon termination of the rollout algorithm is at least as small as the cost $f(x_0)$

of the initial solution x_0 produced by the base heuristic. For further elaboration of the sequential consistency property, we refer to the paper by Bertsekas, Tsitsiklis, and Wu [1997], which also discusses some underlying connections with the policy iteration method of dynamic programming.

A condition that is more general than sequential consistency is that the algorithm be *sequentially improving*, in the sense that at each iteration there holds

$$H(P^+) \leq H(P).$$

This property also guarantees that the cost of the solutions produced by the rollout algorithm is monotonically nonincreasing. The paper by Bertsekas, Tsitsiklis, and Wu [1997] discusses situations where this property holds, and shows that with fairly simple modification, a rollout algorithm can be made sequentially improving (see also Exercise 10.22).

There are a number of variations of the basic rollout algorithm described above. Here are some examples:

(1) We may adapt the rollout framework to use multiple heuristic algorithms. In particular, let us assume that we have K algorithms $\mathcal{H}_1, \ldots, \mathcal{H}_K$. The kth of these algorithms, given an augmented partial solution P_y^+, produces a heuristic cost $H_k(P_y^+)$. We may then use in the flow selection via Eq. (10.35) a heuristic cost of the form

$$H(P_y^+) = \min_{k=1,\ldots,K} H_k(P_y^+),$$

or of the form

$$H(P_y^+) = \sum_{k=1}^{K} r_k H_k(P_y^+),$$

where r_k are some fixed scalar weights obtained by trial and error.

(2) We may incorporate *multistep lookahead* or *selective depth lookahead* into the rollout framework. Here we consider augmenting the current partial solution $P = \{x_{ij} \mid (i,j) \in S\}$ with all possible values for the flows of a finite sequence of arcs that are not in S. We run the base heuristic from each of the corresponding augmented partial solutions, we select the sequence of arc flows with minimum heuristic cost, and then augment the current partial solution P with the first arc flow in this sequence. As an illustration, let us recall the traveling salesman problem with the nearest neighbor method used as the base heuristic. An example rollout algorithm with two-step lookahead operates as follows: We begin each iteration with a path $\{i_1, \ldots, i_k\}$. We run the nearest neighbor heuristic starting from each of the paths $\{i_1, \ldots, i_k, i\}$ with $i \neq i_1, \ldots, i_k$, and obtain a corresponding tour. We then form the subset $\overline{I}$ consisting of the m nodes $i \neq i_1, \ldots, i_k$ that correspond to the m best tours thus obtained. We run the nearest neighbor heuristic starting from each of the paths $\{i_1, \ldots, i_k, i, j\}$

with $i \in \bar{I}$ and $j \neq i_1, \ldots, i_k, i$, and obtain a corresponding tour. We then select as the next node i_{k+1} of the path the node $i \in \bar{I}$ that corresponds to a minimum cost tour.

(3) We may use alternative methods for computing a cost $H(P_y^+)$ of a candidate augmented partial solution P_y^+ for use in the flow selection via Eq. (10.35). For example, instead of generating this cost via the base heuristic, we may calculate it as the optimal or approximately optimal cost of a suitable optimization problem. In particular, it is possible to use a cost derived from Lagrangian relaxation, whereby at a given partial solution, an appropriate dual problem is solved, and its optimal cost is used in place of the heuristic cost H in Eq. (10.35). Alternatively, a complementary solution may be constructed based on minimization of the corresponding Lagrangian function. As another example, one may use as cost of a partial solution, some heuristic measure of quality of the partial solution; this idea forms the basis for computer chess, where various positions are evaluated using a heuristic "position evaluation function."

Let us provide a few examples of rollout algorithms. The first example is very simple, but illustrates well the notions of sequential consistency and sequential improvement.

Example 10.13. (One-Dimensional Walk)

Consider a person who walks on a straight line and at each time period takes either a unit step to the left or a unit step to the right. There is a cost function assigning cost $f(i)$ to each integer i. Given an integer starting point on the line, the person wants to minimize the cost of the point where he will end up after a given and fixed number N of steps.

We can formulate this problem as a problem of selecting a path in a graph (see Fig. 10.15). In particular, without loss of generality, let us assume that the starting point is the origin, so that the person's position after N steps will be some integer in the interval $[-N, N]$. The nodes of the graph are identified with pairs (k, m), where k is the number of steps taken so far $(k = 1, \ldots, N)$ and m is the person's position $(m \in [-k, k])$. A node (k, m) with $k < N$ has two outgoing arcs with end nodes $(k+1, m-1)$ (corresponding to a left step) and $(k+1, m+1)$ (corresponding to a right step). Let us consider paths whose starting node is $(0, 0)$ and the destination node is of the form (N, m), where m is of the form $N - 2l$ and $l \in [0, N]$ is the number of left steps taken. The problem then is to find the path of this type such that $f(m)$ is minimized.

Let the base heuristic be the algorithm, which, starting at a node (k, m), takes $N - k$ successive steps to the right and terminates at the node $(N, m + N - k)$. It can be seen that this algorithm is sequentially consistent [the base heuristic generates the path $(k, m), (k+1, m+1), \ldots, (N, m+N-k)$ starting from (k, m), and also the path $(k+1, m+1), \ldots, (N, m+N-k)$ starting from $(k+1, m+1)$, so the criterion for sequential consistency is fulfilled].

The rollout algorithm, at node (k, m) compares the cost of the destination node $(N, m + N - k)$ (corresponding to taking a step to the right and then following the base heuristic) and the cost of the destination node $(N, m + N - k - 2)$ (corresponding to taking a step to the left and then following the base heuristic). Let us say that an integer $i \in [-N + 2, N - 2]$ is a *local minimum* if $f(i - 2) \geq f(i)$ and $f(i) \leq f(i + 2)$. Let us also say that N (or $-N$) is a local minimum if $f(N - 2) \leq f(N)$ [or $f(-N) \leq f(-N + 2)$, respectively]. Then it can be seen that starting from the origin $(0, 0)$, the rollout algorithm obtains the *local minimum that is closest to* N, (see Fig. 10.15). This is no worse (and typically better) than the integer N obtained by the base heuristic. This example illustrates how the rollout algorithm may exhibit "intelligence" that is totally lacking from the base heuristic.

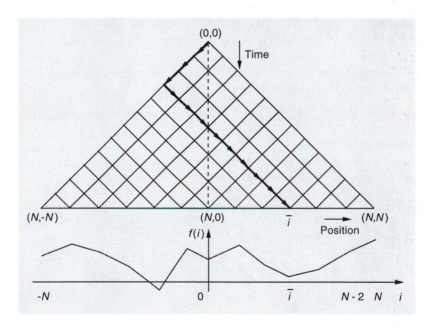

Figure 10.15: Illustration of the path generated by the rollout algorithm in Example 10.13. It keeps moving to the left up to the time where the base heuristic generates two destinations $(N, \bar{i})$ and $(N, \bar{i} - 2)$ with $f(\bar{i}) \leq f(\bar{i} - 2)$. Then it continues to move to the right ending at the destination $(N, \bar{i})$, which corresponds to the local minimum closest to N.

Consider next the case where the base heuristic is the algorithm that, starting at a node (k, m), compares the cost $f(m + N - k)$ (corresponding to taking all of the remaining $N - k$ steps to the right) and the cost $f(m - N + k)$ (corresponding to taking all of the remaining $N - k$ steps to the left), and accordingly moves to node

$$(N, m + N - k) \qquad \text{if} \qquad f(m + N - k) \leq f(m - N + k),$$

or to node

$$(N, m - N + k) \qquad \text{if} \qquad f(m - N + k) < f(m + N - k).$$

It can be seen that this base heuristic is not sequentially consistent, but is instead sequentially improving. It can then be verified that starting from the origin $(0,0)$, the rollout algorithm obtains the *global minimum* of f in the interval $[-N, N]$, while the base heuristic obtains the better of the two points $-N$ and N.

Example 10.14. Constrained Traveling Salesman Problem

Consider the traveling salesman problem of Example 10.1, where we want to minimize the cost

$$\sum_{(i,j) \in T} a_{ij},$$

of a tour T, while satisfying the side constraints

$$\sum_{(i,j) \in T} c_{ij}^k \le d^k, \qquad \forall\, k = 1, \ldots, K.$$

A rollout algorithm starts with the trivial path $P = (s)$, where s is some initial node, progressively constructs a sequence of paths $P = (s, i_1, \ldots, i_m)$, $m = 1, \ldots, N - 1$, consisting of distinct nodes, and then completes a tour by adding the arc (i_{N-1}, s). The rollout procedure is as follows.

We introduce nonnegative penalty coefficients μ^k for the side constraints, and we form modified arc traversal costs $\hat{a}_{ij}$, given by

$$\hat{a}_{ij} = a_{ij} + \sum_{k=1}^{K} \mu^k c_{ij}^k.$$

The method of obtaining μ^k is immaterial for our purposes in this example, but we note that one possibility is to use the Lagrangian relaxation method of Section 10.3. We assume that we have a heuristic algorithm that can complete the current path $P = (s, i_1, \ldots, i_m)$ with a path $(i_{m+1}, \ldots, i_{N-1}, s)$, thereby obtaining a tour $T^*(P)$ that has approximately minimum modified cost. Some of the heuristics mentioned in Example 10.1, including the k-OPT heuristic, can be used for this purpose. Furthermore, we assume that by using another heuristic, we can complete the current path P to a tour $\hat{T}(P)$ that satisfies all the side constraints.

Given the current path $P = (s, i_1, \ldots, i_m)$, the rollout algorithm, considers the set A_m of all arcs $(i_m, j) \in \mathcal{A}$ such that j does not belong to P. For each of the nodes j such that $(i_m, j) \in A_m$, it considers the expanded path $P_e = (s, i_1, \ldots, i_m, j)$ and obtains the tours $T^*(P_e)$ and $\hat{T}(P_e)$, using the heuristics mentioned earlier. The rollout algorithm then adds to the current partial path P the node j for which the tour $T^*(P_e)$ satisfies the side constraints and has minimum cost (with respect to the arc costs a_{ij}); if no path

$T^*(P_e)$ satisfies the side constraints, the algorithm adds to the current path the node j for which the tour $\hat{T}(P_e)$ has minimum cost.

One of the drawbacks of the scheme just described is that it requires the approximate solution of a large number of traveling salesman problems. A faster variant is obtained if the arc set A_m above is restricted to be a suitably chosen subset of the eligible arcs (i_m, j), such for example those whose length does not exceed a certain threshold.

Finally, it is interesting to compare rollout algorithms with the local search methods of the preceding section. Both types of algorithms generate a sequence of solutions, but in the case of a rollout algorithm, the generated solutions are partial (except at termination), while in a local search method, the generated solutions are complete. In both types of algorithms, the next solution is generated from within a neighborhood of the current solution, but the selection criterion in rollout algorithms is the *estimated* cost of the solution as obtained by the base heuristic, while in local search methods, it is typically the *true* cost of the solution. Finally, in rollout algorithms, there is no concern about local minima and cycling, but there is also no provision for improving a complete solution after it is obtained.

There are interesting possibilities for combining a rollout algorithm with a local search method. In particular, one may use a local search method as part of a base heuristic in a rollout algorithm; here, the local search method could be fairly unsophisticated, since one may hope that the rollout process will provide an effective mechanism for solution improvement. Alternatively, one may first use a rollout algorithm to obtain a complete solution, and then use a local search method in an effort to improve this solution.

10.6 NOTES, SOURCES, AND EXERCISES

There is a great variety of integer constrained network flow problems, and the associated methodological and applications literature is vast. For textbook treatments at various levels of sophistication, which also cover broader aspects of integer programming, see Lawler [1976], Zoutendijk [1976], Papadimitriou and Steiglitz [1982], Minoux [1986a], Schrijver [1986], Nemhauser and Wolsey [1988], Bogart [1990], Pulleyblank, Cook, Cunningham, and Schrijver [1993], Cameron [1994], and Cook, Cunningham, Pulleyblank, and Schrijver [1998]. Volumes 7 and 8 of the Handbooks in Operations Research and Management Science, edited by Ball, Magnanti, Monma, and Nemhauser [1995a], [1995b], are devoted to network theory and applications, and include several excellent survey papers with large bibliographies. O'hEigeartaigh, Lenstra, and Rinnoy Kan [1985] provide an extensive bibliography on combinatorial optimization. Von Randow [1982],

[1985] gives an extensive bibliography on integer programming and related subjects.

The traveling salesman problem has been associated with many of the important investigations in discrete optimization. It was first considered in a modern setting by Dantzig, Fulkerson, and Johnson [1954], whose paper stimulated much interest and research. The edited volume by Lawler, Lenstra, Rinnoy Kan, and Shmoys [1985] focuses on the traveling salesman problem and its variations, and the papers by Junger, Reinelt, and Rinaldi [1995], and by Johnson and McGeoch [1997] provide extensive surveys of the subject. There is a large literature on the use of polyhedral approximations to the feasible set of integer programming problems and the traveling salesman problem in particular; see, for example, the papers by Cornuejols, Fonlupt, and Naddef [1985], Grötschel and Padberg [1985], Padberg and Grötschel [1985], Pulleyblank [1983], and the books by Nemhauser and Wolsey [1988], and Schrijver [1986]. The papers by Burkard [1990], Gilmore, Lawler, and Shmoys [1985], and Tsitsiklis [1992] discuss some special cases of the traveling salesman problem and some extensions.

The monograph by Martello and Toth [1990] is devoted to generalized assignment problems, including ones with integer constraints. The book by Kershenbaum [1993] provides a lot of material on tree construction and network design algorithms for data communications; see also Monma and Sheng [1986], Minoux [1989], Bertsekas and Gallager [1992], and Grötschel, Monma, and Stoer [1995]. Exact and heuristic methods for the Steiner tree problem are surveyed by Winter [1987] and Voß [1992].

Matching problems are discussed in detail in the monograph by Lovasz and Plummer [1985], the survey by Gerards [1995], and Chapter 10 of the book by Murty [1992]. For vehicle and arc routing problems, see the surveys by Assad and Golden [1995], Desrosiers, Dumas, Solomon, and Soumis [1995], Eiselt, Gendreau, and Laporte [1995a], [1995b], Federgruen and Simchi-Levi [1995], Fisher [1995], and Powell, Jaillet, and Odoni [1995].

An important application of multidimensional assignment problems arises in the context of multi-target tracking and data association; see Blackman [1986], Bar-Shalom and Fortman [1988], Pattipati, Deb, Bar-Shalom, and Washburn [1992], Poore [1994], Poore and Robertson [1997]. The material on the error bounds for the enforced separation heuristic in three-dimensional assignment problems (Exercise 10.31) is apparently new.

Integer multicommodity flow problems are discussed by Barnhart, Hane, and Vance [1997]. Nonlinear, nonconvex network optimization is discussed by Lamar [1993], Bell and Lamar [1993], as well as in general texts on global optimization; see Pardalos and Rosen [1987], Floudas [1995], and Horst, Pardalos, and Thoai [1995]. For a textbook treatment of scheduling (cf. Exercises 10.23-10.27), see Pinedo [1995].

Branch-and-bound has its origins in the traveling salesman paper by Dantzig, Fulkerson, and Johnson [1954]. Their paper was followed by Croes [1958], Eastman [1958], and Land and Doig [1960], who considered versions of the branch-and-bound method in the context of various integer programming problems. The term "branch-and-bound" was first used by Little, Murty, Sweeney, and Karel [1963], in the context of the traveling salesman problem. Balas and Toth [1985], and Nemhauser and Wolsey [1988] provide extensive surveys of branch-and-bound.

Lagrangian relaxation was suggested in the context of discrete optimization by Held and Karp [1970], [1971]. Subgradient methods were introduced by Shor in the Soviet Union during the middle 60s. The convergence properties of subgradient methods and their variations are discussed in a number of sources, including Auslender [1976], Goffin [1977], Shapiro [1979], Shor [1985], Poljak [1987], Hiriart-Urruty and Lemarechal [1993], Brannlund [1993], Bertsekas [1995b], and Goffin and Kiwiel [1996].

Cutting plane methods were proposed by Cheney and Goldstein [1959], and by Kelley [1960]; see also the book by Goldstein [1967]. Central cutting plane methods were introduced by Elzinga and Moore [1975]. More recent proposals, some of which relate to interior point methods, are discussed in Goffin and Vial [1990], Goffin, Haurie, and Vial [1992], Ye [1992], Kortanek and No [1993], Goffin, Luo, and Ye [1993], [1996], Atkinson and Vaidya [1995], Nesterov [1995], Luo [1996], and Kiwiel [1997b].

Three historically important references on decomposition methods are Dantzig and Wolfe [1960], Benders [1962], and Everett [1963]. An early text on large-scale optimization and decomposition is Lasdon [1970]; see also Geoffrion [1970], [1974]. Subgradient methods have been applied to the solution of multicommodity flow problems using a decomposition framework by Kennington and Shalaby [1977]. The book by Censor and Zenios [1997] discusses several applications of decomposition in a variety of algorithmic contexts.

The literature of local search methods is extensive. The edited volume by Aarts and Lenstra [1997] contains several surveys of broad classes of methods. Osman and Laporte [1996] provide an extensive bibliography.

The book by Goldberg [1989] focuses on genetic algorithms. Tabu search was initiated with the works of Glover [1986] and Hansen [1996]. The book by Glover and Laguna [1997], and the surveys by Glover [1989], [1990], Glover, Taillard, and de Verra [1993] provide detailed expositions and give many references.

Simulated annealing was proposed by Kirkpatrick, Gelatt, and Vecchi [1983] based on earlier suggestions by Metropolis, Rosenbluth, Rosenbluth, Teller, and Teller [1953]; see also Cerny [1985]. The main theoretical convergence properties of the method were established by Hajek [1988] and Tsitsiklis [1989]; see also the papers by Connors and Kumar [1989], Gelfand and Mitter [1989], and Bertsimas and Tsitsiklis [1993], and the book by Korst, Aarts, and Korst [1989]. A framework for integration of local search methods is presented by Fox [1993], [1995].

Rollout algorithms for discrete optimization were proposed in the book by Bertsekas and Tsitsiklis [1996] in the context of the neuro-dynamic programming methodology, and in the paper by Bertsekas, Tsitsiklis, and Wu [1997]. An application to scheduling using the framework of the quiz problem (cf. Exercises 10.28 and 10.29) is described by Bertsekas and Castañon [1998]. The idea of sequential selection of candidates for participation in a solution is implicit in several combinatorial optimization contexts. For example this idea is embodied in the sequential fan candidate list strategy as applied in tabu search (see Glover, Taillard, and de Werra [1993]). A similar idea is also used in the sequential automatic test procedures of Pattipati (see e.g., Pattipati and Alexandridis [1990]).

EXERCISES

10.1

Consider the symmetric traveling salesman problem with the graph shown in Fig. 10.16.

(a) Find a suboptimal solution using the nearest neighbor heuristic starting from node 1.

(b) Find a suboptimal solution by first solving an assignment problem, and by then merging subtours.

(c) Try to improve the solutions found in (a) and (b) by using the 2-OPT heuristic.

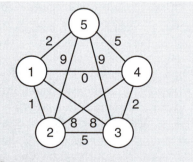

Symmetric Traveling Salesman
Problem Data.
Costs Shown Next to the Arcs.
Each arc is bidirectional.

Figure 10.16: Data for a symmetric traveling salesman problem (cf. Exercise 10.1). The arc costs are shown next to the arcs. Each arc is bidirectional.

10.2 (Minimum Cost Cycles)

Consider a strongly connected graph with a nonnegative cost for each arc. We want to find a forward cycle of minimum cost that contains all nodes but is not necessarily simple; that is, a node or an arc may be traversed multiple times.

(a) Convert this problem into a traveling salesman problem. *Hint*: Construct a complete graph with cost of an arc (i, j) equal to the shortest distance from i to j in the original graph.

(b) Apply your method of part (a) to the graph of Fig. 10.17.

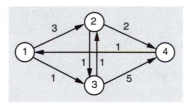

Figure 10.17: Data for a minimum cost cycle problem (cf. Exercise 10.2). The arc costs are shown next to the arcs.

10.3

Consider the problem of checking whether a given graph contains a simple cycle that passes through all the nodes. (The cycle need not be forward.) Formulate this problem as a symmetric traveling salesman problem. *Hint*: Consider a complete graph where the cost of an arc (i, j) is 1 if (i, j) or (j, i) is an arc of the original graph, and is 2 otherwise.

10.4

Show that an asymmetric traveling salesman problem with nodes $1, \ldots, N$ and arc costs a_{ij} can be converted to a symmetric traveling salesman problem involving a graph with nodes $1, \ldots, N, N + 1, \ldots, 2N$, and the arc costs

$$\bar{a}_{i(N+j)} = \begin{cases} a_{ij} & \text{if } i, j = 1, \ldots, N, \ i \neq j, \\ -M & \text{if } i = j, \end{cases}$$

where M is a sufficiently large number. *Hint*: All arcs with cost $-M$ must be included in an optimal tour of the symmetric version.

10.5

Consider the problem of finding a shortest (forward) path from an origin node s to a destination node t of a graph with given arc lengths, subject to the additional constraint that the path passes through every node exactly once.

(a) Show that the problem can be converted to a traveling salesman problem by adding an artificial arc (t, s) of length $-M$, where M is a sufficiently large number.

(b) (Longest Path Problem) Consider the problem of finding a simple forward path from s to t that has a maximum number of arcs. Show that the problem can be converted to a traveling salesman problem.

10.6

Consider the problem of finding a shortest (forward) path in a graph with given arc lengths, subject to the constraint that the path passes through every node exactly once (the choice of start and end nodes of the path is subject to optimization). Formulate the problem as a traveling salesman problem.

10.7 (Traveling Salesman Problem/Triangle Inequality)

Consider a symmetric traveling salesman problem where the arc costs are nonnegative and satisfy the following *triangle inequality*:

$$a_{ij} \le a_{ik} + a_{kj}, \qquad \text{for all nodes } i, j, k.$$

This problem has some special algorithmic properties.

(a) Consider a procedure, which given a cycle $\{i_0, i_1, \ldots, i_K, i_0\}$ that contains all the nodes (but passes through some of them multiple times), obtains a tour by deleting nodes after their first appearance in the cycle; e.g., in a 5-node problem, starting from the cycle $\{1, 3, 5, 2, 3, 4, 2, 1\}$, the procedure produces the tour $\{1, 3, 5, 2, 4, 1\}$. Use the triangle inequality to show that the tour thus obtained has no greater cost than the original cycle.

(b) Starting with a spanning tree of the graph, use the procedure of part (a) to construct a tour with cost equal to at most two times the total cost of the spanning tree. *Hint*: The cycle should cross each arc of the spanning tree exactly once in each direction. "Double" each arc of the spanning tree. Use the fact that if a graph is connected and each of its nodes has even degree, there is a cycle that contains all the arcs of the graph exactly once (cf. Exercise 1.5).

(c) (Double tree heuristic) Start with a minimum cost spanning tree of the graph, and use part (b) to construct a tour with cost equal to at most twice the optimal tour cost.

(d) Verify that the problem of Fig. 10.18 satisfies the triangle inequality. Apply the method of part (c) to this problem.

10.8 (Christofides' Traveling Salesman Heuristic)

Consider a symmetric traveling salesman problem where the arc costs are nonnegative and satisfy the triangle inequality (cf. the preceding exercise). Let R

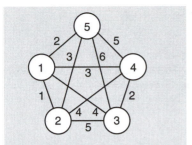

Symmetric Traveling Salesman Problem Data.
Costs Shown Next to the Arcs.
Each arc is bidirectional.

Figure 10.18: Data for a symmetric traveling salesman problem (cf. Exercises 10.7 and 10.8). The arc costs are shown next to the arcs.

be a minimum cost spanning tree of the graph (cf. Exercise 2.30), and let S be the subset of the nodes that has an odd number of incident arcs in R. A *perfect matching* of the nodes of S is a subset of arcs such that every node of S is an end node of exactly one arc of the subset and each arc of the subset has end nodes in S. Suppose that M is a perfect matching of the nodes of S that has minimum sum of arc costs. Construct a tour that consists of the arcs of M and some of the arcs of R, and show that its weight is no more than 3/2 times the optimal tour cost. Solve the problem of Fig. 10.18 using this heuristic, and find the ratio of the solution cost to the optimal tour cost. *Hint*: Note that the total cost of the arcs of M is at most 1/2 the optimal tour cost. Also, use the fact that if a graph is connected and each of its nodes has even degree, there is a cycle that contains all the arcs of the graph exactly once (cf. Exercise 1.5).

10.9 (K-Traveling Salesmen Problem)

Consider the version of the traveling salesman problem where there are K salesmen that start at city 1, return to city 1, and collectively must visit all other cities exactly once. Transform the problem into an ordinary traveling salesman problem. *Hint*: Split city 1 into K cities.

10.10 (Degree-Constrained Minimum Weight Spanning Trees)

Consider the minimum weight spanning tree problem, subject to the additional constraint that the number of tree arcs that are incident to a single given node s should be no greater than a given integer k. Consider adding a nonnegative weight w to the weight of all incident arcs of node s, solving the corresponding unconstrained spanning tree problem, and gradually increasing w until the degree constraint is satisfied.

(a) State a polynomial algorithm for doing this and derive its running time.

(b) Use this algorithm to solve the problem of Fig. 10.19, where the degree of node 1 is required to be no more than 2.

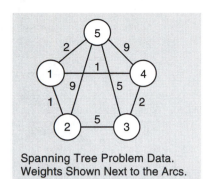

Spanning Tree Problem Data.
Weights Shown Next to the Arcs.

Figure 10.19: Data for a minimum weight spanning tree problem (cf. Exercises 10.10 and 10.11). The arc weights are shown next to the arcs.

10.11 (Steiner Tree Problem Heuristic)

We are given a connected graph G with a nonnegative weight a_{ij} for each arc $(i,j) \in A$. We assume that if an arc (i,j) is present, the reverse arc (j,i) is also present, and $a_{ij} = a_{ji}$. Consider the problem of finding a tree in G that spans a given subset of nodes S and has minimum weight over all such trees.

(a) Let W^* be the weight of this tree. Consider the graph $I(G)$, which has node set S and is complete (has an arc connecting every pair of its nodes). Let the weight for each arc (i,j) of $I(G)$ be equal to the shortest distance in the graph G from the node $i \in S$ to the node $j \in S$. Let T be a minimum weight spanning tree of $I(G)$. Show that the weight of T is no greater than $2W^*$. *Hint*: Consider a minimum weight tour in $I(G)$. Show that the weight of this tour is no less than the weight of T and no more than $2W^*$.

(b) Construct a heuristic based on part (a) and apply it to the problem of Fig. 10.19, where $S = \{1, 3, 5\}$.

10.12 (A General Heuristic for Spanning Tree Problems)

Consider a minimum weight spanning tree problem with an additional side constraint denoted by C (for example, a degree constraint on each node). A general heuristic (given by Deo and Kumar [1997]) is to solve the problem neglecting the constraint C, and then to add a scalar penalty to the cost of the arcs that "contribute most" to violation of C. This is then repeated as many times as desired.

(a) Construct a heuristic of this type for the capacitated spanning tree problem (cf. Example 10.3).

(b) Adapt this heuristic to a capacitated Steiner tree problem.

10.13

Consider the Königsberg bridge problem (cf. Fig. 10.6).

(a) Suppose that there existed a second bridge connecting the islands B and C, and also another bridge connecting the land areas A and D. Construct an Euler cycle that crosses each of the bridges exactly once.

(b) Suppose the bridge connecting the islands B and C has collapsed. Construct an Euler path, i.e., a path (not necessarily a cycle) that passes through each arc of the graph exactly once.

(c) Construct an optimal postman cycle assuming all arcs have cost 1.

10.14

Formulate the capacitated spanning tree problem given in Fig. 10.5 as an integer-constrained network flow problem.

10.15 (Network Formulation of Nonbipartite Matching)

Consider the nonbipartite matching problem of Example 10.4. Replace each node i with a pair of nodes i and i'. For every arc (i, j) of the original problem, introduce an arc (i, j') with value a_{ij} and an arc (j, i') also with value a_{ij}. Show that the problem can be formulated as the assignment-like problem involving the conservation of flow inequalities

$$\sum_{j'} x_{ij'} \le 1, \qquad \forall \, i,$$

$$\sum_{i} x_{ij'} \le 1, \qquad \forall \, j',$$

the integer constraints $x_{ij'} \in \{0, 1\}$, and the side constraints

$$\sum_{\{j|(i,j)\in\mathcal{A}\}} x_{ij} + \sum_{\{j|(j,i)\in\mathcal{A}\}} x_{ji} \le 1, \qquad \forall \, i \in \mathcal{N},$$

or

$$\sum_{\{j|(i,j)\in\mathcal{A}\}} x_{ij} + \sum_{\{j|(j,i)\in\mathcal{A}\}} x_{ji} = 1, \qquad \forall \, i \in \mathcal{N},$$

in the case where a perfect matching is sought.

10.16 (Matching Solution of the Chinese Postman Problem)

Given a Chinese postman problem, delete all nodes of even degree together with all their incident arcs. Find a perfect matching of minimum cost in the remaining graph. Create an expanded version of the original problem's graph by adding an extra copy of each arc of the minimum cost matching. Show that an Euler cycle of the expanded graph is an optimal solution to the Chinese postman problem.

10.17 (Solution of the Directed Chinese Postman Problem)

Consider expanding the graph of the directed Chinese postman problem by duplicating arcs so that the number of incoming arcs to each node is equal to the
number of its outgoing arcs. A forward Euler cycle of the expanded graph corresponds to a solution of the directed Chinese postman problem. Show that the
optimal expanded graph is obtained by minimizing

$$\sum_{(i,j)\in\mathcal{A}} a_{ij} x_{ij}$$

subject to the constraints

$$\sum_{\{j|(i,j)\in\mathcal{A}\}} x_{ij} - \sum_{\{j|(j,i)\in\mathcal{A}\}} x_{ji} = d_i, \qquad \forall\, i \in \mathcal{N},$$

$$0 \le x_{ij}, \qquad \forall\, (i,j) \in \mathcal{A},$$

where d_i is the difference between the number of incoming arcs to i and the
number of outgoing arcs from i.

10.18 (Shortest Paths and Branch-and-Bound)

Consider a general integer-constrained problem of the form

$$\text{minimize} \quad f(x_1,\ldots,x_n)$$
$$\text{subject to} \quad x \in X, \qquad x_i \in \{0,1\}, \quad i = 1,\ldots,n,$$

where X is some set. Construct a branch-and-bound tree that starts with a subproblem where the integer constraints are relaxed, and proceeds with successive
restriction of the variables $x_1,\ldots,x_n$ to the values 0 or 1.

(a) Show that the original integer-constrained problem is equivalent to a single
origin/single destination shortest path problem that involves the branch-
and-bound tree. *Hint:* As an example, for the traveling salesman problem,
nodes of the tree correspond to sequences $(i_1,\ldots,i_k)$ of distinct cities, and
arcs correspond to pairs of nodes $(i_1,\ldots,i_k)$ and $(i_1,\ldots,i_k,i_{k+1})$.

(b) Modify the label correcting method of Section 2.5.2 so that it becomes
similar to the branch-and-bound method (see also the discussion in Section
2.5.2).

10.19

Use the branch-and-bound method to solve the capacitated spanning tree problem
of Fig. 10.5.

10.20 (Simulated Annealing)

In the context of simulated annealing, assume that T is kept constant and let p_{xy} be the probability that when the current solution is x, the next solution sampled is y. Consider the special case where $p_{xy} = p_{yx}$ for all feasible solutions x and y, and assume that the Markov chain defined by the probabilities p_{xy} is irreducible, in the sense that there is positive probability to go from any x to any y, with one or more samples. Show that the steady-state probability of a solution x is

$$\pi_x = \frac{e^{-f(x)/T}}{C},$$

where

$$C = \sum_{x \in F} e^{-f(x)/T}.$$

Hint: This exercise assumes some basic knowledge of the theory of Markov chains. Let q_{xy} be the probability that y is the next solution if x is the current solution, i.e.,

$$q_{xy} = \begin{cases} p_{xy} e^{-\left(f(y) - f(x)\right)/T} & \text{if } f(y) > f(x), \\ p_{xy} & \text{otherwise.} \end{cases}$$

Show that for all x and y we have $\pi_y q_{yx} = \pi_x q_{xy}$, and that $\pi_y = \sum_{x \in F} \pi_x q_{xy}$. This equality together with $\sum_{x \in F} \pi_x = 1$ is sufficient to show the result.

10.21 (Rollout Algorithms Based on Greedy Algorithms)

In the context of the rollout algorithm, suppose that given a partial solution $P = \{x_{ij} \mid (i,j) \in S\}$, we have an estimate $c(P)$ of the optimal cost over all feasible solutions that are consistent with P, in the sense that there exists a complementary solution $\overline{P} = \{x_{ij} \mid (i,j) \notin S\}$ such that $P \cup \overline{P}$ is feasible. Consider a heuristic algorithm, which is *greedy* with respect to $c(P)$, in the sense that it starts from $S = \emptyset$, and given the partial solution $P = \{x_{ij} \mid (i,j) \in S\}$, it selects a set of arcs T, forms the collection F_T of all possible values of the arc flows $y = \{y_{ij} \mid (i,j) \in T\}$, and finds

$$\overline{y} = \arg \min_{y \in F_T} c(P_y^+). \tag{10.36}$$

where

$$P_y^+ = \left\{ \{x_{ij} \mid (i,j) \in S\}, \{y_{ij} \mid (i,j) \in T\} \right\}.$$

It then augments P with the arc flows $\overline{y}$ thus obtained, and repeats up to obtaining a complete solution. Assume that the set of arcs T selected depends only on P. Furthermore, the ties in the minimization of Eq. (10.36) are resolved in a fixed manner that depends only on P. Show that the rollout algorithm that uses the greedy algorithm as a base heuristic is sequentially consistent.

10.22 (Sequentially Improving Rollout Algorithm)

Consider a variant of the rollout algorithm that starts with the empty set of arcs, and maintains, in addition to the current partial solution $P = \{x_{ij} \mid (i,j) \in S\}$, a complementary solution $P' = \{x'_{ij} \mid (i,j) \notin S\}$, and the corresponding (complete) flow vector $x' = P \cup P'$. At the typical iteration, we select a subset T of arcs that are not in S, and we consider the collection F_T of all possible values of the arc flows $y = \{y_{ij} \mid (i,j) \in T\}$. Then, if

$$\min_{y \in F_T} H(P_y^+) < f(x'),$$

we augment the current partial solution $\{x_{ij} \mid (i,j) \in S\}$ with the arc flows $\overline{y} = \{\overline{y}_{ij} \mid (i,j) \in T\}$ that attain the minimum above, and we set x' equal to the complete solution generated by the base heuristic starting from $P_{\overline{y}}^+$. Otherwise, we augment the current partial solution to $\{x_{ij} \mid (i,j) \in S\}$ with the arc flows $\{x'_{ij} \mid (i,j) \in T\}$ and we leave x' unchanged. Prove that this rollout algorithm is sequentially improving in the sense that the heuristic costs of the partial solutions generated are monotonically nonincreasing.

10.23 (Scheduling Problems Viewed as Assignment Problems)

A machine can be used to perform a subset of N given tasks over T time periods. At each time period t, only a subset $A(t)$ of tasks can be performed. Each task j has value $v_j(t)$ when performed at period t.

(a) Formulate the problem of finding the sequence of tasks of maximal total value as an assignment problem. *Hint:* Assign time periods to tasks.

(b) Suppose that there are in addition some precedence constraints of the general form: Task j must be performed before task j' can be performed. Formulate the problem as an assignment problem with side constraints and integer constraints. Give an example where the integer constraints are essential.

(c) Repeat part (b) for the case where there are no precedence constraints, but instead some of the tasks require more than one time period.

10.24 (Scheduling and the Interchange Argument)

In some scheduling problems it is useful to try to characterize a globally optimal solution based on the fact that it is locally optimal with respect to the 2-OPT heuristic. This is known as the *interchange argument*, and amounts to starting with an optimal schedule and checking to see what happens when any two tasks in the schedule are interchanged. As an example, suppose that we have N jobs to process in sequential order with the ith job requiring a given time T_i for its execution. If job i is completed at time t, the reward is $\alpha^t R_i$, where α is a given discount factor with $0 < \alpha < 1$. The problem is to find a schedule that maximizes the total reward. Suppose that $L = (i_0, \ldots, i_{k-1}, i, j, i_{k+2}, \ldots, i_{N-1})$ is an optimal job schedule, and consider the schedule $L' = (i_0, \ldots, i_{k-1}, j, i, i_{k+2}, \ldots, i_{N-1})$ obtained by interchanging i and j. Let t_k be the time of completion of job i_{k-1}. Compare the rewards of the two schedules, and show that

$$\frac{\alpha^{T_i} R_i}{1 - \alpha^{T_i}} \geq \frac{\alpha^{T_j} R_j}{1 - \alpha^{T_j}}.$$

Conclude that scheduling jobs in order of decreasing $\alpha^{T_i} R_i / (1 - \alpha^{T_i})$ is optimal.

10.25 (Weighted Shortest Processing Time First Rule)

We want to schedule N tasks, the ith of which requires T_i time units. Let t_i denote the time of completion of the ith task, i.e.,

$$t_i = T_i + \sum_{\substack{\text{tasks } k \\ \text{completed before } i}} T_k.$$

Let w_i denote a positive weight indicating the importance of early completion of the ith task. Use an interchange argument (cf. Exercise 10.24) to show that in order to minimize the total weighted completion time $\sum_{i=1}^{N} w_i t_i$ we must order the tasks in decreasing order of w_i / T_i.

10.26

A busy professor has to complete N projects. Each project i has a deadline d_i and the time it takes the professor to complete it is T_i. The professor can work on only one project at a time and must complete it before moving on to a new project. For a given order of completion of the projects, denote by t_i the time of completion of project i, i.e.,

$$t_i = T_i + \sum_{\substack{\text{projects } k \\ \text{completed before } i}} T_k.$$

The professor wants to order the projects so as to minimize the maximum tardiness, given by

$$\max_{i \in \{1, \ldots, N\}} \max[0, t_i - d_i].$$

Use an interchange argument (cf. Exercise 10.24) to show that it is optimal to complete the projects in the order of their deadlines (do the project with the closest deadline first).

10.27 (Hardy's Theorem)

Let $\{a_1, \ldots, a_n\}$ and $\{b_1, \ldots, b_n\}$ be monotonically nondecreasing sequences of numbers. Let us associate with each $i = 1, \ldots, n$ a distinct index j_i, and consider the expression $\sum_{i=1}^{n} a_i b_{j_i}$. Use an interchange argument (cf. Exercise 10.24) to show that this expression is maximized when $j_i = i$ for all i, and is minimized when $j_i = n - i + 1$ for all i.

10.28 (The Quiz Problem)

Consider a quiz contest where a person is given a list of N questions and can answer these questions in any order he chooses. Question i will be answered correctly with probability p_i, independently of earlier answers, and the person will then receive a reward R_i. At the first incorrect answer, the quiz terminates and the person is allowed to keep his previous rewards. The problem is to maximize the expected reward by choosing optimally the ordering of the questions.

   (a) Show that to maximize the expected reward, questions should be answered in decreasing order of $p_i R_i/(1 - p_i)$. *Hint*: Use an interchange argument (cf. Exercise 10.24).

   (b) Consider the variant of the problem where there is a maximum number of questions that can be answered, which is smaller than the number of questions that are available. Show that it is not necessarily optimal to answer the questions in order of decreasing $p_i R_i/(1 - p_i)$. *Hint*: Try the case where only one out of two available questions can be answered.

   (c) Give a 2-OPT algorithm to solve the problem where the number of available questions is one more than the maximum number of questions that can be answered.

10.29 (Rollout Algorithm for the Quiz Problem)

Consider the quiz problem of Exercise 10.28 for the case where the maximum number of questions that can be answered is less or equal to the number of questions that are available. Consider the heuristic which answers questions in decreasing order of $p_i R_i/(1 - p_i)$, and use it as a base heuristic in a rollout algorithm. Show that the cost of the rollout algorithm is no worse than the cost of the base heuristic. *Hint*: Prove sequential consistency of the base heuristic.

10.30

This exercise shows that nondifferentiabilities of the dual function given in Section 10.3, often tend to arise at the most interesting points and thus cannot be ignored. Show that if there is a duality gap, then the dual function q is nondifferentiable at every dual optimal solution. *Hint*: Assume that q has a unique subgradient at a dual optimal solution μ^* and derive a contradiction by showing that any vector x_{μ^*} that minimizes $L(x, \mu^*)$ is primal optimal.

10.31 (Enforced Separation in 3-Dimensional Assignment)

Consider the 3-dimensional assignment problem of Example 10.7 that involves a set of jobs J, a set of machines M, and a set of workers W. We assume that each of the sets J, M, and W contains n elements, and that the constraints are equality constraints. Suppose that the problem is ϵ-*separable*, in the sense that for some $\overline{\beta}_{jm}$ and $\overline{\gamma}_{mw}$, and some $\epsilon \geq 0$, we have

$$|\overline{\beta}_{jm} + \overline{\gamma}_{mw} - a_{jmw}| \leq \epsilon, \qquad \forall \, j \in J, \, m \in M, \, w \in W,$$

where a_{jmw} is the value of the triplet (j, m, w).

(a) Show that if the problem is solved with a_{jmw} replaced by $\overline{\beta}_{jm} + \overline{\gamma}_{mw}$, the 3-dimensional assignment obtained achieves the optimal cost of the original problem within $2n\epsilon$.

(b) Suppose that we don't know $\overline{\beta}_{jm}$ and $\overline{\gamma}_{mw}$, and that we use the enforced separation approach of Example 10.7. Thus, we first solve the jobs-to-machines 2-dimensional assignment problem with values

$$b_{jm} = \max_{w \in W} a_{jmw}.$$

Let j_m be the job assigned to machine m, according to the solution of this problem. We then solve the machines-to-workers 2-dimensional assignment problem with values

$$c_{mw} = a_{j_m m w}.$$

Let w_m be the worker assigned to machine m, according to the solution of this problem. Show that the 3-dimensional assignment $\{(j_m, m, w_m) \mid m \in M\}$ achieves the optimal value of the original problem within $4n\epsilon$.

(c) Show that the result of part (b) also holds when b_{jm} is defined by

$$b_{jm} = a_{jm\overline{w}_m},$$

where $\overline{w}_m$ is any worker, instead of $b_{jm} = \max_{w \in W} a_{jmw}$.

(d) Show that the result of parts (b) and (c) also holds if J and W contain more than n elements, and we have the inequality constraints

$$\sum_{m \in M} \sum_{w \in W} x_{jmw} \leq 1, \qquad \forall \, j \in J,$$

$$\sum_{j \in J} \sum_{m \in M} x_{jmw} \leq 1, \qquad \forall \, w \in W,$$

in place of equality constraints.

10.32 (Lagrangian Relaxation in Multidimensional Assignment)

Apply the Lagrangian relaxation method to the multidimensional assignment problem of Example 10.7, in a way that requires the solution of 2-dimensional assignment problems. Derive the form of the corresponding subgradient algorithm.

10.33 (Separable Problems with Integer/Simplex Constraints)

Consider the problem

$$\text{minimize} \quad \sum_{j=1}^{n} f_j(x_j)$$

$$\text{subject to} \quad \sum_{j=1}^{n} x_j \leq A,$$

$$x_j \in \{0, 1, \ldots, m_j\}, \qquad j = 1, \ldots, n,$$

where A and $m_1, \ldots, m_n$ are given positive integers, and each function f_j is convex over the interval $[0, m_j]$. Consider an iterative algorithm (due to Ibaraki and Katoh [1988]) that starts at $(0, \ldots, 0)$ and maintains a feasible vector $(x_1, \ldots, x_n)$. At the typical iteration, we consider the set of indices $J = \{j \mid x_j < m_j\}$. If J is empty or $\sum_{j=1}^{n} x_j = A$, the algorithm terminates. Otherwise, we find an index $\bar{j} \in J$ that maximizes $f_j(x_j) - f_j(x_j + 1)$. If $f_{\bar{j}}(x_{\bar{j}}) - f_{\bar{j}}(x_{\bar{j}} + 1) \leq 0$, the algorithm terminates. Otherwise, we increase $x_{\bar{j}}$ by one unit, and go to the next iteration. Show that upon termination, the algorithm yields an optimal solution. *Note*: The book by Ibaraki and Katoh [1988] contains a lot of material on this problem, and addresses the issues of efficient implementation.

10.34 (Constraint Relaxation and Lagrangian Relaxation)

The purpose of this exercise is to compare the lower bounds obtained by relaxing integer constraints and by dualizing the side constraints. Consider the nonlinear network optimization problem with a cost function $f(x)$, the conservation of flow constraints, and the additional constraint

$$x \in X = \big\{ x \mid x_{ij} \in X_{ij},\ (i,j) \in \mathcal{A},\ g_t(x) \leq 0,\ t = 1, \ldots, r \big\},$$

where X_{ij} are given subsets of the real line and the functions g_t are *linear*. We assume that f is convex over the entire space of flow vectors x. We introduce a Lagrange multiplier μ_t for each of the side constraints $g_t(x) \leq 0$, and we form the corresponding Lagrangian function

$$L(x, \mu) = f(x) + \sum_{t=1}^{r} \mu_t g_t(x).$$

Let C denote the set of all x satisfying the conservation of flow constraints, let f^* denote the optimal primal cost,

$$f^* = \inf_{x \in C,\ x_{ij} \in X_{ij},\ g_t(x) \leq 0} f(x),$$

and let q^* denote the optimal dual cost,

$$q^* = \sup_{\mu \geq 0} q(\mu) = \sup_{\mu \geq 0} \inf_{x \in C,\ x_{ij} \in X_{ij}} L(x, \mu).$$

Let $\hat{X}_{ij}$ denote the interval which is the convex hull of the set X_{ij}, and denote by $\hat{f}$ the optimal cost of the problem, where each set X_{ij} is replaced by $\hat{X}_{ij}$,

$$\hat{f} = \inf_{x \in C,\, x_{ij} \in \hat{X}_{ij},\, g_t(x) \leq 0} f(x). \tag{10.37}$$

Note that this is a convex problem even if X_{ij} embodies integer constraints.

(a) Show that $\hat{f} \leq q^* \leq f^*$. *Hint:* Use Prop. 8.3 to show that problem (10.37) has no duality gap and compare its dual cost with q^*.

(b) Assume that f is linear. Show that $\hat{f} = q^*$. *Hint:* The problem involved in the definition of the dual function of problem (10.37) is a minimum cost flow problem.

(c) Assume that C is a general polyhedron; that is, C is specified by a finite number of linear equality and inequality constraints (rather than the conservation of flow constraints). Provide an example where f is linear and we have $\hat{f} < q^*$.

10.35 (Duality Gap of the Knapsack Problem)

Given objects $i = 1, \ldots, n$ with positive weights w_i and values v_i, we want to assemble a subset of the objects so that the sum of the weights of the subset does not exceed a given $T > 0$, and the sum of the values of the subset is maximized. This is the knapsack problem, which is a special case of a generalized assignment problem (see Example 8.7). The problem can be written as

$$\text{maximize} \quad \sum_{i=1}^{n} v_i x_i$$

$$\text{subject to} \quad \sum_{i=1}^{n} w_i x_i \leq T, \qquad x_i \in \{0,1\}, \quad i = 1, \ldots, n.$$

(a) Let f^* and q^* be the optimal primal and dual costs, respectively. Show that

$$0 \leq q^* - f^* \leq \max_{i=1,\ldots,n} v_i.$$

(b) Consider the problem where T is multiplied by a positive integer k and each object is replaced by k replicas of itself, while the object weights and values stay the same. Let $f^*(k)$ and $q^*(k)$ be the corresponding primal and dual costs. Show that

$$\frac{q^*(k) - f^*(k)}{f^*(k)} \leq \frac{1}{k} \frac{\max_{i=1,\ldots,n} v_i}{f^*},$$

so that the relative value of the duality gap tends to 0 as $k \to \infty$. *Note:* This exercise illustrates a generic property of many separable problems with integer constraints: as the number of variables increases, the duality gap decreases in relative terms (see Bertsekas [1982], Section 5.5, or Bertsekas [1995b], Section 5.1, for an analysis and a geometrical interpretation of this phenomenon).

10.36 (Convergence of the Subgradient Method)

Consider the subgradient method $\mu^{k+1} = [\mu^k + s^k g^k]^+$, where the stepsize is given by

$$s^k = \frac{q^* - q(\mu^k)}{\|g^k\|^2}$$

and q^* is the optimal dual cost (this stepsize requires knowledge of q^*, which is very restrictive, but the following Exercise 10.37 removes this restriction). Assume that there exists at least one optimal dual solution.

(a) Use Eq. (10.16) to show that $\{\mu^k\}$ is bounded.

(b) Use the fact that $\{g^k\}$ is bounded (since the dual function is piecewise linear), and Eq. (10.16) to show that $q(\mu^k) \to q^*$.

10.37 (A Convergent Variation of the Subgradient Method)

This exercise provides a convergence result for a common variation of the subgradient method (the result is due to Brannlund [1993]; see also Goffin and Kiwiel [1996]). Consider the iteration $\mu^{k+1} = [\mu^k + s^k g^k]^+$, where

$$s^k = \frac{\tilde{q} - q(\mu^k)}{\|g^k\|^2}.$$

(a) Suppose that $\tilde{q}$ is an *underestimate* of the optimal dual cost q^* such that $q(\mu^k) < \tilde{q} \leq q^*$. [Here $\tilde{q}$ is fixed and the algorithm stops at μ^k if $q(\mu^k) \geq \tilde{q}$.] Use the fact that $\{g^k\}$ is bounded to show that either for some $\bar{k}$ we have $q(\mu^{\bar{k}}) \geq \tilde{q}$ or else $q(\mu^k) \to \tilde{q}$. *Hint*: Consider the function $\min\{q(\mu), \tilde{q}\}$ and use the results of Exercise 10.36.

(b) Suppose that $\tilde{q}$ is an *overestimate* of the optimal dual cost, that is, $\tilde{q} > q^*$. Use the fact that $\{g^k\}$ is bounded to show that the length of the path traveled by the method is infinite, that is,

$$\sum_{k=0}^{\infty} s^k \|g^k\| = \sum_{k=0}^{\infty} \frac{\tilde{q} - q(\mu^k)}{\|g^k\|} = \infty.$$

(c) Let δ^0 and B be two positive scalars. Consider the following version of the subgradient method. Given μ^k, apply successive subgradient iterations with $\tilde{q} = q(\mu^k) + \delta^k$ in the stepsize formula in place of $q(\mu^*)$, until one of the following two occurs:

  (1) The dual cost exceeds $q(\mu^k) + \delta^k/2$.

  (2) The length of the path traveled starting from μ^k exceeds B.

Then set μ^{k+1} to the iterate with highest dual cost thus far. Furthermore, in case (1), set $\delta^{k+1} = \delta^k$, while in case (2), set $\delta^{k+1} = \delta^k/2$. Use the fact that $\{g^k\}$ is bounded to show that $q(\mu^k) \to q^*$.

10.38 (Convergence Rate of the Subgradient Method)

Consider the subgradient method of Exercise 10.36, and let μ^* be an optimal dual solution.

(a) Show that
$$\liminf_{k \to \infty} \sqrt{k}\big(q(\mu^*) - q(\mu^k)\big) = 0.$$

   Hint: Use Eq. (10.16) to show that $\sum_{k=0}^{\infty}\big(q(\mu^*) - q(\mu^k)\big)^2 < \infty$. Assume that $\sqrt{k}\big(q(\mu^*) - q(\mu^k)\big) \geq \epsilon$ for some $\epsilon > 0$ and arbitrarily large k, and reach a contradiction.

(b) Assume that for some $a > 0$ and all k, we have $q(\mu^*) - q(\mu^k) \geq a\|\mu^* - \mu^k\|$. Use Eq. (10.16) to show that for all k we have

$$\|\mu^{k+1} - \mu^*\| \leq r\|\mu^k - \mu^*\|,$$

   where $r = \sqrt{1 - a^2/b^2}$ and b is an upper bound on $\|g^k\|$.

10.39

Consider the cutting plane method.

(a) Give an example where the generated sequence $q(\mu^k)$ is not monotonically nondecreasing.

(b) Give an example where, at the kth iteration, the method finds an optimal dual solution μ^k but does not terminate because the criterion $q(\mu^k) = Q^k(\mu^k)$ is not satisfied.

10.40 (Computational Rollout Problem)

Consider the rollout algorithm for the traveling salesman problem using as base heuristic the nearest neighbor method, whereby we start from some simple path and at each iteration, we add a node that does not close a cycle and minimizes the cost of the enlarged path (see the paragraph following the description of the rollout algorithm iteration in Section 10.5). Write a computer program to apply this algorithm to the problem involving Hamilton's 20-node graph (Exercise 1.35) for the case where all arcs have randomly chosen costs from the range $[0, 1]$. For node pairs for which there is no arc, introduce an artificial arc with cost randomly chosen from the range $[100, 101]$. Compare the performances of the rollout algorithm and the nearest neighbor heuristic, and compile relevant statistics by running a suitable large collection of randomly generated problem instances. Verify that the rollout algorithm performs at least as well as the nearest neighbor heuristic for each instance (since it is sequentially consistent).

APPENDIX A:
Mathematical Review

The purpose of this appendix is to provide a summary of mathematical notation, terminology, definitions, and results that are used in the text. For a similar but far more extensive summary, we refer to the author's nonlinear programming text [1995b], which contains optimization-oriented appendixes on analysis, linear algebra, and convexity, and supplies many proofs. For textbook presentations, we refer to Hoffman and Kunze [1971], and Strang [1976] (linear algebra), Luenberger [1969], Ortega and Rheinboldt [1970], and Rudin [1976] (analysis), Hiriart-Urruty and Lemarechal [1993], and Rockafellar [1970] (convex analysis).

A.1   SETS

If x is a member of a set S, we write $x \in S$. We write $x \notin S$ if x is not a member of S. A set S may be specified by listing its elements within braces. For example, by writing $S = \{x_1, x_2, \ldots, x_n\}$ we mean that the set S consists of the elements $x_1, x_2, \ldots, x_n$. A set S may also be specified in the generic form

$$S = \{x \mid x \text{ satisfies } P\},$$

as the set of elements satisfying property P. For example,

$$S = \{x \mid x \text{ real}, 0 \leq x \leq 1\},$$

denotes the set of all real numbers x satisfying $0 \leq x \leq 1$. A set S is said to be *finite* if it consists of a finite number of elements.

If S is a subset of T (i.e., if every element of S is also an element of T), we write $S \subset T$ or $T \supset S$. The *union* of two sets S and T is denoted by $S \cup T$, and the *intersection* of S and T is denoted by $S \cap T$. The *difference* between two sets S and T is the set $\{x \mid x \in S, x \notin T\}$, and is denoted by $S - T$. The *Cartesian product* of sets $S_1, \ldots, S_n$ is the set $\big\{(s_1, \ldots, s_n) \mid s_i \in S_i, i = 1, \ldots, n\big\}$, and is denoted by $S_1 \times S_2 \times \cdots \times S_n$.

Sets of Real Numbers

If a and b are real numbers or $+\infty$, $-\infty$, we denote by $[a, b]$ the set of numbers x satisfying $a \leq x \leq b$ (including the possibility $x = +\infty$ or $x = -\infty$). A rounded, instead of square, bracket denotes strict inequality in the definition. Thus $(a, b]$, $[a, b)$, and (a, b) denote the set of all x satisfying $a < x \leq b$, $a \leq x < b$, and $a < x < b$, respectively.

If S is a set of real numbers that is bounded above, there is a smallest real number y such that $x \leq y$ for all $x \in S$. This number is called the *least upper bound or supremum* of S and is denoted by $\sup\{x \mid x \in S\}$. Similarly, the greatest real number z such that $z \leq x$ for all $x \in S$ is called the *greatest lower bound or infimum* of S and is denoted by $\inf\{x \mid x \in S\}$. If S is unbounded above, we write $\sup\{x \mid x \in S\} = +\infty$, and if it is unbounded below, we write $\inf\{x \mid x \in S\} = -\infty$. If S is the empty set, then by convention we write $\inf\{x \mid x \in S\} = +\infty$ and $\sup\{x \mid x \in S\} = -\infty$. If it is known that there exists some $x^* \in S$ that attains the infimum of S, i.e., $x^* = \inf\{x \mid x \in S\}$, we write $\min\{x \mid x \in S\}$ in place of $\inf\{x \mid x \in S\}$. Similarly, if it is known that there exists some $x^* \in S$ that attains the supremum of S, we write $\max\{x \mid x \in S\}$ in place of $\sup\{x \mid x \in S\}$.

A.2   EUCLIDEAN SPACE

The set of all n-tuples of real numbers $x = (x_1, \ldots, x_n)$ constitutes the *n-dimensional Euclidean space*, denoted by $\Re^n$. The elements of $\Re^n$ are referred to as n-dimensional vectors or simply vectors when confusion cannot arise. The one-dimensional Euclidean space $\Re^1$ consists of all the real numbers (also referred to as *scalars*), and is denoted by $\Re$. Vectors in $\Re^n$ can be added by adding their corresponding components. They can be multiplied by some scalar by multiplication of each component by that scalar.

A set of vectors $a_1, a_2, \ldots, a_k$ is said to be *linearly dependent* if there exist scalars $\lambda_1, \lambda_2, \ldots, \lambda_k$, not all zero, such that $\sum_{i=1}^{k} \lambda_i a_i = 0$. If no such set of scalars exists, the vectors are said to be *linearly independent*.

The *inner product* of two vectors $x = (x_1, \ldots, x_n)$ and $y = (y_1, \ldots, y_n)$ is denoted by $x'y$ and is equal to $\sum_{i=1}^{n} x_i y_i$. Two vectors in $\Re^n$ are said to be *orthogonal* if their inner product is equal to zero.

The *Euclidean norm* of a vector $x = (x_1, \ldots, x_n) \in \Re^n$ is denoted by $\|x\|$ and is equal to $(x'x)^{1/2} = \left(\sum_{i=1}^{n} x_i^2\right)^{1/2}$. This norm has the following properties:

(a) $\|x\| \geq 0$ for all $x \in \Re^n$.

(b) $\|cx\| = |c| \cdot \|x\|$ for every $c \in \Re$ and every $x \in \Re^n$.

(c) $\|x\| = 0$ if and only if $x = 0$.

(d) $\|x + y\| \leq \|x\| + \|y\|$ for all $x, y \in \Re^n$ (this is called the *triangle inequality*).

(e) $|x'y| \leq \|x\| \cdot \|y\|$, with equality holding if and only if $x = \alpha y$ for some scalar α (this is called the *Cauchy-Schwartz inequality*).

A subset $S \subset \Re^n$ is said to be *bounded* if for some $M > 0$ we have $\|x\| \leq M$ for all $x \in S$.

A.3   MATRICES

An $m \times n$ *matrix* is a rectangular array of scalars, referred to as *elements* or *components*, which are arranged in m rows and n columns. If $m = n$ the matrix is said to be *square*. The element in the ith row and jth column of a matrix A is denoted by a subscript ij, such as a_{ij}, in which case we write $A = [a_{ij}]$. The $n \times n$ *identity matrix*, denoted by I, is the matrix with elements $a_{ij} = 0$ for $i \neq j$ and $a_{ii} = 1$, for $i = 1, \ldots, n$. The *sum* of two $m \times n$ matrices A and B is written as $A + B$ and is the matrix whose elements are the sum of the corresponding elements in A and B. The *product of a matrix A and a scalar* λ, written as λA or $A\lambda$, is obtained by multiplying each element of A by λ. The *product* AB of an $m \times n$ matrix A and an $n \times p$ matrix B is the $m \times p$ matrix C with elements $c_{ij} = \sum_{k=1}^{n} a_{ik} b_{kj}$. If b is an $n \times 1$ matrix (i.e., an n-dimensional column vector) and A is an $m \times n$ matrix, then Ab is an m-dimensional (column) vector. We follow the convention, that unless otherwise explicitly stated, a vector is treated as a column vector.

The *transpose* of an $m \times n$ matrix A is the $n \times m$ matrix A' with elements $a'_{ij} = a_{ji}$. A square matrix A is *symmetric* if $A' = A$. An $n \times n$ matrix A is called *nonsingular* or *invertible* if there is an $n \times n$ matrix called the *inverse* of A and denoted by A^{-1}, such that $A^{-1}A = I = AA^{-1}$, where I is the $n \times n$ identity matrix. An $n \times n$ matrix is nonsingular if and only if the n vectors that constitute its rows are linearly independent or, equivalently, if the n vectors that constitute its columns are linearly independent. Thus, an $n \times n$ matrix A is nonsingular if and only if the relation $Av = 0$, where $v \in \Re^n$, implies that $v = 0$.

The *rank* of a matrix A is equal to the maximum number of linearly independent rows of A. It is also equal to the maximum number of linearly independent columns. Thus, the rank of an $m \times n$ matrix is at most equal to the minimum of the dimensions m and n. An $m \times n$ matrix is said to be of *full rank* if its rank is maximal, that is, if it is equal to the minimum of m and n. A square matrix is of full rank if and only if it is nonsingular.

A symmetric $n \times n$ matrix A is called *positive definite* if $x'Ax > 0$ for all $x \in \Re^n$, $x \neq 0$. It is called *positive semidefinite* if $x'Ax \geq 0$ for all $x \in \Re^n$. A positive semidefinite symmetric matrix is positive definite if and only if it is invertible.

A.4   ANALYSIS

Convergence of Sequences

A sequence of vectors $x_0, x_1, \ldots, x_k, \ldots$ in $\Re^n$, is denoted by $\{x_k\}$, or sometimes, with a slight abuse of notation, just by x_k. We have no firm convention of using a subscript to denote the index of an element of a sequence; we also use a superscript, i.e., x^k instead of x_k. A sequence $\{x_k\}$ is said to converge to a *limit* x if given any $\epsilon > 0$, there is an N such that for all

$k \geq N$ we have $\|x_k - x\| < \epsilon$. If $\{x_k\}$ converges to x, we write $x_k \to x$ or $\lim_{k \to \infty} x_k = x$. We have $Ax_k + By_k \to Ax + By$ if $x_k \to x$, $y_k \to y$, and A, B are matrices of appropriate dimensions.

A vector x is said to be a *limit point* of a sequence $\{x_k\}$ if there is a subsequence of $\{x_k\}$ that converges to x, that is, if there is an infinite subset $\mathcal{K}$ of the nonnegative integers such that for any $\epsilon > 0$, there is an N such that for all $k \in \mathcal{K}$ with $k \geq N$ we have $\|x_k - x\| < \epsilon$. A sequence $\{x_k\}$ that is bounded (i.e., for some $M > 0$ we have $\|x_k\| \leq M$ for all k) has at least one limit point.

A sequence of real numbers $\{r_k\}$, which is monotonically nondecreasing (nonincreasing), i.e., it satisfies $r_k \leq r_{k+1}$ ($r_k \geq r_{k+1}$) for all k, must either converge to a real number or be unbounded above (below). In the latter case we write $\lim_{k \to \infty} r_k = \infty$ ($-\infty$). Given any bounded sequence of real numbers $\{r_k\}$, we may consider the sequence $\{s_k\}$, where $s_k = \sup\{r_i \,|\, i \geq k\}$. Since this sequence is monotonically nonincreasing and bounded, it must have a limit. This limit is called the *limit superior* of $\{r_k\}$ and is denoted by $\limsup_{k \to \infty} r_k$. The *limit inferior* of $\{r_k\}$ is similarly defined as the limit of the sequence $s_k = \inf\{r_i \,|\, i \geq k\}$, and is denoted by $\liminf_{k \to \infty} r_k$. If $\{r_k\}$ is unbounded above, we write $\limsup_{k \to \infty} r_k = \infty$, and if it is unbounded below, we write $\liminf_{k \to \infty} r_k = -\infty$.

Open, Closed, and Compact Sets

Let S be a subset of $\Re^n$. A vector x is said to be an *interior point* of S if one can find an $\epsilon > 0$ such that $\{z \mid \|z - x\| < \epsilon\} \subset S$. The subset of all interior points of S is called the *interior* of S. We say that:

(a) S is *open* if it coincides with its interior, i.e., every $x \in S$ is an interior point of S.

(b) S is *closed* if its complement, i.e., the set $\{x \mid x \notin S\}$, is open. An alternative and equivalent definition is that S is closed if every convergent sequence $\{x_k\}$ with elements in S converges to a vector that also belongs to S.

(a) S is *compact* if and only if it is both closed and bounded. An alternative and equivalent definition is that S is compact if and only if every sequence $\{x_k\}$ with elements in S has at least one limit point that belongs to S.

Continuous Functions

A function f mapping a set S_1 into a set S_2 is denoted by $f : S_1 \mapsto S_2$. If the set S_2 is a subset of real numbers, then f is called *real-valued*. A function $f : \Re^n \mapsto \Re^m$ is said to be *continuous at a vector* x if $f(x_k) \to f(x)$ whenever $x_k \to x$. If f is continuous at all $x \in \Re^n$, then it is said to be *continuous*. Equivalently, f is continuous if, given $x \in \Re^n$ and $\epsilon > 0$, there is a $\delta > 0$ such that whenever $\|y - x\| < \delta$, we have $\|f(y) - f(x)\| < \epsilon$. The function $a_1 f_1(\cdot) + a_2 f_2(\cdot)$ is continuous for any two scalars a_1, a_2 and any two continuous functions $f_1, f_2 : \Re^n \mapsto \Re^m$. If S_1, S_2, S_3 are any sets and $f_1 : S_1 \mapsto S_2$, $f_2 : S_2 \mapsto S_3$ are functions, the function $f_2 \circ f_1 : S_1 \mapsto S_3$ defined by $(f_2 \circ f_1)(x) = f_2(f_1(x))$ is called the *composition* of f_1 and f_2. If $f_1 : \Re^n \mapsto \Re^m$ and $f_2 : \Re^m \mapsto \Re^p$ are continuous, then $f_2 \circ f_1$ is also continuous. If $f : X \mapsto \Re$ is a function defined on an interval X, and x is an interior point of X, then f is said to be *right-continuous (left-continuous)* at x if $f(x_k) \to f(x)$ for all sequences $\{x_k\} \subset X$ converging to x with $x_k \geq x$ ($x_k \leq x$, respectively) for all k.

Weierstrass' theorem asserts that a continuous function $f : \Re^n \mapsto \Re$ attains a minimum over any nonempty compact set A, i.e., there exists $x^* \in A$ such that $f(x^*) = \inf_{x \in A} f(x)$.

Derivatives

Let $f : \Re^n \mapsto \Re$ be some function. For a fixed $x \in \Re^n$, the first partial derivative of f at the vector x in the ith component is defined by

$$\frac{\partial f(x)}{\partial x_i} = \lim_{\alpha \to 0} \frac{f(x + \alpha e_i) - f(x)}{\alpha},$$

where e_i is the ith unit vector. If the partial derivatives with respect to all components exist, f is called *differentiable at x* and its *gradient* at x is defined to be the column vector

$$\nabla f(x) = \begin{pmatrix} \frac{\partial f(x)}{\partial x_1} \\ \vdots \\ \frac{\partial f(x)}{\partial x_n} \end{pmatrix}.$$

The function f is called *differentiable* if it is differentiable at every $x \in \Re^n$. If $\nabla f(x)$ exists for every x and is a continuous function of x, f is said to be *continuously differentiable*. Such functions admit the first order Taylor expansion

$$f(x + y) = f(x) + y' \nabla f(x) + o(\|y\|),$$

where $o(\|y\|)$ is a function of y with the property $\lim_{\|y\| \to 0} o(\|y\|)/\|y\| \to 0$. A related result is the *mean value theorem*, which states that if $f : \Re^n \mapsto \Re$ is continuously differentiable, then for every $x, y \in \Re^n$, there exists some $\alpha \in [0, 1]$ such that

$$f(y) - f(x) = \nabla f(x + \alpha(y - x))'(y - x).$$

If the partial derivatives $\partial f(x)/\partial x_i$, $i = 1, \ldots, n$, are differentiable functions, then f is said to be *twice differentiable*. We denote by $\nabla^2 f(x)$ the *Hessian matrix* of f at x, that is, the matrix

$$\nabla^2 f(x) = \left[\frac{\partial^2 f(x)}{\partial x_i \partial x_j} \right]$$

the elements of which are the second partial derivatives of f at x.

If f is twice continuously differentiable, that is, if $\nabla^2 f(x)$ exists and is continuous, then we have second order versions of the Taylor expansion and the mean value theorem. In particular, for all x and y, we have

$$f(x + y) = f(x) + y'\nabla f(x) + \tfrac{1}{2}y'\nabla^2 f(x)y + o(\|y\|^2),$$

and there exists some $\alpha \in [0, 1]$ such that

$$f(x + y) = f(x) + y'\nabla f(x) + \tfrac{1}{2}y'\nabla^2 f(x + \alpha y)y.$$

A vector-valued function $f : \Re^n \mapsto \Re^m$ is called differentiable (respectively, continuously differentiable) if each component f_i of f is differentiable (respectively, continuously differentiable). The *gradient matrix* of f, denoted by $\nabla f(x)$, is the $n \times m$ matrix whose ith column is the gradient $\nabla f_i(x)$ of f_i. Thus,

$$\nabla f(x) = \Big[\nabla f_1(x) \cdots \nabla f_m(x)\Big].$$

The transpose of ∇f is the *Jacobian* of f, that is, the matrix whose ijth entry is equal to the partial derivative $\partial f_i / \partial x_j$.

Let $f : \Re^k \mapsto \Re^m$ and $g : \Re^m \mapsto \Re^n$ be continuously differentiable functions, and let $h(x) = g(f(x))$. The *chain rule* for differentiation states that
$$\nabla h(x) = \nabla f(x)\nabla g(f(x)), \qquad \forall\, x \in \Re^k.$$

If $f : \Re^n \mapsto \Re^m$ is of the form $f(x) = Ax$, where A is an $m \times n$ matrix, we have $\nabla f(x) = A'$. Also, if $f : \Re^n \mapsto \Re$ is of the form $f(x) = x'Ax/2$, where A is a symmetric $n \times n$ matrix, we have $\nabla f(x) = Ax$ and $\nabla^2 f(x) = A$.

A.5   CONVEX SETS AND FUNCTIONS

A subset F of $\Re^n$ is said to be *convex* if for every $x, y \in F$ and every scalar α with $0 \le \alpha \le 1$, we have $\alpha x + (1 - \alpha)y \in F$. In words, F is convex if the line segment connecting any two vectors in F belongs to F. The intersection of a collection of convex sets is convex. The *vector sum* of two convex sets F_1 and F_2, defined by $F_1 + F_2 = \{x_1 + x_2 \mid x_1 \in F_1, x_2 \in F_2\}$, is convex. The *scalar multiple* of a convex set is convex, i.e., for a scalar a and a convex set F, the set $aF = \{ax \mid x \in F\}$ is convex. The *convex hull* of a subset F, denoted conv F, is the intersection of all convex sets that contain F. Given a vector x and a closed convex set C, there exists a unique vector $\hat{x}$, called the *projection* of x on C, such that $\|\hat{x} - x\| \le \|y - x\|$ for all $y \in C$.

A nonempty subset of $\Re^n$ is said to be a *polyhedral set* (or *polyhedron*) if it is specified by a finite set of linear inequalities, i.e., it has the form

$$\{x \mid a_j'x \le b_j, \, j = 1, \ldots, r\},$$

where a_j are some vectors and b_j are some scalars. Such a set is closed and convex since it is the intersection of the sets $\{x \mid a_j'x \le b_j\}$, $j = 1, \ldots, r$, which can be seen to be closed and convex. A vector x is said to be an *extreme point* of a convex set F if x belongs to F, and there do not exist vectors $y \in F$ and $z \in F$, with $y \ne x$ and $z \ne x$, and a scalar $\alpha \in (0,1)$ such that $x = \alpha y + (1 - \alpha)z$. A polyhedron has a finite (possibly empty) set of extreme points. A bounded polyhedron can be represented as the convex hull of its extreme points. An important fact, which forms the basis for the simplex method for a general linear programming problem, is that if a linear function f attains a minimum over a polyhedron F having at least one extreme point, then f attains a minimum at some extreme point of F (as well as possibly at some other nonextreme points).

A function $f : F \mapsto \Re$ defined on a convex subset F of $\Re^n$ is said to be *convex* if for every $x, y \in F$ and every scalar α with $0 \le \alpha \le 1$ we have

$$f\big(\alpha x + (1 - \alpha)y\big) \le \alpha f(x) + (1 - \alpha)f(y).$$

The function f is said to be *concave* if $(-f)$ is convex, or, equivalently, if for every $x, y \in F$ and every scalar α with $0 \le \alpha \le 1$, we have

$$f\big(\alpha x + (1 - \alpha)y\big) \ge \alpha f(x) + (1 - \alpha)f(y).$$

The function f is said to be *strictly convex* if for all $x, y \in F$ with $x \ne y$, we have

$$f\big(\alpha x + (1 - \alpha)y\big) < \alpha f(x) + (1 - \alpha)f(y), \qquad \forall \, \alpha \in (0,1).$$

Such a function can have at most one minimizer over F. If $f : F \mapsto \Re$ is convex, then the sets $\Gamma_\lambda = \{x \mid x \in F, \, f(x) \le \lambda\}$ are convex for every scalar λ. An important property is that a convex function $f : \Re^n \mapsto \Re$ is continuous. Furthermore, if $f : \Re^n \mapsto \Re$ is convex and differentiable, its gradient $\nabla f(x)$ is a continuous function of x, i.e., f is continuously differentiable.

Sometimes a function $f : S \mapsto \Re$ is defined on a subset S of $\Re^n$, and f is convex when restricted to a convex subset F of S, i.e., we have for all $x, y \in F$

$$f\big(\alpha x + (1 - \alpha)y\big) \le \alpha f(x) + (1 - \alpha)f(y), \qquad \forall \, \alpha \in [0,1],$$

but the above inequality may not hold for some x or y from S that do not belong to F. In this case, we say that f is *convex over* F.

If $f_1, f_2, \ldots, f_m$ are convex functions over a convex subset F of $\Re^n$ and $\alpha_1, \alpha_2, \ldots, \alpha_m$ are nonnegative scalars, then the function $\alpha_1 f_1 + \cdots + \alpha_m f_m$ is also convex over F. If $f : \Re^m \mapsto \Re$ is convex, A is an $m \times n$ matrix, and b is a vector in $\Re^m$, the function $g : \Re^n \mapsto \Re$ defined by $g(x) = f(Ax + b)$ is also convex.

For functions $f : \Re^n \mapsto \Re$ that are continuously differentiable, there are alternative characterizations of convexity. Thus, the function f is convex over a convex set F if and only if

$$f(y) \geq f(x) + \nabla f(x)'(y - x), \qquad \forall \, x, y \in F.$$

If f is twice continuously differentiable, then f is convex over $\Re^n$ if and only if $\nabla^2 f(x)$ is a positive semidefinite symmetric matrix for every $x \in \Re^n$. In particular, a quadratic function of the form $f(x) = x'Ax + b'x$ is convex if and only if the matrix A is positive semidefinite.

A.6   SUBGRADIENTS

The *directional derivative* $f'(x; y)$ of a convex function $f : \Re^n \mapsto \Re$ at a vector $x \in \Re^n$ in the direction $y \in \Re^n$ is defined by

$$f'(x; y) = \lim_{\alpha \downarrow 0} \frac{f(x + \alpha y) - f(x)}{\alpha}.$$

(The limit in the above equation is guaranteed to exist because from the definition of convexity, it follows that the ratio above is monotonically nondecreasing as a function of α.) If f is differentiable, then we have

$$f'(x; y) = \nabla f(x)'y, \qquad \forall \, x, y \in \Re^n.$$

Given a convex function $f : \Re^n \mapsto \Re$, we say that $d \in \Re^n$ is a *subgradient* of f at a vector $x \in \Re^n$ if

$$f(z) \geq f(x) + (z - x)'d, \qquad \forall \, z \in \Re^n.$$

If instead f is a concave function, we say that d is a subgradient of f at x if $-d$ is a subgradient of the convex function $-f$ at x, or equivalently, if

$$f(z) \leq f(x) + (z - x)'d, \qquad \forall \, z \in \Re^n.$$

The set of all subgradients of a convex (or concave) function f at $x \in \Re^n$ is called the *subdifferential* of f at x, and is denoted by $\partial f(x)$.

If $f : \Re^n \mapsto \Re$ is convex, then for every $x \in \Re^n$, the subdifferential $\partial f(x)$ is a nonempty, convex, and compact set. Furthermore, if X is a bounded set, the set $\cup_{x \in X} \partial f(x)$ is bounded. The subdifferential can also be expressed in terms of the directional derivative of f. In particular, we have

$$f'(x; y) = \max_{d \in \partial f(x)} y'd, \qquad \forall \, y \in \Re^n.$$

This implies that f is differentiable at x with gradient $\nabla f(x)$ if and only if it has $\nabla f(x)$ as its unique subgradient at x.

Danskin's Min-Max Theorem

The dual function of an optimization problem is defined as the pointwise minimum of concave functions, or as the pointwise maximum of convex functions. Danskin's theorem provides a characterization of the directional derivative and the subdifferential of functions of this type.

Let $Z \subset \Re^m$ be a compact set, and let $\phi : \Re^n \times Z \mapsto \Re$ be a continuous function such that $\phi(\cdot, z) : \Re^n \mapsto \Re$, viewed as a function of its first argument, is convex for each $z \in Z$. Then the function $f : \Re^n \mapsto \Re$ given by

$$f(x) = \max_{z \in Z} \phi(x, z)$$

is convex and has directional derivative given by

$$f'(x; y) = \max_{z \in Z(x)} \phi'(x, z; y),$$

where $\phi'(x, z; y)$ is the directional derivative of the function $\phi(\cdot, z)$ at x in the direction y, and $Z(x)$ is the set of maximizers of $\phi(x, z)$:

$$Z(x) = \left\{ \overline{z} \ \middle| \ \phi(x, \overline{z}) = \max_{z \in Z} \phi(x, z) \right\}.$$

In particular, if $Z(x)$ consists of a unique maximizer $\overline{z}$ and $\phi(\cdot, \overline{z})$ is differentiable at x, then f is differentiable at x, and

$$\nabla f(x) = \nabla_x \phi(x, \overline{z}),$$

where $\nabla_x \phi(x, \overline{z})$ is the gradient of ϕ with respect to x, i.e., the vector with components

$$\frac{\partial \phi(x, \overline{z})}{\partial x_i}, \qquad i = 1, \ldots, n,$$

where x_i are the components of x.

In the case where $\phi(\cdot, z)$ is differentiable for all $z \in Z$ and $\nabla_x \phi(x, \cdot)$ is continuous on Z for each x, we have

$$\partial f(x) = \text{conv}\{\nabla_x \phi(x, z) \mid z \in Z(x)\}, \qquad \forall \ x \in \Re^n,$$

where conv denotes convex hull. In particular, if ϕ is linear in x for all $z \in Z$, i.e., it has the form

$$\phi(x, z) = a_z' x + b_z, \qquad \forall \ z \in Z,$$

then

$$\partial f(x) = \text{conv}\{a_z \mid z \in Z(x)\}.$$

References

Aarts, E., and Lenstra, J. K., 1997. Local Search in Combinatorial Optimization, Wiley, N. Y.

Ahuja, R. K., Magnanti, T. L., and Orlin, J. B., 1989. "Network Flows," in Handbooks in Operations Research and Management Science, Vol. 1, Optimization, Nemhauser, G. L., Rinnooy-Kan, A. H. G., and Todd M. J. (eds.), North-Holland, Amsterdam, pp. 211-369.

Ahuja, R. K., Mehlhorn, K., Orlin, J. B., and Tarjan, R. E., 1990. "Faster Algorithms for the Shortest Path Problem," J. ACM, Vol. 37, 1990, pp. 213-223.

Ahuja, R. K., and Orlin, J. B., 1987. Private Communication.

Ahuja, R. K., and Orlin, J. B., 1989. "A Fast and Simple Algorithm for the Maximum Flow Problem," Operations Research, Vol. 37, pp. 748-759.

Amini, M. M., 1994. "Vectorization of an Auction Algorithm for Linear Cost Assignment Problem," Comput. Ind. Eng., Vol. 26, pp. 141-149.

Arezki, Y., and Van Vliet, D., 1990. "A Full Analytical Implementation of the PARTAN/Frank-Wolfe Algorithm for Equilibrium Assignment," Transportation Science, Vol. 24, pp. 58-62.

Assad, A. A., and Golden, B. L., 1995. "Arc Routing Methods and Applications," Handbooks in OR and MS, Ball, M. O., Magnanti, T. L., Monma, C. L., and Nemhauser, G. L., (eds.), Vol. 8, North-Holland, Amsterdam, pp. 375-483.

Atkinson, D. S., and Vaidya, P. M., 1995. "A Cutting Plane Algorithm for Convex Programming that Uses Analytic Centers," Math. Programming, Vol. 69, pp. 1-44.

Auchmuty, G., 1989. "Variational Principles for Variational Inequalities," Numer. Functional Analysis and Optimization, Vol. 10, pp. 863-874.

Auslender, A., 1976. Optimization: Methodes Numeriques, Mason, Paris.

Balas, E., Miller, D., Pekny, J., and Toth, P., 1991. "A Parallel Shortest Path Algorithm for the Assignment Problem," J. ACM, Vol. 38, pp. 985-1004.

Balas, E., and Toth, P., 1985. "Branch and Bound Methods," in The Traveling Salesman Problem, Lawler, E., Lenstra, J. K., Rinnoy Kan, A. H. G., and Shmoys, D. B. (eds.), Wiley, N. Y., pp. 361-401.

Balinski, M. L., 1985. "Signature Methods for the Assignment Problem," Operations Research, Vol. 33, pp. 527-537.

Balinski, M. L., 1986. "A Competitive (Dual) Simplex Method for the Assignment Problem," Math. Programming, Vol. 34, pp. 125-141.

Ball, M. O., Magnanti, T. L., Monma, C. L., and Nemhauser, G. L., 1995a. Network Models, Handbooks in OR and MS, Vol. 7, North-Holland, Amsterdam.

Ball, M. O., Magnanti, T. L., Monma, C. L., and Nemhauser, G. L., 1995b. Network Routing, Handbooks in OR and MS, Vol. 8, North-Holland, Amsterdam.

Bar-Shalom, Y., and Fortman, T. E., 1988. Tracking and Data Association, Academic Press, N. Y.

Barnhart, C., Hane, C. H., and Vance, P. H., 1997. "Integer Multicommodity Flow Problems," in Network Optimization, Pardalos, P. M., Hearn, D. W., and Hager, W. W. (eds.), Springer-Verlag, N. Y., pp. 17-31.

Barr, R., Glover, F., and Klingman, D., 1977. "The Alternating Basis Algorithm for Assignment Problems," Math. Programming, Vol. 13, pp. 1-13.

Barr, R., Glover, F., and Klingman, D., 1978. "Generalized Alternating Path Algorithm for Transportation Problems," European J. of Operations Research, Vol. 2, pp. 137-144.

Barr, R., Glover, F., and Klingman, D., 1979. "Enhancement of Spanning Tree Labeling Procedures for Network Optimization," INFOR, Vol. 17, pp. 16-34.

Barr, R., and Hickman, B. L., 1994. "Parallel Simplex for Large Pure Network Problems - Computational Testing and Sources of Speedup," Operations Research, Vol. 42, pp. 65-80.

Bazaraa, M. S., Jarvis, J. J., and Sherali, H. D., 1990. Linear Programming and Network Flows (2nd Ed.), Wiley, N. Y.

Bazaraa, M. S., Sherali, H. D., and Shetty, C. M., 1993. Nonlinear Programming Theory and Algorithms (2nd Ed.), Wiley, N. Y.

Bell, G. J., and Lamar, B. W., 1997. "Solution Methods for Nonconvex Network Flow Problems," in Network Optimization, Pardalos, P. M., Hearn,

D. W., and Hager, W. W. (eds.), Lecture Notes in Economics and Mathematical Systems, Springer-Verlag, N. Y., pp. 32-50.

Bellman, R., 1957. Dynamic Programming, Princeton Univ. Press, Princeton, N. J.

Benders, J. F., 1962. "Partitioning Procedures for Solving Mixed Variables Programming Problems," Numer. Math., Vol. 4, pp. 238-252.

Beraldi, P., and Guerriero, F., 1997. "A Parallel Asynchronous Implementation of the Epsilon-Relaxation Method for the Linear Minimum Cost Flow Problem," Parallel Computing, Vol. 23, pp. 1021-1044.

Beraldi, P., Guerriero, F., and Musmanno, R., 1996. "Parallel Algorithms for Solving the Convex Minimum Cost Flow Problem," Tech. Report PAR-COLAB No. 8/96, Dept. of Electronics, Informatics, and Systems, Univ. of Calabria.

Beraldi, P., Guerriero, F., and Musmanno, R., 1997. "Efficient Parallel Algorithms for the Minimum Cost Flow Problem," J. of Optimization Theory and Applications, Vol. 95, pp. 501-530.

Berge, C., 1962. The Theory of Graphs and its Applications, Wiley, N. Y.

Berge, C., and Ghouila-Houri, A., 1962. Programming, Games, and Transportation Networks, Wiley, N. Y.

Bertsekas, D. P., 1975a. "Nondifferentiable Optimization via Approximation," Math. Programming Studies, Vol. 3, North-Holland, Amsterdam, pp. 1-25.

Bertsekas, D. P., 1975b. "Necessary and Sufficient Conditions for a Penalty Method to be Exact," Math. Programming, Vol. 9, pp. 87-99.

Bertsekas, D. P., 1979a. "A Distributed Algorithm for the Assignment Problem," Lab. for Information and Decision Systems Working Paper, M.I.T., Cambridge, MA.

Bertsekas, D. P., 1979b. "Algorithms for Nonlinear Multicommodity Network Flow Problems," in International Symposium on Systems Optimization and Analysis, Bensoussan, A., and Lions, J. L. (eds.), Springer-Verlag, N. Y., pp. 210-224.

Bertsekas, D. P., 1980. "A Class of Optimal Routing Algorithms for Communication Networks," Proc. of the Fifth International Conference on Computer Communication, Atlanta, Ga., pp. 71-76.

Bertsekas, D. P., 1981. "A New Algorithm for the Assignment Problem," Math. Programming, Vol. 21, pp. 152-171.

Bertsekas, D. P., 1982. Constrained Optimization and Lagrange Multiplier Methods, Academic Press, N. Y. (republished in 1996 by Athena Scientific, Belmont, MA).

Bertsekas, D. P., 1985. "A Unified Framework for Minimum Cost Network Flow Problems," Math. Programming, Vol. 32, pp. 125-145.

Bertsekas, D. P., 1986a. "Distributed Asynchronous Relaxation Methods for Linear Network Flow Problems," Lab. for Information and Decision Systems Report P-1606, M.I.T., Cambridge, MA.

Bertsekas, D. P., 1986b. "Distributed Relaxation Methods for Linear Network Flow Problems," Proceedings of 25th IEEE Conference on Decision and Control, Athens, Greece, pp. 2101-2106.

Bertsekas, D. P., 1988. "The Auction Algorithm: A Distributed Relaxation Method for the Assignment Problem," Annals of Operations Research, Vol. 14, pp. 105-123.

Bertsekas, D. P., 1990. "The Auction Algorithm for Assignment and Other Network Flow Problems: A Tutorial," Interfaces, Vol. 20, pp. 133-149.

Bertsekas, D. P., 1991a. Linear Network Optimization: Algorithms and Codes, MIT Press, Cambridge, MA.

Bertsekas, D. P., 1991b. "An Auction Algorithm for Shortest Paths," SIAM J. on Optimization, Vol. 1, pp. 425-447.

Bertsekas, D. P., 1992a. "Auction Algorithms for Network Flow Problems: A Tutorial Introduction," Computational Optimization and Applications, Vol. 1, pp. 7-66.

Bertsekas, D. P., 1992b. "Modified Auction Algorithms for Shortest Paths," Lab. for Information and Decision Systems Report P-2150, M.I.T., Cambridge, MA.

Bertsekas, D. P., 1992c. "An Auction Sequential Shortest Path Algorithm for the Minimum Cost Network Flow Problem," Lab. for Information and Decision Systems Report P-2146, M.I.T.

Bertsekas, D. P., 1993a. "A Simple and Fast Label Correcting Algorithm for Shortest Paths," Networks, Vol. 23, pp. 703-709.

Bertsekas, D. P., 1993b. "Mathematical Equivalence of the Auction Algorithm for Assignment and the ϵ-Relaxation (Preflow-Push) Method for Min Cost Flow," in Large Scale Optimization: State of the Art, Hager, W. W., Hearn, D. W., and Pardalos, P. M. (eds.), Kluwer, Boston, pp. 27-46.

Bertsekas, D. P., 1995a. Dynamic Programming and Optimal Control, Vols. I and II, Athena Scientific, Belmont, MA.

Bertsekas, D. P., 1995b. Nonlinear Programming, Athena Scientific, Belmont, MA.

Bertsekas, D. P., 1995c. "An Auction Algorithm for the Max-Flow Problem," J. of Optimization Theory and Applications, Vol. 87, pp. 69-101.

Bertsekas, D. P., 1996. "Thevenin Decomposition and Network Optimization," J. of Optimization Theory and Applications, Vol. 89, pp. 1-15.

Bertsekas, D. P., and Castañon, D. A., 1989. "The Auction Algorithm for Transportation Problems," Annals of Operations Research, Vol. 20, pp. 67-96.

Bertsekas, D. P., and Castañon, D. A., 1991. "Parallel Synchronous and Asynchronous Implementations of the Auction Algorithm," Parallel Computing, Vol. 17, pp. 707-732.

Bertsekas, D. P., and Castañon, D. A., 1992. "A Forward/Reverse Auction Algorithm for Asymmetric Assignment Problems," Computational Optimization and Applications, Vol. 1, pp. 277-297.

Bertsekas, D. P., and Castañon, D. A., 1993a. "Asynchronous Hungarian Methods for the Assignment Problem," ORSA J. on Computing, Vol. 5, pp. 261-274.

Bertsekas, D. P., and Castañon, D. A., 1993b. "Parallel Primal-Dual Methods for the Minimum Cost Flow Problem," Computational Optimization and Applications, Vol. 2, pp. 317-336.

Bertsekas, D. P., and Castañon, D. A., 1993c. "A Generic Auction Algorithm for the Minimum Cost Network Flow Problem," Computational Optimization and Applications, Vol. 2, pp. 229-260.

Bertsekas, D. P., and Castañon, D. A., 1998. "Solving Stochastic Scheduling Problems Using Rollout Algorithms," Lab. for Information and Decision Systems Report P-12413, M.I.T., Cambridge, MA.

Bertsekas, D. P., Castañon, D. A., Eckstein, J., and Zenios, S., 1995. "Parallel Computing in Network Optimization," Handbooks in OR and MS, Ball, M. O., Magnanti, T. L., Monma, C. L., and Nemhauser, G. L. (eds.), Vol. 7, North-Holland, Amsterdam, pp. 331-399.

Bertsekas, D. P., Castañon, D. A., and Tsaknakis, H., 1993. "Reverse Auction and the Solution of Inequality Constrained Assignment Problems," SIAM J. on Optimization, Vol. 3, pp. 268-299.

Bertsekas, D. P., and El Baz, D., 1987. "Distributed Asynchronous Relaxation Methods for Convex Network Flow Problems," SIAM J. on Control and Optimization, Vol. 25, pp. 74-85.

Bertsekas, D. P., and Eckstein, J., 1987. "Distributed Asynchronous Relaxation Methods for Linear Network Flow Problems," Proc. of IFAC '87, Munich, Germany.

Bertsekas, D. P., and Eckstein, J., 1988. "Dual Coordinate Step Methods for Linear Network Flow Problems," Math. Programming, Series B, Vol. 42, pp. 203-243.

Bertsekas, D. P., and Gafni, E. M., 1982. "Projection Methods for Variational Inequalities with Application to the Traffic Assignment Problem," Math. Progr. Studies, Vol. 17, North-Holland, Amsterdam, pp. 139-159.

Bertsekas, D. P., and Gafni, E. M., 1983. "Projected Newton Methods and Optimization of Multicommodity Flows," IEEE Trans. on Auto. Control, Vol. 28, pp. 1090-1096.

Bertsekas, D. P., Gafni, E. M., and Gallager, R. G., 1984. "Second Derivative Algorithms for Minimum Delay Distributed Routing in Networks," IEEE Trans. on Communications, Vol. 32, pp. 911-919.

Bertsekas, D. P., and Gallager, R. G., 1992. Data Networks, (2nd Ed.), Prentice-Hall, Englewood Cliffs, N. J.

Bertsekas, D. P., Guerriero, F., and Musmanno, R., 1996. "Parallel Asynchronous Label Correcting Methods for Shortest Paths," J. of Optimization Theory and Applications, Vol. 88, pp. 297-320.

Bertsekas, D. P., Hosein, P., and Tseng, P., 1987. "Relaxation Methods for Network Flow Problems with Convex Arc Costs," SIAM J. on Control and Optimization, Vol. 25, pp. 1219-1243.

Bertsekas, D. P, and Mitter, S. K., 1971. "Steepest Descent for Optimization Problems with Nondifferentiable Cost Functionals," Proc. 5th Annual Princeton Confer. Inform. Sci. Systems, Princeton, N. J., pp. 347-351.

Bertsekas, D. P., and Mitter, S. K., 1973. "Descent Numerical Methods for Optimization Problems with Nondifferentiable Cost Functions," SIAM J. on Control, Vol. 11, pp. 637-652.

Bertsekas, D. P., Pallottino, S., and Scutellà, M. G., 1995. "Polynomial Auction Algorithms for Shortest Paths," Computational Optimization and Applications, Vol. 4, pp. 99-125.

Bertsekas, D. P., Polymenakos, L. C., and Tseng, P., 1997a. "An ϵ-Relaxation Method for Separable Convex Cost Network Flow Problems," SIAM J. on Optimization, Vol. 7, pp. 853-870.

Bertsekas, D. P., Polymenakos, L. C., and Tseng, P., 1997b. "Epsilon-Relaxation and Auction Methods for Separable Convex Cost Network Flow Problems," in Network Optimization, Pardalos, P. M., Hearn, D. W., and Hager, W. W. (eds.), Lecture Notes in Economics and Mathematical Systems, Springer-Verlag, N. Y., pp. 103-126.

Bertsekas, D. P., and Tseng, P., 1988a. "Relaxation Methods for Minimum Cost Ordinary and Generalized Network Flow Problems," Operations Research, Vol. 36, pp. 93-114.

Bertsekas, D. P., and Tseng, P., 1988b. "RELAX: A Computer Code for Minimum Cost Network Flow Problems," Annals of Operations Research, Vol. 13, pp. 127-190.

Bertsekas, D. P., and Tseng, P., 1990. "RELAXT-III: A New and Improved Version of the RELAX Code," Lab. for Information and Decision Systems Report P-1990, M.I.T., Cambridge, MA.

Bertsekas, D. P., and Tseng, P., 1994. "RELAX-IV: A Faster Version of the RELAX Code for Solving Minimum Cost Flow Problems," Laboratory for Information and Decision Systems Report P-2276, M.I.T., Cambridge, MA.

Bertsekas, D. P., and Tsitsiklis, J. N., 1989. Parallel and Distributed Computation: Numerical Methods, Prentice-Hall, Englewood Cliffs, N. J. (republished in 1997 by Athena Scientific, Belmont, MA).

Bertsekas, D. P., and Tsitsiklis, J. N., 1996. Neuro-Dynamic Programming, Athena Scientific, Belmont, MA.

Bertsekas, D. P., Tsitsiklis, J. N., and Wu, C., 1997. "Rollout Algorithms for Combinatorial Optimization," Heuristics, Vol. 3, pp. 245-262.

Bertsimas, D., and Tsitsiklis, J. N., 1993. "Simulated Annealing," Stat. Sci., Vol. 8, pp. 10-15.

Bertsimas, D., and Tsitsiklis, J. N., 1997. Introduction to Linear Optimization, Athena Scientific, Belmont, MA.

Birkhoff, G., and Diaz, J. B., 1956. "Nonlinear Network Problems," Quart. Appl. Math., Vol. 13, pp. 431-444.

Bland, R. G., and Jensen, D. L., 1985. "On the Computational Behavior of a Polynomial-Time Network Flow Algorithm," Tech. Report 661, School of Operations Research and Industrial Engineering, Cornell University.

Blackman, S. S., 1986. Multi-Target Tracking with Radar Applications, Artech House, Dehdam, MA.

Bogart, K. P., 1990. Introductory Combinatorics, Harcourt Brace Jovanovich, Inc., New York, N. Y.

Bradley, G. H., Brown, G. G., and Graves, G. W., 1977. "Design and Implementation of Large-Scale Primal Transshipment Problems," Management Science, Vol. 24, pp. 1-38.

Brannlund, U., 1993. On Relaxation Methods for Nonsmooth Convex Optimization, Doctoral Thesis, Royal Institute of Technology, Stockhorm, Sweden.

Brown, G. G., and McBride, R. D., 1984. "Solving Generalized Networks," Management Science, Vol. 30, pp. 1497-1523.

Burkard, R. E., 1990. "Special Cases of Traveling Salesman Problems and Heuristics," Acta Math. Appl. Sin., Vol. 6, pp. 273-288.

Busacker, R. G., and Gowen, P. J., 1961. "A Procedure for Determining a

Family of Minimal-Cost Network Flow Patterns," O.R.O. Technical Report No. 15, Operational Research Office, John Hopkins University, Baltimore, MD.

Busacker, R. G., and Saaty, T. L., 1965. Finite Graphs and Networks: An Introduction with Applications, McGraw-Hill, N. Y.

Cameron, P. J., 1994. Combinatorics: Topics, Techniques, Algorithms, Cambridge Univ. Press, Cambridge, England.

Cantor, D. G., and Gerla, M., 1974. "Optimal Routing in a Packet Switched Computer Network," IEEE Trans. on Computers, Vol. 23, pp. 1062-1069.

Carpaneto, G., Martello, S., and Toth, P., 1988. "Algorithms and Codes for the Assignment Problem," Annals of Operations Research, Vol. 13, pp. 193-223.

Carraresi, P., and Sodini, C., 1986. "An Efficient Algorithm for the Bipartite Matching Problem," Eur. J. Operations Research, Vol. 23, pp. 86-93.

Castañon, D. A., 1990. "Efficient Algorithms for Finding the K Best Paths Through a Trellis," IEEE Trans. on Aerospace and Electronic Systems, Vol. 26, pp. 405-410.

Castañon, D. A., 1993. "Reverse Auction Algorithms for Assignment Problems," in Algorithms for Network Flows and Matching, Johnson, D. S., and McGeoch, C. C. (eds.), American Math. Soc., Providence, RI, pp. 407-429.

Censor, Y., and Zenios, S. A., 1992. "The Proximal Minimization Algorithm with D-Functions," J. Opt. Theory and Appl., Vol. 73, pp. 451-464.

Censor, Y., and Zenios, S. A., 1997. Parallel Optimization: Theory, Algorithms, and Applications, Oxford University Press, N. Y.

Cerny, V., 1985. "A Thermodynamical Approach to the Travelling Salesman Problem: An Efficient Simulation Algorithm," J. Opt. Theory and Applications, Vol. 45, pp. 41-51.

Cerulli, R., De Leone, R., and Piacente, G., 1994. "A Modified Auction Algorithm for the Shortest Path Problem," Optimization Methods and Software, Vol. 4, pp. 209-224.

Cerulli, R., Festa, P., and Raiconi, G., 1997a. "Graph Collapsing in Shortest Path Auction Algorithms," Univ. of Salerno Tech. Report n. 6/97.

Cerulli, R., Festa, P., and Raiconi, G., 1997b. "An Efficient Auction Algorithm for the Shortest Path Problem Using Virtual Source Concept," Univ. of Salerno Tech. Report n. 6/97.

Chajakis, E. D., and Zenios, S. A., 1991. "Synchronous and Asynchronous Implementations of Relaxation Algorithms for Nonlinear Network Optimization," Parallel Computing, Vol. 17, pp. 873-894.

Chen, G., and Teboulle, M., 1993. "Convergence Analysis of a Proximal-Like Minimization Algorithm Using Bregman Functions," SIAM J. on Optimization, Vol. 3, pp. 538-543.

Chen, Z. L., and Powell, W. B., 1997. "A Note on Bertsekas' Small-Label-First Strategy," Networks, Vol. 29, pp. 111-116.

Cheney, E. W., and Goldstein, A. A., 1959. "Newton's Method for Convex Programming and Tchebycheff Approximation," Numer. Math., Vol. I, pp. 253-268.

Cheriyan, J., and Maheshwari, S. N., 1989. "Analysis of Preflow Push Algorithms for Maximum Network Flow," SIAM J. Computing, Vol. 18, pp. 1057-1086.

Cherkasky, R. V., 1977. "Algorithm for Construction of Maximum Flow in Networks with Complexity of $O(V^2\sqrt{E})$ Operations," Mathematical Methods of Solution of Economical Problems, Vol. 7, pp. 112-125.

Christofides, N., 1975. Graph Theory: An Algorithmic Approach, Academic Press, N. Y.

Chvatal, V., 1983. Linear Programming, W. H. Freeman and Co., N. Y.

Connors, D. P., and Kumar, P. R., 1989. "Simulated Annealing Type Markov Chains and their Order Balance Equations," SIAM J. on Control and Optimization, Vol. 27, pp. 1440-1461.

Cook, W., Cunningham, W., Pulleyblank, W., and Schrijver, A., 1998. Combinatorial Optimization, Wiley, N. Y.

Cornuejols, G., Fonlupt, J., and Naddef, D., 1985. "The Traveling Salesman Problem on a Graph and Some Related Polyhedra," Math. Programming, Vol. 33, pp. 1-27.

Cottle, R. W., and Pang, J. S., 1982. "On the Convergence of a Block Successive Over-Relaxation Method for a Class of Linear Complementarity Problems," Math. Progr. Studies, Vol. 17, pp. 126-138.

Croes, G. A., 1958. "A Method for Solving Traveling Salesman Problems," Operations Research, Vol. 6, pp. 791-812.

Cunningham, W. H., 1976. "A Network Simplex Method," Math. Programming, Vol. 4, pp. 105-116.

Cunningham, W. H., 1979. "Theoretical Properties of the Network Simplex Method," Math. of Operations Research, Vol. 11, pp. 196-208.

Dafermos, S., 1980. "Traffic Equilibrium and Variational Inequalities," Transportation Science, Vol. 14, pp. 42-54.

Dafermos, S., 1982. "Relaxation Algorithms for the General Asymmetric Traffic Equilibrium Problem," Transportation Science, Vol. 16, pp. 231-240.

Dafermos, S., and Sparrow, F. T., 1969. "The Traffic Assignment Problem for a General Network," J. Res. Nat. Bureau of Standards, Vol. 73B, pp. 91-118.

Dantzig, G. B., 1951. "Application of the Simplex Method to a Transportation Problem," in Activity Analysis of Production and Allocation, T. C. Koopmans (ed.), Wiley, N. Y., pp. 359-373.

Dantzig, G. B., 1960. "On the Shortest Route Problem Through a Network," Management Science, Vol. 6, pp. 187-190.

Dantzig, G. B., 1963. Linear Programming and Extensions, Princeton Univ. Press, Princeton, N. J.

Dantzig, G. B., 1967. "All Shortest Routes in a Graph," in Theory of Graphs, P. Rosenthier (ed.), Gordan and Breach, N. Y., pp. 92-92.

Dantzig, G. B., and Fulkerson, D. R., 1956. "On the Max-Flow Min-Cut Theorem of Networks," in Linear Inequalities and Related Systems, Kuhn, H. W., and Tucker, A. W. (eds.), Annals of Mathematics Study 38, Princeton Univ. Press, pp. 215-221.

Dantzig, G. B., and Wolfe, P., 1960. "Decomposition Principle for Linear Programs," Operations Research, Vol. 8, pp. 101-111.

Dantzig, G. B., Fulkerson, D. R., and Johnson, S. M., 1954. "Solution of a Large-Scale Traveling-Salesman Problem," Operations Research, Vol. 2, pp. 393-410.

De Leone, R., Meyer, R. R., and Zakarian, A., 1995. "An ϵ-Relaxation Algorithm for Convex Network Flow Problems," Computer Sciences Department Technical Report, University of Wisconsin, Madison, WI.

Dembo, R. S., 1987. "A Primal Truncated Newton Algorithm for Large-Scale Unconstrained Optimization," Math. Programming Studies, Vol. 31, pp. 43-72.

Dembo, R. S., and Klincewicz, J. G., 1981. "A Scaled Reduced Gradient Algorithm for Network Flow Problems with Convex Separable Costs," Math. Programming Studies, Vol. 15, pp. 125-147.

Dembo, R. S., and Tulowitzki, U., 1988. "Computing Equilibria on Large Multicommodity Networks: An Application of Truncated Quadratic Programming Algorithms," Networks, Vol. 18, pp. 273-284.

Denardo, E. V., and Fox, B. L., 1979. "Shortest-Route Methods: 1. Reaching, Pruning and Buckets," Operations Research, Vol. 27, pp. 161-186.

Dennis, J. B., 1959. Mathematical Programming and Electical Circuits, Technology Press of M.I.T., Cambridge, MA.

Deo, N., and Kumar, N., 1997. "Computation of Constrained Spanning Trees: A Unified Approach," in Network Optimization, Pardalos, P. M.,

Hearn, D. W., and Hager, W. W. (eds.), Lecture Notes in Economics and Mathematical Systems, Springer-Verlag, N. Y., pp. 194-220.

Deo, N., and Pang, C., 1984. "Shortest Path Algorithms: Taxonomy and Annotation," Networks, Vol. 14, pp. 275-323.

Derigs, U., 1985. "The Shortest Augmenting Path Method for Solving Assignment Problems – Motivation and Computational Experience," Annals of Operations Research, Vol. 4, pp. 57-102.

Derigs, U., and Meier, W., 1989. "Implementing Goldberg's Max-Flow Algorithm – A Computational Investigation," Zeitschrif fur Operations Research, Vol. 33, pp. 383-403.

Desrosiers, J., Dumas, Y., Solomon, M. M., and Soumis, F., 1995. "Time Constrained Routing and Scheduling," Handbooks in OR and MS, Ball, M. O., Magnanti, T. L., Monma, C. L., and Nemhauser, G. L. (eds.), Vol. 8, North-Holland, Amsterdam, pp. 35-139.

Dial, R. B., 1969. "Algorithm 360: Shortest Path Forest with Topological Ordering," Comm. ACM, Vol. 12, pp. 632-633.

Dial, R., Glover, F., Karney, D., and Klingman, D., 1979. "A Computational Analysis of Alternative Algorithms and Labeling Techniques for Finding Shortest Path Trees," Networks, Vol. 9, pp. 215-248.

Dijkstra, E., 1959. "A Note on Two Problems in Connexion with Graphs," Numer. Math., Vol. 1, pp. 269-271.

Dinic, E. A., 1970. "Algorithm for Solution of a Problem of Maximum Flow in Networks with Power Estimation," Soviet Math. Doklady, Vol. 11, pp. 1277-1280.

Dreyfus, S. E., 1969. "An Appraisal of Some Shortest-Path Algorithms," Operations Research, Vol. 17, pp. 395-412.

Duffin, R. J., 1947. "Nonlinear Networks. IIa," Bull. Amer. Math. Soc., Vol. 53, pp. 963-971.

Eastman, W. L., 1958. Linear Programming with Pattern Constraints, Ph.D. Thesis, Harvard University, Cambridge, MA.

Eckstein, J., 1994. "Nonlinear Proximal Point Algorithms Using Bregman Functions, with Applications to Convex Programming," Math. of Operations Research, Vol. 18, pp. 202-226.

Edmonds, J., 1965. "Paths, Trees, and Flowers," Canadian J. of Math., Vol. 17, pp. 449-467.

Edmonds, J., and Johnson, E. L., 1973. "Matching, Euler Tours, and the Chinese Postman," Math. Programming, Vol. 5, pp. 88-124.

Edmonds, J., and Karp, R. M., 1972. "Theoretical Improvements in Algorithmic Efficiency for Network Flow Problems," J. ACM, Vol. 19, pp. 248-264.

Eiselt, H. A., Gendreau, M., and Laporte, G., 1995a. "Arc Routing Problems, Part 1: The Chinese Postman Problem," Operations Research, Vol. 43, pp. 231-242.

Eiselt, H. A., Gendreau, M., and Laporte, G., 1995b. "Arc Routing Problems, Part 2: The Rural Postman Problem," Operations Research, Vol. 43, pp. 399-414.

Elias, P., Feinstein, A., and Shannon, C. E., 1956. "Note on Maximum Flow Through a Network," IRE Trans. Info. Theory, Vol. IT-2, pp. 117-119.

Egervary, J., 1931. "Matrixok Kombinatoricus Tulajonsagairol," Mat. Es Fiz. Lapok, Vol. 38, pp. 16-28.

El Baz, D., 1989. "A Computational Experience with Distributed Asynchronous Iterative Methods for Convex Network Flow Problems," Proc. of the 28th IEEE Conference on Decision and Control, Tampa, Fl., pp. 590-591.

El Baz, D., 1996. "Asynchronous Gradient Algorithms for a Class of Convex Separable Network Flow Problems," Computational Optimization and Applications, Vol. 5, pp. 187-205.

El Baz, D., Spiteri, P., Miellou, J. C., and Gazen, D., 1996. "Asynchronous Iterative Algorithms with Flexible Communication for Nonlinear Network Flow Problems," J. of Parallel and Distributed Computing, Vol. 38, pp. 1-15.

Elam, J., Glover, F., and Klingman, D., 1979. "A Strongly Convergent Primal Simplex Algorithm for Generalized Networks," Math. of Operations Research, Vol. 4, pp. 39-59.

Elmaghraby, S. E., 1978. Activity Networks: Project Planning and Control by Network Models, Wiley, N. Y.

Elzinga, J., and Moore, T. G., 1975. "A Central Cutting Plane Algorithm for the Convex Programming Problem," Math. Programming, Vol. 8, pp. 134-145.

Engquist, M., 1982. "A Successive Shortest Path Algorithm for the Assignment Problem," INFOR, Vol. 20, pp. 370-384.

Ephremides, A., 1986. "The Routing Problem in Computer Networks," in Communication and Networks, Blake, I. F., and Poor, H. V. (eds.), Springer-Verlag, N. Y., pp. 299-325.

Ephremides, A., and Verdu, S., 1989. "Control and Optimization Methods in Communication Network Problems," IEEE Trans. on Automatic Control, Vol. 34, pp. 930-942.

Esau, L. R., and Williams, K. C., 1966. "On Teleprocessing System Design. A Method for Approximating the Optimal Network," IBM System J., Vol. 5, pp. 142-147.

Escudero, L. F., 1985. "Performance Evaluation of Independent Superbasic Sets on Nonlinear Replicated Networks," Eur. J. Operations Research, Vol. 23, pp. 343-355.

Everett, H., 1963. "Generalized Lagrange Multiplier Method for Solving Problems of Optimal Allocation of Resources," Operations Research, Vol. 11, pp. 399-417.

Falcone, M., 1987. "A Numerical Approach to the Infinite Horizon Problem of Deterministic Control Theory," Appl. Math. Opt., Vol. 15, pp. 1-13.

Federgruen, A., and Simchi-Levi, D., 1995. "Analysis of Vehicle and Inventory-Routing Problems," Handbooks in OR and MS, Ball, M. O., Magnanti, T. L., Monma, C. L., and Nemhauser, G. L. (eds.), Vol. 8, North-Holland, Amsterdam, pp. 297-373.

Ferris, M. C., 1991. "Finite Termination of the Proximal Point Algorithm," Math. Programming, Vol. 50, pp. 359-366.

Fisher, M., 1995. "Vehicle Routing," Handbooks in OR and MS, Ball, M. O., Magnanti, T. L., Monma, C. L., and Nemhauser, G. L. (eds.), Vol. 8, North-Holland, Amsterdam, pp. 1-33.

Florian, M., Guélat, J., and Spiess, H., 1987. "An Efficient Implementation of the "PARTAN" Variant of the Linear Approximation Method for the Network Equilibrium Problem," Networks, Vol. 17, pp. 319-339.

Florian, M. S., and Hearn, D., 1995. "Network Equilibrium Models and Algorithms," Handbooks in OR and MS, Ball, M. O., Magnanti, T. L., Monma, C. L., and Nemhauser, G. L. (eds.), Vol. 8, North-Holland, Amsterdam, pp. 485-550.

Florian, M. S., and Nguyen, S., 1974. "A Method for Computing Network Equilibrium with Elastic Demands," Transportation Science, Vol. 8, pp. 321-332.

Florian, M. S., and Nguyen, S., 1976. "An Application and Validation of Equilibrium Trip Assignment Methods," Transportation Science, Vol. 10, pp. 374-390.

Florian, M. S., Nguyen, S., and Pallottino, S., 1981. "A Dual Simplex Algorithm for Finding All Shortest Paths," Networks, Vol. 11, pp. 367-378.

Floudas, C. A., 1995. Nonlinear and Mixed-Integer Optimization: Fundamentals and Applications, Oxford University Press, N. Y.

Floyd, R. W., 1962. "Algorithm 97: Shortest Path," Comm. ACM, Vol. 5, pp. 345.

Ford, L. R., Jr., 1956. "Network Flow Theory," Report P-923, The Rand Corporation, Santa Monica, CA.

Ford, L. R., Jr., and Fulkerson, D. R., 1956a. "Solving the Transportation Problem," Management Science, Vol. 3, pp. 24-32.

Ford, L. R., Jr., and Fulkerson, D. R., 1956b. "Maximal Flow Through a Network," Can. J. of Math., Vol. 8, pp. 339-404.

Ford, L. R., Jr., and Fulkerson, D. R., 1957. "A Primal-Dual Algorithm for the Capacitated Hitchcock Problem," Naval Res. Logist. Quart., Vol. 4, pp. 47-54.

Ford, L. R., Jr., and Fulkerson, D. R., 1962. Flows in Networks, Princeton Univ. Press, Princeton, N. J.

Fox, B. L., 1993. "Integrating and Accelerating Tabu Search, Simulated Annealing, and Genetic Algorithms," Annals of Operations Research, Vol. 41, pp. 47-67.

Fox, B. L., 1995. "Faster Simulated Annealing," SIAM J. Optimization, Vol. 41, pp. 47-67.

Frank, H., and Frisch, I. T., 1970. Communication, Transmission, and Transportation Networks, Addison-Wesley, Reading, MA.

Fratta, L., Gerla, M., and Kleinrock, L., 1973. "The Flow-Deviation Method: An Approach to Store-and-Forward Computer Communication Network Design," Networks, Vol. 3, pp. 97-133.

Fredman, M. L., and Tarjan, R. E., 1984. "Fibonacci Heaps and their Uses in Improved Network Optimization Algorithms," Proc. 25th Annual Symp. on Found. of Comp. Sci., pp. 338-346.

Fukushima, M., 1984a. "A Modified Frank-Wolfe Algorithm for Solving the Traffic Assignment Problem," Transportation Research, Vol. 18B, pp. 169–177.

Fukushima, M., 1984b. "On the Dual Approach to the Traffic Assignment Problem," Transportation Research, Vol. 18B, pp. 235-245.

Fukushima, M., 1992. "Equivalent Differentiable Optimization Problems and Descent Methods for Asymmetric Variational Inequalities," Math. Programming, Vol. 53, pp. 99-110.

Fulkerson, D. R., 1961. "An Out-of-Kilter Method for Minimal Cost Flow Problems," SIAM J. Appl. Math., Vol. 9, pp. 18-27.

Fulkerson, D. R., and Dantzig, G. B., 1955. "Computation of Maximum Flow in Networks," Naval Res. Log. Quart., Vol. 2, pp. 277-283.

Gafni, E. M., 1979. "Convergence of a Routing Algorithm," M.S. Thesis, Dept. of Electrical Engineering, Univ. of Illinois, Urbana, Ill.

Gafni, E. M., and Bertsekas, D. P., 1984. "Two-Metric Projection Methods for Constrained Optimization," SIAM J. on Control and Optimization, Vol. 22, pp. 936-964.

Gale, D., 1957. "A Theorem of Flows in Networks," Pacific J. Math., Vol. 7, pp. 1073-1082.

Gale, D., Kuhn, H. W., and Tucker, A. W., 1951. "Linear Programming and the Theory of Games," in Activity Analysis of Production and Allocation, T. C. Koopmans (ed.), Wiley, N. Y.

Galil, Z., 1980. "$O(V^{5/3}E^{2/3})$ Algorithm for the Maximum Flow Problem," Acta Informatica, Vol. 14, pp. 221-242.

Galil, Z., and Naamad, A., 1980. "$O(VE\log^2 V)$ Algorithm for the Maximum Flow Problem," J. of Comput. Sys. Sci., Vol. 21, pp. 203-217.

Gallager, R. G., 1977. "A Minimum Delay Routing Algorithm Using Distributed Computation," IEEE Trans. on Communications, Vol. 23, pp. 73-85.

Gallo, G. S., and Pallottino, S., 1982. "A New Algorithm to Find the Shortest Paths Between All Pairs of Nodes," Discrete Applied Mathematics, Vol. 4, pp. 23-35.

Gallo, G. S., and Pallottino, S., 1986. "Shortest Path Methods: A Unified Approach," Math. Programming Studies, Vol. 26, pp. 38-64.

Gallo, G. S., and Pallottino, S., 1988. "Shortest Path Algorithms," Annals of Operations Research, Vol. 7, pp. 3-79.

Garey, M. R., and Johnson, D. S., 1979. Computers and Intractability: A Guide to the Theory of NP-Completeness, W. H. Freeman and Co., San Francisco, Ca.

Gartner, N. H., 1980a. "Optimal Traffic Assignment with Elastic Demands: A Review. Part I. Analysis Framework," Transportation Science, Vol. 14, pp. 174-191.

Gartner, N. H., 1980b. "Optimal Traffic Assignment with Elastic Demands: A Review. Part II. Algorithmic Approaches," Transportation Science, Vol. 14, pp. 192-208.

Gavish, B., Schweitzer, P., and Shlifer, E., 1977. "The Zero Pivot Phenomenon in Transportation Problems and its Computational Implications," Math. Programming, Vol. 12, pp. 226-240.

Gelfand, S. B., and Mitter, S. K., 1989. "Simulated Annealing with Noisy or Imprecise Measurements," J. Opt. Theory and Applications, Vol. 69, pp. 49-62.

Geoffrion, A. M., 1970. "Elements of Large-Scale Mathematical Programming, I, II," Management Science, Vol. 16, pp. 652-675, 676-691.

Geoffrion, A. M., 1974. "Lagrangian Relaxation for Integer Programming," Math. Programming Studies, Vol. 2, pp. 82-114.

Gerards, A. M. H., 1995. "Matching," Handbooks in OR and MS, Ball, M. O., Magnanti, T. L., Monma, C. L., and Nemhauser, G. L. (eds.), Vol. 7, North-Holland, Amsterdam, pp. 135-224.

Gibby, D., Glover, F., Klingman, D., and Mead, M., 1983. "A Comparison of Pivot Selection Rules for Primal Simplex Based Network Codes," Operations Research Letters, Vol. 2, pp. 199-202.

Gill, P. E., Murray, W., and Wright, M. H., 1981. Practical Optimization, Academic Press, N. Y.

Gilmore, P. C., Lawler, E. L., and Shmoys, D. B., 1985. "Well-Solved Special Cases," in The Traveling Salesman Problem, Lawler, E., Lenstra, J. K., Rinnoy Kan, A. H. G., and Shmoys, D. B. (eds.), Wiley, N. Y., pp. 87-143.

Glover, F., 1986. "Future Paths for Integer Programming and Links to Artificial Intelligence," Computers and Operations Research, Vol. 13, pp. 533-549.

Glover, F., 1989. "Tabu Search: Part I," ORSA J. on Computing, Vol. 1, pp. 190-206.

Glover, F., 1990. "Tabu Search: Part II," ORSA J. on Computing, Vol. 2, pp. 4-32.

Glover, F., Glover, R., and Klingman, D., 1986. "The Threshold Shortest Path Algorithm," Math. Programming Studies, Vol. 26, pp. 12-37.

Glover, F., Glover, R., and Klingman, D., 1986. "Threshold Assignment Algorithm," Math. Programming Studies, Vol. 26, pp. 12-37.

Glover, F., Karney, D., and Klingman, D., 1974. "Implementation and Computational Comparisons of Primal, Dual, and Primal-Dual Computer Codes for Minimum Cost Network Flow Problem," Networks, Vol. 4, pp. 191-212.

Glover, F., Karney, D., Klingman, D., and Napier, A., 1974. "A Computation Study on Start Procedures, Basis Change Criteria, and Solution Algorithms for Transportation Problems," Management Science, Vol. 20, pp. 793-819.

Glover, F., Klingman, D., Mote, J., and Whitman, D., 1984. "A Primal Simplex Variant for the Maximum Flow Problem," Naval Res. Logist. Quart., Vol. 31, pp. 41-61.

Glover, F., Klingman, D., and Phillips, N., 1985. "A New Polynomially

Bounded Shortest Path Algorithm," Operations Research, Vol. 33, pp. 65-73.

Glover, F., Klingman, D., and Phillips, N., 1992. Network Models in Optimization and Their Applications in Practice, Wiley, N. Y.

Glover, F., Klingman, D., Phillips, N., and Schneider, R. F., 1985. "New Polynomial Shortest Path Algorithms and Their Computational Attributes," Management Science, Vol. 31, pp. 1106-1128.

Glover, F., Klingman, D., and Stutz, J., 1973. "Extension of the Augmented Predecessor Index Method to Generalized Netork Problems," Transportation Science, Vol. 7, pp. 377-384.

Glover, F., Klingman, D., and Stutz, J., 1974. "Augmented Threaded Index Method for Network Optimization," INFOR, Vol. 12, pp. 293-298.

Glover, F., and Laguna, M., 1997. Tabu Search, Kluwer, Boston.

Glover, F., Taillard, E., and de Verra, D., 1993. "A User's Guide to Tabu Search," Annals of Operations Research, Vol. 41, pp. 3-28.

Goffin, J. L., 1977. "On Convergence Rates of Subgradient Optimization Methods," Math. Programming, Vol. 13, pp. 329-347.

Goffin, J. L., Haurie, A., and Vial, J. P., 1992. "Decomposition and Non-differentiable Optimization with the Projective Algorithm," Management Science, Vol. 38, pp. 284-302.

Goffin, J. L., and Kiwiel, K. C, 1996. 'Convergence of a Simple Subgradient Level Method," Unpublished Report, to appear in Math. Programming.

Goffin, J. L., Luo, Z.-Q., and Ye, Y., 1993. "On the Complexity of a Column Generation Algorithm for Convex or Quasiconvex Feasibility Problems," in Large Scale Optimization: State of the Art, Hager, W. W., Hearn, D. W., and Pardalos, P. M. (eds.), Kluwer.

Goffin, J. L., Luo, Z.-Q., and Ye, Y., 1996. "Further Complexity Analysis of a Primal-Dual Column Generation Algorithm for Convex or Quasiconvex Feasibility Problems," SIAM J. on Optimization, Vol. 6, pp. 638-652.

Goffin, J. L., and Vial, J. P., 1990. "Cutting Planes and Column Generation Techniques with the Projective Algorithm," J. Opt. Th. and Appl., Vol. 65, pp. 409-429.

Goldberg, A. V., 1987. "Efficient Graph Algorithms for Sequential and Parallel Computers," Tech. Report TR-374, Laboratory for Computer Science, M.I.T., Cambridge, MA.

Goldberg, A. V., 1993. "An Efficient Implementation of a Scaling Minimum-Cost Flow Algorithm," Proc. 3rd Integer Progr. and Combinatorial Optimization Conf., pp. 251-266.

Goldberg, A. V., and Tarjan, R. E., 1986. "A New Approach to the Maximum Flow Problem," Proc. 18th ACM STOC, pp. 136-146.

Goldberg, A. V., and Tarjan, R. E., 1990. "Solving Minimum Cost Flow Problems by Successive Approximation," Math. of Operations Research, Vol. 15, pp. 430-466.

Goldberg, D. E., 1989. Genetic Algorithms in Search, Optimization, and Machine Learning, Addison Wesley, Reading, MA.

Goldfarb, D., 1985. "Efficient Dual Simplex Algorithms for the Assignment Problem," Math. Programming, Vol. 33, pp. 187-203.

Goldfarb, D., and Hao, J., 1990. "A Primal Simplex Algorithm that Solves the Maximum Flow Problem in at Most nm Pivots and $O(n^2m)$ Time," Math. Programming, Vol. 47, pp. 353-365.

Goldfarb, D., Hao, J., and Kai, S., 1990a. "Anti-Stalling Pivot Rules for the Network Simplex Algorithm," Networks, Vol. 20, pp. 79-91.

Goldfarb, D., Hao, J., and Kai, S., 1990b. "Efficient Shortest Path Simplex Algorithms," Operations Research, Vol. 38, pp. 624-628.

Goldfarb, D., and Reid, J. K., 1977. "A Practicable Steepest Edge Simplex Algorithm," Math. Programming, Vol. 12, pp. 361-371.

Goldstein, A. A., 1967. Constructive Real Analysis, Harper and Row, N. Y.

Gondran, M., and Minoux, M., 1984. Graphs and Algorithms, Wiley, N. Y.

Gonzalez, R., and Rofman, E., 1985. "On Deterministic Control Problems: An Approximation Procedure for the Optimal Cost, Parts I, II," SIAM J. on Control and Optimization, Vol. 23, pp. 242-285.

Graham, R. L., Lawler, E. L., Lenstra, J. K., and Rinnooy Kan, A. H. G., 1979. "Optimization and Approximation in Deterministic Sequencing and Scheduling: A Survey," Annals of Discrete Math., Vol. 5, pp. 287-326.

Grötschel, M., Monma, C. L., and Stoer, M., 1995. "Design of Survivable Networks," Handbooks in OR and MS, Ball, M. O., Magnanti, T. L., Monma, C. L., and Nemhauser, G. L. (eds.), Vol. 7, North-Holland, Amsterdam, pp. 617-672.

Grötschel, M., and Padberg, M. W., 1985. "Polyhedral Theory," in The Traveling Salesman Problem, Lawler, E., Lenstra, J. K., Rinnoy Kan, A. H. G., and Shmoys, D. B. (eds.), Wiley, N. Y., pp. 251-305.

Guerriero, F., Lacagnina, V., Musmanno, R., and Pecorella, A., 1996. "Efficient Node Selection Strategies in Label-Correcting Methods for the K Shortest Paths Problem," Technical Report PARCOLAB No. 6/96, Department of Electronics, Informatics and Systems, University of Calabria.

Guler, O., 1992. "New Proximal Point Algorithms for Convex Minimization," SIAM J. on Optimization, Vol. 2, pp. 649-664.

Hajek, B., 1988. "Cooling Schedules for Optimal Annealing," Math. of Operations Research, Vol. 13, pp. 311-329.

Hall, M., Jr., 1956. "An Algorithm for Distinct Representatives," Amer. Math. Monthly, Vol. 51, pp. 716-717.

Hansen, P., 1986. "The Steepest Ascent Mildest Descent Heuristic for Combinatorial Optimization," Presented at the Congress on Numerical Methods in Combinatorial Optimization, Capri, Italy.

Hearn, D. W., and Lawphongpanich, S., 1990. "A Dual Ascent Algorithm for Traffic Assignment Problems," Transportation Research, Vol. 24B, pp. 423-430.

Hearn, D. W., Lawphongpanish, S., and Nguyen, S., 1984. "Convex Programming Formulation of the Asymmetric Traffic Assignment Problem," Transportation Research, Vol. 18B, pp. 357-365.

Hearn, D. W., Lawphongpanish, S., and Ventura, J. A., 1985. "Finiteness in Restricted Simplicial Decomposition," Operations Research Letters, Vol. 4, pp. 125-130.

Hearn, D. W., Lawphongpanish, S., and Ventura, J. A., 1987. "Restricted Simplicial Decomposition: Computation and Extensions," Math. Programming Studies, Vol. 31, pp. 99-118.

Held, M., and Karp, R. M., 1970. "The Traveling Salesman Problem and Minimum Spanning Trees," Operations Research, Vol. 18, pp. 1138-1162.

Held, M., and Karp, R. M., 1971. "The Traveling Salesman Problem and Minimum Spanning Trees: Part II," Math. Programming, Vol. 1, pp. 6-25.

Helgason, R. V., and Kennington, J. L., 1977. "An Efficient Procedure for Implementing a Dual-Simplex Network Flow Algorithm," AIIE Transactions, Vol. 9, pp. 63-68.

Helgason, R. V., and Kennington, J. L., 1995. "Primal-Simplex Algorithms for Minimum Cost Network Flows," Handbooks in OR and MS, Ball, M. O., Magnanti, T. L., Monma, C. L., and Nemhauser, G. L. (eds.), Vol. 7, North-Holland, Amsterdam, pp. 85-133.

Helgason, R. V., Kennington, J. L., and Stewart, B. D., 1993. "The One-to-One Shortest-Path Problem: An Empirical Analysis with the Two-Tree Dijkstra Algorithm," Computational Optimization and Applications, Vol. 1, pp. 47-75.

Hiriart-Urruty, J.-B., and Lemarechal, C., 1993. Convex Analysis and Minimization Algorithms, Vols. I and II, Springer-Verlag, Berlin and N. Y.

Hochbaum, D. S., and Shantikumar, J. G., 1990. "Convex Separable Optimization is not Much Harder than Linear Optimization," J. ACM, Vol. 37, pp. 843-862.

Hoffman, A. J., 1960. "Some Recent Applications of the Theory of Linear Inequalities to Extremal Combinatorial Analysis," Proc. Symp. Appl. Math., Vol. 10, pp. 113-128.

Hoffman, A. J., and Kuhn, H. W., 1956. "Systems of Distinct Representatives and Linear Programming," Amer. Math. Monthly, Vol. 63, pp. 455-460.

Hoffman, K., and Kunze, R., 1971. Linear Algebra, Prentice-Hall, Englewood Cliffs, N. J.

Holloway, C. A., 1974. "An Extension of the Frank and Wolfe Method of Feasible Directions," Math. Programming, Vol. 6, pp. 14-27.

Hopcroft, J. E., and Karp, R. M., 1973. "A $n^{5/2}$ Algorithm for Maximum Matchings in Bipartite Graphs," SIAM J. on Computing, Vol. 2, pp. 225-231.

Horst, R., Pardalos, P. M., and Thoai, N. V., 1995. Introduction to Global Optimization, Kluwer Academic Publishers, N. Y.

Hu, T. C., 1969. Integer Programming and Network Flows, Addison-Wesley, Reading, MA.

Hung, M., 1983. "A Polynomial Simplex Method for the Assignment Problem," Operations Research, Vol. 31, pp. 595-600.

Ibaraki, T., and Katoh, N., 1988. Resource Allocation Problems: Algorithmic Approaches, M.I.T. Press, Cambridge, MA.

Iri, M., 1969. Network Flows, Transportation, and Scheduling, Academic Press, N. Y.

Iusem, A. N., Svaiter, B., and Teboulle, M., 1994. "Entropy-Like Proximal Methods in Convex Programming," Math. Operations Research, Vol. 19, pp. 790-814.

Jensen, P. A., and Barnes, J. W., 1980. Network Flow Programming, Wiley, N. Y.

Jewell, W. S., 1962. "Optimal Flow Through Networks with Gains," Operations Research, Vol. 10, pp. 476-499.

Johnson, D. B., 1977. "Efficient Algorithms for Shortest Paths in Sparse Networks," J. ACM, Vol. 24, pp. 1-13.

Johnson, D. S., and Papadimitriou, C. H., 1985. "Computational Complexity," in The Traveling Salesman Problem, Lawler, E., Lenstra, J. K., Rinnoy Kan, A. H. G., and Shmoys, D. B. (eds.), Wiley, N. Y., pp. 37-85.

Johnson, D. S., and McGeoch, L., 1997. "The Traveling Salesman Problem:

A Case Study," in Local Search in Combinatorial Optimization, Aarts, E., and Lenstra, J. K. (eds.), Wiley, N. Y.

Johnson, E. L., 1966. "Networks and Basic Solutions," Operations Research, Vol. 14, pp. 619-624.

Johnson, E. L., 1972. "On Shortest Paths and Sorting," Proc. 25th ACM Annual Conference, pp. 510-517.

Jonker, R., and Volgenant, A., 1986. "Improving the Hungarian Assignment Algorithm," Operations Research Letters, Vol. 5, pp. 171-175.

Jonker, R., and Volgenant, A., 1987. "A Shortest Augmenting Path Algorithm for Dense and Sparse Linear Assignment Problems," Computing, Vol. 38, pp. 325-340.

Junger, M., Reinelt, G., and Rinaldi, G., 1995. "The Traveling Salesman Problem," Handbooks in OR and MS, Ball, M. O., Magnanti, T. L., Monma, C. L., and Nemhauser, G. L. (eds.), Vol. 7, North-Holland, Amsterdam, pp. 225-330.

Karzanov, A. V., 1974. "Determining the Maximal Flow in a Network with the Method of Preflows," Soviet Math Dokl., Vol. 15, pp. 1277-1280.

Karzanov, A. V., and McCormick, S. T., 1997. "Polynomial Methods for Separable Convex Optimization in Unimodular Linear Spaces with Applications to Circulations and Co-circulations in Network," SIAM J. on Computing, Vol. 26, pp. 1245-1275.

Kelley, J. E., 1960. "The Cutting-Plane Method for Solving Convex Programs," J. Soc. Indust. Appl. Math., Vol. 8, pp. 703-712.

Kennington, J., and Helgason, R., 1980. Algorithms for Network Programming, Wiley, N. Y.

Kennington, J., and Shalaby, M., 1977. "An Effective Subgradient Procedure for Minimal Cost Multicommodity Flow Problems," Management Science, Vol. 23, pp. 994-1004.

Kernighan, B. W., and Lin, S., 1970. "An Efficient Heuristic Procedure for Partitioning Graphs," Bell System Tech. Journal, Vol. 49, pp. 291-307.

Kershenbaum, A., 1981. "A Note on Finding Shortest Path Trees," Networks, Vol. 11, pp. 399-400.

Kershenbaum, A., 1993. Network Design Algorithms, McGraw-Hill, N. Y.

Kirkpatrick, S., Gelatt, C. D., and Vecchi, M. P., 1983. "Optimization by Simulated Annealing," Science, Vol. 220, pp. 621-680.

Kiwiel, K. C., 1997a. "Proximal Minimization Methods with Generalized Bregman Functions," SIAM J. on Control and Optimization, Vol. 35, pp. 1142-1168.

Kiwiel, K. C., 1997b. "Efficiency of the Analytic Center Cutting Plane Method for Convex Minimization," SIAM J. on Optimization, Vol. 7, pp. 336-346.

Klee, V., and Minty, G. J., 1972. "How Good is the Simplex Algorithm?," in Inequalities III, O. Shisha (ed.), Academic Press, N. Y., pp. 159-175.

Klein, M., 1967. "A Primal Method for Minimal Cost Flow with Applications to the Assignment and Transportation Problems," Management Science, Vol. 14, pp. 205-220.

Klessig, R. W., 1974. "An Algorithm for Nonlinear Multicommodity Flow Problems," Networks, Vol. 4, pp. 343-355.

Klincewitz, J. C., 1989. "Implementing an Exact Newton Method for Separable Convex Transportation Problems," Networks, Vol. 19, pp. 95-105.

König, D., 1931. "Graphok es Matrixok," Mat. Es Fiz. Lapok, Vol. 38, pp. 116-119.

Korst, J., Aarts, E. H., and Korst, A., 1989. Simulated Annealing and Boltzmann Machines: A Stochastic Approach to Combinatorial Optimization and Neural Computing, Wiley, N. Y.

Kortanek, K. O., and No, H., 1993. "A Central Cutting Plane Algorithm for Convex Semi-Infinite Programming Problems," SIAM J. on Optimization, Vol. 3, pp. 901-918.

Kuhn, H. W., 1955. "The Hungarian Method for the Assignment Problem," Naval Research Logistics Quarterly, Vol. 2, pp. 83-97.

Kumar, V., Grama, A., Gupta, A., and Karypis, G., 1994. Introduction to Parallel Computing, Benjamin/Cummings, Redwood City, CA.

Kushner, H. J., 1990. "Numerical Methods for Continuous Control Problems in Continuous Time," SIAM J. on Control and Optimization, Vol. 28, pp. 999-1048.

Kushner, H. J., and Dupuis, P. G., 1992. Numerical Methods for Stochastic Control Problems in Continuous Time, Springer-Verlag, N. Y.

Kwan Mei-Ko, 1962. "Graphic Programming Using Odd or Even Points," Chinese Math., Vol. 1, pp. 273-277.

Lamar, B. W., 1993. "An Improved Branch and Bound Algorithm for Minimum Concave Cost Network Flow Problems," in Network Optimization Problems, Du, D.-Z., and Pardalos, P. M. (eds.), World Scientific Publ., Singapore, pp. 261-287.

Land, A. H., and Doig, A. G., 1960. "An Automatic Method for Solving Discrete Programming Problems," Econometrica, Vol. 28, pp. 497-520.

Larsson, T., and Patricksson, M., 1992. "Simplicial Decomposition with

Disaggregated Representation for the Traffic Assignment Problem," Transportation Science, Vol. 26, pp. 4-17.

Lasdon, L. S., 1970. Optimization Theory for Large Systems, Macmillian, N. Y.

Lawphongpanich, S., and Hearn, D., 1984. "Simplicial Decomposition of the Asymmetric Traffic Assignment Problems," Transportation Research, Vol. 18B, pp. 123-133.

Lawphongpanich, S., and Hearn, D. W., 1986. "Restricted Simplicial Decomposition with Application to the Traffic Assignment Problem," Ricerca Operativa, Vol. 38, pp. 97-120.

Lawler, E., 1976. Combinatorial Optimization: Networks and Matroids, Holt, Reinhart, and Winston, N. Y.

Lawler, E., Lenstra, J. K., Rinnoy Kan, A. H. G., and Shmoys, D. B., 1985. The Traveling Salesman Problem, Wiley, N. Y.

LeBlanc, L. J., Helgason, R. V., and Boyce, D. E., 1985. "Improved Efficiency of the Frank-Wolfe Algorithm for Convex Network Programs," Transportation Science, Vol. 19, pp. 445–462.

LeBlanc, L. J., Morlok, E. K., and Pierskalla, W. P., 1974. "An Accurate and Efficient Approach to Equilibrium Traffic Assignment on Congested Networks," Transportation Research Record, TRB-National Academy of Sciences, Vol. 491, pp. 12-23.

LeBlanc, L. J., Morlok, E. K., and Pierskalla, W. P., 1975. "An Efficient Approach to Solving the Road Network Equilibrium Traffic Assignment Problem," Transportation Research, Vol. 9, pp. 309-318.

Leventhal, T., Nemhauser, G., and Trotter, Jr., L., 1973. "A Column Generation Algorithm for Optimal Traffic Assignment," Transportation Science, Vol. 7, pp. 168-176.

Lemarechal, C., 1974. "An Algorithm for Minimizing Convex Functions," in Information Processing '74, Rosenfeld, J. L. (ed.), North Holland Publ. Co., Amsterdam, pp. 552-556.

Little, J. D. C., Murty, K. G., Sweeney, D. W., and Karel, C., 1963. "An Algorithm for the Traveling Salesman Problem," Operations Research, Vol. 11, pp. 972-989.

Lovasz, L., and Plummer, M. D., 1985. Matching Theory, North-Holland, Amsterdam.

Luenberger, D. G., 1969. Optimization by Vector Space Methods, Wiley, N. Y.

Luenberger, D. G., 1984. Linear and Nonlinear Programming, Addison-Wesley, Reading, MA.

Luo, Z.-Q., 1997. "Analysis of a Cutting Plane Method that Uses Weighted Analytic Center and Multiple Cuts," SIAM J. of Optimization, Vol. 7, pp. 697-716.

Luo, Z.-Q., and Tseng, P., 1994. "On the Rate of Convergence of a Distributed Asynchronous Routing Algorithm," IEEE Trans. on Automatic Control, Vol. 39, pp. 1123-1129.

Malhotra, V. M., Kumar, M. P., and Maheshwari, S. N., 1978. "An $O(|V|^3)$ Algorithm for Finding Maximum Flows in Networks," Inform. Process. Lett., Vol. 7, pp. 277-278.

Marcotte, P., 1985. "A New Algorithm for Solving Variational Inequalities with Application to the Traffic Assignment Problem," Math. Programming Studies, Vol. 33, pp. 339-351.

Marcotte, P., and Dussault, J.-P., 1987. "A Note on a Globally Convergent Newton Method for Solving Monotone Variational Inequalities," Operations Research Letters, Vol. 6, pp. 35-42.

Marcotte, P., and Guélat, J., 1988. "Adaptation of a Modified Newton Method for Solving the Asymmetric Traffic Equilibrium Problem," Transportation Science, Vol. 22, pp. 112-124.

Martello, S., and Toth, P., 1990. Knapsack Problems, Wiley, N. Y.

Martinet, B., 1970. "Regularisation d'Inequations Variationnelles par Approximations Successives," Rev. Francaise Inf. Rech. Oper., Vol. 4, pp. 154-159.

McGinnis, L. F., 1983. "Implementation and Testing of a Primal-Dual Algorithm for the Assignment Problem," Operations Research, Vol. 31, pp. 277-291.

Mendelssohn, N. S., and Dulmage, A. L., 1958. "Some Generalizations of Distinct Representatives," Canad. J. Math., Vol. 10, pp. 230-241.

Metropolis, N., Rosenbluth, A., Rosenbluth, M., Teller, A., and Teller, E., 1953. "Equation of State Calculations by Fast Computing Machines," J. of Chemical Physisc, Vol. 21, pp. 1087-1092.

Meyer, R. R., 1979. "Two-Segment Separable Programming," Management Science, Vol. 25, pp. 385-395.

Miller, D., Pekny, J., and Thompson, G. L., 1990. "Solution of Large Dense Transportation Problems Using a Parallel Primal Algorithm," Operations Research Letters, Vol. 9, pp. 319-324.

Minty, G. J., 1957. "A Comment on the Shortest Route Problem," Operations Research, Vol. 5, p. 724.

Minty, G. J., 1960. "Monotone Networks," Proc. Roy. Soc. London, A, Vol. 257, pp. 194-212.

Minieka, E., 1978. Optimization Algorithms for Networks and Graphs, Marcel Dekker, N. Y.

Minoux, M., 1986a. Mathematical Programming: Theory and Algorithms, Wiley, N. Y.

Minoux, M., 1986b. "Solving Integer Minimum Cost Flows with Separable Convex Cost Objective Polynomially," Math. Programming Studies, Vol. 26, pp. 237-239.

Minoux, M., 1989. "Network Synthesis and Optimum Network Design Problems: Models, Solution Methods,and Applications," Networks, Vol. 19, pp. 313-360.

Monma, C. L., and Sheng, D. D., 1986. "Backbone Network Design and Performance Analysis: A Methodology for Packet Switching Networks," IEEE J. Select. Areas Comm., Vol. SAC-4, pp. 946-965.

Mulvey, J., 1978a. "Pivot Strategies for Primal-Simplex Network Codes," J. ACM, Vol. 25, pp. 266-270.

Mulvey, J., 1978b. "Testing a Large-Scale Network Optimization Program," Math. Programming, Vol. 15, pp. 291-314.

Murty, K. G., 1992. Network Programming, Prentice-Hall, Englewood Cliffs, N. J.

Nagurney, A., 1988. "An Equilibration Scheme for the Traffic Assignment Problem with Elastic Demands," Transportation Research, Vol. 22B, pp. 73-79.

Nagurney, A., 1993. Network Economics: A Variational Inequality Approach, Kluwer, Dordrecht, The Netherlands.

Nemhauser, G. L., and Wolsey, L. A., 1988. Integer and Combinatorial Optimization, Wiley, N. Y.

Nesterov, Y., 1995. "Complexity Estimates of Some Cutting Plane Methods Based on Analytic Barrier," Math. Programming, Vol. 69, pp. 149-176.

Nesterov, Y., and Nemirovskii, A., 1994. Interior Point Polynomial Algorithms in Convex Programming, SIAM, Phila., PA.

Nguyen, S., 1974. "An Algorithm for the Traffic Assignment Problem," Transportation Science, Vol. 8, pp. 203-216.

Nicholson, T., 1966. "Finding the Shortest Route Between Two Points in a Network," The Computer Journal, Vol. 9, pp. 275-280.

Nilsson, N. J., 1971. Problem-Solving Methods in Artificial Intelligence, McGraw-Hill, N. Y.

Nilsson, N. J., 1980. Principles of Artificial Intelligence, Tioga, Palo Alto, CA.

O'hEigeartaigh, M., Lenstra, S. K., and Rinnoy Kan, A. H. G. (eds.), 1985. Combinatorial Optimization: Annotated Bibliographies, Wiley, N. Y.

Ortega, J. M., and Rheinboldt, W. C., 1970. Iterative Solution of Nonlinear Equations in Several Variables, Academic Press, N. Y.

Osman, I. H., and Laporte, G., 1996. "Metaheuristics: A Bibliography," Annals of Operations Research, Vol. 63, pp. 513-628.

Padberg, M. W., and Grötschel, M., 1985. "Polyhedral Computations," in The Traveling Salesman Problem, Lawler, E., Lenstra, J. K., Rinnoy Kan, A. H. G., and Shmoys, D. B. (eds.), Wiley, N. Y., pp. 307-360.

Pallottino, S., 1984. "Shortest Path Methods: Complexity, Interrelations and New Propositions," Networks, Vol. 14, pp. 257-267.

Pallottino, S., and Scutellà, M. G., 1991. "Strongly Polynomial Algorithms for Shortest Paths," Ricerca Operativa, Vol. 60, pp. 33-53.

Pallottino, S., and Scutellà, M. G., 1997a. "Shortest Path Algorithms in Transportation Models: Classical and Innovative Aspects," Proc. of the International Colloquium on Equilibrium in Transportation Models, Montreal, Canada.

Pallottino, S., and Scutellà, M. G., 1997b. "Dual Algorithms for the Shortest Path Tree Problem," Networks, Vol. 29, pp. 125-133.

Pang, J.-S., 1984. "Solution of the General Multicommodity Spatial Equilibrium Problem by Variational and Complementarity Methods," J. of Regional Science, Vol. 24, pp. 403-414.

Pang, J.-S., and Yu, C.-S., 1984. "Linearized Simplicial Decomposition Methods for Computing Traffic Equilibria on Networks," Networks, Vol. 14, pp. 427-438.

Papadimitriou, C. H., and Steiglitz, K., 1982. Combinatorial Optimization: Algorithms and Complexity, Prentice-Hall, Englewood Cliffs, N. J.

Pape, U., 1974. "Implementation and Efficiency of Moore - Algorithms for the Shortest Path Problem," Math. Programming, Vol. 7, pp. 212-222.

Pardalos, P. M., and Rosen, J. B., 1987. Constrained Global Optimization: Algorithms and Applications, Springer-Verlag, N. Y.

Patricksson, M., 1991. "Algorithms for Urban Traffic Network Equilibria," Linköping Studies in Science and Technology, Department of Mathematics, Thesis No. 263, Linköping University, Linköping, Sweden.

Pattipati, K. R., and Alexandridis, M. G., 1990. "Application of Heuristic Search and Information Theory to Sequential Fault Diagnosis," IEEE Trans. on Systems, Man, and Cybernetics, Vol. 20, pp. 872-887.

Pattipati, K. R., Deb, S., Bar-Shalom, Y., and Washburn, R. B., 1992. "A

New Relaxation Algorithm and Passive Sensor Data Association," IEEE Trans. Automatic Control, Vol. 37, pp. 198-213.

Pearl, J., 1984. Heuristics, Addison-Wesley, Reading, MA.

Peters, J., 1990. "The Network Simplex Method on a Multiprocessor," Networks, Vol. 20, pp. 845-859.

Phillips, C., and Zenios, S. A., 1989. "Experiences with Large Scale Network Optimization on the Connection Machine," in The Impact of Recent Computing Advances on Operations Research, Vol. 9, Elsevier, Amsterdam, The Netherlands, pp. 169-180.

Pinar, M. C., and Zenios, S. A., 1992. "Parallel Decomposition of Multicommodity Network Flows Using a Linear-Quadratic Penalty Algorithm," ORSA J. on Computing, Vol. 4, pp. 235-249.

Pinar, M. C., and Zenios, S. A., 1993. "Solving Nonlinear Programs with Embedded Network Structures," in Network Optimization Problems, Du, D.-Z., and Pardalos, P. M. (eds.), World Scientific Publ., Singapore, pp. 177-202.

Pinar, M. C., and Zenios, S. A., 1994. "On Smoothing Exact Penalty Functions for Convex Constrained Optimization," SIAM J. on Optimization, Vol. 4, pp. 486-511.

Pinedo, M., 1995. Scheduling: Theory, Algorithms, and Systems, Prentice-Hall, Englewood Cliffs, N. J.

Poljak, B. T., 1987. Introduction to Optimization, Optimization Software Inc., N. Y.

Polymenakos, L. C., 1995. "ϵ-Relaxation and Auction Algorithms for the Convex Cost Network Flow Problem," Ph.D. Thesis, Electrical Engineering and Computer Science Dept, M.I.T., Cambridge, MA.

Polymenakos, L. C., and Bertsekas, D. P., 1994. "Parallel Shortest Path Auction Algorithms," Parallel Computing, Vol. 20, pp. 1221-1247.

Polymenakos, L. C., Bertsekas, D. P., and Tsitsiklis, J. N., 1998. "Efficient Algorithms for Continuous-Space Shortest Path Problems," IEEE Trans. on Automatic Control, Vol. AC-43, pp. 278-283.

Poore, A. B., 1994. "Multidimensional Assignment Formulation of Data Association Problems Arising from Multitarget Tracking and Multisensor Data Fusion," Computational Optimization and Applications, Vol. 3, pp. 27-57.

Poore, A. B., and Robertson, A. J. A., 1997. New Lagrangian Relaxation Based Algorithm for a Class of Multidimensional Assignment Problems," Computational Optimization and Applications, Vol. 8, pp. 129-150.

Powell, W. B., Jaillet, P., and Odoni, A., 1995. "Stochastic and Dynamic

Networks and Routing," Handbooks in OR and MS, Ball, M. O., Magnanti, T. L., Monma, C. L., and Nemhauser, G. L. (eds.), Vol. 8, North-Holland, Amsterdam, pp. 141-295.

Powell, W. B., Berkkam, E., and Lustig, I. J., 1993. "On Algorithms for Nonlinear Dynamic Networks," in Network Optimization Problems, Du, D.-Z., and Pardalos, P. M. (eds.), World Scientific Publ., Singapore, pp. 177-202.

Pulleyblank, W., 1983. "Polyhedral Combinatorics," in Mathematical Programming: The State of the Art - Bonn 1982, by Bachem, A., Grötschel, M., and Korte, B., (eds.), Springer, Berlin, pp. 312-345.

Pulleyblank, W., Cook, W., Cunningham, W., and Schrijver, A., 1993. An Introduction to Combinatorial Optimization, Wiley, N. Y.

Resende, M. G. C., and Veiga, G., 1993. "An Implementation of the Dual Affine Scaling Algorithm for Minimum-Cost Flow on Bipartite Uncapacitated Networks," SIAM J. on Optimization, Vol. 3, pp. 516-537.

Resende, M. G. C., and Pardalos, P. M., 1996. "Interior Point Algorithms for Network Flow Problems," Advances in Linear and Integer Programming, Oxford Lecture Ser. Math. Appl., Vol. 4, Oxford Univ. Press, New York, pp. 145-185.

Rockafellar, R. T., 1967. "Convex Programming and Systems of Elementary Monotonic Relations," J. of Math. Analysis and Applications, Vol. 19, pp. 543-564.

Rockafellar, R. T., 1969. "The Elementary Vectors of a Subspace of R^N," in Combinatorial Mathematics and its Applications, by Bose, R. C., and Dowling, T. A. (eds.), University of North Carolina Press, pp. 104-127.

Rockafellar, R. T., 1970. Convex Analysis, Princeton Univ. Press, Princeton, N. J.

Rockafellar, R. T., 1976. "Monotone Operators and the Proximal Point Algorithm," SIAM J. on Control and Optimization, Vol. 14, pp. 877-898.

Rockafellar, R. T., 1981. "Monotropic Programming: Descent Algorithms and Duality," in Nonlinear Programming 4, by Mangasarian, O. L., Meyer, R. R., and Robinson, S. M. (eds.), Academic Press, N. Y., pp. 327-366.

Rockafellar, R. T., 1984. Network Flows and Monotropic Programming, Wiley, N. Y.

Rudin, W., 1976. Real Analysis, McGraw Hill, N. Y.

Sahni, S., and Gonzalez, T., 1976. "P-Complete Approximation Problems," J. ACM, Vol. 23, pp. 555-565.

Schwartz, B. L., 1994. "A Computational Analysis of the Auction Algorithm," Eur. J. of Operations Research, Vol. 74, pp. 161-169.

Sheffi, Y., 1985. Urban Transportation Networks. Equilibrium Analysis with Mathematical Programming Methods, Prentice-Hall, Englewood Cliffs, N. J.

Shier, D. R., 1979. "On Algorithms for Finding the K Shortest Paths in a Network," Networks, Vol. 9, pp. 195-214.

Shier, D. R., and Witzgall, C., 1981. "Properties of Labeling Methods for Determining Shortest Path Trees," J. Res. Natl. Bureau of Standards, Vol. 86, pp. 317-330.

Shiloach, Y., and Vishkin, U., 1982. "An $O(n^2 \log n)$ Parallel Max-Flow Algorithm," J. Algorithms, Vol. 3, pp. 128-146.

Schrijver, A., 1986. Theory of Linear and Integer Programming, Wiley, N. Y.

Shapiro, J. E., 1979. Mathematical Programming Structures and Algorithms, Wiley, N. Y.

Shor, N. Z., 1985. Minimization Methods for Nondifferentiable Functions, Springer-Verlag, Berlin.

Srinivasan, V., and Thompson, G. L., 1973. "Benefit-Cost Analysis of Coding Techniques for Primal Transportation Algorithm," J. ACM, Vol. 20, pp. 194-213.

Strang, G., 1976. Linear Algebra and Its Applications, Academic Press, N. Y.

Suchet, C., 1949. Electrical Engineering, Vol. 68, pp. 843-844.

Tabourier, Y., 1973. "All Shortest Distances in a Graph: An Improvement to Dantzig's Inductive Algorithm," Disc. Math., Vol. 4, pp. 83-87.

Tardos, E., 1985. "A Strongly Polynomial Minimum Cost Circulation Algorithm," Combinatorica, Vol. 5, pp. 247-255.

Teboulle, M., 1992. "Entropic Proximal Mappings with Applications to Nonlinear Programming," Math. of Operations Research, Vol. 17, pp. 1-21.

Toint, P. L., and Tuyttens, D., 1990. "On Large Scale Nonlinear Network Optimization," Math. Programming, Vol. 48, pp. 125-159.

Tseng, P., 1986. "Relaxation Methods for Monotropic Programming Problems," Ph.D. Thesis, Dept. of Electrical Engineering and Computer Science, M.I.T., Cambridge, MA.

Tseng, P., 1991. "Relaxation Method for Large Scale Linear Programming Using Decomposition," Math. of Operations Research, Vol. 17, pp. 859-880.

Tseng, P., 1998. "An ϵ-Out-of-Kilter Method for Monotropic Programming," Department of Mathematics Report, Univ. of Washington, Seattle,

Wash.

Tseng, P., and Bertsekas, D. P., 1987. "Relaxation Methods for Linear Programs," Math. of Operations Research, Vol. 12, pp. 569-596.

Tseng, P., and Bertsekas, D. P., 1990. "Relaxation Methods for Monotropic Programs," Math. Programming, Vol. 46, 1990, pp. 127-151.

Tseng, P., and Bertsekas, D. P., 1993. "On the Convergence of the Exponential Multiplier Method for Convex Programming," Math. Programming, Vol. 60, pp. 1-19.

Tseng, P., and Bertsekas, D. P., 1996. "An Epsilon-Relaxation Method for Separable Convex Cost Generalized Network Flow Problems," Lab. for Information and Decision Systems Report P-2374, M.I.T., Cambridge, MA.

Tseng, P., Bertsekas, D. P., and Tsitsiklis, J. N., 1990. "Partially Asynchronous Parallel Algorithms for Network Flow and Other Problems," SIAM J. on Control and Optimization, Vol. 28, pp. 678-710.

Tsitsiklis, J. N., 1989. "Markov Chains with Rare Transitions and Simulated Annealing," Math. of Operations Research, Vol. 14, pp. 70-90.

Tsitsiklis, J. N., 1992. "Special Cases of Traveling Salesman and Repairman Problems with Time Windows," Networks, Vol. 22, pp. 263-282.

Tsitsiklis, J. N., 1995. "Efficient Algorithms for Globally Optimal Trajectories," IEEE Trans. on Automatic Control, Vol. 40, pp. 1528-1538.

Tsitsiklis, J. N., and Bertsekas, D. P., 1986. "Distributed Asynchronous Optimal Routing in Data Networks," IEEE Trans. on Automatic Control, Vol. 31, pp. 325-331.

Ventura, J. A., and Hearn, D. W., 1993. "Restricted Simplicial Decomposition for Convex Constrained Problems," Math. Programming, Vol. 59, pp. 71-85.

Voß, S., 1992. "Steiner's Problem in Graphs: Heuristic Methods,", Discrete Applied Math., Vol. 40, pp. 45-72.

Von Randow, R., 1982. Integer Programming and Related Areas: A Classified Bibliography 1978-1981, Lecture Notes in Economics and Mathematical Systems, Vol. 197, Springer-Verlag, N. Y.

Von Randow, R., 1985. Integer Programming and Related Areas: A Classified Bibliography 1982-1984, Lecture Notes in Economics and Mathematical Systems, Vol. 243, Springer-Verlag, N. Y.

Warshall, S., 1962. "A Theorem on Boolean Matrices," J. ACM, Vol. 9, pp. 11-12.

Wein, J., and Zenios, S. A., 1991. "On the Massively Parallel Solution of the Assignment Problem," J. of Parallel and Distributed Computing, Vol.

13, pp. 228-236.

Whitting, P. D., and Hillier, J. A., 1960. "A Method for Finding the Shortest Route Through a Road Network," Operations Research Quart., Vol. 11, pp. 37-40.

Winter, P., 1987. "Steiner Problem in Networks: A Survey," Networks, Vol. 17, pp. 129-167.

Wright, S. J., 1997. Primal-Dual Interior Point Methods, SIAM, Phila., PA.

Ye, Y., 1992. "A Potential Reduction Algorithm Allowing Column Generation," SIAM J. on Optimization, Vol. 2, pp. 7-20.

Ye, Y., 1997. Interior Point Algorithms: Theory and Analysis, Wiley, N. Y.

Zadeh, N., 1973a. "A Bad Network Problem for the Simplex Method and Other Minimum Cost Flow Algorithms," Math. Programming, Vol. 5, pp. 255-266.

Zadeh, N., 1973b. "More Pathological Examples for Network Flow Problems," Math. Programming, Vol. 5, pp. 217-224.

Zadeh, N., 1979. "Near Equivalence of Network Flow Algorithms," Technical Report No. 26, Dept. of Operations Research, Stanford University, CA.

Zenios, S. A., and Mulvey, J. M., 1986. "Relaxation Techniques for Strictly Convex Network Problems," Annals of Operations Research, Vol. 5, pp. 517-538.

Zoutendijk, G., 1976. Mathematical Programming Methods, North Holland, Amsterdam.

INDEX